SURVIVAL STRATEGIES FOR AMERICAN INDUSTRY

HARVARD BUSINESS REVIEW EXECUTIVE BOOK SERIES

Executive Success: Making It In Management

Survival Strategies for American Industry

Managing Effectively in the World Marketplace

Strategic Management

Financial Management

Catching Up with the Computer Revolution

Marketing Management

Using Logical Techniques for Making Better Decisions

SURVIVAL STRATEGIES FOR AMERICAN INDUSTRY

ALAN M. KANTROW,
Editor

JOHN WILEY & SONS, INC.
New York • Chichester • Brisbane • Toronto • Singapore

All articles reprinted from HBR© by President and fellows of Harvard College; all other materials copyright © 1983 by John Wiley & Sons, Inc.

All rights reserved. Published simultaneously in Canada.

Reproduction or translation of any part of this work beyond that permitted by Section 107 or 108 of the 1976 United States Copyright Act without the permission of the copyright owner is unlawful. Requests for permission or further information should be addressed to the Permissions Department, John Wiley & Sons, Inc.

This publication is designed to provide accurate and authoritative information in regard to the subject matter covered. It is sold with the understanding that the publisher is not engaged in rendering legal, accounting, or other professional service. If legal advice or other expert assistance is required, the services of a competent professional person should be sought. *From a Declaration of Principles jointly adopted by a Committee of the American Bar Association and a Committee of Publishers.*

Library of Congress Cataloging in Publication Data:

Main entry under title:

Survival strategies for American industry.

   (Harvard business review executive book series)
   Includes bibliographical references and index.
   1. Industrial management—United States—Addresses, essays, lectures. 2. Production management—Addresses, essays, lectures. 3. Competition, International—Addresses, essays, lectures. I. Kantrow, Alan M.,
     1947-   . II. Series.

HD70.U5S857 1983   658′ .00973   82-13408
ISBN 0-471-87632-1

Printed in the United States of America

10 9 8 7 6 5 4 3 2 1

Foreword

For sixty years the *Harvard Business Review* has been the farthest reaching executive program of the Harvard Business School. It is devoted to the continuing education of executives and aspiring managers primarily in business organizations, but also in not-for-profit institutions, in government, and in the professions. Through its publishing partners, reprints, and translation programs, it finds an audience in many languages in most countries in the world, occasionally penetrating even the barrier between East and West.

The *Harvard Business Review* draws on the talents of the most creative people in modern business and in management education. About half its content comes from practicing managers, the rest from professional people and university researchers. Everything *HBR* publishes has something to do with the skills, attitudes, and knowledge essential to the competent and ethical practice of management.

Survival Strategies for American Industry consists of 33 articles dealing with the problems and opportunities of production management, its relationship to corporate strategy, and new ways of thinking about the manufacturing function. Neither abstruse nor superficial, the articles chosen for this volume are intended to be usefully analytical, challenging, and carefully prescriptive. Every well-informed business person can follow the exposition in its path away from the obvious and into the territory of independent thought. I hope that readers can adapt these ideas to their own unique situations and thus make their professional careers more productive.

KENNETH R. ANDREWS, Editor
Harvard Business Review

Contents

Introduction, Alan M. Kantrow, 1

Part One   The New Challenge to Industrial Competence

An Overview, 13

1. *Managing Our Way to Economic Decline*, Robert H. Hayes and William J. Abernathy, 15
2. *Managing as if Tomorrow Mattered*, Robert H. Hayes and David A. Garvin, 36
3. *Survival Strategies in a Hostile Environment*, William K. Hall, 52
4. *The New Industrial Competition*, William J. Abernathy, Kim B. Clark, and Alan M. Kantrow, 72

Part Two   Defining a Strategic Role for Production

An Overview, 97

5. *Manufacturing: Missing Link in Corporate Strategy*, Wickham Skinner, 99
6. *Limits of the Learning Curve*, William J. Abernathy and Kenneth Wayne, 114
7. *Link Manufacturing Process and Product Life Cycles*, Robert H. Hayes and Steven C. Wheelwright, 132
8. *The Dynamics of Process-Product Life Cycles*, Robert H. Hayes and Steven C. Wheelwright, 144
9. *Operations Versus Strategy-Trading Tomorrow for Today*, Robert L. Banks and Steven C. Wheelwright, 159

Part Three Manufacturing as a Competitive Weapon

    An Overview, 175
10. *The Focused Factory,* Wickham Skinner, 179
11. *How Should You Organize Manufacturing?* Robert H. Hayes and Roger W. Schmenner, 193
12. *Can Marketing and Manufacturing Coexist?* Benson P. Shapiro, 215
13. *Why Japanese Factories Work,* Robert H. Hayes, 231
14. *The Incline of Quality,* Frank S. Leonard and W. Earl Sasser, Jr., 248

Part Four Integrating the Production System

    An Overview, 263
15. *The Concept of a Production System,* Philip M. Thurston, 265
16. *Logistics Essential to Strategy,* James L. Heskett, 269
17. *Integrating Critical Elements of Production Planning,* John E. Bishop, 289
18. *Production Planning and Control Integrated,* William K. Holstein, 303
19. *Fit Production Systems to the Task,* Jeffrey G. Miller, 334
20. *Do's and Don'ts of Computerized Manufacturing,* Donald Gerwin, 349

Part Five The Factors of Production (Resources, Capacity, and Capital)

    An Overview, 363
21. *Behind the Growth in Materials Requirements Planning,* Jeffrey G. Miller and Linda G. Sprague, 365
22. *Materials Managers: Who Needs Them?* Jeffrey G. Miller and Peter Gilmour, 377
23. *Managing Manufacturing Lead Times,* Ernest L. Huge, 396
24. *Look Beyond the Obvious in Plant Location,* Roger W. Schmenner, 409
25. *Capacity Strategies for the 1980s,* Robert A. Leone and John R. Meyer, 421

Part Six The Factors of Production (Labor)

    An Overview, 433
26. *The Anachronistic Factory,* Wickham Skinner, 435
27. *The Man on the Assembly Line,* Charles R. Walker and Robert H. Guest, 452
28. *'By Days I Make the Cars',* John F. Runcie, 474
29. *How to Counter Alienation in the Plant,* Richard E. Walton, 490
30. *Doing Away with the Factory Blues,* Donald N. Scobel, 510
31. *Work Innovations in the United States,* Richard E. Walton, 526
32. *Quality of Work Life: Learning from Tarrytown,* Robert H. Guest, 545
33. *Let First-level Supervisors Do Their Job,* W. Earl Sasser, Jr. and Frank S. Leonard, 563

About the Authors, 579

Index, 587

Introduction

ALAN M. KANTROW

"It is in America," observed a famous European visitor of the mid-nineteenth century, "that one learns to understand the influence which physical prosperity exercises over political actions." Especially so under a democratic form of government, for "when the people rule, they must be rendered happy or they will overturn the state; and misery stimulates them to those excesses to which ambition rouses kings." Alexis de Tocqueville's keen understanding of the conditions under which a political democracy could flourish had reference not to a booming industrial sector, for that lay several generations in the future, but to the immense natural advantages of the land itself. Among an agricultural and mercantile people with "no neighbors and consequently . . . no great wars, or financial crises, or inroads, or conquest, to dread," it was the economic promise of the land that held the political society together.

Today, that promise still holds; but during the century and a half that separates Tocqueville's day from our own, there has been a profound shift in the center of social gravity. In the latter part of the twentieth century, industry has far surpassed agriculture as the nation's economic bulwark—the source of its wealth and the employer of its people. No wonder, then, that any major challenge to industry's vitality raises disturbing questions for society as a whole—the more so, of course, as the long era of prosperity after World War II accustomed people and institutions to an ever higher standard of economic performance.

In the past, when such challenges arose, they were as a rule thought to be the result of misguided, hence remediable, actions. Did the railroads enjoy an unconscionable stranglehold on the affairs of small producers? If so, an Interstate Commerce Commission could right the balance. Did the barons of Wall Street jeopardize the financial markets with lucrative but unscrupulous shenanigans? If so, a web of new banking laws and securities regulation could remove the threat. Did a few large companies dominate an industry and flout the public interest with their extortionate prices? If so, an active Justice Department backed by strong antimonopoly legislation could repair the competitive situation. In the present, however, when the challenge is not one of malfeasance but of inadequate performance, the remedy is not so easy to define.

For a quarter century and more, a good many American managers have increasingly taken for granted the superiority of the operations under their control to those anywhere else in the world. Protected by a strong dollar, a huge domestic market, relatively low energy costs, and lackluster foreign competition, they became complacent. They had built a system; the system worked; and, as is often the case in such matters, the system appeared as if it would work forever. Companies abroad might enjoy an unusual, perhaps an unfair, degree of support from their governments; they might even be masters of a specific skill or technology. But when it came to the actual work of production—the nuts-and-bolts management of plants and factories—the competence of American managers was second to none. Or so ran the conventional wisdom.

That wisdom dies hard. No small part of the difficulty American industry now faces in coming to grips with the new realities of a weak dollar, relatively high energy costs, world class foreign competition, and increasingly global markets stems from its reluctance to admit that its problem is, at heart, a manufacturing problem. Outrageous interest rates, runaway inflation, excessive regulation, one-sided trade practices, troublesome unions, meddlesome bureaucrats—these must be the reason that the American economy languishes, its vital force spent. If the Japanese played fair or the Federal Reserve behaved or Lane Kirkland were reasonable or OSHA disappeared, then industry could get back to doing its proper job. The refrain is familiar, appealing, even seductive. But it is profoundly misleading.

The root of the problem lies deeper. Where American industry has fallen short is in the strategic determination—and the ability—to make excellence in manufacturing a primary competitive weapon. As we all have too good reason to know, domestic producers of tires, cameras, motorcycles, televisions, radios, machine tools, automobiles, and a host of other products have suddenly found themselves faced with shrinking market shares and aggressive foreign competitors with a knack for turning out goods at low cost and high levels of quality. The inscrutable mysteries of MITI (the Japanese Ministry of International Trade and Industry) notwithstanding, the plain fact remains that Japanese automobile producers can put a compact car on an American dealer's lot for roughly $1500 less (in 1981 dollars) than their American counterparts. Favorable governmental attitude can explain only so much; the rest is a function of differential competence in manufacturing.

INTRODUCTION

Exhibit 1. Balance of Trade

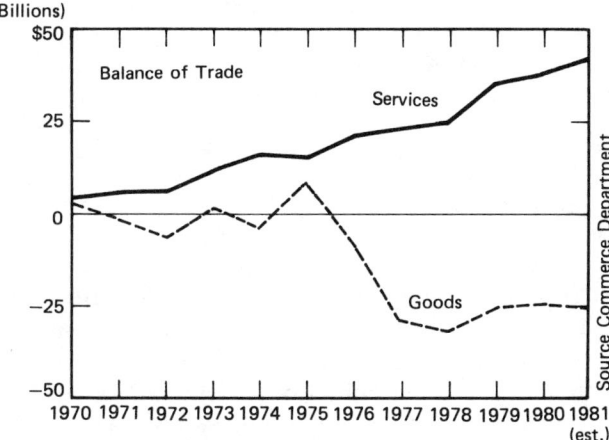

Source: W.S. Journal, 2/10/82.

Overall trade figures drive this unpleasant truth home. As Exhibit 1 indicates, the nation's cumulative trade balance remained favorable in 1981, but this was due largely to activity in the service sector. The margin by which imports of manufactured goods exceeded exports grew in 1981 to some $27.8 billion—as against a positive balance of $2.6 billion in 1970. During the decade of the 1970s, then, a massive shift occurred in the competitive strength of traditional American industry. Or, perhaps, it is more reasonable to say that that decade reaped the sorry harvest of many years of neglect and overconfidence. True, not every manufacturer was guilty of the general failure of performance, and not all industries suffered equally at the hands of foreign producers. Yet so widespread has been the failure and so painful the suffering that followed that it is bootless to seek for causes in this or that limited error of judgment, this or that outdated practice. Something fundamental is wrong.

This is, no doubt, a particularly harsh way to state the case, but it is harsh in order to make a point; a consciousness of the strategic importance of manufacturing has been wanting. As Robert Hayes and William Abernathy succinctly put it, "In our preoccupation with the braking systems and exterior trim, we may have neglected the drive trains of our corporations." More recently, as the evidence of such preoccupation mounted, an answering chorus has drawn managerial attention back to the detailed operation of plants and factories. This "rediscovery of the factory," as Robert Lubar calls it in an article in *Fortune*, is long overdue. "A good many corporate managers," Lubar notes, shocked by faltering productivity and loss of markets to Japanese and other rivals, have begun to perceive a connection between their setbacks and their neglect of the part of their business that actually produces the goods. They have been reminded that in production the *how* can be as important as the *what*, and they are going back to basics—or, in the metaphor of John A. Young, the C.E.O. of Hewlett-Packard, "back to blocking and tackling." As Young observes, "There is a feeling in the business community that managing the fundamentals well is something that has escaped us a bit."

But why this neglect of manufacturing in the first place? In the broadest terms, the international political situation of the United States after World War II, the rapid expansion of its economy, and the unquestioned strength of the dollar bred general confidence in the competitive might of American industry. With the age-old problem of production largely solved, ran the liberal opinion of the era, the nation could safely turn its attention not (as had so often been the experience of other societies) to the allocation of scarcity but, instead, to the equitable sharing of abundance. Americans were, in a famous phrase, a "people of plenty" who lived in an "affluent society."

The essential issue, as John Kenneth Galbraith formulated it in the late 1950s, was conceptual. Although the conditions of life had changed substantially, economic attitudes remained "rooted in the poverty, inequality and economic peril of the past." It was time for those attitudes to come to terms with the realities of affluence. In truth, so pervasive were those new realities that most ordinary citizens had lost sight of the fact that their standard of living was available not even to the rich a century ago.

In the postwar period, according to Galbraith, an implicit consensus developed across all political and social lines that identified the successful production of goods and services as *the* relevant measure of achievement. At the same time, however, little systematic thought was being given—at the individual, corporate, or national levels—to the necessary preconditions for successful production. "Our efforts to increase production," he wrote,

> are stylized. We stress the evils of idleness and bad resource allocation which were relevant to efforts to increase output a century ago. We do little or nothing in peacetime to increase the rate of capital formation or the rate of technological progress in background industries despite the clear indication that these are the dimensions along which large increases in output are to be expected.

How could so important a national goal be left unattended at the level of idea or policy? The answer was simple: in a Keynesian environment, equipped as it was with all the modern instruments of mass persuasion, consumer demand was always available to justify the emphasis on production and to absorb whatever goods were produced. That they could be produced was never in question; all assumed that the necessary machinery was in place. That they could be produced at competitive levels of cost and quality was never in question; all assumed that appropriate consumer demand could be generated at need.

The proper task of management in such a world was to keep adequate manufacturing capacity on line and to sell everything it made. In 1960 *HBR* published an immensely influential repudiation of this interpretation of the managerial task. Drawing on the work of Peter Drucker and others, Theodore Levitt charged American industry with an inexcusable "marketing myopia," the confusion of mere selling activity with a true commitment to marketing. Levitt's argument has lost none of its force with time. Real marketing competence, which was the true measure of sound management, lay in the sophisticated understanding of what products to manufacture, not in the mastery of the selling techniques necessary to move those products off the shelves. The job of organizing for the actual work of production, however, was secondary; it happened in the wings, not on the main stage of corporate activity.

This balance of functional emphasis gained strength, in turn, from other business developments of the time. As Alfred Chandler has shown, for example, the general movement toward a division-based corporate structure, which offered the best hope for managers of ever-larger and more diversified companies to control their varied activities, drove manufacturing issues even further toward the periphery of management attention. Moreover, to the extent that such diversified enterprises required mechanisms of integration more effective than those supplied by past practice, the need was often met through the application of strict quantitative systems of reporting and control. In corporate circles, the relevant data on production was numerical—so many units produced, so great or little a deviation from projections of variable costs, so high or low a return on invested capital—not experiential. Hands-on knowledge of what it took to run a plant or factory was important down the line, not at headquarters, for companies did not really compete on the basis of excellence in manufacturing. Finally, as managers became aware that an essential part of their jobs was to devise and implement a corporate strategy, they commonly took too narrow a view of the kind of thing strategy was. Modern portfolio theories, with their arm's length concern for asset deployment, rearrangement, and divestment, are only the most recent expression of this tendency to view corporate activities as so many disembodied pieces on the strategic chessboard.

We can no longer afford this neglect of manufacturing's competitive importance, nor can we afford its corollary: the belief that mastery of production is a skill easily achieved and maintained. The world is not what it was during the flush days of the early postwar era. Even so, these difficulties are not new or unprecedented. Part of the problem, of course, has to do with the political environment of international trade. But as a Secretary of the Treasury noted shortly after the war,

> The United States are to a certain extent in the situation of a country precluded from foreign Commerce. They can indeed, without difficulty obtain from abroad the manufactured supplies, of which they are in want; but they experience numerous and very injurious impediments to the emission and vent of their own commodities. Nor is this the case in reference to a single foreign nation only. The regulations of several countries, with which we have the most extensive intercourse, throw serious obstructions in the way of the principal staples of the United States.

Then as now, however, most of the problem is attributable to managerial inattention and hidebound allegiance to ineffective practices. As that same Secretary has argued,

> Experience teaches, that men are so much governed by what they are accustomed to see and practice, that the simplest and most obvious improvements, in the most ordinary occupations, are adopted with hesitation, reluctance, and by slow gradations. The spontaneous transition to new pursuits, in a community long habituated to different ones, may be expected to be attended with proportionably greater difficulty. When former occupations ceased to yield a profit adequate to the subsistence of their followers, or when there was an absolute deficiency of employment in them owing to a superabundance of hands, changes would ensue; but these changes would likely be more tardy than might consist with the interest either of individuals or of the Society. In many cases they would not happen, while a bare support could be insured by an adherence to ancient courses; though a resort to a more profitable employment might be practicable.

The language here may sound a bit stilted and old-fashioned, but the argument has aged not at all. In fact, the language should sound a bit out of date, for the war in question was the American Revolution and the Treasury Secretary, Alexander Hamilton.

The present challenge to management is certainly no greater than that posed by Hamilton in his 1791 *Report on Manufactures*. And there is certainly no reason why today's managers, if they are sufficiently determined and clear-sighted, cannot acquit themselves with as much success as did their predecessors nearly two centuries ago. After all, in an important sense, the problem is the same: to acknowledge that the economic world is not what it was a generation earlier, to call familiar but outdated assumptions into question, and to marshal the wit, spirit, and energy to adapt to new competitive realities.

It is to help in this effort that *HBR* makes available the present col-

INTRODUCTION 7

lection of articles from past issues. By bringing together this material in one convenient place, our hope is not to cover all—or even most—of the important aspects of the manufacturing function but, instead, to advance a general thesis and to provide a general framework for thought. The thesis is simply stated: to succeed in the competitive environment of the 1980s and beyond, American managers must be willing to compete on the basis of excellence in manufacturing. The conceptual framework is less easily put on the head of a pin. It grows out of *HBR*'s long association with attempts to define the proper relationship between manufacturing and corporate strategy, and it takes into account the inevitable difficulties in making such a relationship work over time.

We do not see this volume, then, proud as we are of its contents, as an indispensable guide to the day-to-day operation of a production facility. We see it, rather, as a manifesto of sorts, a call to arms. Its readers are not likely to rush into their plants while holding it aloft as if it were a pirated copy of some Japanese organizational chart. Our fondest hope is that its readers will come to look at the world in a different way—that is, will come to a new and enlarged understanding of the nature and importance of their responsibilities.

Accordingly, we have arranged the articles included here into half a dozen sections or groupings, intended to lead the reader through the varied stages of a single broad argument. The first of these, "The New Challenge to Industrial Competence," sounds a note of alarm long felt, but not voiced, by managers about the production-based sluggishness of American industry. But why does this note of alarm have any more useful a purpose to serve than do the countless other lamentations in the business press over current economic ills? In the first place, the four articles in Part One provide a strong, if controversial, rationale for attributing those ills not so much to inflation, high energy costs, government regulation, or tax policy as to a failure of management. Second, they define a range of corporate strategies adequate to the circumstances of today's harsh business environment. Finally, they identify those competitive weapons—enlightened work force management, efficient production processes, technological expertise—with which traditional producers in mature industries can renew themselves.

Together, these articles prepare the ground for everything that follows. Their dogged insistence that present difficulties are the result of shortsighted management attitudes and practices is both troubling and reassuring—*troubling* in that the allocation of blame in such matters is never pleasant; *reassuring* in that the necessary means for re-achieving international competitiveness lie well within the reach of today's managers if only they are willing to use them. Of course, high interest rates and the like have an effect, but it is a mistake to interpret that effect too broadly. Companies abroad have long suffered from higher real energy costs, more extensive government intervention in the market, and less flexible labor policies than their counterparts in the United States, yet many have consistently taken market share away from American producers.

Where domestic producers have fallen short, therefore, is not in the unattractiveness of their business environment but, rather, in their misguided allegiance to certain principles of management. These principles, as Robert Hayes and William Abernathy cogently argue in "Managing Our Way to Economic Decline," work subtly to "encourage a preference for (1) analytic detachment rather than the insight that comes from 'hands-on' experience and (2) short-term cost reduction rather than long-term development of technological competitiveness." When applied to the investments in capital stock on which a company's future depends, these principles can strongly bias managers against investment. Such is the conclusion reached by Robert Hayes and David Garvin in "Managing As If Tomorrow Mattered."

By itself, however, even a long-term "hands-on" managerial orientation is not enough. To be of value in the marketplace, that orientation must be put at the service of a sharply focused competitive strategy. This necessity lies at the heart of William Hall's "Survival Strategies in a Hostile Environment," which distills from research on 64 large manufacturing companies the two basic leadership strategies responsible for above-average performance in today's market. But neither revised managerial orientation nor intelligent business planning is likely to produce beneficial results unless translated into a better understanding of how internationally competitive manufacturing systems actually run. In "The New Industrial Competition," William Abernathy, Kim Clark, and I attempt that translation.

The second group of articles, "Defining a Strategic Role for Production," moves the argument of the book beyond a recognition of production's new importance. It begins, appropriately enough, with Wickham Skinner's influential "Manufacturing—Missing Link in Corporate Strategy," a strongly worded plea for the better integration of manufacturing operations with a company's overall competitive strategy. The three articles that follow, one by William Abernathy and Kenneth Wayne, and two by Robert Hayes and Steven Wheelwright, provide the conceptual basis for that integration. By establishing the process–product life cycle as a useful model for interpreting the joint evolution of product lines and their attendant production processes, these articles demonstrate the nature of the link between operations and strategy. Steven Wheelwright and Robert Banks, whose "Operations vs. Strategy: Trading Tomorrow for Today" closes the section, examine the inevitable tensions in that linkage and suggest realistic controls for minimizing their ill effects.

If the articles in Part Two set out the terms for a workable production-based strategy, they do not explore the key organizational problems that must be solved if a revived manufacturing function is to meet its new strategic responsibilities. This task falls to Part Three, "Manufacturing as a Competitive Weapon," which charts the many pitfalls in the road to developing a manufacturing mission in harmony with corporate goals and resources.

Again, Wickham Skinner provides the lead, this time with "The Focused Factory," a concise statement of what happens when a factory is charged with too varied a range of production tasks. Yet even when those tasks are reasonable and consistent, there remains the job of creating an administrative structure capable of seeing them through. This is the subject of Robert Hayes and Roger Schmenner in "How Should You Organize Manufacturing?" which evaluates the structures best suited to both product- and process-focused operations. Still, as Benson Shapiro argues in "Can Marketing and Manufacturing Coexist?" no force on earth can prevent some interfunctional tension from arising. But that tension need not prove destructive—if, that is, managers share a clear view of necessary areas of cooperation and a firm commitment to resolving conflicts in the manner most beneficial to the company as a whole. With that kind of consensus in place, managers can—and must—turn their attention again to getting the fundamentals of production right. Such, at least, is the lesson drawn by Robert Hayes in "Why Japanese Factories Work" and by Earl Sasser and Frank Leonard in "The Incline of Quality."

There is always a danger, however, that a call for a return to the basics will mean in practice a return to a narrow-minded concern for discrete operation detail. To counterbalance that danger, the fourth group of articles, "Integrating the Production System," insists in a variety of ways on the interconnectedness of all manufacturing-related activities. That they comprise a unified system is the thesis of Philip Thurston's "The Concept of a Production System," an early attempt to visualize the manufacturing function as a coherent whole. In fact, even the simplest logistical choices, as James Heskett maintains in "Logistics—Essential to Strategy," have broad strategic implications and must, therefore, be carefully integrated with a company's distinctive production competence. At a still more basic level, John Bishop's "Integrating Critical Elements of Production Planning" uses the complex real-world interactions among demand, capacity, and inventory to supply a better foundation for management decisions than the tradition EOQ (economic order quantity) formula.

At the forefront of advances in manufacturing, the case is pretty much the same. According to William Holstein, new computer technology both makes possible and underscores the need to have "Production Planning and Control Integrated." In practice, however, the application of computerized systems to production does not always show the happy results intended. When foulups occur, blame flies in a hundred directions, but rarely toward the real culprit: a lack of "fit" between control systems and corporate goals. Hence, it is essential, in Jeffrey Miller's words, to "Fit Production Systems to the Task." Nor are problems of integration absent from the experience of producers with the latest automated process technologies. Donald Gerwin's purpose in "Do's and Don'ts of Computerized Manufacturing" is to identify the tricky problems involved in tying those technologies into a functioning production system.

Part Five, "The Factors of Production (Resources, Capacity, and Capital)," considers the broad implications of the foregoing articles on several of the economists' traditional factors of production. Jeffrey Miller, with Linda Sprague in "Behind the Growth in Materials Requirements Planning" and with Peter Gilmour in "Materials Managers: Who Needs Them?" provides an updated charter for the often neglected materials function. Ernest Huge then discusses the perennial difficulties that follow a lack of adequate attention to "Managing Manufacturing Lead Times"; Roger Schmenner urges managers to "Look Beyond the Obvious in Plant Location"; and in "Capacity Strategies for the 1980s", Robert Leone and John Meyer chart the effects of a rising-cost environment on traditional assumptions about capacity expansion.

The final section, "The Factors of Production (Labor)," is by no means an afterthought or catch-all. Especially in light of Japan's recent success in making its work force into a significant competitive weapon, the experience of American manufacturers with the human side of factory operations is a reliable guide to their success in the market. The importance of effective work force management has never been so clear as it is at present, but a host of practical questions remain.

That the conventional wisdom about factory management is outdated is the inescapable fact to which Wickham Skinner points in "The Anachronistic Factory." But what is that world of work like to the factory employees themselves? Two articles, separated from each other by nearly 30 years, begin to provide an answer: Charles Walker and Robert Guest's "The Man on the Assembly Line" and John Runcie's " 'By Days I Make the Cars.' "

Their answer is troubling because, for too many workers, the factory was and is an alien and alienating environment. What to do? Richard Walton has several suggestions in "How to Counter Alienation in the Plant," as does Donald Scobel in "Doing Away with the Factory Blues." And what has been the record of past attempts to improve working conditions? Richard Walton takes a look at a decade's experience in "Work Innovations in the United States," and Robert Guest reports on a single well-known effort in "Quality of Work Life—Learning from Tarrytown." Other than these broad brush solutions, what organizational choices do managers on the spot have? For one thing, as Earl Sasser and Frank Leonard argue, they should "Let First-Level Supervisors Do Their Job."

INTRODUCTION

The particular merits of this last group of articles, as of the collection as a whole, now await your closer inspection. We offer it to you not by way of *ex cathedra* pronouncement but, rather, in the spirit of helping to move along common discourse about important problems. Our intent is not to preach but to whet an appetite for learning. And our topic is, we believe, a critical one. As Wickham Skinner noted in an article reprinted here, "A company's manufacturing function typically is either a competitive weapon or a corporate millstone. It is seldom neutral." In today's aggressive global marketplace, that sentiment is truer than ever. Learning to manage the manufacturing function well may, in fact, provide the single greatest challenge—individual and institutional—for this generation of managers. It is, at the least, the basis of any realistic hope that they can reverse the decline of American industry.

PART ONE
THE NEW CHALLENGE TO INDUSTRIAL COMPETENCE

AN OVERVIEW

No other article that *HBR* has published in its 60 year history has excited quite the same degree of reaction as Robert Hayes and William Abernathy's "Managing Our Way to Economic Decline." It touched a nerve by putting into words a vague nagging discontent in the back of many managers' minds. Typically concerned with the planning and control systems appropriate to large decentralized organizations, these managers had slowly been losing touch with the manufacturing base of their companies. Their decision-making horizons had grown shorter and shorter, their determination to sustain long-term technological leadership had weakened, and their attention to this year's profits had correspondingly increased. They had mastered all the technical apparatus of professional management, but things had not worked out as planned. Something was terribly wrong, but no one knew precisely where to look for it.

    Not surprisingly, as the competitive performance of American industry grew worse, earlier discontent hardened into dismay and, in some quarters, dismay into paralysis. To many it seemed as if the whole edifice of postwar prosperity were coming unglued, economic logic and institutions both. Signs of disarray were everywhere, yet precious few hands were confidently raised to set things right. In retrospect, this lack of purposeful response makes a certain kind of sense. So great an upheaval in familiar arrangements often has about it the irresistible force of nature; when such winds blow, managers are sorely tempted to batten down the hatches and wait.

"Managing Our Way to Economic Decline" entered a powerful brief against passively riding out the storm. It argued that the real enemy was not the overmastering violence of economic disturbance but, rather, the comfortable practices and guiding assumptions of American managers themselves. This argument is, of course, controversial because it calls into question a generation of accepted wisdom about the way things should be done. But it is hopeful as well because it points toward a reasonable mode of corrective action. By placing responsibility squarely on the shoulders of management, Hayes and Abernathy sound a positive call to arms: what managers do wrong, managers can fix.

The three other articles in this section extend this stern critique of management's shortsightedness, inattention to fundamentals, and strategic indecision. That new investments in capital stock must be made, that strategies exist for performing well even under hostile market conditions, that closer attention to the operation of plants and factories is essential—these ideas must provide the foundation for a revised managerial creed, for managers must again feel themselves in active control of their own destinies. They must genuinely believe that the means for regaining industrial competitiveness lie ready to hand. Such belief never comes easily, and the battering that American companies have taken in recent years has put it at greater distance still.

To break through this predictable reluctance to face the necessity for change, what is needed is an explanation of events, a set of terms for thinking about the new competitive realities, that makes cogent sense. It is the work of these articles to present such an explanation. This is not a frivolous or impractical task. Do not underestimate the value or power of a new way of looking at the world, for ideas can change a landscape every bit as much as can a military occupation. It was the late unlamented Joseph Stalin who, when confronted with the threat of papal displeasure, asked in his ignorance, "How many divisions has the Pope?" We need not repeat the same mistake.

1
Managing Our Way to Economic Decline

ROBERT H. HAYES and WILLIAM J. ABERNATHY

How are we to fix responsibility for the current malaise of American business? Most attribute its weakened condition to the virus of inflation, the paralysis brought on by government regulation and tax policy, or the feverish price escalation by OPEC. Not quite right, say the authors. In their judgment, responsibility rests not with general economic forces alone but also with the failure of American managers to keep their companies technologically competitive over the long run. In advancing their controversial diagnosis, the authors draw on their own extensive work in the production field as well as their recent association with Harvard's International Senior Managers Program in Vevey, Switzerland. Having taken a long hard look from abroad at how American managers operate, they propose some strong medicine for improving the health of American business.

During the past several years American business has experienced a marked deterioration of competitive vigor and a growing unease about its overall economic well-being. This decline in both health and confidence has been attributed by economists and business leaders to such factors as the rapacity of OPEC, deficiencies in government tax and monetary policies, and the proliferation of regulation. We find these explanations inadequate.

They do not explain, for example, why the rate of productivity growth in America has declined both absolutely and relative to that in Europe and Japan. Nor do they explain why in many high-technology as well as mature industries America has lost its leadership position. Although a host of readily named forces—government regulation, inflation, monetary policy, tax laws, labor costs and constraints, fear of a capital shortage, the price of imported oil—have taken their toll on American business, pressures of this sort affect the economic climate abroad just as they do here.

A German executive, for example, will not be convinced by these explanations. Germany imports 95% of its oil (we import 50%), its government's share of gross domestic product is about 37% (ours is about 30%), and workers must be consulted on most major decisions. Yet Germany's rate of productivity growth has actually increased since 1970 and recently rose to more than four times ours. In France the situation is similar, yet today that country's productivity growth in manufacturing (despite current crises in steel and textiles) more than triples ours. No modern industrial nation is immune to the problems and pressures besetting U.S. business. Why then do we find a disproportionate loss of competitive vigor by U.S. companies?

Our experience suggests that, to an unprecedented degree, success in most industries today requires an organizational commitment to compete in the marketplace on technological grounds—that is, to compete over the long run by offering superior products. Yet, guided by what they took to be the newest and best principles of management, American managers have increasingly directed their attention elsewhere. These new principles, despite their sophistication and widespread usefulness, encourage a preference for (1) analytic detachment rather than the insight that comes from "hands-on" experience and (2) short-term cost reduction rather than long-term development of technological competitiveness. It is this new managerial gospel, we feel, that has played a major role in undermining the vigor of American industry.

American management, especially in the two decades after World War II, was universally admired for its strikingly effective performance. But times change. An approach shaped and refined during stable decades may be ill suited to a world characterized by rapid and unpredictable change, scarce energy, global competition for markets, and a constant need for innovation. This is the world of the 1980s and, probably, the rest of this century.

The time is long overdue for earnest, objective self-analysis. What exactly have American managers been doing wrong? What are the critical weaknesses in the ways that they have managed the technological performance of their companies? What is the matter with the long-unquestioned assumptions on which they have based their managerial policies and practices?

A Failure of Management

In the past, American managers earned worldwide respect for their carefully planned yet highly aggressive action across three different time frames:

- ☐ *Short term.* Using existing assets as efficiently as possible.
- ☐ *Medium term.* Replacing labor and other scarce resources with capital equipment.

A FAILURE OF MANAGEMENT   17

☐ *Long term.* Developing new products and processes that open new markets or restructure old ones.

The first of these time frames demanded toughness, determination, and close attention to detail; the second, capital and the willingness to take sizable financial risks; the third, imagination and a certain amount of technological daring.

Our managers still earn generally high marks for their skill in improving short-term efficiency, but their counterparts in Europe and Japan have started to question America's entrepreneurial imagination and willingness to make risky long-term competitive investments. As one such observer remarked to us: "The U.S. companies in my industry act like banks. All they are interested in is return on investment and getting their money back. Sometimes they act as though they are more interested in buying other companies than they are in selling products to customers."

In fact, this curt diagnosis represents a growing body of opinion that openly charges American managers with competitive myopia:

> Somehow or other, American business is losing confidence in itself and especially confidence in its future. Instead of meeting the challenge of the changing world, American business today is making small, short-term adjustments by cutting costs and by turning to the government for temporary relief. . . . Success in trade is the result of patient and meticulous preparations, with a long period of market preparation before the rewards are available. . . . To undertake such commitments is hardly in the interest of a manager who is concerned with his or her next quarterly earnings reports.[1]

More troubling still, American managers themselves often admit the charge with, at most, a rhetorical shrug of their shoulders. In established businesses, notes one senior vice president of research: "We understand how to market, we know the technology, and production problems are not extreme. Why risk money on new businesses when good, profitable low-risk opportunities are on every side?" Says another:

> It's much more difficult to come up with a synthetic meat product than a lemon-lime cake mix. But you work on the lemon-lime cake mix because you know exactly what that return is going to be. A synthetic steak is going to take a lot longer, require a much bigger investment, and the risk of failure will be greater.[2]

These managers are not alone; they speak for many. Why, they ask, should they invest dollars that are hard to earn back when it is so easy—and so much less risky—to make money in other ways? Why ignore a ready-made situation in cake mixes for the deferred and far less certain prospects in synthetic steaks? Why shoulder the competitive risks of making better and more innovative products?

In our judgment, the assumptions underlying these questions are prime evidence of a broad managerial failure—a failure of both vision and leadership—that overtime has eroded both the inclination and the capacity of U.S. companies to innovate.

Familiar Excuses

About the facts themselves there can be little dispute. Exhibits 1–4 document our sorry decline. But the explanations and excuses commonly offered invite a good deal of comment.

It is important to recognize, first of all, that the problem is not new. It has been going on for at least 15 years. The rate of productivity growth in the private sector peaked in the mid-1960s. Nor is the problem confined to a few sectors of our economy; with a few exceptions, it permeates our entire economy. Expenditures on R&D by both business and government, as measured in constant (noninflated) dollars, also peaked in the mid-1960s—both in absolute terms and as a percentage of GNP. During the same period the expenditures on R&D by West Germany and Japan have been rising. More important, American spending on R&D as a percentage of sales in such critical research-intensive industries as machinery, professional and scientific instruments, chemicals, and aircraft had dropped by the mid-1970s

Exhibit 1. Growth in Labor Productivity since 1960 (United States and Abroad)

	Manufacturing 1960–1978	All Industries 1960–1976
United States	2.8%	1.7%
United Kingdom	2.9	2.2
Canada	4.0	2.1
Germany	5.4	4.2
France	5.5	4.3
Italy	5.9	4.9
Belgium	6.9[a]	—
Netherlands	6.9[a]	—
Sweden	5.2	—
Japan	8.2	7.5

Source: Council on Wage and Price Stability, *Report on Productivity* (Washington, DC, Executive Office of the President, July 1979).

[a]1960–1977.

Exhibit 2. Growth of Labor Productivity by Sector, 1948–1978

Time Sector	Growth of Labor Productivity (annual average percent)		
	1948–1965	1965–1973	1973–1978
Private business	3.2%	2.3%	1.1%
Agriculture, forestry, and fisheries	5.5	5.3	2.9
Mining	4.2	2.0	−4.0
Construction	2.9	−2.2	−1.8
Manufacturing	3.1	2.4	1.7
Durable goods	2.8	1.9	1.2
Nondurable goods	3.4	3.2	2.4
Transportation	3.3	2.9	0.9
Communication	5.5	4.8	7.1
Electric, gas, and sanitary services	6.2	4.0	0.1
Trade	2.7	3.0	0.4
Wholesale	3.1	3.9	0.2
Retail	2.4	2.3	0.8
Finance, insurance, and real estate	1.0	−0.3	1.4
Services	1.5	1.9	0.5
Government enterprises	−0.8	0.9	−0.7

Source: Bureau of Labor Statistics.
Note: Productivity data for services, construction, finance, insurance, and real estate are unpublished.

to about half its level in the early 1960s. These are the very industries on which we now depend for the bulk of our manufactured exports.

Investment in plant and equipment in the United States displays the same disturbing trends. As economist Burton G. Malkiel has pointed out:

> From 1948 to 1973 the [net book value of capital equipment] per unit of labor grew at an annual rate of almost 3%. Since 1973, however, lower rates of private investment have ldd to a decline in that growth rate to 1.75%. Moreover, the recent composition of investment [in 1978] has been skewed toward equipment and relatively short-term projects and away from structures and relatively long-lived investments. Thus our industrial plant has tended to age. . . .[3]

Other studies have shown that growth in the incremental capital equipment-to-labor ratio has fallen to about one-third of its value in the early 1960s. By contrast, between 1966 and 1976 capital investment as a percentage

Exhibit 3. National Expenditures for performance of R&D as a Percent of GNP by Country, 1961–1978*

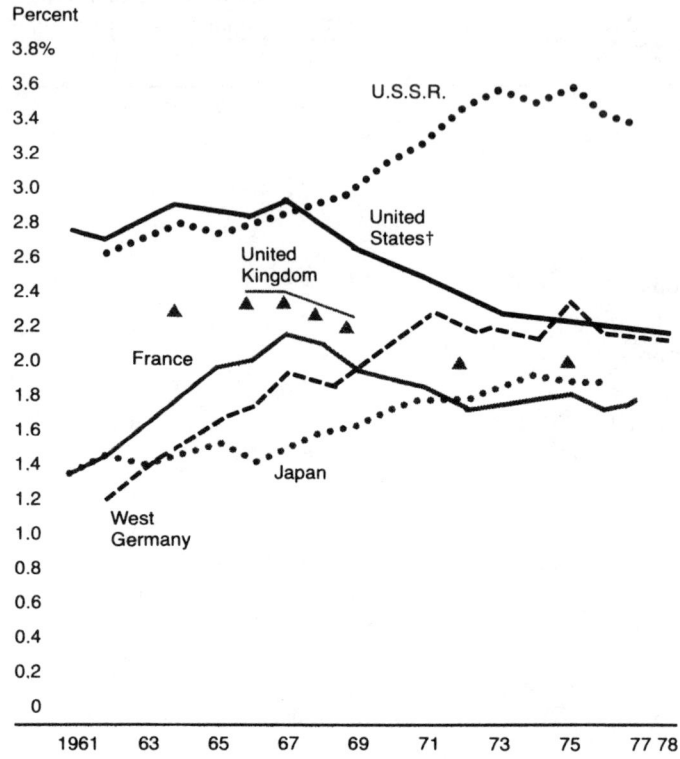

*Gross expenditures for performance of R&D including associated capital expenditures.
†Detailed information on capital expenditures for R&D is not available for the United States. Estimates for the period 1972-1977 show that their inclusion would have an impact of less than one-tenth of 1% for each year.
Source: *Science Indicators – 1978* (Washington, D.C.: National Science Foundation, 1979), p. 6.
Note: The latest data may be preliminary or estimates.

of GNP in France and West Germany was more than 20% greater than that in the United States; in Japan the percentage was almost double ours.

To attribute this relative loss of technological vigor to such things as a shortage of capital in the United States is not justified. As Malkiel and others have shown, the return on equity of American business (out of which comes the capital necessary for investment) is about the same today as 20 years ago, *even after adjusting for inflation*. However, investment in both new equipment and R&D, as a percentage of GNP, was significantly higher 20 years ago than today.

Exhibit 4. Industrial R&D Expenditures for Basic Research, Applied Research, and Development, 1960–1978 (in $ millions)

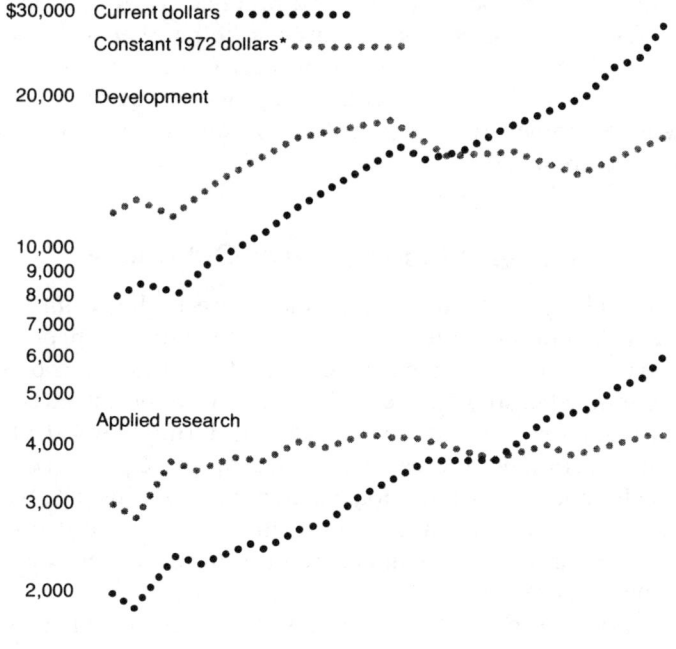

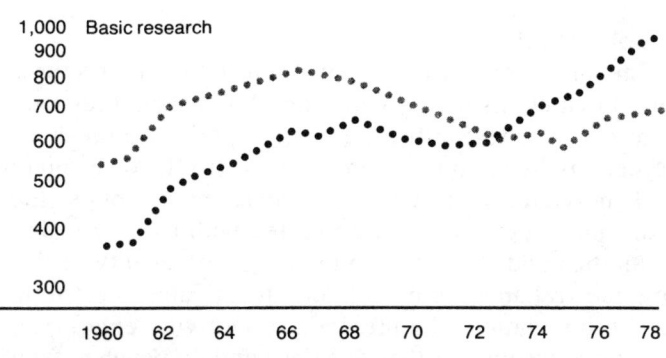

*GNP implicit price deflators used to convert current dollars to constant 1972 dollars.
Source: *Science Indicators – 1978*, p. 87.
Note: Preliminary data are shown for 1977 and estimates for 1978.

The conclusion is painful but must be faced. Responsibility for this competitive listlessness belongs not just to a set of external conditions but also to the attitudes, preoccupations, and practices of American managers. By their preference for servicing existing markets rather than creating new ones and by their devotion to short-term returns and "management by the numbers," many of them have effectively forsworn long-term technological superiority as a competitive weapon. In consequence, they have abdicated their strategic responsibilities.

The New Management Orthodoxy

We refuse to believe that this managerial failure is the result of a sudden psychological shift among American managers toward a "super-safe no risk" mind set. No profound sea change in the character of thousands of individuals could have occurred in so organized a fashion or have produced so consistent a pattern of behavior. Instead we believe that during the past two decades American managers have increasingly relied on principles which prize analytical detachment and methodological elegance over insight, based on experience, into the subtleties and complexities of strategic decisions. As a result, maximum short-term financial returns have become the overriding criteria for many companies.

For purposes of discussion, we may divide this *new* management orthodoxy into three general categories: financial control, corporate portfolio management, and market-driven behavior.

Financial Control

As more companies decentralize their organizational structures, they tend to fix on profit centers as the primary unit of managerial responsibility. This development necessitates, in turn, greater dependence on short-term financial measurements like return on investment (ROI) for evaluating the performance of individual managers and management groups. Increasing the structural distance between those entrusted with exploiting actual competitive opportunities and those who must judge the quality of their work virtually guarantees reliance on objectively quantifiable short-term criteria.

Although innovation, the lifeblood of any vital enterprise, is best encouraged by an environment that does not unduly penalize failure, the predictable result of relying too heavily on short-term financial measures—a sort of managerial remote control—is an environment in which no one feels he or she can afford a failure or even a momentary dip in the bottom line.

Corporate Portfolio Management

This preoccupation with control draws support from modern theories of financial portfolio management. Originally developed to help balance the overall risk and return of stock and bond portfolios, these principles have been applied increasingly to the creation and management of corporate portfolios—that is, a cluster of companies and product lines assembled through various modes of diversification under a single corporate umbrella. When applied by a remote group of dispassionate experts primarily concerned with finance and control and lacking hands-on experience, the analytic formulas of portfolio theory push managers even further toward an extreme of caution in allocating resources.

"Especially in large organizations," reports one manager, "we are observing an increase in management behavior which I would regard as excessively cautious, even passive; certainly overanalytical; and, in general, characterized by a studied unwillingness to assume responsibility and even reasonable risk."

Market-Driven Behavior

In the past 20 years, American companies have perhaps learned too well a lesson they had long been inclined to ignore: businesses should be customer oriented rather than product oriented. Henry Ford's famous dictum that the public could have any color automobile it wished as long as the color was black has since given way to its philosophical opposite: "We have got to stop marketing makeable products and learn to make marketable products."

At last, however, the dangers of too much reliance on this philosophy are becoming apparent. As two Canadian researchers put it:

> Inventors, scientists, engineers, and academics, in the normal pursuit of scientific knowledge, gave the world in recent times the laser, xerography, instant photography, and the transistor. In contrast, worshippers of the marketing concept have bestowed upon mankind such products as new-fangled potato chips, feminine hygiene deodorant, and the pet rock. . . .[4]

The argument that no new product ought to be introduced without managers undertaking a market analysis is common sense. But the argument that consumer analyses and formal market surveys should dominate other considerations when allocating resources to product development is untenable. It may be useful to remember that the initial market estimate for computers in 1945 projected total worldwide sales of only 10 units. Similarly, even the most carefully researched analysis of consumer preferences for gas-guzzling cars in an era of gasoline abundance offers little useful guidance to today's automobile manufacturers in making wise product investment decisions. Customers may know what their needs are, but they often define those needs in terms of existing products, processes, markets, and prices.

Deferring to a market-driven strategy without paying attention to its limitations is, quite possibly, opting for customer satisfaction and lower risk in the short run at the expense of superior products in the future. Satisfied customers are critically important, of course, but not if the strategy for creating them is responsible as well for unnecessary product proliferation, inflated costs, unfocused diversification, and a lagging commitment to new technology and new capital equipment.

Three Managerial Decisions

These are serious charges to make. But the unpleasant fact of the matter is that, however useful these new principles may have been initially, if carried too far they are bad for U.S. business. Consider, for example, their effect on three major kinds of choices regularly faced by corporate managers: the decision between imitative and innovative product design, the decision to integrate backward, and the decision to invest in process development.

Imitative Versus Innovative Product Design

A market-driven strategy requires new product ideas to flow from detailed market analysis or, at least, to be extensively tested for consumer reaction before actual introduction. It is no secret that these requirements add significant delays and costs to the introduction of new products. It is less well known that they also predispose managers toward developing products for existing markets and toward product designs of an imitative rather than an innovative nature. There is increasing evidence that market-driven strategies tend, over time, to dampen the general level of innovation in new product decisions.

Confronted with the choice between innovation and imitation, managers typically ask whether the marketplace shows any consistent preference for innovative products. If so, the additional funding they require may be economically justified; if not, those funds can more properly go to advertising, promoting, or reducing the prices of less advanced products. Though the temptation to allocate resources so as to strengthen performance in existing products and markets is often irresistible, recent studies by J. Hugh Davidson and others confirm the strong market attractiveness of innovative products.[5]

Nonetheless, managers having to decide between innovative and imitative product design face a difficult series of marketing-related trade-offs. Exhibit 5 summarizes these trade-offs.

By its very nature, innovative design is, as Joseph Schumpeter observed a long time ago, initially destructive of capital—whether in the form of labor skills, management systems, technological processes, or capital equipment. It tends to make obsolete existing investments in both marketing and manufacturing organizations. For the managers concerned it represents the choice of uncertainty (about economic returns, timing, etc.) over relative

Exhibit 5. Trade-offs Between Imitative and Innovative Design for an Established Product Line

Imitative Design	Innovative Design
Market demand is relatively well known and predictable.	Potentially large but unpredictable demand; the risk of a flop is also large.
Market recognition and acceptance are rapid.	Market acceptance may be slow initially, but the imitative response of competitors may also be slowed.
Readily adaptable to existing market, sales, and distribution policies.	May require unique, tailored marketing distribution and sales policies to educate customers or because of special repair and warranty problems.
Fits with existing market segmentation and product policies.	Demand may cut across traditional marketing segments, disrupting divisional responsibilities and cannibalizing other products.

predictability, exchanging the reasonable expectation of current income against the promise of high future value. It is the choice of the gambler, the person willing to risk much to gain even more.

Conditioned by a market-driven strategy and held closely to account by a "results now" ROI-oriented control system, American managers have increasingly refused to take the chance on innovative product/market development. As one of them confesses: "In the last year, on the basis of high capital risk, I turned down new products at a rate at least twice what I did a year ago. But in every case I tell my people to go back and bring me some new product ideas."[6] In truth, they have learned caution so well that many are in danger of forgetting that market-driven, follow-the-leader companies usually end up following the rest of the pack as well.

Backward Integration

Sometimes the problem for managers is not their reluctance to take action and make investments but that, when they do so, their action has the unintended result of reinforcing the status quo. In deciding to integrate backward because of apparent short-term rewards, managers often restrict their ability to strike out in innovative directions in the future.

Consider, for example, the case of a manufacturer who purchases a major component from an outside company. Static analysis of production economies may very well show that backward integration offers rather substantial cost benefits. Eliminating certain purchasing and marketing functions, centralizing overhead, pooling R&D efforts and resources, coordinating design and production of both product and component, reducing uncertainty over design changes, allowing for the use of more specialized equipment and labor skills—in all these ways and more, backward integration holds out to management the promise of significant short-term increases in ROI.

These efficiencies may be achieved by companies with commoditylike products. In such industries as ferrous and nonferrous metals or petroleum, backward integration toward raw materials and supplies tends to have a strong positive effect on profits. However, the situation is markedly different for companies in more technologically active industries. Where there is considerable exposure to rapid technological advances, the promised value of backward integration becomes problematic. It may provide a quick short-term boost to ROI figures in the next annual report, but it may also paralyze the long-term ability of a company to keep on top of technological change.

The real competitive threats to technologically active companies arise less from changes in ultimate consumer preference than from abrupt shifts in component technologies, raw materials, or production processes. Hence those managers whose attention is too firmly directed toward the marketplace and near-term profits may suddenly discover that their decision to make rather than buy important parts has locked their companies into an outdated technology.

Further, as supply channels and manufacturing operations become more systematized, the benefits from attempts to "rationalize" production may well be accompanied by unanticipated side effects. For instance, a company may find itself shut off from the R&D efforts of various independent suppliers by becoming their competitor. Similarly, the commitment of time and resources needed to master technology back up the channel of supply may distract a company from doing its own job well. Such was the fate of Bowmar, the pocket calculator pioneer, whose attempt to integrate backward into semiconductor production so consumed management attention that final assembly of the calculators, its core business, did not get the required resources.

Long-term contracts and long-term relationships with suppliers can achieve many of the same cost benefits as backward integration without calling into question a company's ability to innovate or respond to innovation. European automobile manufacturers, for example, have typically chosen to rely on their suppliers in this way; American companies have followed the path of backward integration. The resulting trade-offs between production efficiencies and innovative flexibility should offer a stern warning to those American managers too easily beguiled by the lure of short-term ROI improvement. A case in point: the U.S. auto industry's huge investment in automating the manufacture of cast-iron brake drums probably delayed by more than five years its transition to disc brakes.

Process Development

In an era of management by the numbers, many American managers—especially in mature industries—are reluctant to invest heavily in the development of new manufacturing processes. When asked to explain their reluctance, they tend to respond in fairly predictable ways. "We can't afford to design new capital equipment for just our own manufacturing needs" is one frequent answer. So is: "The capital equipment producers do a much better job, and they can amortize their development costs over sales to many companies." Perhaps most common is: "Let the others experiment in manufacturing; we can learn from their mistakes and do it better."

Each of these comments rests on the assumption that essential advances in process technology can be appropriated more easily through equipment purchase than through in-house equipment design and development. Our extensive conversations with the managers of European (primarily German) technology-based companies have convinced us that this assumption is not as widely shared abroad as in the United States. Virtually across the board, the European managers impressed us with their strong commitment to increasing market share through internal development of advanced process technology—even when their suppliers were highly responsive to technological advances.

By contrast, American managers tend to restrict investments in process development to only those items likely to reduce costs in the short run. Not all are happy with this. As one disgruntled executive told us:

> For too long U.S. managers have been taught to set low priorities on mechanization projects, so that eventually divestment appears to be the best way out of manufacturing difficulties. Why?
>
> The drive for short-term success has prevented managers from looking thoroughly into the matter of special manufacturing equipment, which has to be invented, developed, tested, redesigned, reproduced, improved, and so on. That's a long process, which needs experienced, knowledgeable, and dedicated people who stick to their jobs over a considerable period of time. Merely buying new equipment (even if it is possible) does not often give the company any advantage over competitors.

We agree. Most American managers seem to forget that, even if they produce new products with their existing process technology (the same "cookie cutter" everyone else can buy), their competitors will face a relatively short lead time for introducing similar products. And as Eric von Hipple's studies of industrial innovation show, the innovations on which new industrial equipment is based usually originate with the user of the equipment and not with the equipment producer.[7] In other words, companies can make products more profitable by investing in the development of their own process technology. Proprietary processes are every bit as formidable competitive weapons as proprietary products.

The American Managerial Ideal

Two very important questions remain to be asked: (1) Why should so many American managers have shifted so strongly to this new managerial orthodoxy and (2) why are they not more deeply bothered by the ill effects of those principles on the long-term technological competitiveness of their companies? To answer the first question, we must take a look at the changing career patterns of American managers during the past quarter century; to answer the second, we must understand the way in which they have come to regard their professional roles and responsibilities as managers.

The Road to the Top

During the past 25 years the American manager's road to the top has changed significantly. No longer does the typical career, threading sinuously up and through a corporation with stops in several functional areas, provide future top executives with intimate hands-on knowledge of the company's technologies, customers, and suppliers.

Exhibit 6 summarizes the currently available data on the shift in functional background of newly appointed presidents of the 100 largest U.S. corporations. The immediate significance of these figures is clear. Since the mid-1950s there has been a rather substantial increase in the percentage of new company presidents whose primary interests and expertise lie in the financial and legal areas and not in production. In the view of C. Jackson Grayson, president of the American Productivity Center, American management has for 20 years

> coasted off the great R&D gains made during World War II, and constantly rewarded executives from the marketing, financial, and legal sides of the business while it ignored the production men. Today [in business schools] courses in the production area are almost nonexistent.[8]

In addition, companies are increasingly choosing to fill new top management posts from outside their own ranks. In the opinion of foreign observers, who are still accustomed to long-term careers in the same company or division, "High-level American executives . . . seem to come and go and switch around as if playing a game of musical chairs at an Alice in Wonderland tea party."

Far more important, however, than any absolute change in numbers is the shift in the general sense of what an aspiring manager has to be "smart about" to make it to the top. More important still is the broad change in

Exhibit 6. Changes in the Professional Origins of Corporate Presidents (percent changes from baseline years [1948–1952] for 100 top U.S. companies)

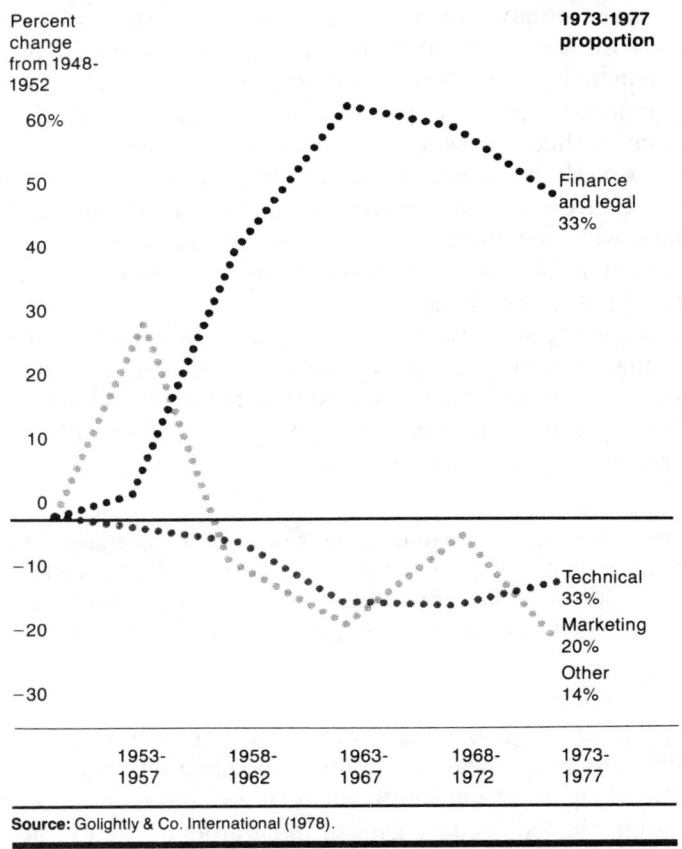

Source: Golightly & Co. International (1978).

attitude such trends both encourage and express. What has developed, in the business community as in academia, is a preoccupation with a false and shallow concept of the professional manager, a "pseudo-professional" really—an individual having no special expertise in any particular industry or technology who nevertheless can step into an unfamiliar company and run it successfully through strict application of financial controls, portfolio concepts, and a market-driven strategy.

The Gospel of Pseudo-Professionalism

In recent years, this idealization of pseudo-professionalism has taken on something of the quality of a corporate religion. Its first doctrine, appropriately enough, is that neither industry experience nor hands-on technological expertise counts for very much. At one level, of course, this doctrine helps to salve the conscience of those who lack them. At another, more disturbing, level it encourages the faithful to make decisions about technological matters simply as if they were adjuncts to finance or marketing decisions. We do not believe that the technological issues facing managers today can be meaningfully addressed without taking into account marketing or financial considerations; on the other hand, neither can they be resolved with the same methodologies applied to these other fields.

Complex modern technology has its own inner logic and developmental imperatives. To treat it as if it were something else—no matter how comfortable one is with that other kind of data—is to base a competitive business on a two-legged stool, which must, no matter how excellent the balancing act, inevitably fall to the ground.

More disturbing still, true believers keep the faith on a day-to-day basis by insisting that as issues rise up the managerial hierarchy for decision they be progressively distilled into easily quantifiable terms. One European manager, in recounting to us his experiences in a joint venture with an American company, recalled with exasperation that

> U.S. managers want everything to be simple. But sometimes business situations are not simple, and they cannot be divided up or looked at in such a way that they become simple. They are messy, and one must try to understand all the facets. This appears to be alien to the American mentality.

The purpose of good organizational design, of course, is to divide responsibilities in such a way that individuals have relatively easy tasks to perform. But then these differentiated responsibilities must be pulled together by sophisticated broadly gauged integrators at the top of the managerial pyramid. If these individuals are interested in but one or two aspects of the total competitive picture, if their training includes a very narrow exposure to the range of functional specialties, or if—worst of all—they are devoted simplifiers themselves, who will do the necessary integration? Who will attempt to resolve complicated issues rather than try to uncomplicate them artificially? At the strategic level there are no such things as pure production problems, pure financial problems, or pure marketing problems.

Merger Mania

When executive suites are dominated by people with financial and legal skills, it is not surprising that top management should increasingly allocate time and energy to such concerns as cash management and the whole process of corporate acquisitions and mergers. This is indeed what has happened. In 1978 alone there were some 80 mergers involving companies with assets in excess of $100 million each; in 1979 there were almost 100. This represents roughly $20 billion in transfers of large companies from one owner to another—two-thirds of the total amount spent on R&D by American industry.

In 1978 *Business Week* ran a cover story on cash management in which it stated that "the 400 largest U.S. companies together have more than $60 billion in cash—almost triple the amount they had at the beginning of the 1970s." The article also described the increasing attention devoted to—and the sophisticated and exotic techniques used for—managing this cash hoard.

There are perfectly good reasons for this flurry of activity. It is entirely natural for financially (or legally) trained managers to concentrate on essentially financial (or legal) activities. It is also natural for managers who subscribe to the portfolio "law of large numbers" to seek to reduce total corporate risk by parceling it out among a sufficiently large number of separate product lines, businesses, or technologies. Under certain conditions it may very well make good economic sense to buy rather than build new plants or modernize existing ones. Mergers are obviously an exciting game; they tend to produce fairly quick and decisive results, and they offer the kind of public recognition that helps careers along. Who can doubt the appeal of the titles awarded by the financial community; being called a "gunslinger," "white knight," or "raider" can quicken anyone's blood.

Unfortunately, the general American penchant for separating and simplifying has tended to encourage a diversification away from core technologies and markets to a much greater degree than is true in Europe or Japan. U.S. managers appear to have an inordinate faith in the portfolio law of large numbers—that is, by amassing enough product lines, technologies, and businesses, one will be cushioned against the random setbacks that occur in life. This might be true for portfolios of stocks and bonds, where there is considerable evidence that setbacks *are* random. Businesses, however, are subject not only to random setbacks such as strikes and shortages but also to carefully orchestrated attacks by competitors, who focus all their resources and energies on one set of activities.

Worse, the great bulk of this merger activity appears to have been absolutely wasted in terms of generating economic benefits for stockholders. Acquisition experts do not necessarily make good managers. Nor can they increase the value of their shares by merging two companies any better than their shareholders could do individually by buying shares of the acquired company on the open market (at a price usually below that required for a takeover attempt).

There appears to be a growing recognition of this fact. A number of U.S. companies are now divesting themselves of previously acquired companies; others (for example, W.R. Grace) are proposing to break themselves up into relatively independent entities. The establishment of a strong competitive position through in-house technological superiority is by nature a long, arduous, and often unglamorous task. But it is what keeps a business vigorous and competitive.

The European Example

Gaining competitive success through technological superiority is a skill much valued by the seasoned European (and Japanese) managers with whom we talked. Although we were able to locate few hard statistics on their actual practice, our extensive investigations of more than 20 companies convinced us that European managers do indeed tend to differ significantly from their American counterparts. In fact, we found that many of them were able to articulate these differences quite clearly.

In the first place, European managers think themselves more pointedly concerned with how to survive over the long run under intensely competitive conditions. Few markets, of course, generate price competition as fierce as in the United States, but European companies face the remorseless necessity of exporting to other national markets or perishing.

The figures here are startling: manufactured product exports represent more than 35% of total manufacturing sales in France and Germany and nearly 60% in the Benelux countries, as against not quite 10% in the United States. In these export markets, moreover, European products must hold their own against "world class" competitors, lower-priced products from developing countries, and American products selling at attractive devalued dollar prices. To survive this competitive squeeze, European managers feel they must place central emphasis on producing technologically superior products.

Further, the kinds of pressures from European labor unions and national governments virtually force them to take a consistently long-term view in decision making. German managers, for example, must negotiate major decisions at the plant level with worker-dominated works councils; in turn, these decisions are subject to review by supervisory boards (roughly equivalent to American boards of directors), half of whose membership is worker elected. Together with strict national legislation, the pervasive influence of labor unions makes it extremely difficult to change employment levels or production locations. Not surprisingly, labor costs in Northern Europe have more than doubled in the past decade and are now the highest in the world.

To be successful in this environment of strictly constrained options, European managers feel they must employ a decision-making apparatus that grinds very fine—and very deliberately. They must simply outthink and outmanage their competitors. Now, American managers also have their strategic options hedged about by all kinds of restrictions. But those restrictions have not yet made them as conscious as their European counterparts of the long-term implications of their day-to-day decisions.

As a result, the Europeans see themselves as investing more heavily in cutting-edge technology than the Americans. More often than not, this investment is made to create new product opportunities in advance of consumer demand and not merely in response to market-driven strategy. In case after case, we found the Europeans striving to develop the products and process capabilities with which to lead markets and not simply responding to the current demands of the marketplace. Moreover, in doing this they seem less inclined to integrate backward and more likely to seek maximum leverage from stable long-term relationships with suppliers.

Having never lost sight of the need to be technologically competitive over the long run, European and Japanese managers are extremely careful to make the necessary arrangements and investments today. And their daily concern with the rather basic issue of long-term survival adds perspective to such matters as short-term ROI or rate of growth. The time line by which they manage is long, and it has made them painstakingly attentive to the means for keeping their companies technologically competitive. Of course they pay attention to the numbers. Their profit margins are usually lower than ours, their debt ratios higher. Every tenth of a percent is critical to them. But they are also aware that tomorrow will be no better unless they constantly try to develop new processes, enter new markets, and offer superior—even unique—products. As one senior German executive phrased it recently, "We look at rates of return, too, but only after we ask 'Is it a good product?' "[9]

Creating Economic Value

Americans traveling in Europe and Asia soon learn they must often deal with criticism of our country. Being forced to respond to such criticism can be healthy, for it requires rethinking some basic issues of principle and practice.

We have much to be proud about and little to be ashamed of relative to most other countries. But sometimes the criticism of others is uncomfortably close to the mark. The comments of our overseas competitors on American business practices contain enough truth to require our thoughtful consideration. What is behind the decline in competitiveness of U.S. business? Why do U.S. companies have such apparent difficulties competing with foreign producers of established products, many of which originated in the United States?

For example, Japanese televisions dominate some market segments, even though many U.S. producers now enjoy the same low labor cost advantages of offshore production. The German machine tool and automotive producers continue their inroads into U.S. domestic markets, even though their labor rates are now higher than those in the United States and the famed German worker in German factories almost as likely to be Turkish or Italian as German.

The responsibility for these problems may rest in part on government policies that either overconstrain or undersupport U.S. producers. But if our foreign critics are correct, the long-term solution to America's problems may not be correctable simply by changing our government's tax laws, monetary policies, and regulatory practices. It will also require some fundamental changes in management attitudes and practices.

It would be an oversimplification to assert that the only reason for the decline in competitiveness of U.S. companies is that our managers devote too much attention and energy to using existing resources more efficiently. It would also oversimplify the issue, although possibly to a lesser extent, to say that it is due purely and simply to their tendency to neglect technology as a competitive weapon.

Companies cannot become more innovative simply by increasing R&D investments or by conducting more basic research. Each of the decisions we have described directly affects several functional areas of management, and major conflicts can only be reconciled at senior executive levels. The benefits favoring the more innovative aggressive option in each case depend more on intangible factors than do their efficiency-oriented alternatives.

Senior managers who are less informed about their industry and its confederation of parts suppliers, equipment suppliers, workers, and customers or who have less time to consider the long-term implications of their interactions are likely to exhibit a noninnovative bias in their choices. Tight financial controls with a short-term emphasis will also bias choices toward the less innovative, less technologically aggressive alternatives.

The key to long-term success—even survival—in business is what it has always been: to invest, to innovate, to lead, to create value where none existed before. Such determination, such striving to excel, requires leaders—not *just* controllers, market analysts, and portfolio managers. In our preoccupation with the braking systems and exterior trim, we may have neglected the drive trains of our corporations.

Notes

1. Ryohei Suzuki, "Worldwide Expansion of U.S. Exports—A Japanese View," *Sloan Management Review*, Spring 1979, p. 1.

2. *Business Week*, February 16, 1976, p. 57.

3. Burton G. Malkiel, "Productivity—The Problem Behind the Headlines," *HBR*, May–June 1979, p. 81.

4. Roger Bennett and Robert Cooper, "Beyond the Marketing Concept," *Business Horizons*, June 1979, p. 76.

5. J. Hugh Davidson, "Why Most New Consumer Brands Fail," *HBR*, March–April 1976, p. 117.

6. *Business Week*, February 16, 1976, p. 57.

7. Eric von Hippel, "The Dominant Role of Users in the Scientific Instrument Innovation Process," MIT Sloan School of Management Working Paper 75-764, January 1975.

8. *Dun's Review*, July 1978, p. 39.

9. *Business Week*, March 3, 1980, p. 76.

2
Managing as if Tomorrow Mattered

ROBERT H. HAYES and DAVID A. GARVIN

In evaluating proposed investments, American managers have turned increasingly to sophisticated analytic techniques. Their goal has been greater rationality in making investment decisions, yet their accomplishment has often been quite different—a serious underinvestment in the capital stock (the productive capacity, technology, and worker skills) on which their companies rest. As a result they have unintentionally jeopardized their companies' futures.

How can these managers have been so misled? Their intentions were commendable: to make investment decisions that responded in an objective, rational fashion to the economic facts of life. But, as the authors of this article claim, they may have placed their confidence in a set of techniques that are, in certain critical ways, profoundly biased against investment.

Few economic decisions are as difficult as those involving the choice between present and future consumption. Some people, unable to place much faith in the future, happily borrow to fund present pleasures; others, with longer time horizons, are wary of such "fly now, pay later" policies. They fear that the required payments, when viewed up close, will be much more burdensome than they appear from a distance.

Investments in plant and equipment are especially sensitive to such differences in outlook and perception. Ethical issues make these decisions more difficult still, for a company's approach to investments in long-lived capital says much about its sense of obligation to future workers, managers, and stockholders.

Highly sophisticated analytic techniques now dominate the capital budgeting process at most companies. Rare is the manager who will make an important investment decision without first carefully calculating its net present value or internal rate of return. Although these methods have been around for years, managers are using them more and more today as aids to rational decision making. A 1971 survey of 184 large manufacturing companies showed that 57% used discounting techniques to evaluate investment projects; only 19% had done so in 1959. A 1975 survey of 33 major corporations indicated even wider acceptance, with 94% of the companies using discounting calculations.[1]

As these techniques have gained ever wider use in investment decision making, the growth of capital investment and R&D spending in this country has slowed. We believe this to be more than a simple coincidence. We submit that the discounting approach has contributed to a decreased willingness to invest for the following reasons: (1) it is often based on misperceptions of the past and present economic environment, and (2) it is biased against investment because of critical errors in the way the theory is applied. Bluntly stated, the willingness of managers to view the future through the reversed telescope of discounted cash flow is shortchanging the futures of their companies.

A Decline in Reinvestment

Raw data on recent capital spending and R&D investment by the private sector tell a tale of modest but steady increase—until, that is, one adjusts for inflation or for changes in GNP and the size of the work force. Then the figures tell a different story. Although gross business investment as a percentage of GNP has remained roughly constant in real terms since the 1950s, the capital invested per labor hour and the share of GNP devoted to net new investment have both declined over the last decade.

Between 1948 and 1973, for example, the ratio of the net book value of capital equipment to the number of labor hours worked grew at about 3% per year. Since then it has increased at only about one-half that rate. Moreover, the growth in the ratio of net capital stock to the number of full-time equivalent employed workers—a figure that adjusts for changes in the hours per week worked by the average employee—reveals an ever greater post-1973 decline.

Spending on R&D presents an equally disturbing picture. Viewed as a percentage of GNP, total U.S. investment in R&D fell steadily between 1967 and 1978. In basic research, which involves longer time horizons, the picture is even bleaker. Measured in constant dollars, investment peaked in the late 1960s, then dipped, and did not regain its earlier level until 1978. As a percentage of GNP, corporate spending on basic research is today only two-thirds of what it was in the mid-1960s.

American managers are also underinvesting in human resource development, especially in critical industrial skills. The average age of experienced tool and die makers, for example, is approaching 50 years. If present trends continue, within the next decade this vital reservoir of skills—necessary in a variety of industries and already in short supply—threatens to dry up. Similarly, the Department of Labor estimates an annual demand for 22,000 skilled machinists during the 1980s, yet only about 2,800 graduate each year from various apprenticeship programs. Much the same is true for skilled assemblers, forging-machine operators, and optical workers.

Taken together, this evidence suggests that business spending on many crucial activities has been lagging badly in recent years. What lies behind this dangerous slowdown in long-term investment?

Searching for Answers

There is no shortage of popular explanations. Most fall into one of the following categories:

1. *Managerial theories.* Blame business itself for the emphasis on near-term profitability that now dominates managerial decision making. Observers attribute this myopia to a variety of causes: the shift to multidivisional organizations, which typically use short-term financial measures as the primary means for evaluating managerial performance; the desire of younger managers for rapid advancement, which tends to limit the time a person spends at any one job; and pressure from the financial community.

2. *Environmental theories.* Cite as culprits inflation, high income and capital gains taxes, rising energy prices, constrictive federal regulations, erratic shifts in public policy, and other features of the business environment.

3. *Financial theories.* Point to the recent increase in mergers and acquisitions as being responsible for the decline in direct investment. According to this view, managers are simply responding rationally to current economic conditions when they purchase inexpensive used assets rather than invest in more expensive—and risky—new assets.

Some of these theories are more persuasive than others. That American managers tend to be more concerned with short-term financial performance than their German and Japanese counterparts is, for example, now widely recognized. So, too, is the effect on investment of dramatic changes in the economic environment, although other developed countries have experienced similar shifts during the past decade without a corresponding slackening of investment.[2] Increases in merger activity and in the funds devoted to corporate acquisitions, however, do not explain this decline in capital spending.

Corporate acquisitions are neither a substitute for direct investment nor a cheap way of acquiring plant and equipment. The bargain-basement character of such activity is an illusion resulting from attention to the wrong

A DECLINE IN REINVESTMENT

set of figures. Typically, analysts cite data that compare the market value of U.S. companies (as measured by the sum of their outstanding debt and equity) with their replacement value to justify the claim that assets can be obtained more cheaply by acquisition than by direct investment.

Government figures do indeed show that market value, measured in this way, has been well below replacement cost in each year since 1972. Most mergers, however, involve acquisition prices substantially above supposed market value because some premium is generally required to entice managers and shareholders to approve the sale. Should a bidding war develop, the acquisition price can escalate dramatically—often to more than double the company's market value.

Focusing only on acquisitions that have actually happened, rather than on the market value-to-replacement cost ratios of all companies, gives a different perspective on the financial attractiveness of mergers. In the 1960s and early 1970s, actual acquisition prices averaged from 20% to 60% *more* than the estimated replacement costs of acquired companies. In recent years, this margin has declined somewhat, but prices have still fallen only to a level about equal to replacement costs. Used assets may have become cheaper over the past few years, but they are not at all the bargain that many managers seem to think they are.

Indeed, even if these assets were underpriced, their attractiveness would not explain America's declining capital investment, for at the national level heightened merger activity does not substitute directly for stepped-up physical investment. Acquisitions, after all, are essentially transfers of funds between two business entities (except, of course, for the small percentage siphoned off by investment bankers, lawyers, and accountants). These transfers, therefore, should not diminish total corporate investment, although they may affect the decisions of particular companies.

Nor can the problem be attributed to a lack of capital caused by inflation, reduced profitability, higher taxes, or government-mandated nonproductive expenditures. During the past 10 years, the inflation-adjusted aftertax return on equity for U.S. corporations has roughly equaled its level in the 1950s. The ratio of shareholder dividends to total corporate operating cash flow, however, was 11% higher in the late 1970s than in the late 1960s—and 30% higher in 1980. The ratio of investment in new capital equipment to corporate cash flow, on the other hand, has generally declined since the 1950s. The problem is not that U.S. business lacks the money to spend; it is simply not spending the money it has in the same ways that it used to.

Is this behavior evidence of a foolish, but unintentional, mistake on the part of American managers? Not necessarily. They appear to believe completely in the legitimacy of their investment decisions and in the techniques on which they are based. These methods, however, have profound conceptual weaknesses that are not always recognized, and the answers they

Discounting the Future

The theory is simple: a dollar received today is worth more than a dollar received tomorrow. How much more depends on the current uses to which the dollar can be put. If it can earn 5% interest, a dollar today will be worth $1.05 after a year; if 10%, $1.10. Conversely, at a 5% interest rate, a dollar received a year from now is worth only $1.00 ÷ 1.05, or 95.2 cents today; at a rate of 10%, 90.9 cents. This determination of a future dollar's present value is, according to accepted theory, the appropriate way to compare future benefits with present costs.

Extending the theory to capital investment is also simple: a company pays a certain amount of money to receive a series of returns stretching off into the future, each of which can be translated into an equivalent amount today. The difference between the amount invested and the sum of the discounted returns determines whether the proposed investment is more attractive than the best alternative use of the funds. Notice that this calculation requires several critical estimates: the size of the anticipated investment, the amount and timing of the resulting cash flows, and the rate of return that could be realized if the capital project were not approved and the funds were directed elsewhere. This last figure is generally termed the company's opportunity rate or, more prosaically, its hurdle rate.

Today such calculations have, because of their apprent rationality, gained the upper hand in the evaluation of new investment proposals. Yet these techniques are as subject to misperceptions and biases in application as are other less formal methods. Consider the following example.

A company with a set of assets—its capital stock—worth $100 million generates an annual aftertax cash flow of $12 million. Here capital stock includes not only operating assets (the net value of plant and equipment, inventories, and accounts receivable) but also the productive value of such intangible assets as human skills and the residual value of the R&D and advertising expenditures that have built up over the years. Now, say this capital stock is deteriorating (that is, slowly losing its capacity to generate earnings) at a rate of 5% per year. Further, any cash not reinvested in the business can be invested in other activities—either directly by management or via dividend payments to stockholders—that will eventually generate cash flows equivalent to an 8% rate of return.

Please note that our use of the term *deterioration* is related to, but not precisely the same as, the usual accounting definition of *depreciation*. We are not concerned with the amortization of previous investments in fixed

DISCOUNTING THE FUTURE   41

assets for the purpose of calculating taxes or reporting profits. Instead, we are interested in the rate of erosion in the earnings-generating power of the company's total capital stock, a rate that in practice is often highly irregular.

Skimping on reinvestment may therefore take other forms than not replacing equipment as it depreciates in value. Managers can, for example, allow the productivity of existing equipment to deteriorate faster than normal by using it more hours per week than before or by replacing it with less productive, and usually less expensive, equipment as it wears out. Or, more subtly, they can replace it with machinery based on dated technology. Similarly, managers can allow spending on R&D, advertising, and personnel development to fall below historical levels.

Back to our example. Simply to preserve the earnings-generating capacity of its capital stock, the company must reinvest $5 million (the annual deterioration, at a rate of 5%, of a $100 million capital base) of its yearly $12 million cash flow. Doing so ensures only that its capital stock will continue to be $100 million and that future earnings will stay at $12 million per year.

The remaining $7 million of cash flow can be invested outside the business, either directly or indirectly via dividends to shareholders. The discounted value of these annual outflows, assuming an opportunity rate of 8%, equals $7 million ÷ .08, or $87.5 million (see Exhibit 1). This $87.5 million is, in a sense, the value today of a goose that will lay each and every year golden eggs that are worth $7 million—providing, of course, that the proceeds from these eggs can be invested in activities earning 8%.

But is this the best way to manage the goose? Could the company raise the present value of these annual cash outflows either by taking more capital out of the business each year and thus cutting its earnings-generating capacity or by taking out less and building up its capital stock?

What would be the effect, for example, of increasing the cash throwoff from 58.3% ($7 million ÷ $12 million) to 70% of the annual cash flow? The first year $8.4 million would be available for outside investment instead of the previous $7 million. This figure could not, however, be sustained over time, for without adequate reinvestment the company's capital stock would gradually deteriorate and thus steadily reduce the value of the cash throwoff.

But what about the present value of the throwoffs resulting from this strategy of "more now, less later"? According to the calculations in Exhibit 2, it actually rises from $87.5 million to $89.36 million.

In other words, present-value calculations support a decision to operate on the goose and remove some of its golden eggs prematurely, even though doing so impairs its future egg-laying ability. In fact, such calculations always justify a policy of progressive disinvestment as long as a company's net return on internal investment (the amount available, after deterioration, for the payment of capital charges and additions to earned surplus—12% minus 5% in our example) is less than its net return from external investment (8%).

Exhibit 1. The Present Value of Different Reinvestment Rates: Maintaining Value of Existing Capital Stock (in $ millions)

Premise:
Company reinvests $5 million every year (maintaining its earnings-generating capability) and invests the remaining $7 million each year outside its existing business.

Year	Present Value Factor @ 8%	Invested in Company	Invested Outside	Present Value of Outside Investment
1	.926	$5	$7	$6.48
2	.857	5	7	6.00
3	.794	5	7	5.56
4	.735	5	7	5.15
5	.681	5	7	4.77
6	.630	5	7	4.41
7	.583	5	7	4.08
8	.540	5	7	3.78
9	.500	5	7	3.50
etc.	.	.	.	.
.	.	.	.	.
.	.	.	.	.

Sum of present values — $87.50

In this simple case, we can calculate discounted present value directly: $\dfrac{\$7}{.08}$ = $87.5 million

Note: There is disagreement over the proper rate for discounting future payments. Some argue that it should be the company's opportunity rate (its average rate of return on alternative investments), while others prefer the company's cost of capital, the rate demanded by the stock market for those in the same risk class. Theoretically, in the long run the two rates should converge because the cost of capital will rise toward the opportunity rate as increasingly risky investments are undertaken. But the long run takes forever to arrive, and in the short run—where the cost of capital is usually less than the opportunity rate—most companies use the rate of return of the minimally acceptable investment (as determined by management) as the discount rate in present value calculations. We have followed this latter practice.

Exhibit 2. Gradual Disinvestment (in $ millions)

Premise:
Company reinvests only 30% of the cash throwoff each year (allowing its earnings-generating capability to deteriorate gradually) and reinvests the remaining 70% outside its existing business.

Year	Beginning-of-Year Capital Stock	Cash Generated During Year	Deterioration During Year	Reinvested in Company	Invested Outside	Present Value of Outside Investment
1	$100.00	$12.00	$5.00	$3.60	$8.40	$7.78
2	98.60	11.83	4.93	3.55	8.28	7.10
3	97.22	11.67	4.86	3.50	8.17	6.48
4	95.86	11.50	4.79	3.45	8.05	5.92
5	94.52	11.34	4.73	3.40	7.94	5.40
6	93.19	11.18	4.66	3.35	7.83	4.93
7	91.89	11.03	4.59	3.31	7.72	4.50
8	90.60	10.87	4.53	3.26	7.61	4.11
9	89.33	10.72	4.47	3.22	7.50	3.75
etc.	.	.	.	.	.	.
.	.	.	.	.	.	.
.	.	.	.	.	.	.

Sum of present values $89.36

We can calculate this discounted present value directly:

$$\frac{(1.0 - 30)(.12)\,100}{.08 + .05 - (.30)(.12)} = \$89.36$$

The Theory's Wobbly Legs

Few managers, of course, view the reinvestment process in quite this stylized fashion. Their job is to evaluate specific investment proposals by discounting the estimated cash flows (after taxes and depreciation) from a proposed investment using a hurdle rate that reflects the minimum acceptable return for proposals of that type. Should a given project not promise to generate profits (after depreciation) equal to those available from investments outside the business, it will be rejected.

According to discounting theory, then, a pattern of progressive disinvestment might make perfect sense. Discounting techniques, however, rest on rather arbitrary assumptions about profitability, asset deterioration, and external investment opportunities. In fact, we believe that much of the decline in investment in capital stock is the result of misperceptions about the changes that have taken place in these three critical variables over the past decade. American managers have acted as though these variables have been moving in such a way as to make direct reinvestment in their existing businesses less and less desirable. But how have these variables actually behaved?

Cash-Generating Rate

Many managers are convinced that the ability of their companies to generate earnings is less today than in the past. They blame global competition, industry maturation, and intrusive government for the decline; yet according to Burton Malkiel and other leading economists, the overall rate of return on equity for U.S. companies, *after adjustment for inflation*, has remained roughly constant for about 30 years.[3] Only during the mid-1960s, when the rate of return rose to double its historical level of about 4.5%, did this pattern change. Even then, the gains were short-lived and earnings soon fell back to their former levels.

Many executives, however, view the rates of return during the mid-1960s as the norm, rather than an aberration. By this standard, things have indeed worsened in recent years. But even though a company's profit margin may have dropped from, say, 10% in 1965 to 5% today, that 10% figure is not a reasonable reference point for historical comparison.

Nor, in fact, is the 5% figure always reliable. When managers attempt to net out the impact of inflation on the profitability of their businesses, they usually address only the asset side of the balance sheet. They reduce profits by the amount that inflation has increased the value of inventories and recalculate depreciation on the basis of the replacement cost, rather than the historical cost, of equipment. Rarely, however, do they acknowledge that their long-term debt also declines in value during an inflationary period. By ignoring the debit side of the balance sheet, many managers have overestimated—perhaps by as much as 50%—the decline in profitability attributable to inflation.[4]

Deterioration Rate

Even if the perception of a long-term decline in corporate profitability is illusory, there is good reason to believe that the rate of deterioation of capital stock has increased. Inflation is partly to blame, for the cost of many capital goods has risen faster than the prices of the products they make; consequently, it is more expensive to replace the fixed assets that a company employs in its business. Between 1970 and 1979, for example, the price of metal-forming machine tools almost tripled, but the price of all manufactured durables increased by little more than a factor of two. Such high prices often deter reinvestment or limit it to some fixed percentage of annual sales.

Also responsible, of course, are rising energy prices, which have so burdened operating costs that some production processes are no longer competitive. The rapid obsolescence of manufacturing equipment—whether because of high energy consumption, restrictive government regulations, or declining efficiency compared with the newer process technologies—can appear prohibitively expensive to remedy. When replacement costs are in the stratosphere, the need to reinvest in capital stock can easily paralyze, not galvanize, a manager's willingness to reinvest in existing businesses.

Hurdle Rate

Despite their perceptions of a decline in the profitability, and an increase in the rate of deterioration, of their companies' assets, American managers have not made a corresponding reduction in the hurdle rates they employ in capital budgeting.

These rates are typically quite high, often in the range of 25% to 40%, and there is some evidence that they have been rising over the past decade. A recent survey, for example, shows that about 25% of American manufacturing companies require expenditures for modernization and replacement of equipment to pay off within three years. Ten years ago only 20% had required that rapid a payoff. Shorter payback periods imply higher hurdle rates, just as higher hurdle rates imply a stronger emphasis on near-term benefits.

As with most of the arbitrary numbers that find their way into a company's systems and procedures, these hurdle rates are often used without question, even by executives who profess to be open minded. The chairman of a leading American equipment manufacturing company recently described himself as an executive who encouraged his managers to take risks; at the same time, he insisted that all new investments produce a 25% return during the first five years.

Such hurdle rates often bear little resemblance either to a company's real cost of capital (even after appropriate adjustment for differences in risk) or to the actual rates of return (net of deterioration replenishment) that the company can reasonably expect to earn from alternative investments. Again and again we have observed the use of pretax hurdle rates of 30% or more in companies whose actual pretax returns on investment were less than 20%.

How do managers normally defend this practice? First, they claim that an artificially high rate helps protect them from unforeseen reductions in cash throwoffs that are triggered by competitors' actions, unexpected inflationary increases in investment costs, and number fudging by subordinates anxious to have a project approved for personal reasons. Second, they argue that high hurdle rates increase motivation and that difficult to achieve targets tend to spur good performance.

As attractive as these explanations appear at first glance, their logic is faulty. Systematic adjustments for risk are quite appropriate when computing present values, but many of the hurdle rates that we have seen contain unreasonably high risk components. Moreover, using such rates as a motivational tool undermines their worth in evaluating investment opportunities. For one thing, they often discourage investment in existing businesses whose risks are known and direct it toward businesses whose risks are less understood.

Such behavior also reflects a growing preference among managers for acquisitions over internal investments. Despite considerable evidence to the contrary, American managers appear to believe that aggressive acquisition programs make possible both higher long-term growth rates and greater profitability. Many are so firmly convinced that the grass is greener in almost any industry other than their own that they are far less tough minded in evaluating acquisition candidates than they are in assessing internal investment proposals.

The key assumptions in this approach for analyzing investment proposals—assumptions about rates of profitability, deterioration, and acceptable return—are highly unreliable and prone to individual bias. Managers may have an accurate sense of their businesses' past profitability, but their beliefs about future profitability depend heavily on their basic optimism and confidence in the economy. They may know to several decimal points the average depreciation rate for their industry, but they are less likely to know the real deterioration rate of their companies' total capital stock. Even more uncertain is their assessment of the profit opportunities and deterioration rates in businesses other than their own.

Bitten, perhaps, by the merger bug and unwilling to adjust their inflated hurdle rates, many American managers have found reinvestment in existing businesses less and less desirable. Under siege in a changing world, they recall the economic Camelot of the 1960s and believe that it still exists somewhere, waiting to be found outside their corporate bunker. Had they placed less faith in the misleading objectivity of their discounting techniques, they might instead be spending their time and resources reinforcing their own bunker's walls.

The Theory's Blind Spots

Discounting methods are biased against investment in new capital stock in still other ways. Present-value comparisons are especially difficult to make if the projects under review have different lifetimes: when projects are of equivalent length, present-value calculations favor those with shorter payback periods; when projects are of unequal length, those with longer lives often appear more attractive than those with shorter lives. Few investments, however, are intended as "doomsday projects" for which there is no successor. Managers usually assume that at the end of a current investment's lifetime, another, involving similar activities, will begin. Thus, unless corrected for, discounting's focus on the profitability of initial projects can lead to a series of absurd decisions.

Narrow use of the present-value criterion will, for example, almost inevitably argue for expanding facilities already in place rather than for building a new plant in a different location. The initial investment is normally much less, the returns more immediate. Over the long run, however, a series of such decisions—each backed by its own impeccable logic—can lead to ponderous, outmoded dinosaurs that are easy prey for the smaller, more modern, and better focused plants of competitors.

Consider the experience of one producer of large machinery that opened a simple assembly operation in the 1920s. As sales increased, the plant kept expanding both the size and number of its processes until today the company finds itself with a mammoth and uneconomical complex. Now it is trying to figure out how to break apart a manufacturing operation that appears to have grown like Topsy over the years, although each addition made perfect sense at the time.

Another manufacturer, which recently focused attention on its home plant, discovered a collection of more than 40 multilevel buildings producing an extraordinary variety of low-demand items using equipment that dated back before World War II. Rather than undertake the immense task of modernizing this outmoded plant, whose condition was the result of a series of apparently rational investment decisions over a long period, the company reluctantly closed it down.

For similar reasons, the present-value criterion will often suggest delaying the replacement of a piece of equipment by another, more modern machine that performs roughly the same function. The economic benefit of delaying purchase for a year, say, is seldom offset by the efficiencies obtained from using the new machine on comparable activities. Less obvious benefits from increased worker skills and capabilities, new products, and a different cost structure are harder to document in advance and so do not fit neatly into a present-value analysis. In fact, to counteract this bias against modernization, some companies are experimenting with a "sunset law" for capital equipment, under which a piece of equipment is automatically replaced at the end of a predetermined period unless a special review process decides otherwise. (See the Appendix following this article for an example of how one company handles its machine replacement.)

The Logic of Disinvestment

The threat implicit in discounting techniques is not limited to misperceptions, too short time horizons, or a bias against major modernization projects. It extends to the very ability—and willingness—of managers to ward off the attacks of aggressive competitors.

Consider, for example, two companies that share the market in a price-sensitive industry. Initially, both use the same production processes and have similar cost structures. A new manufacturing process, however, promises to reduce variable costs significantly. Company A, with a high hurdle rate, rejects the investment out of hand as being insufficiently profitable; Company B, with a lower hurdle rate, decides to buy the new equipment.

Both companies perform similar discounting calculations to weigh the advantages of the proposed investment. They arrive at opposite conclusions because of the differences in the hurdle rates employed and in the importance placed on maintaining competitive vigor. In theory, both should be satisfied with the results.

Company B, once its new equipment is in place, quite naturally proceeds to compete aggressively for market share by lowering prices. Its new manufacturing process, after all, gives it much lower variable costs and requires high production volumes for maximum efficiency.

Can Company A respond? Its outdated equipment places it at a distinct competitive disadvantage. Moreover, its competitor's price reductions have so reduced the profitability of its existing business that the investment required to upgrade its facilities looks even less attractive than before. At the least, Company A will lose market share; at the worst, it could be driven out of the business entirely and, perhaps, be forced to use its remaining capital to acquire another business, one apparently better able to meet its high hurdle rate.

Many American companies today find themselves in a position much like that of Company A. The problem is not that reliance on discounting techniques inevitably leads to inaccurate results but rather that managers can all too easily hide behind the apparent rationality of such financial analyses while sidestepping the hard decisions necessary to keep their companies competitive.

One reason companies so often become trapped in this sort of disinvestment spiral—deferred investment leading to reduced profitability, which further reduces the incentive to invest—is that discounting techniques make the implicit assumption that investment processes are reversible. That is, if one sells an asset, one can always buy it back; if one delays an investment, one can always make it at some later date with no penalty other than that implied by the company's discount rate.

No company, however, can be sure of recovering lost ground quite so easily. To regain its position, a company may have to spend a good deal more than if it had made the investment when first proposed. As time passes, downward spirals become much more difficult to arrest. Moreover, as the experience of both Ford and Chrysler attests, postponed investments (in downsizing in the mid-1970s) may not be reversible; complete recovery may be impossible.

This irreversibility is partly rooted in the dynamics of human organizations. Companies are collections not simply of tangible assets but of people as well, and the bonds among them reflect understandings and commitments developed over a long time. Such bonds need constant support and reinforcement; once they begin to dissolve, an organization loses its sense of movement and often falls prey to a sense of resignation. Morale sags, performance suffers, and employees—generally the best ones—begin to leave. Faced with these circumstances, top management often concludes that a division or product line is unsalvageable and purposely continues the process of disinvestment.

Reversing the Disinvestment Spiral

It is both difficult and costly for a company to extract itself from such a spiral, for usually no single investment can repair the damage. Instead, simultaneous investments in several projects are often necessary to achieve an acceptable return. If managers evaluated each of these projects individually with no attention to the interactions among them, they might reject some as being insufficiently profitable. Unfortunately, the capital budgeting procedures that most companies follow today do not readily accommodate such interdependencies (what economists call "indivisibilities") among investment projects. The same logic that got a company into such a predicament can therefore impede its attempt to extract itself.

No company can break out of a disinvestment spiral by relying on the same financial logic that got it there. The only remedy is to understand the shape of that logic as well as the direction in which it leads—and then to take an opposite course. Managers must be willing to reinvest at the very time such action appears least attractive. They must stop pouring funds into refurbishing their images and upgrade their factories instead. They must resist the lure of unfamiliar businesses and mind their own.

Beyond all else, capital investment represents an act of faith, a belief that the future will be as promising as the present, together with a commitment to making that future happen. Modern financial theory argues that under certain "reasonable" assumptions, disinvestment is a logical and appropriate course of action. Today, the future consequences of a disinvestment strategy, as seen through the reversed telescope of discounting, may appear inconsequential; but once tomorrow arrives, those who must deal with it are certain to feel differently.

Notes

1. See Thomas P. Klammer, *Empirical Evidence of the Adoption of Sophisticated Capital Budgeting Techniques," Journal of Business*, July 1972, p. 393, and Eugene F. Brigham, *Hurdle Rates for Screening Capital Expenditure Proposals," Financial Management*, Autumn 1975, p. 18.

2. Many of these points have been argued earlier in Robert H. Hayes and William J. Abernathy, *Managing Our Way to Economic Decline," HBR,* July–August 1980, p. 67, and Chapter 1, this volume.

3. See Burton G. Malkiel, *The Capital Formation Problem in the United States," Journal of Finance,* May 1979, p. 291, and "Unraveling the Mysteries of Corporate Profits," *Fortune,* August 27, 1979, p. 90.

4. Franco Modigliani and Richard A. Cohn, *Inflation, Rational Valuation, and the Market," Financial Analysts Journal,* March–April 1979, p. 24.

Suggested Readings

Harold Bierman, Jr. and Jerome E. Haas, "Are High Cut-Off Rates a Fallacy?" Financial Executive, *June 1973, p. 90.*

Peter K. Clark, "Investment in the 1970s: Theory, Performance, and Prediction," Brookings Papers on Economic Activity, *Vol. 1, 1979.*

Peter K. Clark, "Issues in the Analysis of Capital Formation and Productivity Growth," Brookings Papers on Economic Activity, *Vol. 2, 1979.*

Economic Report of the President *(Washington, DC: U.S. Government Printing Office, 1981).*

Anthony C. Fisher, John V. Krutilla, and Charles C. Cicchetti, "The Economics of Environmental Preservation: A Theoretical and Empirical Analysis," American Economic Review, *September 1972, p. 605.*

Claude Henry, "Investment Decisions under Uncertainty: The 'Irreversibility Effect'," American Economic Review, *December 1974, p. 1006.*

National Machine Tool Builders' Association, *1980/81 Economic Handbook of the Machine Tool Industry.*

Malcolm S. Salter and Wolf A. Weinhold, "Merger Trends and Prospects for the 1980s" (HBS Working Paper 80–49, October 1980).

F.M. Scherer, "No Boon in the Merger Boom," Business and Society Review, *Winter 1979–1980, p. 17.*

Science Indicators—1978, *report of the National Science Board (Washington, DC: U.S. Government Printing Office, 1979).*

Appendix: Toolmaker Practices What It Preaches*

Machine tool and machinery builders may urge customers to buy the newest and latest, but in their own shops they frequently make do with older equipment. Not Ingersoll Milling Machine Company, Rockford, Illinois. There, each production department manager must annually write a justification to *keep* any machine that's over seven years old. The only generally accepted reason for not replacing equipment is that a new machine doesn't offer any significant improvements over older models. The average age of machines at Ingersoll is six years. In the tool industry as a whole, 76% of the machines are over ten years old, and 40% are over 20 years old.

Industry Week, September 1980, p. 11.

3
Survival Strategies in a Hostile Environment

WILLIAM K. HALL

How are such domestic manufacturing industries as steel, tire and rubber, automotive, heavy-duty truck and construction equipment, home appliance, beer, and cigarette evolving in the face of today's adverse external pressures? Given the lower growth, inflationary, regulatory, and competitive impacts, what business strategies are appropriate? Which strategic choices offer the best chances for survival, growth, and ROI in a hostile environment? This author investigates these issues and presents some preliminary findings from an ongoing research project which explores the strategic and structural changes that took place in the 1970s and that are expected to continue into the 1980s.

As economists, managers, and industry analysts pause to look back on the past decade, there remains little doubt that the business environment in the United States grew increasingly hostile during the 1970s. More important, there is now little doubt that this hostile environment will continue (and perhaps even worsen) during the decade ahead, reflecting the combined effects of:

☐ Slow erratic growth in domestic and world markets.
☐ Intensified inflationary pressures on manufacturing and distribution costs.
☐ Intensified regulatory pressures on business conduct and investment decisions.
☐ Intensified competition, both from traditional domestic competitors and also from the new wave of foreign competitors entering U.S. markets with different objectives and frequently lower ROI expectations.

As a result of these growing pressures, large U.S. manufacturing corporations are witnessing a major evolution in industry structures and competitive behaviors. Many structures that were stable and highly profitable during the "go-go" decade of the 1960s are now moving toward instability and marginal profitability.

Moreover, the broad range of corporate strategies and business "success formulas" which brought prosperity in those earlier years are no longer working. Instead, these are being replaced with a much narrower range of strategic choices that are becoming essential to survive in the hostile environment ahead.

The purpose of this article is to present some preliminary findings from an ongoing research project that my colleagues and I are conducting to explore these strategic and structural changes in more depth. This project is focusing on these broad questions:

1. How are industry structures in the mature markets evolving in the face of the adverse external pressures of the late 1970s?
2. Given this evolution, what business strategies are appropriate? Which strategic choices give the best chances for survival, growth, and return in the hostile environment ahead?

In-Depth Investigation

To examine these issues, I selected eight major domestic manufacturing industries for comprehensive study because of their importance to national and/or regional economic development and also because the adverse external trends of the 1970s have been especially severe in their impact on them. As a result, during the 1970s, all eight industries underwent a significant structural change which is expected to continue into the 1980s. Within these industries, I examined the strategies and evolving competitive positions of the 64 largest companies by using a combination of public data sources and field interviews.

In examining the impact of external pressures on these companies, I found that the eight industries either matured during the 1970s or will mature in the 1980s, resulting in lower growth records and growth expectations as shown in Exhibit 1. Although the industries (on average) exceeded national economic growth rates in the 1950s and 1960s, they grew only slightly faster than the GNP in the 1970s, and they are projected to grow significantly more slowly than the U.S. economy in the 1980s.

During this maturation period, these eight industries, which are capital, raw material, and labor intensive, have been subjected to heavy inflationary pressures that cannot easily be price recovered. All are being forced by regulatory agencies to make major investments to comply with new occu-

Exhibit 1. Compound Annual Real Growth Rates in Demand—United States (eight basic industries)

	1950–1970	1971–1980	1980 Forecast[a]
Industrial goods			
Primary products			
Steel	4.0%	2.2%	1.5%-2.5%
Tire and rubber	4.2	1.4	1.0-1.5
Intermediate products			
Heavy-duty trucks	7.0	2.8	2.5
Construction and materials handling equipment	7.8	3.6	2.3
Consumer goods			
Durable products			
Automotive	4.8	3.5	2.0-3.0
Major home appliances	6.2	2.9	2.3-2.8
Nondurable products			
Beer	3.1	2.5	2.3
Cigarettes	1.6	1.0	0
Average growth rates—eight industries	**4.8%**	**2.4%**	**1.9%**
Average growth rates—U.S. GNP	**3.7%**	**2.3%**	**2.5%**

[a]Based on economic forecasts and industry projections.

pational safety and health regulations and with new product safety, performance, and environmental protection standards.

In addition to the domestic pressures, foreign competition has been harsh in the eight basic industries selected for study. Foreign competitors have achieved significant market shares in three of the industries—steel, tire and rubber, and automotive; moderate shares in two—heavy-duty trucks and construction and materials handling equipment; and entry positions in the other three—major home appliances, beer, and cigarettes.

Because many of these foreign competitors are either nationalized, quasinationalized, or highly salient in their own countries, they are frequently willing to accept lower returns in U.S. markets, offsetting these lower returns against unemployment, balance of payments, and capital gains at home. Although these foreign approaches have been criticized as unfair, the results have altered U.S. domestic industry structures in all eight cases.

Needless to say, the net effect of these adverse trends has made life anything but pleasant for managers and companies in these basic industries.

Profitability and sales growth levels have generally fallen to or below the average manufacturing returns in the U.S. economy (Exhibit 2). And industry spokesmen frequently speak out, urging either public assistance or some type of return to the simpler, less painful world of the 1960s.

As one senior executive I interviewed commented: "Maybe I should have accepted that job as an IBM systems engineer after graduation from college. It sure would be fun to look forward to going to work in the morning." Despite the outcries, the adverse external trends haven't gone away, and structural evolution continues at a slow, but inevitable, pace.

The heavy-duty truck manufacturing industry provides an excellent example of this evolution. In the early 1960s, spurred by rapid growth in the economy and by the completion of the U.S. interstate highway system, the industry grew at more than 8% per year. Eight major manufacturers—International Harvester, General Motors, Ford, Mack, White Motor, Diamond Reo, Chrysler, and Paccar—participated fairly equally in this growth, producing 60 truck models to serve the rapidly growing light-heavy and heavy-duty segments (19,000 pounds and greater gross vehicle weight).

However, by the late 1970s, annual growth had slowed to less than 3%. Emission regulations and inflation had raised unit costs. Investments for new truck model development had slowed to the extent that the number of models had dropped from 60 to 35 by 1979.

As a result of this movement toward a hostile environment, Chrysler

Exhibit 2. Financial Returns and Revenue Growth Rates, 1975–1979 (eight basic industries)

	Return on Equity	Return on Capital	EPS Growth	Revenue Growth
Steel	7.1%	5.7%	5.5%	10.4%
Tire and rubber	7.4	5.9	3.9	9.6
Heavy-duty trucks[a]	15.4	11.6	13.8	13.8
Construction and materials handling equipment	15.4	10.7	16.8	13.0
Automotive[a]	15.4	11.6	13.8	13.8
Major home appliances	10.1	9.0	3.2	6.8
Beer	14.1	10.2	6.2	12.4
Cigarettes	18.2	10.5	8.9	12.2
Average—eight industries	**12.9%**	**9.4%**	**9.0%**	**11.5%**
Average *Fortune* "1,000" company	**15.1%**	**11.0%**	**13.1%**	**13.1%**

[a] All vehicle manufacturers.

closed its heavy-duty truck manufacturing operation, Diamond Reo was in bankruptcy, and White lingered near receivership. Both Mack and International Harvester had lost significant market share and were searching for foreign assistance or major cost-cutting programs to maintain their viability. Of the eight healthy domestic competitors in the early 1960s, only three—General Motors, Ford, and Paccar—maintained free-standing, vibrant, competitive positions as they entered the decade of the 1980s.

Similar moves toward lower profitability and consolidation occurred in all eight industries as the hostile environment took its evolutionary toll. In steel, Bethlehem announced in 1977 the largest corporate quarterly loss in U.S. history up to that time (exceeded by Chrysler two years later and U.S. Steel in late 1979), Jones & Laughlin and Youngstown merged under the failing firm provision of U.S. antitrust laws in 1978, and Kaiser tried to sell its steel-making operation to the Japanese in 1979. In rubber, industry analysts waited impatiently for Uniroyal to exit the industry; and in automotive, Chrysler made front-page headlines in its race against time to achieve federal loan assistance. Words like "dinosaur" and "dog" were coined by industry observers to describe the evolving competitive profiles in all eight industries.

However, the profiles of basic industry problems and corporate failures tell only part of the story. These "disaster" tales need to be juxtaposed against some success stories to see how some companies have survived and even prospered in the same hostile environment. The resulting comparisons provide important insights into survival strategies and industry dynamics not only for general managers in the eight industries under study but also for managers in other industries as they lead their companies into the new decade. For example, a careful comparison of success and problem strategies in the eight industries in this study demonstrates that:

☐ Great success is possible, even in a hostile environment.
☐ Strategies leading to success share common characteristics.
☐ Successful strategies come from purposeful moves toward a leadership position.
☐ Problems come from failure to gain or defend a leadership position.
☐ For a deteriorating position, diversity may not be the proper recovery approach.
☐ Structural evolution moves toward a dynamic equilibrium as basic industries face a hostile environment.

I will amplify and discuss each of these insights in subsequent sections of this article.

IN-DEPTH INVESTIGATION

Great success is possible, even in a hostile environment

When one looks at the eight industries in this study, as well as at other basic manufacturing industries facing the hostile environment of the 1980s, it is easy to slip into generalizations by extrapolating from aggregate industry problems to the individual companies within the industry.

Recent articles in the business press, asking "What Killed the U.S. Steel Industry?," "Is Chrysler the Prototype?," or proclaiming "Tire Industry Goes Flat" or "Last Chances for Cigarette Producers," are typical of those that tend to project adverse trends uniformly onto all competitors in the industry. In fact, however, nothing could be further from the truth. Some of the most vibrant successful companies in the world reside and prosper in these seemingly hostile industry environments.

If one eliminates from my eight-industry sample of 64 companies all competitors who gain a majority of revenues and profits from diversification efforts outside their basic industry (e.g., Armco Steel and General Tire), then the most profitable remaining competitors (the industry leaders) in terms of corporate return on equity are those shown in Exhibit 3.

While some variation in returns exists among these leading competitors (Goodyear and Inland had significantly lower returns and growth rates than the other six), the corporate average return on equity earned over the last

Exhibit 3. Financial Returns and Growth Rates, 1975–1979 (leading companies in eight basic industries)[a]

	Average Return on Equity	Average Return on Capital	Annual Revenue Growth Rate
Goodyear	9.2%	7.0%	10.0%
Inland Steel	10.9	7.9	11.4
Paccar	22.8	20.9	14.9
Caterpillar	23.5	17.3	17.2
General Motors	19.8	18.0	13.2
Maytag	27.2	26.5	9.1
G. Heileman Brewing	25.8	18.9	21.4
Philip Morris	22.7	13.5	20.1
Average	**20.2%**	**16.3%**	**14.7%**
Median *Fortune* "1,000" company (same time period)	**15.1%**	**11.0%**	**13.1%**

[a] Excluding those companies that gained a majority of their returns from diversification efforts.

half of the 1970s easily places these companies in the top 20% of the *Fortune* "1,000" industrials and well ahead of the median *Fortune* company on return on capital and annual growth rate.

Moreover, the average returns on both equity and capital in my sample of industry leaders are well ahead of those earned by the leading international oil company (Phillips Petroleum). These average returns are also well ahead of those earned by companies heralded by the business community as technology leaders (Xerox, Eastman Kodak, Texas Instruments, and Digital Equipment), and these returns are likewise well ahead of those earned by corporations singled out as models of progressive diversification and acquisition planning (General Electric and United Technologies).

In fact, as Exhibit 4 shows, the industry leaders shown in Exhibit 3 outperformed all of the highly touted companies during the most recent five years. In addition, the industry leaders grew faster than premier corporations

Exhibit 4. Financial Returns and Growth Rates, 1975–1979 (leading companies in other and more rapidly growing industries)

	Average Return on Equity	Average Return on Capital	Annual Revenue Growth Rate
International oil			
Phillips Petroleum	19.5%	14.7%	16.6%
Technology leaders			
Xerox	17.8	14.4	15.5
Eastman Kodak	18.8	17.7	11.8
Texas Instruments	17.2	16.3	14.6
Digital Equipment	17.0	15.5	37.4
Diversification leaders			
General Electric	19.4	16.9	10.5
United Technologies	18.3	12.6	19.0
Average of these "high performance" leaders	**18.3%**	**15.4%**	**17.9%**
Average (leading companies in basic industries from Exhibit 3)	**20.2%**	**16.3%**	**14.7%**
"Blue chip" competitors			
IBM	21.9	21.2	13.5
3M	20.7	17.7	13.1

like 3M and IBM, and they returned only slightly less to their shareholders and capital investors than these same "blue chip" competitors in high-growth industries.

In retrospect, perhaps the much publicized article, "TI Shows U.S. Industry How to Compete in the 1980s,"[1] should have been written about one of the leading companies in my sample instead of about Texas Instruments, because 75% of the leaders in the basic industries I studied outperformed TI during the latter half of the 1970s. Moreover, they outperformed TI in industries that averaged only 2.4% real growth during the past decade, significantly less than the 15% to 20% compound growth rates of the semiconductor industry during this same period.

Thus even a cursory analysis of leading companies in the eight basic industries leads to an important observation: survival and prosperity are possible even when the business environment turns hostile and industry trends change from favorable to unfavorable. In this regard, the casual advice frequently offered to competitors in basic industries—that is, diversify, dissolve, or be prepared for below-average returns[2]—seems oversimplified and even erroneous. A hostile environment offers an excellent basic investment opportunity and reinvestment climate, at least for the industry leaders insightful enough to capitalize on their positions.

Strategies leading to success share common characteristics

A more detailed examination of the business strategies employed by the top two performing (nondiversified) companies in each of the eight industries sampled reveals that these success strategies share strong common characteristics, irrespective of the particular industry. Indeed, throughout their modern history, all 16 of these leading companies have demonstrated a continuous, single-minded determination to achieve one or both of the following competitive positions within their respective industries:

☐ Achieve the lowest delivered cost position relative to competition, coupled with both an acceptable delivered quality and a pricing policy to gain profitable volume and market share growth.

☐ Achieve the highest product/service/quality differentiated position relative to competition, coupled with both an acceptable delivered cost structure and a pricing policy to gain margins sufficient to fund reinvestment in product/service differentiation.

A rough categorization of the strategies employed by these 16 companies, based on selective field studies and observed behavior over time, is shown in Exhibit 5. In most cases, the industry growth and profit leaders chose only one of the two strategic approaches, on the basis that the skills and resources necessary to invest in a low-cost position are insufficient or incompatible with those needed to invest simultaneously in a strongly differentiated position.

The rudiments of this strategic trade-off can be found as early as the 1920s in Alfred P. Sloan's statements regarding General Motors' selection of a cost-reduced strategy:

> Management should now direct its energies toward increasing earning power through increased effectiveness and reduced expense. . . . Efforts that have been so lavishly expended on expansion and development should now be directed at economy in operation. . . . This policy is valid if our cars are at least equal to the best of our competitors in a grade, so that it is not necessary to lead in design.[3]

However, in at least three cases, the leading companies in my sample chose to combine the two approaches, and each has had spectacular success.

Caterpillar has combined lowest cost manufacturing with higher cost but truly outstanding distribution and after-market support to differentiate

Exhibit 5. Competitive Strategies Employed by Leading Companies (eight basic industries)

Industry	Achieved Low Delivered Cost Position	Achieved "Meaningful" Differentiation	Simultaneous Employment of Both Strategies
Steel	Inland Steel	National	
Tire and rubber	Goodyear	Michelin (French)	
Heavy-duty trucks	Ford	Paccar	
Construction and materials handling equipment		John Deere	Caterpillar
Automotive	General Motors	Daimler Benz (German)	
Major home appliances	Whirlpool	Maytag	
Beer	Miller	G. Heileman Brewing	
Cigarettes	R.J. Reynolds		Philip Morris

its line of construction equipment. As a result, Caterpillar, ranking as the 24th largest and 39th most profitable company in the United States, is well ahead of its competitors and most of the *Fortune* "500" glamour companies.

Similarly, the U.S. cigarette division of Philip Morris combines the lowest cost fully automated cigarette manufacturing operation in the world with highest cost focused branding and promotion to gain industry profit leadership, even without the benefit of either the largest unit volume or segment market share in both domestic and international markets.

And finally, Daimler Benz operates with elements of both strategies but in different segments, coupling the lowest cost position in heavy-duty truck manufacturing in Western Europe with an exceptionally high quality feature-differentiated car line for European and North American export markets.

A more complete picture of the strategic and performance profiles of all major competitors in these eight hostile environments can be obtained by positioning on a matrix those businesses whose axes reflect the relative delivered cost position and the relative product/service differentiation with respect to other competition. The result is a conceptual diagram like that shown in Exhibit 6.

Although the quantification of competitive profiles in this format is typically inexact—because of the proprietary nature of relevant cost, sector, and performance data—a qualitative attempt to perform this analysis for the heavy-duty truck manufacturing industry is presented in Exhibit 7. This representation, based on an analysis of industry interviews and public records, is imprecise, yet it correlates perfectly with the industry performance profiles over time.

For example, from Exhibit 8, it is clear why Ford and Paccar continually lead the heavy-duty truck industry in growth and financial performance. It is equally clear why White lingers near bankruptcy and also why Freightliner and International Harvester are rethinking their strategies for heavy-duty trucks. (Freightliner entered into a distribution agreement with Volvo in an attempt to differentiate its distribution system in the light-heavy segment, and International Harvester initiated a major cost-reduction effort in truck design and manufacturing in an attempt to improve its weak relative cost position.)

A similar analysis of business-level returns for all 16 leading competitors in the eight industries (Exhibit 8) indicates some interesting aspects of the respective strategies, as the following comparison reveals:

☐ The *lowest delivered cost* leader typically grows more slowly, holding price increases and operating margins down to gain volume, fixed-cost reductions, and improved asset turnover. In addition, this competitor will typically have a lower sales turnover than the differentiated

Exhibit 6. Strategic Profile Analysis (basic mature industries)

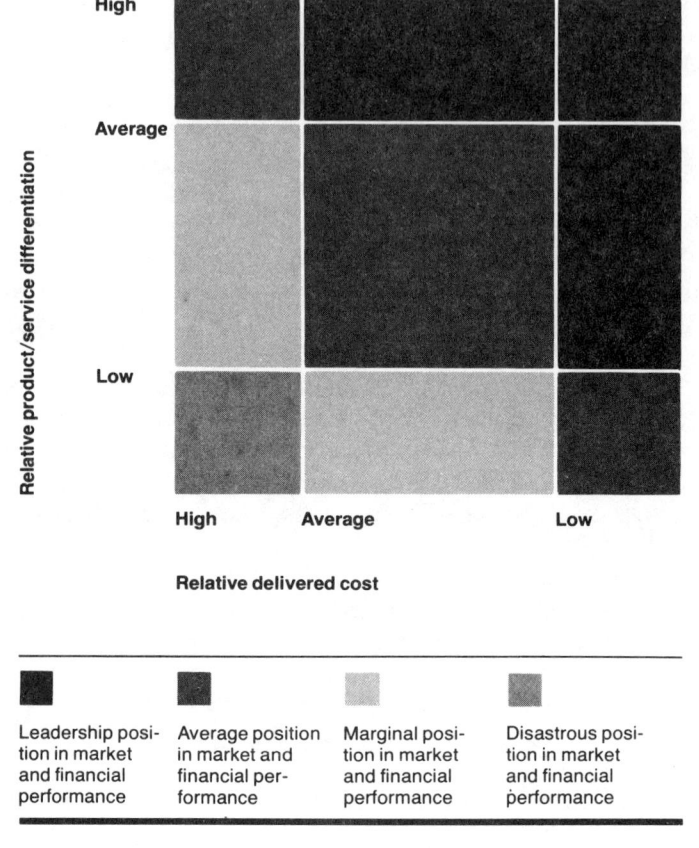

producer, reflecting the higher asset intensity necessary to gain cost reductions in production and distribution.

☐ The *differentiated position* leader typically grows faster, with higher prices and operating margins to cover promotional, research, and other product/service costs. At the same time, this competitor typically operates with lower asset intensity (higher sales turnover), reflecting both higher prices and a lower cost "flexible" asset base.

Successful strategies come from purposeful moves toward a leadership position

In examining the business strategies and subsequent performance of the leading competitors, it becomes clear that purposeful movement toward and defense of a "winning" strategic position—either lowest cost and/or superior

IN-DEPTH INVESTIGATION

Exhibit 7. Strategic Profiles in U.S. Heavy-Duty Truck Manufacturing

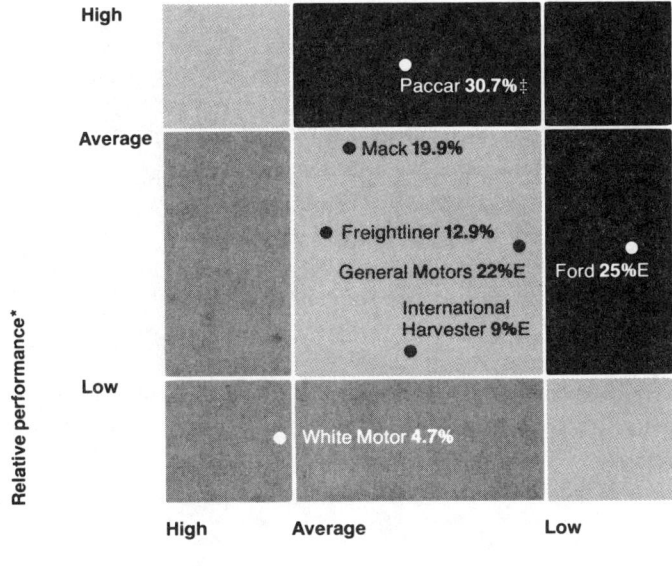

*Based on customer and industry interview data.

†Based on manufacturing and distribution cost analysis, evaluating economies of scale, and vertical integration profiles.

‡ Operating return on assets; E = Estimated from industry sources.

---

price-justified differentiation—has been the fundamental long-term objective of all 16 high performance companies. There is little doubt that consistency and clarity of purpose have helped to mobilize and coordinate internal resources in gaining and defending a leadership position.

It is important to note that the time-phased pattern of investment decisions used to attain and hold these winning positions was based on "doing the right things" to gain leadership in lowest costs and/or differentiation. As a result, all the high performers in my sample used careful strategic analysis to guide their investments, avoiding simplistic adherence to doctrinaire approaches toward strategy formulation which come from the naive application of tools such as:

☐ *Share/growth matrices.* Planning models that suggest that mature market segments should be "milked" or "harvested" for cash flows.

Exhibit 8. Business Level Returns and Revenue Growth Rates

	Operating Margins	Sales Turnover	Operating ROA	Revenue Growth Rates, 1975–1979
Leading Industrial Goods Producers[a] 1978				
Steel				
Inland Steel	8.3%	1.3	10.8%	11.4%
National	12.0	1.5	18.0	12.0
Tire and rubber				
Goodyear	8.6	1.5	12.9	10.5
Michelin	10.0 (est.)	N.A.	N.A.	N.A.
Heavy-duty trucks				
Ford	11.0 (est.)	2.3	25.0 (est.)	12.7
Paccar	12.7	2.4	30.5	15.5
Construction and materials handling equipment				
Caterpillar	15.5	1.8	27.9	14.9
John Deere	10.0	1.3	13.0	17.5
Leading Consumer Goods Producers[a] 1978				
Automotive				
General Motors	9.6%	2.0	19.2%	13.2%
Daimler Benz (automotive)	11.0	2.4	26.4	15.1
Major home appliances				
Whirlpool	8.4	1.0	8.4	5.3
Maytag	21.8	1.8	39.2	9.1
Brewing				
Miller	8.2	1.5	12.3	29.2
G. Heileman Brewing	9.5	3.5	33.3	32.2
Cigarettes				
R.J. Reynolds	17.1	2.3	39.3	15.0
Philip Morris	17.7	1.4	24.8	20.1

[a]Lowest delivered cost producer listed first, followed by most differentiated producer.

☐ *Experience curves and PIMS.*[4]   Planning models that suggest that high market share and/or lowest cost vertically integrated production are keys to success in mature markets.

Instead, based on a case-by-case analysis, the performance leaders made investment decisions that frequently conflicted with these doctrinaire theories:

   1. The leadership positions in mature markets were not being milked by any of the 16 competitors, contrary to the advice of consultants who emphasize the portfolio approach to asset management. In fact, the top managers in two of the leading companies I interviewed laughed when they discussed this concept. They pointed out that their future success and growth opportunities were far greater if they aggressively reinvested in their base business than if they redeployed assets into other (diversified) industries.
   2. Low-cost production is not essential to prosper in mature markets, contrary to the belief of strong proponents of the experience curve. Instead, high sustainable returns also come from reinvesting in an average cost, highly differentiated position, as the data of the previous section and Exhibit 8 demonstrate, and as the ongoing track records of companies like Paccar and Maytag clearly illustrate.
   3. High market share and accumulated experience are not essential for cost leadership in a mature market, as indicated by proponents of the experience curve and some large-sample empirical studies like PIMS. In fact, four of the eight low-cost producers in this study—Inland Steel, Whirlpool, Miller, and Philip Morris—have achieved their lowest cost positions without the benefit of high relative market shares.
   Rather, these producers have focused their plants by emphasizing modern automated process technology, and they have heavily invested in their distribution systems to gain scale economies and other cost reductions in their delivery systems.
   4. Vertical integration is not necessary to exploit cost leadership in mature markets, as suggested by a number of empirical and economic studies. In fact, all of the low-cost producers in the industries under study were less vertically integrated into upstream and downstream activities than at least one other major competitor in their industry.

Instead of emphasizing vertical integration as a policy, all looked for selective integration into high value-added, proprietary componentry, following the type of integration policy first delineated by General Motors in the 1920s of "not investing in general industries of which a comparatively small part of the product is consumed in the manufacture of cars."

Instead of fully integrating, the low-cost leaders invested to have the most efficient process technology in at least one selective stage of the vertical chain. Consider, for example, Ford in truck assembly and Inland in order entry-distribution. The result in all cases is focus—the ability to orient management attention to gain low costs in a partially integrated operation. As one of Ford's major competitors observed:

> Ford is the least integrated of any of the high-volume heavy-duty truck manufacturers in the world, yet it is still the low-cost producer and gains one of the highest ROIs in the industry. In retrospect, Ford's strategy was brilliant; they let the rest of us learn to manufacture componentry while they learned to manufacture profits.

Problems come from failure to gain or defend a leadership position

A more detailed examination of the marginal or failing competitors in each of the eight basic industries (Exhibit 9) also reveals some interesting observations:

1. The historical strategies and policies pursued by these companies have placed them in an unstable position. All are the high-cost producers in their segments, and all have a product that not only is largely undifferentiated in any meaningful sense but also in many cases is below average in quality and performance.

2. The external pressures that these companies complain about—unwarranted regulation and unfair foreign competition—are simply the final blows, sealing a fate that was predestined by improper strategic positioning or repositioning in the 1950s and 1960s, a period when there was still growth and time to maneuver.

3. Many of these marginal producers held low-cost or differentiated positions in these earlier years, and made strategic errors in their reinvestment decisions which contributed to their marginal or failing positions today, as the following examples show.

International Harvester. Led the U.S. heavy-duty truck manufacturing industry in 1965 with a market share of 30%. However, over the next decade, IH failed to reduce costs as rapidly as Ford and GM. As a result, the IH truck division is now a high-cost low-margin producer.

White Motor. A strong number-two truck producer in the mid-1960s, invested in backward integration into cabs, frames, axles, and engine manufacturing, assuming that this would reduce costs. Unfortunately, these investments, all made at suboptimal capacities for efficient scale economies,

Exhibit 9. Marginal or Failing Companies in U.S. Markets

Steel	J&L-Youngstown
	Kaiser
Tire and rubber	Uniroyal
	Mohawk
	Cooper
Heavy-duty trucks	White Motor
Construction and materials handling equipment	Massey Ferguson
	Allis Chalmers
Automotive	Chrysler
Major home appliances	Tappan
Beer	Most regional breweries
	Schlitz
Cigarettes	Liggett & Myers

resulted in a relative high-cost position, adding momentum to White's deteriorating situation.

Tappan. The technology leader in ranges in the early 1960s, chose to broaden that product line, to diversify, to reduce R&D expenditures, and to outsource certain key engineering activities. As a result, it failed to gain the low-cost position in ranges (today held by GE). And by failing to reinvest in technology, it lost its differentiated position in ranges to Caloric (gas), Jenn-Air (electric), and Raytheon (microwave).

Chrysler. The technology leader in the U.S. automotive market in the early 1950s with a 25% market share, chose to make questionable international expansion decisions while adopting a "me too" participatory strategy in the domestic market. The subsequent decline in Chrysler's position and returns was predictable, and this disaster trajectory was certainly accelerated in the early 1970s when its management team announced a revised (but highly inappropriate) strategy to "try to be a General Motors in whatever segments of the market we choose to compete in."

> *For a deteriorating position, diversity may not be the proper recovery approach*

Over the past several years, it has become fashionable to recommend product/market diversification as a way out of an unstable or failing position for mature companies in hostile environments. Unfortunately, in the 64 companies I examined in this research, diversification has "helped" overcome major competitive/performance problems in only three—B.F. Goodrich, General Tire, and Armco Steel (now Armco Group). These three competitors recognized the tenuous nature of their positions early in the maturity cycle and took steps to resegment their base businesses into more advantageous positions by redeploying assets in carefully chosen diversification moves.

Goodrich moved into high-margin, specialty segments of the tire industry while diversifying to attain a low-cost position in PVC and other basic chemicals.

General shifted into low-cost production of tires for commercial vehicles while diversifying to attain a participatory position in very high-growth, fragmented industries such as communications and aerospace.

Armco proceeded into low-cost steel production in selected regional segments like oil country pipe, while diversifying into high-growth markets like oilfield equipment, oil and gas exploration, and financial services. (A recent public relations release from Armco announced that most of its new capital investment would go toward growing these diversification ventures, while maintaining only current capacity levels in steel making.)

These early efforts to resegment and to gain meaningful diversification have paid off. General and Armco lead all competitors in the rubber and steel industries in return on capital and growth, while Goodrich has moved into a stable third place among the surviving tire and rubber producers.

On the other hand, efforts to gain meaningful economic diversification have eluded most of the other problem competitors in the eight industries. By waiting too long to begin diversification efforts, most lack the capital and managerial skills to enter new markets and/or to grow businesses successfully in these markets. Thus their diversification efforts to date have been too small or have been managed in too conservative a fashion to obtain sustainable performance improvements, as witnessed by the very minor performance contribution of U.S. Steel's diversification program into chemicals and the continuing problems of Liggett & Myers despite a 43% diversification program out of the tobacco industry.

As a result of these modest participatory efforts, some of the marginal performers in the eight industries have even divested diversified assets to gain capital and "hang on" for a few more years in the base business. Two notable examples are White Motor's recent sale of its construction equipment operation and Uniroyal's sale of its consumer goods division.

On the whole, it would appear that diversification comes too little and too late for most companies caught in a hostile environment. However, for a courageous few, continued managerial commitment and refocus on the base business to provide a steady flow of capital for promoting meaningful positions in diversified businesses may work to ensure ongoing growth and vitality.

IN-DEPTH INVESTIGATION 69

Exhibit 10. Strategic and Performance Subgroups (basic industries)

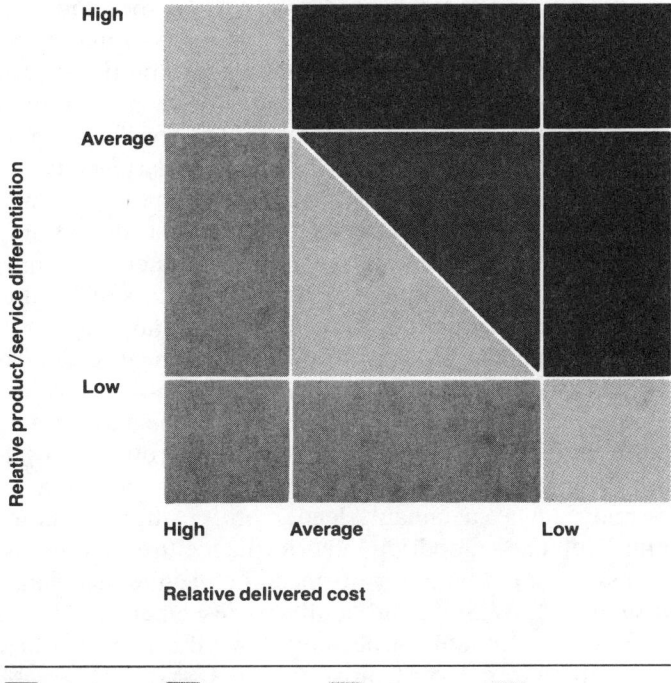

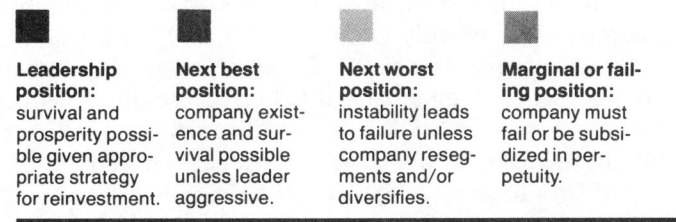

Leadership position: survival and prosperity possible given appropriate strategy for reinvestment.

Next best position: company existence and survival possible unless leader aggressive.

Next worst position: instability leads to failure unless company resegments and/or diversifies.

Marginal or failing position: company must fail or be subsidized in perpetuity.

Structural evolution moves toward a dynamic equilibrium as basic industries face a hostile environment

A summary of the underlying data in my study suggests that basic industries in mature hostile environments are moving through a structural evolution, leading ultimately to four industry and performance subgroups (Exhibit 10):

1. *Leadership position.* Competitors who achieve the lowest delivered cost and/or the highest differentiated position. These positions are gained either on a full product line (Caterpillar) or on an economically viable segment (Whirlpool in washers and dryers). At maturity these competitors will

have the highest growth rates and returns in the industry, the best reinvestment prospects, and they should be able to prosper and coexist in dynamic equilibrium even though external pressures continue.

2. *Next best position.* Competitors who attain the second best position in either cost or differentiation (again on either a full or partial line basis). These companies will have moderate but generally acceptable growth rates and returns, and reinvestments can (and will typically) be made at return levels slightly above the cost of capital. For these companies, vulnerability to strategic and performance deterioration occurs mainly when the industry leaders or a set of externally subsidized competitors choose to attack aggressively. (For example, the recent problems of Ford in the U.S. automotive market can be directly traced to GM's more aggressive market share strategy, coupled with the European and Japanese attacks on U.S. small car markets.)

3. *Next worst position.* Competitors who finish in third place as the industry matures. Given a hostile environment, growth rates and return prospects for these companies are bleak unless they resegment into uncovered niches and gain a sustainable leadership position in these segments (AMC in utility vehicles, Goodrich in performance tires), or unless they can make major asset redeployment into meaningful diversified markets (like Armco and General). Without the ability to resegment or diversify, competitors in this class ultimately will move toward a marginal or failing position. (Chrysler in automotive, Uniroyal in tires, and Schlitz in brewing are examples of companies currently going through such a transition.)

4. *Marginal or failing position.* Competitors who end up last in mature hostile environments ultimately must fail or be subsidized, either through government ownership or aid (Chrysler) or through cash infusions from a diversified parent (Kaiser in steel, Allis Chalmers in construction equipment). Despite efforts to use such subsidies to resegment and refocus their operations, the survey data shows no successful efforts in such turnaround attempts among the 64 competitors in the eight basic industries, raising a fundamental question as to whether there is any real possibility of strategic turnaround. Consequently, a society or a company subsidizing this type of marginal competitor should expect the worst—perpetual subsidies, perhaps slightly offset by infrequent operating returns during high peaks in basic economic cycles.

In Summary

The strategic and performance data from this eight-industry study suggest that both great successes and failures are occurring as basic mature industries move into a hostile business environment created by slower growth, higher inflation, more regulation, and intensified competition. Uniformly, the successes come to those companies that achieve either the lowest cost or most differentiated position. Simultaneously, survival is possible for those companies that have the foresight to downsize their asset commitments into niches in their basic industry and to use their incremental capital for meaningful diversification moves. For the weaker companies, the inability to achieve a lowest cost or most differentiated position results in high vulnerability and ultimate failure or perpetual subsidy.

For general managers guiding their companies into the economic environment of the 1980s, the implications of these findings are clear. The laws of the jungle change as maturity comes and hostility intensifies. In such a jungle, the range of strategic options narrows, requiring both an early warning of the coming hostility and an early strategic repositioning for a company to survive and prosper.

Hence intensified efforts must be made to create internal administrative structures and mechanisms to recognize and efficiently manage this repositioning. (GM's effective organizational restructuring in the early 1970s to respond to the down-sizing imperative stands as a brilliant case study in the use of such an administrative effort to create strategic change.)

For public policymakers monitoring and attempting to influence the business environment, these results suggest that failures will be inevitable as industry structures evolve in the face of maturity and hostility. The currently popular attempts at forced consolidation and subsidies are one way of dealing with these failures. However, these actions should be taken with full knowledge that they will not stop the driving market forces.

The question that remains in the decade ahead is whether the short-run employment, balance of payments, and fiscal stability provided by such public policy actions is worth the long-run cost of maintaining an inefficient industry structure that conflicts with the driving market forces created by a hostile environment.

Notes

1. *Business Week*, September 18, 1978, p. 66.

2. See, e.g., Theodore Levitt, "Dinosaurs among the Bears and Bulls," *HBR*, January–February 1975, p. 41; also the section on basic industries in Richard P. Rumelt, *Strategy, Structure, and Economic Performance* (Boston: Division of Research, Harvard Business School, 1974), pp. 128–139.

3. Alfred P. Sloan, Jr., *My Years with General Motors* (New York, Doubleday, 1964), pp. 65–66, 172.

4. PIMS (Profit Impact of Market Strategies) is a multiple regression model which relates profitability to a number of associative variables. See Sidney Schoeffler, Robert D. Buzzell, and Donald F. Heany, "Impact of Strategic Planning on Profit Performance," *HBR*, March–April 1974, p. 137.

4
The New Industrial Competition

WILLIAM J. ABERNATHY, KIM B. CLARK, and ALAN M. KANTROW

The results of Japanese competition in U.S. markets are evident to all Americans. Repercussions from competitive pressures exerted by European and Japanese manufacturers have been or are being felt by U.S. producers of cars, machine tools, minicomputers, commercial aircraft, textile machinery, and color TV sets, to name a few traditional businesses. Taking auto manufacture as their case example, the authors of this article attribute the Japanese carmakers' success to superiority in the manufacturing plant, especially in their process systems and work force management.

The authors describe the current dilemma of U.S. car manufacturers, who find themselves at a crossroads because this struggle has changed the rules of the game. Now these producers face a situation in which advancing technology and the momentous changes it wreaks—instead of the incremental changes through styling, marketing, and service to which U.S. manufacturers are accustomed—will determine the winners and losers. As often happens in a mature industry when a new phase of competition appears, the auto industry may well undergo a renewal that transforms it. The challenge for U.S. companies in endangered industries is to recognize the altered situation, adjust to it, and learn to manage change.

It is barely possible that in some remote corner of the United States a latter-day Rip Van Winkle awoke this morning fresh with shining images of American industry in the 1950s still fixed in his head. But it is not very likely. Who, after all, during the past few years could have slept undisturbed through the general chorus of lament about the economy? Who could have remained unaware that much of U.S. industry—especially the mature manufacturing sector—has fallen on hard times?

And who did not have a surefire remedy? Born-again supply-siders argued for the massive formation of capital; "new class" advocates of a more systematic industrial policy, for better allocation of existing capital; industrial economists, for enhanced productivity; organized labor, for a coherent effort at reindustrialization; subdued (if unrepentant) Keynesians, for more artful demand management; boisterous Lafferites, for a massive tax cut; congressional experts, for carefully targeted tax breaks on depreciation and investment; Friedmanites, for tight money; and Naderites, for an anticorporate economic democracy.

This loudly divided counsel on the best strategy for managing economic change reflects inadequacy in both perception and understanding: our current industrial malaise defies the usual interpretations and resists the usual prescriptions. Managing change successfully has proved difficult because policymakers in business and government, trained in an old economic calculus, have found it hard to see the new competitive realities for what they are—or to identify the best terms in which to analyze them.

Policymakers fail to understand that the old rules of thumb and worn assumptions no longer hold. Similarly, the traditional structural arrangements in many industries—the familiar relationship between, say, labor and management or producer and supplier—no longer square with the facts of competitive life. As a result, decision makers who continue to act as if nothing has happened are, at best, ineffective and, at worst, inadvertent agents of economic disaster.

Levers of Change

What has happened? The two principal changes have been greater exposure to international competition and technical advances that alter competition. For a start, let's look at two basic major manufacturing industries that have experienced these forces.

- ☐ This industry was confronted with new competitors who emphasized high productivity, reliability, quality, and competent design (but not innovative design, except for Sony).
- ☐ Many competitors—Warwick, Motorola, and Admiral among them—did not survive the foreign thrust and were either taken over or went out of business.
- ☐ Foreign competitors' emphasis on manufacturing, a critical element, was transferred to their U.S. operations—witness Sanyo's management of the previously unsuccessful old Warwick plant, with many of the same employees and U.S. middle managers.
- ☐ Now technological changes have created a situation of potential

renewal of the product life cycle—developments in videocassette recorders, videodiscs, flat high-resolution screens, telecommunications, and computers may combine to revolutionize the television business.

And another is textile machinery:

☐ Before the 1960s a few U.S. manufacturers (e.g., Draper) dominated this business; conglomerates acquired them (e.g., Rockwell International took over Draper).

☐ The U.S. manufacturers began to lose business primarily because of deterioration in product performance relative to European and Japanese models and failure to remain at the cutting edge of new technology.

☐ Because of insufficient investment (conglomerates treated them as cash cows), the once-dominant U.S. manufacturers have lost technical and market leadership to the Swiss, Germans, and Japanese.

Now consider two other industries that are facing the new forces of international competition.

One of them is computers:

☐ Fujitsu has introduced a mainframe computer that attacks IBM where its strength is—service. Fujitsu is doing this by building a high-quality reliable machine that can *guarantee* 99% uptime. In a test run of strategy, Fujitsu has taken on IBM in Australia with this approach and bested the U.S. giant in obtaining some mainframe contracts. The experience there to date: 99.8% uptime.

☐ In minicomputers and home computers the Japanese are entering the U.S. market. Producers like Mitsubishi, Nippon Electric, and Hitachi will soon offer high-quality products that are cost competitive.

And another is machine tools:

☐ Japanese producers have entered this market with a strategy built around a very reliable, high-quality product. Recently, for instance, a U.S. auto producer ordered transfer lines from an established U.S. machine tool manufacturer and from Toyota. The lines arrived at the U.S. plant at the same time. Toyota sent two engineers who had the equipment running and fully debugged in two weeks, while the competitor's team of eight engineers spent several months getting its line operational.

☐ Developments in new technology—electronics, optical and tactile sensors, lasers, and robotics—are creating opportunities for improved metalworking operations and are opening up new applications in areas like assembly and inspection, where mechanization and automation have hardly played a role. Integration of these advances with computerized design and manufacturing could change the very concepts on which traditional machine tools are founded.

A number of other long-stable U.S. manufacturing industries no doubt will be shaken in the not-distant future by these pressures. One is the air compressor field, which a few companies have dominated. A Japanese producer, Hokuetsu, entered its domestic market five years ago and now rules it. Among the companies left in its wake is Ingersoll-Rand, whose market share in Japan plunged from well over 50% to zero. Hokuetsu offers a dependable good-quality product at half the cost of the comparable U.S. compressor.

Still another field is major household appliances, which the Japanese have slated for heavy export activity in this decade. Sanyo, Toshiba, and other companies are setting up U.S. plants and distribution systems. General Electric, for one, is worried; GE has begun a program designed to improve greatly the quality and productivity of its Louisville appliance complex.

The list of endangered industries goes on: jet engines, commercial aircraft, small forklift trucks, steel, electric motors, lawnmowers, and chainsaws, to name just a few.

Character of the New Competition

Let us focus on a single industry to show in detail the character of the conditions that the imperiled U.S. industries face. An inkling of these conditions has entered the consciousness of all Americans as they witnessed Japan's extraordinary success in capturing a large share of the automobile market from the entrenched Big Three domestic producers. In this article we go beyond the previously known facts and show exactly how the Japanese implemented their strategy on the plant floor, on the engineers' design boards, and in the executive offices.

Until recently, developments in the U.S. auto industry were determined mostly by government policies and economic forces peculiar to North America. The sheer extent of the U.S. market and its productive base had long guaranteed the industry a largely self-contained posture. Over the past 15 years, however, the competitive boundaries have expanded drastically until now they are virtually worldwide in scope.

Accompanying this expansion has been a rapid increase in the number of healthy competitors. These new international players, moreover, have quite a different approach from that of the U.S. Big Three; their plan consists of radically new strategies, modes of operation, and production experience.

More to the point, the novel competitive challenge they present cannot be overcome by the familiar responses U.S. companies have long used against each other. Strategically, the Big Three are well prepared to fight not this new war, but the last one.

Many observers believe that the perceived low quality of Detroit's vehicles is a simple function of lethargy and past practice. This view ignores the close connection between poor quality and a disadvantage in costs. The productive capacity of some new entrants, notably the Japanese, enjoys a significant cost advantage over that of the Americans. The Japanese have been especially skillful in exploiting this advantage by adding performance and quality to their cars. This combination of competitive price and high quality has proved tremendously successful in reaching consumers in the American market.

What makes this advantage particularly troublesome is that it does not represent primarily an investment problem; if it did, it would be far easier to remedy. Instead, it arises to some extent from differences in wage rates and, more significant, from differences in productivity and management of operations.

In 1973, when Lee A. Iacocca was asked about the competitive advantage of innovation as perceived by Ford, he responded simply, "Give them [American consumers] leather. They can smell it." In Ford's reading of the U.S. market, innovation did not pay; styling did. Things are quite different today: technology matters.

In the 1950s and 1960s, product technology was competitively neutral. No auto company sought a competitive advantage through significant innovation. In the 1980s, however, the necessity for advantage through innovation is steadily growing. In fact, consumer preference for small fuel-efficient automobiles has developed faster in the United States than it did earlier in Europe or Japan. Beset by unfortunate decisions in the past, the continued absence of a workable long-term energy policy, conflicting regulatory requirements, and the massive financial demands posed by a retooling of production capacity, U.S. producers find themselves at a serious technological disadvantage.

But this is not all. The edge that U.S. companies have long enjoyed in mass production technology and in the resulting economies of scale—an edge long believed essential to competitive success—no longer obtains. Most of the standard U.S. technology is either already widely diffused or easily transferable. Moreover, the process technology for the new smaller autos is subtly but significantly different from that now in place. In other words, changing market preferences and changing rates of technology diffusion have diluted, perhaps destroyed, the established scale economies of U.S. producers.

Premium on Management

Two main distinctions have largely provided the structure for discussions of manufacturing competitiveness. The first is the division between analysis and prescription of a "macro" sort (that is, having to do with such overarching questions of economic management as fiscal and monetary policy and tax incentives) and those of a "micro" sort (that is, having to do with issues relating to the management of particular companies). The second is the division between analysis and prescription based on "hardware" (equipment, buildings, and machinery) and those based on "software" (people management, organizational systems, and corporate strategies).

Considered together, these distinctions form the simple matrix shown in Exhibit 1. Although the distinctions among these quadrants are rough, they are nonetheless useful. In practice, however, they are often neglected, which has left the unfortunate impression in some minds that the current industrial difficulties are composed equally—and indistinguishably—of problems in all the quadrants.

This impression has been mischievous, for these difficulties and their remedies are distributed unevenly about the matrix. In the auto industry the key measures for meeting the new competition fall primarily into Quadrant 4.

Exhibit 1. Key Elements in Manufacturing Competitiveness

	Macro	Micro
Hardware	1. Government fiscal and monetary policies Taxation Capital markets Savings	2. Production capability Plant Equipment
Software	3. Socioeconomic environment Work ethic Regulation Education	4. Corporate management Organization Administration Production systems

Japanese Micromanagement

The Japanese advantage in production costs and product quality in the auto industry, as well as many other established U.S. industries, is not only a fact defining the new competitive reality but also the result of a carefully honed approach to management—the stuff of Quadrant 4. Americans' talk of overregulation, and underdepreciation, pervasive national culture, and markedly absent government support is misplaced.

Costs of Production

Several estimates have placed the landed cost advantage in U.S. markets of Japanese-produced subcompact cars in the $400 to $600 range per vehicle. For example, Abraham Katz, then assistant secretary of commerce for international economic policy, testified last year that "the apparent cost advantage to Japanese producers may have been $560 per car in 1979."[1]

These estimates, in our view, seriously understate the advantage. In the first place, they fail to reflect both current rates of labor compensation and, perhaps more important, the great differences in productivity between Japanese and American manufacturers. Furthermore, they are often based on a narrow definition of the productive units to be compared, for they assume that the relevant comparison is between two original equipment manufacturers—say, Ford and Toyota—even though the really meaningful comparison lies between two productive systems, or "confederations"—that is, an OEM and its constellation of suppliers.

To get a truer picture of the Japanese cost advantage, we must therefore produce estimates that account for productivity differentials, labor costs, and industry structure.

The first step in developing these improved estimates is to update assessments of differential labor productivity. We know that in 1974 output per labor hour in the Japanese auto industry—OEMs and suppliers—was 88% of the level in the United States (that is, the ratio of Japanese to U.S. productivity was 0.88). Published data suggest that growth in labor productivity in the Japanese auto industry (motor vehicles and parts) averaged 8% to 9% in the 1970s; the comparable figure for the United States was 3% to 4%. Using a midrange estimate of the difference (5%), we arrive at a 1980 productivity ratio of 1.18. This means that in 1980 Japanese producers operated at a productivity level almost 20% above that of their American competitors.

This rapid growth was offset in part by higher rates of wage increase: in 1974 Japanese hourly compensation rates were about 37% of those in the United States, while in 1980 they were roughly 50%. Dividing the compensation ratio (0.5) by the productivity ratio (1.18) yields a unit labor cost ratio of 0.424—a figure that has remained more or less constant during the entire 1974–1980 period.

Table A in the Appendix translates this steady labor cost ratio into a Japanese advantage of $1,673. Subtracting $400 for freight and tariff costs yields a landed cost advantage of $1,273 on a 1980 subcompact that sells in the American market for about $5,500—a cost advantage of 23%.

Although the calculations in Table A are based on a number of undocumented assumptions about cost structure and labor content, reasonable adjustment of these assumptions would not affect the order of magnitude of the Japanese cost advantage. Indeed, we were biased conservatively throughout in estimating that cost advantage. Moreover, inclusion of general administrative and selling expenses, as well as the costs of capital and salaried personnel, would leave the Japanese cost advantage intact. So we figure that Japanese producers enjoy a $1,200 landed cost advantage on every small vehicle sold in the United States.

We can to some extent check these numbers against information in the annual reports of major U.S. and Japanese producers. These reports yield data on the costs of nonlabor inputs and salaried personnel but none on the labor embodied in components or materials.

Getting at these data, however, presents several analytic problems. Perhaps the most serious is the great difference between U.S. and Japanese OEMs in their degree of vertical integration and in the nature of their relationships with suppliers. At Toyota, for example, purchases account for almost 80% of the value of sales; but because Toyota holds an equity interest in many of its suppliers, this figure is somewhat misleading. Comparable data for U.S. companies show much less reliance on suppliers; GM, for instance, has a purchase-to-sale ratio of less than 50%.

A second problem is the quite different product mix of U.S. and Japanese OEMs. The data we use come from 1979, when medium-size cars dominated the U.S. Big Three's product lines. The Japanese were producing a much narrower range of vehicles and, of course, were emphasizing the subcompact segment.

Table B in the Appendix shows estimates of total employee costs per vehicle in 1979 at Ford and Toyo Kogyo (Mazda). Our calculations suggest that assembly of the average Ford vehicle required 112.5 employee hours; a Toyo Kogyo vehicle, only 47. Employee costs in building the Ford vehicle were $2,464; for Toyo Kogyo, $491.

As already noted, this sizable cost gap reflects differences in product mix and vertical integration as well as in labor costs and productivity. Information on value added in the annual reports and discussions with industry sources suggest that the Toyo Kogyo results should be increased by 15% to 20% to adjust for vertical integration. Using these higher estimates yields a per-vehicle total of 56 hours instead of 47. (To correct for product mix, we have estimated the cost to Ford of producing the Toyo Kogyo product mix. These calculations are presented in Table C in the Appendix.)

Our analysis of annual report data suggests that in 1979 the difference between Ford and Toyo Kogyo employee costs per small vehicle was about $1,300. Updating this figure to 1980 might increase the absolute dollar amount somewhat, but the evidence we cited on relative growth rates in productivity and compensation implies that the percentage gap would not change much.

Adjustment for changes in exchange rates would also have a negligible effect. Using a rate of 200 yen to the dollar (the approximate rate at the end of 1980) instead of 218 would reduce the gap by only $50. And when we adjust this $1,300 to reflect the U.S. advantage in administrative and selling expenses, the 2.9% tariff with the relevant freight costs for Japanese imports, and the Japanese productivity edge at the supplier level, we emerge with a landed cost advantage for Japanese OEMs of about $1,400.

Exhibit 2. Evidence on Assembly Quality of U.S. Autos Versus Certain Imports

	Vehicle Category	Condition at Delivery[a]	Condition After One Month of Service[b]
	Aggregates	**Domestic**	**Imports**
	Subcompact	6.4	7.9
	Compact	6.2	7.7
	Midsize	6.6	8.1
	Standard	6.8	—
Models	**Domestic**		
	Omni	7.4	4.10
	Chevette	7.2	3.00
	Pinto	6.5	3.70
	Rabbit (U.S.)[a]	7.8	2.13
	Horizon	7.5	NA
	Imports		
	Civic	8.0	1.23[b]
	Fiesta	7.9	NA
	Colt	7.8	NA
	Corolla	7.8	0.71[c]

Source: Aggregates—Rogers National Research, *Buyer Profiles*, 1979; models—industry sources.
[a]Scale of 1–10; 10 is excellent.
[b]Number of defects per vehicle shipped.
[c]European Rabbit averages 1.42 defects per vehicle shipped.
[d]Honda average.
[e]Toyota average.

Contrasts in Product Quality

It is, of course, true that the competitively important dimensions of auto quality are established not by experts but by the market. And many American consumers, who place a high value on quality of assembly workmanship (what the industry calls "fits and finishes"), on reliability, and on durability, seem to believe that Japanese cars are superior in each of these dimensions.

Exhibit 2, which presents industry data on assembly quality, suggests that consumer perceptions are consistent with experience. Buyers rated the imports as a group superior in quality to the domestically produced cars, while the top Japanese models were ranked first and third among the nine rated. Japanese makes also had fewer defects after one month of service.

Similarly, subscribers to *Consumer Reports* gave high ratings to Japanese autos for reliability as measured by the incidence of repairs (see Exhibit 3). Nevertheless, what little evidence exists indicates that U.S.-built vehicles

Exhibit 3. Ratings of Body and Mechanical Repair Frequency[a]

Make All Models	Body 1980	Mechanical 1980
Domestic		
Buick	9.3	9.4
Chevrolet	8.4	8.9
Dodge	10.0	10.0
Ford	7.2	9.2
Lincoln	8.1	8.4
Oldsmobile	8.4	9.3
Volkswagen	11.3	8.6
Imports		
Datsun	15.3	10.8
Honda	16.0	11.1
Mazda	17.5	12.7
Toyota	16.9	12.4
Volkswagen	11.3	10.0
Volvo	11.9	10.5

Source: *Consumer Reports* annual auto issue, April 1981.

[a]Average = 10; maximum = 20; minimum = 0.

The data cover repair frequency of mechanical systems, components, and body (structure and finish). Ratings are given in five categories: average, below average, far below average, above average, and far above average. Beginning with a score of zero for far below average, we have assigned values of 5, 10, 15, and 20 to the other categories. The sum of the scores on body and mechanical systems gives the total score.

Exhibit 4. Customer Loyalty[a]

	Domestic	Imports	Total
Subcompact	77.2	91.6	81.2
Compact	74.2	91.4	72.4
Midsize	75.3	94.5	76.9
Standard	81.8	—	—
Luxury	86.6	94.6	87.2
Weighted average	78.7	91.8	—

Source: Rogers National Research, *Buyer Profiles*, 1979.
[a] Percent who would buy same make/model again.

have superior corrosion protection and longer-lived components and systems.

At any rate, American automobiles enjoy much less customer loyalty than do Japanese imports. Exhibit 4, which summarizes the data on loyalty, gives perhaps the clearest evidence of the differential customer perception of product value for each dollar spent.

Lessons of Quadrant 4

Most explanations of this Japanese advantage in production costs and product quality emphasize the impact of automation, the strong support of the central government, and the pervasive influence of national culture. No doubt these factors have played an important role, but the primary sources of this advantage are found instead in the Japanese producers' mastery of Quadrant 4—that is, in their execution of a well-designed strategy based on the shrewd use of manufacturing excellence.

It may seem odd to think of manufacturing as anything other than a competitive weapon, yet the history of the U.S. auto market shows that by the late 1950s manufacturing had become a competitively neutral factor. It was not, of course, unimportant, but none of the major American producers sought great advantage through superior manufacturing performance. Except perhaps for their reliance on economies of scale, they tended to compete by means of styling, marketing, and dealership networks.

The Japanese cost and quality advantage, however, originates in painstaking strategic management of people, materials, and equipment—that is, in superior manufacturing performance. This approach, in our view, arose from the Japanese pattern of domestic competition and the need for an effective strategy to enter the U.S. market.

At that time the Japanese realized it would be foolish to compete head-on with the established domestic producers' competence in making elaborately (and annually) styled large cars with a "boulevard ride." They lacked the experience, the manufacturing base, and the resources. Instead, taking a lesson from Volkswagen's success, the Japanese concentrated on producing a reliable, high-quality, solid-performance small automobile and on backing it up with a responsible network of dealers.

Exhibit 5 outlines the seven factors most responsible for successful productivity performance and compares the Japanese practice in each with the American. On the basis of extensive discussions with U.S. industry executives, engineers, and consultants, we have ranked these factors in the order of their importance in determining the current state of the industry and have given them approximate relative weights.

Surprisingly, the hardware associated with technology—new automation and product design—proves relatively insignificant in assessing the competitive difficulties of the U.S. manufacturers, although its importance for the future of the industry grows ever larger. Despite the publicity given Japan's experimentation with industrial robots and advanced assembly plants like Nissan's Zama facility, the evidence suggests that U.S. producers have so far maintained roughly comparable levels of process equipment. However appealing they may be, Quadrant 2 explanations cannot themselves account for U.S.–Japanese differentials in manufacturing productivity.

Focus on "Process Yield"

To the contrary, a valid explanation must start with the factor of "process yield," an amalgam of management practices and systems connected with production planning and control. This yield category reflects Japanese superiority in operating processes at high levels of efficiency and output over long periods of time. Although certain engineering considerations (machine cycles, plant layouts, and the like) are significant here, the Japanese advantage has far more to do with the interaction of materials control systems, maintenance practices, and employee involvement. Exhibit 6 attempts to make this interaction clear.

At the heart of the Japanese manufacturing system is the concept of "just in time" production. Often called *Kanban* (after the cards or tickets used to trigger production), the system is designed so that materials, parts, and components are produced or delivered just before they are needed. Tight coupling of the manufacturing stages reduces the need for work-in-process inventory. This reduction helps expose any waste of time or materials, use of defective parts, or improper operation of equipment.[2]

Furthermore, because the system will not work if frequent or lengthy breakdowns occur, it creates inescapable pressure for maximizing uptime and minimizing defects. This pressure, in turn, supports a vigorous maintenance program. Most Japanese plants operate with only two shifts, which allows for thorough servicing of equipment during nonproductive time and

Exhibit 5. Seven Factors Affecting Productivity: Comparison of Technology, Management, and Organization

Factor, with Ranking and Relative Weights	Definition	Comparative Practice, Japan Relative to United States
Process systems		
Process yield 1 (40%)	Output rate variations in conventional manufacturing lines; good parts per hour from a line, press, work group, or process line. Key determinants are machine cycle times, system uptime, and reliability, affected by materials control methods, maintenance practices, and operating patterns.	Production-materials control minimizes inventory, reduces scrap, exposes problems. Line stops highlight problems and help eliminate defects. Operators perform routine maintenance; scheduling of two shifts instead of three leaves time for better maintenance.
Quality systems 5 (9%)	Series of controls and inspection plans to ensure that products are built to specifications.	Japanese use fewer inspectors. Some authority and responsibility are vested in production worker and supervisor; good relationship with supplier and very high standards lead to less incoming inspection.
Technology		
Process automation 4 (10%)	Introduction and adaptation of advanced, state-of-the-art manufacturing equipment.	Overall, state of technology is comparable. Japanese use more robots; their stamping facilities appear somewhat more automated than average U.S. facilities.
Product design 6 (7%)	Differences in the way the car is designed for a given market segment; aspects affecting productivity: tolerances, number of parts, fastening methods, etc.	Japanese have more experience in small car production and have emphasized design for manufacturability (i.e., productivity and quality). Newer U.S. models

Exhibit 5. (*Continued*)

Factor, with Ranking and Relative Weights	Definition	Comparative Practice, Japan Relative to United States
		(Escort, GM J-car) are first models with design/ manufacturing specifications comparable to Japanese.
Work force management		
Absenteeism 3 (12%)	All employee time away from the workplace, including excused, unexcused, medical, personal, contractual and other reasons.	Levels of contractual time off are comparable; unexcused absences are much higher in United States.
Job structure 2 (18%)	Tasks and responsibilities included in job definitions.	Japanese practice is to create jobs with more breadth (more tasks or skill per job) and depth (more involvement in planning and control of operations); labor classifications are broader; regular production workers perform more skilled tasks; management layers are fewer.
Work pace 7 (4%)	Speed at which operators perform tasks.	Evidence is inconclusive; some lines run faster, some appear to run more slowly.

Exhibit 6. Determinants of Process Yield

Rated machine speed	×	**Uptime**	×	**1-Defect Rate**	=	**Annual Output of Good Parts**
Total parts per hour		Hours per year		Good parts/ Total parts		

results in a much lower rate of machine breakdown and failure than in the United States.

Pressure for elimination of defects makes itself felt not in maintenance schedules but in the relationships of producers with suppliers and in work practices on the line. Just-in-time production does not permit extensive inspection of incoming parts. Suppliers must, therefore, maintain consistently high levels of quality, and workers must have the authority to stop operations if they spot defects or other production problems.

Worker-initiated line stoppages are central to the concept of *Jidoka* (making a just-surfaced problem visible to everyone by bringing operations to a halt), which—along with Kanban—helps direct energy and attention to elimination of waste, discovery of problems, and conservation of resources.

It is difficult, of course, to separate the effects of Kanban-Jidoka on process yield from the effects of, say, job structure and quality systems—factors given a somewhat lower ranking by the experts we consulted (see Exhibit 5). It is also difficult to separate them from the benefits of having a loyal work force (Japanese factories have little unexcused absenteeism). Taken together, these aspects of work force management clearly account for much of the Japanese advantage in production.

It is sometimes argued, by the way, that the union–management relationship in the United States helps explain the superior Japanese performance in productivity and product quality. There is no doubt that the industrial relations system in the U.S. auto industry is a critical element in its performance. Nor is there any doubt that many aspects of that system do not square with the new facts of competitive life. Yet to lay these problems at the door of the union—and only there—is misleading.

Employment contracts and collective bargaining relationships do not just happen. Indeed, a contract provision that a company today finds dysfunctional often was initiated by management some time in the past. Moreover, the production philosophy embodied in a contract may have had its origins in the very early days of the industry, long before unionization. Finally, many of the systems and practices that inhibit performance have little to do with a collective bargaining agrement.

Superior manufacturing performance, the key to the Japanese producers' competitive success, is therefore not the fruit of government policy, technical hardware, or national culture (Quadrants 1, 2, and 3). Instead it derives simply from the way people and operations are organized and managed (Quadrant 4).

Technological Renewal

Having looked at causes, we now turn our attention to cures. In a time of expensive energy, by their success in the marketplace Japanese producers have rekindled interest in the automobile—especially the small, fuel-efficient automobile—as a product and thus have opened the way for technology to become the relevant basis of competition in the American market. As one General Motors executive remarked, "We took a look at the Honda Accord and we knew that the game had changed."

But does the American auto industry—or, for that matter, do government bureaucrats, lenders, and suppliers—really understand that the game has changed? Our investigation indicates that it has not—yet. We often hear two interpretations of the current crisis, both of them deeply flawed. By extension, both of these interpretations can apply to other sectors of the U.S. industrial economy.

Misperceptions of Causes

The first of these interpretations, which we call "the natural consequences of maturity," holds that what has happened is the natural consequence of life cycle processes operating internationally on mature industrial sectors. Once an industry reaches the point where its production process has been embodied in equipment available for purchase—that is, once its mode of production is stable and well known—the location of factories becomes a simple matter of exploiting geographic advantages in the relative costs of production. In this view, it makes perfect sense to move these facilities out of the United States as lower cost opportunities become available elsewhere.

Many economists argue that rather than coming to the aid of threatened industries, government and management should follow the path of least resistance, so to speak, and let the life cycle work its will. They recommend a policy not of intervention but, in the phrase of Edward M. Graham, of "positive adjustment." "Government should not," he writes, "protect or subsidize industries that are threatened by imports or [are otherwise] noncompetitive internationally, but should take concrete steps to encourage the transfer of resources from less into more competitive industries."[3]

The question of who is sufficiently infallible to be entrusted with the nasty job of picking winners and losers is, of course, conveniently left unanswered. The evidence to date suggests that no one is.

The second line of interpretation, which we call "transient economic misfortune," is a considerably more optimistic point of view. It holds that the present difficulties with automobiles are temporary, the result of rapid changes in oil prices and consumer preferences. Cost or quality is not the problem, but inappropriate capacity: too many facilities for building big cars.

The forces needed to right the competitive balance are even now locked into place, their happy result merely a matter of time and of bringing the needed capacity on line. Understandably, this view of things appealed strongly to many in the Carter administration, who could use it to rationalize a firm policy of doing nothing.

Both of these interpretive schemes are inadequate—not only because they ignore differences in Quadrant 4 management but also because they count on future stability in technology. Adherents of the maturity thesis assume an irreversible tendency of products to become standardized—that is, technologically stable over time. Adherents of the misfortune thesis, assuming that all outstanding technological problems have been solved, see the industry as needing only to bring the requisite capacity on line to recapture its competitive standing.

Both groups of adherents argue from a set of familiar but outdated assumptions about the relation of technology to industrial development. Looking back on the years since World War II as a period of competition in autos based mainly on economies of scale, styling, and service networks, they persist in viewing the car manufacturers as constituting a typical mature industry, in which any innovation is incremental, never radical, and is thus—in marketing terms—virtually invisible.

Fluidity Versus Stability

Times have changed. Environmental concerns and the escalating price of oil have combined since the oil shock of 1979 to change the structure of market demand fundamentally. Technological innovation—in its radical as well as its incremental forms—again has vital competitive significance.

Changes in product technology have become at once more rapid and more extreme. Unlike most of the postwar period, recent technical advances have spawned a marked diversity in available systems and components. In engines alone, the once dominant V-8 has been joined by engines with four, five, and six cylinders, diesel engines, rotary engines, and engines with turbocharging and computer feedback control.

Moreover, these kinds of product innovation are increasingly radical in their effects on production processes. We have moved from a period in which product innovation focused on the refinement and extension of existing concepts to a period in which completely new concepts are developed and introduced. And this transition from a time of little change in production systems to a time of great turbulence in equipment, processes, skills, and organization is only beginning.

If our assessment is right, this shift in the nature of innovation will have far-reaching implications for the structure of the industry, the strategic decisions of companies, and the character of international trade. The supposedly mature auto industry now has the opportunity to embark on a technology-based process of rejuvenation in which the industry could recover the open-ended dynamics of its youth when competitive advantage was based largely on the ability to innovate.

Research has shown that manufacturing processes, no less than the products turned out, go through a life cycle evolution. As products evolve from low-volume, unstandardized one-of-a-kind items toward high-volume, standardized, commoditylike items, the associated processes likewise evolve from individual job-shop production toward continuous-flow production. In other words, a product–process configuration, or productive unit that is initially fluid (relatively inefficient, flexible, and open to radical change), gradually becomes stable (relatively efficient, inflexible, and open only to incremental change).

This seemingly inexorable movement toward technological stability has long been the fate of the auto industry. Economies of scale on massive production lines have for more than a generation dictated the search for ever-greater product standardization and more streamlined production. Radical change in the underlying technology of either became competitively dysfunctional; the production unit was too finely tuned to wring out the last increment of marginal cost reduction—and its management too focused on organizational coordination and control—to allow the entrepreneurially fertile disruptions caused by radically new technology.[4]

The new industrial competition, however, has dated this older logic by rewarding the ability to compete on technological grounds. It has precipitated a technological ferment, which has in turn been supported by the market's post-1979 willingness to pay a premium for vehicles boasting new technology.

Consider, for example, the rapid market adoption of General Motors' X-bodies with their transaxle and transverse mounted engines, the popularity of enhanced four-cylinder engines like Ford's compound-valve hemispherical head, or the appeal of such fuel-saving materials as graphite fibers, dual-phased steel, and advanced plastics. As a result, the industry has begun to revitalize itself in a movement back to a more fluid process–product configuration in the companies and a more lively technology-based competition among them.

Technology-Driven Strategies

The following factors are the prime elements in the renewal of the auto industry: (1) an increasing premium in the marketplace on innovation, (2) a growing diversity in the technology of components and production processes, and (3) an increasingly radical effect of factors 1 and 2 on long-established configurations in the productive unit as a whole. These developments, in turn, have begun to define the structure and competitive dynamics of the industry in the years ahead—and the corporate strategies best suited to both.

The conventional wisdom about industry structure and strategy accepts an implicit equation between concentration and maturity. When technology-based competition heats up, this logic runs, industry concentration loosens. In such a case, car manufacturers will know how to adjust their strategies accordingly.

To be sure, in a capital-intensive industry with great economies of scale, a period of ferment in product technology often allows manufacturers to offer an increasing variety of products at or below the cost of the old product mix. Especially when the production technology is well understood and easily procurable (in the form of equipment or human skills), companies on the fringe of the industry and fresh entrants can identify and exploit new market niches. Technological activity, market growth, and industry deconcentration usually go hand in hand.

When, however, the ferment in product technology is so extreme that it causes fundamental alterations in process technology, the same degree of activity may have very different results. In this case the immediate effect of a process-linked industry renewal may well be to *increase* the degree and the stability of concentration—that is, as many believe, to push industry structure apparently in the direction of *greater* maturity.

Where these observers go wrong is in failing to distinguish concentration from maturity or, said another way, in assuming that all evidence of frozen or rising concentration is evidence of movement toward maturity. This may, but need not, be the case.

In the auto field, for example, some corporate responses to the prospect of radical process innovation probably will take the industry farther along the road to maturity. Because truly radical product changes are still some years off and because commitments to existing process technology are large (especially in the standard model segment), it is reasonable to expect producers with experience in the older technologies to defend their positions through technical alterations that reduce costs or improve performance but do not make their processes obsolete.

Such a strategy requires the high volumes necessary for scale economies. As a result, the strategy may help concentrate production—either through greater use of joint ventures or, if the scale effects are great enough, through mergers and like forms of mature industry consolidation.

Other corporate responses to process-linked renewal may have the opposite effect. Major innovations in products that are linked to innovations in process technology often permit drastic reductions in production costs or improvements in performance, thus making possible the higher volumes necessary to expand market share. These innovations, however, usually involve large capital outlays as well as development of hard-to-acquire skills on the part of workers and management. So they require large increases in volume to offset the greater investment. As a result, only the leading producers may be able to profit from the process innovations and thus, temporarily at least, enhance their market share and reinforce industry concentration.

Though this pattern of concentration may appear identical to the one we have described, nothing could be further from the truth. Here a consolidation of the market serves to throw the industry into technological ferment that stimulates further technological competition—not to lock it into older process technology.

In time, this upheaval in process technology may even provide the competitive basis for new entrants to the field. Depending on the nature of process advances in auto production, companies in related industries (electronics, for example, or engines or energy) may find invasion of the market an attractive strategic option. But even if a decade from now these new entrants have not materialized, the forces that made their participation possible will have changed the competitive structure of the industry in two fundamental ways:

- ☐ Whatever its immediate tendency, industry concentration will in the long run have become far less stable than at present.
- ☐ The basis of competition will have changed to reflect the now crucial importance of technology-driven strategies.

The Challenge to Management

Once U.S. auto manufacturers understand that energy prices and internationalization of competition have altered the industry's old competitive dynamics, they have to decide how they want to compete under the new rules of the game. It may be best for them to avoid duplicating the Japanese pattern of competition. At any rate, after decades of the maturing process, the basis for competing is in flux for U.S. producers and radical rethinking about strategy—not blind imitation—is in order.

The industrial landscape in America is littered with the remains of once-successful companies that could not adapt their strategic vision to altered conditions of competition. If the automobile producers prove unequal to the new reality that confronts them, their massive, teeming plants will become the ghost towns of late twentieth century America. The same, of course, holds true for all companies, large and small, in those old-line manufacturing industries exposed to assault from abroad. Only those able to see the new industrial competition for what it is and to devise appropriate strategies for participating in it will survive.

Managers must recognize that they have entered a period of competition that requires of them a technology-driven strategy, a mastery of efficient production, and an unprecedented capacity for work force management. They cannot simply copy what others do but must find their own way. No solutions are certain, no strategies assured of success. But the nature of the challenge is clear.

Henry Ford, as Alfred P. Sloan recalled him, was a man who had had

... many brilliant insights in [his] earlier years, [but] seemed never to understand how completely the market had changed from the one in which he had made his name and to which he was accustomed. . . . The old master failed to master change.⁵

That is still the crucial challenge—and opportunity.

Notes

1. Statement before the Subcommittee on Trade of the House Ways and Means Committee, March 18, 1980.

2. See Robert H. Hayes, "Why Japanese Factories Work," *HBR*, July–August 1981, p. 56.

3. Edward M. Graham, "Technological Innovation and the Dynamics of the U.S. Competitive Advantage in International Trade," in *Technological Innovation for a Dynamic Economy*, edited by Christopher T. Hill and James M. Utterback (Elmsford, NY, Pergamon Press, 1979), p. 152.

4. For a discussion of the evolution toward industrial maturity, see James M. Utterback and William J. Abernathy, "A Dynamic Model of Process and Product Innovation," *Omega*, 1975, Vol. 3, p. 639.

5. Alfred P. Sloan, Jr., *My Years with General Motors* (Garden City, NY, Doubleday, 1964), pp. 186–187.

Appendix: The Japanese Cost Advantage

Table A Calculation of U.S. and Japanese Labor Costs for a Subcompact Vehicle

	1 Share in OEM Manufacturing Costs	2 Average OEM Hours per Vehicle	3 Estimated OEM Employee Cost per Hour ($)	4 Estimated Cost per Vehicle ($)	5 Labor Content (%)	6 [4 × 5] Labor Cost per Vehicle ($)	7 [6 × .575] U.S.–Japan Difference ($)
OEM labor Hourly	.24	65	18	1,170	100	1,170	673
Salaried	.08	15	21	315	100	315	181
Purchased components	.39	NA	NA	1,901	66	1,255	721
Purchased materials	.14	NA	NA	683	25	171	98
Total	—	—	—	4,875	NA	2,911	1,673

Notes: OEM hourly labor is defined as total nonexempt and includes direct and indirect production workers. The calculations assume an exchange rate of 218 yen per dollar. The method of calculation and sources of data are as follows:

Column 1 contains estimates of the share of total manufacturing cost accounted for by direct and indirect production labor (at the OEM level), purchased components, and materials. These estimates do not reflect the experience of any one company but approximate an industry average. They are based on data prepared for the National Research Council's Committee on Motor Vehicle Emissions as well as on discussions with industry sources. The latter have also provided us with the data in columns 2, 3, and 5.

We made the calculation of U.S.–Japan cost differences in three steps. We first used the data in columns 2 and 3 to get an OEM labor cost per vehicle of $1,170, then extrapolated using the cost shares (column 1) to arrive at a total manufactured cost and the cost of purchased components and materials (column 4). We next multiplied the cost per vehicle in column 4 by an estimate of the labor content of the three categories presented in column 5. The data imply, for example, that $1,255 of the $1,901 cost of components is labor cost. Finally, we calculated the Japan–U.S. labor cost gap by multiplying the U.S. data in column 6 by 0.575, the adjustment factor derived from our estimate of the Japan-to-U.S. unit labor cost ratio.* Thus column 7 provides an estimate of the difference in the cost of producing a subcompact vehicle in the United States and Japan due to differences in unit labor costs, not only at the OEM level but also at the supplier level.

*Let $C(US)$ and $C(J)$ indicate unit labor costs in the United States and Japan. We estimate $C(J)/C(US) = .425$. We want to know $C(US) - C(J)$. Column 6 gives us $C(US)$. Thus, $C(US)$

$$- C(J) = \left(1 - \frac{C(J)}{C(US)}\right) \times \text{column 6};\text{ this result is in column 7.}$$

Table B Ford and Toyo Kogyo's Estimated Per-Vehicle Employee Costs in 1979

	Ford	Toyo Kogyo
Domestic car and truck production in millions	3,163	0.983
Total domestic employment†		
Automotive	219,599	24,318
Nonautomotive	19,876	2,490
Total domestic employee hours‡		
Automotive in millions	355.75	46.20
Total employee costs§		
Automotive in millions	$7,794.50	$482.20
Employee hours per vehicle	112.5	47.0
Employee cost per vehicle	$2,464	$491

*Ford figure excludes 65,000 imported vehicles; Toyo Kogyo figure is adjusted for production of knock-down assembly kits.

†Data on automotive employment and costs were obtained by assuming that the ratio of automotive employment to total employment was the same as the ratio of sales. The same assumption was made to obtain Ford employment costs.

‡Ford hours were determined by assuming that each employee worked 1,620 hours per year; Toyo Kogyo hours assum 1,900 hours. These adjustments reflect vacations, holidays, leaves, and absences.

§Data include salaries, wages, and fringe benefits. Toyo Kogyo compensation data were derived by updating a 1976 figure using compensation growth rates at Toyota. An exchange rate of 218 yen/$ (1979 average) was used to convert yen.

Table C   Product Mix Adjustment

	Ford	Toyo Kogyo
1. Ratio of car to total vehicle production	0.645	0.652
2. Production shares by size		
Small	0.11	0.83
Medium	0.68	0.17
Large	0.21	—
3. Relative manufacturing cost by size		
Small	1.00	NA
Medium	1.35	NA
Large	1.71	NA
4. Weighted average of relative manufacturing cost small = 1.00	1.38	1.06
5. Production of Toyo Kogyo mix at Ford level of integration		
Employee cost per vehicle	$1,893	$589
Employee hours per vehicle	87	56

Notes: Line 2 for Ford assumes that only Pinto and Bobcat models are small; Mustang and Capri sales were placed in the medium category.

Line 5 for Ford is obtained by multiplying lines 6 and 7 in Exhibit B by (1.06/1.38).

Table B uses the data on manufacturing costs by vehicle size developed for the Committee on Motor Vehicle Emissions of the National Research Council in 1974. We derived estimates of the cost to Ford of producing the Toyo Kogyo mix by first computing a weighted average of the relative manufacturing cost indices with Ford's 1979 production shares by size as weights. The ratio of the comparable Toyo Kogyo weighted average (1.06) to the Ford weighted average (1.38) was used to adjust both costs and productivity as a means of estimating the effect of product mix on Ford's average cost and labor hours per vehicle. After these adjustments we estimate that Ford would require 87 employee hours to produce the average-size vehicle in the Toyo Kogyo product line, compared with 56 hours in the Japanese company. Labor cost per vehicle is just over $1,300 higher at Ford. These comparisons are based on the average-size vehicle at Toyo Kogyo. For a small vehicle (i.e., Pinto vs. Mazda GLC), the Ford estimate is 82 hours per vehicle, while the comparable Toyo Kogyo figure is 53; the corresponding costs per vehicle are $1,785 (Ford) and $566 (Toyo Kogyo). Even this adjustment may overstate costs and hours required to produce the Toyo Kogyo mix at Ford if the trucks and commercial vehicles produced by the two companies differ substantially.

PART TWO
DEFINING A STRATEGIC ROLE FOR PRODUCTION

AN OVERVIEW

Even if managers develop a renewed commitment to manufacturing excellence, nothing guarantees a smooth translation of commitment into improved performance. For the shift in outlook suggested by the first group of articles to be effective, heightened attention to production must be closely linked to broader corporate strategy. Without that linkage, every flurry of activity at the factory level is but another loose cannon rolling around the corporate deck. During the past decade or so, *HBR*—as represented by the articles in this second section—has made a substantial contribution to the work of lashing that cannon down.

At the conceptual level that contribution has largely consisted in the definition of a top-down approach to manufacturing management. Only when managers are agreed on a company's competitive strategy can they establish appropriate manufacturing policies. And, as Wickham Skinner notes, "only when basic manufacturing policies are defined can the technical experts, industrial and manufacturing engineers, labor relations specialists, and computer experts have the necessary guidance to do their work." In a sense, then, the first essential task is to put the cart firmly behind the horse and make sure that it stays there.

But it is not enough just to get the relative positions of horse and cart set correctly. Many possible means exist for yoking them together, and managers must clearly understand the implications of doing it in any particular way. To reach that understanding they require a conceptual framework for thinking about the nature of the relationship between product/market strategies and production processes. It is to building and exploring that framework—the process–product life cycle—that most of these articles address themselves.

As products evolve from one-of-a-kind specialty items toward standardized commoditylike items, their associated production processes evolve from the jobshop of the craftsman toward the flow production system of the chemical refinery. This joint sequence of development reflects the shifting economies of production at different volume levels. It also reflects the changing locus of acceptable innovative activity. In the early stages of a product's life cycle, before market expectations have hardened, substantial variety often exists in product-based technology. Once the nature of the product stabilizes and its "dominant design" gets locked into place, however, the locus of innovation shifts from product to manufacturing process. The key consideration is no longer to supply the market with a slightly different kind of product technology but, rather, to wring as much cost as possible out of the production process. As a result, products become ever more standardized in design—that is, ever more suitable for mass production.

5
Manufacturing: Missing Link in Corporate Strategy

WICKHAM SKINNER

The thesis of this article is that manufacturing has too long been dominated by experts and specialists. For many years these were the industrial engineers; now they are the computer experts. As a result, top executives tend to avoid involvement in manufacturing policy making, manufacturing managers are ignorant of corporate strategy, and a function that *could* be a valuable asset and tool of corporate strategy becomes a liability instead. The author shows how top management can correct this situation by systematically linking up manufacturing with corporate strategy.

A company's manufacturing function typically is either a competitive weapon or a corporate millstone. It is seldom neutral. The connection between manufacturing and corporate success is rarely seen as more than the achievement of high efficiency and low costs. In fact, the connection is much more critical and much more sensitive. Few top managers are aware that what appear to be routine manufacturing decisions frequently come to limit the corporation's strategic options, binding it with facilities, equipment, personnel, and basic controls and policies to a noncompetitive posture which may take years to turn around.

Research I have conducted during the past three years reveals that top management unknowingly delegates a surprisingly large portion of basic policy decisions to lower levels in the manufacturing area. Generally, this abdication of responsibility comes about more through a lack of concern than by intention. And it is partly the reason that many manufacturing policies and procedures developed at lower levels reflect assumptions about corporate strategy that are incorrect or misconstrued.

Millstone Effect

When companies fail to recognize the relationship between manufacturing decisions and corporate strategy, they may become saddled with seriously noncompetitive production systems which are expensive and time-consuming to change. Here are several examples.

Company A entered the combination washer-dryer field after several competitors had failed to achieve successful entries into the field. Company A's executives believed their model would overcome the technical drawbacks that had hurt their competitors and held back the development of any substantial market. The manufacturing managers tooled the new unit on the usual conveyorized assembly line and giant stamping presses used for all company products.

When the washer-dryer failed in the market, the losses amounted to millions. The plant had been "efficient" in the sense that costs were low. But the tooling and production processes did not meet the demands of the marketplace.

Company B produced five kinds of electronic gear for five different groups of customers; the gear ranged from satellite controls to industrial controls and electronic components. In each market a different task was required of the production function. For instance, in the first market, extremely high reliability was demanded; in the second market, rapid introduction of a stream of new products was demanded; in the third market, low costs were of critical importance for competitive survival.

In spite of these highly diverse and contrasting tasks, production management elected to centralize manufacturing facilities in one plant in order to achieve "economies of scale." The result was a failure to achieve high reliability, economies of scale, or an ability to introduce new products quickly. What happened, in short, was that the demands placed on manufacturing by a competitive strategy were ignored by the production group in order to achieve economies of scale. This production group was obsessed with developing "a total system, fully computerized." The manufacturing program satisfied no single division, and the serious marketing problems that resulted choked company progress.

Company C produced plastic molding resins. A new plant under construction was to come onstream in eight months, doubling production. In the meantime, the company had a much higher volume of orders than it could meet.

In a strategic sense, manufacturing's task was to maximize output to satisfy large key customers. Yet the plant's production control system was set up—as it had been for years—to minimize costs. As a result, long runs were emphasized. Although costs were low, many customers had to wait, and many key buyers were lost. Consequently, when the new plant came onstream, it was forced to operate at a low volume.

The mistake of considering low costs and high efficiencies as the key manufacturing objective in each of these examples is typical of the over simplified concept of "a good manufacturing operation." Such criteria frequently get companies into trouble, or at least do not aid in the development of manufacturing into a competitive weapon. Manufacturing affects corporate strategy, and corporate strategy affects manufacturing. Even in an apparently routine operating area such as a production scheduling system, strategic considerations should outweigh technical and conventional industrial engineering factors invoked in the name of "productivity."

Shortsighted Views

The fact is that manufacturing is seen by most top managers as requiring involved technical skills and a morass of petty daily decisions and details. It is seen by many young managers as the gateway to grubby routine, where days are filled with high pressure, packed with details, and limited to low-level decision making—all of which is out of the sight and minds of top-level executives. It is generally taught in graduate schools of business administration as a combination of industrial engineering (time study, plant layout, inventory theory, and so on) and quantitative analysis (linear programming, simulation, queuing theory, and the rest). In total, a manufacturing career is generally perceived as an all-consuming, technically oriented, hectic life that minimizes one's chances of ever reaching the top and maximizes the chances of being buried in minutiae.

In fact, these perceptions are not wholly inaccurate. It is the thesis of this article that the technically oriented concept of manufacturing is all too prevalent; and that it is largely responsible for the typically limited contribution manufacturing makes to a corporation's arsenal of competitive weapons, for manufacturing's failure to attract the top talent it needs and *should* have, and for its failure to attract more young managers with general management interests and broad abilities. In my opinion, manufacturing is generally perceived in the wrong way at the top, managed in the wrong way at the plant level, and taught in the wrong way in the business schools.

These are strong words, but change is needed, and I believe that only a more relevant concept of manufacturing can bring change. I see no sign whatsoever that we have found the means of solving the problems mentioned. The new mathematically based "total systems" approaches to production management offer the promise of new and valuable concepts and techniques, but I doubt that these approaches will overcome the tendency of top management to remove itself from manufacturing. Ten years of development of quantitative techniques have left us each year with the promise of a "great new age" in production management that lies "just ahead." The promise never seems to be realized. Stories of computer and "total systems" fiascoes are available by the dozen; these failures are always expensive, and in almost every case management has delegated the work to experts.

I do not want to demean the promise—and, indeed, some present contributions—of the systems/computer approach. Two years ago I felt more sanguine about it. But, since then, close observation of the problems in U.S. industry has convinced me that the "answer" promised is inadequate. The approach cannot overcome the problems described until it does a far better job of linking manufacturing and corporate strategy. What is needed is some kind of integrative mechanism.

Pattern of Failure

An examination of top management perceptions of manufacturing has led me to some notions about basic causes of many production problems. In each of six industries I have studied, I have found top executives delegating excessive amounts of manufacturing policy to subordinates, avoiding involvement in most production matters, and failing to ask the right questions until their companies are in obvious trouble. This pattern seems to be due to a combination of two factors:

1. A sense of personal inadequacy, on the part of top executives, in managing production. (Often the feeling evolves from a tendency to regard the area as a technical or engineering specialty, or a mundane "nuts and bolts" segment of management.)

2. A lack of awareness among top executives that a production system inevitably involves trade-offs and compromises and so must be designed to perform a limited task well, with that task defined by corporate strategic objectives.

The first factor is, of course, dependent in part on the second, for the sense of inadequacy would not be felt if the strategic role of production were clearer. The second factor is the one we shall concentrate on in the remainder of this article.

Like a building, a vehicle, or a boat, a production system can be designed to do some things well, but always at the expense of other abilities. It appears to be the lack of recognition of these trade-offs and their effects on a corporation's ability to compete that leads top management to delegate often critical decisions to lower technically oriented staff levels, and to allow policy to be made through apparently unimportant operating decisions.

In the balance of this article I would like to:

☐ Sketch out the relationships between production operations and corporate strategy.

STRATEGIC IMPLICATIONS

- [ ] Call attention to the existence of specific trade-offs in production system design.
- [ ] Comment on the inadequacy of computer specialists to deal with these trade-offs.
- [ ] Suggest a new way of looking at manufacturing which might enable the nontechnical manager to understand and manage the manufacturing area.

Strategic Implications

Frequently the interrelationship between production operations and corporate strategy is not easily grasped. The notion is simple enough—namely, that a company's competitive strategy at a given time places particular demands on its manufacturing function, and, conversely, that the company's manufacturing posture and operations should be specifically designed to fulfill the task demanded by strategic plans. What is more elusive is the set of cause-and-effect factors which determine the linkage between strategy and production operations.

Strategy is a set of plans and policies by which a company aims to gain advantages over its competitors. Generally a strategy includes plans for products and the marketing of these products to a particular set of customers. The marketing plans usually include specific approaches and steps to be followed in identifying potential customers, determining why, where, and when they buy, and learning how they can best be reached and convinced to purchase. The company must have an advantage, a particular appeal, a special push or pull created by its products, channels of distribution, advertising, price, packaging, availability, warranties, or other factors.

Contrasting Demands

What is not always realized is that different marketing strategies and approaches to gaining a competitive advantage place different demands on the manufacturing arm of the company. For example, a furniture manufacturer's strategy for broad distribution of a limited low-price line with wide consumer advertising might generally require:

- [ ] Decentralized finished-goods storage.
- [ ] Readily available merchandise.
- [ ] Rock-bottom costs.

The foregoing demands might in turn require:

- [ ] Relatively large lot sizes.

- [ ] Specialized facilities for woodworking and finishing.
- [ ] A large proportion of low and medium-skilled workers in the work force.
- [ ] Concentration of manufacturing in a limited number of large-scale plants.

In contrast, a manufacturer of high-price high-style furniture with more exclusive distribution would require an entirely different set of manufacturing policies. Although higher prices and longer lead times would allow more leeway in the plant, this company would have to contend with the problems implicit in delivering high-quality furniture made of wood (which is a soft dimensionally unstable material whose surface is expensive to finish and easy to damage), a high setup cost relative to running times in most wood-machining operations, and the need to make a large number of nonstandardized parts. Although the first company must work with these problems too, they are more serious to the second company because its marketing strategy forces it to confront the problems head on. The latter's manufacturing policies will probably require:

- [ ] Many model and style changes.
- [ ] Production to order.
- [ ] Extremely reliable high quality.

These demands may in turn require:

- [ ] An organization that can get new models into production quickly.
- [ ] A production control group that can coordinate all activities so as to reduce lead times.
- [ ] Technically trained supervisors and technicians.

Consequently, the second company ought to have a strong manufacturing-methods engineering staff; simple flexible tooling; and a well-trained experienced work force.

In summary, the two manufacturers would need to develop very different policies, personnel, and operations if they were to be equally successful in carrying out their strategies.

Important Choices

In the example described, there are marked contrasts in the two companies. Actually, even small and subtle differences in corporate strategies should be reflected in manufacturing policies. However, my research shows that few companies do in fact carefully and explicitly tailor their production systems to perform the tasks that are vital to corporate success.

Instead of focusing first on strategy, then moving to define the manufacturing task, and next turning to systems design in manufacturing policy, managements tend to employ a concept of production that is much less effective. Most top executives and production managers look at their production systems with the notion of "total productivity" or the equivalent, "efficiency." They seek a kind of blending of low costs, high quality, and acceptable customer service. The view prevails that a plant with reasonably modern equipment, up-to-date methods and procedures, a cooperative work force, a computerized information system, and an enlightened management will be a good plant and will perform efficiently.

But what is "a good plant"? What is "efficient performance"? And what should the computer be programmed to do? Should it minimize lead times or minimize inventories? A company cannot do both. Should the computer minimize direct labor or indirect labor? Again, the company cannot do both. Should investment in equipment be minimized—or should outside purchasing be held to a minimum? One could go on with such choices.

The reader may reply: "What management wants is a combination of both ingredients that results in the lowest *total* cost." But that answer, too, is insufficient. The "lowest total cost" answer leaves out the dimensions of time and customer satisfaction, which must usually be considered too. Because cost *and* time *and* customers are all involved, we have to conclude that what is a "good" plant for Company A may be a poor or mediocre plant for its competitor, Company B, which is in the same industry but pursues a different strategy.

The purpose of manufacturing is to serve the company—to meet its needs for survival, profit, and growth. Manufacturing is part of the strategic concept that relates a company's strengths and resources to opportunities in the market. Each strategy creates a unique manufacturing task. Manufacturing management's ability to meet that task is the key measure of its success.

Trade-Offs in Design

It is curious that most top managements and production people do not state their yardsticks of success more precisely, and instead fall back on such measures as "efficiency," "low cost," and "productivity." My studies suggest that a key reason for this phenomenon is that very few executives realize the existence of trade-offs in designing and operating a production system.

Yet most managers will readily admit that there are compromises or trade-offs to be made in designing an airplane or a truck. In the case of an airplane, trade-offs would involve such matters as cruising speed, takeoff and landing distances, initial cost, maintenance, fuel consumption, passenger comfort, and cargo or passenger capacity. A given stage of technology defines limits as to what can be accomplished in these respects. For instance, no one today can design a 500-passenger plane that can land on a carrier and also break the sonic barrier.

Much the same thing is true of manufacturing. The variables of cost, time, quality, technological constraints, and customer satisfaction place limits on what management can do, force compromises, and demand an explicit recognition of a multitude of trade-offs and choices. Yet everywhere I find plants that have inadvertently emphasized one yardstick at the expense of another more important one.

For example, an electronics manufacturer with dissatisfied customers hired a computer expert and placed manufacturing under a successful engineering design chief to make it a "total system." A year later its computer was spewing out an inch-thick volume of daily information. "We know the location of every part in the plant on any given day," boasted the production manager and the computer systems chief.

Nevertheless, customers were more dissatisfied than ever. Product managers hotly complained that delivery promises were regularly missed—and in almost every case they first heard about failures from their customers. The problem centered on the fact that computer information runs were organized by part numbers and operations. They were designed to facilitate machine scheduling and to aid shop forepersons; they were not organized around end products, which would have facilitated customer service.

How had this come about? Largely, it seemed clear, because the manufacturing managers had become absorbed in their own "systems approach"; the fascination of mechanized data handling had become an end in itself. As for top management, it had more or less abdicated responsibility. Because the company's growth and success had been based on engineering and because top management was R&D-oriented, policy-making executives saw production as a routine requiring a lower level of complexity and brainpower. Top management argued further that the company had production experts who were well paid and who should be able to do their jobs without bothering top-level people.

Recognizing Alternatives

To develop the notion of important trade-off decisions in manufacturing, let us consider Exhibit 1, which shows some examples.

In each decision area—plant and equipment, production planning and control, and so forth—top management needs to recognize the alternatives and become involved in the design of the production system. It needs to become involved to the extent that the alternative selected is appropriate to the manufacturing task determined by the corporate strategy.

Making such choices is, of course, an on-going rather than a once-a-year or once-a-decade task; decisions have to be made constantly in these

Exhibit 1. Some Important Trade-Off Decisions in Manufacturing—or "You Can't Have It Both Ways"

Decision Area	Decision	Alternatives
Plant and equipment	Span of process	Make or buy
	Plant size	One big plant or several smaller ones
	Plant location	Locate near markets or locate near materials
	Investment decisions	Invest mainly in buildings or equipment or inventories or research
	Choice of equipment	General-purpose or special-purpose equipment
	Kind of tooling	Temporary, minimum tooling or "production tooling"
Production planning and control	Frequency of inventory taking	Few or many breaks in production for buffer stocks
	Inventory size	High inventory or a lower inventory
	Degree of inventory control	Control in great detail or in lesser detail
	What to control	Controls designed to minimize machine downtime or labor cost or time in process, or to maximize output of particular products or material usage
	Quality control	High reliability and quality or low costs
	Use of standards	Formal or informal or none at all
Labor and staffing	Job specialization	Highly specialized or not highly specialized
	Supervision	Technically trained first-line supervisors or nontechnically trained supervisors
	Wage system	Many job grades or few job grades; incentive wages or hourly wages
	Supervision	Close supervision or loose supervision
	Industrial engineers	Many or few such people

Exhibit 1. (*Continued*)

Decision Area	Decision	Alternatives
Product design/ engineering	Size of product line	Many customer specials or few specials or none at all
	Design stability	Frozen design or many engineering change orders
	Technological risk	Use of new processes unproved by competitors or follow-the-leader policy
	Engineering	Complete packaged design or design-as-you-go approach
	Use of manufacturing engineering	Few or many manufacturing engineers
Organization and management	Kind of organization	Functional or product focus or geographical or other
	Executive use of time	High involvement in investment or production planning or cost control or quality control or other activities
	Degree of risk assumed	Decisions based on much or little information
	Use of staff	Large or small staff group
	Executive style	Much or little involvement in detail; authoritarian or nondirective style; much or little contact with organization

trade-off areas. Indeed, the real crux of the problem seems to be how to ensure that the continuing process of decision making is not isolated from competitive and strategic facts, when many of the trade-off decisions do not at first appear to bear on company strategy. As long as a technical point of view dominates manufacturing decisions, a degree of isolation from the realities of competition is inevitable. Unfortunately, as we shall see, the technical viewpoint is all too likely to prevail.

Technical Dominance

The similarity between today's emphasis on the technical experts—the computer specialist and the engineering-oriented production technician—and yesterday's emphasis on the efficiency expert–time-study person and industrial engineer—is impossible to escape. For 50 years, U.S. management relied on efficiency experts trained in the techniques of Frederick W. Taylor. Industrial engineers were kings of the factory. Their early approaches and attitudes were often conducive to industrial warfare, strikes, sabotage, and militant unions, but that was not realized then. Also not realized was that their technical emphasis often produced an inward orientation toward cost that ignored the customer, and an engineering point of view that gloried in tools, equipment, and gadgets rather than in markets and service. Most important, the cult of industrial engineering tended to make top executives technically disqualified from involvement in manufacturing decisions.

Since the turn of the century, this efficiency-centered orientation has dogged U.S. manufacturing. It has created that image of "nuts and bolts," of greasy dirty detail jobs in manufacturing. It has dominated "production" courses in most graduate schools of business administration. It has alienated young people with broad management educations from manufacturing careers. It has "buffaloed" top managers.

Several months ago I was asked by a group of industrial engineers to offer an opinion as to why so few industrial engineers were moving up to the top of their companies. My answer was that perhaps a technical point of view cut them off from top management, just as the jargon and hocus-pocus of manufacturing often kept top management from understanding the factory. In their isolation, they could gain only a severely limited sense of market needs and of corporate competitive strategy.

Enter the Computer Expert

Today the industrial engineer is declining in importance in many companies. But a new technical expert, the computer specialist, is taking that place. I use the term "computer specialist" to refer to individuals who specialize in computer systems design and programming.

I do not deny, of course, that computer specialists have a very important job to do. I do object, however, to any notion that computer specialists have more of a top management view than was held by their predecessors, the industrial engineers. In my experience, typical computer experts have been forced to master a complex and all-consuming technology, a fact which frequently makes them parochial rather than catholic in their views. Because they are so preoccupied with the detail of a total system, it is necessary for someone in top management to give them objectives and policy guidance. In the choice of trade-offs and compromises for a computer system, they need to be instructed and not left to their own devices. Or, stated differently, the computer experts need to see the entire corporation as a system, not just one corner of it—that is, the manufacturing plant.

Too often this is not happening. The computer is a nightmare to many top managers because they have let it and its devotees get out of hand. They have let technical experts continue to dominate; the failure of top management truly to manage production goes on.

How *can* top management begin to manage manufacturing instead of turning it over to technicians who, through no fault of their own, are absorbed in their own arts and crafts? How can U.S. production management be helped to cope with the rising pressures of new markets, more rapid product changes, new technologies, larger and riskier equipment decisions, and the swarm of problems we face in industry today? Let us look at some answers.

Better Decision Making

The answers I would like to suggest are not panaceas, nor are they intended to be comprehensive. Indeed, no one can answer all the questions and problems described with one nice formula or point of view. But surely we can improve on the notion that production systems need only be "productive and efficient." Top management can manage manufacturing if it will engage in the making of manufacturing policy, rather than considering it a kind of fifth independent estate beyond the pale of control.

The place to start, I believe, is with the acceptance of a theory of manufacturing that begins with the concept that in any system design there are significant trade-offs (as shown in Exhibit 1) which must be explicitly decided on.

Determining Policy

Executives will also find it helpful to think of manufacturing policy determination as an orderly process or sequence of steps. Exhibit 2 is a schematic portrayal of such a process. It shows that manufacturing policy must stem from corporate strategy, and that the process of determining this policy is the means by which top management can actually manage production. Use of this process can end manufacturing isolation and tie top management and manufacturing together. The sequence is simple but vital.

It begins with an analysis of the competitive situation, of how rival companies are competing in terms of product, markets, policies, and channels of distribution. Management examines the number and kind of competitors and the opportunities open to its company.

Next comes a critical appraisal of the company's skills and resources and of its present facilities and approaches.

The third step is the formulation of company strategy: How is the company to compete successfully, combine its strengths with market opportunities, and define niches in the markets where it can gain advantages?

The fourth step is the point where many top executives cut off their thinking. It is important for them to define the implications or "so-what" effects of company strategy in terms of specific manufacturing tasks. For example, they should ask:

Exhibit 2. Schematic Portrayal of Manufacturing Policy Determination

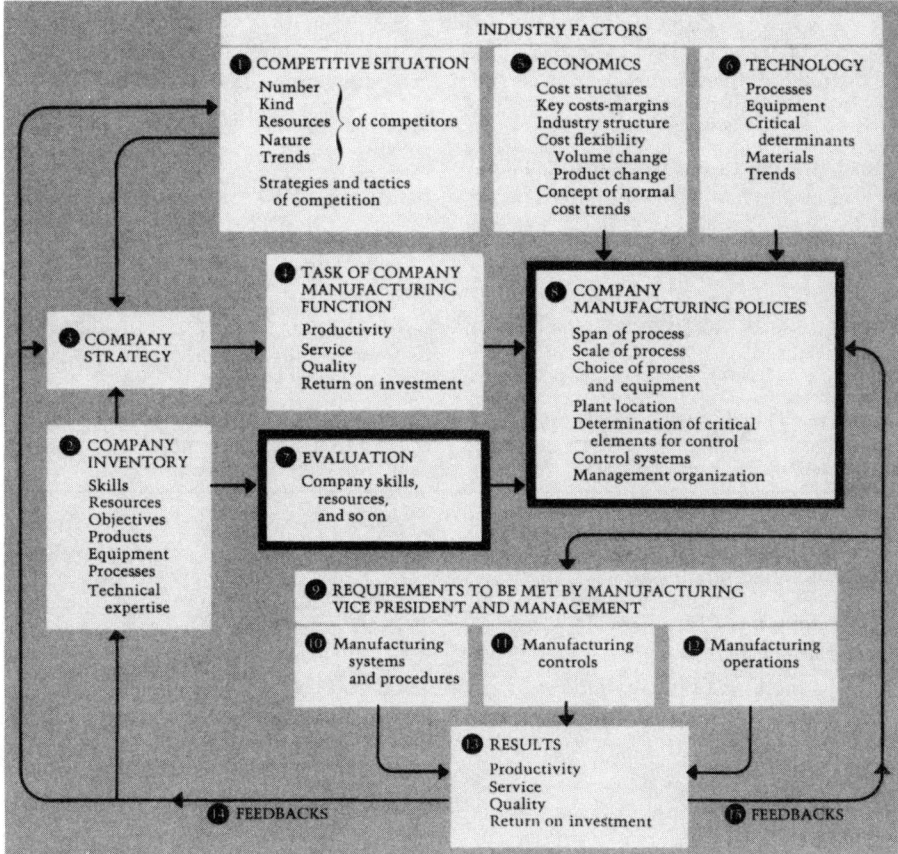

Key:
1. What the others are doing.
2. What we have got or can get to compete with.
3. How we can compete.
4. What we must accomplish in manufacturing in order to compete.
5. Economic constraints and opportunities common to the industry.
6. Constraints and opportunities common to the technology.
7. Our resources evaluated.
8. How we should set ourselves up to match resources, economics, and technology to meet the tasks required by our competitive strategy.
9. The implementation requirements of our manufacturing policies.
10. Basic systems in manufacturing (e.g., production planning, use of inventories, use of standards, and wage systems).
11. Controls of cost, quality, flows, inventory, and time.
12. Selection of operations or ingredients critical to success (e.g., labor skills, equipment utilization, and yields).
13. How we are performing.
14. Changes in what we have got, effects on competitive situation, and review of strategy.
15. Analysis and review of manufacturing operations and policies.

If we are to compete with an X product of Y price for Z customers using certain distribution channels and forms of advertising, what will be demanded of manufacturing in terms of costs, deliveries, lead times, quality levels, and reliability?

These demands should be precisely defined.

The fifth and sixth steps are to study the constraints or limitations imposed by the economics and the technology of the industry. These factors are generally common to all competitors. An explicit recognition of them is a prerequisite to a genuine understanding of the manufacturing problems and opportunities. These are facts that nontechnical managers can develop,

Exhibit 3. Illustrative Constraints or Limitations Which Should Be Studied

A. Economics of the Industry
Labor, burden, material, depreciation costs
Flexibility of production to meet changes in volume
Return on investment, prices, margins
Number and location of plants
Critical control variables
Critical functions (e.g., maintenance, production control, personnel)
Typical financial structures
Typical costs and cost relationships
Typical operating problems
Barriers to entry
Pricing practices
"Maturity" of industry products, markets, production practices, etc.
Importance of economies of scale
Importance of integrated capacities of corporations
Importance of having a certain balance of different types of equipment
Ideal balances of equipment capacities
Nature and type of production control
Government influences

B. Technology of the Industry
Rate of technological change
Scale of processes
Span of processes
Degree of mechanization
Technological sophistication
Time requirements for making changes

study, understand, and put to work. Exhibit 3 contains sample lists of topics for managers to use in doing their homework.

The seventh and eighth steps are the key ones for integrating and synthesizing all the prior ones into a broad manufacturing policy. The question for management is: "Given the facts of the economics and the technology of the industry, how do we set ourselves up to meet the specific manufacturing tasks posed by our particular competitive strategy?" Management must decide what it is going to make and what it will buy; how many plants to have, how big they should be, and where to place them; what processes and equipment to buy; what the key elements are which need to be controlled and how they can be controlled; and what kind of management organization would be most appropriate.

Next come the steps of working out programs of implementation, controls, performance measures, and review procedures (see Steps 9–15 in Exhibit 2).

Conclusion

The process just described is, in my observation, quite different from the usual process of manufacturing management. Conventionally, manufacturing has been managed from the bottom up. The classical process of the age of mass production is to select an operation, break it down into its elements, analyze and improve each element, and put it back together. This approach was contributed years ago by Frederick W. Taylor and other industrial engineers who followed in his footsteps.

What I am suggesting is an entirely different approach, one adapted far better to the current era of more products, shorter runs, vastly accelerated product changes, and increased marketing competition. I am suggesting a kind of "top-down" manufacturing. This approach starts with the company and its competitive strategy; its goal is to define manufacturing policy. Its presumption is that only when basic manufacturing policies are defined can the technical experts, industrial and manufacturing engineers, labor relations specialists, and computer experts have the necessary guidance to do their work.

With its focus on corporate strategy and the manufacturing task, the top-down approach can give top management both its entrée to manufacturing and the concepts it needs to take the initiative and truly manage this function. When this is done, executives previously unfamiliar with manufacturing are likely to find it an exciting activity. The company will have an important addition to its arsenal of competitive weapons.

Limits of the Learning Curve

WILLIAM J. ABERNATHY and KENNETH WAYNE

Two decades ago *HBR* published a pioneering article on a little-known concept, "The Learning Curve as a Production Tool," by Frank J. Andress (January–February 1954). This influential exposition of the learning-curve idea was followed a decade later by a sequel offering some refinements ("Profit From the Learning Curve," by Winfred B. Hirschmann, January–February 1964). Now the concept is much used. Its theory is simple: as workers learn an operation, their efficiency improves and the direct labor input per unit declines. Putting it another way, the learning curve (with variations called the "experience curve" and the "manufacturing progress function") characterizes cost reductions in a product through steady increases in volume. This article looks at the learning curve in a new way. It shows the unforeseen implications of following this strategy single-mindedly: rising fixed costs, a narrowly specialized work group, and a withered capacity for innovation, to name just three consequences. To illustrate their thesis, the authors use the case of Ford Motor Company. This article may be of particular value to manufacturers who think they are reaching the practical limit of cost cutting.

Many companies have built successful marketing and production strategies around the learning curve—the simple but powerful concept that product costs decline systematically by a common percentage each time that volume doubles. The learning-curve relationship is important in planning because it means that increasing a company's product volume and market share will also bring cost advantages over the competition.

However, other results that are not planned, foreseen, or desired may grow out of such a market penetration/cost reduction progression. Reduced

Authors' Note. Support for the research on which this article is based came from the Division of Research and the Associates Fund, Harvard Business School. We greatly appreciate the cooperation of the Ford Archives in providing information.

flexibility, a loss of innovative capability, and higher overhead may accompany efforts to cut costs.

Managers failing to consider the possible outcome of following a cost-minimizing strategy may find themselves with few competitive options once they reach the point where decelerating volume expansion prevents them from obtaining further significant cost reduction.

But if they can identify the likely consequences in advance, they can either anticipate them in their plans or choose an alternative strategy. In this article we analyze those consequences and conclude that management cannot expect to receive the benefits of cost reduction provided by a steep learning-curve projection and at the same time expect to accomplish rapid rates of product innovation and improvement in product performance. Managers should realize that the two achievements are the fruits of different strategies.

Proponents of the learning curve have developed the relationships between volume growth and cost reduction through the use of the following distinct but related approaches:

1. The learning curve (also called the progress function and start-up function) shows that *manufacturing costs* fall as volume rises. It has typically been developed for standardized products like airframes and cameras.

2. The experience curve traces declines in the *total costs* of a product line over extended periods of time as volume grows. Typically, it includes a broader range of costs that are expected to drop than does the learning curve, but disregards any product or process design changes introduced during the period of consideration. Gas ranges and facial tissues are two major product lines on which experience curves have been developed.

The two approaches are sufficiently similar for many purposes of planning and analysis. As we shall demonstrate in due course, however, changes in pricing policy and product design can create significant discrepancies. Care must be exercised in choosing between the two related approaches.

Hard Strategic Questions

Evidence on cost decreases in a wide range of products, including semiconductors, petrochemicals, automobiles, and synthetic fibers, supports the notion that total product costs, as well as manufacturing costs, decline by a constant and predictable percentage each time volume doubles. Because this volume/cost relationship is reliable and quantifiable, it has appeal as a strategic planning tool for use in marketing and financial planning, as well as in production. Moreover, a strategy that seeks the largest possible market share at the earliest possible date can gain not only market penetration but also advantages over competitors who have failed to reach equal volume.

Examples of the economic effects of the learning curve can be found everywhere. The price of ferromagnetic memory cores for computers plunged from 5 cents per bit (unit of memory) in 1965 to less than a half cent in 1973, thereby significantly reducing the costs of computers. In less than two decades of production DuPont reduced the cost of rayon fiber from 53 cents a pound to 17 cents (values not adjusted for inflation). Airframe costs can drop more than 50% per pound during the three to five years of a high-volume production run if the manufacturer can control the rate of modification and sustain volume production.

In considering examples of independent action by one corporation, the most important is that of the Ford Motor Company in its early years. (The Ford example actually shows an experience curve, but the point it makes is equally valid for a learning-curve situation.) During an initial period of less than two years, the average price of a Ford automobile was reduced from more than $5,000 to about $3,000 through the introduction of a dominant product, the Model T. Then, as Exhibit 1 shows on a logarithmic scale, the company cut the price of the Model T to less than $900 following an 85% experience curve. (To underline the contrasts in price, all the figures are translated into 1958 dollars.)

During this time span wages were increased more than threefold, the working day reduced by fiat from ten hours to eight, the moving assembly line invented, and one of the nation's largest industrial complexes (River Rouge) created entirely out of retained earnings. We shall return to the Ford case shortly.

The frequency with which this cost reduction/volume increase pattern is found in practice sometimes leads to the incorrect impression that the learning-curve effect just happens. On the contrary, product design, marketing, purchasing, engineering, and manufacturing must be carefully coordinated and managed. The producer cuts costs with a combination of effects; these include spreading overhead over larger volume, reducing inventory costs as the process becomes more rational and throughput time drops, cutting labor costs with process improvements, achieving greater division of labor, and improving efficiency through greater familiarity with the process on the part of the work force and management. The impetus toward lower costs and higher volume is fragile, however, and if any one of the necessary conditions is removed, a discontinuous return to higher costs may result.

The question management must ask in undertaking such a strategy is whether it fully anticipates or desires the implications that accompany results or that follow execution of the strategy. After the start-up phase, doubling of volume has tremendous implications for the organization. Not all the

Exhibit 1. Price of Model T, 1909–1923 (average list price in 1958 dollars)

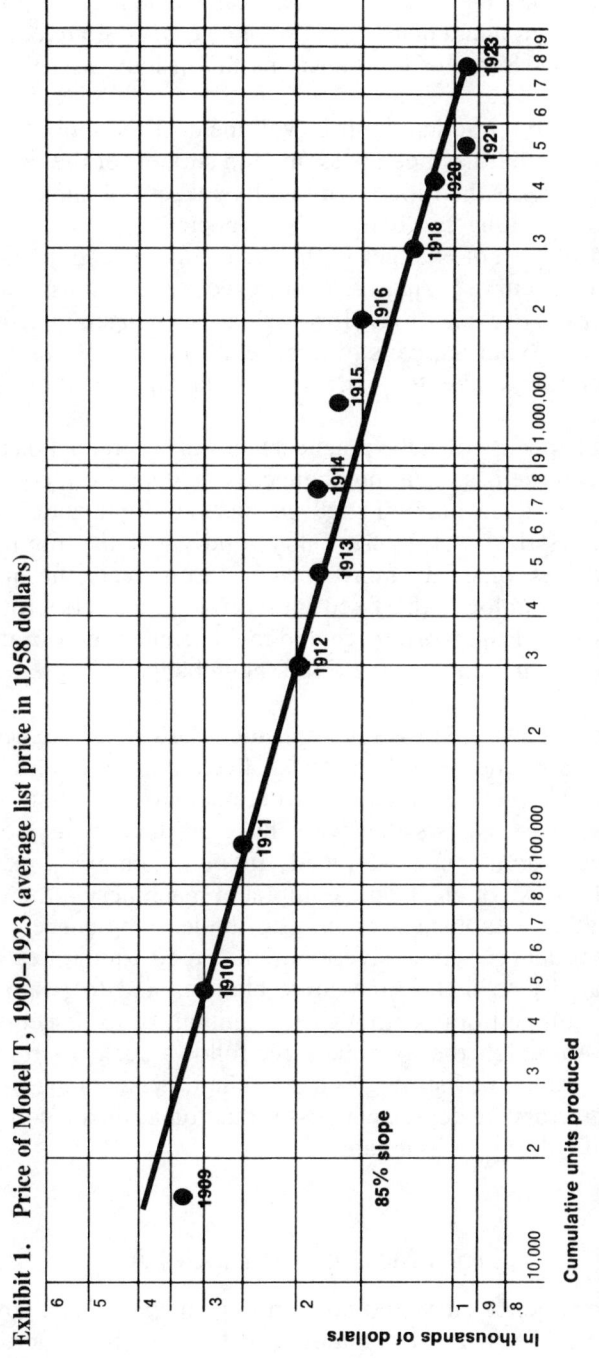

changes it undergoes may be desirable. Management must anticipate the consequences so that it can plan for them, or else it should reject the strategy from the beginning. Some of the questions that it must ask itself are:

1. What is the practical limit to volume/cost reduction? Much of the empirical evidence that has been presented in support of the experience and learning curves ignores their limits, implicitly suggesting that cost reductions go on forever. How long can benefits be expected?

2. What pattern of changes in the organization accompanies progress along the learning curve? Clearly, a long sequence of cost reduction has implications for the organization. How must it be changed to bring such cost reductions about? What happens to overhead, the rate of innovation, manufacturing technology, inventory, the work force, and the investment in plant and equipment?

3. What happens when the practical limits of cost reduction are reached? At this point, can the organization change its strategy from cost minimizing to product-performance maximizing? Or has the organization so changed itself that it loses the vitality, flexibility, and capability for innovation it needs for quick response? In more specific terms, have the quality of the manufacturing technology, the fixed and variable cost structures, and the innovative powers of the work force and management deteriorated so much that the organization cannot make a strategy change?

To explore these questions, we shall consider Ford's early experience, particuarly with the Model T. Then we shall examine other manufacturing cases—such as TV picture tubes, electronic components, and office equipment. The evidence suggests that with those products whose performance can be improved significantly—typically involving complex manufacturing processes such as use of electronic equipment machinery—the incidence of product innovation establishes the limit to the learning curve.

The consequence of intensively pursuing a cost-minimization strategy is a reduced ability to make innovative changes and to respond to those introduced by competitors—although the amount of loss seems to depend on the degree to which the manufacturer follows such a strategy, and its intensity. The problem of strategy choice, then, is balancing the hoped-for advantages from varying degrees of cost reduction against a consequent loss in flexibility and ability to innovate.

From Model T to Model A

At Ford, the experience curve did not continue indefinitely; it governed only the Model T era. Then Ford abandoned it for a performance-maximizing strategy by which the company tried to improve performance year by year at an ever higher product price. The product was the Model A. However, Ford's long devotion to the experience-curve strategy made the transition to another strategy difficult and very costly.

Exhibit 2 shows volume and average prices of the Ford line for some 60 years in an experience-curve format. (The scale of the top part is chronological; the bottom part is logarithmic.) Data on retail price trends, displayed by the two curves, are related to both product-line diversity and the rate of product change. Data on the variety of wheel bases and engines, the horsepower range offered, and the average vehicle weight illustrate how the number of options expanded, contracted, and expanded again. An indicator of the changes in models appears at the top of the exhibit. Taking these three types of information together—product line diversity, the rate of model change, and price trends—one can see that they changed concurrently, whether price is defined on a per-vehicle basis (the upper trend line) or on a per-pound basis (the lower).

Because manufacturing costs vary directly with weight, a comparison of the two trend lines in different periods is revealing. After the Model T was discontinued in 1927, Ford raised the price of its car from year to year, in contrast to the earlier period. The increases were due mainly to design changes which were made to enhance comfort, performance, and safety, but which required more and more expensive materials and caused the price per pound to rise steadily. Considered over a number of years, these systematic annual changes represent a trade-off in favor of size, weight, and performance, as opposed to price.

As the exhibit shows, after an initial period in which several models were offered at the same time, the product line was consolidated in 1909 to the Model T. Ford's objective was to reduce the price of the automobile and thereby increase volume and market share. Before the Model T was conceived, when the least expensive Ford car was priced at $850 and tires alone cost more than $60 a set, Henry Ford announced plans to sell autos at $400—although, he rold reporters, "It will take some time to figure what we can do."

By 1907, after the death of the former company president and the expulsion of dissident stockholder-managers who advocated high-priced cars, attention turned to product cost reduction. The company felt confident in taking this step because of its success with the relatively inexpensive Model N in 1907 and later with the Model T, which was clearly a superior product.[1]

The company accomplished savings by building modern plants, extracting higher volume from the existing plant, obtaining economies in purchased parts, and gaining efficiency through greater division of labor. By 1913 these efforts had reduced production throughput times from 21 days to 14. Later, production was speeded further through major process inno-

Exhibit 2. The Ford Experience Curve (in 1958 constant dollars)

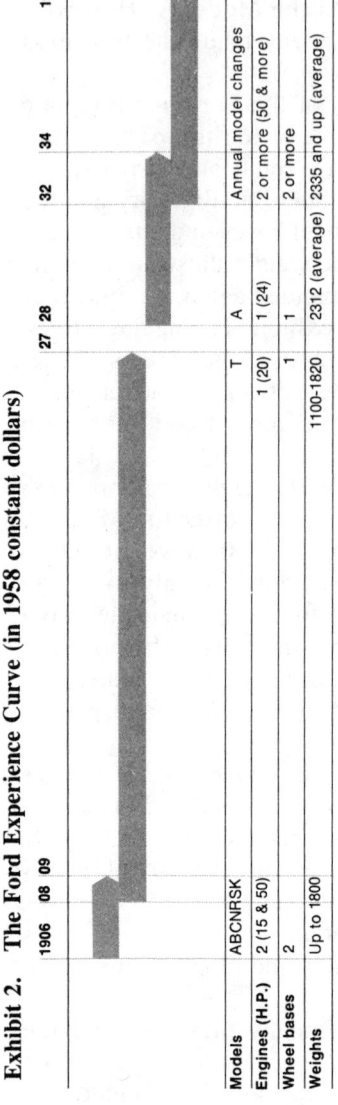
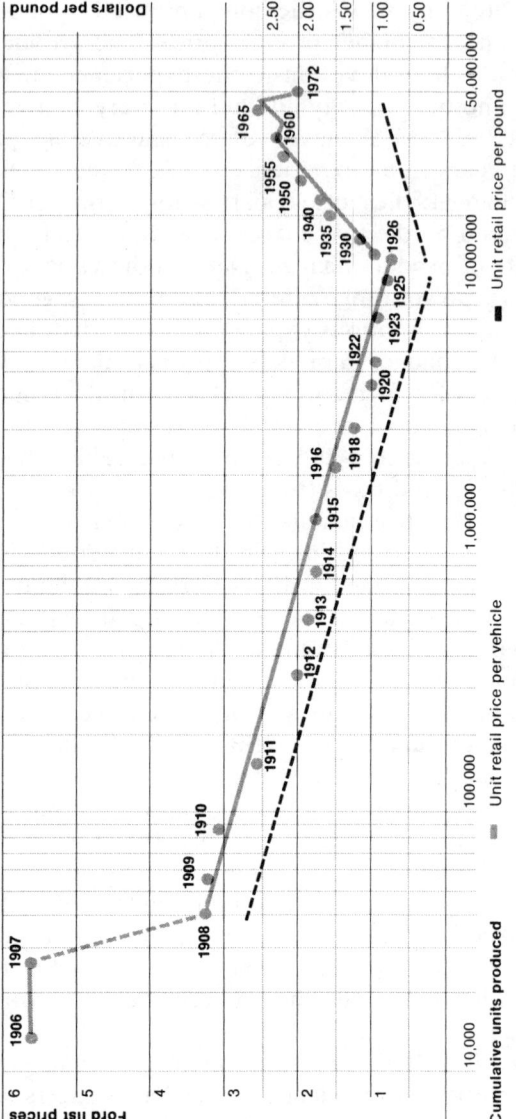

120

vations like the moving assembly line in motors and radiators and branch assembly plants. At times, however, labor turnover reportedly ran as high as 40% per month.[2]

Up to this point, Ford had achieved economies without greatly increasing the rate of capital intensity. To sustain the cost cuts, however, the company embarked on a policy of backward and further forward integration in order to reduce transportation and raw materials costs, improve reliability of supply sources, and control dealer performance. The rate of capital investment showed substantial increases after 1913, rising from 11 cents per sales dollar that year to 22 cents by 1921. The new facilities that were built or acquired included blast furnaces, logging operations and saw mills, a railroad, weaving mills, coke ovens, a paper mill, a glass plant, and a cement plant.

Throughput time was slashed to four days[3] and the inventory level cut in half, despite the addition of large raw materials inventories. The labor hours required of unsalaried employees per 1,000 pounds of vehicle delivered fell correspondingly some 60% during this period, in spite of the additions to the labor force resulting from the backward integration thrust and in spite of substantial use of Ford employees in factory construction.

Constant improvements in the production process made it more integrated, more mechanized, and increasingly paced by conveyors. Consequently, the company felt less need for management in planning and control activities. The percentage of salaried workers was cut from nearly 5% of total employment for 1913 to less than 2% by 1921; these reductions in Ford personnel enabled the company to hold in line the burgeoning fixed-cost and overhead burden.

The strategy of cost minimization single-mindedly followed with the Model T was a spectacular success. But the changes that accompanied it carried the seeds of trouble that affected the organization's ability to vary its product, alter its cost structure, and continue to innovate.

Cost of Transition

In its effort to keep reducing Model T costs while wages were rising, Ford continued to invest heavily in plant, property, and equipment. These facilities even included coal mines, rubber plantations, and forestry operations (to provide wooden car parts). By 1926, nearly 33 cents in such assets backed each dollar of sales, up from 20 cents just four years earlier, thereby increasing fixed costs and raising the break-even point.

In the meantime, the market was changing. In the early 1920s, consumer demand began shifting to a heavier closed body and to more comfort. Ford's chief rival, General Motors, quickly responded to this shift with new designs. Ford's response was to add features to the Model T which gradually increased the weight; between 1915 and 1925 the weight of the car actually gained by nearly 25%, while engine power remained the same.

But the rate of product improvement halted the steady reduction of costs. Nevertheless, to maintain market growth Ford further cut the list price along the experience-curve formula. This created a severe margin squeeze, particularly when unit sales began falling after 1923. As the rate of design changes accelerated and wage levels continued to rise, manufacturing costs loomed ever larger in the retail price. In 1926, the manufacturing costs of some models reached 93% of list price, and some models were actually sold to dealers at prices below costs.

(See Exhibit 3 for sales, manufacturing, and other data on Ford during the critical two decades.) Ford, unbeatable at making one product efficiently, was vulnerable to GM's strategy of quality and competition via superior vehicle performance. As Alfred Sloan, architect of GM's strategy, later wrote:

> Mr. Ford . . . had frozen his policy in the Model T, . . . preeminently an open-car design. With its light chassis, it was unsuited to the heavier closed body, and so in less than two years [by 1923] the closed body made the already obsolescing design of the Model T noncompetitive as an engineering design. . . .
>
> The old [GM] strategic plan of 1921 was vindicated to a "T," so to speak, but in a surprising way as to the particulars. The old master had failed to master change. . . . His precious volume, which was the foundation of his position, was fast disappearing. He could not continue losing sales and maintain his profits. And so, for engineering and market reasons, the Model T fell. . . . In May 1927 . . . he shut down his great River Rouge plant completely and kept it shut down for nearly a year to retool, leaving the field to Chevrolet unopposed and opening it up for Mr. Chrysler's Plymouth. Mr. Ford regained sales leadership again in 1929, 1930, and 1935, but, speaking in terms of generalities, he had lost the lead to General Motors.[4]

A company that had developed and introduced eight new models during a four-year period, before undertaking the cost-minimization strategy, had subsequently so specialized its work force, process technology, and management that it consumed nearly a year in model development and changeover. As an illustration of its specialization, in the course of the model change Ford lost $200 million, replaced 15,000 machine tools and rebuilt 25,000 more, and laid off 60,000 workers in Detroit alone.

So we see that when costs could not be reduced as fast as they were added through design changes, the experience-curve formula became inoperative. Although this sequence should give pause to managers who wish to apply the experience curve to make product-line changes, it does not

Year	Motor Vehicles Sales (in thousands of units)	% of Market Share	% of Employees Salaried	Labor Rate (in $ per hour)	Manufacturing Cost as % of List Price*	Direct Labor Hours per Vehicle*†	Fixed Assets Per $ Sales	Labor Hours Per Vehicle	Profit (loss) (in millions of dollars)‡
1910	32	10.7%	6.9%	$0.25				232	$15
1911	70	20.3	3.5	0.23				265	21
1912	170	22.1	5.5	0.23			$0.10	95	40
1913	203	39.6	4.9	0.27	41%	65	0.11	152	75
1914	308	48.0	5.7	0.55	40	42	0.15	79	90
1915	501	43.4	4.5	0.55			0.19	72	74
1916	735	38.6	4.4	0.55			0.15	84	178
1917	664	46.1	3.2	0.61	79	47	0.16	106	51
1918	498	43.5	3.5	0.66			0.22	133	95
1919	941	46.9	3.0	0.76			0.26	100	140
1920	463		2.9	0.84	70	49	0.27	267	64
1921	971	55.4	1.9	0.87			0.22	102	125
1922	1,307		1.4	0.82	60	31	0.20	125	237
1923	2,019	47.5	1.1	0.85			0.19	125	193
1924	1,929		1.2	0.83	62	35	0.25	140	214
1925	1,920	41.5	1.2				0.27	160	219
1926	1,563		1.4	0.87	93	69	0.33	178	132
1927	424	10.6	1.5	0.87			0.81	475	(65)
1928	750		2.0				0.84	375	(143)
1929	1,870	32.0	2.1	0.92	86	80	0.40	182	175
1930	1,432		2.8				0.54	210	113
1931	731	26.2	4.0		69	40	1.06	290	(97)

Sources: Ford Archives; Federal Trade Commission, *Report on the Motor Vehicle Industry*, 76th Congress, First Session (1940), House Document 468. Missing figures are not available.

*For Model T Touring Car 1913–1926, Model A Tudor 1929 and 1931.
†Computed from direct labor cost for models specified above and from Ford labor rates.
‡In constant 1958 dollars.

invalidate the principle of the learning curve, which assumes a standardized product.

Decline of Innovation

The sequence of evolutionary development in product and process during the period of the cost-minimization strategy and the subsequent strategy transition is paralleled in the pattern of major Ford innovations. Exhibit 4 plots the frequency and significance of Ford-initiated innovations by type of application: product innovation, process innovation, and transfer of process technology to or from associated industries. The new methods and designs are those claimed by Ford. For our analysis, four independent industry experts evaluated the importance of each one and rated it on a scale of 1 to 5. The innovations range in significance from the introduction of the plastic steering wheel (index average of 1) in 1921 to the invention of the power-driven final assembly line (index of 5) in 1914. The vertical axis in Exhibit 4 provides a sum of the average points assigned to significant developments by two-year intervals in Ford's history.

The exhibit indicates that the intensity of innovative activity is closely related to major events in the unfolding of the cost-minimization strategy. During the Model T period the activity shows a ripple effect. Installation of new product applications occurs in clusters with new model development and then declines in frequency as the design is standardized, efficiency is refined, and the process is integrated into operations. Process innovations rise to a peak after the period of product innovation, as the manufacturer rationalizes the process and reduces costs. (Compare the peak designated circled 1 with the peak designated squared 1, circled 2 with squared 2, and so on.) As the manufacturer works out these problems, process technology is transferred following the thrust into backward integration, and a third peak of activity occurs (triangled 2, triangled 3, etc.).

The exhibit suggests not only that the nature of innovation changes, but also that the intensity of innovative activity diminishes. Ford produced only one new product application or process technique during the seven years after 1932 that rated as high on the scale as 4—the development of transfer machines. This step toward further automation took place in 1937.

The changes introduced to trim costs altered the innovative activity in two ways. First, after 1926 the types of innovation peaked coincidentally. As operations became more elaborate and systemslike, product and process change developed intimate linkages; many different elements had to be altered simultaneously to introduce change. This relationship implies a high cost of change. Secondly, the nature of product innovation shifted. In the early years, a new model meant a complete transformation involving major innovation. Later, model change became an annual affair, and innovation centered on new features available across model lines rather than on new

Exhibit 4. Innovation and Process Change at Ford

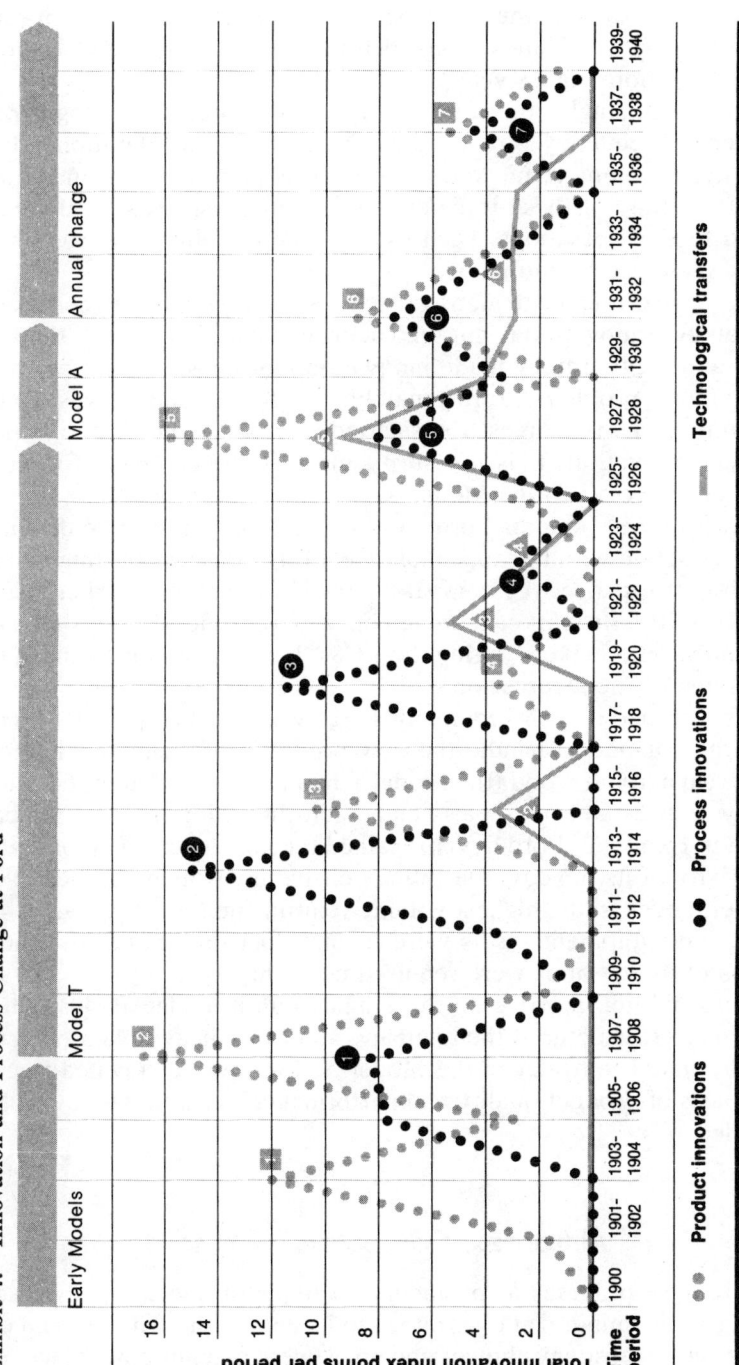

models. For instance, the V-8 engine, whose development appears as a substantial cluster of innovations in Exhibit 4, was produced without substantial alterations for 18 years.

Not surprisingly, the third class of innovation, technology transfers, increased in frequency through the period under consideration. This class had particularly long-term value at Ford since it improved the manufacturing capability. Many of these transfers were accomplished in Ford's newly integrated feeder operations, such as one where technology was applied to produce plate glass continuously.

Ford's experience demonstrates the important link between innovation and strategy. Innovation is not the pacing element; it is part of the strategy. Ford's choice of strategy made innovation more costly and a more serious organizational problem. Unfortunately, the cost-cutting drives also led to weakening of the resources (the salaried employees) needed to initiate and carry out innovation. It is not surprising that the company took nearly a year to change over to the Model A.

With its new model, Ford rose again. Combining the old philosophy of cost reduction with the appeal of an entirely new car boasting demonstrably high performance, the company wrestled the major market share from GM in 1930. But its market share fell once more. Indeed, Chrysler, a distinct third among auto makers during the 1920s, held second place ahead of Ford during most of the Depression.

As it turned out, the company's highly specialized production process lacked the balance to handle the new product; for example, the company had overcapacity in wood (the Model T had many wooden parts) but undercapacity in glass and body parts manufacturing. Moreover, as indicated by the data in Exhibit 3, Ford never regained the high levels of labor and capital productivity of its heyday. Despite extensive investments in new plant and equipment, even in the highest volume year for the Model A (1929), 40 cents in plant and equipment assets were required per dollar of sales, and nearly 80 hours of direct labor were required per vehicle.

Ford did not improve on these figures until the late 1940s, when new management restructured the company and made heavy plant investments. From the time it introduced the Model A, Ford was compelled to compete on the basis of product quality and performance—a strategy in which it was not skilled.

Airframes, Computers, and so on

The Ford case provides a spectacular example of one company's action in pursuing a cost-minimization strategy to its end. Although this is an extreme case in terms of strategy choices and investment magnitudes, the same forces and consequences can be found at stake in other industries. In some cases these forces and consequences are evident when a rapid rate of product change retards the inauguration of the learning curve, and in other cases the difficulties terminate the downward trend as in the following examples.

Douglas Aircraft, once an extremely successful, high-volume aircraft manufacturer, was forced into a merger in 1967 with the McDonnell Company by financial problems whose roots lay in poor control of airframe production costs under fast-shifting conditions. On the assumption that it could reduce the costs of its new jet model following a learning-curve formula, Douglas had made certain commitments on delivery dates and prices to airline customers. But continued modification of its plans disrupted, as *Fortune* put it, "the normal evolution of the all-important learning curve."[5]

International Business Machines' schedules to deliver its new 360 series of computers a decade ago were thrown out of kilter. IBM's 1965 annual report described the situation this way:

> Although our production of System/360 is building up rapidly and equipment shipped has been performing well, we had problems. . . . As a result we found it necessary in October to advise customers of delays from our originally planned delivery schedules. The basic building blocks in the System/360 circuitry are advanced new microelectronic circuit modules requiring totally new manufacturing concepts.

The snag was attributable to the company's efforts to attain high-volume production while it was undertaking major product innovation.

The price of TV picture tubes followed the experience-curve pattern from the introduction of television in the late 1940s until 1963, the average unit price dropping from $34 to $8 (in terms of 1958 dollars). The advent of color TV ended the pattern, as the price for both black-and-white and color TV tubes shot up to $51 by 1966. Then the experience curve reasserted itself; the price dropped to $48 in 1968, $37 in 1970, and $36 in 1972. The transition was less traumatic than is sometimes the case because the innovation was foreseen and the new product was sufficiently similar to the old one that manufacturers could apply their established techniques and facilities in making the color tube.

In some cases radically new technology or the cost of transition has forced many of the "old" manufacturers out of the business. Such has been the case in the shift from vacuum tubes to transistors, from manual to electric typewriters, and from mechanical calculators to electronic machines. The major producers of textile machinery for rug manufacturing, like Lansdowne and Crompton & Knowles, found their markets taken from them by the advent of the new tufting technology in carpets.

The contrary relationship between product innovation and efficiency exists not only in instances where the impetus for change comes about after a long and successful production run, as in the Ford case and in that of Volkswagen more recently. It can also be found when the change is an unintended continuation of uncertainty following new model introduction, as happened in the foregoing airframe and computer examples.

Common Elements of Change

To consider the sort of changes that can accompany a cost-minimizing strategy, it is useful to abstract that aspect of the Ford case. The kinds of changes that took place can be grouped into six categories—product, capital equipment and process technology, task characteristics and process structure, scale, material inputs, and labor.

Product. Standardization increases, models change less frequently, and the product line offers less diversity. As the implementation of the strategy continues, the total contribution improves with acceptance of lower margins accompanying larger volume.

Capital Equipment and Process Technology. Vertical integration expands and specialization in process equipment, machine tools, and facilities increases. The rate of capital investment rises while the flexibility of these investments declines.

Task Characteristics and Process Structure. The throughput time improves and the division of labor is extended as the production process is rationalized and oriented more toward a line-flow operation. The amount of direct supervision decreases as the labor input falls.

Scale. The process is segmented to take advantage of economies of scale. Facilities offering economies of scale, such as engine plants, are centralized as volume rises, while others, like assembly plants, are dispersed to trim transportation costs. Spreading the higher overhead over larger volume gains savings.

Material Inputs. Through either vertical integration or capture of sources of supply, material inputs come under control. Costs are reduced by forcing suppliers to develop materials that meet process needs and by directly reducing processing costs.

Labor. The heightening rationalization of the process leads to greater specialization in labor skills and may ultimately lessen workers' pride in their jobs and concern for product quality. Process changes alter the skills requirements from the flexibility of the craftsman to the dexterity of the operative.

The same pattern of change in the six categories that characterizes the Ford history also describes periods of major cost reduction in other industries. For example, as light-bulb manufacturing progressed from a manual process to an almost entirely automated one, a similar pattern of product development, process elaboration, increase in capital intensity, and so on, was evident.[6] In areas as diverse as furniture manufacturing and commercial building construction, the problems of improving productivity and achieving innovation often hinge on changes similar in thrust to those at Ford. Life cycle studies of international trade in many products, such as chemicals and petrochemicals, demonstrate a coordinated pattern of change involving product characteristics, scale, and price competition that is consistent with the Ford case.

Studies of manufacturing technology yield a common finding for electronics, chemical, and metal-working companies, among others, that certain conditions in a company, like its supervisory structure, product-line diversity, and utilization of technology, relate to characteristics of the manufacturing process. More specifically, manufacturers with more efficient line flows have different ratios of supervisory personnel to the work force, different levels of authority, less product diversity, and greater product standardization than manufacturers with more flexible production process structures.

Risks of Success

In analyzing the difficulties of Ford and other companies, we are not arguing that the pursuit of a cost-minimization strategy is inappropriate. The failure of many companies, particularly small innovative ones, can be traced to their inability to make the transition to high volume and cost efficiency. Nevertheless, management needs to recognize that conditions stimulating innovation are different from those favoring efficient high-volume established operations.

Although there must be a theoretical limit to the amount by which costs can utlimately be reduced, a manufacturer reaches the practical limit first. However, the practical limit is not reached because the means of cutting costs has been exhausted; it is rather determined by the market's demand for product change, the rate of technological innovation in the industry, and competitors' ability to use product performance as the basis for competing.

In determining how the learning-curve strategy should be pursued, management must realize that the risk of misjudging the limit rises directly with the successful continuation of the strategy. There are reasons for this seemingly paradoxical development: first, the market becomes increasingly vulnerable to performance competition and second, attempts to continue reducing costs diminish the organization's ability to respond to this kind of competition.

The market becomes more vulnerable to performance competition because the company must stake out an ever-larger market share to maintain a constant significant rate of cost cutting. Demand must be doubled each time in order to realize the same proportional cost reduction. As the market expands, it becomes harder to hold together and the competition is better able to segment it "from the top," with a superior product or customized options. Once this action is taken, the company on the learning curve must either abandon the all-important volume bases of scale or introduce a major product improvement. Either step, or both, ends the cost-reduction sequence.

The unfortunate implication is that product innovation is the enemy of cost efficiency, and vice versa. To make the learning curve evolve successfully, the manufacturer needs a standard product. Under conditions of rapid product change, unit output costs cannot be slashed.

Managing Technology

The role expected of technology is critical in the formulation of manufacturing strategy. Many a company has sailed into the unknown, trailing glowing reports about the R&D under way in its laboratories and the new products it is developing. Yet too often the promises in annual reports to stockholders and in news releases are never realized. The problem hinges on difficulties in recognizing that a shift in strategy has a pervasive effect *across* the organization's functional areas. The production department cannot follow a program of cost reduction along the learning curve at the same time that R&D or the marketing people are going full steam ahead into new ventures that change the nature of the product.

When a new product born of technology fails, management is often chided because it assertedly marketed the product poorly. The problem may have come, however, from management's failure to realize that its capabilities to handle innovation had weakened. Foresight is a matter of judging the challenge in terms of altered capabilities as well as technological changes and market forces. In the Ford case the difficulties arose as much from what the organization did to itself as from GM's actions. The ability to switch to a different strategy seems to depend on the extent to which the organization has become specialized in following one strategy and on the magnitude of change it must face. An extreme in either factor can spell trouble.

Very little is known about how to plan for this type of technological change. But we can point to two courses of action that some major companies have followed in avoiding the problems we have described. One is to maintain efforts to continue development of the existing high-volume product lines.

This requires setting the industry pace in periodically inaugurating major product changes while stressing cost reduction via the learning curve between model changes. This course of action—which IBM has followed in computers—is obviously a costly option which only companies with large resources should undertake. It amounts to a decision to maintain comparatively less efficient operations overall.

The second course of action is to take a decentralized approach in which separate organizations or plants in the corporate framework adopt different strategies within the same line of business. Several corporations in high-technology industries have taken this approach with success. One organization in the company will pursue profits with a traditional product, like rayon, to the limit of the experience curve. At the same time a new, different organization will undertake the development of innovative (perhaps even competitive) products or processes, such as nylon. In taking this tack, some companies have shut down old plants and started up new ones instead of mingling different capabilities that are at various stages of their development.[7]

Neither of these courses of action will suit the needs of every organization, but some means of dealing with the issue of technological change and strategy transitions should be included in strategic planning.

Notes

1. Allan Nevins, *Ford: The Times, the Man, the Company* (New York, Scribner, 1954), Chapter XII.

2. Keith Sward, *The Legend of Henry Ford* (New York, Rinehart, 1948), p. 51.

3. See *Factory Facts From Ford* (Detroit, Ford Motor Company, 1924).

4. Alfred P. Sloan, Jr., *My Years With General Motors* (New York, Doubleday, 1964), pp. 162–163.

5. John Mecklin, "Douglas Aircraft's Stormy Flight Plan," *Fortune*, December 1966, p. 258.

6. See James R. Bright, *Automation and Management* (Boston, Division of Research, Harvard Business School, 1958).

7. For more on this approach, see Wickham Skinner, "The Focused Factory," *HBR*, May–June 1974, p. 113. Chapter 10, this volume.

7
Link Manufacturing Process and Product Life Cycles

ROBERT H. HAYES and STEVEN C. WHEELWRIGHT

Although the product life cycle concept may have value for managers, its emphasis on marketing can make it inadequate for strategic planners. These authors point out that using a process life cycle can help a company choose among its various manufacturing and marketing options. Using the concept of a "product–process matrix," they show how a company's position reflects its weaknesses and strengths, and they discuss the implications for corporate strategy.

The regularity of the growth cycles of living organisms has always fascinated thoughtful observers and has invited a variety of attempts to apply the same principles—of a predictable sequence of rapid growth followed by maturation, decline, and death—to companies and selected industries. One such concept, known as the "product life cycle," has been studied in a wide range of organizational settings.[1] However, there are sufficient opposing theories to raise the doubts of people like N.K. Dhalla and S. Yuspeh, who argued a few years ago that businessmen should forget the product life cycle concept.[2]

Irrespective of whether the product life cycle pattern is a general rule or holds only for specific cases, it does provide a useful and provocative framework for thinking about the growth and development of a new product, a company, or an entire industry. One of the major shortcomings of this approach, however, is that it concentrates on the marketing implications of the life cycle pattern. In so doing, it implies that other aspects of the business and industry environment move in concert with the market life cycle. Although such a view may help one to think back on the kinds of changes that occur in different industries, an individual company will often find it too simplistic for use in its strategic planning. In fact, the concept may even be misleading in strategic planning.

In this article we suggest that separating the product life concept from a related but distinct phenomenon that we will call the "process life cycle" facilitates the understanding of the strategic options available to a company, particularly with regard to its manufacturing function.

The Product–Process Matrix

The process life cycle has been attracting increasing attention from business managers and researchers over the past several years.[3] Just as a product and market pass through a series of major stages, so does the production process used in the manufacture of that product. The process evolution typically begins with a "fluid" process—one that is highly flexible, but not very cost efficient—and proceeds toward increasing standardization, mechanization, and automation. This evolution culminates in a "systemic process" that is very efficient but much more capital intensive, interrelated, and hence less flexible than the original fluid process.

Using a product–process matrix, Exhibit 1 suggests one way in which the interaction of both the product and the process life cycle stages can be represented. The rows of this matrix represent the major stages through which a production process tends to pass in going from the fluid form in the top row to the systemic form in the bottom row. The columns represent the product life cycle phases, going from the great variety associated with startup on the left-hand side to standardized commodity products on the right-hand side.

Diagonal Position

A company (or a business unit within a diversified company) can be characterized as occupying a particular region in the matrix, determined by the stage of the product life cycle and its choice of production process for that product. Some simple examples may clarify this. Typical of a company positioned in the upper left-hand corner is a commercial printer. In such a company, each job is unique and a jumbled flow or jobshop process is usually selected as being most effective in meeting those product requirements. In such a jobshop, jobs arrive in different forms and require different tasks, and thus the equipment tends to be relatively general purpose. Also, that equipment is seldom used at 100% capacity, the workers typically have a wide range of production skills, and each job takes much longer to go through the plant than the labor hours required by that job.

Exhibit 1. Matching Major Stages of Product and Process Life Cycles

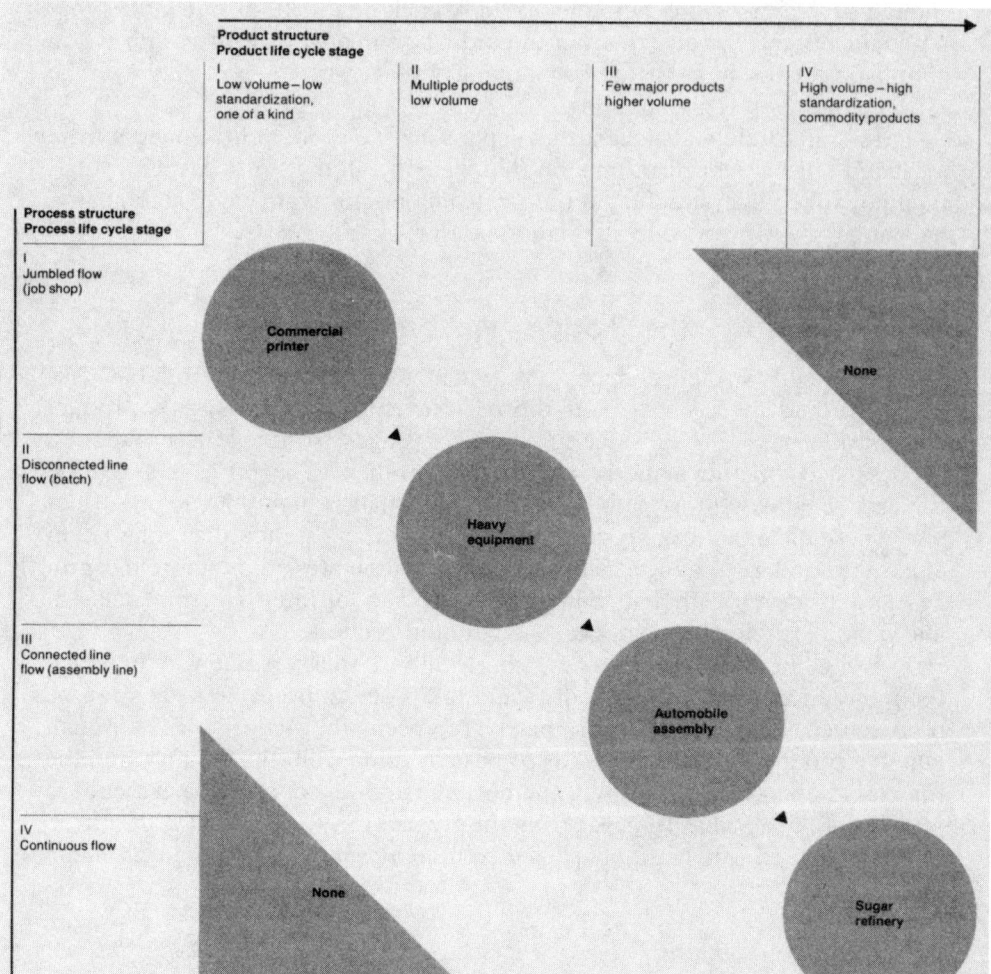

Further down the diagonal in this matrix, the manufacturer of heavy equipment usually chooses a production structure characterized as a "disconnected line flow" process. Although the company may make a number of products (a customer may even be able to order a somewhat customized unit), economies of scale in manufacturing usually lead such companies to offer several basic models with a variety of options. This enables manufacturing to move from a jobshop to a flow pattern in which batches of a given model proceed irregularly through a series of work stations, or possibly even a low-volume assembly line.

Even further down the diagonal, for a product like automobiles or major home appliances, a company will generally choose to make only a few models and use a relatively mechanized and connected production process, such as a moving assembly line. Such a process matches the product life cycle requirements that the automobile companies must satisfy with the economies available from a standardized and automated process.

Finally, down in the far right-hand corner of the matrix, one would find refinery operations, such as oil or sugar processing, where the product is a commodity and the process is continuous. Although such operations are highly specialized, inflexible, and capital intensive, their disadvantages are more than offset by the low variable costs arising from a high volume passing through a standardized process.

In Exhibit 1, two corners in the matrix are void of industries or individual companies. The upper right-hand corner characterizes a commodity product produced by a jobshop process that is simply not economical. Thus there are no companies or industries located in that sector. Similarly, the lower left-hand corner represents a one-of-a-kind product that is made by continuous or very specific processes. Such processes are simply too inflexible for such unique product requirements.

Off the Diagonal

The examples cited thus far have been the more familiar "diagonal cases," in which a certain kind of product structure is matched with its "natural" process structure. But a company may seek a position off the diagonal instead of right on it, to its competitive advantage. Rolls-Royce Ltd. still makes a limited product line of motor cars using a process that is more like a jobshop than an assembly line. A company that allows itself to drift from the diagonal without understanding the likely implications of such a shift is asking for trouble. This is apparently the case with several companies in the factory housing industry that allowed their manufacturing operations to become too capital intensive and too dependent on stable high-volume production in the early 1970s.

As one might expect, when a company moves too far away from the diagonal, it becomes increasingly dissimilar from its competitors. This may or may not, depending on its success in achieving focus and exploiting the advantages of its niche, make it more vulnerable to attack. Coordinating marketing and manufacturing may become more difficult as the two areas confront increasingly different opportunities and pressures. Not infrequently, companies find that either inadvertently or by conscious choice they are at positions on the matrix very dissimilar from those of their competitors and must consider drastic remedial action. Most small companies that enter a mature industry start off this way, of course, which provides one explanation of both the strengths and the weaknesses of their situation.

One example of a company's matching its movements on these two dimensions with changes in its industry is that of Zenith Radio Corporation in the mid-1960s. Zenith had generally followed a strategy of maintaining a high degree of flexibility in its manufacturing facilities for color television receivers. We would characterize this process structure at that time as being stage 2. When planning additional capacity for color TV manufacturing in 1966 (during the height of the rapid growth in the market), however, Zenith chose to expand production capacity in a way that represented a clear move down the process dimension, toward the matrix diagonal, by consolidating color TV assembly in two large plants. One of these was in a relatively low-cost labor area in the United States. Although Zenith continued to have facilities that were more flexible than those of other companies in the industry, this decision reflected corporate management's assessment of the need to stay within range of the industry on the process dimension so that its excellent marketing strategy would not be constrained by inefficient manufacturing.

It is interesting that seven years later Zenith made a similar decision to keep all of its production of color television chassis in the United States, rather than lose the flexibility and incur the costs of moving production to the Far East. This decision, in conjunction with others made in the past five years, is now being called into question. Using our terminology, Zenith again finds itself too far above the diagonal, in comparison with its large, primarily Japanese, competitors, most of whom have mechanized their production processes, positioned them in low-wage countries, and embarked on other cost-reduction programs.

Incorporating this additional dimension into strategic planning encourages more creative thinking about organizational competence and competitive advantage. It also can lead to more informed predictions about the changes that are likely to occur in a particular industry and to consideration of the strategies that might be followed in responding to such changes. Finally, it provides a natural way to involve manufacturing managers in the planning process so that they can relate their opportunities and decisions more effectively with marketing strategy and corporate goals. The experience of the late 1960s and early 1970s suggests that major competitive advantages can accrue to companies that are able to integrate their manufacturing and marketing organization with a common strategy.[4]

Using the Concept

We will explore the following issues that follow from the product–process life cycle: (1) the concept of distinctive competence, (2) the management implications of selecting a particular product–process combination, considering the competition, and (3) the organizing of different operating units so that they can specialize on separate portions of the total manufacturing task while still maintaining overall coordination.

USING THE CONCEPT

Distinctive Competence

Most companies like to think of themselves as being particularly good relative to their competitors in certain areas, and they try to avoid competition in others. Their objective is to guard this distinctive competence against outside attacks or internal aimlessness and to exploit it where possible. From time to time, unfortunately, management becomes preoccupied with marketing concerns and loses sight of the value of manufacturing abilities. When this happens, it thinks about strategy in terms only of the product and market dimension within a product life cycle context. In effect, management concentrates resources and planning efforts on a relatively narrow column of the matrix shown in Exhibit 1.

The advantage of the two-dimensional point of view is that it permits a company to be more precise about what its distinctive competence really is and to concentrate its attentions on a restricted set of process decisions and alternatives, as well as a restricted set of marketing alternatives. Real focus is maintained only when the emphasis is on a single "patch" in the matrix—a process focus as well as a product or market focus. As suggested by Wickham Skinner, narrowing the focus of the business unit's activities and the supporting manufacturing plant's activities may greatly increase the chance of success for the organization.[5]

Thinking about both process and product dimensions can affect the way a company defines its "product." For example, we recently explored the case of a specialized manufacturer of printed circuit boards. Management's initial assessment of its position on the matrix was that it was producing a low-volume one-of-a-kind product using a highly connected assembly line process. (This would place it in the lower left corner of the matrix.) On further reflection, however, management decided that while the company specialized in small production batches, the "product" it really was offering was a design capability for special purpose circuit boards. In a sense, then, it was mass producing designs rather than boards. Hence, the company was not far off the diagonal after all. This knowledge of the company's distinctive competence was helpful to management as it considered different projects and decisions, only some of which were supportive of the company's actual position on the matrix.

Effects of Position

As a company undertakes different combinations of product and process, management problems change. It is the interaction between these two that determines which tasks will be critical for a given company or industry. Along the process structure dimension, for example, the key competitive advantage of a jumbled flow operation is its flexibility to both product and volume changes. As one moves toward more standardized processes, the competitive emphasis generally shifts from flexibility and quality (measured in terms of product specialization) to reliability, predictability, and cost. A similar sequence of competitive emphases occurs as a company moves along the product structure dimension. These movements in priorities are illustrated in Exhibit 2.

For a given product structure, a company whose competitive emphasis is on quality or new product development would choose a much more flexible production operation than would a competitor who has the same product structure but who follows a cost-minimizing strategy. Alternatively, a company that chooses a given process structure reinforces the characteristics

Exhibit 2. Expanded Product–Process Matrix

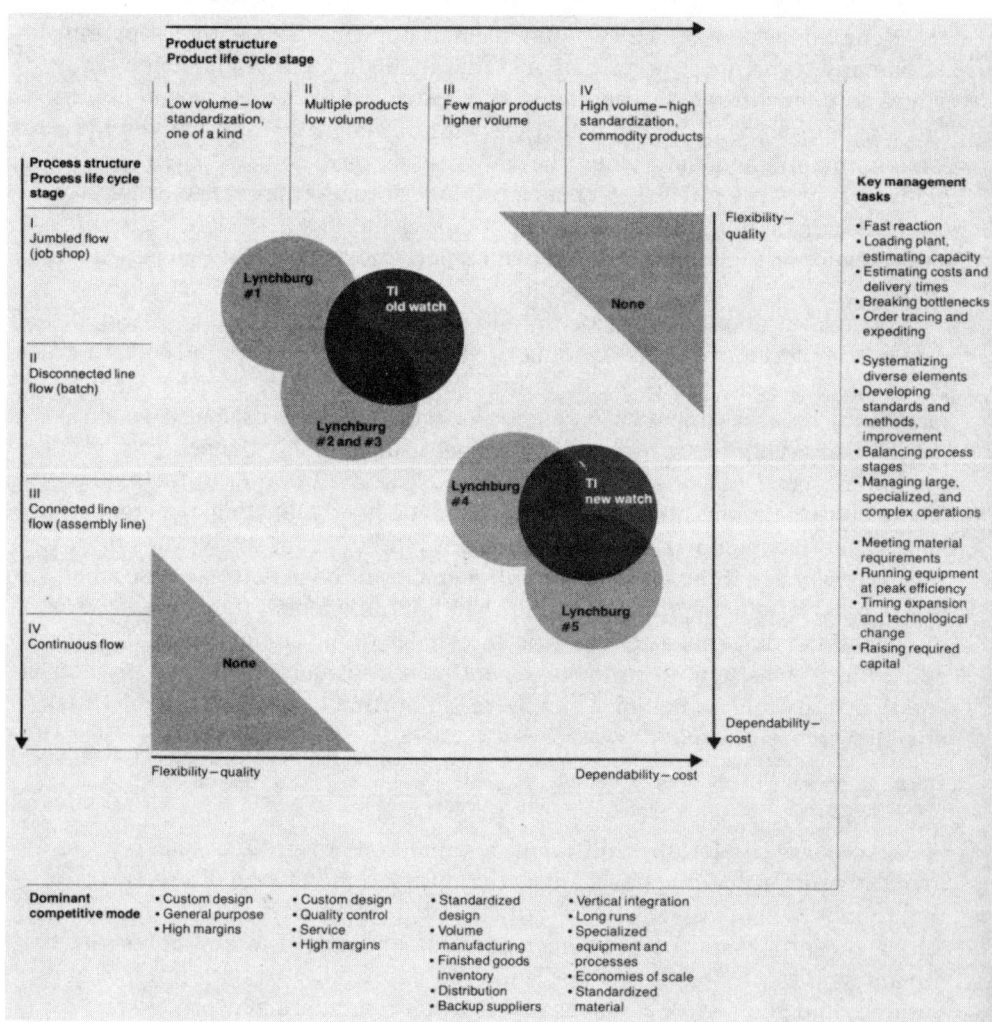

USING THE CONCEPT

of that structure by adopting the corresponding product structure. The former approach positions the company above the diagonal, whereas the latter positions it somewhere along it.

A company's location on the matrix should take into account its traditional orientation. Many companies tend to be relatively aggressive along the dimension—product or process—where they feel most competent and take the other dimension as "given" by the industry and environment. For example, a marketing-oriented company seeking to be responsive to the needs of a given market is more likely to emphasize flexibility and quality than the manufacturing-oriented company that seeks to mold the market to its cost or process leadership.

An example of these two competitive approaches in the electric motor industry is provided by the contrast between Reliance Electric and Emerson Electric. Reliance, on the one hand, has apparently chosen production processes that place it above the diagonal for a given product and market, and the company emphasizes product customizing and performance. Emerson, on the other hand, tends to position itself below the diagonal and emphasizes cost reduction. As a result of this difference in emphasis, the majority of Reliance's products are in the upper left quadrant, whereas Emerson's products tend to be in the lower right quadrant. Even where the two companies' product lines overlap, Reliance is likely to use a more fluid process for that product, whereas Emerson is more likely to use a standardized process.

Each company has sought to develop a set of competitive skills in manufacturing and marketing that will make it more effective within its selected quadrants.

Concentrating on the upper left versus the lower right quadrant has many additional implications for a company. The management that chooses to compete primarily in the upper left has to decide when to drop or abandon a product or market, whereas for the management choosing to compete in the lower right a major decision is when to enter the market. In the latter case, the company can watch the market develop and does not have as much need for flexibility as do companies that position themselves in the upper left, since product and market changes typically occur less frequently during the later phases of the product life cycle.

Such thinking about both product and process expertise is particularly useful in selecting the match of these two dimensions for a new product. Those familiar with the digital watch industry may recall that in the early 1970s Texas Instruments introduced a jewelry line digital watch. This product represented a matrix combination in the upper left-hand quadrant, as shown in Exhibit 2. Unfortunately, this line of watches was disappointing to Texas Instruments, in terms of both volume and profitability. Early in 1976, therefore, TI introduced a digital watch selling for $19.95. With only one electronic module and a connected line flow production process, this watch represented a combination of product and process further down the diagonal and much more in keeping with TI's traditional strengths and emphases.

Organizing Operations

If management considers the process structure dimension of organizational competence and strategy, it can usually focus its operating units much more effectively on their individual tasks. For example, many companies face the problem of how to organize production of spare parts for their primary products. Although increasing volume of the primary products may have caused the company to move down the diagonal, the follow-on demand for spare parts may require a combination of product and process structures more toward the upper left-hand corner of the matrix. There are many more items to be manufactured, each in smaller volume, and the appropriate process tends to be more flexible than may be the case for the primary product.

To accommodate the specific requirements of spare parts production, a company might develop a separate facility for them or simply separate their production within the same facility. Probably the least appropriate approach is to leave such production undifferentiated from the production of the basic product, since this would require the plant to span too broad a range of both product and process, making it less efficient and less effective for both categories of product.

The choice of product and process structures will determine the kind of manufacturing problems that will be important for management. Some of the key tasks related to a particular process structure are indicated on the right side of Exhibit 2. Recognizing the impact that the company's position on the matrix has on these important tasks will often suggest changes in various aspects of the policies and procedures the company uses in managing its manufacturing function, particularly in its manufacturing control system. Also, measures used to monitor and evaluate the company's manufacturing performance must reflect the matrix position selected if such measures are to be both useful and consistent with the corporate goals and strategy.

Such a task-oriented analysis might help a company avoid the loss of control over manufacturing that often results when a standard set of control mechanisms is applied to all products and processes. It also suggests the need for different types of management skills (and managers), depending on the company's major manufacturing tasks and dominant competitive modes.

Although a fairly narrow focus may be required for success in any single product market, companies that are large enough can (and do) effectively produce multiple products in multiple markets. These are often in different stages of the product life cycle. However, for such an operation to be successful, a company must separate and organize its manufacturing facilities to best meet the needs of each product and then develop sales volumes that are large enough to make those manufacturing units competitive.

An example of separating a company's total manufacturing capability into specialized units is provided by the Lynchburg Foundry, a wholly owned subsidiary of the Mead Corporation. This foundry has five plants in Virginia. As Exhibit 2 shows, these plants represent different positions on the matrix. One plant is a jobshop, making mostly one-of-a-kind products. Two plants use a decoupled batch process and make several major products. A fourth plant is a paced assembly line operation that makes only a few products, mainly for the automotive market. The fifth plant is a highly automated pipe plant, making what is largely a commodity item.

Although the basic technology is somewhat different in each plant, there are many similarities. However, the production layout, the manufacturing processes, and the control systems are very different. This company chose to design its plants so that each would meet the needs of a specific segment of the market in the most competitive manner. Its success would suggest that this has been an effective way to match manufacturing capabilities with market demand.

Companies that specialize their operating units according to the needs of specific narrowly defined patches on the matrix will often encounter problems in integrating those units into a coordinated whole. A recent article suggested that a company can be most successful by organizing its manufacturing function around either a product-market focus or a process focus.[6] That is, individual units will either manage themselves relatively autonomously, responding directly to the needs of the markets they serve, or they will be divided according to process stages (for example, fabrication, subassembly, and final assembly), all coordinated by a central staff.

Companies in the major materials industries—steel companies and oil companies, for example—provide classic examples of process-organized manufacturing organizations. Most companies that broaden the span of their process through vertical integration tend to adopt such an organization, at least initially. Then again, companies that adopt a product or market-oriented organization in manufacturing tend to have a strong market orientation and are unwilling to accept the organizational rigidity and lengthened response time that usually accompany centralized coordination.

Most companies in the packaging industry provide examples of such product and market-focused manufacturing organizations. Regional plants that serve geographical market areas are set up to reduce transportation costs and provide better response to market requirements.

A number of companies that historically have organized themselves around products or markets have found that, as their products matured and as they have moved to become more vertically integrated, a conflict has arisen between their original product-organized manufacturing facilities and the needs of their process-oriented internal supply units.

As the competitive emphasis has shifted toward cost, companies moving along the diagonal have tended to evolve from a product-oriented manufacturing organization to a process-oriented one. However, at some point, such companies often discover that their operations have become so complex with increased volume and increased stages of in-house production that they defy centralized coordination and management must revert to a more product-oriented organization within a divisionalized structure.

Strategy Implications

We can now pull together a number of threads and summarize their implications for corporate strategy. Companies must make a series of interrelated marketing and manufacturing decisions. These choices must be continually reviewed and sometimes changed as the company's products and competitors evolve and mature. A company may choose a product or marketing strategy that gives it a broader or narrower product line than its principal competitors. Such a choice positions it to the left or right of its competitors, along the horizontal dimension of our matrix.

Having made this decision, the company has a further choice to make: Should it produce this product line with a manufacturing system—a set of people, plants, equipment, technology, policies, and control procedures—that will permit a relatively high degree of flexibility and a relatively low capital intensity? Or should it prefer a system that will permit lower cost production with a loss of some flexibility to change (in products, production volumes, and equipment) and usually a higher degree of capital intensity? This choice will position the company above or below its competitors along the vertical dimension of our matrix.

There are, of course, several dynamic aspects of corporate competitiveness where the concepts of matching the product life cycle with the process life cycle can be applied. In this article, however, we have dealt only with the more static aspects of selecting a position on the matrix. We will discuss in a forthcoming article how a company's position on the product–process matrix might change over time and the traps that it can fall into if the implications of such moves are not carefully evaluated.

Notes

1. *The Product Life Cycle and International Trade*, Louis T. Wells, Jr., ed. (Cambridge, MA, Harvard University Press, 1972), for example, provides evidence from a number of industries that argues for broad application of this concept.

2. N.K. Dhalla and S. Yuspeh, "Forget the Product Life Cycle Concept!" *HBR*, January–February 1976, p. 102.

3. For example, William J. Abernathy and Philip L. Townsend, "Technology, Productivity, and Process Changes," in *Technological Forecasting and Social Change*, Volume VII, No. 4, 1975, p. 379; Abernathy and James Utterback, "Dynamic Model of Process and Product Innovation," *Omega*, Vol. III, No. 6, 1975, p. 639; Abernathy and Utterback, "Innovation and the Evolution of Technology in the Firm," Harvard Business School Working Paper (*HBS* 75-18R, Revised June 1975).

4. See "Manufacturing—Missing Link in Corporate Strategy," by Wickham Skinner, *HBR*, May–June 1969, p. 136. Chapter 5, this volume.

5. "The Focused Factory," *HBR*, May–June 1974, p. 113. Chapter 10, this volume.

6. Robert H. Hayes and Roger W. Schmenner, "How Should You Organize Manufacturing?" *HBR*, January–February 1978, p. 105. Chapter 11, this volume.

The Dynamics of Process-Product Life Cycles

ROBERT H. HAYES and STEVEN C. WHEELWRIGHT

Using the process–product life cycle they described in a previous issue of *HBR*, these authors examine the possible effects on a company of change in either its products or its production processes. If a company ignores the changes brought about by maturing markets, technological developments, or even the effects of the learning curve, serious internal problems can result. The authors explore different types of growth, such as product proliferation and vertical integration, to show how they affect manufacturing and marketing, pointing out the various strategic choices that are open to a company as a result.

In a previous issue of *HBR* we reviewed the concept of the "process life cycle," in contrast with the more familiar "product life cycle," and suggested that a framework that incorporates both concepts provides a more useful vehicle for exploring strategy options than does a framework based on only one of them.[1] We proposed the "product–process matrix" as a way of combining these concepts into a framework for describing alternative business strategies and examining their implications for the company's manufacturing organization.

In our earlier article, we limited ourselves essentially to exploring issues related to corporate "positioning" on the matrix; that is, to choosing how a company prefers to compete (see Exhibit 1, Chapter 7).

☐ To the left or to the right of the matrix diagonal (implying, respectively, greater product diversity and more rapid product change, or fewer more stable products).

☐ Above or below the matrix diagonal (implying either flexible, less capital-intensive processes or more mechanized, cost-efficient, and rigid processes).

We next examined the familiar concept of distinctive competence—the notion that each company should identify and exploit those resources, skills, and organizational characteristics that give it a comparative advantage over its competitors—and we used this concept to link a company's manufacturing competence with its product and market competence.

We also considered the management implications of selecting a product and a process position vis-à-vis others in the industry. Although related to a company's distinctive competence, this choice reflects the added dimension of viability and dominance in considering various positions on the matrix.

Finally, we explored the problems that multidivisional companies face when their different divisions position themselves in different areas of the matrix. We suggested ways in which such companies might organize their manufacturing functions to better cope with such diversity.

If nothing changed in the world, this matrix framework might serve only as an interesting adjunct to more traditional strategy formulation models—adding a nuance here and some extra insight there. The problem for corporate management is that everything is always changing, and simultaneously. Markets are evolving and maturing, processes are undergoing technological change, and costs and prices are continually being buffeted by forces ranging from the Organization of Petroleum Exporting Countries (OPEC) to the operating changes that result in the learning curve.

The impact of such external forces is often to change a company's position on the matrix, relative to many of its competitors, whether or not the company makes any changes in its own product or process structures. If such changes and their implications go unrecognized, the result can be a series of severe internal problems. These problems cannot be "managed away," typically, since they arise out of basic structural inconsistencies and inadequacies. Good managers who are assigned to deal with them may become sacrificial lambs.

In our observation of a number of manufacturing companies that have gotten into trouble, we have been struck by the sense of aimlessness, the low esprit de corps, and the lack of perspective that usually tend to permeate them. Although there may be a variety of causes for their problems, two stand out as being particularly important. The first is that coordination and mutual understanding between the marketing and manufacturing functions have broken down. Second, one or both functions have lost their sense of focus; they no longer feel the sense of competence and the implicit understanding of priorities that come when both marketing and manufacturing know they are doing something that the company is particularly good at and that the market desires.

Change in Position

The framework of the product–process matrix concept provides an excellent vehicle for understanding why these problems occur and how they can be minimized. No matter how tightly focused and coordinated a company might be, any change in the relative positioning of either its products or its production processes will expose it to two kinds of danger.

The first follows a change in either dimension without a corresponding change in the other so that there is a reduction in focus and increased difficulty in coordinating manufacturing and marketing.

A company that automates its production process without understanding the problems that such automation is likely to cause for its marketing organization is laying the groundwork for a potentially acrimonious future relationship between the two functions. It is also impairing its ability to compete as effectively as can companies that have coordinated and matched more closely the changes in their product and process structures.

The second difficulty, possibly even more dangerous than the first, follows when a company tries to respond to a change on one dimension by broadening its activity on the other; such as responding to a product shift, not with a corresponding shift in the production process but by adding an additional process.

Loss of Focus

The need for focus is quite well understood by marketing people. They segment markets and design products, prices, promotional strategies, and sales organizations to meet the specific imperatives of each segment. If the needs of one segment are quite different from those of another, they do not hesitate to pursue different strategies, and they often use different people in responding to these needs. Concentrating on a restricted segment of activities is just as important in manufacturing, but unfortunately the resistance to piecemeal changes and incremental expansion tends often to be lower there.

The packaging operation of a major consumer products manufacturer provides an illustration of this latter difficulty. The sole reason for the division's existence in the corporation was to offer a low-cost source for a highly specialized packaging product. This division, which was evaluated as a profit center, found that it could increase its revenues and profits considerably if it augmented its basic product lines with some new less standardized higher priced products. However, as the division pursued this additional business, it encountered pressure to change its process so that it could better meet the needs of its new customers. Responding to such pressures, the division began to dilute the focus it had maintained for several years.

Another example is a company that found its standardized product line being challenged by other more marketing-oriented companies that were seeking to segment the market and target specialized forms of the product for each segment. When the company responded by expanding its own line to offer specialized products, it found that its high-volume, standardized production processes were not economical at those lower volumes and that it could not compete effectively with other companies which had designed their processes for the specific volume and product standardization of their segments of the market.

In both of these examples, if the company had considered coordinated, compensating changes in both the product and the process dimensions, it would have selected options that maintained or increased its competitive competence rather than simply tried to broaden its activity on one dimension or the other, which diluted its past competence.

While the matrix concept can explain the causes of many failures in previously healthy companies, it can provide even more useful insights for planning product and process changes. Since planning for growth concentrates management attention on decisions regarding both product and process activities, growth is a natural framework for the next segment of this discussion.

Planning for Growth

Companies typically pursue four major types of growth. Going from the simpler types to the more complex, these can be summarized as follows:

1 Simple growth of sales volume within an existing product line and market.
2 Expansion of the product line within a single market, using an existing process structure (often called product proliferation).
3 Expansion of the process structure (usually termed vertical integration).
4 Expansion into new products and markets.

Although other forms of growth exist, they can generally be viewed as variations or combinations of these four types. Thus an understanding of the demands that each might place on manufacturing and marketing can do much to aid in planning for continued coordination and focus of these functions.

Type 1: Simple Growth

The simplest form of growth consists of increased volume that is met with an existing product line and existing production process. This type of growth opportunity requires that extremely stable conditions exist—in terms of competitors, technology, and market tastes—with the only change occurring in the size of the market. Unfortunately, such conditions are the exception rather than the rule, and thus even when a company limits itself to fairly narrow product and process activities, periodic changes will be required as markets and technologies mature.

In the context of a single product line and a single process structure, incremental changes in each reflect a type of simple growth. However, the company must now make two kinds of decisions. The first relates to both the entrance and the exit strategies for a specific market, and the second to the strategy to be pursued while the company is participating in that market. The matrix concept is useful for examining and planning for both of these.

Entrance–Exit Strategies. In the first area, the company tends to follow one of four entrance–exit strategies. In summary, the company:

A Enters early and then, when technology stabilizes, profit margins narrow, and the larger companies following strategy C begin to appear, it leaves that product and attempts to exploit the company's superior flexibility and technological skills in the introductory phases of some new product.

B Enters early and grows up with the industry, seeking to be a major factor in the business throughout the product's entire life cycle.

C Waits on the sidelines until some degree of product and process stabilization has occurred and then enters the industry, so that it can better exploit its more massive production, distribution, and marketing resources.

D Waits to enter, anticipating that it is following strategy C, but when it does enter, fails to gain a sustainable market position and consequently chooses to withdraw without having made an adequate return on its investment.

As shown in Exhibit 1, the four segments of the product-market dimension of the matrix can be used to form a Latin square representing the combinations of entrance and exit strategies available to a company.

Until relatively recently, strategy B was considered the "normal" or most desirable, whereas A and C were examples of either lost nerve or lucky accidents, respectively. The model of a successful company was one that developed a new product that became the basis for a major industry and then "rode on its back" to success. Polaroid and Xerox provide classic examples.

Exhibit 1. Combinations of Entrance and Exit Strategies

	Exit Strategy	
Entrance Strategy	Maturity	Decline
Rapid growth	**D** Mistake	**C** Efficient, standardized, high volume
Start-up	**A** Innovative, flexible	**B** Starts flexible, shifts to standardized and high volume

But such a strategy can put an enormous strain on a company, particularly when its industry matures rapidly. The same people who managed the introduction of the new product may be called on to manage its evolution into a commodity item. The type of production process, the level of capital intensity, the marketing skills, the distribution channels, in fact the whole personality of the company, must undergo profound change in the space of a relatively few years.

An example of such change is provided by the microwave oven business. As the market leader since the early 1960s, Litton Industries Atherton Division has emphasized flexibility in its production facilities to respond to the frequent product changes required by a young rapidly growing market.

With the maturing of the market expected in the late 1970s, however, the entry of more traditional appliance manufacturers, and increased competition from Japanese imports, Litton recently has been forced to review its earlier policies as to how far it should move toward vertical integration and more automated production processes. By the early 1980s, Litton-Atherton will be a very different company, requiring different skills, organizational practices, and probably a different management style if it is to continue to mature with the market successfully and maintain its earlier position.

Strategy C is particularly favored by large national or multinational companies whose production systems emphasize high stable volumes and low variable costs. These companies can exploit their large sales forces' distribution channels, advertising expertise, and overall "market clout," and they have easy access to capital markets for the funds required by the scale and capital intensity of their mode of competition.

A number of large companies that were seduced by the "go go" atmosphere of the late 1960s into entering small rapidly changing markets found to their regret that they simply were not very good—or, at best, no better—than the smaller companies that were competing in the same markets. Most of them have since retreated to doing the things they can do best.

Although strategy A is still regarded largely as a strategy for the "little guys," it is becoming increasingly attractive to companies that prefer not to compete in high-volume–low-margin businesses, and to many highly diversified companies whose managers look on their job as one of managing a portfolio of assets. The managers of such companies are willing to use the cash flow from mature products, at the end of their product life cycles, to finance the growth and success of products or subsidiaries in earlier stages, and to liquidate such products (and often their associated companies) entirely when they can no longer meet the company's profitability goals.

Strategy D, of entering late and leaving early, is probably never pursued intentionally, since there is not sufficient time to reap the rewards necessary to justify the initial investment. Nevertheless, this strategy is seen from time to time, as illustrated by the experience in calculators of Rockwell International.

In 1974 Rockwell entered the calculator business but exited only a couple of years later, having failed to gain a tenable position in that industry. Rockwell had several problems, but these may simply represent the cumulative challenges a company faces by waiting to enter a business until the industry has proceeded far down the diagonal. Even with relative success, the costs associated with starting up a high-volume operation at that stage can be substantial, as Kodak's entry into instant photography illustrates.

A further form of late entry difficulty that the matrix concept clarifies is entry into the lower right quadrant with a totally new production process. Since the product is already a commodity item, the process must be continuous and highly efficient to be competitive. Successful entry at this point would be extremely challenging with a proved process but is doubly so if a new process must be developed without the benefit of passing incrementally through the early stages of the process life cycle. Recent efforts at coal gasification and oil shale processing appear to be examples of this.

Paths on the Matrix. Once a company selects an entrance–exit strategy for a market, management must select a strategy for both product and process developments. Although these must be based in part on assessments of how the market will develop and competitors will react, management should consider a variety of strategies. One way to view these options is as possible paths on the matrix.

An industry usually progresses down the diagonal of the matrix. Of course, if this always occurred, it would be possible to collapse the two-dimensional matrix into a single dimension and to base analyses and projections on either a product life cycle or a process life cycle footing. But, even though movement along the diagonal is the composite pattern (the industry average, in a sense), it is a much less likely pattern for any individual company to follow. This is because companies tend to make only one kind of change at a time—either a product structure change or a process structure change.

At a given point a company will usually face a clear choice either between alternative product structres, given an existing production process structure, or between alternative process structures for producing an existing product structure. Progression down the diagonal, *if* it occurs, therefore usually involves a series of roughly alternating vertical and horizontal steps.

Moreover, both the size and the frequency of these steps are dictated more by the rate of product maturation and technological innovation than by corporate wishes. As a result, it is seldom possible to move smoothly down the diagonal. A company can, however, through consistency in its decisions over time, "lean" in one direction or the other—moving roughly parallel to the diagonal but either above or below it—or attempt to stay as close to the diagonal as possible.

There is no best choice; it is simply a matter of corporate preference for one mode of competitive behavior or another. Maintaining a position above the diagonal will maintain flexibility to change products, production volumes, and processes quickly, and will reduce the company's capital needs. However, it will make the company vulnerable to competitors who can undercut its price, offer greater delivery dependability and, possibly, tighter product specifications as well.

If the product life cycle moves too rapidly toward fewer, more standard products, such companies may suddenly find themselves too far above the diagonal, with old, outmoded, inefficient, high-cost plants and unneeded product and volume flexibility.

Nor is it necessarily preferable for a company to try to position itself below the diagonal. The appropriateness of such a strategy depends highly on how rapid and inexorable the product's evolution along the product life cycle is. Moving vertically down the process dimension usually implies a reduction in cost per unit but an increase in capital investment and the breakeven point. As long as there is no major change in the design of individual products, or the volume mix across products in the product line, a company may achieve a significant competitive advantage from such a decision.

Conversely, seeking to maintain a position below the diagonal can lock the company into a set of facilities and manufacturing capabilities that will make it difficult to respond to the market changes that usually accompany movement along the product life cycle. Moreover, if the product progresses too rapidly, the company may not receive its expected return from an investment in increased mechanization until after the next step in product evolution renders it obsolete. This explains why the required investment payback period in the electronics industry is typically less than 18 months and sometimes as low as 6 months, while it is typically 8 years or more in the steel and oil industries.

A company also has to protect itself against the possibility of the product life cycle "reversing direction" after it has moved toward a more standardized production process. This is the familiar phenomenon of product proliferation that companies often succumb to when trying to stimulate sales in a relatively mature market. This can cause a company's manufacturing strengths to become incompatible with its marketing strategy, particularly if it was already below the diagonal before the shift.

William Abernathy's research in the automobile industry has suggested that product innovation tends to lead in the early stages of the product's progression through the product life cycle, while process innovation takes the lead later on.[2] Although this analysis may hold in the majority of cases, a number of counterexamples can be identified. These suggest that innovation may follow a much more intricate pattern, with process and product interchanging leadership roles more than once.

An example of such a pattern in the electronics industry is the radio. It followed the standard life cycle until about 1955, when a process innovation (printed circuit boards using transistors) produced the miniature battery-powered radio, and product innovation (FM and stereo receivers) followed. Recently, another process innovation (microcircuitry) has resulted in the development of another product, the low-cost CB radio (a transmitter as well as a receiver). For the radio, maturity appears to have been a transitory phenomenon.

The Model T Ford provides another example of a product that was rushed to maturity. When Alfred P. Sloan of General Motors competed against this commodity product by offering product variety, he caused the industry to be reborn. An *HBR* article argues that such rebirth—the ability to create variety in a standard product, which in effect is moving it back along the product life cycle continuum—is the key to success for marketing organizations.[3]

A related issue that is perhaps even more interesting is determining why some products never seem to complete their progression down the matrix diagonal. Instead, they appear to have stalled at some point. Classic examples are home building and furniture, both of which seem to be victims of an arrested product development. Processes already exist that would carry both products further down the diagonal if increased product standardization were to be allowed by the consumer. In the case of home building, this appeared to become possible with the popularization of the mobile home, but, if anything, this product has become *less* standardized over the past decade. The mobile home industry now finds itself in the same frustrating predicament as the more traditional home industry.

Once an industry stops progressing (other examples include construction equipment, sailboats, and clothing), a key question is how it can get started again. The answer to that question does not appear to lie in process innovation, given the abortive attempts in both home building (modular homes built from plastic or metal components) and furniture (molded or pressed plastic forms). The failure of these industries to achieve the systematic efficiency of the auto industry is not due to the lack of process opportunities but to the inability of the market to standardize.

As might be expected, as a company moves too far away from the matrix diagonal in either direction, it becomes increasingly dissimilar from its competitors. This may or may not (depending on its success in exploiting the advantages of its niche), make it more vulnerable to their attacks. This position may also make coordinating marketing with manufacturing more difficult, since the two functions will develop different skills and priorities and will tend to respond to different sorts of opportunities.

Not infrequently, companies find that, either inadvertently or by conscious choice, they have become "outliers" on the matrix and must consider drastic remedial action. Most small companies that enter a mature industry start off as outliers, of course, and therefore they have to solve the problems associated with moving closer to the matrix diagonal at the same time they are coping with the usual small company problems of lack of working capital, lack of management depth, and the conflict between entrepreneurial and bureaucratic management styles.

Learning Curve. A final aspect of the movement along both the product and the process dimensions of the matrix that is particularly relevant for a company planning the simple Type 1 growth is the notion of learning. Some companies have used the so-called experience effect, or learning curve, which argues that product costs (in constant dollars) should decline at a steady rate every time cumulative production volume doubles, as the basis for their competitive strategy.[4] This learning phenomenon explains, for example, why companies with higher market shares tend to be more profitable (as measured in terms of return on investment) than their competitors.[5] Unfortunately, the term *learning-curve strategy* suggests a black-or-white choice: one either follows it or one does not.

Progression along the product life cycle alone, without any change in the process used (i.e., proceeding horizontally across the matrix), would still provide numerous opportunities for cost reduction—through product redesign, product-line simplification, development of improved raw materials and parts, increased sales volume, use of less costly distribution channels, and the fact that over time the whole organization simply learns to do its job better.

Similarly, moving vertically down the matrix provides other cost-reduction opportunities, through economies of scale, improved materials-handling technology, and better tools and equipment as well as reduced labor costs through automation. What is called the experience curve is simply the combination of these two effects resulting in movement down the matrix diagonal. In other words, the experience curve depicts the total improvement in unit costs obtainable by combining product evolution with process evolution.

A company that prefers to follow a path above the diagonal (see Exhibit 2) will thereby limit its cost-reduction opportunities, so that, when it reaches a given level of product standardization, it may be able to reduce its unit cost only 90% of its previous value after each doubling of cumulative volume. It will, however, preserve its flexibility to follow market movements quickly, and it will limit its capital investment.

A company that chooses to follow a path below the diagonal may achieve even greater cost reductions for a given level of product standardization than those pursuing a path on the diagonal. The danger of this strategy is that those cost reductions may make the company very inflexible to product changes, and the benefits may be short lived.

A company that follows a more balanced progression of product and process changes so as to remain near the matrix diagonal can often achieve faster rates of learning than those consistently above it but slower rates of

Exhibit 2. Possible Learning Curve Strategies

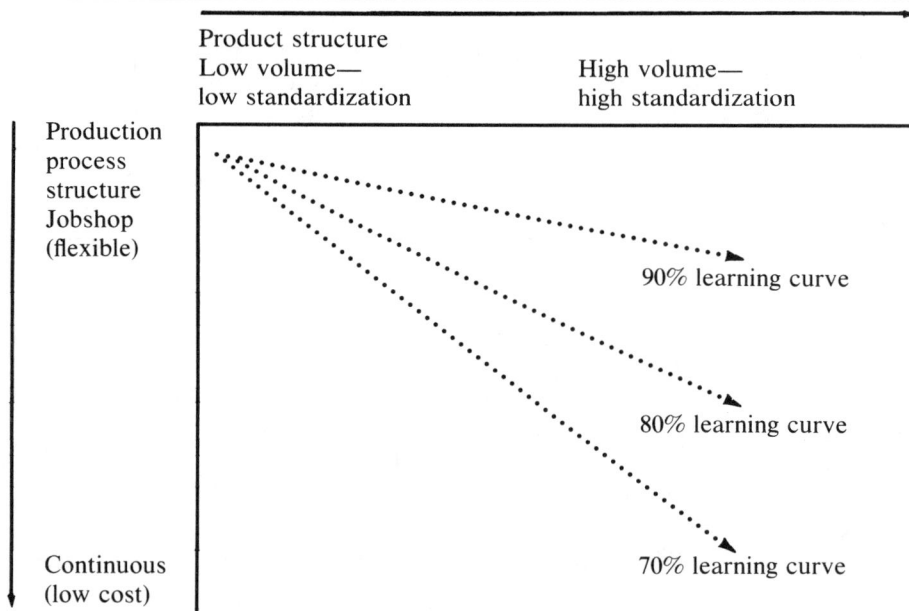

Note: An 80% learning curve implies that unit costs will be reduced to 80% of their previous value each time cumulative volume doubles.

learning than those below it. However, such an approach takes advantage of potential cost improvements coming from both dimensions while maintaining flexibility to respond to market shifts. For many companies, this flexibility is worth the forgone cost improvements available through more aggressive pursuit of process standardization.

As with the other aspects of strategy examined in this article, no single answer fits all companies. The best strategy for a given company will depend on its resources, skills, market situation, competitive pressures, and general business philosophy.

The real issue is not whether learning improvements will be pursued as *the* driving force for marketing and production decisions but rather the degree to which such improvement possibilities will guide management's actions. Depending on whether a company seeks simple Type 1 growth by pursuing product and process movements on the diagonal, rather than above or below it, will largely determine the learning improvements that are likely to be realized.

Type 2: Product Growth

In the context of our matrix, this type of growth represents a broadening of the product line. Such growth can occur in two ways. One is by adding more standardized products while maintaining existing less standardized products. The addition of new products, combined with a reluctance to drop a part of the product line, represents a shift to the left on the product dimension. Marketing believes that "good service" requires a "full line." Manufacturing thinks that almost any sale can be shown to make a net contribution to overhead and fixed costs. As a result, even when a company is at capacity, it can sometimes be extremely difficult to get a consensus on a decision to narrow the product line.

The other way that this type of growth can occur is to add special features to an existing more standardized product line. Such product expansion also represents movement on the matrix from right to left that goes against the prevailing current of the product life cycle (which assumes continual standardization of products). This is often a cyclical problem in capital intensive industries as companies seek to use existing capacity to meet the specialized needs of a number of secondary markets.

The real danger of such product proliferation growth, as many companies know too well, is that it may cause the company's product structure to put unreasonable strains on its production processes. To avoid such problems, management must add products selectively and take actions related to physical facilities, organizational structures, and operating procedures that will compensate for many of these strains. (We discussed these and other actions in our earlier article; see Chapter 7.)

Type 3: Vertical Integration

Growth based on broadening the scope of the production process (vertical integration) can also be udnerstood more clearly by using our matrix. In a manner analogous to product proliferation, this form of growth occurs when a company maintains existing processes and adds either less standardized more flexible processes (forward integration) or more standardized less flexible processes (backward integration) in hopes of either increasing sales volume and market responsiveness or reducing costs and improving dependability.

The problems that companies often encounter when they vertically integrate, even in the simplest case where they begin making a part that they formerly bought from an outside supplier, can be significant. What is usually involved is not simply an expansion of the company's processes but the production of a completely different product that may be at a very different point on the matrix.

In other words, the company may have to think in terms of an additional matrix for that component part or raw material and develop strategies for it that are very different from those selected for the original end product. If this is not done, the company may be tempted to produce the new part with a process and an organizational structure that are completely inappropriate.

An example of one approach to this problem is provided by the experience of the Trus Joist Corporation, which manufactures custom floor and roof support systems for both residential and commercial construction.

Before 1970, the company used sawed lumber as the major raw material in its joist products, which were fabricated and assembled in a number of regional plants. These small flexible plants were consistent with the company's product line and markets and its made-to-order strategy. However, when it developed and introduced Micro-Lam, a unique laminated structural material, as a replacement to sawed lumber in many of its products, the company's span of process became much broader than it had been.

Given the capital intensity of the Micro-Lam production process and its high degree of standardization, Trus Joist chose to separate the two stages of its production process and to organize itself as if it were in two separate markets, even though it anticipated using all of its Micro-Lam output as raw material for its joist plants.

Type 4: New Markets

Growth through expansion into new markets, Type 4, is even more difficult to deal with than the other three types, because it may follow any of several paths. If the company can avoid product proliferation, for example, market expansion may simply imply an increase in scale (Type 1 growth). Alternatively, a company may want to reflect the individual requirements of the new market by creating a new matrix for it and plotting a separate strategy for that market. This mirrors the approach followed by Trus Joist when it broadened its process.

More commonly, a company's involvement in a new market subjects it to pressures to expand its product line—in effect, to retreat horizontally on the matrix. This creates a situation that most companies find particularly difficult to deal with, because both the production and the marketing sides of the business encounter problems (different, but complementary) at about the same time—marketing because it is trying to adapt itself to a new market for which its process is not adequately suited, and production because it is trying to adapt to new products that put analogous strains on its process.

This situation often leads to what can be described as the "creeping breakeven" phenomenon. In an effort to stimulate demand, a company enters a new market or introduces a new product. This step is successful at first, but the existing process is incapable of meeting the added scale and complexity without additional investment (more capacity, different equipment, more make rather than buy, or a more powerful inventory control system). Success tends to breed failure. The increased investment raises the company's breakeven point, offsetting the expected gains from the increased sales volume. This motivates the company to pursue additional markets and products so as to break out of the box in which it finds itself.

In Summary

In this article and its predecessor, we have attempted to introduce and apply a framework that can help a company to conduct a diagnosis of its strategic evolution, think creatively about possible future strategic directions, and explicitly involve both marketing and manufacturing in coordinating and implementing its competitive goals. Moreover, in analyzing the various opportunities and pressures that companies face as markets and technologies evolve, the approach we describe illustrates why companies can so easily lose their way.

Another advantage of this approach is that it encourages a company's managers to think creatively about their strategy for process evolution: What kinds of process changes are appropriate and when should they occur? The managers can then use this framework to position themselves along these two dimensions so that both marketing and manufacturing are responsible for a restricted or focused set of products and process characteristics.

The concepts outlined both in this and in our earlier article can be useful in the following ways:

1. Determining the appropriate mix of manufacturing facilities, identifying the key manufacturing objectives for each plant, and monitoring progress on those objectives at the corporate level.

2 Reviewing investment decisions for plant and equipment in terms of their consistency with product and process plans.
3 Determining the direction and timing of major changes in a company's production processes.
4 Evaluating product and market opportunities in light of the company's manufacturing capabilities.
5 Selecting an appropriate process and product structure for entry into a new market.

Notes

1. "Link Manufacturing Process and Product Life Cycles," *HBR*, January–February 1979, p. 133. Chapter 7, this volume.

2. See William J. Abernathy and Phillip L. Townsend, "Technology, Productivity, and Process Change," *Technological Forecasting and Social Change*, Vol. 7, 1975, p. 379; and James Utterback and William J. Abernathy, "A Dynamic Model of Process and Product Innovation," *Omega*, December 1975, p. 639.

3. Nariman K. Dhalla and Sonia Yuspeh, "Forget the Product Life Cycle Concept," *HBR*, January–February 1976, p. 102.

4. Winfred B. Hirschmann, "Profit from the Learning Curve," *HBR*, January–February 1964, p. 125.

5. The research done by the Marketing Science Institute, and reported in this magazine, tends to confirm this; see Sidney Schoeffler, Robert D. Buzzell, and Donald F. Heany, "Impact of Strategic Planning on Profit Performance," *HBR*, March–April 1974, p. 137.

9
Operations Versus Strategy: Trading Tomorrow for Today

ROBERT L. BANKS and STEVEN C. WHEELWRIGHT

Often in decision making, operating managers face alternatives that not only affect immediate profits but also touch on the long-term strategic objectives of their corporations. Frequently, managers opt for the alternative that improves short-run performance at the expense—sometimes considerable—of the timely achievement of long-term corporate goals. This article examines the prevalence and nature of trade-offs between short-term and long-term objectives. The analysis is based on a study of six major corporations. The authors also look at the question of what controls can be used to ensure that conflicts between short and long-term goals are handled with a balanced perspective.

The end of the year was approaching with frightening speed. Sales were off because of an unexpected downturn in the economy, and profits were below projection. The pressure was on from top management. "You'd better make your profit projections, George, or you'll never make the spring cuts," was how the boss had described the situation.

What to do? Only one thing was possible. Dramatically cut costs by laying off a third of the work force. If the downturn continues, George reasoned, we'll be in good shape to ride it out. If it isn't as bad as we think it will be, then after the holidays we can rehire many of the workers laid off. Most important, my division will make its last-quarter profit goals. Considering the kind of year it has been, that could mean a bonus *and* a promotion!

No doubt managers everywhere have sweated over this kind of pressure at one time or another and have reacted as well as they knew how in the face of adversity to salvage profits—and maybe, like George, even their careers. In this particular case, as so often happens, George was hailed as a hero for saving the company's profits, a significant feat in the light of top management's optimistic promises to stockholders and the financial community.

But George's decision turned out to have devastating consequences for his company later on. A crucial building block in the company's strategy had long been to remain nonunion in order to avoid the costs associated with stringent work rules, restrictive hiring and promotion covenants, wildcat strikes, and the like—problems which plagued most major competitors. But not long after George's Christmas layoff, angry workers held a representation election, and by May the company had been unionized—not just George's division, but the entire company. George had made his short-term profit goals, but in the process had traded away one of the company's strategic competitive advantages.

Continual Tug-of-War

Although this example is extreme, the occurrence of detrimental trade-offs is an everday reality. In a study of six major U.S. companies, we documented numerous examples of short-term operating decisions that adversely affected long-term goal achievement. The tug-of-war between short-term and long-term goals is a dilemma that corporations face recurrently.

The conflict is basic. The attainment of long-range goals often involves resource commitments that may adversely affect profits in the current period, even though these investments may provide significant returns in later years. Additionally, achievement of long-range goals may require adherence to a specific strategy—such as a market, product, or labor relations strategy—that in certain economically difficult years might cause higher-than-normal expenses. In the short run, these expenses reduce profits, but, in the long run, they are "investments" designed to pay off.

There is constant pressure on operating management to produce ever-increasing annual profits regardless of long-term strategic implications. Sometimes the pressure is a result of overoptimistic promises made by top management to stockholders and to the financial community. At other times it is a matter of poor forecasting, either by the corporation or by the manager. Occasionally, a sister division fails to make its targets and another division must make up the difference in profits. However, regardless of the cause, the pressure is always there.

Our study shows that, compared with 10 or 15 years ago, there is growing awareness of the problem of short-term versus long-term conflicts in operating decisions—what we shall call, for ease of reference, the S/L trade-off. Our finding is consistent with the results of a recent study by the Conference Board.[1] (See the Appendix following this article for elaboration on our research methods.)

For one thing, S/L trade-offs are now more obvious than they used to be. Through the expansion and development of formal strategic planning processes during the past decade, top managers have become more aware of where their corporations should be going, and deviations from the prescribed course are more noticeable. For another, the consequences of inappropriate S/L trade-offs can be more significant as companies continue to grow in size and complexity. Managers receive greater authority and responsibility, especially in highly diversified firms, and decisions made favoring the short run over strategic goal achievement may have serious financial consequences.

In addition, it appears that the effects of unrelated S/L trade-offs can be cumulative. When viewed independently, many S/L trade-offs appear to have relatively mild consequences for a company. But even apparently minor S/L trade-offs may adversely affect a corporate strategy. Moreover, they can have a serious effect on the entire corporation. For instance, in the example about George, there had been earlier layoffs at certain divisions. George's decision provided the proverbial straw that broke the camel's back.

Many managers and planners we interviewed also feel that changes in the external business environment are occurring at a more rapid pace than in the past. These changes create increased pressure for short-term performance and make accurate forecasting more difficult. Compounding this problem, competition in U.S. and foreign markets seems greater. With slower growth rates in major economies of the world, many companies find themselves having to compete more vigorously to meet short and long-term goals than was the case in years past. This intensified competition stretches divisional management capabilities. As short-term profit commitments become more difficult to make, strategic objectives can suffer.

Where Trade-Offs Occur

The need to make trade-offs can arise at almost any level of the corporate structure and can affect a multitude of operating areas. In all of the six companies we studied, executives were able to contribute problematic examples of actual or potential S/L trade-offs. The problems can be divided into four categories, each of which we will discuss. For each category we will also give a detailed example of a trade-off situation. Sometimes, since the divisions are necessarily arbitrary, an example overlaps a couple of categories.

Postponing Capital Outlays

Capital expenditure programs are one of the most vulnerable areas for detrimental S/L trade-offs. The horizons for returns are more than a year off; yet the costs associated with implementing the programs can easily reduce near-term profits. Postponements can almost always free up capital and manpower resources needed to produce immediate operating profits.

Since almost any capital program is susceptible to this dilemma, we studied examples concerning new plant construction, additions to existing plant, new equipment purchases, upgrading of old equipment, production-process improvements, cost-reduction investments, and long-term product-development projects. A timely example is investing in energy efficiency. Capital projects involving needs like pollution control are highly vulnerable to the S/L trade-off problem, since the investments are generally capital-consuming rather than capital-generating. Consider this case.

One of the companies studied recently faced the prospect of replacing several relatively new and very expensive steam boilers with more efficient onces, since the company had projected a doubling of its already sizable fuel costs over the next five years. The current boiler costs were acceptable. The division manager knew that if she waited to replace the boilers until their efficiency became a serious liability in three or four years, her operating profits would remain higher in the meantime and her record would look better.

On the other hand, waiting would significantly increase the long-term cost to the company because of inflation, declining cost efficiency, and the fact that competitors (whose boilers were aging anyway) planned to add more fuel-efficient equipment within two years. Consequently, a difficult S/L trade-off had to be made.

This particular example, fortunately, had a happy ending. The division manager chose to install the new boilers right away. But suppose that a division manager in a similar situation knew that tenure would be short (for instance, the manager might be expecting a promotion or a transfer). Then the manager would be strongly tempted to decide the other way.

Deferring Operating Expenses

Many operating expenses for the current period can be postponed without causing undue harm to long-term goals. But other operating expenses can be vital to the timely accomplishment of strategic objectives. It usually is easy for a manager to postpone such expenses, since they are directly under his or her control and are often not monitored closely, if at all.

Indeed, some managers we interviewed indicated that they always overbudgeted certain operating expenses to provide a contingency fund which could be shifted around if the need arose. Only one of the six companies tightly locked managers into budgets and required formal approval of any transfers of expenses from one budget category to another. In the other companies, managers reported postponing expenses related to manpower development, advertising and public relations, maintenance, research and development, and marketing and product research.

Product-development expenses are a particularly choice target for cuts, leading frequently to detrimental S/L trade-offs.

1. At one company, division managers often postponed small product-development expenses, regardless of the possible significance to a marketing strategy, in order to achieve profit goals. However, these managers did not defer costs for larger projects under their responsibility because the latter had greater corporatewide visibility.

2. In another company, one with several lines of well-established products, managers often had to decide whether to continue to milk existing products for maximum profit or make the commitment required to develop new products. The latter meant some sacrifice of current earnings.

The historical tendency at this company had been for the managers to favor current products, because managerial performance was measured largely on the basis of short-term profits. Only recently had the company begun to substantially fund and require performance on the development of new products.

3. In a third company, the inertia of the status quo was so strong that, in order to ensure successful development of new markets for an old product line, management had to create a new division rather than attempt to encourage product development in the existing organization. Managers simply were unwilling to trade off any part of the present for the future (though of course they did not put it so baldly).

Reducing Operating Expenses

Expenses vital to long-term goals can be pared down as well as postponed. From a strategic standpoint, this can be equally dangerous. An expense often may be postponed without forgoing the associated benefits forever. A delay in incurring the expense slows down the product development, engineering, marketing, or other objective, but does not kill it.

On the other hand, eliminating some expenses in order to salvage profits can do irreparable damage to a company's position. In the example at the beginning, George translated pressure for short-term profit into layoffs that ultimately cost his company a significant strategic advantage in labor relations. In our study, we came across other such examples in marketing, field sales, quality control, and materials purchasing.

One area that can be of critical strategic importance is customer service; yet expenses for future improvements in service are all too easy to cut when the pressure for earnings is on. In an industrial products company, for example, customer service might include having the engineering staff work closely with customers on equipment installation and operation. If this extra effort is part of the company's long-term competitive advantage, cutbacks in it can permanently damage customer relations. So, too, can cuts in warranty terms and claims handling.

Another example is the classic production-versus-marketing trade-off, either minimizing inventories to lower costs or increasing them to improve product selection and delivery time. Again, in a hotel or restaurant chain, cuts in staffing and training to achieve short-term profits can be fatal in the long run. Any such moves can easily drive customers away and into the arms of a waiting competitor.

Other Operating Changes

Current profits can be improved at the expense of long-term goals in still other ways. Common methods include changes in the product mix, delivery, suppliers, marketing strategy, and pricing (both market pricing and intra-company-transfer pricing).

Price changes, in particular, are a simple way to make a trade-off. For example, one division manager's market was extremely sensitive to price changes, and management tightly controlled pricing actions by means of a multilayered approval process. Nevertheless, the manager admitted to having successfully used price changes to boost sales and reduce inventories, improving current operations but hurting customer service and goodwill.

Price increases can disproportionately affect market share. On the other hand, price decreases can mistakenly signal changes in strategic direction to competitors. Depending on the company and its industry, price reductions can even bring down the wrath of the federal government.

Why Managers Make Trade-Offs

When a division manager decides to favor short-term profits over long-term strategic goals, the manager has likely been influenced by two considerations. The first, and perhaps more influential, is the manner in which his or her performance is measured by the corporation. The second is a combination of a clear lack of balance between the short and long run as emphasized in corporate communications, linkages between the long-range plan and the operating budget, and the general "culture" of the company.

Evaluation of Performance

Although our study did not delve deeply into psychological factors, it is clear that performance evaluation is a key motivating factor in S/L trade-offs.[2] Naturally, managers are motivated to take actions that will reflect favorably on them personally, either immediately or in the future. Division managers at major corporations hold their positions largely because they have succeeded over time in managing their tasks the way the company decreed they should. They are very aware of how success is measured in their organization in terms of both status (e.g., peer evaluation, supervisor evaluation, rank, perquisites) and compensation (e.g., salary, commission, or bonus).

At the companies studied, it appears that the more important of the two performance evaluation motivators is status. Trade-offs appear to be made not so much with remuneration in mind (although it is important in a few instances) as with a careful eye on how the decision will be viewed by peers and superiors.

It comes as no surprise that, in general, the more a company emphasizes performance in the short run as a determinant for reward, the greater the tendency for managers to favor the near term. However, if a company allocates equal emphasis to both short-term and long-term goals, decisions appear to put the short and long terms in better balance. Two of the companies studied fell in the latter category and benefited from such a perspective:

☐ One assigned specific responsibilities to managers for strategic goal accomplishment (along with operating responsibilities) and measured the managers frequently on performance in both areas.

☐ The other company divided the annual bonus for a manager between specific strategic and operational objectives (e.g., 60% of bonus on operational goals; 40% on strategic ones). It also examined the manager's performance on both measures periodically during the operating year.

Imbalance in Emphasis

In the absence of other controls, there appears to be a natural tendency for operating managers to lean toward achieving short-term goals instead of long-term ones. Short-term goals are visible and easily comprehended. Clearly, they become dominant unless firm measures are taken to put them in perspective.

In most of the companies studied, this perspective is not fostered in communications. Division and lower-level managers are not always fully aware of their corporation's strategic aims. Most important, the managers do not always understand exactly how their operations fit into the company's grand plans.

Methods for communicating a balanced emphasis can take a variety of forms, such as publications about goals and meetings with upper and lower-level managers to discuss strategy. Whatever the method, several managers told us that "well-informed managers make good decisions, decisions that take into account the long-term good of the corporation."

Managerial perspectives are influenced also by the linkages between operating budgets and long-range financial plans. Considerable research has been done on the relative merits of loose and tight linkages.[3] We find that a tight link between the two appears to favor a balanced decision process.

The question of linkage usually arose during our interviews when we were probing weaknesses in planning processes. Generally, the long-range plan is the essential financial manifestation of the corporation's strategic objectives and is its intended accomplishment over a span of five or ten years. The operating budget, meanwhile, does double duty. It is the operating manager's road map for a small part of that time span. Also, it is an instrument to assist in the accomplishment of the long-term financial performance levels described in the long-range plan.

However, at three of the companies examined, the operating budgets were not developed as a specific part of the long-term plan. In fact, in one case, the operating budget was developed and locked into operations before the long-range plan (including the current year) was finalized.

Operating managers indicated to us that when the operating budget was developed peripherally to the long-range financial plan, they found it difficult to relate their performance to the company's long-term goals and objectives. In short, they lacked a sense of belonging to the larger and more important effort of attaining the strategic objectives.

Finally, imbalance in short and long-term emphasis is affected by top management pressure to produce current earnings. By applying pressure, top management may virtually force division-level managers to make S/L trade-offs that may have adverse results later. In the companies studied, a division suffered from top-down pressure about earnings most commonly when a sister division did not perform according to plan, leading top management to attempt to squeeze more profits from other divisions.

Controlling Trade-Offs

The number and importance of S/L trade-offs that managers make depend on two conditions, one given and one the direct result of top management action.

Structural controls are the "facts of life"—the internal and external conditions that affect managerial perceptions. Some of them cannot be altered at all; others can be altered over time. Examples of structural controls outside the organization are the capital intensity of the industry, rates of technological change, rates of new-product introduction, end-consumer product orientation, industry maturity, and other factors. Examples of internal structural controls are the nature of the organization (e.g., the formal and informal power structure) and the basic culture or operating climate (e.g., workload norms and peer pressures).

In short, structural controls are the "givens" under which a company elects to operate, and they appear to determine the frequency with which managers encounter significant S/L trade-off decisions.

By contrast, *variable* controls are the product of managerial decisions. We found many of them in our study. It became clear that the companies most satisfied with their S/L trade-off balance had systematically considered the extent, type, and basic causes of trade-offs likely to occur and then had tailored their selection of variable controls to the needs of the situation. Before taking action the top executives usually considered questions such as the following:

1 Is the necessity for S/L trade-offs recognized as a major problem at the company? If not, is it because executives are unaware of the occurrence of such trade-offs, or because they already have sufficient controls on them?
2 Do controls exist to minimize the likelihood of detrimental S/L trade-offs?
3 Is top management getting the proper information it needs regarding both the long and short-term consequences of the alternatives faced by division managers?
4 Does the planning and review system motivate managers to keep long-term corporate goals in sight?
5 Does the planning and review process of each division take into account the structural controls that affect decision making there?

To assist managers in assessing their own corporate situations, Exhibit 1 shows the many types of variable controls observed and indicates at what stages of planning and review development the controls are most effective. The designated development stages are somewhat arbitrary, but they serve to identify the course of evolution that companies are likely to experience and they offer some insight into the uses of variable controls. As for the controls themselves, they can be grouped under five headings.

Realistic Goals

The most frequent situation in which detrimental S/L trade-offs occur arises when operating managers fail to meet the budget goals agreed on for their divisions or cost centers. In our study, several companies found that one way to reduce the frequency of such trade-offs was simply to establish more realistic goals for the managers, either during the initial goal setting or in later periods when goals or plans of action are adjusted.[4] Indeed, as is evident from Exhibit 1, establishing realistic goals is the step that appears most

Exhibit 1. Most Effective Controls on S/L Trade-Offs

	Typical characteristics of stage of planning	I. Preplanning Top management does strategy Narrow product/market segmentation Largely centralized decision making Some pressure from division level for long-term planning	II. Initial Long-range planning largely financial Staff develops system; does most of work Some lower management resistance Planning accompanies decentralization	III. Intermediate Long-range planning system in place and accepted More emphasis on issues Large staff involvement Not used at lower management levels for decision making	IV. More complete Decisions made and performance evaluated according to accomplishment of plan High commitment to plan Short- and long-term performance tied directly to plan in reviews Line management does planning Postaudits utilized	V. Advanced Explicit contingency planning Tactical operating plans used Lower management levels involved in planning System encourages creativity in identifying opportunities Rolling financial forecasts
Method of control or influence						
Establishment of realistic goals						
Top management revises and adjusts submitted budget figures as needed to assure realism						
Incorporate economic-cycle predictions in budgets to avoid undue profit pressure						
Incorporate historical-trend analysis in budget-setting process						
Establish appropriate time horizons for fixed portion of budget and keep up to date						
Allow some flexibility in budget beyond fixed time horizons for unforeseen events						
Establishment of management performance measures that reflect S/L considerations						
Split goals, performance evaluation, rewards into discrete short- and long-term components						
Establish quarterly performance reviews for accomplishment of long-term strategic goals						
Perform postaudits on capital expenditures and other projects						
Limit time horizons on capital spending authorizations to minimize postponements						
Increased managerial knowledge of long-term strategy goals						
Increase lower-level management involvement in strategy formulation						
Increase discussions about strategic goals between top- and lower-level management						
Line management develops long- and short-range plans						
Hold explicit discussions on S/L trade-offs and the need for balanced decision making						
Establishment of planning and review process elements that reflect S/L trade-off considerations						
Top management reviews lower-level decision alternatives and recommendations						
Analyze industry, other long-term trends to judge the "reasonableness" of plan						
Increase linkage between operating budget and first year of strategic long-term plan						
Use planning process as integral part of management decision-making process						
Utilize monthly closings and reviews to minimize adverse S/L trade-offs						
Disseminate planning "issues" from the top down; build issue-based plans bottom up						
Develop explicit tactical operating plans for operational goal accomplishment						
Use explicit contingency plans with well-defined "trigger points" for implementation						
Implementation of organization and staffing changes						
Create new strategic business units to focus on strategic goals						
Undertake long-term commitments and joint ventures with other firms						
Replace managers who consistently miss achievement of operating goals						
Change managers when long-range strategies change						

applicable to companies in any stage of development of their planning processes.

More realistic goals can be developed in several ways. Increased accuracy in the budget numbers themselves can be achieved by incorporating economic-cycle predictions and historical-trend analysis in setting budgets. Additionally, since budgets are little more than sophisticated guesses of what will happen in the future, an allowance of some flexibility for unforeseen problems can ease short-term pressures on managers.

Most businesses can predict accurately for, say, a few months away, but beyond that the crystal ball gets hazy. Several companies studied compensated for this difficulty by making a short portion of the budget—for instance, three months—inflexible but by allowing for some fluctuation in performance beyond that time. Concurrently, the budget was updated on a regular basis.

Finally, at a few companies the "final" budget numbers submitted by divisions were altered by top management to reflect either perceived optimism or conservatism on the part of division managers. In one case, the chief executive even lowered the budget projections for presentation to the board of directors while leaving the higher numbers as goals for the divisional personnel.

Longer-Range Evaluations

Another way of minimizing detrimental S/L trade-offs is to increase the emphasis on long-term goals in measurement of managerial performance. This helps to compensate for the inevitable pressure to produce short-term results. In the goal-setting process, for example, objectives can be split into discrete short and long-term portions, with performance evaluation and rewards likewise divided.

To ensure performance on long-range objectives, management can conduct milestone reviews on a regular basis (e.g., quarterly) along with normal operating reviews. Management can also review important capital projects to ensure they are developed according to plan. In addition, it can make audits to verify the timely expenditure of funds and conduct "postaudits" to examine returns on the projects after they are completed.

Several companies in our study impose time limits on capital spending authorizations in order to prevent postponements. If a manager does not spend the funds authorized before the deadline, he or she must reapply for funds.

Awareness of Strategies

Closely related to the establishment of performance measures that reflect both long and short-term considerations are attempts to make lower-level managers knowledgeable about long-term corporate goals and how operating managers contribute to the achievement of those goals. The underlying philosophy for these actions appears to be that good managers more likely will make appropriate trade-offs when they have a sound understanding of long-term plans.

To achieve this increased involvement, the companies emphasize the development of strategic and operating plans by line management and not by planning staffs. Additionally, some managements attempt to involve lower-level managers more in creating long-range plans (normally the lower levels merely concentrate on short-term budgets).

To improve communications, some companies increase the number of meetings between top and lower-level managers to discuss the corporate goals and how each person fits into the grand plan and to focus attention on S/L trade-off problems and the need for balanced decisions.

Planning and Review

The companies in our study use the planning and review process to stimulate better S/L trade-off decisions. Companies that have reached the intermediate development stage (see Exhibit 1) are the ones most likely to develop more balance in this way. The actions they take can be classified as follows:

1. *Philosophical.* Management may stress the use of planning as an integral part of managing the business rather than as an adjunct of managing per se. It may evaluate the overall "reasonableness" of the long-range plan by analyzing long-term industrial and other trends. It may set a policy of reviewing managers' recommended actions on given decisions as well as the alternatives considered.

2. *Specific.* At a more workaday level, management may take advantage of monthly closings and reviews to keep short-range concerns from dominating S/L trade-offs. It may increase the linkages between the first year of the long-range plan and the operating budget. It may develop explicit how-to tactical plans to ensure accomplishment of goals. It may design carefully delineated contingency plans with clearly defined "trigger points" for switching to alternate programs and strategies.

Staffing Changes

As pointed out earlier, the managements in our study do not try to influence S/L trade-offs by changing the organization scheme—it takes too long. However, management can make headway with revisions and variations of the organization plan. As also noted, one company, in an attempt to focus more narrowly on objectives when conditions changed, set up new strategic business units to manage new projects instead of working through the old organizations.

Similarly, this company changed managers when the long-term strategies of an operation changed, a move which helped avoid a tendency to emphasize historical trade-off considerations and the status quo. Another obvious—but not always used—action was to replace managers who consistently missed their operating goals. Poor performance tends to increase short-term emphasis in decision trade-offs, and the longer such performance continues, the higher the probability of poor decisions.

Finally, one of the managements set up joint ventures and made other long-range commitments with outside companies. By so doing, it limited the options and possibilities for making detrimental S/L trade-offs. For instance, the schedule of production commitments to a joint venture might make it difficult for managers to manipulate their budgets for the sake of strong short-term profit showings.

Conclusion

The tendency toward achieving short-run gains at the expense of timely accomplishment of long-term strategic objectives is a significant and surprisingly common problem, our study shows. Clearly, though, there are steps that top executives can take to identify the extent of the problem in their companies and to ensure that managers make decisions with a view toward the proper balance between long and short-term goals.

We have described some of these steps. Which one or ones should be selected depends on the relative maturity of a company's planning and review process. Some of the steps help to counterbalance the tendency to emphasize the short term in decision making. Others limit the frequency and severity of pressure on managers to achieve short-term earnings regardless of long-term considerations.

Together, these steps provide a basic pool of tactics for managers to use in developing their plans of action. There is a "George" at every company, but he or she *can* be encouraged to keep the company's long-term objectives in sight when making operating decisions.

Notes

1. See Rochell O'Connor, *Planning under Uncertainty: Multiple Scenarios and Contingency Planning*, Conference Board Report No. 741 (1978), p. 23.

2. For a detailed analysis of executive compensation and performance evaluation, see Alfred Rappaport, "Executive Incentives vs. Corporate Growth," *HBR*, July–August 1978, p. 81.

3. For example, see John K. Shank, Edward G. Niblock, and William T. Sandalls, Jr., "Balance 'Creativity' and 'Practicality' in Formal Planning," *HBR*, January–February 1973, p. 87.

4. See Ronald N. Paul, Neil B. Donavan, and James W. Taylor, "The Reality Gap in Strategic Planning," *HBR*, May–June 1978, p. 124.

Appendix

Research Methods

This article is based primarily on in-depth interviews with managers and planners at different organization levels in six major U.S. companies. We chose the interview approach because it provides the best opportunity to examine many examples of short-term and long-term conflicts in decisions made under widely varying circumstances but within the limited time frame of the study.

We selected the companies to provide a broad sampling of current planning and management review systems, along with a diversity of such significant characteristics as capital intensity, nature of industry, nature of production process, type of products sold, type of market served, organizational structure, and competitive strength. Because of the subjective nature of our interviews, we could not make statistical comparisons of the companies, their planning processes, or their relative success in their industries.

Companies participating in the study included two natural resource-based organizations, each serving a different industry; a large (more than $10 billion in sales) diversified corporation with worldwide distribution of products to industrial and consumer markets; a large diversified company serving electronics-related markets; a medium-sized industrial products company; and a smaller ($200 million sales) manufacturer of limited lines of consumer and industrial products. Since certain of the data gathered are confidential, only those data that preserve anonymity are included in the article.

In the interviews, we focused on the S/L trade-off problem largely at the *business level*—that is, at the level where a whole area of related products is managed. However, some of our talks concerned planning at the corporate or strategic level and the *activity* or *functional* levels.*

The business level corresponds closely to the division level at the participating companies and includes managers with responsibility for the profit center or significant-cost center. The corporate or strategic level is where the corporation's long-term strategy is determined; at some of the companies studied this means the chief executive, at others it means the

---

*See Richard F. Vancil, "Strategy Formulation in Complex Organizations," *Sloan Management Review*, Winter 1976, p. 1.

group vice president. The activity or functional level (e.g., plant or marketing managers) is where most decision making becomes shorter term and operational in nature.

In addition, we held interviews at two staff levels: the corporate staff level, which includes high-level planners and staff consultants, and the functional staff level, which includes mostly persons (e.g., division controllers) who assist division managers with staff responsibilities. In total, we conducted more than 50 interviews.

To provide information beneficial to corporate managers, we have attempted to pinpoint in what areas and under what circumstances adverse S/L trade-offs are likely to be made by identifying examples of several different types of trade-off decisions at the companies. In addition, we have examined those elements of the planning and review process, as well as structural constraints imposed by the industry and the organization, which work to minimize the number of suboptimal trade-offs actually made. From this information, we have formulated recommendations as to how corporations in various stages of planning and review might approach S/L trade-off problems, determine their significance, and design actions to improve decision making.

This study was funded by an Associate of the Harvard Business School, the Mead Corporation. We gratefully acknowledge its assistance.

PART THREE
MANUFACTURING AS A COMPETITIVE WEAPON

AN OVERVIEW

It is not enough for managers to identify the current strategic role for their manufacturing operations. They must also have a clear understanding of the best way to use those operations for competitive advantage. Said another way, they must not only keep larger corporate goals in view but also distill those goals into a manufacturing mission well fitted to their organization's distinctive competence in production. As the experience of many companies attests, lack of precision in the statement of mission can play havoc with the efficient operation of plants and factories.

Perhaps the most common mistake is to assign too wide a variety of tasks to a given factory. Caught between often conflicting demands and forced to make necessary trade-offs with no guiding principles on which to rely, manufacturing managers have long been asked to serve too many masters. Not surprisingly, the result has been that plants run at far from peak efficiency, morale sags, forward planning never gets done, productivity declines, and a valuable corporate resource is mindlessly wasted. No one factory can do everything, nor is there only one way to compete in terms of production competence. Hard choices must be made about what each manufacturing facility should try to do well.

Lacking such a focus, factories inevitably develop, as Wickham Skinner so rightly observes, a complex, heterogeneous mixture of general and special-purpose equipment, long- and short-run operations, high and low tolerances, new and old products, off-the-shelf items and customer specials, stable and changing designs, markets with reliable forecasts and unpredictable ones, seasonal and nonseasonal sales, short and long lead times, and high and low skills.

In the midst of so great a babble of production orientation, competitive advantage is well and truly lost.

Accordingly, the articles in this third section concern themselves with the proper definition of manufacturing focus at the plant or factory level, which includes, of course, the problem of integrating manufacturing tasks with other functional responsibilities. There is, after all, no one best way to organize production. What counts is not the effort to apply some general formula but, rather, the effort to identify and then provide for a particular set of manufacturing needs.

On balance, then, the argument is for a relativistic approach to production. It is essential to remember, however, that some rules *do* apply in all cases, that not everything is to be sacrificed to the press of local circumstances. Whatever a plant's chosen focus, the importance of paying attention to the fundamentals of manufacturing—the management of inventory, the rate of defects, the motivation of the work force, the assurance of quality, and so on—never changes. For too long now, American managers have tended to let many of the fundamentals go in their preoccupation with meeting abstract target schedules, quotas, or performance levels. And given the way they were evaluated by their own superiors, who could blame them? Only in retrospect does it become clear how disastrous a course they have followed.

These articles are not concerned with allocating blame for slipshod or shortsighted performance; there is enough to go around. Their purpose is of a different sort: to provide a stern reminder of those facts about running a manufacturing system that are not subject to this year's fashion, that are never out of date, that are always safe guides to action. Much of this is but common sense, but then *HBR* has always believed strongly in the value of common sense—not of exotic gimmickry, secret formulas, or faddish cure-alls. Good manufacturing management is what it always has been: disciplined attention to the basics within a clearly defined and sharply focused strategic framework.

There is, then, an inherent logic to the way products and processes develop, and this logic has an important role to play in integrating corporate strategy with manufacturing operations. Mundane operational decisions can have major repercussions at the strategic level, for they can either enhance or hinder the achievement of an effective balance between products and processes. Just as it would be wrong to make rare, top-of-the-line pieces of jewelry by mass production techniques, so it would be wrong to support the needs of an ethical drug manufacturer with the inventory and control systems suitable to a maker of highly specialized machine tools. True, operational decisions may, from a distance, appear almost invisible on the strategic horizon, but their cumulative effect on a company's ability to compete as planned is substantial.

No corporate strategy, whatever its merits, will be successful unless translated into coordinated activity at the operational level. Similarly, no operational decision, whatever its immediate appeal, will prove beneficial if it achieves short-term advantage by sacrificing longer-term goals. The managerial challenge, of course, is to keep each firmly in harness with the other.

The Focused Factory

WICKHAM SKINNER

The conventional factory attempts to do too many conflicting production tasks within one inconsistent set of manufacturing policies. The chief result is that the plant is likely to be noncompetitive because its policies are not focused on the one key manufacturing task essential to successfully competing in its industry. In this article, the author discusses the concept of focused manufacturing, which offers the opportunity both to stop compromising each element of the production system and to build on competitive strength.

The threat posed by foreign competition, the problem of industries suffering from "blue-collar blues," and the increasing complexity and frustration of life in the factory have forced public attention back to the industrial sector of the economy. Many years of taking our industrial health and leadership for granted abruptly ended in the 1970s when our declining position in world markets weakened the dollar and became a national issue.

In the popular press and at the policy level in government, the issue has been seen as a "productivity crisis." The National Commission on Productivity was established in 1971. The concern with productivity has appealed to many managers who have firsthand experience with our problems of high costs and low efficiency.

So pessimism now pervades the outlook of many managers and analysts of the U.S. manufacturing scene. The recurring theme of this gloomy view is that (1) U.S. labor is the most expensive in the world, (2) its productivity has been growing at a slower rate than that of most of its competitors, and

---

Author's Note. This article is an analysis based on my cases written in the electronics, plastics, textile, steel, and industrial equipment industries, supplemented by recent project research in the furniture industry. Financial support for this work provided by the Harvard Business School Division of Research and course development funds is gratefully acknowledged.

therefore, (3) our industries sicken one by one as imports mushroom and unemployment becomes chronic in our industrial population centers.

In this article, I shall offer a more optimistic view of the productivity dilemma, suggesting that we need not feel powerless in competing against cheaper foreign labor. Rather, we have the opportunity to effect basic changes in the management of manufacturing, which could shift the competitive balance in our favor in many industries. What are these basic changes? I can identify four:

1. Seeing the problem not as "How can we increase productivity?" but as "How can we compete?"
2. Seeing the problem as encompassing the efficiency of the *entire* manufacturing organization, not only the efficiency of the direct labor and the work force. (In most plants, direct labor and the work force represent only a small percentage of total costs.)
3. Learning to focus each plant on a limited concise manageable set of products, technologies, volumes, and markets.
4. Learning to structure basic manufacturing policies and supporting services so that they focus on one explicit manufacturing task instead of on many inconsistent, conflicting, implicit tasks.

A factory that focuses on a narrow product mix for a particular market niche will outperform the conventional plant, which attempts a broader mission. Because its equipment, supporting systems, and procedures can concentrate on a limited task for one set of customers, its costs and especially its overhead are likely to be lower than those of the conventional plant. But, more important, such a plant can become a competitive weapon because its entire apparatus is focused to accomplish the particular manufacturing task demanded by the company's overall strategy and marketing objective.

In spite of their advantages, my research indicates that focused manufacturing plants are surprisingly rare. Instead, the conventional factory produces many products for numerous customers in a variety of markets, thereby demanding the performance of a multiplicity of manufacturing tasks all at once from one set of assets and people. Its rationale is "economy of scale" and lower capital investment.

However, the result more often than not is a hodge-podge of compromises, a high overhead, and a manufacturing organization that is constantly in hot water with top management, marketing management, the controller, and customers.

A simple but telling example of a failure to focus is uncovered in this case study of a manufacturer, the American Printed Circuit Company (APC).

APC was a small company that had been growing rapidly and successfully. Its printed circuits were custom-built in lots of one to 100 for about

20 principal customers and were used for engineering tests and development work. APC's process consisted of about 15 operations using simple equipment, such as hand-dipping tanks, drill presses, and manual touch-ups. There was considerable variation in the sequence and processes for different products. Delivery was a major element for success, and price was not a key factor.

APC's president accepted an order from a large computer company to manufacture 20,000 printed circuit boards—a new product for the company—at a price equivalent to about one third of its average mix of products. APC made the decision to produce these circuit boards in order to build volume, broaden the company's range of markets, and diversify the line. The new product was produced in the existing plant.

The result was disastrous. The old products were no longer delivered on time. The costs of the new printed circuit boards were substantially in excess of the bid price. The quality on all items suffered as the organization frenetically attempted to meet deliveries. Old customers grew bitter over missed deliveries, and the new customer returned one third of the merchandise for below-spec quality. Such heavy losses ensued that the APC company had to recapitalize. Subsequently, the ownership of the company changed hands.

The purpose of this article is to set forth the advantages of focused manufacturing. I shall begin with the basic concepts of the focused factory, then follow with an analysis of the productivity phenomenon, which tends to prevent the adoption of the focused plant concept. Finally, I shall offer some specific steps for managing manufacturing to accomplish and take advantage of focus.

Basic Concepts

From my study of approximately 50 plants in six industries, I can pinpoint three basic concepts underlying focused manufacturing. Consider:

1. *There are many ways to compete besides by producing at low cost.* This statement may be self-evident to the reader (particularly, to one in an industry that has been badly hit by low-priced foreign imports and has been attempting to compete with better products, quality, or customer service and delivery). Nevertheless, it still needs saying for two reasons. One is simply the persistent attitude that ways of competing other than on the basis of price are second best. The other is that a company that starts out with higher manufacturing costs than its competitors is in trouble regardless of whatever else it does. Although these assumptions may be true of industries with mature products and technologies, they are not at all true of

products in earlier stages of their life cycles. In fact, in many U.S. industries, companies are being forced to shift to products in which technological innovation in the form of advanced features is a more critical element of competitive advantage than cost.

2. *A factory cannot perform well on every yardstick.* There are a number of common standards for measuring manufacturing performance. Among these are short delivery cycles, superior product quality and reliability, dependable delivery promises, ability to produce new products quickly, flexibility in adjusting to volume changes, low investment and hence higher return on investment, and low costs. These measures of manufacturing performance necessitate trade-offs—certain tasks must be compromised to meet others. They cannot all be accomplished equally well because of the inevitable limitations of equipment and process technology. Such trade-offs as costs versus quality or short delivery cycles versus low inventory investment are fairly obvious. Other trade-offs, while less obvious, are equally real. They involve implicit choices in establishing manufacturing policies. Within the factory, managers can make the manufacturing function a competitive weapon by outstanding accomplishment of one or more of the measures of manufacturing performance. But managers need to know: "What must we be especially good at? Cost, quality, lead times, reliability, changing schedules, new-product introduction, or low investment?" Focused manufacturing must be derived from an explicitly defined corporate strategy that has its roots in a corporate marketing plan. Therefore, the choice of focus cannot be made independently by production people. Instead, it has to be a result of a comprehensive analysis of the company's resources, strengths and weaknesses, position in the industry, assessment of competitors' moves, and forecast of future customer motives and behavior. Conversely, the choice of focus cannot be made without considering the existing factory, because a given set of facilities, systems, and people skills can do only certain things well within a given time period.

3. *Simplicity and repetition breed competence.* Focused manufacturing is based on the concept that simplicity, repetition, experience, and homogeneity of tasks breed competence. Furthermore, each key functional area in manufacturing must have the same objective, derived from corporate strategy. Such congruence of tasks can produce a manufacturing system that does limited things very well, thus creating a formidable competitive weapon.

Major Characteristics

Key characteristics of the focused factory are:

1. *Process technologies.* Typically, unproven and uncertain technologies are limited to one per factory. Proven mature technologies are limited to what their managers can easily handle, typically two or three (e.g., a foundry, metal working, and metal finishing).

2. *Market demands.* These consist of a set of demands including quality, price, lead times, and reliability specifications. A given plant can usually only do a superb job on one or two demands at any given period of time.

3. *Product volumes.* Generally, these are of comparable levels, such that tooling, order quantities, materials handling techniques, and job contents can be approached with a consistent philosophy. But what about the inevitable short runs, customer specials, and one-of-a-kind orders that every factory must handle? The answer is usually to segregate them. This is discussed later.

4. *Quality levels.* These employ a common attitude and set of approaches so as to neither overspecify nor overcontrol quality and specifications. One frame of mind and set of mental assumptions suffice for equipment, tooling, inspection, training, supervision, job content, materials handling.

5. *Manufacturing tools.* These are limited to only one (or two at the most) at any given time. The task at which the plant must excel in order to be competitive focuses on one set of internally consistent, doable, and noncompromised criteria for success.

My research evidence makes it clear that the focused factory will outproduce, undersell, and quickly gain competitive advantage over the complex factory. The focused factory does a better job because repetition and concentration in one area allow its work force and managers to become effective and experienced in the task required for success. The focused factory is manageable and controllable. Its problems are demanding, but limited in scope.

Productivity Phenomenon

The conventional wisdom of manufacturing management has been and continues to be that the measure of success is productivity. Now that U.S. companies in many industries are getting beaten hands down by overseas competitors with lower unit costs, we mistakenly cling to the old notion that "a good plant is a low-cost plant." This is simply not so. A low-cost plant may be a disaster if the company has sacrificed too much in the way of quality, delivery, flexibility, and so forth, in order to get its costs down.

Too many companies attempt to do too many things with one plant and one organization. In the name of low investment in facilities and spreading their overheads, they add products, markets, technologies, processes, quality levels, and supporting services that conflict and compete with each other and compound expense. They then hire more staff to regulate and control the unmanageable mixture of problems.

In desperation, many companies are now "banging away" at anything to reduce the resulting high costs. But we can only regain competitive strength by stopping this process of increasing complexity and overstaffing.

This behavior is so illogical that the phenomenon needs further explanation. Our plants are generally managed by extremely able people; yet the failure to focus manufacturing on a limited objective is a common managerial blind spot. What happens to produce this defect in competent managers? Engineers know what can and cannot be designed into planes, boats, and building structures. Engineers accept design objectives that will accomplish a specific set of tasks which are possible, although difficult.

In contrast, most of the manufacturing plants in my study attempted a complex heterogeneous mixture of general and special-purpose equipment, long and short-run operations, high and low tolerances, new and old products, off-the-shelf items and customer specials, stable and changing designs, markets with reliable forecasts and unpredictable ones, seasonal and nonseasonal sales, short and long lead times, and high and low skills.

Lack of Consistent Policies

It is not understood, I think, that each of the contrasting features just noted generally demands conflicting manufacturing tasks and hence different manufacturing policies. The particular mix of these features should determine the elements of manufacturing policy. Some of these elements are the following:

- ☐ Size of plant and its capacity.
- ☐ Location of plant.
- ☐ Choice of equipment.
- ☐ Plant layout.
- ☐ Selection of production process.
- ☐ Production scheduling system.
- ☐ Use of inventories.
- ☐ Wage system.
- ☐ Training and supervisory approaches.
- ☐ Control systems.
- ☐ Organizational structure.

Instead of designing elements of manufacturing policy around one manufacturing task, what usually happens? Consider, for example, that the wage system may be set up to emphasize high productivity, production control to maximize short lead times, inventory to minimize stock levels, order quantities to minimize setup times, plant layout to minimize materials handling costs, and process design to maximize quality.

While each of these decisions probably looks sensible to the professional specialist in each field, the conventional factory consists of six or more inconsistent elements of manufacturing structure, each of which is designed to achieve a different implicit objective.

Such inconsistency usually results in high costs. One or another element may be excessively staffed or operated inefficiently because its task is being exaggerated or misdirected. Or several functions may require excess staff in order to control or manage a plant which is unduly complex.

But often the result is even more serious. My study shows that the chief negative effect is not on productivity but on ability to compete. The plant's manufacturing policies are not designed, tuned, and focused as a whole on that one key strategic manufacturing task essential to the company's success in its industry.

Reasons for Inconsistency

Noncongruent manufacturing structures appear to be common in U.S. industry. In fact, my research revealed that a fully consistent set of manufacturing policies resulting in a congruent system is highly rare. Why does this situation occur so often? In the cases I studied, it seemed to come about essentially for one or more of these reasons:

1 Professionals in each field attempted to achieve goals which, although valid and traditional in their fields, were not congruent with goals of other areas.
2 The manufacturing task for the plant subtly changed while most operating and service departments kept on the same course as before.
3 The manufacturing task was never made explicit.
4 The inconsistencies were never recognized.
5 More and more products were piled into existing plants, resulting in an often futile attempt to meet the manufacturing tasks of a variety of markets, technologies, and competitive strategies.

Let me elaborate on the first and last set of causes we have just noted.

"Professionalism" in the Plant.   Production system elements are now set up or managed by professionals in their respective fields, such as quality control, personnel, labor relations, engineering, inventory management, materials handling, systems design, and so forth.

These professionals, quite naturally, seek to maximize their contributions and justify their positions. They have conventional views of success in each of their particular fields. Of course, these objectives are generally in conflict.

I say "of course" not to be cynical. These fields of specialty have come into existence for many different reasons—some to reduce costs, others to save time, others to minimize capital investments, still others to promote human cooperation and happiness, and so on. So it is perfectly normal for them to pull in different directions, which is exactly what happens in many plants.

This problem is not totally new. But it is changing because professionalism is increasing; we have more and more experts at work in different parts of the factory. So it is a growing problem.

Product Proliferation. The combination of increasing foreign and domestic competition plus an accelerating rate of technological innovation has resulted in product proliferation in many factories. Shorter product life, more new products, shorter runs, lower unit volumes, and more customer specials are becoming increasingly common. The same factory which five years ago produced 25 products may today be producing 50 to 100.

The inconsistent production system grows up, not simply because there are more products to make—which is, of course, likely to increase direct and indirect costs and add complexity and confusion—but also because new products often call for different manufacturing tasks. To succeed in some tasks may require superb technological competence and focus, others may demand extremely short delivery, and still others, extremely low costs.

Yet, almost always, new products are added into the existing mix in the same plant, even though some new equipment may be necessary. The rationale for this decision is usually that the plant is operating at less than full capacity. Thus the logic is, "If we put the new products into the present plant, we can save capital investment and avoid duplicating overheads."

The result is complexity, confusion, and, worst of all, a production organization which, because it is spun out in all directions by a kind of centrifugal force, lacks focus and a doable manufacturing task. The factory is asked to perform a mission for Product A that conflicts with that of Product B. Thus the result is a hodgepodge of compromises.

When we may have, in fact, four tasks and four markets, we make the mistake of trying to force them into one plant, one set of equipment, one factory organization, one set of manufacturing policies, and so on. We try to cram into one operating system the ability to compete in an impossible mix of demands. Each element of the system attempts to adjust to these demands with variation, special sections, complex procedures, more people, and added paperwork.

In my opinion this syndrome, starting with added market demands and ending with incongruent internal structures, to a large extent accounts for the human frustrations, high costs, and low competitive abilities we see so often in U.S. industry today.

Who gets the blame? The manufacturing executive, of course, gets it from corporate headquarters for high costs, poor productivity, low quality and reliability, and missed deliveries. In turn the executive tends to blame the situation on anything that makes sense, such as poor market forecasts, subpar labor, unconcern over quality, inept engineering designs, faulty equipment, and so forth.

Probably all such factors contribute and, undoubtedly, they all add to the pressure on production people. But what is not perceived is that a given production organization, as we noted earlier, can only do certain things well; trade-offs are inevitable.

Experience accomplishes wonders, but a diffused organization with conflicting structural elements and competing manufacturing tasks accumulates experience and specialized competence very slowly.

Toward Manufacturing Focus

A new management approach is needed in industries where diverse products and markets require companies to manufacture a broad mix of items, volumes, specifications, and customer demand patterns. Its emphasis must be on building competitive strength. One way to compete is to focus the entire manufacturing system on a limited task precisely defined by the company's competitive strategy and the realities of its technology and economics. A common objective produces synergistic effects rather than internal power struggles between professionalized departments. This approach can be assisted by these guiding rules:

1. Centralize the factory's focus on relative competitive ability.
2. Avoid the common tendency to add staff and overhead in order to save on direct labor and capital investment.
3. Let each manufacturing unit work on a limited task instead of the usual complex mix of conflicting objectives, products, and technologies.

This management approach can be thought of as focused manufacturing, for it is the opposite of the under-one-roof diffusion process of the conventional factory. Instead of permitting the whirling diversity of tasks and ingredients, top management applies a centripetal force that constantly pulls inward toward one central focus—the one key manufacturing task. The result is greater simplicity, lower costs, and a manufacturing and support organization that is directed toward successful competition.

Achieving the Focused Plant

In my experience, manufacturing managers are generally astounded at the internal inconsistencies and compromises they discover once they put the concept of focused manufacturing to work in analyzing their own plants.

Then, when they begin to discern what the company strategy and market situation are implicitly demanding and to compare these implicit demands with what they have been trying to achieve, many submerged conflicts surface.

Finally, when they ask themselves what a certain element of the structure or of the manufacturing policy was designed to maximize, the built-in cross-purposes become apparent.

At the risk of seeming to take a cookbook approach to an inevitably complex set of issues, let me offer a recipe for the focused factory based on an actual but disguised example of an industrial manufacturing company which attempted to adapt its operations to this concept.

Consider this four-step approach of, say, the WXY Company, a producer of mechanical equipment.

1. *Develop an explicit brief statement of corporate objectives and strategy.* The statement should cover the next three to five years, and it should have the substantial involvement of top management, including marketing, finance, and control executives. In its statement, the top management of the WXY Company agreed to the following:

> Our corporate objective is directed toward increasing market share during the next five years via a strategy of (1) tailoring our product to individual customer needs, (2) offering advanced and special product features at a modest price increment, and (3) gaining competitive advantage via rapid product development and service orientation to customers of all sizes.

2. *Translate the objectives-and-strategy statement into "what this means to manufacturing."* What must the factory do especially well in order to carry out and support this corporate strategy? What is going to be the most difficult task it will face? If the manufacturing function is not sharp and capable, where is the company most likely to fail? It may fail in any one of the elements of the production structure, but it will probably do so in a combination of some of them. To carry on with the WXY Company example, such a manufacturing task might be defined explicitly as follows:

> Our manufacturing task for the next three years will be to introduce specialized, customer-tailored new products into production, with lead times which are substantially less than those of our competitors.
>
> Since the technology in our industry is changing rapidly, and since product reliability can be extremely serious for customers, our most difficult problems will be to control the new-product introduction process, so as to solve technical problems promptly and to maintain reliability amid rapid changes in the product itself.

3. *Make a careful examination of each element of the production system.* How is it now set up, organized, focused, and manned? What is

TOWARD MANUFACTURING FOCUS

it now especially good at? How must it be changed to implement the key manufacturing task?

4. *Reorganize the elements of structure to produce a congruent focus.* This reorganization focuses on the ability to do those limited things well that are of utmost importance to the accomplishment of the manufacturing task.

To complete the example of the WXY Company, Exhibit 1 lists each major element of the manufacturing system of the company, describes its present focus in terms of that task for which it was implicitly or inadvertently aimed,

Exhibit 1. Conflicting Manufacturing Tasks Implied by Incongruent Elements of the Present Production System

Production System Elements	Present Approach (conventional factory)	Implicit Manufacturing Tasks of Present Approach	Changed Approach (focused factory)
Equipment and process policies	One large plant; special purpose equipment; high-volume tooling; balanced capacity with functional layout.	Low manufacturing costs on steady runs of a few large products with minimal investment.	Separate old, standardized products and new customized products into two plants within a plant (PWP). For new PWP, provide general purpose equipment, temporary tooling, and modest excess capacity with product-oriented layout.
Work-force management policies	Specialized jobs with narrow job content; incentive wages; few supervisors; focus on volume of production per hour.	Low costs and efficiency.	Create fewer jobs with more versatility. Pay for breadth of skills and ability to perform a variety of jobs. Provide more foremen for solving technical problems at workplace.
Production scheduling and control	Detailed, frequent sales forecasts; produce for	Short delivery lead times.	Produce to order special parts and stock of common

Exhibit 1. (*Continued*)

Production System Elements	Present Approach (conventional factory)	Implicit Manufacturing Tasks of Present Approach	Changed Approach (focused factory)
	inventory economic lot sizes of finished goods; small decentralized production scheduling group.		parts based on semi-annual forecast. Staff production control to closely schedule and centralize parts movements.
Quality control	Control engineers and large inspection groups in each department.	Extremely reliable quality.	No change.
Organizational structure	Functional; production control under superintendents of each area; inspection reports to top.	Top performance of the objectives of each functional department, i.e., many tasks.	Organize each PWP by program and project in order to focus organizational effort on bringing new products into production smoothly and on time.

and lists a new approach designed to bring consistency, focus, and power to its manufacturing arm.

What stands out most in this exhibit is the number of substantial changes in manufacturing policies required to bring the production system into a total consistency. The exhibit also features the implicit conflicts between many manufacturing tasks in the present approach, which are the result of the failure to define one task for the whole plant.

The reader may perceive a disturbing implication of the focused plant concept—namely, that it seems to call for major investments in new plants, new equipment, and new tooling, in order to break down the present complexity.

For example, if the company is currently involved in five different products, technologies, markets, or volumes, does it need five plants, five sets of equipment, five processes, five technologies, and five organizational structures? The answer is probably *yes*. But the practical solution need not involve selling the big multipurpose facility and decentralizing into five small facilities.

In fact, the few companies that have adopted the focused plant concept have approached the solution quite differently. There is no need to build five plants, which would involve unnecessary investment and overhead expenses.

The more practical approach is the "plant within a plant" (PWP) notion in which the existing facility is divided both organizationally and physically into, in this case, five PWPs. Each PWP has its own facilities in which it can concentrate on its particular manufacturing task, using its own workforce management approaches, production control, organization structure, and so forth. Quality and volume levels are not mixed; worker training and incentives have a clear focus; engineering of processes, equipment, and materials handling are specialized as needed.

Each PWP gains experience readily by focusing and concentrating every element of its work on those limited essential objectives that constitute its manufacturing task. Since a manufacturing task is an offspring of a corporate strategy and marketing program, it is susceptible to either gradual or sweeping change. The PWP approach makes it easier to perform realignment of essential operations and system elements over time as the task changes.

Conclusion

The prevalent use of "cost" and "efficiency" as the conventional yardsticks for planning, controlling, and evaluating U.S. plants played a large part in the increasing inability of many of the approximately 50 companies included in my research to compete successfully. However, such goals are no longer adequate because competition is getting rougher and in particular, because a strictly low-cost high-efficiency strategy is apparently becoming less viable in many industries.

Although the economy has moved toward an era of more advanced technologies and shorter product lives, we have not readjusted our concepts of production to keep up with these changes. Instead, we have continued to use "productivity" and "economies of scale" as guiding objectives. Both feature only one element of competition (i.e., costs), and both are now obsolete as general all-purpose guides in manufacturing management.

But I have concluded that the focused plant is a rarity. With the mistaken rationale that the keys to success are limited investment, economies of scale, and full utilization of existing plant resources to achieve low costs, we keep adding new products to plants which were once focused, manageable, and competitive.

Reversing the process, however, is not impossible. In most of the cases I have studied, capital investment in facilities is not difficult to justify when payoffs that will result from organizational simplicity are taken into account. Resources for simplifying the focus of a manufacturing complex are not hard to acquire when the expected payoff is the ability to compete successfully, using manufacturing as a competitive weapon.

Moreover, better customer service and competitive position typically support higher margins to cover capital investments. And when studied carefully, the economies of scale and the effects of less than full utilization of plant equipment are seldom found to be as critical to productivity and efficiency as classical economic approaches often predict.

The U.S. problem of "productivity" is real indeed. But seeing the problem as one of "how to compete" can broaden management's horizon. The focused factory approach offers the opportunity to stop compromising each element of the production system in the typical general-purpose do-all plant that satisfies no strategy, no market, and no task.

Not only does focus provide punch and power, but it also provides clear goals that can be readily understood and assimilated by members of an organization. It provides, too, a mechanism for reappraising what is needed for success, and for readjusting and shaking up old tired manufacturing organizations with welcome change and a clear sense of direction.

In many sectors of U.S. industry, such change and such a new sense of direction are needed to shift the competitive balance in our favor.

11
How Should You Organize Manufacturing?

ROBERT H. HAYES and ROGER W. SCHMENNER

Among the characteristics of a company that shape corporate and, therefore, manufacturing strategy are its dominant orientation (market or product), pattern of diversification (product, market, or process), attitude toward growth (acceptance of low growth rate), and choice between competitive strategies (high profit margins versus high output volumes). Once the basic attitudes or priorities are established, the manufacturing arm of a company must arrange its structure and management so as to reinforce these corporate aims. Examining the extremes of "product-focused" and "process-focused" organizations, the authors illustrate the development of a "manufacturing mission" whereby the organization of manufacturing supports management's needs.

Manufacturing organizations tend to attract the attention of general managers the way airlines do: one only notices them when they're late, when ticket prices rise, or when there's a crash. When they are operating smoothly, they are almost invisible. But manufacturing is getting increasing attention from business managers who, only a few years ago, were preoccupied with marketing or financial matters.

    The fact is that in most companies the great bulk of the assets used—the capital invested, the people employed, and management time—are in the operations side of the business. This is true of both manufacturing and service organizations, in both the private and public sectors of our economy. These resources have to be deployed, coordinated, and managed in such a way that they strengthen the institution's purpose; if not, they will almost certainly cripple it.

The problems and pressures facing manufacturing companies ultimately find their way to the factory floor, where managers have to deal with them through some sort of organizational structure. Unfortunately, this structure often is itself part of the problem. Moreover, problems in a corporation's manufacturing organization frequently surface at about the same time as problems in the rest of the company, and they surface in a variety of ways. For example:

A fast-growing, high-technology company had quadrupled in size in a 10-year period. Its manufacturing organization was essentially the same at the end of that period as before, dominated by a powerful vice president for manufacturing and a strong central staff, despite the fact that its product line had broadened considerably, that the company was beginning to make many more of the components it formerly purchased, and that the number of plants had both increased and spread into four countries. A sluggishness and sense of lost direction began to afflict the manufacturing organization, as overhead and logistics costs soared.

A conglomerate had put together a group of four major divisions that made sense in terms of their financial and marketing synergy. But these divisions' manufacturing organizations had little in common, little internal direction, and no overall coordination. The parent company was confronted with a series of major capital appropriation requests and had little understanding of either their absolute merits or the priorities that should be attached to them.

A fast-growing company in a new industry had for a number of years operated in a seller's market, where competition was based on quality and service rather than price. Its manufacturing organization was highly decentralized and adept at new product introduction and fast product mix changes. In the 1970s severe industry overcapacity and price competition caused corporate sales to level off and profit to decline for the first time in its history. Manufacturing efficiency and dependability clearly had to be improved, but there was fear of "upsetting the corporate culture" and "crippling the golden goose."

Why did these companies' manufacturing arms get into trouble? And to what extent were these problems the outgrowth of poorly designed organizational structures? In attempting an answer to these questions, we will begin with a review of the concepts of "manufacturing mission" and "manufacturing focus" that were first defined and explored in a series of articles by Wickham Skinner beginning in 1969.[1] These concepts, and the conclusions that flow logically from them, have since been polished, elaborated, and tested by him and a number of his colleagues in conjunction with various manufacturing companies over the past several years.

After this review we will evaluate the advantages and disadvantages of different approaches to organizing a company's manufacturing function and then apply our concepts to recommending the type of organizational design that is most appropriate for a given company. Finally, we will discuss the various kinds of growth that companies can experience and how these expectations should affect the organization of the manufacturing function.

Basic Elements of Strategy

The concept of manufacturing strategy is a natural extension of the concept of corporate strategy, although the latter need not be as rational and explicit as management theorists usually require.[2] As we use the term, a corporate strategy simply implies a consistency, over time, in the company's preferences for and biases against certain management choices as shown in Exhibit 1. We use the term company to refer to a business unit that has a relatively homogeneous product line, considerable autonomy, and enough of a history to establish the kind of track record we refer to here. Such a "company" could, of course, be a relatively independent division within a larger enterprise. The following "attitudes" shape those aspects of a company's corporate strategy that are relevant to manufacturing.

Exhibit 1. Corporate Attitudes that Imply Strategic Preferences

Dominant orientation
Market
Product or material
Technology

Pattern of diversification
Product
Market (geographic or consumer group)
Process (vertical integration)
Unrelated horizontal (conglomerate)

Corporate attitude toward growth
Growth sought explicitly
Growth viewed as a by-product of successful management of the "core" business

Competitive priorities
Dependability
Price
Product flexibility
Quality
Volume flexibility

1. *Dominant orientation.* Some companies are clearly market oriented. They consider their primary expertise to be the ability to understand and respond effectively to the needs of a particular market or consumer group. In exploiting this market knowledge, they use a variety of products, materials, and technologies. Gillette and Head Ski are examples of such companies. Other companies are clearly oriented to materials or products; they are so-called steel companies, rubber companies, or oil companies (or, more recently, energy companies). They develop multiple uses for their product or material and follow these uses into a variety of markets. Corning Glass, Firestone, DuPont, and Conoco come to mind. Still other companies are technology-oriented—most electronics companies fall into this class—and they follow the lead of their technology into various materials and markets. A common characteristic of a company with such a dominant orientation is that it seldom ventures outside that orientation, is uncomfortable when doing so, often does not appreciate the differences and complexities associated with operating the new business, and then often fails because it hesitates to commit the resources necessary to succeed. A recent example of a company that ventured, with considerable trauma, outside its dominant orientation was Texas Instruments' entry into consumer marketing of electronic calculators and digital watches.

2. *Pattern of diversification.* Diversification can be accomplished in several ways: (1) product diversification within a given market, (2) market diversification (geographic or consumer group) using a given product line, (3) process or vertical diversification (increasing the span of the process so as to gain more control over vendors and/or customers) with a given mix of products and markets, and (4) unrelated (horizontal) diversification, as exemplified by conglomerates. Decisions about diversification are closely interrelated with a company's dominant orientation, of course, but they also reflect its preference for concentrating on a relatively narrow set of activities or, alternatively, its willingness to enter into a wide variety of activities, products, and/or markets—and which ones it will enter.

3. *Corporate attitude toward growth.* Does growth represent an input to or an output of the company's planning process? Every company continually confronts a variety of growth opportunities. Its decisions about which to accept and which to reject signal, in a profound way, the kind of company it prefers to be. Some companies, in their concentration on a particular market, geographic area, or material, essentially accept the growth permitted by that market or area or material consumption. A company's acceptance of a low rate of growth reflects a decision, conscious or unconscious, to retain a set of priorities in which a given orientation and pattern of diversification are more highly valued than growth. Other companies, however, are so structured and managed that a certain rate of growth is required in order for the organization to function properly. If its current set

of products and markets will not permit this desired rate of growth, it will seek new ones to "fill the gap." Again, this decision will closely reflect its attitudes regarding dominant orientation and diversification. One obvious indication of a company's relative emphasis on growth is how growth is treated in its planning, budgeting, and performance evaluation cycle, and particularly the importance that is placed on annual growth rate, compared with such other measures as return on sales or return on assets. It is necessary to differentiate between a company's stated goals—words on paper—and what actually moves it to action.

4. *Choice of competitive priorities.* In its simplest form this choice is between seeking high profit margins or high output volumes. Some companies consistently prefer high margin products, even when this limits them to relatively low market shares. Others feel more comfortable with a high-volume business, despite the fact that this commits them to severe cost-reduction pressure and often implies low margins. An interesting article describes David Packard's attempts to redirect Hewlett-Packard away from the latter approach, where it was nose-to-nose with Texas Instruments, and back toward the former approach.[3] This concept can be expanded and enriched, however, since companies can compete in ways other than simply through the prices of their products. Some compete on the basis of superior quality—either by providing higher quality in a standard product (for example, Mercedes-Benz) or by providing a product that has features or performance characteristics unavailable in competing products. We intend here to differentiate between an actual quality differential and a perceived difference, which is much more a function of selling and advertising strategy. Other companies compete by promising utter dependability; their product may be priced higher and may not have some of the competitive products' features or workmanship. It will, however, work as specified, is delivered on time, and any failures are immediately corrected. IBM has been cited as an example of a company that competes on this basis; in a sense, so do AT&T and Sears, Roebuck. Still others compete on the basis of product flexibility, their ability to handle difficult nonstandard orders and to lead in new product introduction. This is a competitive strategy that smaller companies in many industries often adopt. And, finally, others compete through volume flexibility, being able to accelerate or decelerate production quickly. Successful companies in cyclical industries like housing or furniture often exhibit this trait. In summary, within most industries different companies emphasize one of these five competitive dimensions—price, quality, dependability, product flexibility, and volume flexibility. It is both difficult and potentially dangerous for a company to try to compete by offering superior performance along several competitive dimensions. Instead, a company must attach definite priorities to each that describe how it chooses to position itself relative to its competitors.

Practically every decision a senior manager makes will have a different impact on each of these dimensions, and the organization will thus have to make trade-offs between them. Unless these trade-offs are made consistently over time, the company will slowly lose its competitive distinctiveness.

Without such consistency, it does not matter how much effort a company puts into formulating and expounding on its "strategy"—it essentially does not have one. One test of whether a company has a strategy is that it is clear not only about what it wants to do but also about what it does *not* want to do—to what proposals it will consistently say no.

Toward a Manufacturing Mission

Once such attitudes and competitive priorities are identified, the task for manufacturing is to arrange its structure and management so as to mesh with and reinforce this strategy. Manufacturing should be capable of helping the company do what it wants to do without wasting resources in lesser pursuits. This is what we call the company's "manufacturing mission."

It is surprising that general managers sometimes tend to lose sight of this concept, since the need for priorities permeates all other arenas of management. For example, marketing managers segment markets and focus product design, and promotional and pricing effects around the needs of particular segments, often at the expense of the needs of other segments. And management information systems must be designed to emphasize particular kinds of information at the expense of others.

Although it is possible to chalk up to inexperience the belief of many general managers that manufacturing should be capable of doing everything well, it is harder to explain why many manufacturing managers themselves either try to be good at everything at once or focus on the wrong thing. They know that all-purpose tools generally are used only when a specific tool is not available. Perhaps they fall into this trap because of pride, too little time, or because they are reluctant to say no to their superiors.

All these factors enter into the following scenario. A manufacturing manager has nicely aligned the organization according to corporate priorities when suddenly the manager is subjected to pressure from marketing because of "customer complaints" about product quality or delivery times. Under duress, and without sufficient time to examine the trade-offs involved, the manager attempts to shore up performance along these dimensions. Then the manager is confronted with pressure from finance to reduce costs or investment or both. Again, in the attempt to respond to the "corporate will," or at least to oil the squeaky wheel, the manager reacts. Step by step, priorities and focus disappear, each lagging dimension being brought into line by some function's self-interest.

Falling into such a trap can be devastating, however, because a manufacturing mission that is inconsistent with corporate strategy is just as dangerous as not having any manufacturing mission at all. The more top management delegates key manufacturing decisions to "manufacturing specialists" (usually engineers), the more likely it is that manufacturing's priorities will be different from corporate priorities. They will reflect engineering priorities, or operating simplicity (often the goal of those who have worked their way up from the bottom of the organization)—not the needs of the business.

Using Structural Decisions

Translating a set of manufacturing priorities into an appropriate collection of plant, people, and policies requires resources, time, and management perseverance. As we mentioned earlier, the great bulk of most companies' assets (capital, human, and managerial) is found in manufacturing. Moreover, these assets tend to be massive, highly interrelated, and long lived—in comparison with marketing and most financial assets. As a result, it is difficult to redirect them, and "fine-tuning" is almost impossible. Once a change is made, its impact is felt throughout the system and cannot be undone easily.

Such manufacturing inertia is made worse by many manufacturing managers' reluctance to change. And it is further compounded by many top managers' lack of understanding of the kind of changes that are needed, as well as by their unwillingness to commit the resources to effect such changes.

The decisions that implement a set of manufacturing priorities are structural; for a given company or business they are made infrequently and at various intervals. They fall into two broad categories: facilities decisions and infrastructure decisions.

Facilities decisions involve the following considerations:

1 The total amount of manufacturing and logistics capacity to provide for each product line over time.
2 How this capacity is broken up into operating units (plants, warehouses, etc.), their size and form (a few large plants versus many small ones), their location, and the degree or manner of their specialization (e.g., according to product, process, etc.).
3 The kind of equipment and production technology used in these plants.
4 The span of the process—that is, the direction of vertical integration (toward control either of markets or of suppliers), its extent (as reflected roughly by value added as a percentage of sales), and the degree of balance among the capacities of the production stages.

Infrastructure decisions involve the following considerations:

1. Policies that control the loading of the factory or factories—raw material purchasing, inventory, and logistics policies.
2. Policies that control the movement of goods through the factory or factories—process design, work-force policies and practices, production scheduling, quality control, logistics policies, inventory control.
3. The manufacturing organizational design that coordinates and directs all of the foregoing.

These two sets of decisions are closely intertwined, of course. A plant's total annual capacity (a facilities decision) depends on whether the production rate is kept as constant as possible over time or, alternatively, changed frequently in an attempt to "chase demand" (an infrastructure decision). Similarly, work-force policies interact with location and process choices, and purchasing policies interact with vertical integration choices. Decisions regarding organizational design also will be highly dependent on vertical integration decisions, as well as on the company's decisions regarding how various plants are located, specialized, and interrelated.

Each of these structural decisions places before the manager a variety of choices, and each choice puts somewhat different weights on the five competitive dimensions. For example, an assembly line is highly interdependent and inflexible but generally promises lower costs and higher predictability than a loosely coupled line or batch-flow operation or a jobshop. Similarly, a company that attempts to adjust production rates so as to chase demand will generally have higher costs and lower quality than a company that tries to maintain more level production and absorb demand fluctuations through inventories.

If consistent priorities are to be maintained, as a company's strategy and manufacturing mission change, then change usually becomes necessary in *all* of these structural categories. Again and again the root of a manufacturing crisis is that a company's manufacturing policies and people—workers, supervisors, and managers—become incompatible with its plant and equipment, or both become incompatible with its competitive needs.

Even more subtly, plant may be consistent with policies, but the manufacturing organization that attempts to coordinate them all no longer does its job effectively. For, in a sense, the organization is the glue that keeps manufacturing priorities in place and welds the manufacturing function into a competitive weapon. It also must embody the corporate attitudes and biases already discussed.

In addition, the way manufacturing chooses to organize itself has direct implications for the relative emphasis placed on the five competitive dimensions. Certain types of organizational structures are characterized by high flexibility; others encourage efficiency and tight control; still others promote dependable promises.

Approaching the Design

How are the appropriate corporate priorities to be maintained in a manufacturing organization that is characterized by a broad mix of products, specifications, process technologies, production volumes, skill levels, and customer demand patterns? To answer this question, we must begin by differentiating between the administrative burden on the managements of individual plants and that on the central manufacturing staff. Each alternative approach for organizing a total manufacturing system will place different demands on each of these groups. In a rough sense, the same amount of "control" must be exercised over the system, no matter how responsibilities are divided between the two.

At one extreme, one could lump all production for all products into a single plant. This makes the job of the central staff relatively easy (in some respects it becomes almost nonexistent), but the job of the plant management becomes horrendous. At the other extreme, one could simplify the job of each plant (or operating unit within a given plant), so that each concentrates on a more restricted set of activities (products, processes, volume levels, etc.), in which case the coordinating job of the central organization becomes much more difficult.

Although many companies adopt the first approach by either design or default, in our experience it becomes increasingly unworkable as more and more complexity is put under one roof. At some point a single large plant, or a contiguous plant complex, breaks down as more products, processes, skill levels, and market demands are added to it. Skinner has argued against this approach and for the other extreme in an article in which he advocates dividing up the total manufacturing job into a number of *focused* units, each of which is responsible for a limited set of activities and objectives:

> Each [manufacturing unit should have] its own facilities in which it can concentrate on its particular manufacturing task, using its own workforce management approaches, production control, organization structure, and so forth. Quality and volume levels are not mixed; worker training and incentives have a clear focus; and engineering of processes, equipment, and materials handling are specialized as needed. Each [unit] gains experience readily by focusing and concentrating every element of its work on those limited essential objectives which constitute its manufacturing task.[4]

If we adopt this sensible (but radical) approach, we are left with the problem of organizing the central manufacturing staff in such a way that it can effectively manage the resulting diversity of units and tasks. It must somehow maintain the total organization's sense of priorities and manufacturing mission, even though individual units may have quite different tasks and focuses. It carries out this responsibility both directly, by establishing and monitoring the structural policies we mentioned earlier (for example, process design, capacity planning, work force management, inventory control, logistics, purchasing, and the like), and indirectly, by measuring, evaluating, and rewarding individual plants and managers, and through the recruitment and systematic development of those managers.

These basic duties can be performed in a variety of ways, however, and each will communicate a slightly different sense of mission. To illustrate this, let us consider two polar examples—a "product-focused organization" and a "process-focused organization." To clarify this discussion, look at the two highly simplified organizations shown in Exhibit 2 and think about what the tasks of the corporate manufacturing staff and plant managers would be in each.

Exhibit 2.   Product-Focused and Process-Focused Organization
Product-focused organization

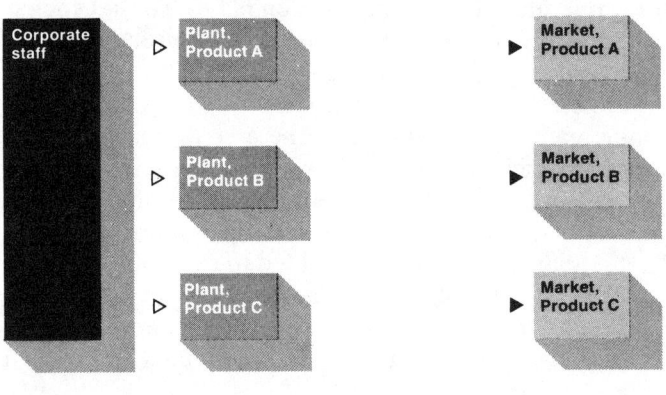

Process-focused organization

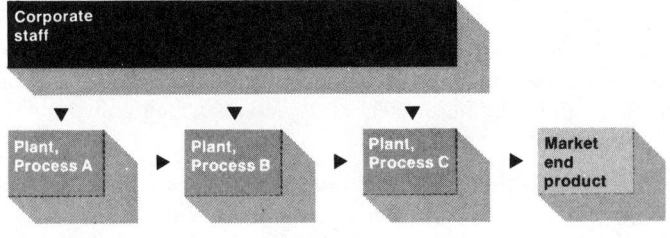

APPROACHING THE DESIGN

The corporate staff clearly must play a much more active role in making the second organization work. Logistics movements have to be carefully coordinated, and a change in any of the plants (or the market) can have repercussions throughout the system.

Only at the last stage (Process C), can the plant manager be measured on a profitability basis, and even that measure depends greatly on negotiated transfer prices and the smooth functioning of the rest of the system. The manager will not have much opportunity to exercise independent decision making, since most variables under his or her control (capacity, output, specifications, and so on) will affect everybody else. Thus the manager will probably be regarded as a "cost center" and be measured in large part on his or her ability to work smoothly within this highly interdependent system.

The distinction between such product-focused and process-focused manufacturing organizations should not be confused with the distinction between traditional functional and divisional corporate organizations. In fact, it is entirely possible that two divisions within a divisionally organized company would choose to organize their manufacturing groups differently. The important distinction has less to do with the organization chart than with the role and responsibilities of the central manufacturing staff and how far authority is pushed down the organization. In a sense, the distinction is more between centralized control and decentralized control.

With this brief overview, let us turn to more realistic product and process organizations.

Product-Focused Organization

Basically, the product-focused organization resembles a traditional plant-with-staff organization, which then replicates itself at higher levels to handle groups of plants and then groups of products and product lines. Authority in the product-focused organization is highly decentralized, which contributes to the flexibility of this type of organization in new product introduction. Each product group is essentially an independent small company, and thus it can react quickly to product development considerations.

A product focus tends to be better suited to less complex less capital-intensive process technologies, where the capital investment required is generally not high, where economies of scale do not demand large common production facilities, and where flexibility and innovation are more important than careful planning and tight control. A product-focused organization is a "clean" one, with responsibilities well delineated, and profit or return on investment the primary measures. Such an organization tends to appeal most to companies that have a high need and tolerance for diversity, and whose dominant orientation is to a market or consumer group, as opposed to a technology or a material.

The responsibility for decisions on capital, technology, and product development are thrust down from the corporate level to lower levels of management. Plant managers become very important people. This places special burdens on the organization. Product focus demands talented entrepreneurially minded junior managers and thus much concern for recruiting and managerial development. Junior managers must be tracked carefully through the system, and this implies devoting considerable resources to the company's evaluation and reward system.

And, because staff functions are isolated in individual product lines, the corporate staff must coordinate general policies, goals, and personnel across all the product lines. The corporate level central staff is well removed from day-to-day operations, but it is instrumental in communications and coordination across groups regarding such issues as personnel policies, manpower availability, special services (from computer assistance to training programs), capital appropriation requests, and purchasing.

Process-Focused Organization

Within a process-focused organization, individual plants are typically dedicated to a variety of different products. Sometimes a product is produced entirely by a single plant in such an organization, but more often the plant is only one of several that add value to the product.

Responsibilities throughout the plant and also throughout the upper management hierarchy are delineated, not by product line, but by segment of the full manufacturing process. Plants tend to be cost centers, not profit centers, and measurement is based on historical or technologically derived standards. An organization with this division of responsibility can properly be called process-focused.

Process focus tends to be better suited to companies with complex (and divisible) processes and with large capital requirements, companies we earlier called material or technology-oriented companies.

Questions of capacity, balance, logistics, and technological change and its impact on the process are critical for such companies and absorb much of top management's energies. A process focus is not conducive to the rapid introduction of new products, since it does not assign authority along product lines. Nor is it flexible in altering the output levels of existing products, because of the "pipeline momentum" in the system. But it can facilitate low-cost production if there are cost advantages deriving from the scale, continuity, and technology of the process.

A process-focused organization demands tremendous attention to coordinating functional responsibilities to ensure smooth changes in the product mix. And, because control is exercised centrally, young managers must ensure a long and generally a more technical apprenticeship with less decision-making responsibility. This places a burden on upper level management to keep junior managers motivated and learning.

Despite the strong centralization of control in a process-focused organization, it may not be more efficient (in terms of total manufacturing costs) than a well-managed product-focused organization. The central overhead and logistics costs required by a process focus can sometimes offset any variable cost reductions because of tight control and economies of scale. A product focus, however, is inherently easier to manage because of its small scale and singlemindedness. This usually results in shorter cycle times, less inventories, lower logistics costs, and, of course, lower overhead.[5]

The plants in a process organization can be expected to undertake one task that the central staff in a product organization cannot adequately perform, however. Since these plants are technologically based, they tend to be staffed with people who are highly expert and up to date in that technology. They will be aware of technological alternatives and trends, current research, and the operating experience of different technologies at other plants. Operating people in such a plant are more likely to transfer to a similar plant of a competitor's than they are to move to one of the other plants in their own company.

In a product organization, each product–plant complex will involve a number of technologies, and there may not be a sufficient mass of technical expertise to keep abreast of the changing state of the art in that technology. This becomes, then, more a responsibility of the corporate staff or, possibly, of a separate research group in the corporation, which may not even be under the aegis of the manufacturing organization. For this reason, businesses that use highly complex and evolving technologies are often forced to gravitate toward process organizations.

A process organization tends to manage purchasing somewhat better than a product organization does. If purchasing becomes too fragmented because of decentralization, the company as a whole tends to lose economies of scale as well as "clout" with suppliers. Conversely, centralized purchasing tends to be more bureaucratic and less responsive to local or market needs. The result is usually a combination of both, where through some decision rule the product organizations are given responsibility for certain purchases and a central purchasing department handles the procurement and distribution of the remainder.

Exhibit 3 gives a summary of the important differences between product-focused and process-focused organizations.

Product or Process Focus?

The polar extremes of manufacturing organization—product and process focus—place fundamentally different demands and opportunities on a company, and the choice of manufacturing organization should essentially be a choice *between* them. That is, manufacturing confronts a very definite either/

Exhibit 3. Differences Between Product-Focused and Process-Focused Manufacturing Organizations

	Product Focus	Process Focus
Profit or cost responsibility: where located	Product groups	Central organization
Size of corporate staff	Relatively small	Relatively large

Major functions of corporate staff	(a) Review capital appropriation requests
	(b) Communicate corporate changes and requests
	(c) Act as clearinghouse for
	   personnel information
	   management recruiting
	   purchasing
	   used equipment
	   management
	   development programs
	(d) Evaluate and reward plant managers
	(e) Select plant managers and manage career paths—possibly across product group lines
		(a) Coordination with marketing
		(b) Facilities decisions
		(c) Personnel policies
		(d) Purchasing
		(e) Logistics-inventory management
		(f) Coordination of production schedules
		(g) Make versus buy, vertical integration decisions
		(h) Recruit future plant managers
		(i) Review plant performance, cost center basis

Major responsibilities of plant organizations	(a) Coordination with marketing (b) Facilities decisions (subject to marketing) (c) Purchasing and logistics (d) Production scheduling and inventory control (e) Make versus buy (f) Recruit management	(a) Use materials and facilities efficiently (b) Recruit production, clerical, and lower management workers (c) Training and development of future department and plant managers (d) Respond to special requests from marketing, within limited ranges

PRODUCT OR PROCESS FOCUS?

or choice of organization—either product-focused or process-focused. Just as individual plants must have a clear focus, so must a central manufacturing organization.

Because the demands of a process-focused organization are so different from those of a product-focused organization—as to policies and practices, measurement and control systems, managerial attitudes, kinds of people, and career paths—it is extremely difficult for a mixed manufacturing organization with a single central staff to achieve the kind of policy consistency and organizational stability that can both compete effectively in a given market and cope with growth and change.

A mixed or composite production focus will only invite confusion and a weakening of the corporation's ability to maintain consistency among its manufacturing policies, and between them and its various corporate attitudes. If different manufacturing groups within the same company have different focuses, they should be separated as much as possible—each with its own central staff.

To illustrate, we can examine some mixed organizational focuses and the difficulties they might encounter.

A process-focused factory producing for two distinct product groups would have the organization chart shown in Exhibit 4. Here the corporation is trying to serve two different markets and product lines from the same factory, whose process technology appears to meet the needs of both (it may, in fact, consist of a series of linked process stages operating under tight central control). This kind of organization invites the now-classic problems of Skinner's unfocused factory. The manufacturing mission required by each market may be vastly different, and a plant that tries to carry out both at the same time is likely to do neither well.

Exhibit 4. Process-Focused Factory Serving Two Different Product Markets

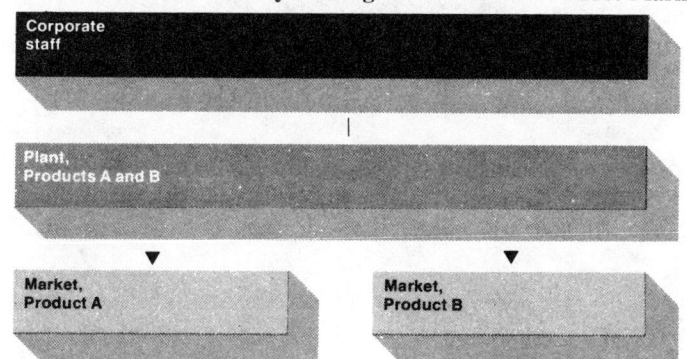

Similarly, an organization that uses the manufacturing facilities of one of its product groups to supply a major portion of the needs of another product group's market would be risking the same kind of confusion—that is, a nominally product-focused organization with an organization chart like the one in Exhibit 5.

A process-focused factory supplying parts or materials to two distinct product groups would have the organization chart shown in Exhibit 6. In this instance a corporate staff oversees two independent product groups, which serve two distinct markets, *and* a process-focused plant that supplies both product groups. The usual argument for an independent supplier plant is that economies of scale are possible from combining the requirements of both product groups. No matter what the reason, the supplier plant is coordinated by the same staff that oversees the product groups. One vice president of manufacturing directs a corporate manufacturing staff with one materials manager, one chief of individual engineering, one head of purchasing, one personnel director—all supervising the activities of two product-focused organizations and a process-focused organization.

Another variant of this difficulty is for the captive supplier plant for one product group to supply a major portion of the requirements of another product group's plant. Or a plant belonging to a product-focused division might act as a supplier to one of the plants within a process-focused division.

How else can a company organize around such situations? The important notion is that a plant that attaches certain priorities to different competitive dimensions is likely to prefer suppliers who have the same priorities. This suggests that a company should erect managerial dividing lines between its product and process-focused manufacturing segments. In

Exhibit 5. One Product Group Serving Another Product Group's Market

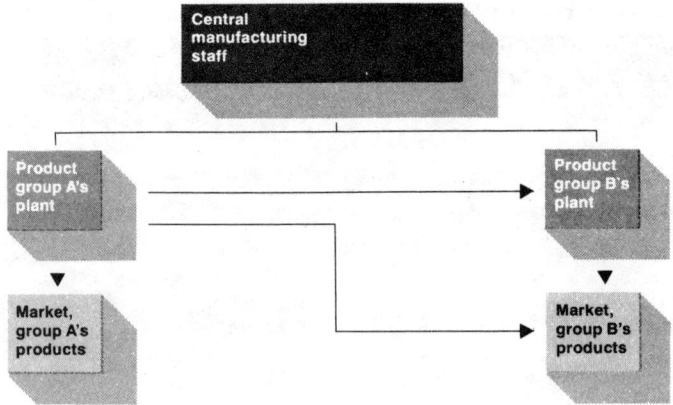

TEST FOR ORGANIZATIONAL FOCUS

Exhibit 6. Two Product Groups and a Supplier Plant

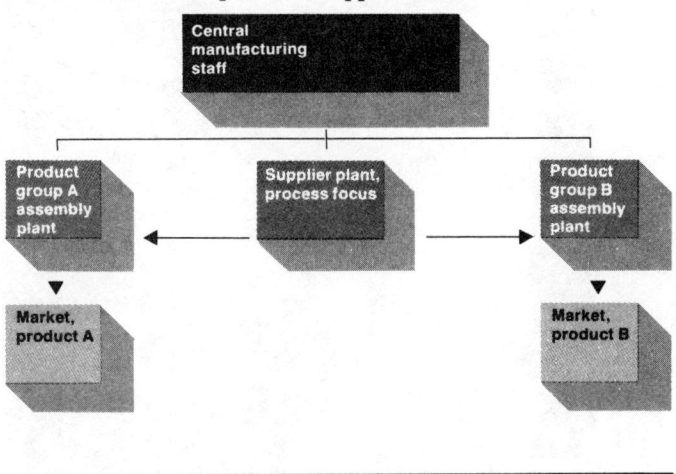

particular, transfer of products between product and process-focused plant groups should not be coordinated by a central staff group but handled through arm's-length bargaining, as if, in effect, they had independent "subsidiary" relationships within the parent company.

Such an in-house supplier would then be treated like any other supplier, able to resist demands that violate the integrity of its manufacturing mission just as the customer plant is free to select suppliers that are more attuned to its own mission. The organization chart might look something like that shown in Exhibit 7.

Such an arrangement may appear to be needlessly complex and add to the manufacturing's administrative overhead without clear financial benefits. However, combining two dissimilar activities does not reduce complexity; it simply camouflages it and is likely to destroy the focus and distinctiveness of both. Our position is not that both product and process focus cannot exist within the same company but simply that separating them as much as possible will result in less confusion and less danger that different segments of manufacturing will be working at cross purposes.

Test for Organizational Focus

Many companies, consciously or unconsciously, have moved toward precisely this kind of wide separation. In some cases it is explicit, with two or more different staff groups operating relatively autonomously; in others, although a single central staff appears on the organization chart, subgroups within this staff operate independently. One way for a company to test the

Exhibit 7. Product-Focused Division Supplying to Process-Focused Division

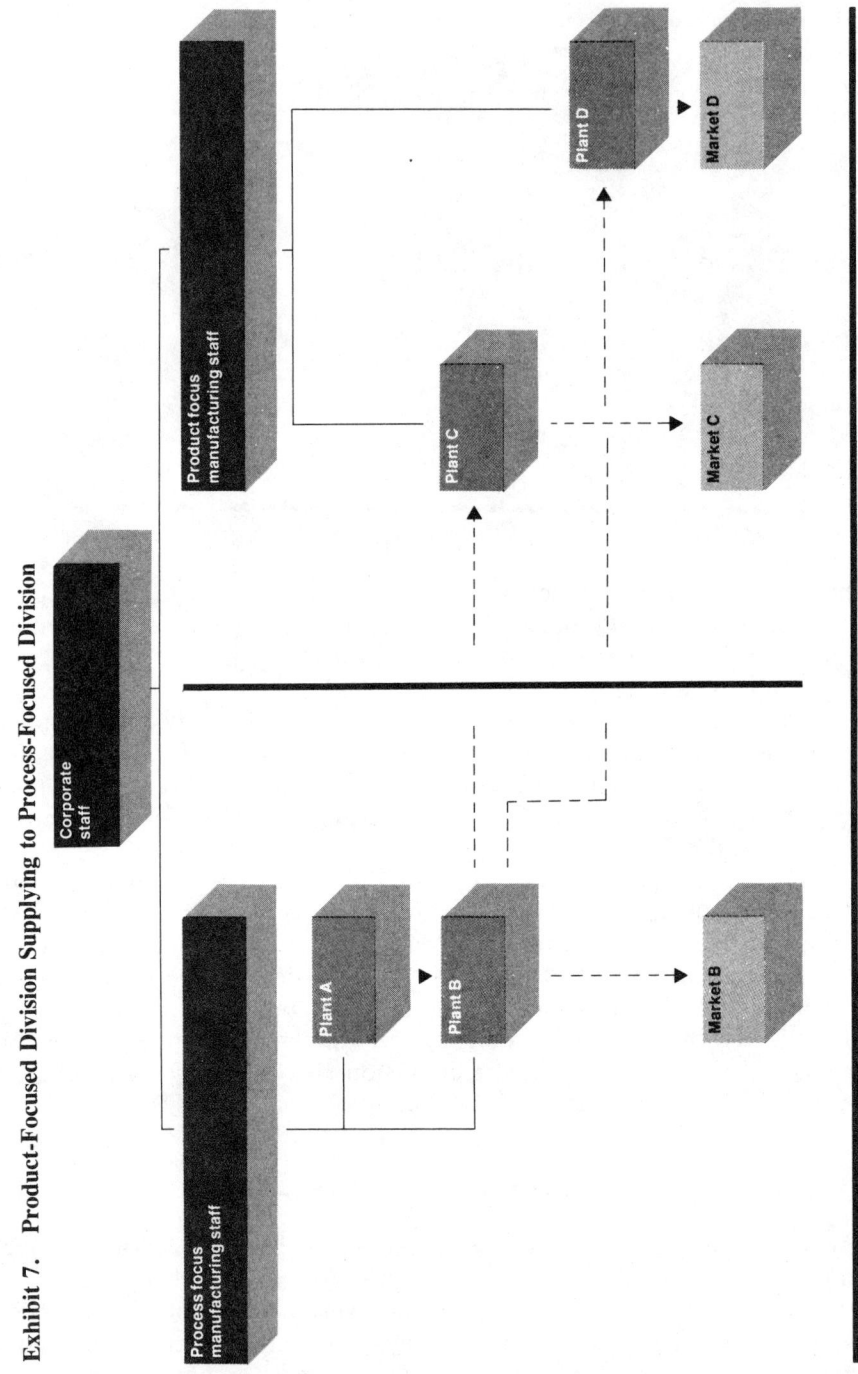

degree of organizational focus in its manufacturing arm, and whether adequate insulation between product and process-focused plant groups exists, is to contemplate how it would fragment itself if forced to (by the Antitrust Division of the Department of Justice, for example). A segmented and focused organization should be able to divide itself up cleanly and naturally, with no substantial organizational changes.

Consider the large auto companies. From the point of view of the marketplace, they are organized by product groups (Oldsmobile, Lincoln, Mercury, Chevrolet, etc.), but this organization is essentially cosmetic. In reality, the auto companies are classic examples of large process-focused organizations. Any effort by the Department of Justice to sever these companies by product group is foolish because it cuts across the grain of their manufacturing organization. If the companies had to divest themselves, it could only be by process segment. But the point is that divestiture could be accomplished readily, and this is the acid test of an effective and focused manufacturing organization.

The Impact of Growth

Up to this point we have been arguing that a company's manufacturing function must structure and organize itself so as to conform to the company's priorities for certain competitive dimensions. Moreover, the choice of manufacturing organizational structure—which provides most of the key linkages between the manufacturing group and the company's other people and functions—must also fit with the basic attitudes, preferences, and traditions that shape and drive the remainder of the company.

But companies change and grow over time. Unless a manufacturing organization is designed so that it can grow with the company, it will become increasingly unstable and inappropriate to the company's needs. Therefore, simplicity and focus are not sufficient criteria; the organizational design must somehow also incorporate the possibility of growth.

In fact, growth is an enemy of focus and can subvert a healthy manufacturing operation—not all at once, but bit by bit. For example, growth can move a company up against a different set of competitors at the same time it is acquiring new resources and thus force a change in its competitive strategy. The strategy change may be aggressive and deliberate or unconscious and barely perceived. In either case, however, success for the company may now require different skills from those already mastered—a different manufacturing mission and focus to complement a new corporate strategy.

Even without a change of strategy, growth can diminish a manufacturing organization's ability to maintain its original focus. Especially if growth is rapid, top-level managers will be pressed continually to decide on capital acquisitions and deployment, and to relinquish some authority over operational issues in existing plants. Slowly, focus disintegrates.

To cope with growth, we believe that first one must identify and understand the type of growth being experienced and the demands it will place on the organization. Growth has the following important dimensions:

1. A broadening of the products or product lines being offered.
2. An extended span of the production process for existing products to increase value added (commonly referred to as vertical integration).
3. An increased product acceptance within an existing market area.
4. Expansion of the geographic sales territory serviced by the company.

These types of growth are very different, but it is important to distinguish among them so that the organization design can reflect the *kind* of growth experienced, not simply the fact of growth. This means keeping the organization as stable and focused as possible as growth proceeds.

If growth is predominantly a broadening of product lines, a product-focused organization is probably best suited to the demands for flexibility that such a broadening requires. With such organizations, other aspects of manufacturing, particularly the production of the traditional product lines, need change only little as growth proceeds.

Alternatively, if growth is chiefly toward increasing the span of the process (that is, vertical integration), a process-focused organization can probably best introduce and manage the added segments of the full production process. In this fashion, the separate pieces of the process can be coordinated effectively and confusion can be reduced in the traditional process segments.

Then again, if growth is realized through increased product acceptance, the product becomes more and more a commodity and, as acceptance grows, the company is usually pressed to compete on price. Such pressure generally implies changes in the production process itself: more specialization of equipment and tasks, an increasing ratio of capital to labor expenses, a more standard and rigid flow of the product through the process. The management of such changes in the process is probably best accomplished by an organization that is focused on the process, willing to forsake the flexibilities of a more decentralized product focus.

Growth realized through geographic expansion is more problematic. Sometimes such growth can be met with existing facilities. But frequently, as with many multinational companies, expansion in foreign countries is best met with an entirely separate manufacturing organization that can be organized along either a product or a process focus.

Recognizing Common Pitfalls

As we examined a number of manufacturing organizations that had "lost their way"—become unfocused or whose focus was no longer congruent with corporate needs—it became apparent that in most cases the culprit was growth. Problems due to growth often surface with the apparent breakdown of the relationship between the central manufacturing staff and division or plant management. For example, many companies that have had a strong central manufacturing organization find that as their sales and product offerings grow in size and complexity, the central staff simply cannot continue to perform the same functions as well as before. A tenuous mandate for changing the manufacturing organization surfaces.

Sometimes, product divisions are broken out. But the natural inclination is to strengthen the central staff functions instead, which usually diminishes the decision-making capabilities of plant managers.

As the central staff becomes stronger, it begins to siphon authority and people from the plant organization. Thus the strong tend to get stronger and the weak weaker. At some point this vicious cycle breaks down under the strain of increasing complexity, and then a simple executive order cannot accomplish the profound changes—in people, policies, and attitudes—that are necessary to reverse the process and cause decentralization.

We do not mean to imply that decentralizing manufacturing management is always the best path to follow as an organization grows. It may be preferable in some cases to split it apart geographically, with two strong central staffs coordinating the efforts of two independent plant organizations.

However, it is sometimes dangerous to delegate too much responsibility for capacity-expansion decisions to product-oriented manufacturing managers. To keep their own tasks as simple as possible, they may tend to "expand in place"—continually expanding current plants or building nearby satellite plants. Over time they may create a set of huge tightly interconnected plants that exhibit many of the same characteristics as a process organization: tight central control, inflexibility, and constraints on further incremental expansion.

Such a situation could occur in spite of the fact that the corporation as a whole continues to emphasize market flexibility, decentralized responsibility, and technological opportunism. The new managers trained in such a complex will have to be different in personality and skills from those in other parts of the company, and a different motivation and compensation system is required. Such a situation can be remedied either by dismembering and reorganizing this product organization or by uncoupling it from the rest of the company so that it has more of an independent subsidiary status, as described earlier.

Product focus can also encroach on an avowed process focus. For example, a company offering several complex products whose manufacture takes these products through very definite process stages in which the avowed focus is process-oriented, and with separate divisions for stages of the process all subject to strong central direction, must resist the temptation to alter manufacturing so that it can "get closer to the market." If the various product lines were allowed to make uncoordinated requests for product design changes or new product introductions, the tightly coupled process pipeline could then crumble. Encroaching product focus would subvert it.

Concluding Remarks

Manufacturing functions best when its facilities, technology, and policies are consistent with recognized priorities of corporate strategy. Only then can manufacturing gain efficiency without wasting resources by "improving" operations that do not count.

The manufacturing organization itself must be similarly consistent with corporate priorities. Such organizational focus is aided by simplicity of design. This simplicity in turn requires either a product or a process-focused form of organization. The proper choice between these two organizational types can smooth company's growth by lending stability to its operations.

Notes

1. See, for example, Wickham Skinner, "Manufacturing—Missing Link in Corporate Strategy," *HBR*, May–June 1969, p. 136, and "The Focused Factory," *HBR*, May–June 1974, p. 113. Chapters 5 and 10, this volume.

2. Two representative texts are: Kenneth R. Andrews, *The Concept of Corporate Strategy* (Homewood, IL, Dow Jones–Irwin, 1971), and H. Igor Ansoff, *Corporate Strategy* (New York, McGraw-Hill, 1965).

3. "Hewlett-Packard: Where Slower Growth Is Smarter Management," *Business Week*, June 9, 1975, p. 50.

4. See Wickham Skinner, "The Focused Factory," *HBR*, May–June 1974, p. 121. Chapter 10, this volume.

5. E.F. Schumacher has eloquently argued a similar point in a somewhat different context in his provocative book *Small Is Beautiful* (New York, Harper & Row, 1975).

Can Marketing and Manufacturing Coexist?

BENSON P. SHAPIRO

This article deals with the familiar but classic problem that afflicts every manufacturing company—namely, conflict between these two functional areas. It can be dysfunctional in that the day-to-day abrasion can lead to open warfare. This situation is particularly dangerous because rather than walking a tightrope between marketing orientation and production orientation, the company can become so sales minded that manufacturing can't operate effectively. Or else it can become so manufacturing focused that the customer is forgotten in the name of smooth operations. In managing the conflict, the author suggests that marketing develop its programs to take advantage of the company's manufacturing capability, that manufacturing adapt its capability in response to the needs of selected market segments, and that top management emphasize approaches that foster cooperation between the two functions.

Marketing personnel in companies that manufacture industrial goods often complain about the activities and attitudes of their manufacturing counterparts with laments such as: "Why can't they become market-oriented or customer-oriented?" "Why are they so provincial?" The manufacturing people, on the other hand, lament like this: "The marketing people have no understanding of costs, profits, plants, or operations. They are just a bunch of dumb peddlers."

Although some consumer goods companies, particularly those in fashion industries with broad product lines (e.g., apparel, furniture), experience

---

Author's Note. The study on which this article is based was financed by the Marketing Science Institute, the Associates of the Harvard Business School, and the *Harvard Business Review*. Their support, as well as the constructive suggestions of Robert H. Hayes, Wickham Skinner, and John P. Kotter, is gratefully acknowledged.

antagonism between these two key functions, the need for cooperation is much greater in the typical industrial goods company.

In this article I will begin by detailing the areas of necessary cooperation but potential conflict. Then, I will consider the causes of conflict. Next, I will suggest ways of managing the conflict by increasing cooperation and minimizing antagonism between the marketing and manufacturing functions. Finally, I will recommend an approach for strengthening the two functions.

The Problem Areas

Exhibit 1 lists eight general areas in which there is a strong likelihood of conflict in managing the marketing/manufacturing interface in an industrial company. Let us start by taking a closer look at each of these problem areas.

Capacity Planning and Long-Range Sales Forecasts

Beyond the day-to-day issue of what product do we make tomorrow or next week, one of the strategic areas of cooperation is capacity planning and long-range sales forecasting. It often takes a long time for a company to change its manufacturing capacity. If such a change requires a new or enlarged building, design and construction can take several years. The addition of new equipment can take up to two years in most industries. Even the hiring and training of additional employees to staff existing physical capacity can take as long as from one year in fairly typical industries to several years in fields requiring great skill and experience such as tool and die making or advanced welding.

The problem is further exacerbated by the business cycle. Usually, most companies want to build plants, buy equipment, and hire employees at the very time when the construction industry is busiest, the equipment backlogs longest, and the labor market tightest. In addition, excess capacity is expensive. Mortgage payments, rent, taxes, depreciation, unemployment benefits, wasted training, and so on eat into profits when sales are lowest.

Thus the solution is clear: have exactly the right capacity at the right time.

But that requires precise long-term sales forecasting. And, because sales forecasting is not a science, the marketing and sales executives who forecast sales can't be expected to be right every time. In many companies, the problem is much more complex than just a gross sales forecast. In these situations, either capacity is a function of product mix, or different manufacturing processes require different facilities or labor input. Here the sales forecast must not only be precise in total, but each part must also be precise.

Capacity planning is an area in which both marketing and manufacturing are seldom perfect. The sales forecasts are often wrong partly because of

Exhibit 1. Marketing Manufacturing Areas of Necessary Cooperation but Potential Conflict

Problem Area	Typical Marketing Comment	Typical Manufacturing Comment
Capacity planning and long-range sales forecasting	"Why don't we have enough capacity?"	"Why didn't we have accurate sales forecasts?"
Production scheduling and short-range sales forecasting	"We need faster response. Our lead times are ridiculous."	"We need realistic customer commitments and sales forecasts that don't change like wind direction."
Delivery and physical distribution	"Why don't we ever have the right merchandise in inventory?"	"We can't keep everything in inventory."
Quality assurance	"Why can't we have reasonable quality at reasonable cost?"	"Why must we always offer options that are too hard to manufacture and that offer little customer utility?"
Breadth of product line	"Our customers demand variety."	"The product line is too broad—all we get are short uneconomical runs."
Cost control	"Our costs are so high that we are not competitive in the marketplace."	"We can't provide fast delivery, broad variety, rapid response to change, and high quality at low cost."
New product introduction	"New products are our life blood."	"Unnecessary design changes are prohibitively expensive."
Adjunct services such as spare parts inventory support, installation, and repair	"Field service costs are too high."	"Products are being used in ways for which they weren't designed."

the inexactness of the forecasting act itself and partly because the salespeople who are closest to the customer often react emotionally to market prospects. When business is down, the salespeople perceive it as even worse than it is; when business is good, they become ebullient.

In self-defense, manufacturing people often second-guess the marketers and operate from revised forecasts. Since the manufacturing people are insulated from the marketplace, their forecasts are often no better, and are sometimes even worse.

If capacity is too low, marketers are upset because they are losing sales. If capacity is too high relative to sales, they are upset because costs are too high.

Production Scheduling and Short-Range Sales Forecasting

This problem area is a short-term mirror image of the longer-term situation. It is more operational and thus less likely to involve top level line executives, but the conflict between the production scheduler and the sales manager can be intense, especially due to the fact that specific customer relationships and orders are involved.

In addition, the people active in this fray usually have less perspective on the company as well as less experience and judgment. They are, therefore, likely to be insular in their viewpoints. Also, as in the longer term, perfection is unlikely to be achieved. The forecasts aren't perfect, and the schedules are not totally flexible. In addition, the scheduler must be responsive to needs beyond those of the sales manager and his or her customers. Schedulers often are attempting to maximize total output, minimize cost, and maintain labor stability so that they are almost forced to schedule at the convenience of the plant managers as well as of the marketers.

Delivery and Physical Distribution

This area is like the previous two in that it involves sales forecasts going from marketing to manufacturing and manufacturing's response through the management of a capability. In this instance, the response is determined by inventory availability instead of manufacturing capacity.

The nature of the company's industrial business largely determines the importance of this problem area and the degree of conflict related to it. If the company manufactures a broad line of proprietary items (as opposed to custom-designed and built items) and if customers require rapid response, the inventory/distribution system is of major concern. Companies that provide replacement parts for capital equipment, for example, usually find delivery and inventory control crucial because their customers' operations are dependent on their ability to ship orders quickly.

In many companies physical distribution has been a traditional area of conflict involving frequent organizational shuffling. Usually the sequence

THE PROBLEM AREAS

works something like this: marketing runs physical distribution and inventory control and, while customer service is good, inventories are too high. Yet manufacturing does not gain the benefits it thinks it needs from using the inventory to smooth production and lengthen runs because marketing is always demanding small batches on short notice to keep inventories balanced.

In response to this problem, management shifts the physical distribution function from marketing to manufacturing. The result is better inventory management and coordination with production scheduling, but poorer customer service. Then, after months of organizational backbiting and bickering, management settles on a third option. It creates a separate physical distribution function. Finally, this arrangement satisfies neither marketing nor manufacturing and lasts only until the pressure gets too high, and the organization is reshuffled again.

Quality Assurance

Because production and inspection operations are seldom perfect, products have quality problems that are obvious to customers and sources of aggravation and embarrassment to salespeople. The typical marketing expectation is that if the plant were run correctly, problems would be nonexistent or at least minimal. Sometimes that is true—quality problems are caused by poor manufacturing management.

On the other hand, quality levels are closely related to other marketing interests that involve manufacturing complexity, variety, cost, and field service. Marketers often perceive customers as desiring "advanced" features and options. These complicate the manufacturing task and increase the probability of quality and field service problems. In addition, the broader the product line, the more opportunity there is for the manufacturing operation to fail in some way because of employee unfamiliarity or system error.

Finally, because meticulous manufacturing and quality assurance are expensive, in some situations it is cheaper to fix a few problems in the field than to raise manufacturing and inspection standards throughout the production process.

Breadth of Product Line

Folklore has it that the marketers want a broad product line whereas manufacturers respond with the classic line attributed to Henry Ford, "You can have any color you want as long as it's black." The source of the conflict is understandable when one compares the cost (to the company) of a product line broader than optimum (from the total company's viewpoint) to one narrower than optimum.

The product line that is too narrow results in lost sales through (1) loss of competitive position as a "full line" supplier or in particular product areas and market segments, (2) loss of distributor and sales force support, and (3) loss of economies of scale.

The line that is too broad results in (1) added inventory cost of raw material on hand, work in process, and finished goods, (2) increased cost of manufacturing changeover due to loss of capacity, setup changes, scrap generation, and stress and strain on equipment and employees, (3) added order processing and transportation costs, and (4) possible sales force, distributor, and customer confusion and displeasure.

Most of the costs of the narrow product line and all of the *measurable* (as distinct from actual) costs are in the marketing area. For the broader than optimum line the situation is reversed—all of the measurable costs and almost all of the actual costs are in the manufacturing area. There is, therefore, a natural rational basis for conflict.

Cost Control

Most marketers view cost as a prime determinant of price as well as, of course, of profits. Marketers tend to attribute costs that are too high to inept manufacturing management. Manufacturing personnel tend to relate high costs to "unreasonable" marketing demands such as rapid delivery, high quality, a broad line, and facile introduction of new products. Because it is inherently difficult to precisely assess either the costs or the benefits of such demands and to know what is "just enough" quality and so forth, there is often little factual data to support or refute such biases.

New Product Introduction

Although they are a prime competitive weapon in the marketplace, new products can greatly upset the manufacturing operation. They require new processes, employee training, new equipment, and trial-and-error operation until they are integrated into existing operations.

Furthermore, what is only a minor modification to a marketer may be a major operating change to a manufacturing person. Ideally, innovative new products should offer great customer benefit and little upset in the plant. All too often, the manufacturing personnel perceive little customer benefit and great upset in the plant.

Adjunct Services

Finally, there is a range of services, which often include installation and field service or repair, that concern both marketing and manufacturing. As in the preceding areas, interests and perceptions differ, and conflict is frequent. Factory people, for example, tend to view installation as the final manufacturing operation whereas marketers view it as a customer service function.

The Basic Causes

The explainable reasons for conflict in the problem areas just discussed fall into two categories. One consists of basic causes found in almost every industrial goods producer. The other is complicating factors that exacerbate the basic causes in certain situations. Here, I will confine my discussion to a review of the basic causes. Then, in the following section, I will examine the complicating factors.

Evaluation and Reward

One prime reason for the marketing/manufacturing conflict is that the two functions are evaluated on the basis of different criteria and receive rewards for different activities. On the one hand, the marketing people are judged on the basis of profitable growth of the company in terms of sales, market share, and new markets entered. Unfortunately, the marketers are sometimes more sales-oriented than profit-oriented. On the other hand, the manufacturing people are often evaluated on running a smooth operation at minimum cost. Similarly unfortunately, they are sometimes more cost-oriented than profit-oriented.

This system of evaluation and reward means that the marketers are encouraged to generate change, which is one hallmark of the competitive marketplace. To be rewarded, they must generate new products, enter new markets, and develop new programs. But the manufacturing people are clearly rewarded for accepting change only when it significantly lowers their costs.

Because the marketers and manufacturers both want to be evaluated positively and rewarded well, each function responds as the system asks it to in order to protect its self-interest.

The nature of the costs involving the problem areas magnifies the differences in the evaluation and reward system. The prior discussion about breadth of product line is a good example. Because the costs of a broader line are primarily in the manufacturing area, the manufacturing manager emphasizes the advantages of a narrower line. The reverse is true for the marketer. Thus the situation literally forces each manager into an adversary position. Each creates pressure for the policy that minimizes costs, maximizes benefits, and leads to a positive evaluation and an appropriate reward.

Inherent Complexity

Many of the problem areas help to engender conflict by the very nature of their inherent complexity. Because they involve at least two different functions, they usually need data from two different sources. Furthermore, the data are typically a mixture of "soft" (i.e., qualitative) marketing data and "hard" (i.e., quantified) manufacturing data. With regard to capacity expansion, it is fairly easy to determine the costs of facilities and equipment but hard to forecast sales and capacity utilization.

The problem areas are also complex because of the amount of the organization they involve. In many ways, the sales and the manufacturing operations represent the real horsepower of a company. They are the line functions that support the planning, financial, control, and administrative staffs. Thus any issue at this interface involves the core of the company.

Moreover, there is inherent complexity both conceptually and operationally at the analysis, policy formulation, and implementation levels. The data are in both sides of the house. The people responsible for formulating and implementing the policies are in both places. And the effects are felt in both.

Orientation and Experience

Another basic cause of conflict relates to the exposure, both current and past, of the managers involved. By and large, industrial marketers are most likely to have come up through the sales route. They began as salespersons who "lived and died" by their customers, and their work experience has always emphasized the customer. As sales managers and even as marketing managers, they deal with customer problems. The problems may be broader and the accounts larger, but their orientation remains the same—the customer.

The top marketing people usually have offices near the more operationally oriented salespeople, work with them on an intimate basis, and even visit field sales locations and customers. Their early biases are thus magnified by the people and situations they deal with on a day-to-day basis.

Their counterparts in manufacturing often began as forepersons and worked up through the production operation. They are aware of factory problems. They understand them, and they are exposed to them every day. Even the top manufacturing executives interact with their close (organizationally and geographically) associates whose prime concern is the plant. They visit manufacturing operations much more frequently than they do customers.

Each marketing and each manufacturing manager is more aware of his or her own organizational situation and problems. Each is more at ease with his or own function. Each is also more in tune with his or her own subordinates. The manager hires and trains them, shares their experiences and viewpoints, understands their orientations and attitudes. How could they be anything but right?

Cultural Differences

In most situations, the top level marketing and manufacturing managers literally live differently. As an example, consider two executives at an actual but disguised company that I will call here the Stopem Startem Controller Company (SSC). This company is a medium-sized midwestern producer of electronic flow controllers for liquids and gases sold to original equipment manufacturers, engineering contractors, and end-users in process industries such as chemicals, paper, and petroleum refining.

Sandra Sell, who is vice president of sales and marketing, received a bachelor's degree in chemical engineering from Drexel Institute in Philadelphia. She began her career as a salesperson and worked for several other companies before joining SSC. Bob Build, vice president of manufacturing, received a bachelor's degree in mechanical engineering from Purdue University and a master's in industrial engineering from Illinois Institute of Technology. He began as a foreperson with SSC and worked his way up through line and staff production positions.

These two executives differ literally in the way they live as well as in the way in which they manage. Sandra Sell has much greater ego drive and empathy (the typical salesperson's personality structure) than Bob Build. Sell drives an Oldsmobile 98 and enjoys golf, tennis, and bridge. Build drives a Porsche, which he maintains himself, and his hobbies are his car, gardening, and woodworking. He is a meticulous craftsman. In short, they fulfill their different marketing and manufacturing stereotypes. But they are real people. And they are the rule rather than the exception.

In fact, despite the belief among some academics I have talked with that the differences just cited are too strongly drawn, there are data to support them. Paul R. Lawrence and Jay W. Lorsch, for example, have found significant differences in the task and social concerns of sales and production managers.[1]

It is not unlikely that Sandra Sell's and Bob Build's cultural differences alone would make it hard for them to work together intimately. When this subtle but equally important source of conflict is added to the other previously described basic causes, it is easy to understand why the marketing and manufacturing people don't always see eye-to-eye.

Complicating Factors

The situation can be even more complex because there are some additional factors that have an impact on most companies as well as a more limited set of factors that affect some companies. Let us first consider the more limited factors. In some industrial companies, the marketing and manufacturing people must also interface with either the R&D function or the engineering function, or both. The two-party situation thus becomes a three or four-party situation.

This interface is especially difficult in the new product area where R&D and engineering are key functions. In many companies that manufacture electrical or mechanical components and/or equipment (e.g., machine tools, drives, hydraulics), the engineering manager plays a role that coordinates manufacturing and marketing and in some cases even subordinates these functions. At times, the nature of the business and its strategy dictate that ascendency. At other times, the engineering manager by virtue of technical knowledge and/or political strength is the only person who can manage the marketing/manufacturing interface.

Other functions enter the picture to add complexity to certain decision areas. The finance people, for example, are almost always intimately involved with capacity planning decisions. Control personnel are usually active in cost control and often in inventory control/physical distribution decisions.

Companies with large and diverse product lines have a particularly difficult job in managing the marketing/manufacturing interface. Rapidly growing companies also encounter special difficulties because the pressures for performance are greater, the resources more strained, and the organizational mechanisms often less developed. Thus, although the need for cooperation is greater, the capabilities to cooperate are sometimes more limited.

These situations affect only some companies. Almost all manufacturers, however, feel the effects of environmental changes. The economy has been more erratic than in the recent past. Since the sales cycles of most industrial goods companies are closely related to the general business cycle, they are greatly affected. Sales forecasting is more difficult, product planning is harder, and mistakes are more costly. Mistakes also contribute to long-term counterproductive antagonisms.

Technology is changing more rapidly. Products more quickly become obsolete, and then processes need to be replaced. This environmental change puts tremendous burdens on both marketers and manufacturers.

Closely related to technological change is the proliferation of automated operations, which are often much harder to change than more labor-intensive operations. Mistakes are more expensive and response to marketing needs slower. However, even newer technologies utilizing minicomputers may allow more flexible response. But until these are developed, automation apparently makes the marketing/manufacturing interface less fluid and thus more exasperating.

Capital constraints and the high cost of capital make major manufacturing changes expensive and redeployment of plant facilities difficult. Mistakes are visible, and poor response and poor coordination can't be easily covered over by committing more dollars.

Finally, the sheer increase in the size of companies makes the marketing/manufacturing interface more difficult to manage. More people are involved. For example, if it is a multidivision corporation, both the marketing and the manufacturing managers must coordinate not only with one another, but also with divisional functional managers, the division general manager, and their corporate counterparts.

The situation is, however, not all bleak.

Managing the Conflict

Like market competition, conflict can ensure effectiveness and efficiency. Top management's task is to maintain a constructive amount of tension by making sure that both marketing and manufacturing understand the need for a balanced situation but still strongly represent their own interests.

Explicit Policies

Top management can balance the interface with more than the traditional techniques of mediation and arbitration, which are useful and necessary. A good beginning is the development and promulgation of clear straightforward corporate policies. For example, marketing and manufacturing are much less likely to argue about product line breadth if, as a conscious policy, the company decides to be a full-line producer, to emphasize only high-volume items, or to concentrate on some other category of products. Such policies provide a set of rules within which the marketing and manufacturing people can operate, and they encompass most, if not all, of the problem areas delineated earlier.

Illustrative Examples. Let me demonstrate the importance of explicit corporate policies covering the marketing/manufacturing interface by offering two examples.

In one situation, a manufacturer sold replacement parts for heavy construction equipment to distributors and large end-users. To the marketing people, the essence of their strategy was rapid response to orders and on-time delivery because lack of a part could keep an expensive piece of equipment out of operation. To the manufacturing people, the basis of their approach was effective asset management, which meant low inventories and high capacity utilization.

However, manufacturing's low inventories made it impossible for the company to provide rapid response to orders. High capacity utilization implied undercapacity when the highly cyclical construction industry was busiest.

Vocal dissatisfaction from key distributors and large end-users finally reached top management. After several meetings involving both marketing and manufacturing people, a task force was formed to study the issue. The task force approach had two happy results. First, the people involved developed personal cross-functional relationships. Second, explicit corporate guidelines accepted by top management included the measurement of manufacturing people on service levels stressing percentage of orders shipped complete and percentage shipped on time.

In short, the guidelines clarified the trade-off between service level on the one hand and inventory size and capacity utilization on the other. The conflict problem was not "solved," but the tension was brought under control.

In the other situation, a manufacturer of office furniture was subject to frequent hassles concerning length of product line. Because no explicit goal had been established, the manufacturing vice president constantly fought to reduce the line and the marketing vice president fought to expand it. They found it impossible to jointly analyze the financial impact of changes in product line length, and they became more strongly committed to their own beliefs.

The sales manager, who reported to the marketing vice president, provided ample evidence of "lost sales" because the line lacked additional "popular" styles. Similarly, the plant manager supported the manufacturing vice president with reams of data on the "cost" of the "overly long" product line. No light but much heat was generated by quarterly "planning" meetings.

Subsequently, in desperation, a team of outside experts was handed the problem. The team clarified costs, studied the market, and—as in the previous example—made explicit the trade-off between a broader product line more attuned to customer needs and a smaller product line more responsive to manufacturing constraints. In this particular example, the management decision to contract the product line in particular areas was incorporated into a revised strategic plan. Nobody was totally pleased with the solution but both functional sides viewed the result as a "sensible compromise."

Over time, the management guidelines have been adjusted to changes in customer needs, competitive activities, manufacturing capabilities, and technology. In fact, product line length is now a major parameter of the corporate business plan.

Each function should also be responsible for developing policies that relate to the total corporate strategy and to the needs of its sister function. Thus, if the manufacturing schedule and corporate policies are oriented toward large orders, the sales force can have policies limiting small orders. Or, on the other hand, if delivery is a key part of corporate and marketing policy, the manufacturing operation can emphasize high finished and semifinished inventory. Although it is poor policy to have the marketing function stressing delivery while manufacturing stresses low finished goods inventory, it is not unusual to find such situations.

Modified Measurements

To bolster common policies, the evaluation and reward system can be modified to stress interfunctional cooperation. Marketing managers might, for example, be judged on those variables viewed as important to the manufacturing operation. Good sales forecasting might be rewarded instead of going over the sales quota. If the sales people are judged on their ability to beat the quota, they will keep it low rather than realistic.

Manufacturing people might be judged on a combination of inventory size, delivery response time, and the ability to meet delivery commitment dates rather than just on asset management. Cost goals should be spelled out not only in terms of lower costs but also in terms of improved performance in quality, implementation of new product introduction, and so forth.

A common evaluation and reward system can be effective only if there are policies on which the criteria can be based and data that enable measurement against a plan. Many companies don't, for example, have planned or actual breadth of line data. All that is known is that marketing thinks the line is too narrow and manufacturing is just as sure that it is too broad.

The gathering and analysis of data concerning interfunctional problems are useful for more than measuring performance against a plan. Data are necessary to relieve some of the inherent complexity of the interfunctional situations. As an example, if a company were concerned with field service, it would have to have good data on service costs, frequency of failure, impact on the customer and/or prospects, and even the cost of tighter quality control.

It is important for the data to include quantified plans and budgets, as well as actual performance. The best way to evaluate sales forecasting is to record the forecast and compare it with actual sales. The same is true of the other problem areas.

The data to be gathered will vary with the type of industry and the situation but should, in general, focus as closely as possible on the basic desired parameters. As well as cost performance, these data will often emphasize customer needs such as inventory support, rapid repair service, and the like.

In fact, it is quite realistic to survey customers concerning their perceptions and to use these as a basis for analysis, planning, and evaluation. For example, although it is important to measure the cost of a service operation, average frequency of repair, and maximum time from request to repair, it is also useful to ask customers to rate the service quality, helpfulness of repair people, and so on.

People Concerns

Several people-oriented approaches can be taken, the simplest of which is to encourage informal interfunctional contact. The best sales meetings, for example, include manufacturing managers and representatives from other functional areas. This enables the manufacturers to meet informally with the marketers in both work and recreational settings. Experiences and concerns can be shared. Perhaps even more important, personal relationships can be developed. These generate mutual respect and understanding, which are particularly useful when difficult interfunctional problems are confronted.

Another people-oriented approach involves mixed career paths. If more managers cross over functional lines during their development, they will better understand the activities, concerns, and values of their sister functions. It will also lead to better balanced top managers. Most companies shy away from this approach because they fear the upset or cost. Concerns include, "I don't want a foreperson-type to ruin a good customer" or "That sales-type will be eaten alive by the union."

Although such concerns are valid, the problems are clearly not insurmountable—especially if the program is begun fairly early in career development and fairly low in the organization where risks are minimal. This career path approach requires a strong management commitment but the benefits can be high because it provides a solution to the orientation, experience, and cultural differences discussed earlier.

A major side benefit is the development of broad-experienced general managers. A surprisingly large proportion of outstanding division general managers has risen this way. In the past such a path often came about haphazardly. In the future, it should be part of a combined executive development program and method of coping with interfunctional conflict.

Still another people-oriented approach is less drastic than mixed career paths and perhaps less effective. Many opportunities present themselves for interfunctional task forces and committees. If these are well-developed and involve people at lower levels in the organization, they can be effective in helping each function to learn from the other. The informal contact engendered by such a program can often be as useful as the purely task-related interaction.

Mediation and arbitration cannot be neglected as useful tools in managing the interface. They are really a part of the broader more focused program recommended here. Top management can gain much by bringing marketing and manufacturing people together in an air of cooperation to analyze, plan, and implement approaches to problem areas. These sessions will be particularly useful if, as previously mentioned, goals are explicitly specified and credible data are available.

Strengthening the Functions

In order to lessen the amount of marketing/manufacturing conflict, management can make each function more responsive to the other's needs. Mar-

STRENGTHENING THE FUNCTIONS

keters should build their programs around the operational strengths of their manufacturing unit. Thus marketing executives must not only analyze customers and prospects to understand their needs, but also analyze the manufacturing capability to understand its competitive strengths and constraints. Then, they must divide their markets into segments and select for penetration those segments whose needs they can fill. Finally, they must develop a product policy that builds on the manufacturing unit's ability to service customers in the chosen segments.

This kind of strategy is a great deal easier to describe than to implement. Few companies have explicit policies that provide a clear definition of the products and services they will offer and the benefits they will provide to the customer. Thus a product policy might state, "We will provide large volumes of a limited line of utilitarian items at low cost to customers who are capable of buying such volumes and willing to accept little variety and infrequent design change."

It requires a great deal of top management discipline to select market segments and develop product policies. Without such an explicit strategy, the company begins to be "all things to all people" and eventually becomes "nothing to everybody." The marketing function is thus given the task of selecting customers who need the company's products.

The manufacturing function should not offer the marketers a fixed capability. Instead, the productive capacity of the company should become a well-honed marketing tool. In the past 12 years two main concepts have been developed by manufacturing scholars to help to accomplish this.

Martin K. Starr suggested that products can be designed so that they can be made of interchangeable modules. With the appropriate production process, this modular approach enables the manufacturing function to provide substantial variety to the customer at limited cost. In such a situation, argues Starr, "Marketing management supplies the consumer with apparent variety even though the production output is based on the concepts of mass production."[2]

Careful design of the manufacturing system can do even more. Wickham Skinner has shown that improved competitiveness can result from "learning to focus each plant on a limited, concise, manageable set of products, technologies, volumes, and markets" and from "learning to structure basic manufacturing policies and supporting services so that they focus on one explicit manufacturing task instead of on many inconsistent, conflicting, implicit tasks."[3]

This approach enables a company to build its manufacturing capability in response to the specific needs of a clearly defined market segment. In a sales sense, customer benefits are maximized whereas manufacturing costs are minimized.

Recent suggestions that large factories are not necessarily efficient make the Skinner concept even more implementable.[4] One large auto parts supplier, for example, has committed itself to the construction of small (no more than 500 employees) plants designed around specific customer needs and production technologies. This focused approach is a far cry from the consolidated manufacturing operations of the past.

Concluding Note

The following advertisement appeared in a recent issue of the *Saturday Review*:

> Semantic difficulty with our Osaka, Japan branch factory has resulted in 468 Concert Grand Pianos, with tonal dynamics in reverse of normal. For particulars write Weaver Piano Company, East Grand Forks, SR Box G.P.R.[5]

Although this particular ad was obviously written in jest, actual problems such as this are quite common. But they can be addressed if top management understands that:

1. The problems of marketing and manufacturing conflict are real and important.
2. The causes are complex but understandable.
3. The situation can be improved through carefully developed programs to foster cooperation.
4. The company will prosper when the marketing and manufacturing functions operate in an atmosphere of cooperation with the realization that each has its role to play and its needs to fill. Neither function can subvert the other.

Notes

1. Paul R. Lawrence and Jay W. Lorsch, "Differentiation and Integration in Complex Organizations," *Administrative Quarterly*, June 1967, p. 1.

2. Martin K. Starr, "Modular Production—A New Concept," *HBR*, November–December 1965, p. 137.

3. Wickham Skinner, "The Focused Factory," *HBR*, May–June 1974, p. 114. Chapter 10, this volume.

4. See Roger W. Schmenner, "Before You Build a *Big* Factory," *HBR*, July–August 1976, p. 100.

5. *Saturday Review*, October 30, 1976, p. 60.

13
Why Japanese Factories Work

ROBERT H. HAYES

Japan's rapid evolution into a major industrial power has aroused in U.S. managers both awe and the wish to discover the "secret" of Japanese manufacturing success. Contrary to popular opinion, this evolution has not come about through the use of techniques like quality circles and advanced technologies such as robots. What Japan has created is the factory of the present, operating as it should. Japanese managers have never stopped emphasizing the basics. To them, every stage of the manufacturing process—from product design to distribution—is equally important. They constantly work to improve equipment design, inventory control systems, and worker skills through cooperation at all levels. The ultimate goal? Perfect products and error-free operations.

U.S. industry can also redress the decline in its manufacturing competitiveness, says the author, by using its enormous resources and talents to do the basics better. As always, this—and not some magical solution—is the route to manufacturing success.

Twenty years ago, most Americans pictured the Japanese factory as a sweatshop, teeming with legions of low-paid low-skilled workers trying to imitate by hand, with great effort and infrequent success, what skilled American and European workers were doing with sophisticated equipment and procedures. Today, shocked and awed by the worldwide success of Japanese

Author's Note. In the course of my work, I visited the manufacturing facilities of six Japanese companies (all located in or near Tokyo): Toshiba, Sanyo, Yokogawa Electric, TRW Tokai (a subsidiary of TRW Inc., where I toured three separate plants), Mitsubishi Melcom Computer Works, and Molex Japan (a U.S. subsidiary). These variously-sized companies represent a broad range of industries and ownership histories. I made the first three plant visits with a group of about 25 manufacturing managers from General Electric; the last three tours I made on my own.

products, Americans tend to rationalize Japan's industrial prowess by imagining gleaming factories peopled by skillful robots—both human and otherwise—all under the benevolent sponsorship of "Japan, Inc."

My research (see my note for a detailed description) suggests that this new stereotype is probably as incorrect as the old one. The modern Japanese factory is not, as many Americans believe, a prototype of the factory of the future. If it were, it might be, curiously, far less of a threat. We in the United States, with our technical ability and resources, ought then to be able to duplicate it. Instead, it is something much more difficult for us to copy; it is the factory of *today* running as it should.

The Japanese have achieved their current level of manufacturing excellence mostly by doing simple things but doing them very well and slowly improving them all the time. "The nail that sticks up is hammered down," says the Japanese proverb. In the factories I visited, all the nails appeared to have been hammered down.

In describing some of the ways in which this "hammering" has been done, I shall not discuss the effect of Japanese cultural or social norms on management behavior, the distinctive aspects of Japanese management systems, or the virtues of Japanese industrial policy. They are all important topics, but all have been the subject of innumerable books and articles. (See the end of this article for a list of related reading.) Instead, I will focus simply on how the Japanese manage their manufacturing functions.

What I Did *Not* See

For the most part, Japanese factories are *not* the modern structures filled with highly sophisticated equipment that I (and others in the group) expected them to be. The few "intelligent" robots I encountered were largely still experimental; the general level of technological sophistication that I observed was not superior to (and was usually lower than) that found in comparable U.S. plants.

Automation consisted mainly of simple materials-handling equipment used in conjunction with standard processing equipment—just as it is here. Nor do the Japanese run this equipment at higher rates or for longer hours than U.S. factories do. Because of government regulations against women working after 10 P.M., very few Japanese facilities operate more than two shifts a day.

Similarly, the famed "quality circles" did not appear as influential as I expected. They were not widely adopted until several years after the Japanese Union of Scientists and Engineers had given them its official support in the mid-1960s. Most of the plants I visited had, in fact, experienced problems with QCs for three to four years after their introduction. Moreover, most of the companies I talked to already had enviable reputations for high-quality products by the time they adopted QCs.

One company treated quality circles as secondary peripheral activities; another had eliminated them altogether ("temporarily," it said). But the quality levels at these plants were just as high as at others where QCs were active.

Finally, I did not observe the use of uniform compensation systems. I had been led to expect wage systems based strictly on seniority, bonuses based on corporate profitability, no incentives based on individual performance, and no time clocks. Yet at one plant I found wages based on level of skill and commuting distance as well as on seniority. At another, by agreement with the union, bonuses equaled a certain number of months of regular salary independent of recent corporate profitability. At a third, the general manager wanted to tie compensation more directly to individual performance measurement—almost on a piecework basis. And I did see a few time clocks in operation. In short, there appeared to be few general rules covering employee compensation.

What I *Did* See

Although I found no exotic strikingly different Japanese way of doing things, I did notice several areas to which the Japanese had directed special attention.

Creating a Clean, Orderly Workplace

The factories I visited were exceptionally quiet and orderly, regardless of the type of industry, the age of a company, its location, or whether it was a U.S. subsidiary. Clearly, this orderliness was not accidental. The meticulousness of the Japanese worker was not, in my opinion, the major reason for the pervasive sense of order that I observed but seemed instead to result from the attitudes, practices, and systems that plant managers had carefully put into place over a long period.

The workers' uniforms (provided, of course, by the company) were clean, their machines were clean, and so were the floors around their machines. Sources of litter and grime were carefully controlled: boxes placed to catch metal shavings, plastic tubs and pipes positioned to catch and direct oil away from the workplace, spare parts and raw materials carefully stored in specified areas. The rest areas were centrally located, tastefully decorated (often with plants and flowers), and immaculate. As one American manager observed, "If you clean up the factory floor, you tend to clean up the thought processes of the people on it too."

Keeping their workplaces and machines in good order was a responsibility assigned to the workers themselves, along with maintaining output and quality and helping fellow workers. Moreover, each worker was trained to correct the minor problems that often arose in the course of the day, to conduct regular preventive maintenance, to monitor and adjust equipment, and to search continually for ways to eliminate potential disruptions and improve efficiency. The object was simple: to avoid any breakdown of equipment during working hours.

Eliminating 'the Root of All Evil'

In the factories I saw, the sense of order also resulted from an almost total absence of inventory on the plant floor. Raw materials were doled out in small batches only as needed. In many cases, vendors maintained stores of materials and purchased parts that the company "called off" periodically. Suppliers often made three or four deliveries a day to avoid excess stock in the plant. Finished goods were removed immediately from the floor and either transferred to a separate warehouse or shipped directly to customers or distributors. The little inventory I did observe was carefully piled in boxes in specified places around the plant—marked, as were the aisles, with painted stripes.

Even work-in-process inventory was minimal. Material moved along steadily, assisted by materials handlers, by automated equipment, and by the workers themselves. Buffer inventories of partially completed work at various stations were unnecessary, for stoppages caused by breakdowns at earlier process stages almost never occurred. Because the incidence of rejects was very low, rejects did not pile up in baskets or on the floor (I discuss this at length in the next section). In short, most of the plants I saw appeared to have instituted materials movement systems similar to Toyota's famous "just in time" system: inventory is minimized if every part arrives precisely when needed or when a machine is available.

Why do U.S. companies have such large work-in-process inventories? One major reason is their emphasis on producing "economic batches," which seek to balance inventory costs against the setup costs created by changing from one item to another. In contrast, the Japanese believe that inventory is by definition bad, and they therefore seek to avoid the rationale for large-batch production by directing their attention and ingenuity to reducing setup costs. Toyota, for example, estimated that one U.S. auto company took six hours to change the presses in its hood and fender-stamping department. Volvo and a German competitor took four hours. Toyota's changeover time was 12 minutes.

As one senior manager phrased it:

> We feel that inventory is the root of all evil. You would be surprised how much you simplify problems and reduce costs when there are no inventories. For example, you don't need any inventory managers or sophisticated inventory control systems. Nor do you need expediters, because you can't expedite. And, finally, when something goes wrong, the system stops. Immediately the whole organization becomes aware of the problem and works quickly to resolve it. If you have buffer in-

ventories, these potential problems stay hidden and may never get corrected.

Keeping Murphy Out of the Plant

The inventory control system I describe requires iron discipline, not just on the plant floor but, more important, throughout the plant's managerial infrastructure: vendor relations, production planning, industrial engineering, manufacturing/process engineering, and quality assurance. Everywhere I saw evidence of Japanese managers' determination to prevent Murphy's law ("If something can go wrong, it will go wrong") from taking effect and to make sure that problems which do arise are resolved before they get to the plant floor.

"Before you can increase productivity or improve quality, you must have stability and continuity in your manufacturing process," argued one manager. "How can you have stability when crises are occurring? Our job is to keep crises from developing on the production floor so that our production workers can focus their attention on quality and productivity."

Preventing Machine Overload. Tools, dies, and production equipment were not overloaded. In fact, machines often operated at slower rates than they were designed for—and at less than the usual rate in U.S. factories. This practice reduced the possibility of jams and breakdowns as well as the wear on machine parts and dies.

Along with regular preventive maintenance, constant cleaning, and adjustment, machines last longer with reduced rates of use. I expected to be impressed by the newness of Japanese machine tools compared with those used in the same industries in the United States. (The average age of machine tools in U.S. industry is about 20 years; in Japan, 10 to 12.) But the machines were not really that much newer; they just *looked* newer. And they *ran* newer.

One American manager who has studied closely the Japanese companies in his industry estimated that, even though they used equipment similar to that found in the United States, it lasted two to three times longer. Another summarized the difference as follows: "They use their machines; we abuse ours."

Monitoring Systems. Most factories I saw used comprehensive equipment monitoring and early warning systems. These devices checked the process flow, signaled when jams occurred, measured dimensions and other characteristics of finished parts, indicated when these characteristics approached tolerance limits, and kept track of rates of use (number of strokes, shots, or impressions) of tools and dies and indicated when to adjust or regrind them.

These monitoring systems, together with the widespread use of simple materials-handling equipment, allowed Japanese workers to oversee the operation of more machines than their U.S. counterparts. American managers, when walking around the floor of a Japanese factory, are often struck by the sense of being in a virtually untended forest of machines. Sometimes they *are* untended. The Japanese have such trust in the error-free functioning of their equipment that they often load up a machine with work at the end of the last shift and let it run through the night.

No-Crisis Atmosphere. Production schedules were based on capacity measures derived from actual performance data (not, as one often sees in the United States, from theoretical or obsolete standards). They were established at least a day in advance—generally several days. And unlike U.S. companies, where manufacturing is expected—with good grace and a can-do attitude—to react to last-minute changes imposed by marketing personnel, these schedules were ironclad. (How can you change a production schedule when the inventory required to produce something different is not available?)

No expediting and no overloading were allowed. Work was meted out to the plant in careful doses instead of being, as one U.S. manager put it, "dumped on the floor so the foreperson can figure out what to do with it." In short, I never detected an atmosphere of crisis in any of the plants I visited or anything like the "end-of-the-month push" and the "Friday afternoon crisis" so familiar to many American factories.

One plant I visited, which produced electronic instruments in low volume, had a different approach. Production schedules were made up two weeks in advance, and at the beginning of each two-week period all the materials required to meet that schedule were distributed along the production line. At the end of the period, the inventory was used up and a new batch brought in. Workers, therefore, had the satisfaction of cleaning up the plant floor every two weeks and were exposed to continual controlled pressure to meet production quotas.

Another company with a very broad product line imposed a simple constraint on production schedulers to reduce the frequency of equipment changeovers: it allowed no more than eight product changes a day. Salespeople might complain and schedulers might be pushed to the limits of their ingenuity, but the rule was firm. If it became impossible to operate within the constraints of this rule, the company reduced its product line or increased the minimum size of customer orders—but the factory did not become burdened with confusion over additional product changes.

The crisis prevention programs like those I have just described generally extended to a company's suppliers as well. A company often informed a supplier several months in advance of its schedule of deliveries to a plant.

Any change in the plant's production schedule was translated automatically into a revised delivery schedule for its supplier. The fact that Japanese companies tend to favor nearby suppliers reinforced this tight linkage.

As one American manager put it, "Doesn't Murphy's law work here?" Perhaps one reason Murphy lives in America is that American managers actually *enjoy* crises; they often get their greatest personal satisfaction, the most recognition, and their biggest rewards from solving crises. Crises are part of what makes work fun. To Japanese managers, however, a crisis is evidence of failure. Their objective is disruption-free error-free operation—operation that doesn't require dramatic fixes.

Management and Manufacturing

It became clear to me that what sets Japanese factories apart is not so much what managers do but, rather, how well they do the things they have decided to do—that is, how they view their roles and responsibilities.

"Pursuing the Last Grain of Rice"

Japanese products have a worldwide reputation for precision, reliability, and durability. Many Americans still find this reputation somewhat incongruous because "Made in Japan" used to mean cheap and shoddy products. The important point, however, is *not* that the Japanese have made a remarkable transition but that it took 25 years of hard work to do it.

"Pursuing the last grain of rice in the corner of the lunchbox" is a Japanese saying that describes, somewhat disparagingly, a person's tendency to be overscrupulous. But it conveys volumes about the Japanese character. As managers and as workers, the Japanese are smart and industrious—and never satisfied. They regard *all* problems as important.

Their concept of "zero defects" is a good case in point. As one Japanese scholar phrased it:

> If you do an economic analysis, you will usually find that it is advantageous to reduce your defect rate from 10% to 5%. If you repeat that analysis, it may or may not make sense to reduce it further to 1%. The Japanese, however, will reduce it. Having accomplished this, they will attempt to reduce it to 0.1%. And then 0.01%. You might claim that this obsession is costly, that it makes no economic sense. They are heedless. They will not be satisfied with less than perfection.

Indeed, in most of the Japanese factories I visited, the quality charts on the walls measured the defect rate not in percentages but in parts per million: 1,000 ppm represents a 0.1% defect rate. These companies' current defect rate was 300 to 500 ppm, and their "near-term goal" was 100 to 200 ppm. And the long term? "Zero, of course."

"It's not just that we are idealistic," one Japanese manager stated, "but we realize that your willingness to stop at 95%, coupled with our unwillingness to accept 95%, is what makes us able competitors." Another, with perfect sincerity, informed me that "a defect is a treasure." So few of them turned up in that manager's company that each could be studied individually and mined for the information it contained about the remaining bugs in the production process.

It is important to add that a Japanese manager who talks about a quality problem in an operation is as likely to be talking about a design problem, a productivity problem, an inventory problem, a delivery problem, or an absenteeism problem as about defective products. Quality, to the Japanese, means error-free operation. Any defect in any part of the manufacturing operation, therefore, becomes a quality problem in management's view—another "grain of rice" to be pursued and eliminated.

High quality, after all, is not achieved by a few random management decisions but by a complex all-encompassing interactive management system that has the uncompromising long-term support of top management. The basis of this system is not simply an appropriate arrangement of people and machines. It is a way of thinking.

"Thinking Quality In." Japanese managers have taken the familiar American slogan, "You don't inspect quality into a product, you have to build it in," one step further: "Before you build it in, you must *think* it in."

1. *Planning.* Managers think it in, first, by careful planning in the product design stage. Interminable discussions among engineering, production, quality assurance, and sales personnel take place before the design is made final. Right from the start, manufacturing and industrial engineers help in developing machine specifications, methods, and standards. Product design is viewed as part of a total product-process system.

2. *Training.* Once production begins, managers concentrate on holding to these standards. Therefore, they think quality in by training workers to deliver consistently high-quality products while developing in them expectations of producing high quality. Japanese production workers automatically check the parts they receive to make sure that they are defect-free. They work meticulously, knowing that any defects arising from their operation will be spotted and ultimately—and embarrassingly—tracked to them. When the system works well, making high-quality products becomes a source of pride, and management attitudes and actions constantly reinforce this feeling.

3. *Feedback.* Managers encourage production workers and quality inspectors to identify and correct any quality problems that arise (even when they are so minor that the product still passes final inspection). Everybody

works together to ascertain the causes of problems and to eliminate them. By contrast, in many U.S. companies a "we against them" attitude prevails between production workers and quality inspectors. As a result, workers keep potential problems hidden and shunt off defects to be reworked, and the pressure to meet delivery deadlines makes quality inspectors reluctant to delay delivery because of minor quality problems. In Japanese companies "we" is everybody and "them" are defects. Feedback from production workers, quality inspectors, salesmen, vendors, and customers is encouraged. Field service organizations often report directly to the manufacturing manager rather than, as in most U.S. companies, to the sales manager.

4. *Materials.* Managers also think quality in by recognizing that even the most carefully designed and stable production process cannot maintain high quality if the materials that enter the process are defective. Japanese companies, therefore, devote intensive effort to screening incoming parts and materials and to feeding the results back to suppliers. One hundred percent inspection is often the rule until a supplier proves its reliability. The pressure put on suppliers to improve the quality of their own materials is incredible to an American, but Japanese manufacturers do not think that simple pressure is sufficient. Instead, they work with suppliers to ascertain why problems arise and to help solve them. They even conduct seminars for employees of supplier companies. The message: "If you follow these steps, you will learn to meet our requirements." Given the long-term relationships between suppliers and customers in Japan, suppliers cannot refuse or take lightly such assistance and advice.

Benefits of the System. Driving this quality consciousness—long before Japan's determined assault on export markets—are the realities of the Japanese domestic market. As one senior government official put it:

> A 1% defect rate means that if you sell 100,000 units of a product, 1,000 of them will be defective. In a country as small geographically and as crowded as ours is, it is simply unacceptable to have that many dissatisfied customers 'unselling' your product to their friends.

Moreover, the practice in some U.S. companies of shipping off-spec products to remote or less favored customers is unthinkable.

The Japanese have learned how to exploit the inevitable. They have come to realize that the same conditions that promote defect-free manufacturing operations also increase productivity. The apparent relationship between productivity and quality is supported by one American expert—Robert Lynas, group vice president at TRW—who notes that "a 2% reduction in defects is usually accompanied by a 10% increase in productivity."

This finding may simply be due to the fact that fewer defects mean more output without a corresponding increase in costs. As one Japanese manager pointed out:

> If you eliminate the production of defective items, things become much simpler and less costly to manage. You don't need as many inspectors as before. You don't need to have production workers doing rework, or systems that manage the detection and flow of rework through the process. Waste goes down. Inventory goes down. But morale goes up. Everybody feels very proud when you produce only perfect products.

Time Consciousness

In my tour, I was confronted time and again with concrete evidence of Japanese managers' emphasis on long-term commitments. The managers of U.S. companies jealously guard their "flexibility" and "reaction time" and, therefore, think in terms of "sales," "hourly workers," "vendors," and "stockholders." Japanese managers, on the other hand, are likely to think in terms of "everlasting customers," "lifetime employees," "supplier-partners," and "owners." This difference has enormous implications for both action and attitude.

Partnership. One simply does not develop a relationship with an everlasting customer in the same way that one makes a one-time sale—the two require completely different expectations and approaches. Nor does one disappoint an everlasting customer by delivering defective products or by failing to meet delivery schedules. One does not disappoint a supplier-partner by not buying from him if his prices are somewhat out of line, although one certainly works with him to help him get prices back in line with those of competitors. The objective, as in all partnerships, is a mutually beneficial long-term relationship—what many Japanese companies refer to as "codestiny."

American managers usually operate quite differently. One marketing vice president, for example, observed:

> When I visit a U.S. customer, I am allowed to present my product and then out I go. When recently I visited [a Japanese customer], on the other hand, I was told we would meet with a group of 4 people—which turned into a group of 12. I was told we would probably be there for an hour, but we were there for four hours as they questioned and probed me for information on what was happening in other areas and with other manufacturers.
>
> All the time I was speaking they were making notes frantically; after I finished, they had a discussion in Japanese to ensure that they had all the necessary information. I was then asked to tour their factory and make suggestions and recommendations to improve their product. I think that the Japanese approach is more fruitful.

When asked to comment on this difference in U.S. and Japanese companies' treatment of vendors, American managers usually justified their short directed meetings on the grounds that they were too busy to spend time in meetings like the one just described. But where do Japanese managers find time to be so thorough? Perhaps they do such a good job of creating error-free operations that their plants can run without their active supervision and intervention. Or perhaps they have a different notion of how important their suppliers are to the ultimate success of their businesses and therefore allocate time differently.

Lifetime Employment. The Japanese custom of lifetime employment, which has attracted much attention in the West, dates in its current form only from the end of World War II and is still not the rule in all Japanese companies. Even today, less than a third of all Japanese workers are lifetime employees. Only the elite companies (that is, the biggest and most successful, whose products typically appear in international markets) usually practice it—and even they dilute it by using both subcontractors and large numbers of temporary workers hired on a monthly or yearly basis.

The impact of lifetime employment on these companies is enormous, for it both expresses and forces a certain kind of management thinking about workers. "I get the impression," remarked one Japanese visitor to the United States,

> that American managers spend more time worrying about the well-being and loyalty of their stockholders, whom they don't know, than they do about their workers, whom they do know. This is very puzzling. The Japanese manager is always asking himself how he can share the company's success with his workers.

Lifetime employees are, in the Japanese view of things, "human capital"—and expensive capital at that. A Japanese worker will earn about 100 million yen ($500,000 in 1980 dollars) in salary and bonuses during the worker's life employment and another 30 to 50 million yen ($200,000) in fringe benefits—not too much less than U.S. workers.

As a U.S. manufacturing manager pointed out:

> U.S. managers analyze, rationalize, and agonize until their office walls are covered with paper before committing to a piece of equipment requiring an investment of $500,000—and therefore an annual depreciation charge of $50,000. Yet the process of evaluating and making recommendations regarding the training, compensation, and career path of a $50,000 a year (including benefits) engineer typically requires one-half of a piece of paper, reluctantly prepared in one-half hour once a year!

This difference in priorities is puzzling, particularly when one recognizes that a machine is simply the embodiment of an engineer's skill.

As with all expensive capital investments, choosing lifetime employees requires considerable management planning and screening. Because a company limits the number of its lifetime employees, it must increase their value through training programs, skill-enriching job assignments, and the like. Then, whenever a problem arises, managers have an additional source of expert advice on which to rely: the workers. After all, insisted the managers we met, "They are the experts." This is neither lip service nor false modesty, for management has seen to it that they are.

Such emphasis on continually developing the skills and, thus, the productivity of workers made an enormous impression on the American managers who confronted it. As one commented:

> Our whole philosophy has been to "deskill" our work force through automation, so we end up having relatively unskilled people overseeing highly sophisticated machines. The Japanese put highly skilled people together with highly sophisticated machines and end up with something better than either.

Another observed:

> U.S. industry has divided up the total work that has to be done and assigned various parts of it to specialists. This has resulted in production jobs that are repetitive and uninteresting, while the skilled jobs are centralized and moved away from the production floor where they are needed and where corrective action must be taken.

It is important to remember that a company's commitment to its lifetime employees also leads to a reciprocal commitment from employees to the company. Recognizing that a no-layoff policy requires a work force level that lags behind sales demand, Japanese workers in the companies I visited willingly worked up to 60 hours of overtime per month (3 hours per day) when demand was high.

Their willingness to do so was encouraged by their knowledge that management understood intimately the difficulties and pressures under which they operated and was working just as hard as they were. Workers know that potential managers typically begin their careers with a year or so in relatively low-level occupations—the shop floor or the trading desk—to learn about the day-to-day concerns of operating people. Over time they work their way up the ladder, but a sense of identification with the workers remains. In the plants I visited, everybody—from the most junior production worker to the plant manager—wore the same company uniform.

Equipment Independence

Another aspect of management thinking in Japan that surprised and, at first, perplexed me was the insistence on designing and fabricating production equipment in-house. Most of the companies I visited claimed that at least 50% of their production equipment was built by their own engineers and machinists and that most of the remainder was designed in-house as well. One Japanese magazine has estimated that roughly 40% of Japanese R&D goes for process or equipment improvement.

By contrast, the conventional management wisdom in the United States, where a much smaller percentage of process equipment is developed in-house, says that equipment manufacture is best left to experts. Equipment producers, so the reasoning goes, can afford the high fixed costs of using specialized engineers and can amortize these and other developmental expenses over long production runs, thus reducing the cost of their product.

The Japanese will have none of this. "Every machine represents a compromise among various users and, therefore, various uses," one manager told us. "We prefer to design equipment that is directed toward our own needs. Not only do we get better equipment, but our costs are lower and our delivery times less."

Why is this so? One reason is that machines designed in-house cost less because they do not need the safety margins and "design cushions" that equipment manufacturers build into their general-purpose machines. More to the point, the same manager informed us:

> We always need machines when business conditions are good—which is when everybody else wants machines. The equipment manufacturing industry is notorious for its cyclical behavior. During these periods of high demand, they stretch out their lead times and they raise prices. If you are dependent on them, you soon regret it.

But what about the slack times, when companies must carry underused manufacturing engineers and skilled machinists? Then Japanese managers use these skilled resources to upgrade the company's existing equipment and perfect the new drive mechanisms, computerized controls, materials-handling equipment, and the equipment monitoring and warning devices mentioned earlier. Observed one manager, "The advantage of having highly skilled people (like manufacturing engineers) around is that they can always find something useful to do!"

Re-Solving "The Problem of Production"

During the past 15 to 20 years, a number of important U.S. manufacturing industries have acted as if they had entered into a tacit agreement to compete on grounds other than manufacturing ability. They appeared to think they had, as John Kenneth Galbraith phrased it, "solved the problem of production" and, therefore, directed attention and resources to mass distribution, packaging, advertising, and developing incremental new products (to round out product lines or attack specific market segments)—but neglected to upgrade continually their manufacturing capabilities.

As a result, U.S. plant and equipment have been allowed to age. Our technological advantage has eroded because of reduced expenditures on new-product R&D and on new process technologies. Our best managerial talent has been directed toward fast tracks that often do not include direct manufacturing experience. At the same time, promotions to top corporate positions have increasingly favored specialists in finance, marketing, accounting, and law.

This complacent attitude toward the problem of production did not impair the competitiveness of U.S. manufacturers for a number of years—until, that is, they began to encounter companies (like those in Japan) that *did* compete on such mundane grounds as reliable low-cost defect-free products and dependable delivery. Then U.S. businesses found themselves increasingly displaced in international markets and, more recently, in their home markets as well. This sudden weakness has come as a shock to many American managers who, in searching belatedly for causes and explanations, have often looked for dramatic, easily imitated, or purchased solutions: quality circles, government assistance, and the use of intelligent robots.

The Japanese have never considered the production problem solved, never underestimated the challenge of building and improving the "factory of the present." There are no magic formulas—just steady progress in small steps and focusing attention on manufacturing fundamentals. This is why their example will be so hard for American companies—and American managers—to emulate.

Yet it is not beyond our capabilities. Many of the attributes that characterize Japanese manufacturing management are valued in America too. Although we emphasize our "rugged individualism" (and criticize, in the same breath, the fact that "everybody is out for himself"), Americans love to work in smoothly functioning teams.

Nor is the Japanese concept of self-reliance—by which they refer to the importance of developing their own production equipment in-house and of modifying purchased equipment to meet their own specific needs—foreign to us. Americans are inveterate tinkerers with a tradition of self-reliance that springs from frontier roots. Our dependence on "off-the-shelf" solutions developed by outside experts—whether these individuals be equipment producers, company-hopping executives, or consultants—is a recent phenomenon.

Nor is the concept of lifetime employment so strange. In most large U.S. companies, 30% to 40% of the work force has lifetime employment, in the sense that any production worker who has worked for more than 10 years is almost never laid off. Rather than making that fact explicit, however, and using it to increase workers' sense of self-worth and their commitment to the company, we continue to refer to them as "hourly workers." We thereby imply they are expendable—which they aren't.

And we blind ourselves to the opportunities for increasing their skills (and thus their value to the company) that we routinely employ to upgrade the capabilities of expensive capital goods—which in a sense employees are. We complain about workers who have no commitment to their company and conveniently ignore the fact that most companies make no commitment to their workers.

The "we're all in this together" attitude of Japanese companies is also reminiscent of the American management tradition of "let's roll up our sleeves and get it done." The lack of managerial elitism in the United States used to be a source of wonder to Europeans, whose managerial traditions reflected the deep divisions between social classes. With some shock, we recognize the emergence of elitism and lack of trust in the United States—managers who isolate themselves from workers, both physically and emotionally; who have no direct experience in the businesses they manage; who see their role as managing resource allocation and other organizational processes rather than as leadership by example.

Improving our manufacturing competitiveness does not lie with the "last-quarter touchdowns," the "technological fixes," or the "strategic coups" that we love so much. Instead, we must compete with the Japanese as they do with us: by always putting our best resources and talent to work doing the basic things a little better every day over a long period of time. It is that simple—and that difficult.

Related Reading

Articles

Peter F. Drucker, "What We Can Learn From Japanese Management," *HBR*, March–April 1971, p. 110.

Peter F. Drucker, "Japan Gets Ready for Tougher Times," *Fortune*, November 3, 1980, p. 108.

Peter F. Drucker, "The Price of Success: Japan Revisited," *Foreign Affairs*, August 1978, p. 28.

Byron K. Marshall, "Japanese Business Ideology and Labor Policy," *Columbia Journal of World Business*, Spring 1977, p. 22.

Richard Tanner Pascale, "Zen and the Art of Management," *HBR*, March–April 1978, p. 153.

Howard F. Van Zandt, "How to Negotiate in Japan," *HBR*, November–December 1970, p. 45.

Ezra F. Vogel, "Guided Free Enterprise in Japan," *HBR*, May–June 1978, p. 161.

Books

Robert Cole, Japanese Blue Collar: The Changing Tradition (Berkeley, CA, University of California Press, 1971).

Chie Nakane, Japanese Society (Berkeley, CA, University of California Press, 1970).

Ezra F. Vogel, Japan as Number One: Lessons for America (New York, Harper & Row, 1979).

Appendix

Innovation, Not Imitation*

. . . A U.S. company attempting to introduce an alien management style in an adverse cultural environment may be inviting rigid bureaucratization without realizing the benefits of higher productivity. It may be better off leaving the fundamentals of the organization and company culture alone and instead attempt to change the characteristics of the industry. A successful change will bring the industry in harmony with the strengths of the U.S. environment, and will force the Japanese to defend their weaknesses.

For example, the U.S. company can invest in an industry, not in process improvements or in going down the learning curve, but to fundamentally change the nature of the product. This is what aircraft manufacturers have done. Such investments, if made boldly, can create enough uncertainty about the future of the industry that the community of Japanese decision makers is unable to tolerate the level of risk.

Another option is to shift technological innovation away from the factory floor where Japanese work culture provides advantages and into the design room or laboratory. This may involve willingness to scrap reliable

*From Tino Puri and Amar Bhide, McKinsey & Company, "The Crucial Weaknesses of Japan Inc.," the *Wall Street Journal*, June 8, 1981. Reprinted with permission of the *Wall Street Journal* © 1981, Dow Jones & Co., Inc.

existing technologies, hire seemingly unproductive PhDs, acquire the tangible and intangible assets of entrepreneurial companies and sell the soundness of the strategy to the financial community.

A third option is to set up global organizations that use local manufacturing and local marketing. The United States is a melting pot and its multinational corporations contain diverse nationalities and talents. . . . With few exceptions Japanese strengths have come from manufacturing operations located in Japan. A truly multinationally staffed and operated global business will give non-Japanese competitors significant advantages of market access and responsiveness in numerous international markets.

None of these options is without risks, but the ability to innovate and explore the uncharted is precisely what separates the leader from the industry follower. The Japanese system has shown great strengths in coming up from behind. But the kind of organizational skills that were needed for catching up are probably not appropriate for being at the cutting edge. In time, Japanese society and industrial organizations may transform themselves in order to fulfill these new tasks. Until then, non-Japanese competitors have real opportunities to hold their own by exploiting Japanese institutional rigidities.

14
The Incline of Quality

FRANK S. LEONARD and W. EARL SASSER

There was a time when engineers designed products, manufacturing people built them, quality personnel inspected them as they came off the line, and marketers sold them. If a problem existed, manufacturing was expected to correct it, to make things "right." Quality was not an overall approach to doing business but an after-the-fact-measurement of production success in statistical terms: so many defects per thousand units, so many deviations from the specs, so high or low a rate of failure in the field. And managing quality was the responsibility of a handful of low-ranking, not very well-respected measurement-takers in each company. As the authors suggest, in today's competitive environment, where a demonstrated edge in quality has immense strategic value, that archaic view of things is no longer tolerable.

Managing quality well requires total organizational commitment. It requires attention to the quality-related implications of every decision at every stage of the product development continuum—from design to sales. And it requires careful identification of the most effective levers for improving the quality of each individual product line. Adopting this changed perspective on what it means to manage quality well is, of course, not easy, but it can be done. In the face of stiff foreign competition, companies that choose not to make the effort are preparing the way for their own demise.

Many consumer advocates, government bureaucrats, management consultants, business writers, and even business executives are now convinced that "Made in Japan" has replaced "Made in the USA" as a label guaranteeing quality. In fact, however, this assumption of a decline in the quality of American goods and services is dead wrong. On an absolute scale, their quality has never been higher—witness, for example, the television sets produced by RCA and Zenith, the computers built by Digital Equipment Corporation and IBM, the jeans made by Levi Strauss and Wrangler, and the telephone service provided by AT&T.

Why, then, this widely shared perception of a quality decline? For one thing, the foreign competitors that have taken market share away from domestic producers have largely based their attack not on the poor quality of American goods and services but on the superiority of their own. These competitors, mostly Japanese but also European manufacturers like Volkswagen and Philips, have for 20 years relentlessly pursued quality improvement as an integral part of a national strategy to build an export economy.

In particular, the Japanese determined to sell worldwide products of comparable or higher quality than those of their competitors—and at the same or lower prices. In the past, American companies competed against each other for the U.S. mass market and left the top end open to expensive, high-performance imports (Mercedes cars, Omega and Seiko watches, Nikon and Hasselblad cameras) and the low end to cheap, low-quality imports. Today, however, many American manufacturers see the Japanese as their most serious competitors for both consumer and industrial markets. General Motors and Ford watch Toyota carefully; Caterpillar keeps a close eye on Komatsu; IBM follows Fujitsu's Facom subsidiary with great interest; and RCA monitors Sony's and Philips' every move.

The success of Japan's export strategy has changed the basis of competition in both American and world markets. Quality has become a major strategic variable in the battle for market share. But this is not the whole story. The perception of a decline in the quality of American goods and services stems not only from Japanese manufacturing successes but also from increased demand for quality products. In our opinion, several crucial developments have effected this change in the nature of demand:

1. Rates of inflation have dramatically increased; consumers are more attracted by durable products with long useful lives than by disposable items.
2. Energy costs have skyrocketed; consumers are shifting to energy-efficient goods and services.
3. Repair and maintenance costs have risen; consumers are increasingly concerned about warranties and frequency-of-repair records.

Manufacturers in Europe and especially in Japan have adjusted to these conditions faster than U.S. producers and, as a result, have been able to capitalize in the United States on their advantage in product quality. These competitive pressures have, in turn, made themselves felt at each stage of the production chain. As demand for more reliable, durable, and energy-efficient products increases, so does the demand for high-quality components, parts, and materials.

Changing Nature of Quality Management

Given the new strategic importance of quality, American managers must start asking themselves some tough, perhaps embarrassing, questions. What are the rules by which the competitive quality game must now be played? Are American managers sensitive to those rules? And to compete more effectively, do they have to change the ways they manage?

To track managers' responses, we conducted extensive field research and interviews in more than 30 corporations and administered a questionnaire on quality to a group of manufacturing executives from many of the *Fortune* "500" companies. The perceived sources of quality problems broke down as follows:

Workmanship/work force	21.5%
Materials/purchases of parts	20.6
Maintenance of process equipment	11.3
Design of process equipment	7.3
Product design	12.2
Control Systems	13.9
Management	5.9
Other	7.0
	100.0%

(On further discussion, it became clear that most of the executives thought management a much larger cause of the problem than the 6% response indicates; for, as they correctly pointed out, management is responsible for all the other causes listed.)

Even taking these figures as a rough approximation, we can see that the seeds of quality problems are widely distributed and that no simple attention to one or another aspect of a company's operations can keep them from sprouting. Only a determined effort to manage quality throughout an organization promises to be competively effective, but such an effort requires fundamental changes in the way American executives address the whole quality issue. Happily, we have begun to see such adjustments take shape.

The first of these, at the general management level, is a shift from an inspection-oriented, manufacturing-focused approach toward a defect-prevention and company-focused strategy. Even at companies such as the major pharmaceutical producers, which have traditionally paid close attention to quality, the management of quality is broadening and placing new responsibilities and duties on general managers. Exhibit 1 suggests the implications of this change for organizational structures and management systems and styles.

The second is a change from quality personnel being seen as technically

Exhibit 1. Changes in American Manufacturers' Views of Quality for the General Manager

Past	Present
General managers are *not* evaluated on quality.	Quality performance is part of general manager's review.
Manufacturing focus is on product quality.	Organizational focus is on process quality.
Historical dilution and budgeting hunches made on the cost of quality (i.e., scrap, rejects, returns).	Cost of quality measurement made by systems and reporting.
Functional view of quality predominates.	Matrix view of quality predominates.
Quality is quality department's responsibility.	Quality is line management's responsibility.
Quality is predominantly blue-collar related (direct labor).	Quality is predominantly white-collar related (indirect, overhead, staff).
Defects should be hidden.	Defects should be highlighted.
Problems lead to blame, excuses, justifications.	Problems lead to cooperative solutions.

and problem oriented, defensive, powerless, responsible for inspecting and "fixing" failures, and not well respected to their being seen as managerially oriented, planning and prevention oriented, assertive, powerful, responsible for preventing failures, and well respected. Quality managers, then, are growing out of their narrow administrator or technician roles and becoming crossfunctional.

By no means have both these changes been widely accepted. Few of the 30 companies we studied have taken them beyond the idea stage. We are, however, encountering more and more companies that are willing to experiment with different approaches. But where are these changes leading?

New Direction

To better understand the thrust of these changes, consider an industrial company's product introduction cycle, presented in Exhibit 2. As new products develop, they generally pass through four separate but overlapping stages: product design, process design, manufacturing, and sales/service. At each stage different kinds of people, possessing varying personalities and technical skills and operating under diverse constraints and priorities, make decisions that cumulatively affect the quality of the final product.

The old way of managing quality occurred almost entirely at the man-

Exhibit 2. Quality Impact: the Product Design to Sales Continuum (some types of decisions that affect quality)

Product Design

Performance	Layout
Components	Features
Materials	Documentation
Configuration	

Process Design

Capacity	Maintenance levels
Cycle times	Operator skills
Construction times	Production tolerances
Cost structures	Materials
Environmental impacts	

Manufacturing

Equipment adjustment	Maintenance
Operator training	Equipment operation
Documentation, controls	Supervision
Quality control	Rework

Sales/Service

Quality image	Training
Customer expectations	Returns
Field changes	Returns
Installations	Repairs

Vendors

Materials	Construction, installation
Equipment	Components, parts

People Involved at Specific Times

Two to Ten Years Ago	One to Six Years Ago	Now	Up to Three Years from Now
Engineering	Industrial engineering	Production workers	Sales offices
R & D	Process engineering	Production management	Retail outlets

Exhibit 2. (*Continued*)
People Involved at Specific Times

Two to Ten Years Ago	One to Six Years Ago	Now	Up to Three Years from Now
Package engineering	Consultants	Maintenance	Sales representatives
		Manufacturing, engineering	Service centers
		Quality	Distribution centers

ufacturing stage. Here was where quality problems surfaced—machine maladjustment, operator error, poor training, inadequate supervision, poor sampling techniques, insufficient controls, mechanical malfunctions, and lack of preventive maintenance. Inasmuch as this was the stage at which assembled products first came together, here was where these problems had to be "solved." Although manufacturing people might complain about "this awful piece of equipment" or be convinced that "this crazy design can't possibly be made," it was their job to "make it right with what you have, now!" Quality people merely culled the output to indicate when it had passed the appropriate tests and was acceptable.

By no means should we paint manufacturing managers as the quality saints, or martyrs, of the industrial era. They not only inherit problems caused elsewhere; they themselves make decisions that influence product quality. In practice, however, they have often had most of the responsibility for—but not much control over—quality, which was often determined by the many actions and decisions taken prior to the manufacturing stage. Even the advances in statistical quality control did not make the placement of responsibility more equitable. These techniques were used primarily to pinpoint what manufacturing could do to solve the problems it was blithely expected to solve.

Under the traditional scheme of product development, product design engineers would first come up with a prototype or model which, of course, embodied a number of explicit and implicit decisions on performance, components, materials, configuration, layout, and product features. Process design engineers would then either create a new process from top to bottom or modify the existing process and equipment. Whatever course the designers followed inevitably contained further decisions—about cycle times, capacities, construction times, cost structures (both fixed and variable), environmental impacts, maintenance levels, downtime, necessary operator skills, production tolerance levels, and substitutability of raw materials. At both these stages, there was little understanding of how these decisions affected final product quality.

After the manufacturing department tried its best to make the product as designed on the equipment as designed, sales/service managers would be responsible for selling, installing, and servicing the product. Influenced by such market-related factors as irate customers, commissions and bonuses, competitive market practices, and geographical separation between the manufacturing and design stages, sales/service managers naturally had a lot to do with setting expectations about quality and performance levels, determining product image, and establishing obligations concerning product failure.

Note, again, that responsibility for—but not control over—quality seldom ventured out of the manufacturing stage. The reasons for this are many:

1. Differences in the kind of people who work at the various stages of development.
2. Geographic distances (product R&D is usually located at corporate headquarters, process design at divisional or corporate headquarters, and sales/service at local field offices).
3. Time lags (it often takes years to move a product from design to market).
4. The sheer amount of information needed to trace quality problems in a complex organizational setting.
5. Ways in which managers are trained to solve functional, as opposed to systems, problems.
6. An organization's understanding of who has the power to make inviolable decisions.

Shifting competitive realities and expanding world markets have, however, created increasing pressures for change. Managers are at last recognizing the importance of upstream design decisions and downstream sales-service decisions in establishing product quality. Moreover, many companies are now demanding overall responsibility for quality from their general managers who, along with quality managers at all organizational levels, continually review the entire product-process-operations-service continuum to discover the most significant areas for quality improvement.

In these developments we can see the long overdue emergence of a systematic approach to quality management. That is, the realization is finally taking hold that the design and production of high-quality goods and services is not just a quality manager's technical problem on the factory floor, but a general manager's problem throughout the entire corporation. It leads everywhere and touches everything.

As one executive put it,

Of all our quality problems, about 20% are in manufacturing, 40% are with our vendors, and 40% are in design aspects. I had to start with the 20% in manufacturing, though, to find the others. I had to work backward to solve the problems. Rather than send staff engineers into the plants, I started sending manufacturing people back to the labs.

The companies most successful in changing their approach to quality management use an incremental approach, working backward and forward through the various stages of product development as well as outward to include vendors and customers. Managers are starting to recognize that getting their vendors to provide a consistently reliable supply of parts and materials is of critical importance to their own quality programs. They are also asking customers to participate in various product specification programs.

Levers for Quality

An electronics company specializing in hand-assembled customer-monitoring equipment devoted two thirds of its design staff to redesigning the product so that it could be assembled and tested more easily. Then it put all its operators and assemblers through a series of training courses tied to the new design.

A specialty chemicals outfit solved a lot of its contamination problems by installing piping that could be easily flushed and cleaned and by changing to a valving system that could not be incorrectly aligned.

A fast-food chain altered its raw material purchases so that all grill items were of the same thickness. As a result, heat settings never had to be changed, which equalized cooking time for all grill items—and thus eliminated overcooking and undercooking.

A major credit card company, besieged by increasing cost and competitive pressures, redesigned information and process flows to solve customer service problems and curtail processing errors.

As these examples show, a company can improve its product or service quality in many ways. Like most managerial choices, deciding what to do and how to do it depends on many things—for example, the product in question, the relevant process technology, the company's strategy, and its corporate culture. In each instance, the first managerial task is to identify the appropriate quality levers—that is, the exact location, cause, and pattern of distribution of each problem and the best way to resolve it.

The next step—selecting the right quality levers—requires management to evaluate the expected return from different ways of spending its time, effort, and money. Many American managers operate under the mistaken assumption that improved quality is always costly. Most such managers are detection and rework oriented. "I only add units of inspection and rework," they would say, "as long as the expected benefits from higher quality are greater than the expected costs of additional inspection and rework. To spend more is foolish." There is nothing wrong with their reasoning; the problem is that they often stop there. The real challenge to management is to discover investments that will yield higher quality at lower unit costs.

Such an investment might, for instance, take the form of adopting a more participative style of management as a way to change workers' attitudes toward quality. Or it might entail the purchase and installation of a numerically controlled milling machine or even a CAD/CAM system. To choose investments with the best return, managers must first ask:

☐ Where on the product development continuum is the most improvement possible? What are the quality levers?

☐ Do any of these levers require prior action? For example, must operators be trained before new equipment is installed?

☐ What improvements will follow the exercise of each quality lever? How far down the quality–cost relationship does it move a company's operations?

☐ What is the cost of exercising any one quality lever?

Identifying the different quality levers, understanding their effect on the quality–cost curve, and determining both the investment needed to apply each lever and its payback in product quality—these must be the first order of business for all quality conscious managers.

A Handle on Productivity

When evaluating the various levers on quality, do not overlook the close connection between quality and productivity. Among the examples we have seen or studied are the following.

1. One company's installation of a new "clean room" reduced the contaminants on printed circuit boards and boosted output by almost 35%.

2. Elimination of rework stations at one television factory forced assembly workers to find and solve their own quality mistakes. These adjustments resulted in an increased production rate per hour of direct labor and in the elimination of thousands of dollars of rework costs.

3. One company using precision assembly equipment designed components that would not fit together unless they were "right." This arrangement raised production rates as well as distribution efficiencies. It also improved the productivity of the sales force since it no longer had to spend time collecting, boxing, and replacing returned components.

In our experience, efforts to raise quality almost always result in heightened productivity. We have found that the reverse also holds true: efforts to raise productivity usually pay off in better quality. Traditional wisdom, however, has viewed quality and productivity as being inversely related. For years managers have believed that, for instance, because it requires more time to do a high-quality job, increases in quality can only come at the expense of productivity. This is simply not true.

Better quality does not automatically mean more machine time, more labor hours, greater skill levels, or higher-cost materials. More often than not, better quality can mean better productivity—but *only* if managers move their companies to a new and lower quality–cost curve.

In practice, though, American managers have often taken their product development systems as a given, in which productivity or quality could be improved, but not both. They have treated the decision before them as an "either/or" choice: either reduce costs or raise quality. What our research suggests—and what Japanese producers have known for the last 20 years—is that the relevant decision is an "and/also" choice: both productivity and quality can be enhanced if managers are willing to make systemic adjustments to their operations and not just to this or that particular detail.

What is needed, then, is a revolution in the way managers think about the continuum of product development activities. By this we do not mean a shift only in their conventional approaches to quality problems but also in their readiness to make the long-term investments in people and equipment necessary to reach a lower cost–quality curve.

Getting There From Here

None of the dozens of quality programs now being marketed, written up, discussed, debated, and hailed as cure-alls can be universally successful in solving quality problems. These problems and the levers for correcting them differ too much from company to company and even product to product or location to location. Further, since both problems and solutions are often systemic, any technique that focuses on a single activity or function is suspect. The failure rate of the quality programs that have been sanctimoniously shoved down middle management's throat by well-intentioned or merely desperate executives argues strongly that techniques rarely solve complex organizational problems.

For a quality program to have a real chance of success, it must have the following attributes.

Top Management's Strategic Support

Top management must be openly and actively committed to improving quality as a strategic necessity. Quality considerations must figure centrally in their strategic planning, in the trade-offs they make among demands for resources, in the risks they are willing to take, in the kinds of corporate performance they find acceptable (off-spec product is off-spec product— whether it is the beginning or the end of the month), and in their evaluation and reward systems for subordinates. In sum, top management should treat quality as an integral part of all corporate review processes.

Organizational Analysis

Managers need to improve their ability to analyze the decisions, work flows, and organizational structures that influence product quality and to anticipate the downstream effects of quality-related decisions. When the analysis is completed, a manager should be able to identify confidently the relevant quality levers for each product in question.

Responsibility

Far too often American companies have treated quality as a functional responsibility when, in fact, it should be an organizational goal. Because most quality problems are caused by managerial action or inaction, the challenge of improving product quality should be the task not only of workers and quality departments but of everyone in an organization, regardless of the person's authority or responsibility.

Open Participation

The successful efforts to improve product quality that we observed shared some form of participative management that cut across traditional organizational boundaries (functional, geographic, social, and temporal). This participation was open and fluid (and thus was not confined to certain times of the week, or certain people, topics, or situations.

Although we do not like the current American addiction to quality circles, we certainly do see that many such programs have made positive contributions. What works best, however, are not the slickly packaged QC concepts now being peddled by a number of consultants but rather the simple formation of groups of people who share information, interests, skills, resources, and a stake in solving all quality problems. In fact, the most effective groups we encountered acted more like quality "webs" than circles. That is, they did not limit themselves to officially designated quality problems but traced them back to issues in design or whatever. Whether these groups were informal and spontaneous or formal and planned, they accomplished two things: they opened up and helped integrate their parent organizations.

Quality Calculus

Managers should also reexamine the calculus by which they measure, estimate, and account for quality-related decisions. Most of the measurement and performance systems we encountered simply ignored quality issues. Those that did explicitly consider quality were often biased toward short-term measures of performance and thus grossly understated the costs of not getting quality right the first time. Many capital appropriation processes, for example, downplayed the benefits of improved quality as "probabilistic," "subjective," or "qualitative." These benefits are indeed long-term and highly uncertain (an increase in market share, say, or customer loyalty; a reduction in warranty costs), but any movement to a lower cost, higher quality position requires at some point a leap of faith. What a good quality measurement system should do is provide a diving board.

Quality Assurance and Control

To say that quality is a managerial responsibility does not deny the need for quality professionals. Well-run quality departments, when used as organizational consultants to prevent defects, monitor testing, supervise process checks, and assist line managers in establishing good quality practices and procedures, can provide a valuable perspective. They should not, however, become involved in the direct implementation of activities that fall rightfully under line management's discretion.

The tendency to build empires, to waste energy justifying the exercise of professional knowledge, to become mesmerized by intricate and complicated systems, and to confuse corporate with functional goals is a real and present danger. The proper size of the quality function, its place in the organization, the breadth of its mission, and the nature of its role in the strategic process are all issues that a general manager has to confront. The burning question is, "How can the quality area best perform its service role to the line operations?" And the answer, simply put, depends on the situation.

Training and Development

To produce significant results, efforts to improve quality require an enormous and sustained investment of energy and resources. Ideally, every person in the company should accept responsibility for product quality; employees, suppliers, and even customers require special training to achieve this goal. One of the remarkable things about the Japanese is the amount of training that they have provided for years at all levels of their organizations. Good quality-related training extends far beyond what we normally think of as "quality topics" (statistical methods, sampling techniques, or inspection procedures) and includes equipment operation, advanced milling techniques, preventive maintenance, setups and breakdowns, gauging, computer-aided design, and interpersonal communication.

American managers must think more broadly about this kind of long-term investment in training and encourage it in areas where the leverage on quality is greatest. Of course, as improvements are made, as new people come into the organization and others are promoted, and as product and process technologies change, the nature of the training will itself shift.

Personal Attributes

As Philip Crosby, author of *Quality Is Free*, has argued, improving quality is not a motivational consideration but a matter of managerial style or personal leadership attributes. Quality oriented managers tend to share a number of characteristics.

The best managers we observed paid attention to detail and were never caught short because of incomplete planning. They always kept track of problems and items that might turn into problems, were conscientious in their striving for quality and had the dignity and integrity to set—and then hold to—high personal standards, never sought personal glory at the expense of product quality, had the personal resolve to keep up their arduous efforts, were modest enough to acknowledge that their achievements were always the work of many, managed with gentleness and finesse—not with a sledgehammer, and were trustworthy so that their employees, suppliers, and customers had complete confidence in their actions and intent.

By no means is this list exhaustive, nor can any of these attributes substitute for deep technical knowledge or administrative ability. We simply mean to suggest that America's difficulties in competing on quality grounds may, to some extent, be a function of the character of its managers. In the battle for industrial survival, managers with good instincts in adversarial situations have usually come out on top. When management battles workers, suppliers attempt to outwit customers, engineering departments make life miserable for manufacturing departments, and business and government officials distrust every move made by the other, it is these managers who are most in their element. But are their personal characteristics suitable for the competitive environment of the future? We think not—and we hope not.

A Final Word

Most observers of American business would have entitled this article "The Decline of Quality." We have not. Doomsayers have proclaimed that the quality gap between the United States and Japan signals the end of America's dominance of world markets. We have not. Admittedly, many American companies have lost world market share in the last decade, but their vital signs remain strong. The steps we outlined above can make them even stronger.

A number of U.S. companies have already made tremendous progress in improving their competitive positions by discovering that higher quality and lower costs can be achieved through prudent investments in people, product design, and process improvement. The keystone of each of these success stories is that managers understand the systemic nature of quality and make a commitment to improving the quality of their company's products. The more we observe, the more firmly we are convinced that quality improvement is the most fruitful path to higher productivity and competitive success.

Readings

Quality Is Free: The Art of Making Quality Certain, by Philip B. Crosby, New York: McGraw-Hill, 1979.

Elementary Principles of Statistical Control of Quality, by Edward W. Deming, Nippon Kagaku Gijutsu Renmei, Tokyo, 1950.

Total Quality Control, by A.V. Feigenbaum, *HBR*, November–December 1956.

Quality Control Handbook, 3d ed., by Joseph M. Juran, New York: McGraw-Hill, 1974.

Quality Planning and Analysis from Product Development Through Use, 2d ed., by Joseph M. Juran, New York: McGraw-Hill, 1980.

PART FOUR
INTEGRATING THE PRODUCTION SYSTEM

AN OVERVIEW

No effort to make excellence in manufacturing a competitive weapon can succeed if, in their haste to repair past neglect of the fundamentals, managers forget that production is, above all, a system. Tinkering with any one aspect will inevitably have effects on the rest, and no tactical issues—however minor—are without some cumulative influence on overall strategic competence. In fact, taking this "systems" view seriously and acting on it deliberately are essential to the work of management.

The articles in this fourth section have less a common theme than a common concern for the ways in which managers, intent on solving a particular functional problem, often lose sight of how that problem ties in with others. It is all too easy in, for example, sifting through the complex mathematics of inventory levels or service availability or control systems to overlook the fact that neither inventory nor service levels nor financial controls are an end in themselves. Figuring out the most appropriate way to manage them cannot—and should not—be an isolated activity. Textbooks, to be sure, are chock-a-block with formulas designed to provide infallibly correct answers to carefully specified functional questions. Real-world problems, however, rarely admit of so neat or so contained a definition.

When issues reach a manufacturing manager's desk, they require more insight and understanding than a simple determination of the best possible quantitative results. One can, for example, do wonders with the abstractions of ROI by never replacing old or worn out equipment, but it does little good to find cures that guarantee a relapse of the original disease—or worse. To define a manager's job as, first and foremost, the maximization of a certain set of numbers is to define it too narrowly, too inflexibly, too simplemindedly. In almost every instance, the true managerial task is to deal with inventory, service availability, or whatever in such a way that it supports the rest of the production system. There is, after all, little value in arranging technically perfect operations if the patient dies or begins to suffer from another, equally painful ailment.

However unglamorous, integrated decisions about the nuts-and-bolts logistics of production systems are essential to any company's health. And never more so than at present. "If," as James Heskett notes,

> general management inevitably will have to spend an increasing proportion of its time dealing with low or no-growth situations, it is not too early to put in place a process to ensure that logistical considerations will not be overlooked in formulating strategy.

In good times, some managerial inattention can be tolerated without ill effect; in bad times, that slack vanishes. But at no time can attention lavished on a company's strategy make up for operational decisions that ignore it at every turn, for no strategy—no matter how elegant—is worth a fig unless it actively shapes and, in turn, is shaped by the integrated management of operational detail.

New technological advances in data processing, which make possible elaborate manufacturing control systems and extensive automation of production processes, merely underscore this point. The more closely tied the various aspects of production are to each other and to the rest of the organization, the greater the benefits to be derived from intelligent coordination—and the greater the dangers from a failure of coordination. Just as a high degree of financial leverage makes a company's profit performance more volatile, so a high degree of communications leverage makes its production performance more volatile. A person with a contagious virus in the middle of nowhere is a danger to no one else; in the heart of a crowded city, that person is a danger to all.

15
The Concept of a Production System

PHILIP H. THURSTON

How can a general concept of production as a whole be visualized?

How can such a concept help managers in the analysis of specific production problems?

What is the penalty for overlooking the interrelationships of the various elements in a production system when managing operations?

To function successfully, a company's manufacturing operations must be organized to secure the efficient flow of materials through various processing steps. Only when each aspect of that process is treated as part of a single integrated production system can managers intelligently approach whatever individual problems arise.

A manager of production deals with the design of products, rate of flow of material, level of training of workers, machine capacity, and a host of other important factors. But he or she does not deal with each of these separately. The redesign of a product can call for additional training in the work force, and the level of training influences the rate of flow of material. These and more complicated interrelationships suggest that productive operations may be usefully thought of as *production systems*. The word "system" has been used to describe integrated bodies, both mechanical and human, in a number of different settings and is appropriate here.

My objective in this article is to present one concept of a production system that should be useful in considering a wide variety of productive operations. However, I must add a disclaimer. Although I will identify the factors that appear over and over again in varying degrees and in different combinations in all productive systems and although I will describe the common core elements, I will go only a short distance in building a general concept of production. Much will remain undone. The all-important steps of identifying which factors are of greatest importance to a particular situation and of determining how these factors interrelate must be taken by the manager concerned, case by case. I doubt that the relative importance and specific pattern of interrelationships of the factors of production ever can be structured in a universal rigorous model. That is, no theorist can present a general how-to-do-it blueprint to replace the analytical thinking of operating managers.

Core and Other Elements

Basic to any productive operation is a process for changing materials. The materials may be thought of as flowing through the one or more steps of a process. Whether they actually flow as do petroleum products in a refinery or move intermittently as do parts in a machine shop does not matter; in both instances management is concerned with the efficient movement or flow of the materials through the process steps.

For this to take place, however, there is a prior requirement of design—design of both the product to be made and the process for making it. Thus within any productive operation there are three basic elements:

- ☐ Product design.
- ☐ Process design.
- ☐ Material flow.

Influencing these core elements are a number of other factors, and my next step is to identify the many factors present in a production system. Rather than simply list them, I find it useful to picture them around a process and flow of material, as in the main section of the pullout chart (Exhibit 1). This is intended as more than a touch of showmanship. It should emphasize that the many activities of production exist primarily to facilitate the efficient movement of material through a well-designed process. The main chart presents such a grouping of all the factors of production. The selection for this diagram of three process steps and a single path for material flow is arbitrary, intended simply to convey a basic idea.

Interrelationships

In every production problem some of the factors shown are involved in an interrelated pattern. The smaller charts, lettered A, B, and C, are intended to illustrate this through three different examples. Each shows the particular

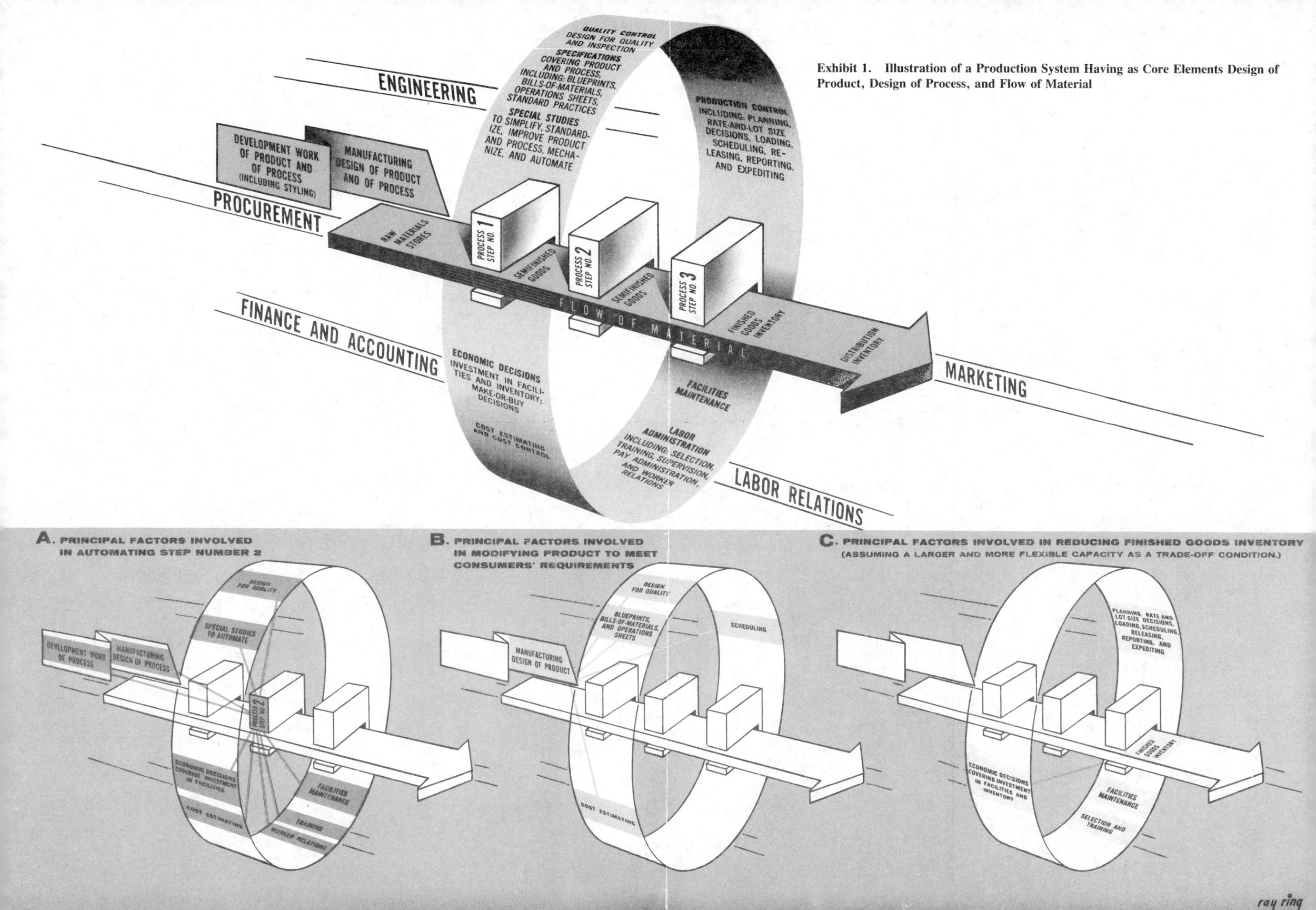

Exhibit 1. Illustration of a Production System Having as Core Elements Design of Product, Design of Process, and Flow of Material

CONCLUSION

network of major interrelationships associated with a given production situation.

The manager faced with a problem has the initial task of identifying the relevant factors and assessing their interrelationships. In a somewhat curious fashion all relevant factors are bound to attract attention sooner or later; if the manager fails initially to recognize them, they will, because of the highly integrated nature of production, create sore points. Let me illustrate with some very brief examples:

- ☐ If the material specifications for a plastic toy are changed (design change) and if provision is not made for a longer "cure time" required by the new material (process change), the reject rate will climb.

- ☐ If a manufacturer of electrical controls increases the ratio of special products to standard products but does not plan further, the manufacturer may not wait long before being faced with an overload in the design section, confusion in production control, and a reduction in the number of units manufactured.

The moral is clear. The competent manager is the one who integrates those factors shown on the rings of the charts to good advantage for the design, process, and material flow of the product.

Corrective mechanisms are an important aspect of any system. Within a production system, feedback is achieved through cost control, quality control, and production control.

Relation to Other Systems

The main chart, besides emphasizing the factors within the area of production, shows at the periphery relationships with other business areas. In theoretical terms, any system interacts with other external systems.

A misreading of the diagrams might suggest that I consider production to be the most important, the central part of a business operation. The charts do focus on production—but only for the immediate objective of better understanding of that functional area. The truth is that production systems are highly interrelated with other business functions, such as finance and marketing, and the relative importance of each to any single business operation depends on the nature of the industry and the competitive position of the individual company.

Conclusion

The heart of this article lies in the charts. They present the core and the scope of production and suggest the integrated nature of the factors shown.

Other writers have dealt in useful ways with production systems for particular industries or with segments of production systems, and some have presented models in which a few of the parts are related mathematically. My attempt here has been more general—to present an over-all concept of production, one that should be valuable in thinking about production as a whole and in developing a background understanding for the analysis of specific production problems.

A Retrospective Note

Twenty years ago I wrote that "no theorist can present a general how-to-do-it blueprint to replace the analytical thinking of operating managers." I feel precisely the same way today; for, as I have been increasingly aware over the years, the value in thinking of a production system *as* a system comes not from the elegance of the concept but from the quality of the managers directly involved.

Able managers do analyze their operations in this fashion, sometimes intuitively and sometimes not. In practice, whatever their balance of intuition with more formal thought, the individuals best able to manage a particular operation are those with an enhanced understanding of how its various components fit together. If this be no more than a truism, I point out that it is often the simple things that escape us.

How would I write the article differently today? Instead of giving greater emphasis to physical things, the flows of material and the tools of production, I would place equal emphasis on human "systems" and on information "systems." At a time of ever more rapid technological change and shifts in people's expectations, it is the critical interrelationships of all factors that determine a given operation's success or failure.

My strongest advice to manufacturing managers remains what it was twenty years ago: step back from whatever parts of your operations are giving you trouble in order to formulate a coherent overall understanding of how the pieces of your production system fit together. More than that, to quote the original article, ". . . production systems are highly interrelated with other business functions. . . ." Manufacturing managers who understand the systems they control have an essential contribution to make to their companies' identifying strategic opportunities and avoiding competitive pitfalls.

16
Logistics—
Essential to Strategy

JAMES L. HESKETT

Logistical considerations have always played a strategic role in business. Among retailers and wholesalers, they transcend inventory management and transportation to include one of the most critical factors in business success—location in relation to markets or sources of supply. Among manufacturers, logistics concerns itself with matters as basic as plant location, sourcing of raw materials, and standards of customer service. In recent years, changes in the business environment have forced companies both large and small to pay particularly close attention to how this function relates to others. Government regulation, the health of the nation's transportation system, energy restrictions, and technological developments all represent important considerations in the formulation of a business strategy. As the author shows in this article, many companies have responded to these challenges by developing competitive strategies based in part on such concepts as postponement and speculation, standardization, consolidation, and differentiation. These are companies in which management has conducted either formal or informal logistics audits, has redesigned systems to provide more effective support for corporate strategies, and has taken steps to ensure continued appraisal of opportunities over the long run.

Logistics can spell the difference between success and failure in business. For example, a few years ago a young engineer-entrepreneur began to build a company from scratch. His first product was liquid bleach. Actually, he didn't know much about the business at the time. He knew that liquid bleach is nearly all water and that the U.S. market is divided among two large manufacturers, Clorox and Purex, and a number of smaller producers that sell branded and private-label bleach on a regional basis. He also knew that the market for private-label bleach in New England, where he wanted to be, was dominated by a manufacturer located in New Jersey.

So the entrepreneur decided to found a private-label bleach manufacturing company near Boston. This location provided his company with a distinct transport cost advantage over its chief competitor. But he didn't stop there. He located his plant near a concentration of grocery chain retail outlets. This enabled him to sell his bleach under an arrangement in which retailers' trucks were loaded with his bleach after making their retail deliveries and before returning to their respective distribution centers. Given this double cost advantage, he was able to go one step further. By adding other items to his product line, he was able to obtain efficient truckload orders from his retail chain customers.

Another new venture in which logistics plays a major role was set up by two honors students. On their graduation from business school, they devised an innovative low-cost way to distribute a high volume of milk and other products. Building a retail "store" that consisted of a convenience-oriented self-service front end and a large truck dock in the rear, they have raw milk delivered by tank trucks and put into vats in the rear of the store. Milk and cream is then separated, homogenized, and bottled on site for sale direct to consumers at significantly lower prices than through traditional channels. Having expanded its line to include other food items often purchased in large quantities, this retailer now enjoys one of the highest sales-per-square-foot ratios of any retailer in the United States and does a volume of sales through its relatively small outlet that many supermarket operators would be pleased to achieve.

Logistics-oriented strategies are also important in large companies. As an example, one of the world's largest chemical manufacturers recently had to replace its ships. The ships carried materials in bulk from plants in the Caribbean to Gulf and East Coast ports for subsequent transfer to barges and rail cars for delivery to terminals at which customers' orders were packed into containers for final delivery by rail and truck. Instead of merely replacing its ships with more modern versions of the same design, the company instead is converting its entire distribution system to one using containers.

This system requires that orders processed in Puerto Rico be shipped in containers that will be delivered direct to customers in the eastern United States by a combination of river barge, rail, and truck. As a result (1) repackaging at all inland terminals eventually will be eliminated, (2) material handling costs and capacities at Gulf and East Coast port facilities will be greatly reduced, and (3) because of the increased frequency of departures of ocean-going container barges from plants, orders will be delivered to customers with little or no increase in order response time and only a small increase in total inventory in the system. Because of the company's sales volume, it is unlikely that competitors will be able to emulate the program even though their geographic production and transport patterns are similar.

What do these examples have in common? They all involve decisions that are long-term in their implications. All involve actions that are big-dollar in relation to the overall size of the companies in which they are implemented. All provide a competitive advantage that, unlike pricing or other actions, is hard for competitors to duplicate. And they all are based on nontraditional approaches to logistics, encompassing those activities that facilitate product movement and the coordination of supply and demand in accomplishing specified cost and service objectives, as suggested in Exhibit 1.

Exhibit 1. The Logistics Process

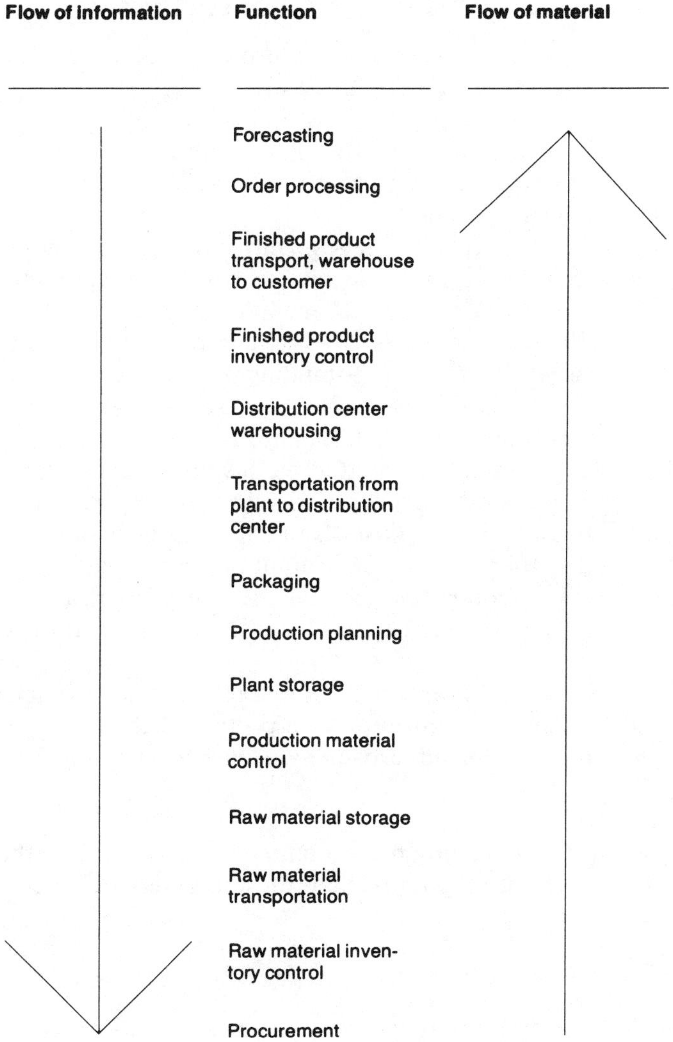

Flow of information	Function	Flow of material
↓	Forecasting	↑
	Order processing	
	Finished product transport, warehouse to customer	
	Finished product inventory control	
	Distribution center warehousing	
	Transportation from plant to distribution center	
	Packaging	
	Production planning	
	Plant storage	
	Production material control	
	Raw material storage	
	Raw material transportation	
	Raw material inventory control	
	Procurement	

These are but three of a growing number of companies that place major reliance on logistics in their business strategies. In this article I shall explore the reasons behind the rebirth of interest in this method of developing competitive advantages, the common elements of successful logistics-oriented strategies, the questions to be asked in auditing the extent to which your management has taken advantage of opportunities for making logistics an integral part of its strategy, and the ways of factoring logistics into strategy formulation.

Growing Influence of Logistics

There are a number of reasons for the growing influence of logistics in business strategy. Included among these are:

1. An increasing number of alternatives for meeting cost and service standards—containerization, minicomputers, air freight, and worldwide satellite communications systems.

2. The threat of energy shortages. During periods of energy shortages, transport costs may figure more heavily in plant and warehouse location decisions. And the locations of retail facilities from resorts to department stores may be influenced more strongly by their proximity to major markets.

3. Closer scrutiny of the long-standing trend toward complex product lines. To a greater extent, the threat of material shortages is injecting logistics as opposed to marketing considerations into product-line decisions.

4. The recent emphasis on effective inventory management through wide swings in business cycles characterized by varying rates of increase in labor costs, fluctuating interest costs, and changing rates of sale. This pressure has been accompanied by the assumption on the part of management that developments in computer-oriented inventory control methods have more than kept pace with user needs—an assumption not always borne out in practice.

5. The increasing involvement of federal and state agencies in issues ranging from the seminationalization of a portion of the transportation network to the availability of advertised sale merchandise on the shelves of retail establishments.

All these pressures are leading many companies to reexamine their view of logistics. What types of responses have these pressures elicited?

Patterns in Uncommon Responses

The increased size and complexity of business operations combined with the application of problem-solving techniques and computer technology have made it possible for many companies to consider less common logistical responses to perceived competitive cost or service disadvantages. Among these are strategies that involve postponement and speculation, standardization, consolidation, and differentiation.

Postpone and Speculate

Although they have done it intuitively for years, many companies are more systematically reviewing ways of postponing their commitment of resources to specific end products as long as possible in channels of distribution in order to reduce the risks of accumulating obsolete or unusable stocks. Others are willingly incurring the risks of speculation, involving the preparation of stocks in advance of need, in order to achieve economies of scale and lower the costs of production. Automobile manufacturers, for example, have pursued strategies of both postponement and speculation at different production and distribution stages.

Automakers practice postponement by operating market-oriented distribution centers at which relatively light manufacturing takes place. Although these facilities commonly are called assembly plants, they really are distribution centers equipped to receive orders, assemble automobiles to the individual desires of millions of prospective auto owners from stocks of standard components, and deliver individually designed autos to dealers and customers in a reasonable period of time.

Similarly, steel service (distribution) centers have become important distribution links for fabricated steel by bending, cutting, shaping, and even welding basic steel products to order. The wave of decentralized packaging of standard products shipped in bulk to distribution centers suggests that postponement will continue to be an effective means of providing a wide array of desired items from a smaller number of mass-produced and bulk-shipped finished components or ingredients.

In fact, postponement at one level in the distribution channel with an attendant uncoupling of functions from those performed "upstream" has enabled automakers to enjoy the benefits of speculation from the mass production of a relatively small number of standard engines, bodies, and other major components, often at locations some distance from end markets. Steel manufacturers have been able to concentrate on mass production because of the growth of steel service centers. And canners of private-label food products process and pack their wares in "bright," unlabeled forms for labeling-to-order in response to later orders from hundreds of retailers.

Standardize Products

It stands to reason that standardization within product lines can reduce production costs, cut inventories, and increase field stock coverage while nevertheless providing the basis for differentiating end products. For example, General Motors is able to produce an endless number of lines, brands, and models of automobiles from its standard A, B, and C auto bodies.

Manufacturers of both consumer and industrial electronic products have created a standardized response to a variety of potential product failures by designing products around modules composed of several components. Given the failure of one or another of these components, the module composed of both operative and defective components can be replaced quickly and with little expertise.

In purchasing, a technique called value analysis has led on occasion to decisions to purchase fewer items and in larger quantities. This has resulted in price discounts and logistical savings that more than compensate for the application of standard components to tasks for which smaller less expensive components might be suited under programs not emphasizing standardization.

The potential for product standardization represents an important element of "slack" in the productive capacity of many companies. As an illustration, after it had cut its product line in half late in 1973 in response to soaring demand and restricted capacity, one manufacturer of white papers found that it could achieve 116% of the theoretical capacity of its mills through reduced machine setups. This discovery has led to more stringent guidelines in this company for the evaluation of new-product proposals.

Consolidate Services

For the most part, consolidation involves practices that encourage the simultaneous storage, long-haul transportation, or delivery of two or more products or orders to achieve economies of scale. It does not have to be achieved at the cost of reduced customer service. An example is that during the most recent recession many companies began to schedule orders for delivery on a once or twice-per-week basis rather than whenever they were received. Suppliers could maintain speed of service for many customers under these programs by advising them of scheduled shipping dates so that those located in particular areas to which consolidated shipments were destined could time their orders to coincide with the schedules. This practice provided an acceptable level of service while maximizing use of limited fuel and lowering delivery costs significantly.

The use of shared or pooled services such as common carrier transport, shippers' cooperatives, and public warehouses is another form of consolidation.[1] Potential savings from the use of shared services have led many manufacturers to consider joint efforts with makers of complementary products requiring similar logistical efforts. In one case, a large manufacturer of grocery products recently sought out other companies selling products to identical kinds of customers to explore joint approaches to distribution for one of its product line's "problem children," a limited-volume item with somewhat distinctive distribution needs.

In another case, a pasta manufacturing company distributed its product daily in Manhattan by using trucks that could only be loaded partially because of the small number of deliveries possible in a given day in the city. Thus, it sought to find another grocery-product manufacturer desiring frequent deliveries in Manhattan for a joint distribution venture. And beer manufacturers in Canada have for some years maintained a joint venture for the retail delivery of their products. Many of these efforts have resulted from the realization that once a delivery vehicle stops, the costs of delivery are relatively insensitive to the size of the delivery.

Consolidation programs require products with homogeneous characteristics or logistics needs. Thus it is no surprise that the most successful consolidation programs undertaken with other manufacturers have been achieved in the distribution of product groupings such as frozen foods, drug products, and dry grocery products. Many of these programs have been able to reduce the actual costs of distribution beyond the field warehouse by as much as 40%.

Differentiate Distribution

For some years, many managers intuitively have recognized potential economies from the differentiated treatment of various product-line items in their distribution. For example, using ABC inventory methods, managers establish more restrictive inventory rules for high-value low-sales-volume items than for others in a product line. This effort reduces inventory holding costs in relation to a given sales volume. It represents a way in which the "80/20" relationship can be used effectively as an integral part of a company's strategy.

How the "80/20" Relationship Applies to Logistics Strategy

It is a well-accepted fact that a few employees file most of the labor grievances or experience most of the lost-time accidents, that a minority of policyholders file most of the insurance policy claims, and that a small proportion of product-line items produce a majority of the sales in most organizations. These "80/20" relationships can help management determine where the greatest opportunities for improvement in performance lie.

A few years ago I examined the inventory turnover rates (unit sales per year compared with average inventories in units) for a sample of fast, moderately, and slow-selling items in a wide variety of manufacturing companies. The results, shown in Table 16.1, suggest that items with the highest volume of unit sales turn over from two to eight times faster than those with the lowest volume of unit sales in the same respective product lines. Each of the companies surveyed used roughly the same inventory management and item location rules for all items measured within a particular line.

Thus a company with half of its stock tied up in items representing only 20% of unit sales and with its highest-sales-volume items selling four

Table 16.1 Relationships Between Sales Volume and Inventory Turnover Rates

Product Line Measured	Annual Turnover Rate*		
	Fast-Moving Items	Moderately Moving Items	Slow-Moving Items
Cereal-based food	64.8	13.5	8.8
Wire and cable, tubing	8.5	9.8	6.4
Small appliances	5.5	4.5	1.6
Small appliance parts	1.6	1.9	1.4
Grocery paper	21.3	19.3	8.9
Writing paper	21.9	7.0	5.4
Automotive window glass	4.7	1.7	0.5
Grinding wheels	2.6	2.3	0.7
Chemicals	24.4	4.1	7.0

Source: James L. Heskett, Nicholas A. Glaskowsky, Jr., and Robert M. Ivie, *Business Logistics* (New York, The Ronald Press Company, 1973), p. 457.

*Rates are based on an average of annual turnover for three selected items falling into each volume sales category for each product line. Fast-moving items are defined as those falling among the 20% of the items in the line selling the largest volume of units; moderately moving items are those among the next 30%; slow-moving items are those among the bottom 50%.

times faster than the lowest-sales-volume items has a great deal to gain by reducing inventories of slow sellers to the point where their turnover rates approach those of fast sellers. It can reduce inventories of its slow-moving items by 75%, for an overall reduction of 37.5%.

How can this be done? One way is to reduce inventories of slow-moving items at all locations at which they are stocked. This, of course, greatly reduces the availability of each item and the overall service level.

An alternative is to concentrate all available stocks of slow-moving items at a single location. This requires only one reserve stock for unusually large customer demands and offers greater control over a greatly reduced inventory. In effect, this approach creates a higher volume of sales per *stock-keeping unit location* (SKUL) for each item by reducing the number of locations at which stock-keeping units are maintained.

Some of the savings in inventory provided by a differentiated approach to the location and availability of slow-moving items can be devoted to providing a higher level of in-stock coverage for fast-moving items. As a result, such efforts might produce a profile of coverage and location such as the one shown in Table 16.2.

This type of differentiation recognizes that customers hold varying

Table 16.2 Differentiated Service Levels

	Units Volume (percent of total)	Sales Volume (percent of total)	Number of SKULs	In-Stock Availability	Days to Service Order (cycle order)
Fast-moving items	20%	80%	16	97.0%	3.0
Moderately moving items	30	15	4	80.0	5.0
Slow-moving items	50	5	1	60.0	7.0
Average service level				92.6%	3.5

levels of expectations. Fast-moving items often are standardized models or parts that customers expect will be in stock and supplied rapidly. Slow-moving items often are odd-sized or nonstandard items for which many customers will expect to wait longer periods of time.

As one appliance retailer told me, "If manufacturers would recognize the fact that customers expect to wait up to six weeks for nonstandard appliances with unusual features, they could save a lot of money. Instead, they provide the same level of service on orders for all items in the line."

Of course, this philosophy has to be applied selectively, depending on the characteristics of a particular product line. Certain automotive parts, for example, call for a high level of service regardless of sales volume because they are critical in the repair of idle equipment. Differentiation in this type of business may have to be based on categories of items measured in terms of both unit sales volume and the criticality of the part.

However, it is possible to achieve a required service level for low-volume critical parts using high-speed communication and transportation methods instead of a large number of market-oriented inventories. The added amounts spent for these methods often are more than offset by (1) the reduced costs of carrying inventory at one as opposed to many locations, (2) increased sales achieved by the creation of one central backup stock capable of providing a higher level of in-stock availability than could be achieved by means of decentralized inventories, and (3) greatly reduced costs of communication otherwise required by searches through many decentralized stocks to find the desired item.

Given the increasing number of logistical choices available to competing companies, opportunities for the development of more extensive programs for differentiated product distribution present themselves. As an illustration, several years ago a major farm equipment manufacturer, confronted with a growing line of replacement parts and with deteriorating service to its dealers and customers, revamped its parts distribution strategy.

Up to that time, its logistics system for parts consisted of a mail and phone order program in which a dealer would contact the manufacturer's nearest regional parts depot of 12 located throughout the United States. Regional depots would either fill all or part of an order and refer the remainder to a sister depot, which might or might not have those items that were found to be out of stock at the first location.

The weekly update of regional depot inventories often produced inaccurate knowledge of inventory availability on the part of order takers. So-called "standard" orders were shipped to dealers by surface methods. Dealers could designate emergency orders, which were then shipped by the fastest method with transportation costs billed to the dealer. One indicator of the ineffectiveness of the system was that a growing proportion of orders were emergencies.

As a result of its review, the company decided to reduce the number of items stocked in its regional depots and to create a complete stock of all items at a master depot located near Chicago. A real-time method of inventory accounting was created. Electronic terminals were provided for many dealers. On receipt of an order, a regional depot would ship those high-sales-volume items in its stock by surface methods to its dealer. Items not in stock were ordered from Chicago. These items were packed immediately for next-morning shipment by air in containers destined for each regional depot.

As a result of this program, dealers were assured of nearly complete order availability in a short period of time, reductions in inventory holding costs more than compensated the company for increased transportation costs, and customer goodwill improved significantly. In fact, the manufacturer gained a reputation throughout the industry for having an outstanding parts supply program achieved by means of a differentiated distribution system.

Although postponement and speculation, standardization, consolidation, and differentiation are all means of achieving strategic competitive advantage, a conscious program of review must be maintained to ensure that they are not overlooked in formulating strategy.

Factoring Logistics into Strategy

To employ logistics as an effective competitive lever and as a significant component of strategy, management must take two actions. First, it must adapt logistics programs to support ongoing corporate strategies in the short term. Second, it must factor logistics into the design of business operating strategies on a continuing long-term basis. Steps necessary to ensure this include the performance of a logistics strategy audit, possible logistics system redesign, and the maintenance of procedures to ensure continued attention to logistics as an integral element of corporate strategy.

Strategy Audit

A first step in achieving this objective can begin immediately in the form of an audit to explore strategic questions such as the following:

What Levels of Service (1) Do Our Customers Expect? (2) Do Our Competitors Provide? Factors influencing answers to these questions include the degree of loyalty that customers exhibit in the purchase of the company's products and of its competitors', the criticality of the company's products to customers, the influence of its service on sales, and the costs of supplying varying levels of service. As I mentioned earlier, customer expectations and competitive levels of service may vary from product to product and from one geographic area to another.

It is not surprising that perhaps the highest levels of product support services are provided by manufacturers who maintain ownership of products they distribute. Revenues of the Xerox Corporation, largely derived from royalties assessed on each page of copy produced by its machines, immediately reflect machine downtime. As a result, Xerox's army of service personnel has reached division size (about 12,000) and its parts distribution system has received a great deal of scrutiny in its effort to maintain a service program that can put a disabled machine anywhere in the continental United States back into operation within three hours after it ceases production.

At a time when their technological leadership is being threatened by expiring patents and eager competitors, companies like Xerox and IBM may well have to rely on their service programs to maintain the strategic advantage that they have enjoyed in their respective industries for years.

Wholesalers and retailers must ask themselves the same questions. Answers may lead to alterations in buying and stocking policies as well as in warehouse and store location. For traders and manufacturers alike, service goals will influence inventory levels and locations as well as transport and customer order-processing methods employed.

How Do Competitors Achieve the Service Levels That We Think They Achieve? Answers to this question require the preparation of a competitive product flow plan, based on information about competitors' plant locations, production strategies, warehouse locations, and methods of transportation. Most if not all of this information exists in the collective unrecorded knowledge of members of the organization who spend a great deal of their time in the field in contact with customers and others. It need only be collected and organized in a systematic fashion.

There is little reason today why a competitor's logistical product flows and attendant costs cannot be simulated in the same manner as those of in-house logistics operations. In an informal poll of logistics managers in attendance at a professional seminar, I found that managers from about 15% of the companies with representatives at the meeting already collect these data on an informal basis. Information of this type is important in responding to the next two questions.

Through How Many Outlets Should We Distribute Our Products? Of What Type? Where? Retailers have long since identified location as a major element of service and sales in their businesses. The area from which a retail outlet draws its business depends on the type of goods sold, the size of the store, the degree to which competing stores sell identical or comparable merchandise, and the importance associated with the purchase of its products by consumers. These factors determine the density of retail locations and the geographic intensity with which various types of retail goods are offered for sale.

The number and type of wholesale outlets for a product are determined by customer service needs ranging from those associated with sales assistance to product availability. Some wholesalers may concentrate on promotional effort while performing no logistical (product-stocking) function, leaving it to retailers or manufacturers to supply the latter.

Among manufacturers, there has been a general reduction in the number of warehouses through which products of any one company are distributed. This probably has resulted from a combination of factors, including increased attention to costs of distributing through too many warehouses, improved methods of order processing and transportation, and a vastly improved highway system, which has extended the territory that can be served from a given warehouse location.

Are Our Plants Located and Focused Properly to Support Corporate Strategy? By definition, a plant location becomes outdated before the paint is dry on the facility. This question of location becomes important only when an existing location is at such odds with the company's logistical needs that economic savings from a move are more than enough to compensate for the economic psychic costs of the move.

Of greatest interest in the logistics study audit, however, is the extent to which the location of producing facilities can provide the very core of a corporate strategy, as in the case of the private-label bleach manufacturing business cited earlier. Production processes that rely heavily on ubiquitous raw materials such as water will require market-oriented facilities. Those involving large weight reductions (as in the production of metal from ore) will logically be located near sources of raw materials. Those requiring large sources of inexpensive power (such as the smelting of aluminum from alumina) may obtain competitive advantage by locating producing facilities near such power sources.

The degree to which plants are focused on the production of one or a limited number of products in a larger product line may be influenced by the economies of scale in production, the extent to which production can be concentrated in a small number of product modules or components for subsequent assembly to order, and the overall volume of demand for the output of one plant from a given customer. An examination of the benefits of a focused production strategy may require an analysis of the logistical costs of mixing (assorting) required by focused plant operations as opposed to the costs of small shipment and mixed shipment transportation and handling required by an unfocused plant production strategy. This leads naturally to the next question in the audit.

Where Is Our Company on the Logistics Life Cycle for All or a Portion of Its Business? A manufacturing company may begin its life cycle by scheduling small quantities of production at a single facility for local or regional distribution. As sales volumes increase, more efficient production and shipment quantities are achieved, reducing costs of logistics in the cost profile of the company. At this point, additional plants may be established, each of which may be focused on a portion of the product line. Sales territories are extended. Logistics networks become more complicated, often involving the operation of large numbers of market-oriented warehouses to minimize the cost of delivering small orders. Product-line extensions and customer orders of increasing size may, at some point, permit the mixing of carload and truckload orders at locations intermediate to plants and markets through the use of distribution centers, such as those established by General Foods.

With the continued growth of individual customer orders, it may once again become possible to ship directly from plants to customers, as in the initial stage of the company's life cycle. But this time the shipments may comprise single products moving in vehicle-load quantities.

Each stage of the logistics life cycle may require different manufacturing policies, plant and warehouse locations, and transportation and order-processing methods. Awareness of the logistics life cycle can reduce the lag between needs produced by changes in corporate strategy and appropriate logistical responses.

Have We Taken Advantage of the Full Potential for Postponement and Speculation, Standardization, Consolidation, and Differentiation in Our Logistics Programs? Opportunities associated with these strategies were discussed earlier.

To What Extent Have We Assured Ourselves That Our Strategy Meets Desired Levels of Costs and Services Where it Counts Most, to the End-User? Earlier I described a logistics program that improved one farm equipment manufacturer's ability to respond to its dealers' needs for replacement parts and that enabled the company to establish a reputation for logistics leadership. Recently, a competing manufacturer decided to measure the level of service delivered by its own much-maligned system and that provided by the well-publicized system of its competitor.

Its survey revealed that end-users perceived no significant differences in the levels of service delivered by the two systems. Puzzled by these results, the study team decided to investigate comparative dealer practices as well. This investigation revealed that its competitors' dealers had come to rely on the company's excellent system so heavily that they had reduced their inventories of spare parts below the levels required to maintain a high level of service to customers. The concerned manufacturer's dealers, on the other hand, had experienced such poor support from their supplier that they maintained a much larger stock of parts on their premises, thus taking up the slack in the system.

This suggests the need to ask the next question as part of the audit.

To What Extent Have We Employed "Channel Vision" in Determining Who Should Do What, When, Where, and How in Our Channels of Distribution? Have We Taken Steps to Ensure That All Parties Carry Out Their Functions as Planned? A good example of "channel vision" is provided by Theodore Levitt's description of the Honeywell Tradeline program, implemented several years ago.[2] At that time the company was distributing its 18,000 separate catalog parts and pieces through 100 company warehouses to some 5,000 distributors, few of whom carried adequate replacement parts stock. Distributors instead were relying on Honeywell to maintain their inventory. As a result, the manufacturer was losing a lot of business and so it devised the Tradeline program.

In essence, the program transformed the inventory maintenance function to distributors through (1) redesigning original equipment with standard interchangeable parts, some of which were compatible with competitors' products, (2) closing all Honeywell field parts warehouses, and (3) requiring distributors to maintain full stocks of all Honeywell replacement modules. Although Honeywell lost most of its distributors in implementing the Tradeline program, the stronger ones who remained formed the nucleus of a group that helped Honeywell achieve rapidly increasing sales in the years following initiation of the program.

In this way, Honeywell was better able to control the level of service and sales to its end-customers.

What Implications Do Technological Trends Have for Our Company? In my previous article, to which I referred earlier, I suggested that the rate of technological change in logistics may not keep pace in the intermediate-term future with that of the recent past. However, logistics is a technology-prone activity. Investments in technology often yield handsome returns, suggesting continued efforts of significant magnitude.

Research expenditures today may be reasonably good predictors of the direction of technological development. Because the government plays such an active role in funding research into logistics technology, government budget allocations may provide clues for strategic planning. For example, it is a pretty good bet that a larger proportion of attention will be devoted to the development of methods and energy sources providing for the uninterrupted flow of goods *at any cost* rather than to the most cost-effective technologies. As environmental constraints close in on us, larger shares of effort will be redirected in this manner. To the extent that they favor one method of transportation over another, technological developments may raise logical questions about the proper orientation of a company's facilities in relation to those of its competitors.

What Implications Do Regulatory Trends Have for Us? In the past, much regulatory activity in the field of logistics has been of an economic nature, particularly associated with transportation rates and operating rights. The recent ground swell of support for economic deregulation of various aspects of logistics has been accompanied by more laws stipulating noneconomic restrictions concerning matters as diverse as housekeeping procedures in the maintenance of sanitation standards in warehouses (with at least one chief executive indicted under this law) to restrictions on the movement of hazardous materials.

The future may bring even more attention to matters of a more strategic nature, including the legality of certain geographic practices that discourage freight-on-board (as opposed to destination or market-oriented) pricing. In several instances, the Federal Trade Commission has even become interested in the quantities of advertised merchandise maintained in stock in support of special promotional efforts.

Does Our Logistics Strategy Support Our Corporate Strategy? To What Extent Should Our Strategy Be Logistics-Oriented? On what markets and market segments does the corporate strategy rely most heavily? Is this reflected in the program of differentiation (if one exists) practiced in the corporation's logistics efforts?

Does the corporate strategy envision important compromises in, for example, the uncoupling of manufacturing processes to achieve lower costs through the creation of larger in-process or finished product inventories? Will the logistics system accommodate this strategy?

What does the financial plan imply for the ownership of transport equipment, warehouses, inventories, and order-processing and other communication facilities?

Does the relative importance of logistics cost or service levels in the total "package" offered to customers suggest an important means for differentiating the company from its competitors? To what extent can the ideas suggested earlier be applied to accomplish this in formulating corporate strategy?

System Redesign

A strategic audit may reveal so much conflict between corporate strategy and logistics methods that a logistics system redesign is called for. Although the audit may provide some of the data necessary for the preparation of a systems analysis effort dealing with specific customer service standards, product flows, and the like, other questions will have to be answered to supply the information needed for system redesign. Such questions, along with techniques for system redesign, have been described extensively in these pages and elsewhere.[3]

This is not to suggest that the impact of a strategy audit will be only on the design of the logistics system. It should also lead to the establishment of a vehicle to ensure continued attention to the potential for achieving strategic advantages through logistics when corporate strategy is being formulated or altered.

Longer-Term Actions

The strategy audit and any resulting logistics system redesign or corporate strategy adjustment will serve to bring logistics efforts into alignment with corporate needs in the short term. Unless some formalization of the process takes place, however, there is little guarantee that logistical considerations will continue to be taken into account in the strategy formulation process. The examples that I cited at the outset of this article serve to suggest ways by which this may be accomplished.

First, top management holds nearly all of the cards in the process. Managers responsible for various logistics functions have not, in the course of their work, had access to the goals and strategies formulated by top management. Quite appropriately, their goals and views have been relatively short-range and nonstrategic in nature. Ironically, they have participated least in decisions that have had the greatest long-run impact on their performance, as suggested in Exhibit 2. All of this indicates that if a vehicle is to be found to raise logistical considerations to an appropriate level of awareness in the strategy formulation process, top management will have to take the initiative.

FACTORING LOGISTICS INTO STRATEGY

Exhibit 2. Participation in Strategic Decision Making

Degree of participation by logistics management	Nature of decision	Degree and length of impact of decision on operations
Least (↓ to Most)	Locating a new plant	Most (↑ to Least)
	Setting customer service standards	
	Changing geographic pricing policies	
	Recombining products to be produced at various plants	
	Changing marketing territories	
	Establishing long-term purchase contracts with major suppliers	
	Introducing a new product line	
	Redesigning inventory control procedures	
	Redesigning order-processing procedures	
	Selecting a method of transportation	
	Locating a warehouse	
	Changing the allocation of business to carriers, public warehousers, or other suppliers	

Second, entrepreneurs have formulated some of the most remarkable logistics-oriented business strategies. The entrepreneur wears so many hats that he or she embodies the wedding between top management and logistical considerations in the strategy formulation process. But what of the large corporation in which organizational differentiation necessarily has created both specialized responsibility and a widening gulf between top functional logistics management?

Here the experience of the large chemical manufacturer may be enlightening. This producer carefully maintains a liaison between functional and long-range planning personnel. Members of logistics groups in operating divisions that are responsible for shorter-range planning and for maintaining an awareness of current problems are kept informed of those elements of corporate strategy that might influence their thinking. Conversely, a member of the corporate long-range planning group purposely maintains both an acquaintance with trends in the logistics "environment" and a line of communication with members of the logistics planning groups found in the operating divisions of the company as well as at the corporate level.

By this means, a member of the logistics planning group was able to sense the need and appropriate timing for the proposed system that required a major revision in the business strategy employed by one of the corporation's divisions. Because of the open lines of communication between long-range planning, logistics planning, and operating managers within the division, it was possible to "sell" the concept both to the division management and to top management.

Given the focus of attention among larger companies on the reorganization of management for logistics activities in recent years, a growing number of companies have staffed their logistics-oriented departments with managers capable of being included in the process of formulating strategy in this manner.

Finally, those companies that have achieved some success in structuring some part of their strategies around logistical considerations have, in many cases, been the same ones that have (1) staffed senior positions in logistics with individuals capable of being promoted to general management positions, (2) viewed logistics as an important step in a program to produce well-rounded general managers, and (3) looked to logistics to provide its share of general managers along with marketing, finance, production, engineering, control, and other major functions.

It is no surprise that members of general management at companies such as PPG, Eastman Kodak, Xerox, General Foods, and Johnson & Johnson have consistently maintained a high level of awareness of the potential for developing competitive strategies based to a substantial degree on logistical considerations.

Corporate Strategy of the Future

If the arguments for the systematic consideration of logistics in formulating corporate strategy in a healthy company primarily serving domestic markets are not sufficiently appealing, there are compelling reasons for considering them more seriously in the future. The reasons include a decline in the growth rate of domestic markets, large incremental costs of energy, and an increasing emphasis on multinational markets in corporate strategies.

Rapid corporate growth conceals many blemishes of poor decision making and operating inefficiencies. And although individual organizations will continue to wax and wane in the future, in general there will be fewer growth opportunities on which to rely in a stable population increasingly concerned about its consumption rates. This will lead to a shift from emphasis on growth per se to what might be called the quality of earnings, obtained through the prudent control of costs required to serve relatively slow-growing markets and sales bases. Logistical considerations will weigh heavily in programs designed to improve the quality of earnings.

There is little doubt now that the most rapidly growing cost of doing business in the foreseeable future will be that of energy. Inevitable energy allocation and conservation programs will involve significantly higher costs of one sort or another. Energy-intensive activities of transportation and materials handling will represent increasingly important methods of gaining competitive advantage in costs and of improving the quality of earnings. The most effective means of obtaining such results will not be through tactical decisions such as a shift from one method of transportation to another. Rather, strategic facility locations, for example, will be primary determinants of the quality of earnings produced from logistics cost advantages.

With the inevitable slowing of certain domestic markets, U.S. producers will look abroad to a growing involvement in multinational business. To the extent that this will involve importation and exportation of goods, whether as part of an export program or as a truly multinational production and distribution strategy, multinational business can be much more logistics-intensive than can domestic business.

Attention to logistics can support expanded product lines in good times or provide a basis for gaining a competitive profit edge during periods of slow growth. Whether the goal is increased market shares or increased profits from existing or smaller market shares, logistics considerations can be basic to these accomplishments. If, as many have predicted, general management inevitably will have to spend an increasing proportion of its time dealing with low or no-growth situations, it is not too early to put in place a process to ensure that logistical considerations will not be overlooked in formulating strategy.

For Want of a Nail . . .*

During World War II, General George S. Patton, Jr. had little time or patience for the function of physical distribution (logistics). General of the Army Omar N. Bradley, who served under Patton at one point, has noted:

---

*From *A Soldier's Story*, by Omar N. Bradley. Copyright 1951 by Holt, Rinehart and Winston. Reprinted by permission of Holt, Rinehart and Winston, publishers.

"On the several occasions I appealed to Patton for more supply support, he would respond as though I had come to chide him on a minor detail and he would brush my complaint aside. Although Patton bossed his Army tactically with an iron hand, he remained almost completely indifferent to its logistical needs. In war as Patton knew it then, there was little time for logistics in the busy day of a field commander."

Nevertheless, Patton felt the sting of inadequate physical distribution support when his attacking Third Army was stopped dead in its tracks for lack of fuel. Patton called this situation the "iron grip of logistics." Bradley referred to it as the "tyranny of supplies."

Notes

1. Walter F. Friedman has described many of these services in *Physical Distribution: The Concept of Shared Services* (Thinking Ahead), *HBR*, March–April 1975, p. 24; for a discussion of other examples, see my article, "Sweeping Changes in Distribution," *HBR*, March–April 1973, p. 123.

2. Theodore Levitt, "Production-Line Approach to Service," *HBR*, September–October 1972, p. 41.

3. See, for example, John F. Magee, "The Logistics of Distribution," *HBR*, July–August 1960, p. 89.

17
Integrating Critical Elements of Production Planning

JOHN E. BISHOP

The many managers who use the so-called economic lot size formula in planning their production have often been disappointed with the results. This author examines the deficiencies of that much-used approach and explains a new point of view which considers not only the demand but also the production facilities and the competition among products for the use of those facilities.

The formula known as the economic lot size—the economic order quantity (EOQ, for short)—has been used in the production planning process for well over 50 years. It has been used too much. In many cases, such obviously poor decisions have resulted that operating managers at the foreperson level quietly ignore the formula and make decisions they know intuitively are better.

I think the reason these managers do so is that they realize that use of the formula, even if it results, as it was designed to, in the control of inventories, may lead to a use of capacity that is quite ineffective. My purpose in this article is to describe an alternative approach, one that can yield substantive payoffs because it leads to better use of capacity.

I will show that an understanding of the interaction among demand, capacity, and inventory can lead to balanced and reduced investment both in capacities and in inventories. I will provide tools to help in planning what level of capacity to have and in scheduling the use of that capacity. These rules, at the same time, control inventory levels and demonstrate how inventory turnover is related to capacity and demand and why it cannot be used by itself as a measure of performance.

It would not be fruitful for me to guess why so many of us have become enamored with the EOQ formula nor to refute the arguments of those who insist on using it (the typical operations research expert's defense is that "it is close to everything"). My purpose is to provide a substitute; not, I hasten to add, a substitute formula but a substitute point of view. I will use this point of view to examine only a few of the problems of production planning. I do not claim for it the universality that the economic lot size formula has achieved.

The situations where this point of view is useful have two essential features. The first is that the items produced are more than less catalogable as commodities, in that they are not customer-specific but tend to be more general purpose, and they have a long shelf life. They may be used in later stages in the company's manufacturing process or sold directly. What is important is that management will consider building to inventory. The second is that there is equipment used in common in the production of these items, so that the items, in effect, compete for the use of that equipment. The ongoing management decisions are how many to make of an item and when.

Economic Lot Size Model

If managers are going to use an operations research analysis, they must know what the starting point of that analysis is. The modus operandi of the operations researcher is to abstract from some real-world problem a mathematical problem for which an answer can be found. That answer is then touted as a guidepost to the manager.

The abstraction that leads to the EOQ formula is as follows.

Consider the product line one item at a time. Though demand for the items under consideration may fluctuate throughout the year, it does no harm to suppose that the demand occurs at a steady rate. (For a product with a short shelf life it is not likely that this is possible.)

The option of producing lots (the production rate must be higher than the average demand rate) is thus a feasible one. And so the next question is: "How big should the lots be?" To answer this question, we argue that if the lots are too big and only a few are produced in the year, the cost of carrying the inventory is too high. To get the famous EOQ formula, we suppose the total carrying cost for the year goes up proportionally with the size of the lots. However, if the lots are too small, too many of them are produced, and if the setup cost per lot is the same regardless of its size, then the total setup cost is too high. The right lot size is the one where these two costs are in balance.

What was the point of view taken by the operations researcher in this abstraction? I think the crucial choice that was made was to look at the product line *one item at a time* and consequently to make the decision on its lot size separately from and independently of the decisions made on the lot sizes of other items.

What is wrong with this point of view? I claim that, as an aid to planning manufacturing, just about everything is wrong with it. It is far too simplistic, as I will now show, and because of this it cannot help in the circumstances where it is currently so commonly used.

If we look again at the preceding scenario, which led to the economic lot size formula, we will see that management paid careful attention to demand but did not even mention production facilities. It is as if a genie emerges and waves a wand, and presto! the product is there. Or, at least, a salesperson picks up the phone and, by placing an order, has on hand, whenever needed, any quantity of the item desired.

But, in manufacturing, it is not enough to consider only the demand. It is equally important that the analysis also involves the capacity of the production process. When management decides how much to invest in plant and equipment, it does so partly in terms of its expectation of the market, but it is much aware at the same time of the economies of trying to meet that demand and of the day-to-day decisions in managing the plant to produce the goods.

In the analysis that follows, I will discuss decisions of these two types—namely, how much equipment to have, and what will be produced and when. My analysis will involve manufacturing processes where a single machine, line, or facility is used for the manufacture of several items. From the point of view of management, the products compete for the common capacity that has been provided to meet the joint demand. The task for operating managers is to make, in some sense, the best use of that capacity. In making its decisions, management is willing to build any of the items in the line for inventory.

A New Point of View

If we were to observe the production system at any time, we would see an inventory of finished goods of the various items on hand, and one of them being produced. At some time soon, management will have to decide whether to keep making the current product or to switch to another. What are the guidelines for making this decision? If management lets things continue as they are, an excessive amount of inventory can be built up in one product and there will be a shortage in some other. The inventory is there but in the wrong product.

In most cases, it takes time to switch over from one product to another. During that downtime there is no production, and so effective capacity is lost. (If, of course, there is so much capacity available that this is of no concern, there are problems elsewhere in the enterprise.) We can push this argument and resulting decision to an extreme. If the lots are too small, then so much capacity can be lost in changeovers that the total time remaining for the production of the items is not sufficient to meet their demand.

The point of view I take here leads inevitably to the conclusion that there has to be an interaction between the size of lots produced and the productive capacity. And since the productive capacity is not considered in the derivation of the EOQ formula, we can bet that it would be only by the most unlikely coincidence that this formula would yield a number useful for making a manufacturing decision where capacity was anything less than so extravagant in quantity that such a large investment had not already been regretted.

What are the relations among demand, lot size, inventory, and capacity? I shall develop here, in a simple situation, precisely what they are: the way of thinking is useful in planning the amount of capacity to have and for what inventories to plan, in other situations as well.

A hypothetical company produces two very similar products on a single line. The annual requirements of both have been forecast, and management agrees as to the amount of production for which it wants to plan. The production rates of the two products are known, and the total runtime for them is found to be less than a year. In other words, there is spare capacity.

To be specific, suppose the plan is to produce to the forecast of 120,000 units of each product for the year. For convenience, let the year be 250 days. The line produces at the rate of 1,000 units per day for either product. The time lost in changeover from one product to the other is always one day.

Where the EOQ Fails

We need some further information to calculate the economic lot size formula. If both products have the selling price of $20 per unit and a variable cost per unit of $10, and the cost of capital is 30%, suppose the inventory carrying cost is $3 per unit per year. The lost contribution from the one-day changeover is $10,000. Suppose that the cost of the crew that does the changeover is $800 for each changeover and the nonproductive operators' cost is $2,200 for the day they are idle during each changeover.

To obtain the economic lot size, we must know the setup cost. The possible costs are: $800 directly attributable to the changeover, or $3,000 to include the nonproductive wages, or $13,000 to cover also the lost contribution.

For each of these three costs, there will be a different economic lot size, a different runtime, and a different number of days required in the year to produce the year's demand (see the Technical Appendix following this article). The number of days required in the work year may be more or less than a year (see Exhibit 1).

It may appear from Exhibit 1 that the best choice of setup cost is to take all the costs and the forgone contribution as the cost of a changeover but to do so is to miss the point. The contribution depends partly on the selling price, and all that needs to be asked is why a small change in the selling price of the output should have such a dramatic effect on the actual capacity of the plant. Thus it is easy to see that the plant can be put from an over to an undercapacity position by a small change in the contribution from the items.

Effect of Demand on Inventory

We need a different way of looking at such planning decisions. The decisions on lot size cannot be made one at a time because, if they are, there is no way to guarantee production of the year's needs within the year. And, even if the year's needs are met, they may be produced very early in the year: it clearly does not pay to produce too early and have the equipment idle toward the end of the year, because inventory is on hand for too long before it is needed. Hence the line should run continuously throughout the year so that production days plus changeover days will equal total days in the year.

The production lot sizes resulting from the action just described are determined as follows. The number of days required to produce each item is found by dividing the output required by the production rate in units per day. The total number of production days required is found by adding these numbers. The remaining days in the year are used for changeovers.

In the case of two products, the next lot to be produced is always that of the item not now in production, and the year will be a set of cycles, each cycle consisting of a production lot of each item and the two changeovers. (If there are more than two products, the cycle may be more complicated than a simple cycling through the product line.) The number of cycles in a year is determined by dividing the days in the year available for changeovers

Exhibit 1. Economic Lot Size and Required Production Time vs. Setup Cost

Setup Cost	Economic Lot Size	Number of Lots	Days per Lot	Days Required per Year
$ 800	8,000	15	9	270
3,000	15,492	7.75	16.5	255
13,000	32,249	3.7	33	245

by the days required for changeovers in a cycle. The lot sizes are then determined by dividing the item demands by the number of cycles in a year.

How does the lot size determined this way differ from that of the classic EOQ formula? Primarily, it takes into account not only the demand but also the production facilities and the competition among the products for the use of these facilities. Most important, the required output will certainly be produced if only there is enough capacity. Further, this determination guarantees that among those choices of lot sizes for which the requirements are met none has lower inventory carrying costs.

What has happened to the setup costs? I claim that using them results in poor decisions and focuses the attention of managers away from the crucial decisions and control they should exercise in managing the manufacturing process.

It is more useful to consider the kind and the sequence of decisions that management makes. We can easily imagine that, in our example, the demand for the two products has been increasing over time and that, at some widely and unequally spaced points in time, management has decided to add capacity. After each of these decisions, the operating management has decided more regularly how much of each item to produce and the timing of that production.

At some time, as demand has grown, capacity has not seemed adequate to the operating manager and he or she has appealed for more capacity. In deciding whether to add capacity, managers will consider, among other issues, alternate uses of funds in other projects, the convenience of more flexibility in planning, and their level of confidence in their forecasts. I think that management should regard—and this is certainly not a novel thought—inventories as a substitute for capacity.

But if capacity and inventory substitute for each other, management should think out *how* they do. For if they do not, either inventories or capacities become too large and make manufacturing costs less competitive. Consider, in this regard, what happens in our example with the same plant, and where the demand for each item has been 80,000; 100,000; and 120,000 units per year. The calculations of lot size and inventory levels are shown in Exhibit 2.

We can draw a dramatic conclusion from Exhibit 2. The device of observing inventory turnover and using that index as an evaluation and control mechanism can lead to costly and harmful decisions. In the situation described in this exhibit, the number of cycles a year can be used as a measure of inventory turnover. The exhibit shows that, when demand is low relative to capacity, a high turnover ratio should be expected. However, the ratio decreases very rapidly as the demand closes in on the capacity.

So these conclusions are inescapable: there is no such thing as an industry turnover ratio that is universally good, and there is also no such

A NEW POINT OF VIEW 295

Exhibit 2. Inventory vs. Demand, Capacity Fixed

Demand (units)	Runtime (days)	Changeover Days	Cycles (number)	Average Inventory
80,000	160	90	45	1,210
100,000	200	50	25	2,400
120,000	240	10	5	12,480
125,000	250	0	—	—

thing as a permanently good company inventory turnover ratio. If management wants to use inventory turnover as an evaluative or control measure in manufacturing, it must set the base in terms of both the demand for the products and the capacity it has provided.

Exhibit 2 permits another conclusion: as the demand for the product line gets closer to the capacity of the plant, management must resist all pressures to produce small lots to meet small stock-outs. To do so will reduce effective capacity still further and worsen the situation. Soon every job will be expedited and nothing will get done.

Effect of Capacity on Inventory

In the preceding few paragraphs, I have explored the relationship between demand and inventory for a given plant capacity. I did this by keeping the plant size fixed and by watching what happened as demand increased. New lessons emerge if we look at the relation between capacity and inventory for a given level of demand. In what follows, the demand will always be the same, namely, 120,000 units of each product for the year. As available capacity is increased, I will examine the inventory resulting from decisions on lot size.

In Exhibit 3, the capacity of 960 units a day is chosen as the starting point. It is the minimum capacity necessary to meet the demand if there were no capacity lost in changeovers. For every doubling of the amount of capacity added (not total capacity), the run is halved as is the corresponding inventory buildup. Exhibit 4 shows the numbers.

Only the last two columns in Exhibit 4 contain new information; the first three columns are from Exhibit 3. The fourth column shows the average number of units in inventory for both products combined. We can find the numbers in that column in the following manner. The average inventory level for an item is one-half the maximum. The maximum occurs at the end of the run for that item and just covers the changeover days (both of them) and the runtime for the other item. For the first line in the exhibit, the number

Exhibit 3. Run Length vs. Capacity, Demand Fixed

Capacity (units/day)	Run Days Required	Changeover Days	Number of Cycles	Run Length (days/item)
960	250	0		
1,000	240	10	5	24
1,040	230.8	19.2	9.6	12
1,120	214.3	35.7	17.9	6
1,280	187.5	62.5	31.3	3
1,600	150	100	50	1.5

is (2 + 24) times 960—that is, 24,960 units. The average level for each item is half that, and so, for the two items together, is exactly that number.

The numbers in the last column are less than the corresponding ones in the fourth by the same amount—that is, 1,920. This is the number of units required to cover one day's downtime and hence is the absolute minimum amount of inventory to have on hand.

A comparison of the second and last columns of Exhibit 4 shows that, as one set of numbers keeps doubling, the other keeps halving. Hence row by row the product of the two remains the same:

$$\begin{array}{c} \text{Capacity above minimum} \\ \text{required to meet demand} \\ \times \\ \text{Inventory above minimum} \\ \text{required to cover changeovers} \end{array} = \text{Constant}$$

Exhibit 4. Inventory vs. Capacity, Demand Fixed

Capacity	Capacity above Minimum	Runtime per Cycle per Item (days)	Average Inventory	Average Inventory above Minimum
1,000	40	24	24,960	23,040
1,040	80	12	13,440	11,520
1,120	160	6	7,680	5,760
1,280	320	3	4,800	2,880
1,600	640	1.5	3,360	1,440

A NEW POINT OF VIEW

The value of this formula is that it is the fundamental fact on which is based the choice of capacity level (see the Technical Appendix).

We have already seen that when demand is high relative to capacity, investment in inventory goes up dramatically. Conversely, inventores can be kept low by having a large investment in capacity. Since efficiency in the use of funds is important, management clearly has to choose between investment in more capacity and investment in more inventory. In our example, we try to see how management would make this choice if its desire is to keep the combined investment in capacity and inventory as small as possible.

The variable cost per unit of either item is $10. Suppose that the investment in a unit of capacity is $1,440. Exhibit 5 updates Exhibit 4 by introducing these dollar amounts.

In Exhibit 5, we see that the smallest investment occurs at that capacity level where the investment in capacity above the minimum investment required equals the investment in inventory above the minimum investment required there. This exemplifies the basic rule: the lowest total investment is that for which the investment in capacity above the minimum required to meet the demand equals the investment in inventory above the minimum required to cover changeovers.

This rule provides an investment guideline for management. When management considers further investment in capacity, it should compare the discretionary investment currently held in capacity with that in inventories. If the investment in inventories appears to be much higher, investment in capacity of such an amount as to balance the two investments should be considered. Of course, I recognize that there is a longer term commitment to investment in capacity and the amount of the investment cannot usually be chosen so as to be exactly equal.

The foregoing analysis suits those situations where management has the option of building to inventory but, at the same time, the fact that several

Exhibit 5. Investments in Inventory and Capacity, Demand Fixed

Capacity above Minimum	Investment above Minimum	Inventory above Minimum	Investment in Inventory	Total Investment
40	$ 57,600	23,040	$230,400	$288,000
80	115,200	11,520	115,200	230,400
160	230,400	5,760	57,600	288,000
320	460,800	2,880	28,800	497,600
640	921,600	1,440	14,400	936,000

items use the same facilities restricts the timing and amount of production. Within those bounds, two types of guidelines emerge: one, an aid in evaluating the desirability of adding more capacity; and two, a scheduling procedure for making good use of the capacity on hand.

There are, of course, many auxiliary questions. One is the complication that arises when there are more than two items in the product line, with different economics and different production rates. Another is how to plan against the uncertainty inevitable in the forecast of demand, how to monitor what actually happens, and when to take action. The first of these problems is purely technical. If, however, the second turns out to be overwhelmingly important, it sets a limit on the type of planning for which this point of view is useful.

The view I take in the discussion and analysis here is that, in deciding how much capacity for which to plan and then how to use it, management cannot look only at the demand for the items in the product line, or only at the production process. What management has to consider as more important than either is the interaction between them—capacity and demand must be considered together when lot sizes are chosen.

When arithmetic was painful and tedious (before computers), management could not as readily take into account the interaction among parts of the enterprise and had to analyze one part at a time. Consequently, there was a time when management had to look primarily at the demand and had to attempt to capture the involvement of the production process through the setup cost. But, even then, it was poor economics to select and put together costs as it was generally done. Managers should have regarded the setup cost as a price, in the economists' meaning of the word, and they ought to have chosen that price at which the year's production would have used up exactly the year's capacity.

In Conclusion

The theme of interaction should be played out once more here. It is common in many production planning exercises to use the following steps.

First, managers make an analysis that leads to the choice of level of production. The result of this analysis is called the aggregate plan, and, in effect, it sets the capacity availabile.[1]

After this, the next step is to schedule into production the various products that use the capacity. Note that the level of detail now is product rather than product line and the corresponding plan is called the master schedule. Generally, the master schedule defines when final assembly takes place.

At the third stage in the planning process, the products consist of components and subassemblies that must be on hand at appropriate times

TECHNICAL APPENDIX

to meet the requirements of the master schedule. It is common practice at this point to use a materials requirement planning device in order to purchase or schedule into production early enough the products necessary for later use in production.[2]

Clearly, the decisions at these three levels cannot be made separately. For, if they are, it will turn out either that the plans are impossible (in material requirements planning, capacities are not usually taken directly into account) or that the planning has not duly recognized the economics of the situation. The strength and the value of the point of view and analysis demonstrated here are that it ties together the aggregate plan and the master schedule. This combination leads to balanced and reduced investment both in capacities and in inventories.

Notes

1. Melvin Anshen et al., "Mathematics for Production Scheduling," *HBR*, March–April 1958, p. 51.

2. Philip H. Thurston, "Requirements Planning for Inventory Control," *HBR*, May–June 1972, p. 67.

Technical Appendix

1. The general formula for the economic lot size is obtained in the following way. Denote the demand for the product D (units per year); let the setup cost be $\$S$ per setup and the inventory carrying cost be $\$C$ per unit per year. If the size of the lots is chosen to be Q units, there are D/Q lots per year with a total setup cost of $\$S(D/Q)$. The average inventory level is taken to be $Q/2$ units and the cost of carrying inventory is $\$C(Q/2)$. The total cost is the sum

$$S(D/Q) + C(Q/2).$$

The technical task of finding the lot size for which this cost is smallest is the same as that of solving the following commonly described problem: of all rectangles of the same area (length × width = constant) find the shape of the one with the smallest perimeter (length + width is minimum).

A reasonable way to think of this problem is to observe that if we were to start with a long narrow rectangle with dimensions, say, of 16 and 1, the product is 16 × 1 = 16 and the sum is 16 + 1 = 17. Cut the rectangle in two, forming two rectangles each 8 × 1 and join them together to form an

8 × 2 rectangle. The product remains the same, 8 × 2 = 16, but the sum gets smaller, 8 + 2 = 10. Repeating the process gives 4 × 4 = 16 and 4 + 4 = 8. The procedure is not as tidy if we do not start with a multiple of 2, but the result is the same. Anyone is willing to generalize that the sum is smallest when the length equals the width.

Returning to the lot size problem, note again that we want the lot size Q for which the sum of $S(D/Q)$ and $C(Q/2)$ is smallest. We observe that the product $S(D/Q)$ times $C(Q/2)$ is $SDC/2$, and so remains the same no matter what Q is. We conclude that the smallest value for the sum occurs when the two quantities are equal, that is, when $S(D/Q) = C(Q/2)$. A little algebraic manipulation puts this in the form

$$Q^2 = 2SD/C$$

and so

$$Q = \sqrt{2SD/C}$$

2. A very similar argument and formula hold true for the decisions analyzed in this article. The similarity in formalism should not, however, lead anyone to think that the decisions have much in common.

Denote by N_c the number of units of capacity above the minimum required to meet the year's demand, and by N_I the number of units of inventory above the amount required for one changeover. These quantities so identified can, at least partially, be controlled by management.

We have seen that these numbers are related such that as one goes up the other goes down, keeping their product constant. We observe that the minimum capacity—that is, the amount required to meet the demand if there were no capacity lost in changeover—has the value $2D$, where D is the annual demand for each item. If the capacity available is $2D + N_c$, the fraction of the year required for runtime is $2D/(2D + N_c)$ and the remainder, $N_c/(2D + N_c)$ is used for changeovers. If each changeover requires S years (actually a fraction of a year), the number of cycles in a year is $N_c/[(2D + N_c)(2S)]$. The runtime per item per cycle is the fraction of the year devoted to running the item divided by the number of cycles in a year. Carrying out the division yields the number $2DS/N_c$. This quantity is the inventory level N_I above minimum, associated with a capacity N_c above the minimum. The product of these two numbers is $2DS$, a number that remains the same regardless of what N_c is chosen to be.

Next consider the investment required. If each unit of capacity requires an investment of $\$c$ and each unit of inventory an investment of $\$I$, the total discretionary investment is

$$\$(cN_c + IN_I).$$

TECHNICAL APPENDIX

We take as our task the selection of N_c (and the concomitant N_I) for which this investment is smallest.

The product of the two investments is $(cN_c)(IN_I)$, which equals $(cI)(2DS)$, and remains constant no matter what the choice of N_c or N_I is. We deduce that the sum is smallest when the parts are equal. The theoretically best choices of capacity and of inventory above their minima satisfy $cN_c = IN_I$. In a different form, this is the same as

$$\frac{N_c}{N_i} = \frac{I}{c}$$

stating that the quantities are in inverse proportion to their unit costs. Or, if it is preferred, either N_c or N_I can be eliminated from the equation by using the fact the $N_c N_I = 2DS$, yielding in one case

$$N_I = \sqrt{\frac{2DSc}{I}}$$

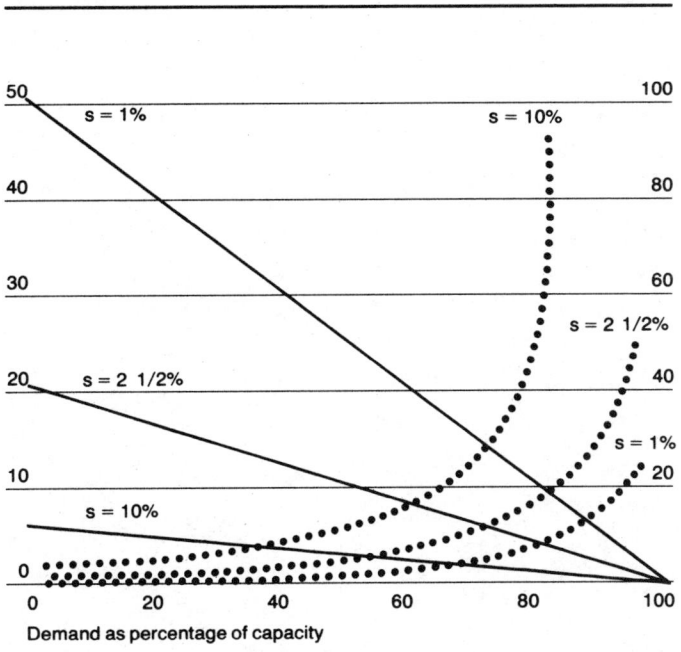

Exhibit A.1. Relationship Between Inventory Turnover and Inventory

3. By considering the demand as a percentage of available capacity, the average inventory level can also be calculated as a percentage of capacity.

Denote the ratio formed by dividing the demand by the capacity available by d; d is then the portion of the year it required for the runtime. Let s be the portion of a year lost in a changeover; $2s$ is the portion lost per cycle. Since the portion $1 - d$ of a year is available for changeovers, the number of cycles is $(1 - d)/(2s)$. This number measures also the inventory turnover. The lot size is about twice the average inventory, and so the average units in inventory for both items is the demand of one during a cycle, namely

$$\frac{(d/2)}{(1 - d)/2s} = \frac{sd}{(1 - d)}.$$

Exhibit A.1 shows the relationship between inventory turnovers and inventory levels.

18
Production Planning and Control Integrated

WILLIAM K. HOLSTEIN

Although much has been written about the individual segments of production planning and control systems, little has appeared in the literature to help practitioners develop an integrated view of the whole process. Many complaints about department overloads or poor delivery performances—particularly in fabrication and assembly operations—focus on scheduling or control. Actually, the basic cause may be unbalanced capacity or an unrealistic sales commitment made months previously. Thus managers must not only look at decision making at all levels, but must also recognize that good short-term performances result from an integrated set of decisions made over a long time span.

- ☐ Where did that huge pile of work in the turret lathe department come from?
- ☐ Why can't we get the Ajax Bearing job done before next week?
- ☐ Should we accept such a large order for delivery in eight weeks?
- ☐ We're up to our armpits in castings on the shop floor. What can be done to reduce this congestion?
- ☐ Why in the devil are we still working overtime in the assembly area?

These questions are representative of real and pressing questions that many production managers face. They are also symptomatic of basic management problems in running numerous production operations.

In this article I shall discuss the contributions that modern, computer-based production planning and control systems can make to aid in the solution of these kinds of problems. I am particularly interested in identifying and tying together the various parts of a production planning and control system, and in so doing I shall focus on tasks to be fulfilled rather than on detailed methods. The systems I shall discuss are applicable to a broad range of industries, but apply most directly to fabrication and assembly operations that make a large number of parts in relatively small lots either for assembly into finished products or for sale to outside customers.

Much has been written about individual segments of production planning and control systems and the specific analytical tools and techniques for handling these separate parts. However, little has been done to help the practitioner use the many tools and techniques that are applicable to the situation in such a way that they relate to one another. Managers are frequently heard to complain about department overloads or poor delivery performances and to blame these on "poor scheduling" or "poor control." The real cause, however, may be unbalanced capacity or an unrealistic sales commitment that was made months ago.

This article is designed, therefore, to help the manager relate the various parts of production planning and control, and to develop an integrated view of the whole process. I shall present the parts in a sequence that begins with long-term planning and ends with day-to-day control of shop floor activity, using exhibits to clarify the individual parts and the way they relate to one another. I shall also cite examples of companies that have made excellent progress on one specific part of a production planning and control system and those that have been successful in tying together two or more of the parts. All of the examples are based on actual situations.

Toward Better Control

Webster's dictionary definition of a system includes "a regularly interacting or interdependent group of items forming a unified whole." The items or parts in a production planning and control system fit together in a time dimension and interact in a certain way. Long-term strategic plans that commit the company to a configuration of manpower, skills, plant, and equipment are based on very crude information and analysis. Moreover, these plans constrain the development of more complete detailed plans closer to actual production dates. Long-term plans are made by high-level management, and, as the time span shortens and the time of actual production approaches, decision making is passed down to lower-level managers. Within the guidelines formed by long-term plans, tactical control must be exercised over the "uncontrollable" variation in product mix and productivity in the short term.

In the very short term this control involves putting employees in the right places, working on the right jobs, and regulating inventory levels. The criteria against which management's production planning and control performance is measured include inventory investment, labor cost, manufacturing cycle time (time to get work through the shop), equipment utilization, and meeting delivery deadlines.

Need for Flexibility

In my view, the most important task in designing any production planning and control system which will measure up well against these criteria is to ensure that the plans and guidelines from higher levels guide, but do not unduly restrict, decision making at lower levels. Flexibility to react to new information and significant deviations from higher-level plans must be built into the system at all levels. Also, feedback information on actual conditions and performance must flow upward through the system to ensure that long-term plans are based on a realistic assessment of the production organization's ability to produce.

Production managers usually do not see their job roles in these clear general terms. Since the "moment of truth"—that is, when poor performance becomes obvious—occurs at the time of actual production, there is a tendency to find fault in the shortest time dimension and thus focus largely on problems at the lowest level. Many production managers spend their time in a continuous, and at times frantic, search for information. In the face of a stream of demanding problems calling for immediate attention and decisions, and because of the sometimes chaotic nature of work flow and clerical decision making on the shop floor, production managers often find themselves chained to an endless sequence of routine decision making.

The consequence is little time to think about next week's or next month's possible problems and to lay plans for solving those problems. Nor is there time to evaluate recent performance and to seek ways of improving it. Despite the fact that managers often spend a great deal of time in the short term, because of the tremendous number of jobs in process, they still must delegate many seemingly small detailed decisions to their first-line supervisors, clerical assistants, or even to the workers themselves. Management thus loses control over decisions that, taken together, may have a great impact on how efficiently the plant is run.

But things can be much better. Recently, many production managers have changed the way they manage, utilizing new systems for production planning and control. New systems do not eliminate all the crises, but they do point the way toward better control with less management involvement at the detail level. Thus they are making it possible for management to plan, redesign, and execute in a more rational manner.

Long-Term Capacity Planning

Plant facilities, equipment, skilled labor, and working capital to support inventory investments usually cannot be made available to production managers on short notice. Consequently, most organizations must be concerned with laying long-term plans for future capacities. In a sense, long-term planning is the starting point for production planning and control; thus it is the logical starting point for our consideration of production planning and control systems.

Forecasts of Future Demand

The production organization competes with engineering and marketing for the company's limited resources, so production plans must be developed, refined, and defended. The long lead times on new construction and equipment acquisition require that some major expansion plans be developed years in advance of actual installation. Analyses of future market conditions and forecasts of future demands thus become important inputs in long-term planning. Even in make-to-order shops where no formal forecasts of future demands are developed, top management's collective hunch about the state of the economy and its impact on the company's future business is a vital ingredient in plans for the future. In some cases the forecasted demand will exceed existing production capacity. When this occurs, sales forecasts must be predicated on capacity plans.

Generation of long-term forecasts of demand, sales, and economic activity is often the responsibility of marketing. The approach utilized by one major U.S. appliance manufacturing company provides a case illustration:

The marketing research manager spends two or three days a month reviewing the economic indicators that might aid in projecting cyclical turning points, predicting the economic climate likely to prevail during the forecast period, and factoring in industry information on inventories, product innovations, and so on, to yield a forecast of industry sales. This forecast is then compared and reconciled with the forecast developed by a senior marketing manager who generates company sales forecasts from detailed company information on consumer surveys; product, marketing, and pricing plans; and estimates of competitors' activities.

As another example of such forecasting, a large food products company is obtaining excellent results with a computer model that generates forecasts for grocery product sales.

Forecasts are developed that show expected sales by regions for existing products and new products not yet on the market. As the time period covered by the forecasts approaches, more and more detail is added.

For instance, the program used to generate quarterly forecasts contains information about planned advertising promotions and seasonal consumer habits. The computer-generated forecasts are carefully scrutinized by marketing managers and production planners, who may revise them to reflect such things as expected price trends, or perhaps a conviction that a given product will have a particularly strong regional appeal.

LONG-TERM CAPACITY PLANNING

Subsequent computer runs reorganize the revised forecasts to provide a breakdown of sales by warehouse territories. These warehouse territory forecasts form the basis of comprehensive production planning for the company's manufacturing plants, pointing up situations where additional capacity will be needed in the future.

Although forecasts come in many varieties (e.g., some cover different time periods, others contain different levels of detail), they are used by manufacturing mainly in setting future capacities. Examples of long-term capacity decisions based on forecasts are plant expansion, equipment acquisition, large work force additions, and major changes in inventory investment. (Inventory is included here, since it can be viewed as comprising stored capacity. A part on the shelf represents so many hours of capacity from a past period and eliminates the need for holding the same number of hours ready to serve a future demand.)

Continual Adjustment

Given forecasts of future demand, planning of capacity is not a one-shot problem that calls for one decision per year, but, rather, a problem that calls for constant review, fiddling, and adjusting. A well-designed system will provide many buffers to soften the impact of variations in demand, but even the best buffered systems will require basic adjustment from time to time through the purchase of plant and equipment, changes in the size of the work force, and major changes in inventory investment.

For a given company, a review of its recent history and current forecasts can often provide the guidelines for future action. A shop that has been choked with work for several months, that is having increasing difficulties meeting delivery deadlines, but nevertheless still has good labor efficiencies and control procedures, probably needs a boost in capacity. Well-organized information from a production planning and control system can provide a clue as to where the capacity is most needed, and the data can even aid in analyzing the effectiveness of alternative courses of action for providing capacity.

A large Connecticut company keeps details on its purchasing requirements and shop loads as far as three years ahead. This information enables management to consider carefully the long-range planning of inventory investment as well as production capacity. The use of shop load forecasts for inventory planning is an excellent example of what I referred to earlier as fitting together the parts of a production planning and control system.

Inventory control, when considered as a separate function, deals largely with individual item levels, order quantities, safety stocks, reorder points, and so forth. Yet one of the most important aspects of inventory management concerns the control of aggregate investment in all finished goods, subassemblies, work in process, and raw materials. The manager who understands the relationship of aggregate inventory investment to capacity, and who also has access to meaningful information on forecasted capacity requirements, can do a more effective capacity planning job than the manager who views the task as unrelated to other parts of the system.

The information flows in the capacity planning process are shown in Exhibit 1. Capacity planning is a high-level long-term planning activity that involves not only production managers, but also marketing, financial, and engineering managers. The element labeled "Production plan—capacity requirements to meet the plan" is the heart of this process of (1) developing long-term production plans on the basis of demand forecasts, and (2) determining the capacity required to support the plans.

At present, this task is normally not performed by a computer, but the computer can provide some of the input information. The general problem

Exhibit 1. Information Flows for Long-Term Capacity Planning

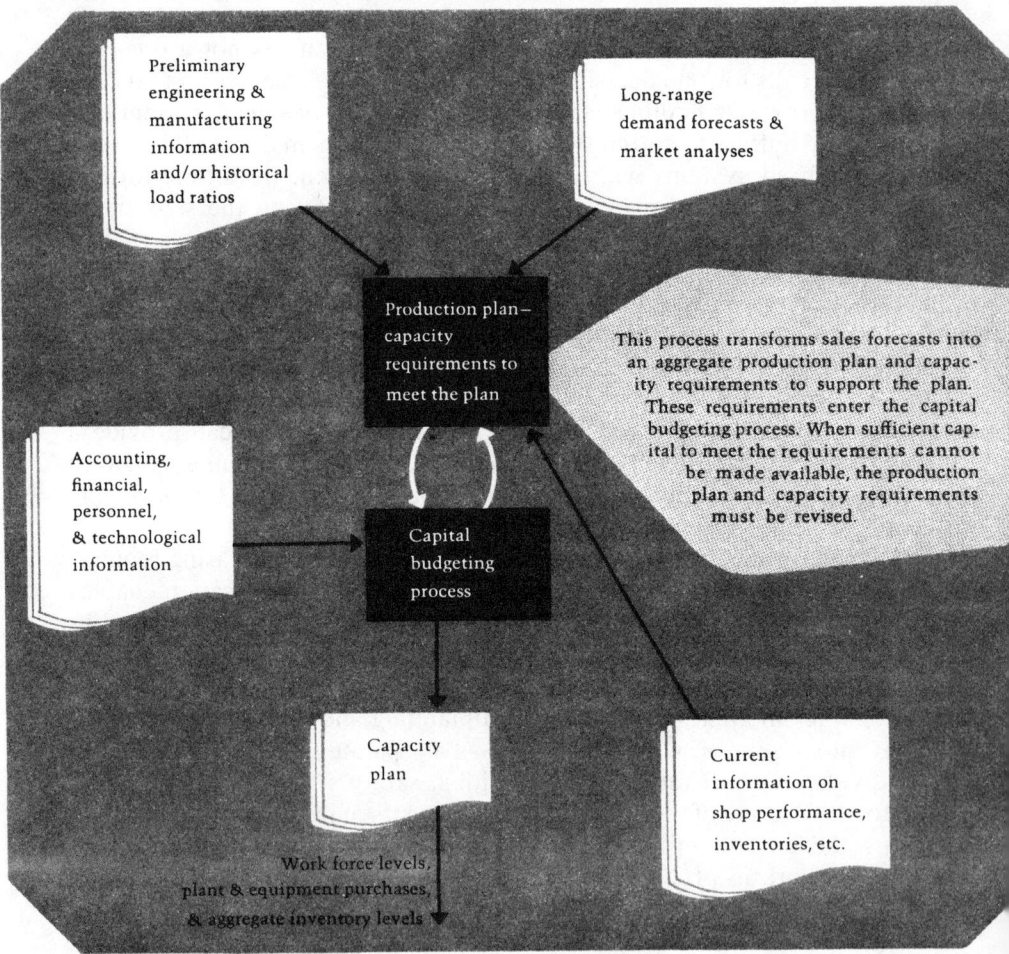

of capacity planning has attracted researchers working at the theoretical level, and it seems likely that within a few years computer-oriented approaches will be available for many practical situations.

The next section concerns the development of rough production plans from sales forecasts and capacity plans.

Master Scheduling

This is the activity that determines the overall production plan for the next several months. After forecasts of future sales have been given and capacity and aggregate inventory levels have been pretty well fixed, master scheduling assigns productive capacity to individual end products or customer orders. Space terminology provides an analogy. A space rocket, if it is to hit the moon, must be launched within a "window" of a few hours and miles per hour. The limits on the window at launching are much rougher than they are at the other end, when the rocket nears the moon; if the launch falls outside the window, the target will be missed.

Similarly, master scheduling is done within coarse limits, but the objective is to ensure that the actual load in the shop two or three months hence will fall within rather narrow limits. Shop load is usually expressed in hours per time period, but the limits I am referring to have an added dimension. An example should help to clarify this concept.

In a two-machine shop that works a regular 40-hour week, the optimum load scheduled for a given week should be 80 machine-hours of work. If more than 80 machine-hours of work are scheduled, overtime can be used, or some of the current week's work can be pushed ahead into the following week. If less than 80 machine-hours of work are scheduled, some work can be pulled back from the next week's schedule to fill up the currently available capacity. Importantly, since master scheduling is done considerably ahead of the time of production, the actual load in the shop will not fit the shop's capacity exactly, and some "push-ahead" or "pull-back" will inevitably exist.

If, on the one hand, considerable push-ahead is required because the master schedule calls for more production in a given time period than the shop is able to produce, work in process will build up, most jobs will fall behind schedule, and almost all work in the shop will become "rush" or high priority. On the other hand, if the shop is not scheduled to capacity, pull-back will result in some jobs being completed ahead of schedule and may result in subsequent unused capacity.

Thus the lower limit on a master schedule should be a load that in hours of work and delivery date requirements will keep the shop's capacity efficiently utilized on current jobs that are neither far ahead nor behind schedule. The upper limit should be the highest load in hours and the tightest load in delivery requirements that can be handled by the shop and still allow for the inevitable rush job from a highly regarded customer, the last minute engineering change or rerun because of scrap losses, and the other occurrences which cannot be predicted in advance.

Estimating Shop Loads

The key to successful master scheduling lies in the ability to forecast the lead times that will translate existing or prospective orders into an approximate shop load and delivery schedule. Often this is done by management intuition based, for example, on the knowledge that the shop cannot produce more than 20 model A machines per month, or that the shop load generated by a model B machine is approximately equal to the load created by two model A's. Intuitive planning is adequate for many situations, but the computer is making possible more sophisticated approaches.

Existing shop loads, or the forecasted load for orders already on the books, can often be a helpful input for determining the lead times required for master scheduling. The computer's ability to store a tremendous amount of detailed information in many instances means that approximate measures of aggregate shop load can be replaced with more detailed estimates of department, work center, or even machine load.

For example, a Midwestern manufacturer of metalworking presses has a program that compiles—from the master schedule for finished presses—weekly estimates of the total load in each work center that will be contributed by the individual component parts. This load information gives management a "20-week peek into the future, an ample length of time for problem solving."[1] With such an advance notice, not only can future master schedules be planned on the basis of recent actual performance, but potential capacity bottlenecks can be spotted and avoided through subcontracting or other capacity adjustments.

To assist in developing master schedules, a manufacturer of complex electronic and mechanical measuring equipment has a computer program that converts sales information on new or proposed orders into shop load long before detailed manufacturing information is available. The program is the result of a careful statistical analysis of the shop load contributed per sales dollar by various product classes. Although not 100% reliable in predicting the load consequences of a given order, this program is of great value in narrowing the limits on master scheduling and in making better estimates of the actual load hours and tightness in delivery times that the shop will encounter.

Master scheduling is graphically portrayed in Exhibit 2 as a two-step process. Sales forecasts and orders already on hand are first broken down into approximate shop loads, and then compared with the capacity plan and current shop information. The feedback information shown coming up from lower levels is a vital input to master scheduling.

Exhibit 2.   Information Flows for Master Scheduling

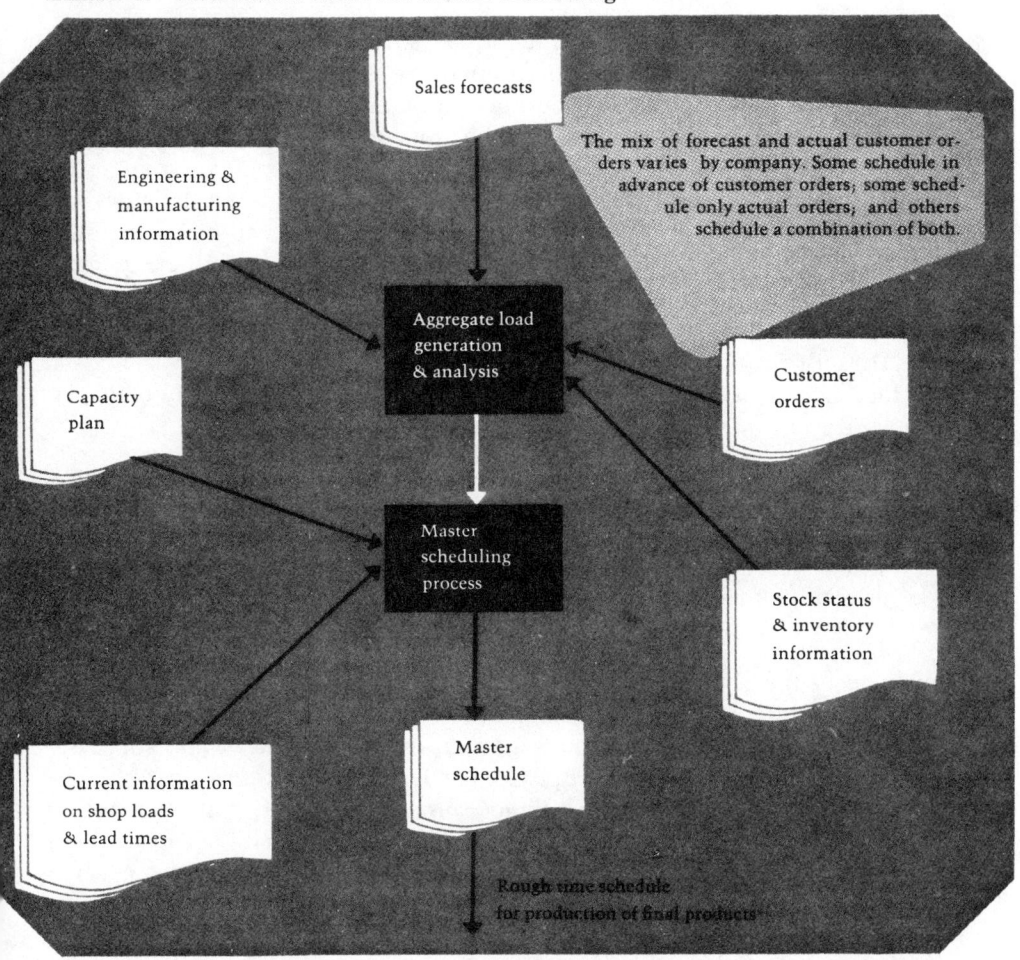

One illustration of the importance of this information is its application in modifying the standard lead times used to convert orders into shop load. Lead times vary directly with shop loads. Thus, on the one hand, a master scheduling system that overlooks actual shop loads and simply uses standard lead times may make commitments that exceed the shop's capacity to produce. On the other hand, the increasing of lead times when shop loads go up and no capacity adjustments are made may cause total manufacturing cycle times to rise beyond the point where the company can compete effectively. Here, again, we see a relationship between two elements of a system that calls for careful management consideration.

Inventory Control

Thus far inventories have been mentioned several times, and this is as it should be. Inventory control is not a separate entity but, rather, a pervasive factor that runs throughout any production planning and control system. A common system for the control of item inventories involves ordering replenishments in economic lots calculated according to one of a number of well-known "square root" formulas.[2] The lot is ordered when the stock on hand reaches a previously determined reorder point based both on estimates of the lead time required to fill the replenishment order and on the expected variability in demand during the lead time.

EOQ-Reorder Point System . . .

Not long ago, I had a conversation with a machine tool company manager who said,

> If we are in error on the economic order quantity [EOQ] figure, we are in no great trouble; but, if we are in error on our reorder point, we can be in serious difficulty. We'll run out of parts needed to meet our assembly schedule, or, equally bad, we will be carrying an unnecessary inventory of parts.

Unfortunately, because the reorder point is directly related to what is going on in the shop, it is difficult to get straight. A typical development occurs at a time of sharply rising sales, when stock items hit their reorder points sooner than normal, resulting in an increased load on the shop. As shop load rises, lead times go up. Longer lead times, in turn, yield higher reorder points that trigger replenishment orders still faster. If all such orders are allowed to get onto the shop floor, a spiraling situation can develop where nothing gets through the shop on time. When sales drop, the reverse spiral is just as bad, or even worse, to deal with.

. . . Versus Time-Phased Requirements

An alternative to the EOQ-reorder point system is time-phased requirements planning; this ties the control of piece parts and subassemblies to the assembly schedule of final products. With this system, parts can be manufactured in economic lots; but the timing of parts orders is based on a date that is exploded back from the date of the final product assembly, rather than on a reorder point.

In the simplest version of time-phased requirements planning, a parts order is placed a standard lead time ahead of the time when assembly is expected to deplete the stock on hand. As shown in Exhibit 3, the current supply of part #47469 is expected to run out during week 7 if no new replenishment orders are placed for the part. To prevent this stock-out and

INVENTORY CONTROL

Exhibit 3. Example of Time-Phased Requirements Planning

Week →	1	2	3	4	5	6	7	8	9	10	11	12	13	14	15	16	17	18	19	20
Master schedule			20				20		(40)	20				30						
Expected usage			40				40		(80)	40				60						
Stock on hand	64	64	24	24	24	24														
Planned parts order release (Lead time = 4 weeks; EOQ = 87 units)			87							87										
Planned receipts							87							87						
Planned stock on hand	64	64	24	24	24	24	71	71	71	71	31	31	31	31	58	58				

Milling machine
(2 required per machine)

"Try proposed order here"

"Additional usage contributed by proposed order"

"Expected run-out"

"Possible action to cover proposed order: place parts order for 49 units in week 5"

"Run out here if proposed order is accepted; need 9 units by week 9 and 40 more by week 11"

still allow the standard 4-week lead time for parts manufacturing, an order must be placed during week 3. This replenishment order for an economic lot of 87 units, along with a similar order during week 11, is shown in the exhibit.

Exhibit 3 also illustrates what can be accomplished when systems that support requirements planning, such as a bill-of-material processor and an inventory record system, are automated. The circled figures show how the system could handle the question: "What action is necessary if we accept an order for 40 #3A milling machines to be delivered in week 9?" Working through the bill of material for these milling machines, the system could identify all the parts required, check on-hand and on-order inventory status, and determine what action would be necessary to have the parts ready in time.

The action to handle the addition of the proposed order is triggered by an expected shortage of part #47469 in week 9. To cover this shortage, a parts order would have to be placed in week 5. More sophisticated logic could explore other alternatives, such as increasing the parts order placed in week 3, or moving the assembly lot in week 11 to a later week.

The automated bill-of-material handling also makes possible time-phased requirements planning by assembly level. Here, the due date for each component part of the final assembly is not the same, but reflects the actual time during the assembly and subassembly process when the part will be required. Thus a component part for a low-level (early in the assembly sequence) subassembly would be noted as being required several weeks ahead of an attachment to be installed late in the assembly process.

Replenishment Problem

A major difficulty with any inventory system is the variability of the load placed on the production facility. Replenishment orders—whether determined by assembly schedules, reorder points, or other rules—tend to arrive without regard to the shop's capacity to handle them. Because these orders represent shop load, the inventory system is linked directly to master scheduling and lower-level systems. Although most companies attempt to provide some protection against variable demand by providing buffer inventories and safety factors in lead time estimates, a more direct approach that ties inventory control to master scheduling and short-term scheduling can greatly assist in smoothing out the load caused by inventory replenishment orders.

An example of such an approach, which squarely faces the problem of tying together the control of item inventories and shop loads, is that developed by a Wisconsin industrial goods manufacturer.

Working from forecasts, shop load reports, and other information, company managers develop a monthly manpower plan that extends six months into the future. The manpower plan sets the basic capacity, whereas detailed machine load reports provide information for short-term capacity adjustments through personnel shifts and overtime. When the inventory system does not generate enough orders to maintain production at the planned rate, the company's computer can identify jobs that will bring the plant's load up to desired levels and still maintain a well-balanced inventory.[3]

This is a good example of how the computer has helped with shop load planning for the intermediate time range between long-term capacity planning and short-term scheduling. Later we will see how the computer, by focusing attention on critical jobs on the shop floor, can also provide help during actual production.

Short-Term Scheduling

As we have seen, master scheduling entails an aggregate plan that ensures that the demands on the shop's capacity will be reasonable. I use the phrase "short-term scheduling" to describe the activity that develops the detailed plans necessary to meet the delivery commitments represented by the master schedule.

The result of short-term scheduling is a set start and completion time for every component part for final products. If, for example, a particular lot of 20 milling machines is to be assembled during week 15, 40 feed levers may be scheduled to start in the shop at the beginning of week 11 and to be completed by the end of week 14. Parts for stock would be scheduled for completion by the time the current supply is expected to be depleted.

One other important output of short-term scheduling is an estimate of the load for the next few weeks or months for each machine or work center in the shop. Indeed, *machine loading* is a term often used for the activity I call short-term scheduling. Machine load estimates can be used to assist management in (1) assigning men to machines to balance the capacities of various work centers, (2) spotting and reducing bottlenecks in work flow, and (3) planning activities on the shop floor.

Short-term scheduling is an activity that is very much like master scheduling, but it has a shorter time horizon and involves considerably more detail. The distinction between master and short-term scheduling is academic in some companies, especially those specializing in made-to-order items or products with short manufacturing cycle times. Also, the computer's ability to make large quantities of detailed information easily available tends to encourage the use of detailed information at higher levels and thus blur the distinction even more.

The foregoing discussion brings us to a level in the production planning process where the information required is often extensive and detailed. The data generally include such things as a bill of materials, showing all component parts and assembly sequences; routings or operations sheets for all parts to be manufactured; lists of raw materials, tools, and fixtures required, as well as information on their availability and their condition; estimates of existing loads already scheduled against machines or work centers in the shop, or estimates of expected lead times or delays to be encountered as work moves through the shop; and estimates of the machining and setup time for each operation on each part.

The concern here is with developing a schedule for each component part and subassembly so that (1) all raw materials arrive on time, and (2) all parts and subassemblies arrive at the appropriate assembly or stock area in time to ensure that the final product will be ready for shipment on schedule. Short-term scheduling is usually accomplished by one of two basic approaches—capacity loading and loading to infinite capacity. I will discuss each of these approaches in turn.

Capacity Loading . . .

This fundamental approach begins with the specification of capacity for the scheduling period. Usually, capacity loading involves stating the number of machines to be manned in each department or work center and the number of shifts to be worked. (At a later date, individual decisions on overtime and so on may change these capacities slightly, but a reasonable estimate is good enough to start.) In the process of capacity loading, component parts requirements are exploded from a bill of materials, and the due date for each part is determined by backdating from the master schedule's due date for the final product.

After a due date has been assigned for each part, standard times for the individual manufacturing operations on the components are scheduled (loaded) in the appropriate work centers, starting with the last operation and allowing for normal material movement and delays. As each job's machining and setup time is added to a particular work center's load, a check is made to ensure that the addition of that job does not cause the total load to exceed the capacity of the work center. If the capacity is exceeded, the job is moved to another time period. If no available capacity can be found within the time required to get the job done on time, either the due date must be changed or capacity adjustments must be made through subcontracting or overtime.

Although this capacity loading approach is simple to describe, it is in fact quite difficult to implement. What about the important job that cannot find room because other less important jobs have been loaded ahead of it? How do you shift the loads around when capacity is exceeded? A point to keep in mind is that it is not necessarily the last job (the cause of the overload) that should be shifted to another week.

Several companies have developed imaginative approaches to capacity loading that deal with problems of this kind. One of the best programs reported is used by a large electronics company.[4] Its computer program loads to actual work-center capacity by scheduling backward, but the person using the program can exert considerable control over how the schedules are developed. Rush jobs can be specially coded, and instructions can be varied from "use full move and wait times" to "use no move and wait times," or even to "use more than one machine where possible." The program develops a provisional timetable according to the rules given by the scheduler, and prints a brief report that shows the scheduler whether the job can be handled within the time period originally specified.

However, if the job cannot be accommodated as desired, the scheduler has several alternative courses of action available such as the following:

SHORT-TERM SCHEDULING

☐ Try another priority.
☐ Cut the lot size (i.e., break the job into two lots).
☐ Try an earlier start time (if tools, material, and so on are available).
☐ Negotiate a later delivery date.
☐ Allow the program to overload one or more work centers after agreeing with the manufacturing superintendent and the foreman on an overtime plan or other capacity adjustment to handle the overload.

... Versus Infinite Capacity

The second common approach to short-term scheduling is a method whereby jobs are scheduled forward, beginning with the first operation at the earliest start date. Using standard move and delay times, load is accumulated as in capacity loading. The load is allowed to fall where it may, and no consideration is given to overloads that may develop. Such overloads are called to the attention of production planners, who attempt to adjust shop capacity to handle the work as scheduled or to rework the schedule to eliminate the overloads.

Loading to infinite capacity is definitely easier to program and implement than capacity loading schemes. There are other advantages, too. Infinite capacity loading focuses attention on bottlenecks and forces action when problems develop. Furthermore, scheduled manufacturing cycle times normally have less variance because the lead times used in developing the schedules never change. If actual manufacturing cycle times are to have low variance as well, however, the shop must have good procedures for adjusting capacity to handle overloads.

Capacity loading, on the other hand, usually presents the shop with a more level load and cuts down on the need for continual capacity adjustments. The price, however, is variance in the manufacturing cycle time or poorer delivery performance that will occasionally result from smoothing the peaks and valleys in demand. The feedback from capacity loading is better than that from infinite capacity schedules because the actual lead times accurately reflect what is likely to develop in the shop. This information on expected lead times can be passed upward to revise master schedules and other higher-level plans.

One problem with any loading approach is that unloading is a difficult task when plans are changed. When a customer cancels an order for a large machine, for example, all the individual loads contributed by the hundreds of piece parts already scheduled must be erased. This may leave idle capacity in several work centers, and questions then arise as to what to do with that capacity. A similar problem crops up when a customer changes the desired delivery date on a large order. These kinds of problems can be overcome only with great difficulty with manual systems, but the versatility of the computer makes possible the rapid readjustment of shop loads when changes are required.

A Statistical View

It is one thing to develop schedules, but quite another to run the shop so work will be accomplished according to schedule. I shall say more about this in the next section, dispatching and shop floor control, but for the time being let me state that the schedules resulting from the kinds of loading programs just described are usually not sufficient to determine how work will be done in the shop. This is so because of machine breakdowns, engineering changes, delivery promise changes, personnel absences, missing tooling, missing raw materials, and other roadblocks to following the schedule exactly as planned.

Thus the short-term schedule is at best a close approximation of what will transpire in the shop itself. This leads one to think about the level of detail required in short-term scheduling and to wonder whether rough, approximate procedures might be used to generate schedules, especially if production is carefully controlled on the shop floor.

Stanley Reiter, a former Purdue University economics professor now at Northwestern University, and I have developed a short-term scheduling program that takes a statistical view of the shop and attempts to ensure that promised delivery dates on new orders take into account the congestion the job is going to encounter as it works its way through the shop. The program was developed as part of a larger production planning and control system for a gear company whose scheduling problem differs somewhat from other problems I have described here in that virtually all work in the shop is for a specific customer order. Master scheduling to forecasts is not done. Instead, a promise date must be generated for each order accepted.

The program works from two basic data files: (1) estimated load by work center (about 200) and by week (six months ahead), and (2) estimated delay (waiting time) that a job will encounter in each work center for each week. The delays are calculated from both the load estimates and manpower (capacity) plans by mathematical formula. When a new order is received, the promise date is determined by (1) estimating the start date for the job, and (2) adding the setup, machining, and delay times for each operation in the job. The delay estimates are taken from the computer file for the appropriate work center and week, and—as the job is scheduled—the setup and machine hours are added to the existing load already in the file.

Every week new delay estimates are calculated on the basis of updated load estimates. If an order is loaded and then subsequently canceled, no unloading is done. Although this introduces known error into the system, there are probably other unknown errors that are at least as important. This does not mean that accuracy is unimportant. Rather, my point is that a quick approximate approach to setting promise dates is useful if the basic sentiments of the approach are in the right direction. To me, "in the right direction" means that a scheduling program lengthens delivery times when shop loads increase, and the output of the program gives management information for making capacity adjustments when necessary.

The delays generated by the program just described can provide management with a picture of where overloads are likely to develop. Thus management can take corrective action before the overload occurs. In fact, management can test the effect of adding capacity through overtime or extra shifts by recalculating the delays on the basis of proposed capacity additions in bottleneck work centers. Again—just so this point is not overlooked—general approximating methods may be adequate in some situations if the methods are properly designed and controlled, and if the shop is not constrained so tightly that it cannot respond to occasional errors in scheduling.

The general process of short-term scheduling is shown in Exhibit 4. Although the information flows may appear to be similar to those shown in Exhibit 2, the short-term scheduling process is based on considerably more detail than the master scheduling process and requires the handling of more supporting data. For example, the combining of master schedule information and customer order detail with engineering, manufacturing, and inventory information to yield data on net component parts requirements for short-term scheduling requires the processing of vast amounts of information. Although this supporting data processing task is large and complex, it should not draw management's eyes away from the main management task that is being supported—namely, the generation of a time schedule for the processing of orders in the shop to make efficient use of the company's capacity and to meet customer demands.

Dispatching Rules

Here are representative examples of the many different dispatching rules currently in use. In each case the rule is used to select the particular job to run next out of a group of jobs waiting for an available machine. Each rule is accompanied by a brief statement about the properties of the schedules that will result from its use.*

Simple Rules

1. *Earliest due date.* Run the job with the earliest due date. Results in good due date performance.

---

*For more complete performance results with several dispatching rules, see "The Development of a Factory Simulation System Using Actual Operating Data," *Management Technology*, May 1963, p. 1.

Exhibit 4. Information Flows for Short-Term Scheduling

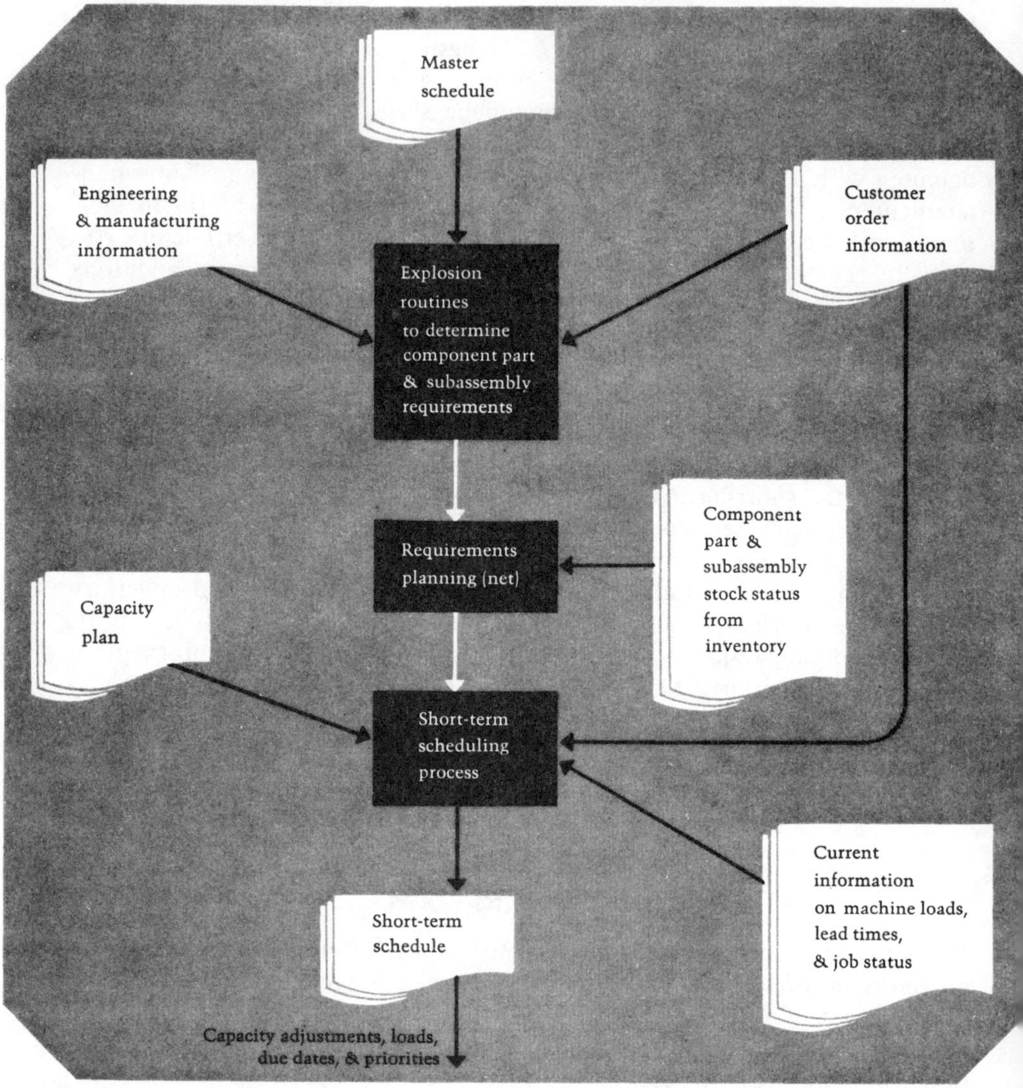

```
                        Master
                        schedule
                           |
  Engineering              |                    Customer
  & manufacturing          v                    order
  information  -----> Explosion      <--------  information
                      routines
                      to determine
                      component part
                      & subassembly
                      requirements
                           |
                           v
                                                Component
                      Requirements  <---------  part &
                      planning (net)            subassembly
                           |                    stock status
  Capacity                 |                    from
  plan  ------------>      v                    inventory
                      Short-term    <---------
                      scheduling
                      process       <---------  Current
                           |                    information
                           v                    on machine loads,
                      Short-term                lead times,
                      schedule                  & job status
                           |
                           v
                Capacity adjustments, loads,
                due dates, & priorities
```

    2. *First come, first served.* Run the job that arrived in the waiting line first. Results in low variance of manufacturing cycle time.

    3. *Shortest processing time.* Run the job that has the shortest setup plus machining time for the current work center. One of the best of the simple rules. Results in low in-process inventory, low average manufacturing cycle times, and good due date performance.

Combination Rules

1. *Minimum slack.* Slack equals calendar time remaining minus processing time remaining; or, slack equals due date minus present time minus setup and machining time for all remaining operations. Run the job with the least slack. Results in a very good due date performance.

2. *Critical ratio.* The critical ratio for made-to-order work is a slack-type rule. Critical ratio equals due date minus present time, divided by number of days required to complete the job order. (The figure for days required to complete the job includes setup, machining, move, and wait times.)

The rule for parts manufactured for inventory is critical ratio equals available stock over reorder point quantity, divided by standard lead time remaining over total manufacturing lead time.

This ratio compares the rate at which stock on hand is being depleted with the rate at which total lead time is being used up. The inventory part ratio is consistent with the made-to-order part ratio; one of its great advantages is that it allows a relative ranking of both kinds of work in any queue.†

Dispatching and Shop Control

The scheduling and control of work actually on the shop floor is a complex and demanding task. In most large shops there are thousands, or even tens of thousands, of job orders in process at any given time. Thus there is not only the problem of limited capacity, but also the problem of what individual operation can be done next, due to sequence constraints and material, tool, and machine availability. Even though every job order in the shop may have a scheduled start and finish time, the particular sequence for the individual machine operations remains to be determined.

Many management problems are caused by a lack of up-to-date information on the status of jobs in the shop. Often even the location of a job is not known, let alone whether it is ahead or behind schedule and what work remains to be done. In this section we shall see how a well-designed dispatching and shop floor control system can help to organize and rationalize the flow of work through the shop, and to ensure that the right jobs are being worked on at all times. We shall also see how timely reports can greatly assist management in the continuous decision-making process that is required to keep a shop going—that is, in controlling the level of in-process

---

†For more detail, see "How to Prevent Stockouts," *American Machinist/Metalworking Manufacturing*, February 17, 1964, p. 97.

inventory, tracking down troublesome jobs, and spotting difficult situations before they develop.

Importance of Timing

Dispatching is the shortest-term scheduling activity performed, because the scheduling takes place right in the shop where the decision has to be made on what job to do next. Some companies with good short-term scheduling or loading systems develop start dates for each individual operation to be performed on the job, and then dispatch on the basis of these scheduled start dates. In other words, when a machine becomes available, then, out of all the jobs waiting for it, the one with the earliest scheduled start time is chosen to be worked on next.

This approach works well if (1) the shop is able to follow the schedule with reasonable accuracy—that is, the jobs move through the shop without holdups for such things as missing material, tools, documents, or machine breakdowns; or if (2) the delay, move, processing, and setup times used to generate the schedule accurately reflect what is happening in the shop. Usually this is difficult, however, and the shop "drifts" off the short-term schedule between the time the schedule was generated and the time the job is actually run. This drift is caused by changes in the specification or timing of the job that may not have been rerun in the short-term schedule, the addition of last-minute rush work not included in the original schedule, and the previously cited random occurrences in the shop that prevent jobs from being run exactly according to the schedule.

To state it simply, time is the all-important ingredient in a production schedule. When timing of a schedule reflects the up-to-the-minute condition of the shop, materials flow smoothly through the shop, in-process work is completed and leaves the shipping dock at the right time, and machines are utilized efficiently.

Because of the vital importance of proper timing in the execution of work in the shop, dispatching has received considerable attention, and several companies have automated this function. All dispatching programs schedule work from a preplanned priority scheme that allows each job in queue for an available machine to be given a priority ranking relative to all other jobs competing for the same capacity.

The particular method for determining priority can vary from a simple ranking by due date to complex rankings that consider not only the scheduled completion date, but also the calendar and processing time remaining, the time required for the next operation, future congestion likely to be encountered, priority codes imposed by management, and even the current inventory status of the part.

The use of any dynamic dispatching rule—that is, one in which prior-

DISPATCHING AND SHOP CONTROL

ities change with the passage of time or the completion of work—requires that up-to-date information be maintained to keep priorities current. This inevitably means that data on each job must be maintained in computer files. With current information on job status and priority available in machine-readable form, dispatchers or forepersons can be provided with lists showing the current location and priority of all jobs in the shop. If these lists are sorted by work center, the person on the shop floor has not only a picture of all the work in each work-center queue, but also information that will enable good decisions to be made on which job to run next. Some companies are already going beyond supplying queue lists in particular work centers. I shall discuss two examples.

Daily Status System

A West Coast company that manufactures electronic systems has a dispatching system that captures up-to-the-minute information on job status and works ahead to predict what will happen during the next shift.[5] Two daily reports are prepared. The first (simplified in Exhibit 5) shows the jobs that are already in each work center at the beginning of the day and the jobs that are expected to arrive during the day. Jobs classified as "hot" or "rush" are listed before regular jobs. Within these categories, jobs are listed by priority (minimum slack per remaining operation).

Knowing what orders are already on hand and their relative priorities, and what jobs to expect throughout the day, the foreperson can plan work in an orderly fashion rather than simply react to a continuous stream of requests and demands from expediters, engineers, project managers, and other interested parties. As the day is planned, the foreperson can sequence the work in terms of efficiently matching the capacity and skill of the work center to the demands and the priorities of the individual job orders.

The second daily report (simplified in Exhibit 6) shows the operations to be performed on "hot" jobs that the computer's dispatching program predicts will be completed during the day. With this "hot order report" in hand, personnel from production control can identify and locate orders that should be expedited, assess their actual versus planned progress throughout the day, and ensure that the high-priority work at the top of the queues moves as rapidly as possible.

In order to generate reports similar to those shown in Exhibits 5 and 6, a dispatching program must actually simulate the operation of the shop for one day, keeping track of what jobs are assigned to which machines, move times, queues, priorities, and so forth. This is necessary, since the program must predict not only which orders will arrive in a given work center, but also when during the day they will actually arrive.

Exhibit 5. Sample Report of Orders on Hand, Their Relative Priorities, and Jobs Expected During the Day

```
                              ORDER STATUS REPORT
                              MACHINE GROUP 62-01
                              MANUFACTURING DAY 212

PRIORITY    PART     PREVIOUS   ARRIVAL   ORDER    PROCESSING   OPERATIONS   PROCESSING
           NUMBER    LOCATION    TIME      QTY        TIME         LEFT      TIME LEFT

         (ORDERS IN STATION)

HOT -3.8   324409     61-03     INSTA      212        2.3          03          8.6
HOT -1.9   448305     60-06     INSTA      172        3.4          02         12.3
    -5.5   104961     72-08     INSTA       53        1.3          13        147.2
    -2.3   665128     61-11     INSTA       87        2.4          06         38.9
    -1.2   401759     72-08     INSTA      200       12.1          00         38.0

         (INCOMING ORDERS)

HOT -9.2   489618     61-03     8-30       137        2.9          02         12.6
HOT -1.6   393474     72-07     9-00        52        0.8          01          5.5
HOT -0.3   506632     60-03     8-30       217       13.1          00
    -2.1   170300     72-08    10-30        62        3.2          06         24.2
    -2.5   463218     60-03    11-30        72        3.7          09        126.
```

Exhibit 6. Sample Report of Operations To Be Performed on "Hot" Jobs During the Day

```
                              HOT ORDER REPORT
                              DEPARTMENT 62-00
                           MANUFACTURING DAY 212

      PART                   ARRIVAL   PREVIOUS  ORDER  PROCESSING  OPERATIONS  PROCESSING  PRIORITY
      NUMBER   LOCATION      TIME      LOCATION  QTY    TIME        LEFT        TIME LEFT

HOT   324409   62-01         INSTA     61-03     212    2.3         03          8.6         -3.8
               68-02         8-30      62-01            6.5         02          2.1         -4.2
               72-08         1-00      68-02            1.8         01                      -6.8
HOT   432186   62-02         INSTA     68-03     57     1.2         06          13.4        -2.1
               72-08         1-30      62-02            1.4         05          12.0        -6.3
HOT   448305   62-01         INSTA     60-06     172    3.4         02          5.8         -1.9
               72-02         9-00      62-01            3.2         01          2.6         -0.2
                             2-30                                   00
```

Job Sequence Schedule

The gear company that I mentioned earlier, in the section on short-term scheduling, also has an interesting dispatching system.[6] Its program develops a schedule that specifies a detailed sequence of jobs by simulating the operation of the shop three days ahead, according to a minimum-slack dispatching rule. In most of the company's work centers, average setup times are used to develop the schedule, but in certain other work centers, where setup sequences are critically important (e.g., continuous heat treating furnaces), the program develops a schedule that takes into account the cost, in time, of going from one setup to another.

A simplified example of the output of this dispatching program is shown in Exhibit 7. Although the foreperson can work directly from the schedule without having to sequence the jobs on the available machines, there may be times when he or she wishes to change the suggested work sequence. If savings can be obtained on setup time, or personnel or machine capabilities better matched to the available jobs by changing the suggested sequence, the foreperson is encouraged to do so.

The question is: How much will such a change affect other parts of the schedule for this job? To answer that question, the foreperson is provided with information on where the job is coming from, when it is expected to be completed in the previous work center, where the job is going, and when it is expected to start at the next work center. With these data, the foreperson can negotiate backward and forward along the job's route, if necessary, or make a change based on the information at hand that will not affect the scheduling in other work centers.

The sharp-eyed reader may have noted a seeming discrepancy in the first line of the sample schedule in Exhibit 7. The job is not only scheduled to start in work center 1612 before it finishes its previous operation in work center 2483, but it is scheduled to start the next operation before it finishes in work center 1612. This is the result of a "line scheduling" feature whereby the first pieces in the lot of a high-priority job are allowed to move ahead to the next operation before the last pieces in the lot are completed in the current operation. This feature requires no outside control and ensures that high-priority work will move through the shop quickly.

In conversations with production managers who have installed successful new production control systems, one big advantage is invariably mentioned: the ability to keep constant tabs on job location and status. The tighter schedules, better delivery performances, and more efficient uses of personnel and machines that result from such systems are acknowledged and appreciated, but the big breakthrough for most managers is the readily available current information on job location and status.

However, this information does not come at zero cost, and again a supporting system must be considered. Job location and status information

Exhibit 7. Sample of Schedule That Specifies Detailed Sequence of Jobs

```
                          SCHEDULE
                       WORK CENTER 1612
                           4/10/68

                                              PREVIOUS          NEXT
PART      ORDER   START       FINISH  PROCESSING  WORK CENTER   WORK CENTER
NUMBER    QTY     TIME         TIME      TIME    + FINISH TIME  + START TIME

ADH1722    53   W  7-40A   W  9-00A    1.33    2483 W  8-00A   3053 W  8-50A
822185R   126   W 10-00A   W 11-00A    1.0     2514 M 10-30A   3024 TH 4-20P
AV859     235   W 10-00P   W 11-40P     .67    2482 W 10-30P   3031 F  3-10P
51619Y    525   TH 5-10P   TH 9-40P    4.5     2632 W  9-20P   3053 F  8-20A
ASF8231    27   F  1-50P   F  2-20P     .33    2483 F  9-30A   3023 F  4-00P
590874_    9_   F  2-20P   _          4.33     24__   __
```

is obtained in many companies through the use of remote data-collection devices on the shop floor. Data are entered into a remote device and transmitted to a central location, where they are usually punched into cards or paper tape that can then be read by a computer at frequent intervals to update the job information in the computer's files. Although such collection devices speed the process of data acquisition, they are not necessarily essential in all applicataions. Many companies obtain job location and status information from handwritten cards or forms from the shop that are key punched before entering the computer.

Profitable Payoffs

A well-designed dispatching system can do the following:

- [ ] Greatly reduce the amount of clerical work required to maintain current records.
- [ ] Implement dynamic priorities that can be updated without laborious hand calculation, sorting, and refiling.
- [ ] Improve the expediting function.

Nonetheless, the large dollar payoff often comes not from these advantages, but from other areas of activity on the shop floor. One important saving is the control of in-process inventory. Work in process consists largely of jobs in queues waiting for an available machine. These waiting lines are desirable for two reasons: (1) to provide a pool of work from which good setup sequences can be developed; and (2) to provide a cushion of work to prevent machine idleness. But, when the queues get too long, unnecessary investment in inventory is tied up, and the time required to get work through the shop rises.

A study at the New England plant of a large manufacturing company has shown that careful control of the amount of work in waiting lines can have a dramatic impact on overall shop performance.[7] The analysts who conducted the study convinced the shop's management and work force that a backlog on paper is just as real as a backlog in iron on the shop floor. (Several authors have stressed the importance of this step.)[8] Then, many jobs were removed from waiting lines in the shop and later were released to the shop a short time ahead of their due date. In addition, all new work was released in tight relation to due date. This control of work releasing and the use of a shortest-processing-time dispatching rule resulted in a one-third reduction in work-in-process inventory levels. Moreover, manufacturing cycle times were cut in half, much more reliable delivery time performance was obtained, and less finished goods inventory was required to satisfy the customer demand.

Another New England company which uses critical ratios for dispatching decided to hold back on releasing all new orders until the ratio indicated that the job was behind schedule. This action forced priority work ahead of jobs that were already on the shop floor and that were ahead of schedule because of early releasing under the old system, or because of due date and engineering changes. Although, at first, it may seem unwise to hold job orders until they are behind schedule, the critical ratio priorities and the considerably reduced work-in-process inventories have enabled the company to follow and expedite jobs, and still maintain a satisfactory performance on deliveries.

Another area of big payoff as a result of improved dispatching is capacity control. Reliable information on the work and priority content of waiting lines in the shop, and the current location and status of individual jobs, can greatly improve management's ability to make short-term capacity adjustments. The control of overtime is perhaps the best example. One company president recently stated that the yearly cost of the computer required to implement a new production planning and control system in the company easily has been paid by the savings in cutting excess overtime.[9]

Other capacity adjustments that can be made more efficiently with good location and job status information include moving an employee from one work center to another, routing a job to an alternate work center for a given operation, and changing the sequence in which the various job operations are performed. All these alternatives are designed to balance the flow of work through the shop and to minimize the number of bottlenecks in work flow at machines where large backlogs have piled up.

We should have clearly in mind, however, that the short-term capacity adjustments under discussion here are the finest of the fine-tuning operations. Remember that initial capacity plans should be laid months, and even years, ahead of actual production, and that opportunities to update and revise those plans to better fit actual conditions should exist at several levels above the shop floor control level.

Viewed in this manner, short-term capacity adjustment becomes a management opportunity (1) to make small moves in reacting to occasional mishaps and requests for unusual service, and (2) to remedy, in some degree, errors in high-level planning and scheduling. In other words, the shop will have the flexibility to move a few important jobs quickly, but not enough leeway to overcome the major shortcomings in plans from higher levels.

The Integrated System

At the beginning of this article, I emphasized the goal of tying together the component parts of production planning and control systems. This is done in Exhibit 8, which not only shows the various elements of a production planning and control system (and their relation to the enlarged parts pre-

Exhibit 8. Information Flows in a Production Planning and Control System

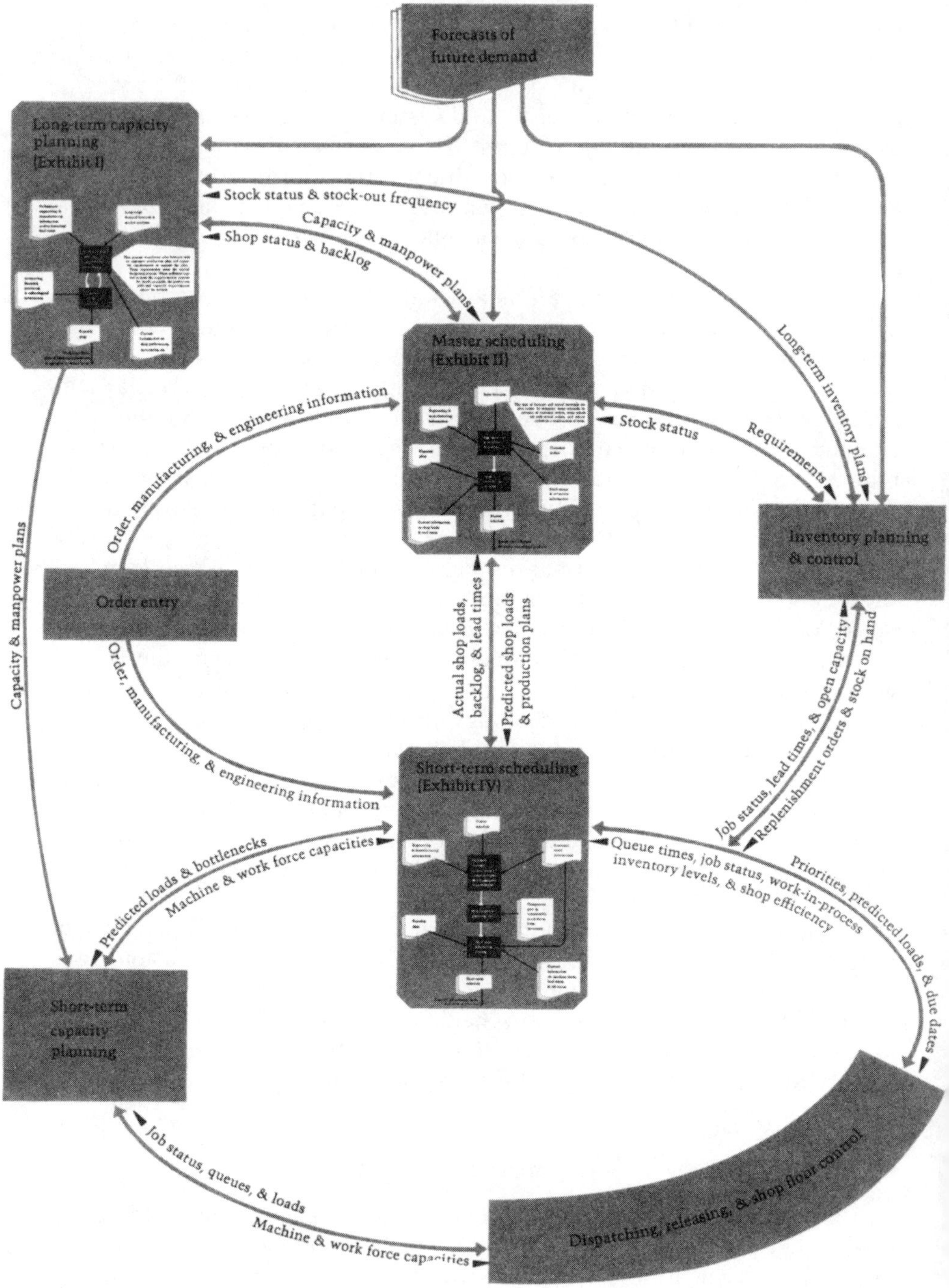

viously illustrated in Exhibits 1, 2, and 4), but also highlights the major information flows that tie the parts together. In studying Exhibit 8, keep in mind my early statement about high-level plans providing guidelines for lower-level planning and the importance of an upward flow of information to ensure that high-level plans are realistic.

Starting at the top of Exhibit 8, long-range forecasts are transformed into capacity plans to guide master scheduling. I use the term "guide" in this instance to mean the setting of approximate limits within which master schedules can be developed. As an example, consider a company whose capacity plans involve an expansion of facilities for turning large work pieces, such as generator shafts or steel mill rolls, with a simultaneous contraction in the milling and heat treating of small forged parts.

Master scheduling would be expected to begin to supply a load for the new facilities and gradually build up that load to utilize the new equipment efficiently. At the same time, master scheduling would act as a filter to keep some of the milling and heat treating work out of the system.

If the demand for milling and heat treating job orders continued, strong action would be needed. Either subcontracting could be used, or marketing could be urged to discourage some orders, so as to keep actual production within the guidelines of the capacity plan. In the opposite direction, information describing growing backlogs, lengthening manufacturing cycle times, and increasing difficulty in maintaining adequate inventories could signal the need for more capacity.

Toward the bottom of Exhibit 8, scheduling, dispatching, capacity adjusting, and inventory control are shown to be highly interrelated. Loads from short-term scheduling provide an advance warning of conditions that may develop in the shop, which releasing and short-term capacity planning may be able to heed. Dispatching information on the length, work content, and priority content of queues, and on the status of individual jobs, can signal situations where previous planning has not taken care of all bottlenecks and where immediate action is called for. In addition, dispatching information can be used in short-term scheduling to compare lead times, loads, and the shop's efficiency or actual performance against planned processing times or output expectations, and then to revise them as necessary.

Significant Progress

At this point in the discussion, some managers may well be thinking: If a production planning and control system is so fine a management tool, then why doesn't every production operation use an integrated approach like this?

Actually, from what I can see, recent progress has been significant, and many companies have made great strides in production planning and control. Much of this progress has been due (1) to the development of computer hardware and software that can handle vast quantities of information rapidly and inexpensively, and (2) to practical developments on parts of the system, such as forecasting, capacity planning, and dispatching.

Despite the impressive progress in fixing up the parts, however, few companies have developed systems that tie the parts together as well as they might. There are roadblocks to overcome. The information requirements for a comprehensive system are a major problem. Data on routings, standards, tooling, materials, and engineering changes must be not only available, but also reliable and accurate. The production planning and control system exists in relationship to other systems—financial, accounting, engineering, quality control, material handling, purchasing—and the coordination and standardization required to tie into these other systems is substantial.

But, again based on what I see, progress in the design and implementation of systems that support production planning and control is proceeding faster than progress on production planning and control systems themselves. Thus, as the pressures mount for better planning and tighter control, the roadblocks to a good system are getting easier to overcome.

Although not addressed specifically to production planning and control systems, a recent article gives evidence that many companies are committing substantial resources to this area.[10] In a comparison of computer use today and forecasted use three to five years in the future, the article shows "planning and control" applications more than doubling from a present [1968] 3% of total usage to a forecasted 7%. "Production" applications are also expected to grow from a current 19% of computer usage to 24% three to five years hence.

Conclusion

At the beginning of this article, I stated that the approaches I would discuss would relate to fabrication and assembly operations. Since this term encompasses a variety of organizations, some readers may have found significant differences between my charts and their own operations. Although there are differences in individual situations, each must deal with the basic problems of planning for capacity, such as setting delivery or due dates, developing and interpreting information on shop loads, scheduling the flow of work through the shop, and providing continuous, timely, and accurate reports for the comparison of planned and actual results.

My major point is that managers must look at decision making at all levels in seeking solutions to these problems. They must also recognize that good short-term performance results from an integrated and coherent set of decisions made over a long time span and not solely from more attention to short-term detail. The manager who translates general ideas and approaches into concrete specifications for the plant, and who then launches a well-planned and well-directed systems development effort, will be able to report such things as "on-time delivery performance up from 10% to 90%," "overtime savings which more than pay for the computer," "number of expediters decreased from nine to three," and "productivity jump of one third."

Notes

1. "Company Profits from Simple Data Processing System," *Foundry*, September 1965, p. 78.

2. See, for example, John F. Magee, "Guides to Inventory Policy: I. Functions and Lot Sizes," *HBR*, January–February 1956, p. 49.

3. See "Job Lot Scheduling: The Best of What's New," *Modern Materials Handling*, October 1966, p. 48.

4. See "Simplified Computer Control: The Mechanics of the New Production Control System," *Factory*, October 1966, p. 98.

5. *Ibid.*

6. C.E. Kramer, "Job Shop Finds Route to Smoother Delivery, Better Maintenance with New Scheduling," *Mill & Factory*, April 1966, p. 76.

7. "Small Backlogs—Big Control," *Executives Bulletin*, Issue #228, April 30, 1965.

8. See, for example, Earl R. Gomersall, "The Backlog Syndrome," *HBR*, September–October 1964, p. 105.

9. "Computer Planning Unsnarls the Job Shop," *Business Week*, April 2, 1966, p. 60.

10. Neal J. Dean, "The Computer Comes of Age," *HBR*, January–February 1968, p. 83.

19
Fit Production Systems to the Task

JEFFREY G. MILLER

Managers seeking ways to improve their manufacturing operations often look to computerized systems for solutions. Typically, though, expected benefits fail to materialize even after the computer systems are installed. The failure of these systems to yield expected benefits is usually ascribed to any of a number of causes, such as inaccurate data or an absence of top management commitment. In actuality, the problems that plague most manufacturing control systems can usually be traced to the failure of managers to match their companies' manufacturing control approach to overall organizational structures and company goals. Simply revamping manufacturing systems is not enough; the relationship of the manufacturing control process to the rest of the company must be recognized. The author identifies those aspects of manufacturing control processes that require the closest attention in coordinating manufacturing with other company requirements. He also provides guidance for overcoming common problems and improving manufacturing control systems.

Rising concern about such problems as declines in productivity, excess inventories, missed shipments, customer complaints, materials shortages, and cost inflation has encouraged manufacturers to develop integrated computer-based systems to help control inventory levels and materials flows. But for many companies, these supposedly modern systems offer little improvement over the manual systems that preceded them.

According to one survey, only 44% of the respondents felt that their new computerized manufacturing control systems were cost-effective.[1] Other estimates of the percentage of companies that have expressed disappointment over their newly installed systems are as high as 50%.[2] Some professionals in the field express doubt that the track record is even that good.

The high failure rates for manufacturing and materials control systems have been ascribed to such problems as bad forecasts, a lack of management commitment, and the use of either too much or too little prepackaged software. The thesis of this article is that the basic causes of failure are far deeper and more fundamental, stemming from a failure by managers to carefully examine the implications of design decisions about manufacturing control processes for their companies. Managers have discounted the impact these decisions have on organization structure, performance measurement, and the role of manufacturing in companies' competitive strategies. When these factors are ignored, system design and implementation tend to become futile exercises in changing the strategic manufacturing task to fit some textbook view of the correct system.

This article addresses the role of general management—general managers and top functional managers in manufacturing, finance, engineering, and marketing—in ensuring the successful design and implementation of manufacturing and materials control systems. (I shall refer to these integrated systems collectively as manufacturing control systems.) The article focuses on ways of fitting the system to the task by discussing how systems, strategy, and organization are related; identifying some key design decisions that often require management's close attention; and reviewing one company's approach to organizing and managing a successful manufacturing system.

Anatomy of Failure

The causes of manufacturing control systems failures are often elusive. Sometimes, major problems in achieving stated cost, shipping, and inventory reduction goals are obvious signals that a system has failed to achieve what was planned. But more often, the individual problems with systems are small but voluminous, contributing to a feeling that manufacturing somehow just isn't working right, that it is vulnerable to any small disturbance that may knock it into a tailspin—that no one is truly in control. Postmortems of these failures typically lead to the following litany:

☐ *Poor inventory record accuracy.* "We all know the adage 'garbage in, garbage out' (GIGO) as it applies to basic data for computer-based systems."

☐ *Bad forecasts.* "Marketing provided poor or delayed forecasts."

☐ *Poor engineering data.* "The design engineers were too busy interfering with our vendors or with manufacturing to provide bills of material needed to drive the system."

☐ *Lack of top management commitment.* "I can't talk my boss into making the marketing forecast better and engineering into giving us good bills of material."

☐ *Unreliable vendors.* "We can't get them to deliver on time or change their schedules, no matter how good our system is."

☐ *Lack of involvement.* "The systems department didn't get the right people involved."

☐ *Prepackaged software.* "We're unique; our mistake was to use prepackaged software that didn't fit our business well."

☐ *Customized software.* "We never got the system off the ground; we spent all that time and money reinventing the wheel."

☐ *Poor organization.* "No one person had responsibility or power to solve the 'whole problem.'"

☐ *No education.* "We didn't spend enough time or effort in training."

Like the blind men with the elephant, managers and specialists try to pinpoint the true identity of their problems—to find out why, after spending all that money, things are no better than they were before. But on close analysis, it usually becomes apparent that this long list of supposed causes of failure is really a list of symptoms for a larger problem—a problem that can be traced to the failure of managers to ensure that the systems developed are consistent with the strategic and organizational requirements of the company. To illustrate, consider the following examples.

A medium-sized components manufacturer installed a sophisticated materials requirements planning system designed to identify the due-date priority of work flowing through the factory. But the company continued to be troubled by poor delivery performance, high inventories, and low productivity. At first, the problem was blamed on unreliable vendors and poor data accuracy. But close analysis showed that forepersons and supervisors were simply not using the due-date priorities to sequence the work. Since the individual factory departments were measured on the dollar value of completed work, they ignored the due-date needs of customers and downstream departments to work first on the jobs with the highest dollar value. It's little wonder forepersons and supervisors failed to keep accurate data—due dates didn't count, dollar value did.

An electronics company implemented a new manufacturing and materials control system designed to make schedule commitments on a first-come, first-served basis that favored the company's numerous small and often unprofitable accounts. But the marketing strategy was oriented to serving a few selected key accounts that provided high volume and market potential. The resulting fiasco led to serious marketing problems. Yet, when these problems first appeared, the blame for them was ascribed to the inability of marketing to make accurate forecasts. The company lost valuable time working on the wrong solutions before the real problems became apparent.

ANATOMY OF FAILURE

A heavy equipment manufacturer started up a new plant to make a new product using a new process technology. It borrowed computer software from a sister division and tried to replicate the other division's approach to manufacturing control. When the new plant started to fall behind in its delivery commitments, the blame was initially placed on start-up problems that included equipment failures, labor difficulties, and so on.

After suffering through a disastrous period of sharply curtailed earnings directly due to the delivery problems at the new plant, management began to change its assessment of the problem. In retrospect, it saw many of the start-up problems as normal for any new operation. Management concluded instead that the problem was in the manufacturing control system, which had been designed for use in a stable labor-intensive line flow type of operation. When used in an unstable capital-intensive jobshop environment, it gave off false signals and, after the inevitable start-up problems occurred, proved unresponsive in helping steer the operation back on course.

Underlying Factors

These examples show why management commitment to effective control systems development is not enough, for beyond the computers and the software of manufacturing systems is the manufacturing control process itself. Here, the relevant variables are not bits and bytes and other technical trivia but reward structures, decision points, motivation, the assignment of responsibility, strategic goals, and basic manufacturing policies. The first company's systems were fine; people weren't motivated to make the right decisions. In the second example, general management hadn't bothered to make its market strategy explicit at operating levels. In the third example, the company tried to change its task to fit an existing system.

Effective manufacturing control systems can't exist where there are ineffective manufacturing control decision processes. Effective processes are those that are consistent with company goals and organizational mechanisms. I believe that it is management's job to define these administrative processes and to ensure that they are consistent with the company's objectives and organization. It is the job of the systems and functional specialists to ensure that the systems support the execution of these processes.

Too often, both general management and systems and functional specialists fail to do their part of the job. General management is typically reluctant to provide more than moral support to systems and process design efforts. Perhaps this occurs because, as Wickham Skinner has pointed out, manufacturing is perceived as "requiring involved technical skills and a morass of petty daily decisions and details,"[3] presumably beyond the scope of high-level managers. When this happens, the specialists are left to cope with organizational and strategic connections in systems and process design that are beyond their scope, with predictably tragic results. Just as tragic are those instances where the specialists are at fault for designing a system to support a set of idealized decision processes that are based more on the parochial views of software vendors and how-to books than on the strategic imperatives of the businesses they serve.

An Array of Choices

General managers and systems specialists play important roles in ensuring the development and implementation of successful manufacturing control systems. These roles both require a broad view of manufacturing control systems as support mechanisms for administrative processes that should be tightly linked to the manufacturing policies, organization, and competitive posture a company has chosen. Both must understand and carefully consider the important array of choices involved in setting out the specifications for any manufacturing planning and control processes and systems. These choices include decisions about architecture, priorities, reflexes, focus, technology, and organization.

Systems Architecture

The first choice in developing systems specifications involves the basic architecture of information and decision flows in relation to the physical flows being controlled. Exhibit 1 shows two different types of architecture that illustrate the extremes over which alternatives might range.

At one extreme are completely decoupled architectures, characterized by semiautonomous processes for each major subunit within the supply chain and very often by large "decoupling" work-in-process inventories among subunits. Coordination across these subunits in decoupled architecture is usually achieved by an overall "global" process.

In contrast, coupled architectures process nearly all manufacturing information and decisions through a global coordinating system; little, if any, local autonomy exists. (The direct communication lines through to vendors and distributors shown in part B of Exhibit 1 illustrate the extremes to which some companies carry the concept of coupled architecture.)

It is not unusual for specialists to see architectural decisions as technical ones (in their lingo, "bill-of-materials structuring decisions"). But choosing an architectural structure usually involves difficult trade-offs of concern to general management. For example, sometimes the choice is closely related to intangible aspects of management style. Companies that grant much autonomy to individuals, divisions, and plants find attempts to centralize control difficult to accept.

In other cases, the trade-offs involved in making architectural decisions affect the basic performance characteristics of the company. For example, one manufacturing company—let's call it Company A—based its competitive strategy on charging a premium price for custom-designed products while

Exhibit 1. System Architecture

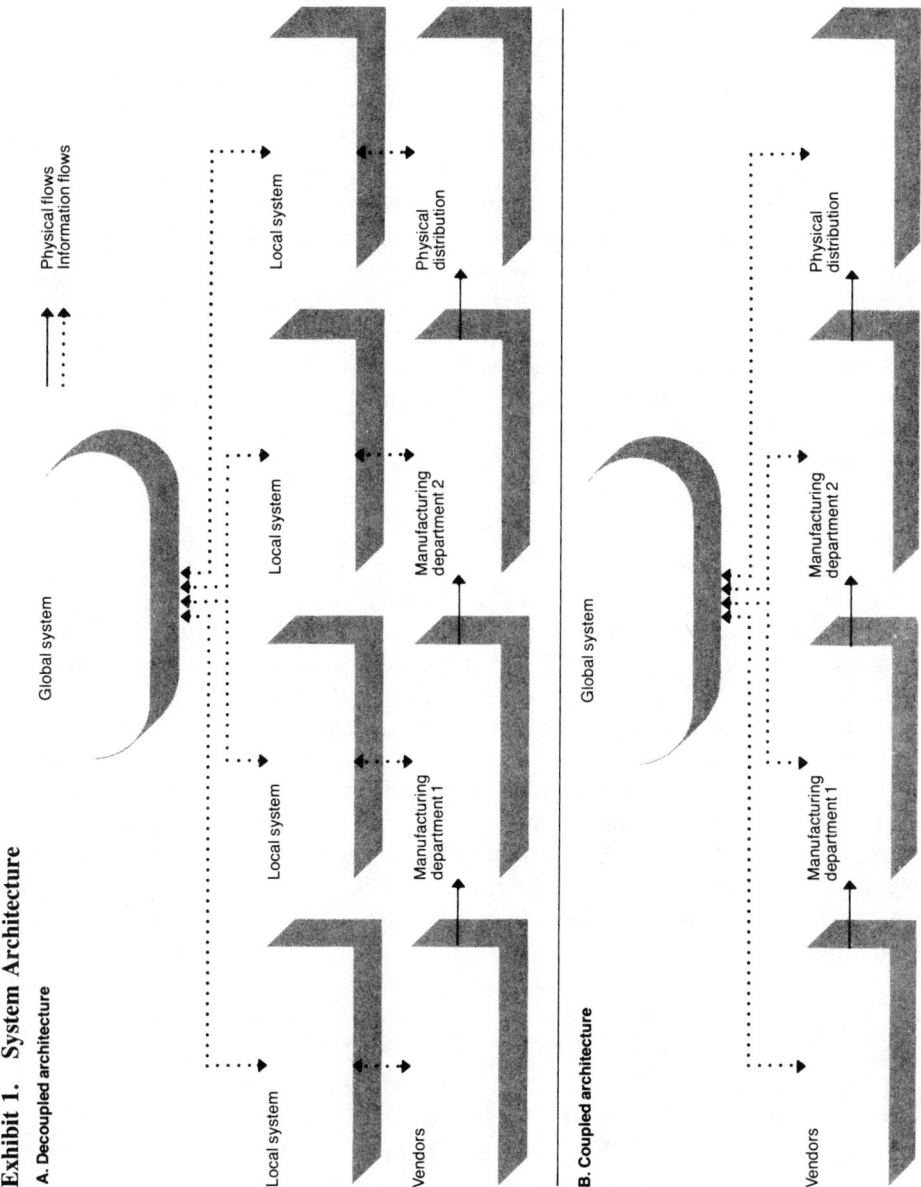

providing rapid response to customer design, due-date, and quantity changes. To obtain the flexibility required to make these rapid changes, the company's processes and systems were designed to tightly link parts requirements as they flowed through its multistage manufacturing operation. In this way, the impact of a due-date change on a finished product was immediately transmitted into a due-date change for up to 15 intermittent process steps and directly through to a vendor's casting plant located 100 miles away.

In contrast, a second manufacturer—Company B—competed by emphasizing low costs instead of service. But its system was designed to decouple the production departments within its factory from one another. Proposed due-date changes for a final product were not necessarily transmitted into due-date changes in downstream departments. Although this company was far less responsive to customer due-date changes, its costs were very low because the cost penalties associated with disruptions and schedule changes were minimized.

Setting Priorities

In plants and warehouses around the world, staff analysts, forepersons, supervisors, and sometimes workers are faced with a recurring decision: which of the various jobs, work tickets, orders, batches, lots, shipments, or whatever else that *could* be worked on *should* be worked on next? The people on the front line of manufacturing management who make the flow of goods and products happen must somehow assign priorities to the tasks.

Sometimes the determination of priorities is simple. On high-volume assembly lines, for example, the only choice is to work on the line's next item. But in the typical batch-oriented factory and even in the shipping and stockroom operations of high-volume assembly plants, literally hundreds of different ways exist for assigning priorities to the work, among them the following:

☐ *Most important customer.* "Complete work first for the most important customer, especially if the work might be late."

☐ *Highest sales value.* "It's the end of the month! Ship items with the highest sales value so we'll meet the financial projections."

☐ *Least cost.* "Work on a job that can use the same machine setup to save labor and use capacity more effectively."

☐ *Earliest due date.* "Work on the jobs in order of their due dates to get every job done on time (or done equally late)."

☐ *Satisfy the most customers.* "Work on all jobs or orders that take the least time so that we will be able to satisfy the most customers."

AN ARRAY OF CHOICES

Although priority work decisions are often made at low levels in an organization, general management's interest in them is obvious. The sum total of the thousands of priority work decisions that may be made each day in a large factory determines that factory's output. And the way in which priorities are set helps determine plants' performance characteristics—whether they are best at producing products on time, producing them at least cost, or meeting budgetary goals.

General management has two main roles in linking priority considerations to systems design decisions. The first ensures that the manufacturing control system is structured so that priorities are set at the proper organizational level. To distinguish this decision from the architectural decision referred to earlier, note that an organizational hierarchy is not necessarily the same as a hierarchy of subsystems and plans. In some companies, changing environments and the importance of the trade-offs involved might argue for flexible priority setting at the very highest organizational levels. In others, company size and operational complexity might make data collection and centralized scheduling so arduous that priority setting is pushed down to lower levels in the hierarchy. The approach decided on will certainly affect the type of information that is developed to support and execute priority decisions.

The second part of the general manager's role ensures that both the company's manufacturing control and performance measurement systems reinforce the use of priority-setting mechanisms that facilitate the accomplishment of competitive strategies. What is most important? Lowest costs? Dependability in delivery? Speedy delivery? Meeting the budget? It is impossible to be a superior performer in all these areas simultaneously. Trade-offs are involved and that is what assigning priorities is all about.

Consider the two companies—A and B—used previously to illustrate different approaches to architecture. They incorporated their strategic needs and goals into the priority-setting mechanisms provided by their systems in different but predictable ways.

In Company A, which emphasized fast response and customer service, decisions about scheduling priorities were based on customer needs. Forepersons used a due-date-based priority rule to schedule work. The rule was programmed on-line into the computer so that a change in customer due dates could immediately be communicated to the shop floor to allow for revised priority decisions. This use of due dates to sequence work was quite consistent with the driving force in this company's competitive strategy—the emphasis on customer service. The fact that this company's priority rules were fixed in the computer software was also consistent; the approach offered a very fast and efficient way of making rescheduling decisions.

The scheduling priority decisions in Company B were made in a substantially different way but in a manner consistent with its competitive posture. Its prime concerns were ensuring low costs and meeting budgeted efficiency goals. Customer needs were a lesser consideration. Rather than employ programmed decision rules to make fast responsive decisions at low levels, this company used a rather ponderous process of discussion, negotiation, and occasional modeling at higher organizational levels to ensure the development of least-cost schedules. Instead of using Company A's narrow base of information for making these decisions, Company B's system generated a broad base of cost and schedule information to aid in its priority-setting tasks.

Differing Reflexes

The two examples just discussed were opposites with respect to a third important choice in manufacturing control systems design—reflexes. Company A could turn on a dime. It could shift directions rapidly in response to customer requests, for two reasons. The first reason was physical—the company had sufficient extra capacity, inventories, and other physical resources so that it was positioned to respond to almost any physical request. The second reason related to the reflexes of the manufacturing control system. They were fast, conditioned by on-line computer capabilities and the short planning cycles that were employed.

In contrast, the reflexes of Company B's manufacturing control system were purposefully slowed to protect manufacturing from costly changes. The planning cycle here was relatively slow. Manufacturing plans were reviewed each month and manufacturing schedules were reviewed weekly; in Company A both plans and schedules were reviewed almost continuously. Company B did not have an on-line computer system to instantaneously report changes throughout; it instead employed a less expensive but more cumbersome batch computer system.

Finally, Company B protected itself from costly market-initiated changes by employing so-called planning fences in conjunction with its manufacturing control system. A planning fence of a certain duration, say, 12 weeks, meant that no changes in production schedules were allowed within that period. The frozen schedules within the planning fence horizon provided manufacturing with the ability to level out work loads and the stability required to work on attaining the lowest possible costs.

Issue of Focus

A fourth important choice in manufacturing control systems design is the way the decision process and information system is adapted to the needs of individual product lines or groups. The issue here, as with the architectural decision (for a coupled or decoupled system), is centralization versus decentralization. The difference is that while focus addresses the extent of decentralization horizontally, across product lines, architecture addresses the extent of decentralization vertically, between sequential steps in the procurement-production-distribution chain.

Ideally, focus decisions for manufacturing control systems would not be an issue. The ideal "focused factory"[4] would be designed to build only one product or product group so that the compromises which result when many product lines with different needs are built in one plant could be avoided. Unfortunately, real economies of scale as well as the fixed nature of production facilities often make such ideals difficult to realize over the short run. For many companies, the best that can be accomplished is to control manufacturing within the same facility to meet the requirements of individual product lines as closely as possible. This is where focused manufacturing control comes in.

Managers must first decide on the critical needs of individual product lines. Once these needs are clearly established, they must then decide how to set out the design of the system to reflect important differences. Many options are available. Some companies develop independent systems for major product lines or groups. For example, one successful company that emphasizes new product development has one system for new products and another for mature products (both produced in the same factory). Other businesses may ignore focus to obtain economies of scale, if these are important.

A third approach compromises by partially focusing on one or more features of architecture, priority decisions, or reflexes in systems design. For example, Company A (with a customer-oriented market strategy referred to previously) had six product lines produced in the same factory. Each line focused on a different type of customer, who often had different needs and ordering patterns. This company focused its systems by creating six essentially independent order entry/assembly scheduling systems whose main common feature from a computer standpoint was a shared database. Company B, in contrast, treated all its customers the same from an order entry/assembly scheduling system standpoint. It sought economies of scale at the expense of differentiation.

Importance of Technology

Computers offer only one so-called technology available for manufacturing planning and control. They can, for example, provide a fast method of centralizing information about demands and the current status of manufacturing departments and purchase orders. Given the proper assumptions, computers can develop plans and time-phased lists of required activities.

However, "organizational technologies" are also used in manufacturing control systems. Examples of these technologies might include regular meetings in which department supervisors informally compare information and negotiate requirements and plans. These technologies are often far more than what might be referred to as "manual" systems. Such approaches can usually accomplish a more diverse set of tasks than computers. Often, one technology dominates in one part of the system, whereas another dominates elsewhere. Typically, both organizational and mechanical, or computerized, technologies are used simultaneously in the same part of the system.

An important factor in determining high or low use of organizational technologies in manufacturing control systems is the relative uncertainty and complexity of the manufacturing environment (see Exhibit 2).[5] Two types of technologies can be described as follows:

1. Systems that emphasize organizational technologies seem to be most useful when suppliers, specifications, demands, production performance, or production goals are unpredictable and uncertain. In these instances, one may assume that the simple planning assumptions on which computers must rely are too unstable for effective computerization. Systems for stable environments are less likely to emphasize the use of organizational techniques such as meetings or informal liaisons, although all systems must, of course, employ them to some extent.

2. Systems that emphasize mechanical, or computerized, technologies seem to be most useful when the manufacturing environment is highly complex (many parts, suppliers, products, processes). When there are fewer things to coordinate in manufacturing and procurement, mechanical systems are less likely to dominate.

In most companies, both types of technology are employed with different degrees of emphasis at various junctures in the manufacturing control sys-

Exhibit 2. Complexity and Uncertainty and the Use of Mechanical or Organizational Technologies

		Complexity	
		High	Low
Uncertainty	High	Systems are: 1 Highly mechanical 2 Highly organizational	Systems are: 1 Less mechanical 2 More organizational
	Low	Systems are: 1 Highly mechanical 2 Less organizational	Systems are: 1 Less mechanical 2 Less organizational

tem. Both Company A and Company B, to continue the previous examples, used both approaches extensively but differently. Both companies made use of computer technology to handle the immense amount of data required to track the many vendors, customers, orders, and parts. Both companies also faced significant uncertainties from differing sources and tried differing solutions.

Company A's major source of uncertainty was external—from those customers whose demands were considered to have top priority. To accommodate the varying demands of these customers, this company continually hedged on equipment and materials acquisitions. Top management dealt with the uncertainty involved in making these facilities and materials decisions through a planning process that made heavy use of organizational technologies. On the shop floor, though, the instructions of the computer dominated.

In contrast, Company B's use of organizational technologies was almost reversed; they were extensively used in low-level shop floor decisions and not very heavily used in higher-level facilities and materials decisions. The company's low-cost-oriented policies effectively insulated the factory from external uncertainties. The uncertainty was generated internally at lower levels as departments negotiated their priorities and cost trade-offs around scarce resources.

Organizational Responsibilities

A detailed discussion of general responsibility assignment patterns for manufacturing personnel and the relationship of these patterns to systems and performance measures is beyond the scope of this article. The previous discussion should have convinced the reader that all these issues are related in important ways. One organizational issue deserves some special attention, however, since it is directly related to manufacturing systems. The issue concerns assigning responsibility for the integrity of the control process per se.

A system, by definition, is more than a grab bag of ad hoc activities. It is a well-defined and interrelated set of administrative processes that are individually incapable of holding themselves together. The pieces of a system must be held together by individuals with responsibility for ensuring its proper operation or integrity. Controllers are usually responsible for cost systems, financial officers for financial planning systems. Who should be responsible for manufacturing control systems?

A recent analysis of the behavior of a number of manufacturing companies shows that many have joined the trend toward developing materials management departments for maintaining systems integrity.[6] In contrast to more decentralized approaches to managing manufacturing operations, such as parceling out responsibility to production planning, purchasing, distribution, engineering, and other departments, materials management organizations provide a way of integrating the many parts of a manufacturing control process.

However, when the effectiveness of important relationships handled outside the context of a manufacturing control system, such as purchasing-engineering relationships to develop product specifications, is very important to company success, the centralization of responsibility in the hands of an integrated materials management department can be counterproductive. Here again, we see the need to consider the trade-offs before deciding on a key element in the control process.

Anatomy of Success

Exhibit 3 contrasts the important design choices of the two companies used throughout this article to illustrate how individual companies adapt their systems and control processes to meet strategic requirements. A technical analysis of their approaches to controlling manufacturing shows that both employ a materials requirements planning (MRP) system. In fact, both companies could feasibly employ some of the same computer software. But the fundamental differences in the systems each company uses demonstrate how very superficial such narrow technical definitions can be.

In addition to the six important design choices for manufacturing systems discussed in the previous section, nearly every manufacturing company has other unique choices that are central to the effectiveness of its systems. The presence of these other idiosyncratic choices suggests that general management cannot focus only on the six areas discussed in this article. Indeed, their presence suggests that general management must develop a process for identifying all the key design issues that should be brought to their attention.

The particulars of the systems design process for involving top management at appropriate junctures vary from company to company. But the experience of a division of a large electronics company that was successful in its system efforts illustrates what I see as the key features of effective processes and management's role in them.

First, the general manager developed an explicit statement of the division's competitive strategy and identified the areas in which manufacturing performance had to excel for this strategy to succeed.

Second, the general manager and top functional managers developed the general specifications for the manufacturing control process. Several important design decisions had to be made. The most difficult ones were related to architecture, reflexes, focus, and organization. The company decided to confront some difficult cost and competitive problems by coupling the stages of manufacture more tightly while sacrificing individual product line sensitivity (focus). These choices were made and implemented with due

Exhibit 3. Contrasting Strategic Choices

	Company A	Company B
Competitive strategy	Customer service strategy	"Price" strategy
Key manufacturing task	Position resources to respond rapidly to customer requests and changes	Produce products at lowest costs; emphasize labor efficiencies
Architecture	Coupled system; control of flows highly centralized	Decoupled system; control of flows decentralized
Priorities	Schedule priority rules based on customer due dates	Schedule priority decisions based on negotiation and analysis rather than simple rules. Priorities heavily weighted to low-cost schedules at expense of responsiveness
Reflexes	Fast; on-line system, short planning cycles, no planning fences	Slow; batch system, long planning cycles, uses planning fences
Focus	Highly focused; six product area subsystems at assembly	Unfocused; sacrifies individual product line differences to economies of scale
Technology	Highly mechanical except at highest levels where uncertainty is absorbed	Uses mechanical technologies throughout, but mainly relies on organizational technologies even at lower levels
Responsibilities	Responsibility for system integrity and maintenance highly centralized with a materials manager	Responsibility for system integrity and maintenance diffused

allowance for required changes in performance measures, budgetary and forecasting procedures, and other cross-functional concerns.

The design process for information systems was begun only after the above steps to design the administrative process were completed. General management was not as directly involved here, but the detailed design process was formulated so that it could be alerted when its direct involvement was required. Task forces were formed to develop and implement detailed specifications and policies for the major subsystems corresponding to major manufacturing control processes such as master scheduling, materials requirements planning, inventory control, capacity management, and shop floor control. The task forces were composed of a variety of managers experienced in manufacturing, materials, systems, and sometimes marketing and finance. The specifications and policies developed for each of these processes were forced through an approval mechanism that involved obtaining sign-offs from those directly involved in them. This mechanism helped in identifying problem areas that required higher-level management attention and, supplemented by periodic progress reports, served to identify the unique choices requiring top management input.

The organization had a clear understanding of what the task, or strategy, was to be. General management understood that the development of a manufacturing control system raised important concerns about the administrative processes managers used to make decisions, set priorities, and control performance; it acted first to address these. General management then developed a process for seeking out and dealing with key design choices, cross-functional issues, and inconsistencies in organizational and reward structures. This division operates with a manufacturing control system that helps the division achieve its strategic goals.

It fit the production systems to the task.

Notes

1. R.F. Sirny, "The Job of the P&IC Manager—1975," *Production and Inventory Management*, September 1977, p. 100.

2. Robert J. Shaw and M.O. Regentz, "How to Prepare Users for a New System," *Management Focus* (New York, Peat, Marwick Mitchell & Co.), March–April 1980, p. 33.

3. Wickham Skinner, "Manufacturing—Missing Link in Corporate Strategy," *HBR*, May–June 1969, p. 136. Chapter 5, this volume.

4. See Wickham Skinner, "The Focused Factory," *HBR*, May–June 1974, p. 113. Chapter 10, this volume.

5. R. Van Dierdonck and J.G. Miller, "Designing Production Planning and Control Systems," *Journal of Operations Management*, Fall 1980, p. 37; and R. Van Dierdonck and J.G. Miller, "Uncertainty and Complexity in Materials Management Systems" (Boston, Division of Research, Harvard Business School, Working Paper No. 80-22, 1980).

6. Jeffrey G. Miller and Peter Gilmour, "Materials Managers: Who Needs Them?" *HBR*, July–August 1979, p. 143. Chapter 22, this volume.

20
Do's and Don'ts of Computerized Manufacturing

DONALD GERWIN

A decade ago it was common for American managers, flush from their successes in the market, to think they had licked the problem of production for good. Today the sterling performance of global competitors has with a vengeance burst that bubble of complacency. In fact, to hold their own against world class competition, American manufacturers have had to relearn how to compete on the basis of excellence in production. When they turned for help to automated production machinery, more often than not they found that lower unit costs and higher quality could be achieved only by sacrificing flexibility. For companies in flow or mass-production industries, this was not a crippling problem; for batch manufacturers, however, it was a nightmare. They could get their costs in line only by giving up the ability to shift machinery quickly from one task to another—the very essence of their production system.

No wonder, then, that batch manufacturers look on recent developments in flexible computerized production technology as if they were pieces of the true cross. But in their haste and excitement to bring this equipment on-line, they are apt to overlook the many questions it raises for the rest of a production system. It is precisely to these questions that the author addresses himself.

The lagging growth in productivity of American industry has at last captured public attention. Many observers attribute the problem, at least in part, to management's reluctance to invest in the capital equipment necessary to automate production systems at fully competitive levels. Not all such investment, however, carries equivalent benefits. Of the three primary methods of manufacture—flow production of liquids and gases, mass production of discrete parts, and batch production of discrete parts—industry probably stands to gain the most from stimulating automation in the last category: batch manufacturing operations.

In both flow and mass production, which are appropriate to large-volume single products or a few standardized products, operations are continuous, follow a cost-efficient predetermined sequence, require specialized equipment, and are already heavily automated. By contrast, batch production, which applies to the manufacture of several different products each with relatively low volume and low standardization, is intermittent, follows no invariable sequence, requires general-purpose equipment, forces work to remain in process for considerably longer intervals, has higher unit costs—and is much less automated.

Improvement here would translate quickly into productivity gains, for batch manufacturing represents more than 35% of the U.S. manufacturing base and constitutes 36% of manufacturing's share of GNP. Moreover, that improvement is almost at hand. Recent developments in the technology of computer-aided manufacturing (CAM) may well provide batch manufacturers with the efficiencies long enjoyed by flow and mass-production systems, although many companies in non-defense-related industries still do not know enough about CAM technology—its potential or its limitations—to justify the investment it requires.[1] Thus, for managers concerned with the productivity of their batch manufacturing operations, a number of critical issues require attention. What exactly is CAM? For whom is it appropriate? By what criteria is it best to evaluate a proposal to adopt CAM technology? What problems are likely to arise after installation? Do effective strategies exist with which to solve these problems? From intensive interviews in companies both here and abroad, I have begun to obtain answers to these and similar questions. Some of the answers are quite surprising.

CAM—What Is It?

Normally, batch producers had two kinds of equipment from which to choose. The first, dedicated machinery such as transfer lines, is best suited for mass production of a single part at an annual volume of 20,000 units or more. This process specialization permits low unit costs, but it also inhibits flexibility. The second—unautomated general-purpose machine tools such as conventional lathes, milling machines, and drill presses—is best suited for one-of-a-kind or very small batch production of many different parts at an annual volume of, say, 200 units or less. Costs per unit tend to be high, but the flexibility of the process can accommodate engineering changes, fluctuations in demand, and shifts in product mix.

For those batch producers making several parts at annual volumes between 200 and 20,000 units each, neither alternative is quite right: general-purpose equipment is too costly, and dedicated machinery lacks flexibility. Today, however, computer-aided manufacturing offers batch producers a third choice—one with more flexibility than transfer lines and lower unit costs than general-purpose machine tools.

Forerunners

To understand the potential of CAM technology, it is important to view this new equipment as but the latest step in the evolution of numerical control (NC) machine tools. Developed after World War II, numerical control was first applied to milling and other metal-cutting operations—drilling, boring, turning, grinding, and sawing—in the production of jet aircraft. More recently, its range of application has grown to include tube bending, shearing, torch cutting, and fabric-cloth cutting.

The significance of an NC system is that it runs according to a detailed set of coded instructions on punched paper tape. Compared with conventional equipment, NC machines offer increased accuracy, flexibility, and uniformity even with highly complex parts. Design changes and special adjustments require only a change of instructions, nothing more. One helicopter manufacturer, for example, used NC to machine a transmission housing whose geometry was such that tolerances could not be met with conventional equipment. Another company using NC made in one year more than a hundred alterations in the design of a new product. These experiences are not unusual.

Problems do exist, however. NC equipment usually costs more than conventional machinery that performs the same function. It also affects the control of factory operations. Because NC systems employ parts programmers to translate engineering drawings into punched-tape code, machine operators no longer actually control machine motion, and thus less-skilled workers can do the job. Forepersons, as always, are caught in the middle. They lose some control over the production process to staff and service personnel at the same time that the cost of NC machines puts them under increased pressure to boost manufacturing performance.

Machining centers, which first appeared in 1959, combine very efficiently NC operations that previously occupied separate machines; in fact, such centers can reduce setups and floor space by as much as two-thirds, direct labor by half, and in-process inventories by nine-tenths. With tool changing automatically controlled by instructions on the tape, as many as 90 tools can be changed in a few seconds.

In 1969 computer numerical control (CNC) replaced the hard-wired control unit of the NC system with a stored-program minicomputer. By 1974 less expensive microcomputers were also available to act as control units. With its programs stored in the computer's memory and not on fragile paper tape, a CNC machine or machining center is more reliable than NC equipment. It is also more flexible. Once a program is in memory, editing and revision are simple tasks, as is the addition of new systems options. The minicomputer can also be used, of course, for machine monitoring, scheduling, and the reporting of performance data.

The Current Version

Computer-aided manufacturing proper, the CAM system, also first appeared around 1969. Known as direct numerical control (DNC), it consists of a battery of NC and/or CNC equipment that is connected to a central computer, which usually controls from five to 20 machine tools but may control up to 250.

By providing a centralized source of information and by extending computational ability, DNC helps managers control shop operations. When, for example, its parts programs were stored at the machine tools themselves, an aircraft company faced with frequent changes in component design had no way of knowing whether the latest updated program for a part was in use. When it switched to a central DNC computer, the company could make sure that all the programs were correct.

In the early 1970s, a second generation of CAM system technology—the flexible manufacturing systems (FMS)—appeared (see Exhibit 1). Combining DNC capabilities with automated materials handling, these systems can machine parts in any sequence at any time and can automatically reroute parts to other machines when one breaks down. This further reduces materials-handling time—in one company, from 160 minutes per part to 20.

Problems of Adoption

Given the immense promise of this technology, why have American companies been slow to adopt it? One major reason, according to the Comptroller General's survey of some 200 U.S. metalworking corporations, is that one in five simply lack the necessary understanding of advanced process technology. Sadly, American industry here faces a chicken-and-egg problem. If, as another recent study suggests, many small and medium-sized companies cannot properly evaluate whether they need NC, their lack of expertise will likely keep them from buying the sophisticated equipment on which their technical experts could acquire the needed experience.[2]

Finding a Champion

At the companies I interviewed, breaking this vicious circle required a "process champion"—a committed individual willing to take chances in selling management on a new concept.[3] When slumping sales led one division of an American manufacturer to invest in a new product line and replace antiquated shop equipment, it was the engineering head's tenacious commit-

Exhibit 1. Layout of a Flexible Manufacturing System

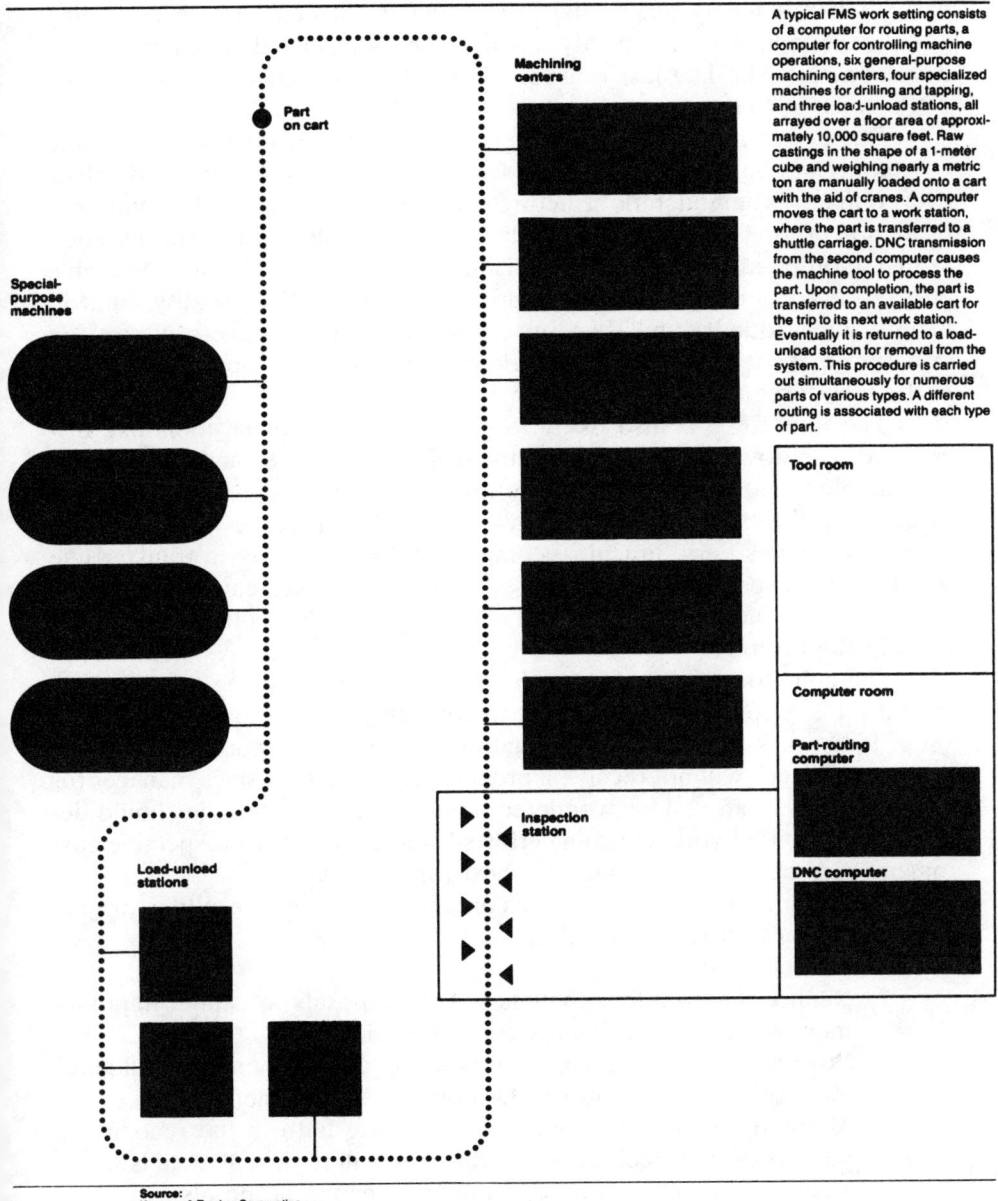

A typical FMS work setting consists of a computer for routing parts, a computer for controlling machine operations, six general-purpose machining centers, four specialized machines for drilling and tapping, and three load-unload stations, all arrayed over a floor area of approximately 10,000 square feet. Raw castings in the shape of a 1-meter cube and weighing nearly a metric ton are manually loaded onto a cart with the aid of cranes. A computer moves the cart to a work station, where the part is transferred to a shuttle carriage. DNC transmission from the second computer causes the machine tool to process the part. Upon completion, the part is transferred to an available cart for the trip to its next work station. Eventually it is returned to a load-unload station for removal from the system. This procedure is carried out simultaneously for numerous parts of various types. A different routing is associated with each type of part.

Source:
Kearney & Trecker Corporation

ment to purchasing an FMS that finally overcame internal resistance. Similarly, when a newly acquired British company decided to replace aging equipment and increase capacity, it was the previous head of manufacturing development (who had just retired) whose plan for modernization sold the DNC concept to management.

But even when a process champion wins the campaign, the task force commonly appointed to investigate designs and vendors is often led astray by a company's bureaucratic structure and power centers. Usually composed of manufacturing engineers, the task force will likely treat CAM adoption as just another capital budgeting decision, which it is not. CAM's inevitable effects on accounting procedures, production scheduling, quality control, maintenance, foundry and assembly operations, plant management, and job structure make it important that workers and functional experts participate in the task force or at least consult with it.

The task force is also likely to discover that financial tools like discounted cash flow analysis do not help much. Either not enough information is available to support estimates of future net returns or the problem of how to quantify the benefits of flexibility—especially where new products are involved—makes very difficult a comparison between, say, a transfer line that machines specified parts at low cost and a CAM system that machines the same parts at higher cost but that can also produce other unspecified parts in the future.

Difficult, too, is quantifying the benefits of centralizing operating information in a computer as opposed to collecting it at various points in the shop. If the task force is under the gun to demonstrate short-term returns, these advantages will not receive a proper weighting. One sales manager for a leading American vendor wondered aloud to me whether she should de-emphasize flexibility in her selling efforts because so many prospective customers were concentrating only on short-run returns.

When faced with pressures for concrete, short-term results, a project champion on a task force should:

1 **Reduce the visibility.** Include CAM proposals in capital improvement programs involving scores of machines.
2 **Project a confident image.** Unswerving commitment can influence managers who lack information on costs and benefits.
3 **Maintain credibility.** Once managers lose faith in the recommendations of their technical experts, they will review all details intensively and more than likely wind up rejecting proposals.
4 **Appear to be rational.** Preparing rudimentary financial analyses of CAM and a written evaluation of its merits—however inexact such statements must be—helps satisfy corporate guidelines for rationality in capital budgeting.

Avoiding the Numbers Trap

As Robert H. Hayes and William J. Abernathy, two authorities on process technology, have warned, an undue emphasis on analytic techniques biases decisions against the purchase of advanced manufacturing equipment that promotes long-term technical superiority.[4] Among the companies I've studied, those that have adopted CAM technology did so on the basis of experience rather than estimated profits. At least three of them did not even conduct sophisticated financial analyses.

One made its selection on the basis of the technology's flexibility, reasoning that a new product line was bound to involve considerable design change and that an FMS could accommodate these changes more readily than could transfer equipment. Another was influenced by its favorable experience with stand-alone NC equipment, by the proven superiority of the NC concept in the aerospace industry, and by a work-piece analysis that showed that an integrated system would reduce waiting times.

Implementing CAM Technology

The unfamiliar complexity of an integrated CAM system is virtually guaranteed to produce novel problems when it comes to implementation. My interviews clearly show that bringing a CAM system on-line has major effects on the blue-collar workers who operate it, the staff who control it, and the managers responsible for strategy development.

Worker Attitudes

My colleague Mel Blumberg and I found that most blue-collar participants in the American company's FMS—especially those who were loaders and operators—felt that their jobs were stressful and offered little motivation. In particular, they regretted the lack in their work of both autonomy (the opportunity to exercise discretion) and task identity (the chance to complete an identifiable piece of work). At the same time, they had a great need for personal growth and development that was not met at work. Not surprisingly, then, most workers (with the exception of forepersons and repairpersons) were dissatisfied with several important aspects of their jobs: comfort (as well as challenge and security), coworker relations, adequacy of resources, clarity of expectations about performance, promotion opportunities, and financial rewards.

If these findings are typical, they indicate a pressing need to redesign the jobs in CAM systems. One possibility is a joint work group that does away with separate jobs for operators and loaders. Given the self-contained nature of tasks in an integrated system, the group can as a whole be responsible for loading, monitoring, unloading, routine repairs, and tool setting. When each member can participate in several tasks and in decisions on such matters as job rotation, motivation is apt to increase and dissatisfaction to decline.

Management and Control

Another common effect of CAM system technology is to call into question the validity of the traditional standards for monitoring quality and financial performance. One quality control unit, for example, wanted quickly to identify the source of defects in order to limit damage to the smallest number of expensive parts. But because quality checks could be made only at the end of the machining process or between machining sequences, two hours might elapse before the unit caught a defective part. Moreover, because defects could arise from problems in the machine tools, the computers, the loading and materials-handling systems, or the parts themselves, the unit had such a hard time knowing where to look that it finally lowered the original quality standards.

CAM system implementation can also play havoc with a factory's accounting standards. Since direct labor hours do not vary with the cost of the part being processed, cost standards must be restated in terms of machining hours while the rest of the shop maintains direct labor hours. Manufacturing managers cannot, therefore, rely on their informal procedures (based on experience with direct labor hours) to control the operation of the new system.

Further, little of the usual data for calculating standard costs is available. For so new a process, no factory in the country can yet provide all the needed historical information. Consequently, standards have to be set largely by intuitive estimate, which experience has shown to be an unreliable benchmark for such major cost components as rework and maintenance. By the same token, revised accounting procedures and radically new process capabilities can make a comparison between data on pre and post-adoption costs virtually useless.

Living with Flexibility

Those batch manufacturers who switch from transfer lines to CAM systems invert the normal developmental course of productive units (as sketched by Abernathy and others) from a fluid to a rigid state—that is, from customized products made on general-purpose equipment to standardized products made on specialized equipment.[5] As a result, the primary strategic significance of CAM lies in its potential for reversing the trend toward more cost-efficient but inflexible productive units. This potential stems from its ability to loosen the ever-tighter integration of product with process.

Unfortunately, manufacturers have to date only a limited understanding of the problems involved in moving backward to more fluid—and thus more uncertain—conditions.⁶ With transfer lines, for example, calculating production time per unit is a fairly easy matter; with a CAM system, production depends on a host of interrelated factors, the effects of which are hard to know in advance.

Moreover, managers are not even agreed among themselves about what flexibility means. My interviews show they use the term in at least five different senses:

1. **Mix flexibility.** The processing at any one time of a mix of different parts loosely related to each other.
2. **Parts flexibility.** The addition of parts to the mix and removal of parts from the mix over time.
3. **Routing flexibility.** The dynamic assignment of parts to machines—that is, the rerouting of a given part if a machine used in its manufacture is incapacitated.
4. **Design-change flexibility.** The fast implementation of engineering design changes for a particular part.
5. **Volume flexibility.** The accommodation of shifts in volume for a given part.

The potential for conflict among the different sources of flexibility makes it imperative for a company to decide early on which kinds of flexibility it values most. Setting these priorities accurately, however, requires a prior strategic consensus formulated by top management. Whether, for example, a company needs parts flexibility will depend to some extent on its plans to engage in new-product development. Without a firm decision on a new-product orientation, top management simply cannot give its manufacturing operations a well-defined mission.

One manufacturer in my sample made a strategic decision to invest in a new product line for which it needed new process equipment. Believing that engineering changes and perhaps even abandonment of the line might be necessary, it put a high priority on both design-change flexibility and parts flexibility.

A second company, planning for a gradual buildup in production, stressed volume flexibility. A third, which intended to produce a large number of products at different volume levels, sought to minimize the costs of frequent setups by focusing on mix flexibility. Each purchased a CAM system well suited to its needs.

Consider, by contrast, an American company that adopted CAM technology to manufacture a new part without understanding the equipment's potential for machining several parts. When demand for the new part fell off, management was unprepared and had to rush to come up with new tooling, fixtures, and parts programs while idle time mounted. Had the company's strategy identified mix flexibility as an important ingredient in its business environment, the problem would have been far less serious.

Curiously enough, the very flexibility of CAM may introduce some undesirable rigidities to decision making. Its ability to machine a variety of parts often makes it indispensable to a company's manufacturing process. Once CAM becomes indispensable, however, it tends to displace all other production equipment and to make subcontracting difficult. These developments, in turn, render any disruption in its normal functioning intolerable.

Building an Infrastructure

All these considerations underscore the importance of the fit between CAM and the manufacturing system it serves. A good fit is the result of a company's having developed not only a coherent strategy but also a human and technical infrastructure to support its manufacturing equipment. This infrastructure includes:

☐ *Skills.* Quality control personnel must have experience in diagnosing the defects that occur in CAM machinery.

☐ *Attitudes.* Skilled maintenance people must be willing to work second and third shifts.

☐ *Systems and procedures.* Accounting systems must adapt to the peculiarities of CAM machinery.

The state of a company's support system is closely related to its stage of manufacturing development. The more experience a company has with NC—converting its cost standards from direct labor to machine hours, for example—the more its support activities will be able to cope with additional advances.[7]

The companies I studied varied markedly in their exposure to NC and, therefore, in their degree of infrastructure development. This had a profound impact on the nature of their implementation plans. One British company, with almost no NC experience except with a balky NC lathe installed in one of its shops, had to forge from scratch a comprehensive human-development and technical-development plan to accompany installation of CAM equipment. A German manufacturer, by contrast, was able to install its CAM system immediately in its main machine shop because the shop already had experience with NC. Quite different was the second British company in my sample, which planned to establish its CAM system in an autonomous unit staffed with new personnel in a new location. With virtually no NC and no infrastructure, the company thought it necessary to insulate the system from the attitudes of existing foremen and workers, who were dedicated to hand skills.

Developing an infrastructure is an easier task when management installs

CAM equipment in stages. This approach keeps problems to a manageable size and allows the company time to gain experience in solving problems. In fact, all the companies that I studied have installed or are installing both machinery and software in stages. As a rule, companies starting from scratch may want to prove out one machine at a time, whereas companies with NC experience may prefer to install an integrated system in modules.

No experience with stand-alone equipment, however, can fully prepare a manufacturer to cope with the complexities of a CAM system. Indeed, my interviews suggest that there is a qualitative leap in complexity between stand-alone machines and integrated systems. Novel problems in control and strategy are compounded by the lack of opportunity to prove out a large integrated system before installation. Later, when manufacturing people press to use the equipment, support personnel must learn about the new system while it is in daily use.

This leap in complexity also prompts some companies to rely too heavily on vendors to solve problems, even though vendors are not completely knowledgeable about what new technology can and cannot do. Turnkey projects, in which vendors assume all responsibility for making the system work, are particularly dangerous. Building up in-house experience is critical. How to avoid the pitfalls of dependence? Begin to worry the very moment your manufacturing people tell you with reference to some problem or other, "Don't worry, that's the vendor's responsibility."

Research Methodology

My research included detailed interviews with 35 managers—in the United States, Great Britain, and West Germany. Meanwhile, my colleague Jean-Claude Tarondeau obtained written responses to the same interview questions from a French company. Also, a questionnaire tapped workers' reactions in one American company. H. Thomas Klahorst of Kearney & Trecker provided helpful advice throughout the project. Among the companies studied were:

1. A diversified American manufacturer (1980 sales, $2 billion) that has a division making a product line for which the major housings are machined on a flexible manufacturing system.
2. A British producer of medium-sized and large electrical motors and generators (1980 sales, $86 million) that was in the process of installing a direct numerical control system for the machining of prime components.
3. A British manufacturer of plain bearings for industrial engines that has a rudimentary direct numerical control system for machining thin wall bearings.

4. A German aircraft manufacturer (1980 sales, $420 million) that was installing a flexible manufacturing system designed to machine over 200 different parts.
5. A German producer of transmission systems for industrial and agricultural vehicles (1979 sales, $750 million) that is developing its own flexible manufacturing system to machine gears and other rotary parts.
6. A French manufacturer of industrial vehicles that began installing a flexible manufacturing system for gear boxes in 1981.

Do's and Don'ts

From my interviews I have compiled a summary list of "do's" and "don'ts" for management to consider when adopting and implementing CAM technology.

Do	Don't
Identify knowledgeable technical people and provide them with the time and resources to evaluate alternatives.	Bank on analytic financial techniques to provide the last word on whether to adopt.
Bring all potentially affected parties—including staff, operating managers, and workers—into the adoption decision.	Expect that the standards used to control CAM operations will be as trustworthy as those for conventional equipment, at least for the first few years.
Develop an infrastructure that will be ready to support a CAM system as it is installed.	Consider CAM just another collection of equipment with no implications for strategy.
Install in stages.	Allow CAM to become indispensable in the production process.
Consider organizing a CAM system work force on a group basis, with job switching allowed and encouraged.	Expect vendors to be completely knowledgeable about operating problems in a CAM system.

This checklist cannot, of course, provide all the answers, but it can give you a sensible starting point for dealing effectively with advanced manufacturing technology. The rest is up to you.

Suggested Reading

Advisory Committee on Industrial Innovation, *Final Report* (Washington, DC, Department of Commerce, 1979).

A.J. Burge and R.E. Goforth, *Survey of Numerical Control Equipment Application in Texas Manufacturing Plants* (College Station, TX, Texas Engineering Experiment Station, Texas A&M University, 1976).

Nathan H. Cook, "Computer-Managed Parts Manufacture," *Scientific American,* Vol. 232, 1975, p. 22.

John J. Hughes, George K. Hutchinson, and Kenneth E. Gross, "Flexible Manufacturing Systems for Improved Mid-Volume Productivity," in *Understanding Manufacturing Systems* (Milwaukee, WI, Kearney & Trecker Corporation, 1976).

George K. Hutchinson, "Advanced Batch Machining Systems" (Working paper, School of Business Administration, University of Wisconsin at Milwaukee, 1979).

Alan M. Kantrow, "The Strategy–Technology Connection," *HBR*, July–August 1980, p. 6.

Notes

1. Comptroller General of the United States, *Report to the Congress: Manufacturing Technology—A Changing Challenge to Improved Productivity* (Washington, DC, U.S. General Accounting Office, 1976).

2. George P. Putnam, "Why More NC Isn't Being Used," *Machine and Tool Blue Book*, September 1978, p. 98.

3. Alok K. Chakrobarti, "The Role of Champion in Product Innovation," *California Management Review,* Winter 1974, p. 58.

4. Robert H. Hayes and William J. Abernathy, "Managing Our Way to Economic Decline," *HBR*, July–August 1980, p. 67. Chapter 1, this volume.

5. William J. Abernathy, *The Productivity Dilemma* (Baltimore, Johns Hopkins University Press, 1978); Robert H. Hayes and Steven C. Wheelwright, "Link Manufacturing Process and Product Life Cycles," *HBR*, January–February 1979, p. 133; Chapter 7, this volume; and Robert

H. Hayes and Steven C. Wheelwright, "The Dynamics of Process–Product Life Cycles," *HBR*, March–April 1979, p. 127. Chapter 8, this volume.

6. William J. Abernathy, Kim B. Clark, and Alan M. Kantrow, "The New Industrial Competition," *HBR*, September–October 1981, p. 68. Chapter 4, this volume.

7. John Ettlie, "Technology Transfer—From Innovators to Users," *Industrial Engineering*, June 1973, p. 16.

PART FIVE
THE FACTORS OF PRODUCTION (RESOURCES, CAPACITY, AND CAPITAL)

AN OVERVIEW

Considered together, the articles in the preceding sections advance an *ex parte* argument in defense of the renewed competitive importance of manufacturing. Their angle of vision has been, for the most part, that suggested by a decade and more of research into the shaping and implementation of corporate strategy. Said another way, they have used the by now familiar premises of strategic thinking to ask pointed questions of the manufacturing function. In this fifth section, by contrast, although the strategy focus is not entirely absent, it has receded. Here the main concern is to consider the implications of what has gone before on what economists speak of as the traditional factors of production.

However well defined a company's manufacturing mission might be and however finely integrated its production system, neither mission nor system can produce worthwhile effects if not supplied with the necessary raw materials, plant capacity, and investment capital. In the competitive environment likely to exist in the 1980s and beyond, sophisticated management of factor inputs will be every bit as important to a company as its achievement of firm strategic oversight. If anything, conditions of resource scarcity may prove the more difficult to adjust to, for they violate the comfortable planning assumptions of several generations of management.

Faced with the need to improve manufacturing performance, managers typically look first to purge their operations of obvious sloppiness, poor integration, and bad organization. This, of course, is all to the good, for today's markets do not deal kindly with bloated or inefficient producers. In their haste to make the most accessible marginal improvements in productivity, however, these same managers are inclined to ignore what Wickham Skinner has called the deeper "structural inefficiencies" in the way companies and industries do business.

In many cases the largest contributor to lackluster performance is not the less than optimal management of ongoing operations but, rather, the incorrect understanding of just what the bases for competition in an industry really are—and of how they have changed from what they were but a few years ago. There is a risk in managing a production system poorly; there is also a risk, perhaps a greater one, in managing it with the wrong set of rules in mind. And one way for managers to get a more accurate fix on what the new rules of competition really are is for them to rethink their approach to the major factors of production.

21
Behind the Growth in Materials Requirements Planning

JEFFREY G. MILLER and LINDA G. SPRAGUE

Until recently, the production manager has found getting the right quantities of supplies and components to the right places at the right times to be a complex and frustrating task. Here the authors discuss how advances in materials requirements planning systems can make the task an easier one. They explain how the MRP system works and discuss what its advantages are likely to be under most circumstances. They then explore its applicability in a variety of manufacturing environments such as basic assembly operations and general machine shops.

Materials requirements planning (MRP) hardly seems a phrase to create much of a furor or evoke much enthusiasm. But in the past few years, hundreds of manufacturing companies have brought MRP systems for production/inventory control on line, or are now doing so, and many more are seriously considering it. APICS (the 11,000-member American Production/Inventory Control Society) has recently finished a massive crusade to inform corporate users of the benefits of MRP systems. Almost all the major computer manufacturers have developed and are pushing software packages to support such systems, and virtually every major industrial consulting firm is advising on them.

So the prospect of your running into an MRP system is growing: many of your suppliers may now be explaining to your purchasing department changes in their delivery promising procedures because they are on MRP; your customers may be insisting on new ways of setting delivery schedules because they are on MRP. And within your own company, you may already be hearing from your manufacturing divisions about proposals for installation of an MRP system, recommendations for analysis of its feasibility, requests to send members of your manufacturing group off to MRP seminars and workshops.

The interest is there; the question is why. Leaving aside the natural propensity of computer manufacturers to tout new systems that use lots of computer time, there is a good reason: *the cost balance in manufacturing control is shifting*. Much of the MRP logic has always been available but, primarily because of high data-processing costs, its use has been expensive. Now, however, computation costs are declining while inventory costs are rising. The result is that a sophisticated computerized production/inventory control system is easier to justify.

Moreover, the economic situation has pushed manufacturing control into the limelight. Unstable interest rates, materials shortages, rising finished goods inventories, order cancellations, the impact of scheduling inefficiencies on profits, and the like are making clear the need for tighter operational control and more rapid and flexible response to change.

Now, although these are benefits whose value few would question, there have been many questions raised as to whether they can actually be achieved through an MRP system. And it is precisely these questions that the manager must seek to answer in light of his or her own organization's particular needs. Our objective here is to provide some answers to them:

- [ ] What is MRP?
- [ ] What are its advantages?
- [ ] Will MRP work for your manufacturing operations?
- [ ] Is MRP worth it?

What Is Materials Requirements Planning?

MRP is a new name applied to an old concept, but it is a concept that has come of age with currently available data processing capabilities. This synthesis of modern computers and some old (and some new) concepts has resulted in a system that can be used effectively to both plan and control production and materials flows. The logic of MRP is based on the fact that the demand for materials, parts, and components depends on the demand for an end product. This distinction is vital since it explains both the behavior of parts orders and, ultimately, inventories.

Dependent Versus Independent Demands[1]

In manufacturing it is reasonable (in fact, perhaps desirable) to want absolutely *no* inventory of a part for, say, ten months and exactly 200 each day for the next two months. Why? Because that exactly corresponds to the demand for the part—the part goes into a finished product that is batch assembled. This "lumpy" demand (zero for several weeks, then 1,000 needed this morning) is a common fact of manufacturing life, even when lot size economies and allowances for scrap are taken into account. It occurs because the demand for parts and components is directly *dependent* on the demand for some higher-order assembly or manufacturing step that is carried out in batches. For example, the demand for steering columns on automobiles is directly dependent on demand for the end products—the cars themselves.

Distribution inventories, on the other hand, often do not experience the "lumpiness" caused by higher-order batching. This is because the demand for finished goods and spare parts is *independent* of the demand for other items produced in manufacturing.

So for manufacturing, where "we want what we want when we want it," keeping "average" numbers of parts on hand, as we might be able to in distribution, will lead to either excess inventories or the inability to produce on time. Manufacturing inventory control systems must incorporate the dependent demand concept to work effectively.

How MRP Works

Exhibit 1 illustrates the four central elements in an MRP system: the master production schedule that "drives" the system, the bill of materials file, the inventory status file that provides the necessary data, and the materials requirements planning package that contains the necessary logic.

The concept of dependent demand is built into the bill of materials file. This file contains information about every part, including its relationship to subassemblies and/or finished products. Managers familiar with indented parts lists for assembled products will recognize this type of information—and will also be familiar with its value. If there is independent demand for any part (e.g., one sold as a replacement), the file can reflect that fact in order to maintain the distinction between dependent and independent demand.

The inventory status file is exactly what its name implies, a record of the actual inventory level of each item and part. It also contains other important data, such as lead times.

The master schedule is analogous to, but not necessarily identical to, an assembly schedule. It indicates when end items (finished products) should be assembled so that customer orders or finished goods inventory requirements can be met. The construction of a master schedule, then, requires

Exhibit 1. Elements of a Materials Requirements Planning System

```
                    Customer orders              Forecasts
                           │                         │
                           ▼                         ▼
                    ┌──────────────────────────────────┐
                    │ Master production schedule:      │
                    │                                  │
 Engineering        │ What should be produced?         │      Inventory
 changes            │                                  │      transaction data
                    │ When is it needed?               │
                    └──────────────────────────────────┘
     │                           │                           │
     ▼                           ▼                           ▼
┌──────────────┐         ┌──────────────────┐         ┌──────────────────┐
│ Bill of      │         │ MRP package:     │         │ Inventory status │
│ materials    │         │                  │         │ file:            │
│ file:        │         │ performs the     │         │                  │
│              │────────▶│ logic            │◀────────│ on hand balance  │
│ product      │         │ explodes         │         │ open orders      │
│ structure    │         │ requirements     │         │ lead times       │
│ data         │         │ offsets lead     │         │                  │
│              │         │ times            │         │                  │
│              │         │ nets out on hand │         │                  │
│              │         │ and order        │         │                  │
│              │         │ balances         │         │                  │
└──────────────┘         └──────────────────┘         └──────────────────┘
                                 │
                                 ▼
                         ┌──────────────────┐
                         │ Exception        │
                         │ reports:         │
                         │                  │
                         │ What should be   │
                         │ ordered?         │
                         │                  │
                         │ What should be   │
                         │ expedited?       │
                         │                  │
                         │ What orders      │
                         │ should be        │
                         │ cancelled?       │
                         │                  │
                         │ What should be   │
                         │ de-expedited?    │
                         │                  │
                         │ Is the master    │
                         │ schedule         │
                         │ realistic?       │
                         └──────────────────┘
```

WHAT IS MATERIALS REQUIREMENTS PLANNING?

forecasts of future demand as well as data on current finished goods inventory levels or firm order commitments.

An Example

In order to understand how the logic of an MRP system works, suppose that, in accordance with a master schedule made out for the next year, we find that we want to deliver a yo-yo in seven weeks to a customer.

We know from the bill of materials that we will require these parts: two wooden sides, one wooden peg, a piece of string, and a cardboard box with printed instructions. A check of the inventory status file shows that we have neither inventories nor open orders for these parts, except that we have one wooden side on hand. We know that the procurement lead times are: sides, five weeks; pegs, one week; string, one week; boxes, four weeks. And we know that it will take one week to actually assemble the toy. To ship during the seventh week then, we will need everything in time for assembly during the sixth.

We could easily place the orders for all these parts right now, but what would happen if we did? We would have string and a peg next week that would sit in inventory for five weeks. Not very important with one toy, but what if this were an order for 50,000?

So instead of ordering everything now, let's work back from the hypothetical delivery date. We will need all of the components in the sixth week, so we can simply calculate when to place our orders by subtracting lead times. This lead-time offsetting, although netting out current inventory balances, will result in planned orders for one wooden side next week, a box the following week, and the peg and string three weeks after that. If, in turn, the sides require red paint that has a three-week lead time, and no paint is on hand, we can see that our delivery would be two weeks late. If this were the case, we could either expedite the paint and side or negotiage for later delivery of the yo-yo's. In either event, we would *not* expedite any of the other components.

Driven by Change

The reader who is familiar with PERT or critical path methods for controlling large projects may see some similarity between the logic of these tools and that of MRP. All operate by working backward through time from some desired end point to determine a starting time for related activities, such as ordering parts. But the analogy is incomplete, because MRP involves far more than just working backward through time. PERT is a planning tool applied to single projects, whereas MRP is a tool for planning and controlling a great number of products and parts that may interact with one another. More important, MRP considers not only the time dimension in planning but also the current and planned quantities of parts and products in inventories. The power of the MRP concept is its ability to take account of the dynamics of both time and quantity for interrelated parts and products.

The logic of MRP makes good sense, but the question inevitably arises: Why hasn't it been done before? Well, it has to some extent. But unless rapid computation is available, the principle breaks down with anything but an extremely simple single product. This explains why some of the older systems that used a bill of materials to derive (or explode) parts requirements used the concept only as a rough *planning* tool for obtaining annual or monthly gross material requirements. Such systems typically did not take current inventories and open orders into account, and the resulting plans were often obsolete before they could be implemented.

A modern MRP system extends the concept of explosion: it is now used in conjunction with lead-time offsetting for both planning *and* control purposes in both the long and the short run. That is, such a system can now inexpensively and rapidly update order priorities weekly or even daily if changes in plans and expectations so dictate. Rapid computation is needed to explode parts requirements from a schedule while simultaneously referencing inventory files to check stock status and lead times, and to keep the entire plan current enough to be useful in spite of broken schedules and late material arrivals. MRP is a tool that is driven by change rather than destroyed by it.

If the computational power is there, MRP can plan, release, and control orders so that materials arrive when they are needed. The system integrates the concept of dependent demand (embodied in the BOM file), the principle of lead-time offsetting (with the MRP package itself), the principle of inventory balancing, and high-speed computation. The result is a manufacturing planning and control system whose objectives are inventory minimization and delivery schedule maintenance.

What Are the Advantages?

The rapid update capability of computers, coupled with the MRP logic and the appropriate data, makes it possible for managers to cope intelligently with the thousands of changes that inevitably occur between the planning and execution of primary tasks.

Keeping Priorities Straight

Consider, for example, a machine breakdown that throws a component two weeks off schedule, ultimately affecting an end-product delivery by two weeks. Because of the delayed delivery date, there is no reason to hurry along other components as planned. (They would probably just show up two weeks early and needlessly sit in inventory.) Instead, these related components could be *de-expedited* (due dates relaxed by two weeks).

You've heard of expediting a needed part to get it in a hurry. Have you ever heard of anyone de-expediting a part when it no longer is urgently needed? MRP provides the ability to change, and keeps priorities straight.

De-expediting and expediting to keep priorities straight has three important effects: (1) it frees up time and capacity for other jobs if the item is produced internally, (2) it prevents the "hurry up and wait" syndrome that is all too common in manufacturing operations and that is responsible for much of the excess in-process and raw materials inventories found in industry, and (3) it can result in rescheduled vendor deliveries for purchased parts, thus reducing purchased materials inventories.

Keeping Inventories Low

Correct priorities can cut average lead times, and lower lead times mean lower in-process inventories. For example, a major original equipment manufacturer (OEM) decreased average lead times from 16 weeks to 12 weeks with a corresponding 25% inventory level decrease. This was possible because, as in most fabrication/assembly companies, the actual time to produce a product amounted to only a small fraction of the time it was on the shop floor; the bulk of the time was consumed waiting for other parts and materials to catch up. With correct priorities provided by MRP, the needed parts are available at the same time. Less waiting means less lead time means less inventory.

It is possible to lower inventories in other ways as well, as the following example shows. A major television manufacturer was faced with substantial writeoffs every year because engineering design changes appeared so frequently that they could not be phased into production in time to prevent the manufacture of obsolete parts. MRP, with its reliance on a bill of materials file that reflected planned engineering changes, allowed the manufacturer to time these changeovers to coincide with the depletion of obsolete parts and thus to decrease writeoffs substantially.

Early Warning

Since an MRP system functions essentially as a simulation of manufacturing activity, it can also be used to examine the feasibility of meeting delivery dates *before* promises are made. Should a component go so far off schedule that it cannot be expedited back on, the affected end-products can be identified well in advance, thus permitting you to warn your customers of impending problems.

Long-Range Planning

Finally, besides being an effective method for controlling materials in the short run, these planning systems have also proved to be important in budgeting and long-range planning. A major electric utilities equipment supplier, for instance, uses the bill of materials, the inventory files, and an annual schedule to simulate various annual production plans and derive budgeting information. The same company uses MRP to plan manpower needs, facilities capacity, and major purchase commitments for several years—a clear advantage of an MRP "model" of manufacturing operations.

Will MRP Work for You?

Our experience shows that, although MRP has universally applicable elements, its ultimate success is intimately related to some important aspects of your overall manufacturing operations, which must be carefully analyzed. It is not a question of whether its basic logic applies—in most cases, it does. The question is how you can best incorporate this logic into your own manufacturing system, given (1) its key control variables, and (2) its key production/inventory tasks. Others have detailed the importance of developing a well thought out manufacturing policy, and this question refers to just that. The answer provides the background for an analysis of what MRP can and cannot do for you.

Let us use the following general examples to illustrate such an analysis:

1. Company A is a basic assembly operation. Almost all parts and subassemblies are purchased externally; there are long production runs of a few models; the finished goods inventory is kept in an extensive distribution system.
2. Company B is a general machine shop. Products are made to order and customer specification; there are complex flows in manufacturing; and there are large in-process inventories.
3. Company C is a fabrication/assembly operation. Most parts are manufactured in a general machine shop and assembled in small quantities to customer order and specification.

Link between Manufacturing and Distribution

For Company A, where a few products are assembled to stock in long production runs, MRP seems a natural. The assembly or master schedule can be used with a bill of materials and inventory file to explode requirements and offset lead times for purchased parts and subassemblies.

But consider the key production/inventory control tasks for this organization. Factory cycle times and in-process inventories are likely to be almost nonexistent. In-process inventory control, though important, is not the key task in this case. Inventories are more likely to be concentrated in the distribution system. Hence, Company A's key production/inventory tasks focus on planning intermediate-term (three to twelve months) production while controlling distribution system inventories and purchase orders. Its key control variables are the avoidance of stockouts at distribution centers, the smoothness of production rates, and the maintenance of a supply of purchased components for the assembly lines to avoid shutdowns.

If MRP is to be used effectively in this kind of manufacturing environment, it must interface well with distribution. The master schedule is important since it links the current stock position at distribution centers with the assembly schedules. Moreover, the master schedule in this case incorporates the intermediate-term production plan by which the manager can smooth peaks and valleys in production levels.

By exploding as well as time-phasing components requirements from this master schedule, an MRP system can give purchasing the information it needs to control its acquisitions. MRP can then maintain priorities as schedules change, stockouts threaten, and deliveries slip. But here its focus is on distribution, production smoothing, and purchasing as the key tasks and control variables of the system. This focus in turn requires, of course, that the organization have a well-developed and rapid distribution and purchasing communications system.

Shop Floor Control

Company B provides a substantially different view of MRP's usefulness. Given the general machine shop's piece-part, make-to-order environment, management must be able to promise realistic due dates to customers, coordinate the design, manufacturing, and engineering functions with production, and schedule the flow of material and work from one machine center to another. Its important control variables are likely to be the percentage of deliveries made on time, the level of in-process inventories, the length of time between customer orders and delivery time, and the utilization of machines and manpower.

But, in contrast to Company A, Company B's manufacturing (in-process) inventory and scheduling control is a critical activity. In fact, most of Company B's inventories are likely to be in-process inventories. Consequently, a reporting and scheduling system must be available in the shop so that production can proceed in accordance with the priorities obtained from the MRP system. Keeping priorities straight here means making maximum use of available capacity. The MRP and shop floor control systems must be carefully coordinated and integrated to be useful.

In this kind of environment an MRP system can also perform two other important functions. First, by offsetting lead times for material requirements, it can help determine realistic due dates for customers. There is little payoff in promising the delivery of a part in 10 weeks if it takes 15 weeks to acquire the necessary materials. Second, it can help control the acquisition of this material. By updating the receipts of materials and other new information, purchasing personnel can quickly focus on the priorities of these items and expedite and de-expedite materials accordingly. Moreover, with such a system it becomes immediately apparent when materials will arrive too late to meet a due date, and management can notify customers early or make other arrangements.

Buffer Stocks and Work Center Priorities

The previous examples illustrate the important role the MRP concept can play in many types of companies. However, there are few in which it has made as great an impact as in the ubiquitous fabrication/assembly type of operation typified by Company C. From a historical perspective, this is easy to understand.

Fabrication/assembly companies, characterized by a general machine shop for fabricating parts and components that are used in downstream assembly operations, have frequently separated these two widely divergent kinds of processes with large buffer inventories. These inventories have served two purposes: to segregate the management of the two kinds of manufacturing for organizational and technical reasons, and to ensure enough of the many parts required to keep assembly operations supplied and to process orders in time.

But these buffer inventories were usually controlled by classical reorder point methods that assumed that the demands for individual components were independent of one another and of the demand for assembled items; they never have been. The result has been large inventories and a great deal of intraorganizational struggle anyway, because the assembly department has constantly interfered with fabrication activities to get all the parts it needed to complete an assembly. For many such companies, a computer-based MRP system has become the answer. But, as before, the special requirements of fabrication/assembly operations mean that the way it has become the answer for them differs from that found to be suitable for others.

Company C's fabrication/assembly operation must simultaneously complete the key tasks of both the assembly operation (like Company A's) and the general machine shop operation (like Company B's). In other words, it must simultaneously be responsive to stockouts and customer due dates, keep assembly operations supplied, and maintain priorities and schedule equipment in the fabrication area. To accomplish this, MRP must serve as the link between fabrication and assembly, as well as between assembly and distribution.

The master schedule serves, as before, to link assembly and distribution, but a fabrication shop floor control system is the link between fabrication and assembly. The shop floor control system accomplishes this by translating the master schedule, via MRP, into priorities that can be used to determine which parts will be worked on at a particular work center. In some companies, "capacity requirements planning" is a second link between fabrication and assembly. This is a technique that can project fabrication shop loads from the master schedule and can also help determine labor requirements, subcontracting needs, or equipment needs.

In fabrication assembly operations, MRP and associated systems allow a company to maintain the separation between two different types of processes, but they also allow such a company to substitute current and timely information from a centralized source for large intraorganizational inventories.

Is MRP Worth It?

Unfortunately, determining the value of MRP is not easy, because the answer depends on your starting point. For one thing, the benefits of the system depend on how well your current production control system is working. The costs depend on the stage of development of your current manufacturing control system as well as on the skills and attitudes of the people in your organization.

To illustrate, a $5 million fabrication/assembly company implemented a simple MRP system in six months with a small computer, the part-time efforts of the factory superintendent, and one (the only) systems analyst in data processing. Another company, which has sales in excess of $20 million and which both fabricates and assembles similarly complex products, is just now reaping the benefits of an integrated MRP-based production control system after five years of stop-and-start evolutionary effort on MRP and associated systems, a new larger computer, and a great deal of data processing support.

Is the point that smaller companies or smaller manufacturing departments can use MRP more effectively and efficiently than larger ones? We think not. More likely, the anomaly stems from the differences between the level of skills, the adequacy of related systems, and the organizational support available in the two companies.

The first company had two skilled and dedicated people to design and implement the system; the second did not and had to hire them from outside and develop them from within. The first company had a reasonably good, though informal, shop floor control and reporting system; the second had to develop such a system from scratch. The first company benefited from good relationships among forepersons, workers, engineers, and marketing personnel; the second did not consult these people in their original design of the system, experienced organizational problems in implementing it, and had to restart with an extensive training and selling program. The first company had accurate bills of material and the organizational commitment and mechanisms to keep them up to date; the second had to develop the bills and convince people that accurate record keeping was an important part of their job.

Realistic Expectations

Clearly, these companies started with different sets of skills, support systems, and levels of organizational commitment. And just as clearly, what was essentially a routine job for one was a major long-term effort for the other. Their experiences show the necessity of beginning with a realistic set of expectations about what it will take and how long it will take to implement such a system.

What results can you expect? On the one hand, if your current production control system is resulting in extremely high inventories and/or poor delivery performance, the net result of an MRP installation is likely to be very rewarding. For example, one company recorded a 12% reduction in finished inventories, a work-in-process inventory reduction of 30%, and a 35% increase in their number of on-time deliveries. But this company had some serious problems to begin with.

On the other hand, if industry and internal standards indicate that your performance is good, the results of an MRP system may not be as dramatic. But a lack of dramatic results can itself be deceiving. For instance, one large company adopted MRP during a period of explosive sales growth that resulted in pressures on its capacity. Even though its inventories did not go down (they actually increased), its turnover remained at about the same level. It is unlikely that this company's old production control system would have withstood these strains.

The interest generated by the MRP concept is indicative of the promise this type of control system offers. The realization of its potential for your organization, however, depends on an analysis of the way it must be focused. Moreover, since implementing such a system can include problems that belie the simplicity of its underlying logic, it is essential that management formulate realistic expectations about its associated costs and benefits.

Notes

1. See Joseph Orlicky, *Materials Requirements Planning, The New Way of Life in Production and Inventory Management* (New York, McGraw-Hill, 1975), for an exposition of dependent versus independent demand.

22
Materials Managers: Who Needs Them?

JEFFREY G. MILLER and PETER GILMOUR

Sharp rises in materials costs and concerns about inventories during the 1970s have caused many companies to reassess their overall materials flow management. As a consequence, many companies have created new materials overseers known as materials managers. The decision to reorganize the functions of production planning, purchasing, and distribution around materials managers, however, is not a simple one. A complex combination of internal and external forces must be considered before a company determines the best way to organize its materials functions. Using survey techniques, the authors have documented the sharp rise in the number of companies using materials managers. In this article, they trace the evolution of the materials management concept, describe companies that did and did not adopt it, and outline the trade-offs companies considering the concept must make. They also describe variations in the materials management approach between divisional and corporate levels.

Concerned with rising purchasing, transportation, distribution, and inventory costs, the new president of a domestic billion dollar industrial company told a meeting of division general managers:

> We are buying, shipping, and inventorying something like $400 million worth of materials. Who do we have in charge of these costs and assets? A bunch of outcasts from engineering, production, marketing, and accounting. In our 25 divisions, we do not have one purchasing, production control, or distribution manager who is promotable to general management levels. Only one is paid enough to be on our key management incentive program. None have been professionally educated.
>
> Now if you really want to get scared, you should remember that we spend $12 million a year on new product R&D. Do you know the easiest way to bomb a new product? Poor materials management—you can't

get the right materials, or the quality is off, or you can't get the product through the factory, or you can't coordinate transportation and distribution to get the product into the hands of the customer.

In response to these concerns, this company created new management positions known as materials managers at both corporate and divisional levels. These materials managers were established professionals who were made responsible for purchasing, production planning, and transportation and distribution. Their charge was to attack the cost and delivery problems plaguing many of the company's major divisions and to upgrade the materials flow management quality.

This company is not alone in turning to materials managers. It proceeded much as a large number of corporations have over the last decade. Nearly half the manufacturers responding to our survey now have materials managers playing important corporate and/or divisional roles, compared with a scant 3% reported in a 1967 survey.[1] (For more details on the survey, see the Appendix to this article.) Even allowing for considerable confusion over job titles and other differences in survey methodology, the increase is substantial.

The emergence of materials managers in such numbers in just 12 years raises several significant questions:

☐ What caused the increase in the numbers of materials managers?

☐ How does the manager decide whether to adopt the materials management concept?

☐ Is this a concept mainly for individual business units, such as divisions of large companies or single product firms, or does it have a place at the corporate level?

Our research over the past year has attempted to answer these and other questions about this new trend. Using large-scale survey methods, coupled with in-depth case studies of representative companies, we have found the forces behind the emergence of the materials manager to be similar across industries.

We also found, however, that the materials management approach is not for all companies. Even when it is right for a company, it may be necessary to tailor it to specific needs. Our major conclusion is that the trade-offs companies face are an important determinant of the best materials organization structure.

Emergence of the Materials Manager

For years manufacturers and scholars have discussed the materials manager concept. Until recently, it had been used on a limited basis in only a few industries under various labels, such as materials management and logistics management.

Theoretically, the materials manager oversees the materials functions of purchasing, production planning and control, and distribution (including traffic). The manager also reports at high and visible levels in the organization, preferably to the president or general manager.[2] Such reporting relationships differ substantially from those in more traditional real-life organizations in which purchasing, for example, reports to the president, production planning reports to manufacturing, and distribution and traffic report to marketing (see Exhibit 1.A).

The emergence of the theoretical materials manager into real-world organizations coincides with significant changes in the business environment between 1968 and 1978.

Forces of Change

The 1973 Arab oil embargo and the subsequent shortages and escalating fuel and materials costs first focused the attention of many manufacturing companies on the importance of materials and transport. The subsequent ballooning inventories that characterized the resulting recession solidified their worries.

In addition to these dramatic, but nonetheless transient events, many companies discovered that long-term cost structures have shifted and that they could achieve much leverage by concentrating on materials, transport, and inventory costs. Evidence of such shifts includes the following.

Data from the *Census of Manufactures* indicate that during the decade in which the materials management organization form has increased in popularity, materials and transport costs for the average American manufacturing company have increased from 53% to nearly 58% of sales. This means that more profit leverage can be obtained by focusing on materials and transport costs. For example, the average company now has to increase sales by more than 10% (a resource consuming activity) in order to generate the same contribution to profit and overhead that a 5% reduction in materials and transport costs (a resource conserving activity) would bring.

American manufacturers annually reinvest four or five times more capital in inventories than they do in new plants and equipment, according to the *Census of Manufactures*. Owing to weak capital markets and the inflation of the 1970s, inventory reductions provide the cheapest and perhaps the most flexible form of financing available.

Pressure on inventories has led many manufacturers to demand increased responsiveness and shorter lead times from their suppliers. But this is a two-way street because the manufacturers' customers have often used the same strategy. The result for suppliers has been an increased emphasis on customer service: on-time deliveries and fast response. For many, customer service has become an important competitive weapon.

Exhibit 1.A. Reporting Relationships in Traditional Organizations

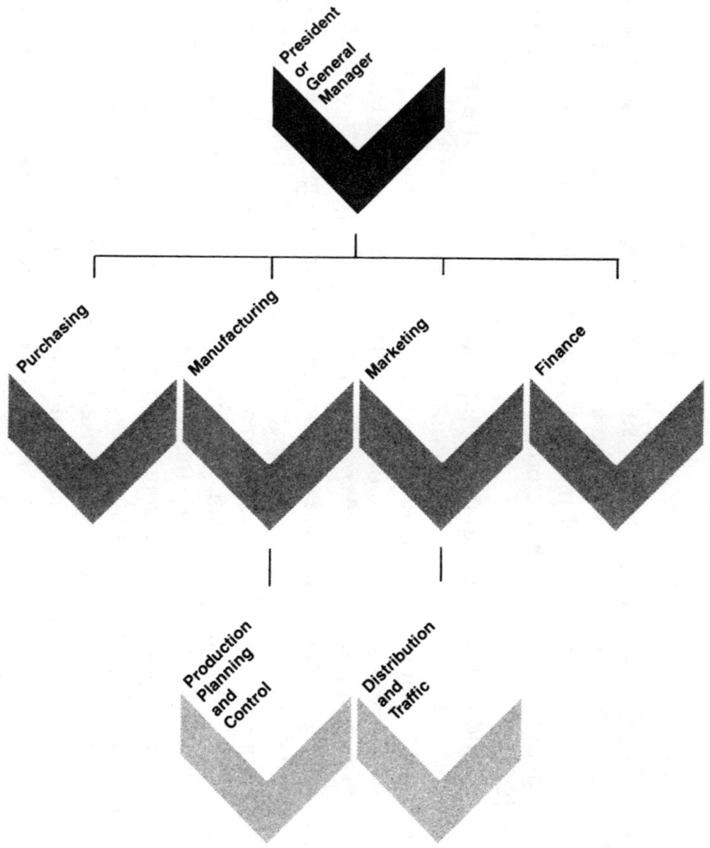

Exhibit 1.B. Reporting Relationships in Materials Management Organizations.

Part B
Materials Management Organizations

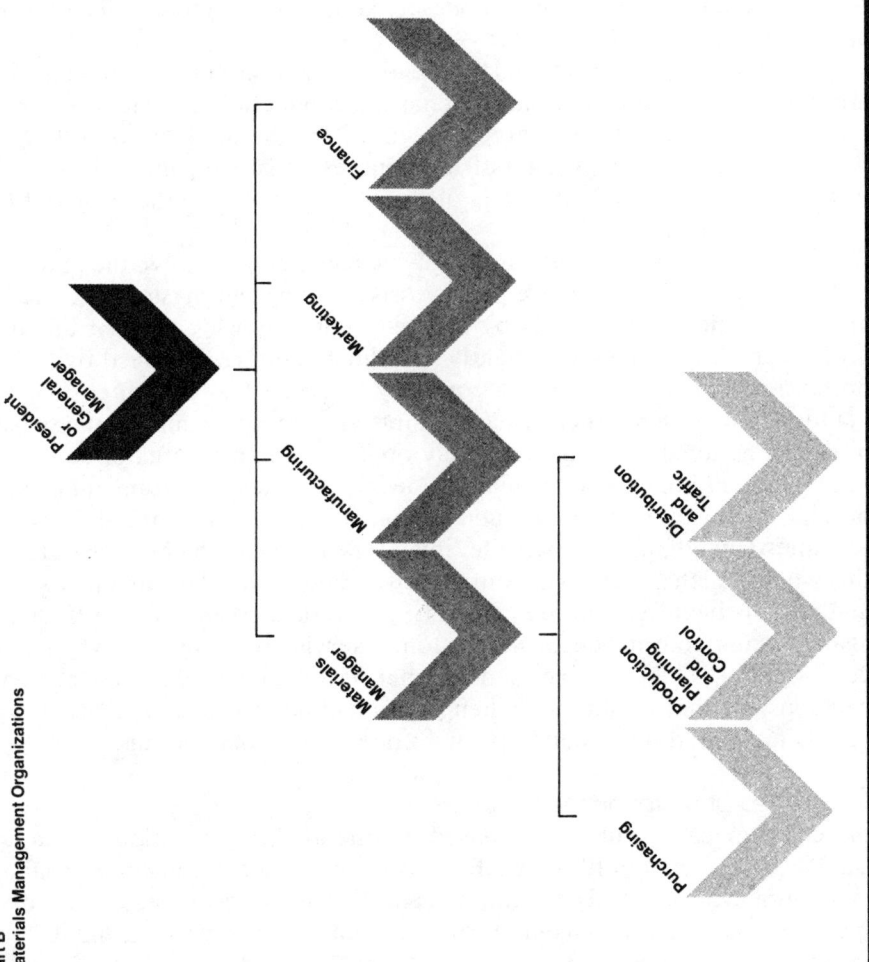

Seen in isolation, these forces might have led manufacturers to attack each problem individually—to call on purchasing departments to reduce materials costs; to give production planning departments responsibility for decreasing inventories; to ask distribution departments to improve customer service. Many manufacturers decided instead to integrate the materials functions into materials management groups designed to attack all of the problems simultaneously. This result is quite consistent with the classical theory of materials management, which implies a major change in traditional reporting and control relationships.

The theoretical arguments for creating a materials management position are tied to the proposition that purchasing, production, and distribution are not separate activities but three aspects of one basic task: controlling the flow of materials and products from sources of supply, through manufacturing, and out through channels of distribution and into the hands of customers.

Proponents argue that a materials manager helps resolve the parochial, self-serving conflicts that frequently arise among purchasing, production, and distribution departments by forcing a companywide view of this flow. Moreover, they argue that a tightly coordinated effort, managed by a single professional manager, allows a company to take advantage of cost and inventory reduction and performance improvement opportunities unavailable if each functional area focuses solely on its own limited area of concern.

These arguments seem tailor-made for a business environment in which purchasing costs, inventories, and customer service levels are all important and interdependent. For example, inventory levels are highly dependent on the way in which materials are purchased and on the level of customer service and responsiveness required. Similarly, materials costs must be traded off against manufacturing costs and customer service requirements when a low-cost supplier is less reliable than a higher cost supplier. Materials managers can consider these trade-offs when implementing changes. With other types of organizations, these conflicts might be swept under the rug.

Types of Materials Manager

Materials management can be based on one ideal organizational structure, such as that shown in Exhibit 1.B. In practice, however, materials management organizations tend to be more versatile. Our survey revealed four major types of materials management organizations as shown in Exhibit 2. Although the four types differ structurally, each includes a specialist carrying a title such as materials manager or equivalent. (Less common titles included logistics manager, physical distribution manager, planning manager, supply manager, and so on. Had we included these titles in our original count of materials managers, about 72% of the survey respondents would have indicated the existence of a materials manager in their organizations.)

Our definition of a materials specialist was a manager whose sole responsibility was for two or more of the materials functions of distribution, purchasing, or production planning. He or she could not oversee these areas as a sideline or by default. Thus a plant manager to whom all three materials functions happened to directly report was not counted as a materials manager.

Exhibit 2 shows the classical integrated materials management structure along with three partially integrated structures that are also prevalent. The completely integrated structure accounts for 31% of the companies in which a materials manager is said to exist. We can break down other structures as follows:

☐ *Distribution oriented.* These are partially integrated organizations in which the distribution and traffic function and the production planning and inventory control function report together. Companies with such structures, which accounted for 23% of the companies with materials managers, tended to integrate those materials functions that were closer to markets than to sources of supply in orientation.

☐ *Supply oriented.* These are partially integrated organizations in which the purchasing function and the production planning and inventory control function report together. In such companies, the two materials functions that report to the same boss are closer to the supply end of the materials pipeline. This type of materials management organization accounted for 18% of the cases in which a materials manager or equivalent existed.

☐ *Manufacturing oriented.* This type of structure is organized around manufacturing, which is in the middle of the materials flow; it accounted for 28% of the materials managers in our survey.

Organize for Materials Management?

Our survey of representative manufacturers indicates that the issue of whether to employ a materials management organization is more complex than it at first appears.

First, the company must decide if it needs and wants such an organization. Second, it must examine the possible structures for a materials management organization. The experiences of two companies that considered materials management and came to different conclusions about it should clarify some of the issues that arise in making those decisions. One company hired a materials manager, and the other did not.

Exhibit 2. Four Major Materials Management Organization Structures

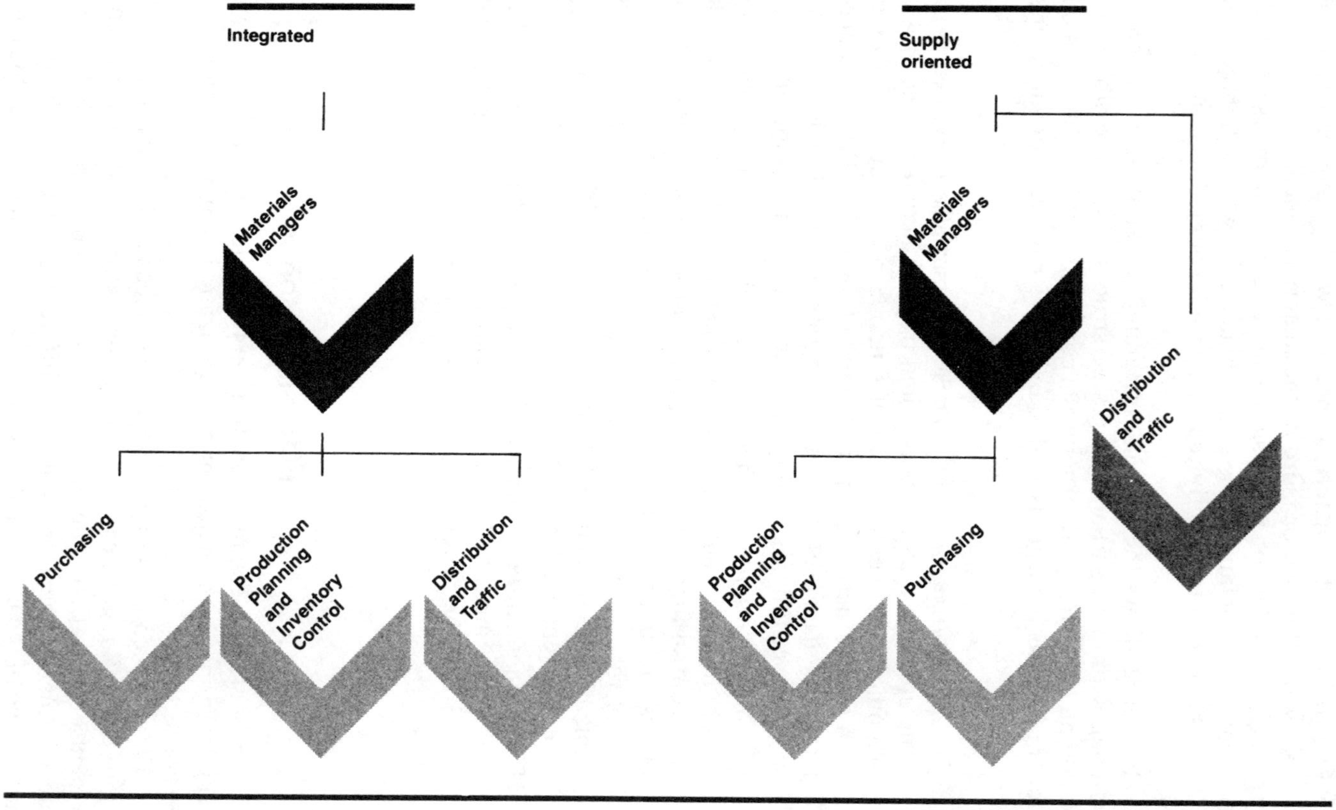

Integrated

Materials Managers

- Purchasing
- Production Planning and Inventory Control
- Distribution and Traffic

Supply oriented

Materials Managers

- Purchasing
- Production Planning and Inventory Control

Distribution and Traffic

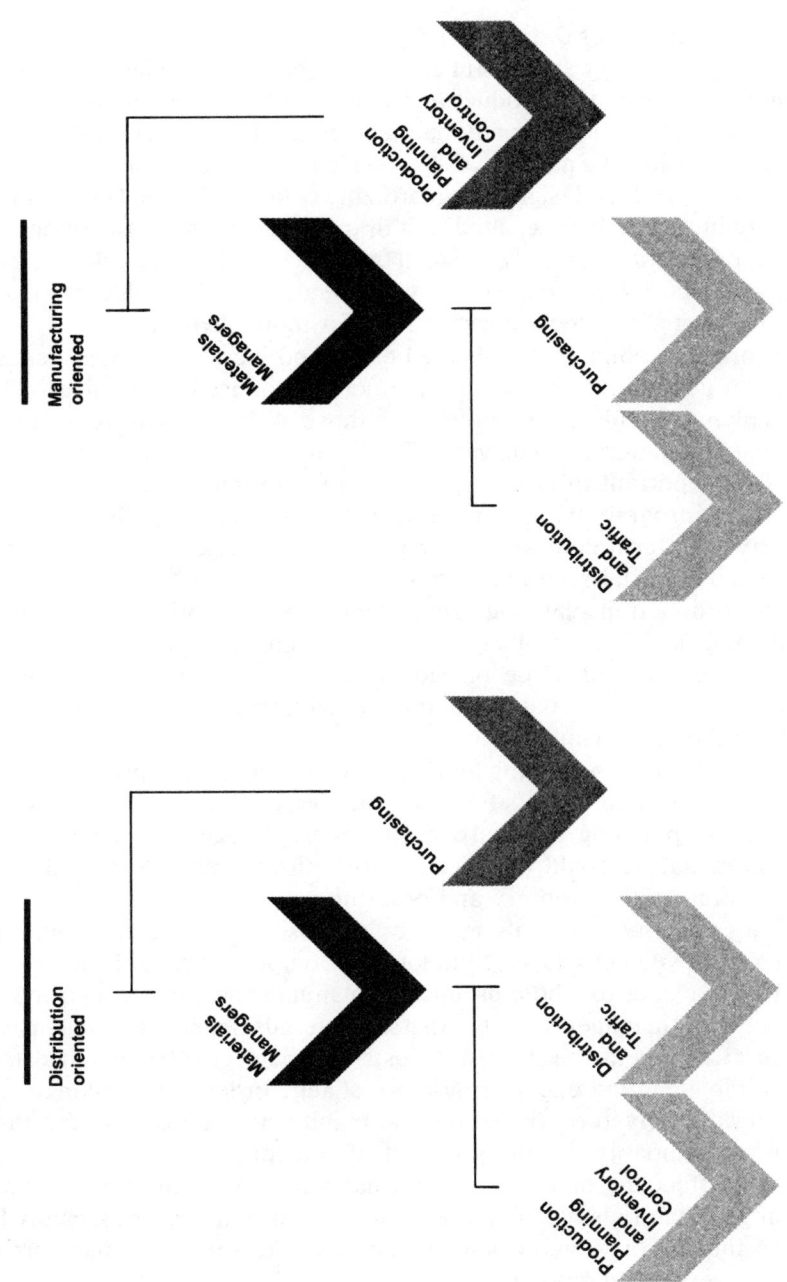

A Company That Did

A substantial and very successful electronics division of a large corporation was entering a period of product and market maturation. In contrast to its earlier days, when the company had grown rapidly with virtually no competition, it now faced a number of aggressive price competitors. It responded by stabilizing product designs, standardizing components, and concentrating on cost reductions. This resulted in a dramatic decrease in the direct labor costs of production, already a small percentage of manufacturing costs. Materials costs, which comprised over 50% of the sales value of the company's products, became a place to look for more savings.

In order to eliminate duplicated effort and increase responsiveness to changes in demand, some company officials proposed combining the production planning and control duties with those of the purchasing department under a single materials manager.

Most important in justifying this reorganization was a plan for a new procurement program that promised to save the company millions of dollars a year by long-term contracting for groups of related materials instead of buying each material separately on a spot basis.

The production planning group figured prominently in the proposed program because it controlled materials inventories and thus determined when releases needed to be placed against the new contracts. Thus the production controllers would be in contact with vendors on a more frequent basis than the purchasing department.

Through their expediting and ordering decisions, the production planners could also significantly affect contract prices. Some managers felt that if production planning and purchasing reported together, their boss, the materials manager, could be sensitive to both materials costs and vendor relations along with inventory and ordering costs.

Critics of this materials manager proposal argued their points quite vociferously. Needless to say, the loudest complaints came from the manufacturing manager to whom production planning and control reported. The manufacturing manager worried that a materials manager would pay inordinate attention to the materials costs and neglect other detailed tasks, such as implementing engineering parts change orders and making certain that materials arrived on time. And the manufacturing manager felt threatened, understandably, by the prospect of someone else controlling affairs that might affect the manager's performance. Without careful attention to the timing of materials receipts, the manufacturing manager's assembly lines could be shut down, which would mean idle workers until late parts arrived, and then overtime to catch up.

This company, after carefully examining both sides of the issue, hired the materials manager.

A Company That Did Not

The operations director of a large manufacturer's consumer products division worried about rising inventory levels of both materials and finished goods, as well as about rising costs and increasing requirements for outside warehouse space.

The division manufactured in two plants—one in the Northeast, the other in the Midwest—a new product that competed vigorously with established manufacturers for market share. To build market share, the company adopted a strategy of selling a prime quality product at a premium price, supported by superior customer service. The company was about to extend distribution to new markets; at issue was whether a materials manager would facilitate better inventory management without interfering with other critical tasks.

The distribution manager felt that an integrated materials management organization made sense. He argued that purchasing, plant management, and distribution needed to collaborate to solve the excess inventory problem. He also felt that without a materials boss, this problem would aggravate internal tensions as the materials functions attempted to put blame on one another.

The purchasing manager opposed the materials manager proposal. She argued that the proposal meant a demotion for purchasing. She also maintained that the materials problem was more than one of excess inventories, since vendors had accepted only 5% of the raw materials specifications for the new product and thus materials rejects represented a serious potential problem.

The plant managers, trying to sort out the problems associated with a relatively new process technology and unstable demand patterns, felt negatively about the proposal, too. One manager argued:

> Plant activity begins with the receipt of a sales forecast and ends with the shipment of a customer order. Plant activities should be under the control of the plant manager in order to reduce the number of communication steps required to achieve plant goals.

The director of operations carefully examined all sides of the issue and decided not to establish a materials management position. Instead, all of the materials functions continued to report directly to the operations director.

A Matter of Trade-Offs

To gain some insights into how a company can adapt a materials organization to its particular needs, it is useful to examine, first, the general nature of the materials trade-offs in each of the preceding companies and, second, how the ranking of these trade-offs helped determine the best way to organize.

Exhibit 3 is a matrix that depicts basic trade-offs within and between materials functions in the typical manufacturing company. The trade-offs on the diagonal are those that usually bring the materials functions in contact with other parts of the organization, whereas the off-diagonal cells show trade-offs that raise concerns between two or more of the materials functions.

For example, purchasing in the consumer products division involved trade-offs between procurement costs and the quality of the item being purchased. In managing the procurement cost-quality trade-off, it is generally necessary for purchasing to interact with engineering, marketing, and other nonmaterials functions to perform value analyses of materials and vendors. Similarly, the linkages between distribution and marketing, and production inventory control and manufacturing, are implied by other diagonal trade-offs.

Off-diagonal trade-offs are exemplified by the inventory cost versus purchasing cost trade-off of concern to the electronics company. Such a situation might encourage production planning and control to order materials in small quantities with assurance of quick deliveries in order to minimize inventories. Purchasing, however, might want order releases to be large to take advantage of the quantity discounts written into the contracts, and thus to minimize materials and ordering costs. Managing this off-diagonal trade-off and conflict requires communication between the two materials functions of production planning and purchasing.

Traditionally organized companies, such as the one shown in Exhibit 1.A, are usually well suited to managing the diagonal trade-offs, which re-

Exhibit 3. Trade-Offs Among Materials Functions

	Purchasing	Production Planning and Inventory Control	Distribution
Purchasing	Procurement cost vs. quality	Inventory costs vs. procurement costs	Transport costs vs. procurement costs
Production planning and inventory control	Procurement costs vs. inventory costs	Inventory costs vs. manufacturing costs	Transport costs vs. inventory costs
Distribution	Procurement costs vs. transportation costs	Inventory costs vs. transport costs	Transport costs vs. customer service

quire communication between one of the materials functions and other functional areas. In contrast, the off-diagonal trade-offs call for communication links between materials functions. The materials management organization shown in Exhibit 1.B tends to facilitate communications that support effective off-diagonal trade-off decisions.

Consistent with the theoretical arguments for the classical materials management structure, a materials manager in the electronics company, for example, could more easily resolve conflicts between production inventory control and purchasing about lot sizing or expediting decisions affecting both inventory costs and materials costs if both reported to that person.

Naturally, every company wants all the trade-offs in its particular matrix to be well managed. However, different organization structures tend to favor particular types of trade-offs. For example, the classic materials management organization in Exhibit 1.B tends to facilitate the management of the off-diagonal trade-offs but to impair the management of the diagonal trade-offs.

For example, when both purchasing and production inventory control report to a materials manager charged with managing the procurement cost versus inventory cost trade-off, the communication lines are likely to be cleared to manage this trade-off well. More obstacles are likely, however, between production inventory control and manufacturing. In this instance, responsibility for managing the trade-off between manufacturing and inventory costs is likely to be split; and with an organization such as that shown in Exhibit 1.B, serious conflicts must go all the way up to the general manager for resolution.

The same reasoning implies, conversely, that a traditional organization structure, such as that shown in Exhibit 1.A, tends to facilitate the management of diagonal trade-offs while, at the same time, inhibiting the management of the off-diagonal trade-offs.

The relationship between materials organization structure and trade-off management suggests that company officials must decide which trade-offs are most important when organizing the materials functions.

For example, the consumer products manufacturer felt that the most important trade-offs were the procurement cost versus quality trade-offs and the delivery cost versus customer service trade-off. The high priorities given these trade-offs coincide with the company's competitive strategy, emphasizing quality and customer service, and the company's plans to build a third regional plant. The relatively traditional organization (sans materials manager) on which this company decided was consistent with these priorities.

The electronics manufacturer felt that the procurement cost versus inventory cost trade-off was most important because of the company's emphasis on cost and inventory reductions. Thus it hired a materials manager to oversee this off-diagonal trade-off. The second most important trade-off for this company was diagonal—the delivery cost versus customer service trade-off. Thus the organization structure most consistent with this company's strategy and environment was not the theoretical materials management organization but instead of partially integrated supply oriented structure.

We feel that the high proportion of partially integrated structures indicated by our survey stems from analyses that rank off-diagonal and diagonal trade-offs first and second, respectively.

Other Options

Managers should keep in mind that there are alternatives to reorganization for managing important trade-offs. Among the alternatives to materials management structures are what organizational theorists call "lateral relations" and also the use of computer-based systems.[3]

Lateral relations involve using informal communications, meetings, joint committees, and similar devices to integrate common concerns across organizational boundaries. In many companies, this approach has enabled purchasing, production control, and distribution people to coexist for years, although it is typically employed to deal with a materials function crisis. Many companies used lateral relations to cope with the severe shortages that accompanied the Arab oil embargo of 1973.

The real challenge facing companies inclined to employ lateral relations is to use the procedure before a crisis develops. The consumer goods manufacturer described earlier decided to rely on lateral relations over the short term, while considering the materials manager approach for the future, after markets and vendors had stabilized.

Many materials manager tasks can be accomplished, at least partially, with the aid of computer-based systems and procedures. This is particularly true in stable environments in which certain materials functions, such as the translation of production plans into materials requirements, can be incorporated into the kind of fixed decision rules and data flows that computers handle so well.

Our data show that some companies tend to substitute computer-based systems for materials managers. Of companies making medium to high use of computer systems to coordinate materials tasks, 78% had no materials manager. And conversely, of companies making little use of computer systems, 60% had a materials manager. Also, many companies use materials managers primarily to implement computer-based systems for materials control. However, companies attempting to completely substitute computer systems for materials managers face a danger, we believe, of carrying the process too far. That is because computer-based systems may come to be viewed as total substitutes for organization, which they are not. Each com-

Matching Trade-Offs and Tools

Organizational design is a complex undertaking and we have no desire to oversimplify it here. Personalities, skill availabilities, personnel policies, and other factors are important in deciding on the best materials organization. The main rationale for an organization structure, however, must be the tasks to be accomplished and the trade-offs to be made.

In organizing for materials management, companies should identify and rank the materials function trade-offs and then match the trade-offs with the best management tools possible. If these key trade-offs are on the diagonal, a traditional organization can be used. If the off-diagonal trade-offs are important, a materials management organization may be most appropriate. If the key concerns are a combination of diagonal and off-diagonal trade-offs, then a partial materials management organization may be best. The tools applied to manage the less important trade-offs could include alternative approaches, such as lateral relations or computer-based systems.

At the Corporate Level

The issues discussed thus far relate to those most often faced by individual divisions of decentralized companies with single markets or product lines, or smaller companies. At the corporate level of companies with several markets or products, the issues differ somewhat because the objective is usually more narrowly defined—whether to provide economies through consolidation of effort.

One way to generate economies is through centralized procurement.[4] For example, a large industrial company established a corporate materials group to handle the materials activities of its many divisions. Although this group could not force divisional participation in its programs, participation eventually occurred because of clearly documented cost savings.

One such program involved establishing "commodity teams" for key materials groups. Any division that purchased a commodity and wished to participate was invited to designate a representative for the team, with the largest divisional user providing the team leader. These commodity teams arranged corporatewide national purchase agreements with commodity suppliers resulting in substantial procurement cost savings.

Another way to generate economies is to consolidate the distribution activity. The same company established a corporate fleet, which led to more efficient trucking of raw materials and finished products to and from divisions as well as to reduced trucking charges. The corporate materials group also reduced costs by establishing a systems section that developed computer-based systems for production planning and inventory control tailored to the specific requirements of a particular division.

Such cost-cutting programs are not the only contribution that a corporate materials management group can make. It can also help develop on a companywide basis an awareness of the importance of integrating materials tasks.

Finally, the corporate materials management group benefited the same large industrial company in the following ways:

☐ By developing a pool of managers who received training across the traditional functional boundaries because the managers performed consulting assignments for the corporate materials group within the divisions.

☐ By disseminating profitable materials-related ideas and developments throughout the company. In the first years of operation, this profit improvement program identified several ways to save $16 million.

☐ By helping to develop links between the various materials activities within divisions. For example, while implementing an inventory management system within a division, the corporate materials consultant helped identify ways the system might be used to coordinate vendor communications and to schedule distribution activities.

☐ By starting a personnel data bank consisting of all materials management personnel currently working for the company as well as bright prospects from outside. This aided development of an integrated materials management operation for interested divisions.

In addition to such functions of a corporate materials group, the mere existence of the group emphasizes to divisions that management considers the area important.

The key question for a corporate materials management structure is whether the economies generated outweigh the effects of the loss of direct control of materials activities by the divisions. If, for example, a division's market depends on its ability to provide rapid delivery service on short notice, the gains from the corporate fleet might not outweigh the loss of customer goodwill that inevitably follows drops in service levels. The division might also need to maintain a high level of manufacturing flexibility, and the economies from a centralized procurement program could reduce that flexibility.

Thus the decision to establish a corporate materials manager is as complex as the decision to establish a divisional materials manager. The pivotal issue at the corporate level is the trade-off between the potential economies of a corporate materials group versus a possible loss of divisional focus.

Organization as a Tool

The trend toward materials managers is an important one. Materials managers have emerged from obscurity and are major forces on the industrial scene. But each company must thoroughly examine its own mission and strategy, its basic priorities, and the necessary trade-offs before deciding for or against using a materials manager and how its organization should be structured.

Perhaps the most important lesson of the materials management approach is that organization can be an important tool for attacking materials problems. A new weapon—the materials manager—has been added to the array of systems, modeling, negotiating, and other approaches that have traditionally been applied to inventory control, production planning, purchasing, and distribution problems. As always, though, creating the weapons for the armory is only half the battle. Just as important is judiciously selecting and using the right weapon for the battle at hand.

Notes

1. Gregory V. Schultz, "The Real Low-Down on Materials Management," *Factory*, December 1967, p. 49.

2. See Dean Ammer, "Materials Management as a Profit Center," *HBR*, January–February 1969, p. 72.

3. For a more complete discussion of these issues, see Paul R. Lawrence and Jay W. Lorsch *Organization and Environment* (Homewood, IL, Irwin, 1969); and Jay Galbraith, *Designing Complex Organizations* (Reading, MA, Addison-Wesley, 1973).

4. See E. Raymond Corey, "Should Companies Centralize Procurement?" *HBR*, November–December 1978, p. 102.

Appendix

The Materials Management Survey

We sent the materials management survey questionnaire to 206 managers in manufacturing companies of all types, and received 137 valid responses. Respondents included capital and industrial goods producers as well as consumer durable and nondurable producers in about the same proportions as they exist in the country. The typical company sampled had sales of $200 million annually, although companies of all sizes were represented (41% of responding companies had sales of less than $100 million and 59% had sales of more than $100 million).

Table A.1 Who Reports to the Materials Manager

	Percent
Purchasing	69
Production planning	77
Distribution	39*
Traffic	55

*The distribution function existed as an identifiable organizational entity in less than 50% of the companies in the sample. In most other cases, finished goods inventories, if any, were located at the factory, or distribution and traffic were synonymous.

It is interesting to note that whether a company has a materials management function appears to be unrelated to company size; the percentage of companies with materials manager posts and less than $20 million of sales is the same as the percentage of companies with more than $200 million sales.

The survey also provided indications of how materials managers fit into their company organizations and the scope of their responsibilities.

Table A.1 indicates, for example, the frequency with which the materials functions report directly to a materials manager when one exists. Even allowing for the considerable ambiguity of terms such as "distribution" and "production planning," the data show that the range of responsibility for most materials managers usually encompasses the nerve center function of production planning, and most often includes at least one other materials function, such as purchasing or traffic.

Table A.2 shows where materials managers reported organizationally. Although a surprisingly high proportion report to a division general manager or the president of a company, the data show that manufacturing is still the most common home for the materials manager. The organizational visibility of most materials managers in the sample is high, however—within two levels of the head of the company or division.

Table A.2 To Whom the Materials Manager Reports

	Percent
General manager or president	22
Manufacturing manager	43
Control or finance	4
Other*	31

*Various positions such as executive vice president, vice president of administration, etc.

Table A.3 Evaluation of Materials Managers

Performance Measure	Percent of Materials Managers Evaluated on This Measure
On-time deliveries	80
Stockouts	71
Customer complaints	27
Inventory levels	87
Profitability	20
Purchased materials costs	69
Warehousing costs	29
Transportation costs	53
Manufacturing costs	7
Other	16

Table A.3 provides another view of the scope of responsibility of materials managers. It indicates how their performance is measured. Not surprisingly, the major performance indicators—customer service, inventories, raw materials, and transport costs—common to most materials managers encompass the same areas of concern as the major forces for change that we have identified.

23
Managing Manufacturing Lead Times

ERNEST C. HUGE

Managers in manufacturing organizations often fail to grasp fully the interrelationships between production lead times and the objectives of schedule performance, inventory, and product cost. Shorter lead times improve responsiveness to schedule changes, thereby softening the effects of economic cycles and forecasting errors. Management can use the cumulative product lead period to determine whether to accept schedule changes—which helps minimize the perennial conflict between the marketing and manufacturing functions. This article describes a program for controlling and reducing lead times. The author discusses work-in-process inventories and ways to handle vendors' lead times.

As a rule, manufacturing managers do not try to reduce production lead times systematically. They accept the existing times and often add a little "pad" for contingency. When the economy inflates and lead times increase significantly, managers automatically put longer lead times into their production and material planning and control systems. In other words, they let lead times happen.

Because of their effects on manufacturing-marketing relationships, production plans, and distribution performance, lead times are highly important to a company's success. Shortening them can improve customer service, reduce inventory costs, and shave product costs.

To a large degree, marketing and manufacturing objectives are opposed. Marketing, on the one hand, wants a fast response to shifting demand that often causes quick production schedule changes and greater expense in overhead and in premiums to vendors to accelerate their deliveries. Manufacturing, on the other hand, wants gradual schedule changes in order to minimize product cost and inventory and overhead expenses, and to maximize output. But this posture reduces responsiveness. The answer is to trade off these conflicting objectives in a way that optimizes results for the company.

Unfortunately, such a trade-off is difficult to quantify. Maintaining objectivity in a trade-off analysis of schedule changes is also difficult because of the psychological pressures when demand is strong; few companies like to turn down or delay new business. Even though the probability of attaining schedule increases may be low, the urge to schedule them anyway is usually overwhelming.

When management succumbs to this urge, inventory and product cost objectives are bound to suffer. The answer to this problem is to maintain the shortest possible lead times for assemblies and component parts in order to allow maximum responsiveness to product schedule increases and decreases without harming inventory and product cost objectives.

If the lead times in a company's system are valid, the cumulative lead time of parts and assemblies on the critical path of product fabrication can be used to determine whether to accept schedule changes. Moreover, the manufacturing manager can evaluate more precisely the effects of any schedule changes that violate the cumulative lead time (and may order the product to be built in less than the cumulative lead time).

How practical is it to apply a rule that cumulative lead time cannot be violated even if you know that your lead times are valid? The answer hinges on several things. First of all, it depends on how effective the materials management organization is. If the organization has met its materials availability objectives consistently, it can probably handle expediting. A key measure of how well availability objectives are being met is the percentage of shop orders that are released on schedule.

Another consideration is whether the requested increase follows a recent reduction affecting the same product or a similar product with a high degree of commonality. Maybe a trade-off is feasible with another product whose completion can be scheduled for a later date. Commonality of parts in two products, however, does not guarantee successful support of a schedule increase.

The inviolability of cumulative lead time, like most policies, does not apply in every situation. But it is an effective starting point when the company is sure of the soundness of the existing production lead times.

Facets of the Problem

Obviously, if lead times are inflated, schedule increases can be easily accommodated. Unfortunately, however, you do not know how many increases you can accept before the pad disappears and costs begin to accelerate.

An organization using a computerized materials planning system faces another problem when it allows several violations in succession: the items that must be expedited soon exceed a manageable quantity. So the integrity of the computerized system deteriorates. Overhead and direct labor costs rise geometrically because determinations now have to be made manually instead of through the computer.

When inflated cumulative product lead times prevail, deciding whether to accept an increase is usually subjective and can be very costly. If the product is complex, a lot of manual analysis is necessary. When time is short, the analysis may cover only unique parts—that is, those used only in the product whose schedule is being evaluated—on the assumption that parts common to other products will pose no problem. This assumption is usually false, because the common parts must also be expedited.

An analysis must deal in the probabilities of expediting components on time. In actuality, the probability of expediting a single part on time is usually less than 95%; and, of course, the probability of having all necessary parts on hand on time declines with the number of parts. Exhibit 1 diagrams the situation.

Even if one assumes near perfection and expects a 95% probability of successfully accelerating the availability of as few as 10 needed parts, the cumulative probability of having all parts on hand in timely fashion is: $(.95)^{10} = .60 = 60\%$.

If only five parts need to be expedited but the probability that each can be delivered on schedule is 50%, then the probability that all can be speeded up is: $(.5)^5 = .03 = 3\%$.

The size of work-in-process (WIP) inventory is related to manufacturing lead times. Therefore, reduction of lead times reduces this inventory and may improve schedule performance and customer service.

Whether it does help schedule performance depends on how much WIP inventory the organization is carrying. If it is excessive, the priorities of work in process probably change frequently. Those shifts are very disruptive, not only because they oblige the production function to spend time finding the right materials to work on, but also because they force excessive setups and teardowns, which reduce throughput and raise product cost.

If a manufacturer or a vendor faces a capacity problem, there is a strong temptation to increase lead time. But this move would only result in a larger WIP inventory, which would probably be counterproductive. The answer is to solve the capacity problem, not lengthen lead times.

The manager should consider carrying an extra inventory of items on the critical path to permit a fast response to schedule increases. A rather small investment in extra inventory may permit a considerably shorter lead time. As with many investments, however, sooner or later it reaches a point

FACETS OF THE PROBLEM

Exhibit 1. Probability that All Parts Will Be Available on Time vs. Number of Parts

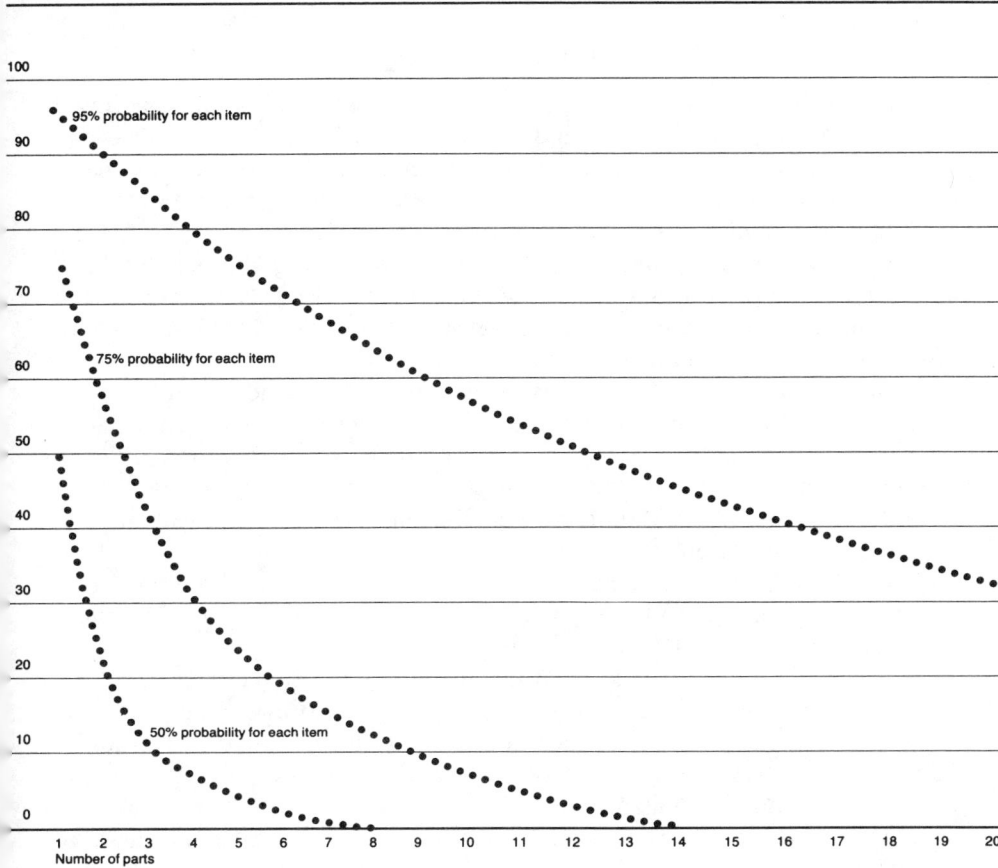

of diminishing returns. When the investment is substantial, for instance, carrying extra finished goods inventory is better. If Operations carries a lot of items on the critical path, the manager will find this approach to be less practical because of the additional manual analysis necessary to determine the acceptable amount of cumulative lead time violation.

(If the product has as many as 50 parts or assemblies, a computer program to determine the critical path is probably worth the effort and expense. Use of a computer program, replacing manual analysis, also permits the user to simulate various plans. If, say, the production function reduces the lead times on parts B, D, and J, what would be the effect on the cumulative lead time?)

Carrying extra stock also increases vulnerability to inventory gluts if the product schedule increases or designs change. Clearly, shorter lead times offer a better alternative.

A Management Program

Companies often emphasize schedule objectives when demand is high and inventory objectives when demand is low and interest rates are up. A lead time management program can facilitate attainment of schedule and inventory objectives simultaneously during all phases of the economic cycle.

It is essential to establish objectives for lead time reduction for the directors of purchasing and manufacturing and to hold these individuals accountable for their attainment. One big advantage of this program is the complementary nature of the objectives at all levels of the organization, down to the production planner.

Industrial Engineering, Production Operations, and Manufacturing Control are all functions that must be held accountable for assembly lead time objectives, for two reasons: (1) each affects lead times, and (2) each provides a check and balance against the other. The primary missions of Production Operations, Manufacturing Control, and Industrial Engineering are, respectively, attaining schedule, making production plans and controlling inventory, and minimizing direct labor costs. If the lead time reduction objective is given only to Industrial Engineering, say, that department might take action at the expense of the schedule.

At first, set the objective rather arbitrarily to reduce a certain percentage of lead time. Once you have set a target and everyone is driving toward it, you can get a better idea of how valid the objective is. Do not be surprised if you change the objective several times before you settle on one that poses a realistic challenge.

The time spent in processing orders can assume great importance in the effort to control lead times. Because almost everyone along the line seems to pad, here is a good opportunity to make improvements at no extra cost. Scrutinize the time it takes:

- ☐ A distribution warehouse or service center to analyze its demand and place orders with the manufacturing plant.
- ☐ Manufacturing to insert an order in its planning and scheduling system, such as the time to write a shop order for in-house assemblies.
- ☐ Materials Planning to authorize Purchasing to procure material.
- ☐ Purchasing to write the purchase order.

Dealing with Vendors

When possible, the organization should negotiate maximum lead times with a vendor, so that the vendor will guarantee to ship a part by a certain date, if not earlier. Prior to negotiations, analyze your experience with this supplier. The vendor may quote a lead time of four months; if, however, you have consistently induced the vendor to give you one-month delivery without extra cost, then one month is the actual lead time. In your negotiations, go after the one-month period, get it in the contract, and tie performance to price.

A good selling point in getting the vendor to agree to a short lead time is that it will minimize the times the vendor is rescheduled (which is another negotiable item). In Exhibit 2, which plots the probability of a schedule change over time, note the very low likelihood until month six.

Superimposed on this plot is the critical path of a typical product, totaling six and one-half months. Observe that if the supplier of a component can reduce the lead time from three months to two, the probability of a schedule change that violates cumulative lead time tumbles from nearly 40% to 5%.

Purchased parts usually have many different lead times, depending on the source and the priorities given them. Consider, for example, a part that can be ordered from the OEM vendor and obtained in two months. It is, however, available from a distributor's shelf on a routine basis in a week

Exhibit 2. Probability of a Future Schedule Change

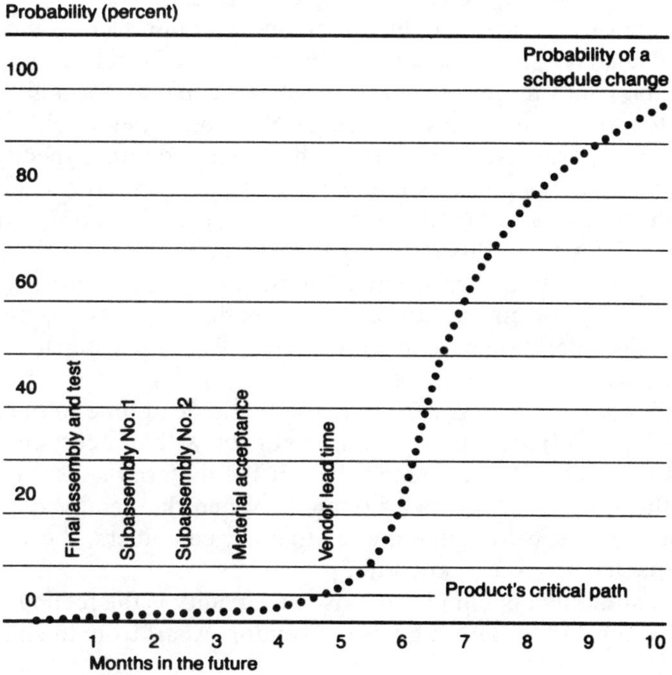

(although probably at great cost) and on an emergency basis in a day (when cost is no object).

In your planning system, incorporate lead times that are short enough to be feasible without resorting to special effort from vendors, such as expediting, taking premium time, and using special transport arrangements. For a sole-sourced part, however, you may find it difficult to negotiate a short lead time. As a rule, it is wise to obtain more vendors before seeking such a reduction.

Vendor's Capacity. A vendor's lead time is, of course, directly related to order backlog and capacity. If the vendor has a backlog of 1,000 parts and a capacity of 200 parts per week, the lead time will be 5 weeks. That is:

$$\text{Lead time} = \frac{\text{backlog}}{\text{capacity}} = \frac{1{,}000 \text{ parts}}{200 \text{ parts per week}} = 5 \text{ weeks}$$

If the vendor's backlog rises or a capacity problem is encountered, the supplier will probably quote a longer lead time. If the period is raised by two weeks, the vendor can expect two weeks' worth of additional orders from customers. These orders, in turn, may justify another lead time increase, and the process goes on ad infinitum. When demand is very strong, a quoted lead time of six months is not unusual, even though the product or process may take only one month to complete.

If a vendor increases the lead time and you don't place more orders, someone else may get ahead of you in line. To forestall a supplier from stretching the lead time, reserve the supplier's capacity for a given volume of output for a certain duration (such as X castings per week). Then, just before the vendor releases the work to the production line, specify the item configurations you want that will make use of the reserved capacity. In this fashion you can make your lead time the supplier's production process time instead of process time plus "stand in line" time.

This is probably the best way to control purchased-part lead periods. The ultimate way, of course, to purchase vendor capacity is either to purchase the entire operation or to integrate vertically. Either step may be logical for critical parts.

Another way of buying capacity is to tie the lead time to the price paid to the supplier, so that if delivery fails to occur within a certain period the supplier is paid less. By the same token, if the material is delivered before deadline, the supplier receives a premium. When the vendor quotes a lead time to you that is less than that quoted to other customers, the vendor must reserve capacity for you to keep the promise.

An outstanding benefit of purchase of capacity is the feeling of security that the long-term relationship gives the vendor. Apart from the higher prior-

A MANAGEMENT PROGRAM 403

ity accorded your orders, the vendor may well suggest ideas that will save money and improve quality. When you make a greater commitment to the supplier, the supplier makes a greater commitment to you in time and resources—perhaps even undertaking a substantial capital outlay in order to meet obligations.[1]

Having established such a relationship, you may be in a position to ask the supplier to help you in other ways. One is having the supplier keep "bonded stock" for you. This is an arrangement in which the vendor maintains a certain quantity of finished parts, perhaps at no extra cost. If, however, the carrying cost of the bonded stock is included in the cost of the part, the result is the same as carrying extra parts in your inventory.

Work in Process

The technique of input-output control is a solid foundation for managing your own capacity and lead times.[2] With this approach the production manager monitors the actual output from a work center versus the planned output, and the actual material input to the work center versus the planned material input. Here are the principles underlying the technique:

☐ The lead time stretches as the backlog grows. As I discussed previously, the lead time lengthens when added time is necessary to manage more material and excessive setups and teardowns due to priority changes.

☐ To control the lead time, therefore, control the backlog.

☐ To control the backlog, release no more work into a center than it has recently shown that it can turn out.

☐ When a work center's output consistently falls short of the input to it, initiate either an expansion of capacity or a reduction of input in order to relieve the capacity constraint.

Exhibit 3 shows a typical input-output format applicable to a work center, operation, or person. As the actual output of this center has consistently fallen short of planned output, at the end of week 4 the cumulative variance stands at minus 95 hours. However, the actual input has proceeded nearly according to plan. So the work center suffers from a capacity constraint.

A key to using the input-output technique is to establish a planned backlog and a tolerance level, such as ±10%, for each work center. When the backlog tolerance level is exceeded, the work center's capacity should be altered.

Assembly Lead Times. In their belief that the correct lead time is what has actually been required in the past, many managers average the data from

Exhibit 3. Sample Input-Output Format (in hours)

		Weeks				
		1	2	3	4	5
Output	Planned	100	100	100	100	100
	Actual	75	85	75	70	
	Cumulative variance	−25	−40	−65	−95	
Input	Planned	100	100	100	100	100
	Actual	110	105	95	95	
	Cumulative variance	+10	+15	+10	+5	
Backlog (200 at start)		235	255	275	300	

experience (and pad it a bit in case of slippage). In reality, the right length of time is often a lot less than "average actuals."

In a continuous-flow production process like that of a chemicals manufacturer, WIP lead time is equal to the actual operation or hands-on time. In a job-shop environment, where different assemblies are processed in the same operation, the total lead time is usually much longer. It consists of hands-on time (setup and actual operation) plus queue time (waiting to be worked on). The latter often accounts for as much as 60% to 90% of the total. In such cases, determining the minimum total duration obviously depends primarily on establishing the minimum queue time.

To understand the basis for the minimum queue time, compare a work center to a bucket with a spigot (Exhibit 4). The fluid in the bucket is work in process. To produce maximum output through the spigot, the operator must maintain the fluid at Point A or higher. If the rate of fluid input exactly equals the rate of output, the fluid level does not have to be higher than Point A.

In all processes other than a continuous flow, however, the materials usually come in at a different rate from the goods going out. Consequently, in the diagrammed case extra queue time is required (the difference between Points A and B) to ensure that the fluid does not fall below Point A. In short, the purpose of queue time is to adjust to variations in the input and output rates.

The important question is: How much excess over Point A is needed to maintain the minimum output required? The answer is: whatever is the maximum variation in flow rates between the two work centers. The variation is determined by looking at the history of variations in queue time.

Exhibit 5 is a simplified table showing this procedure. Note that for

A MANAGEMENT PROGRAM 405

Exhibit 4. Input to and Output from a Work Center, Showing Queue

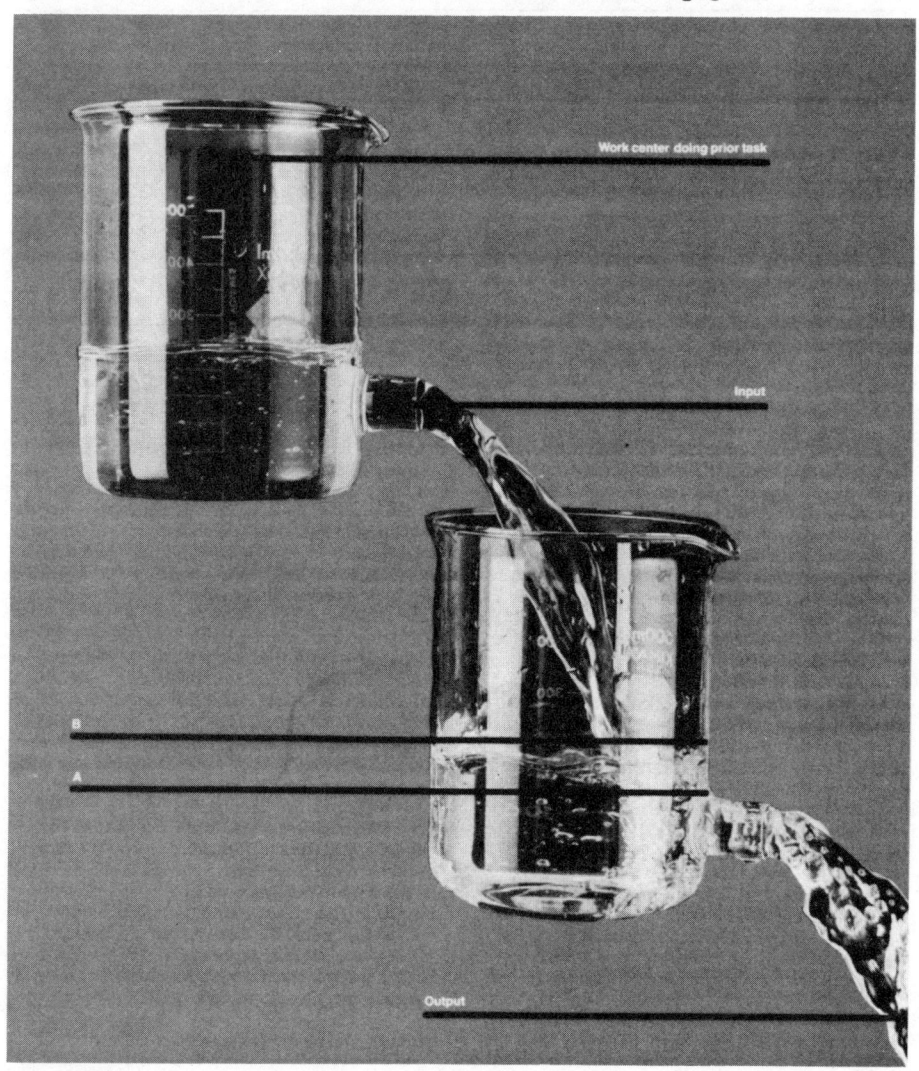

the five shop orders analyzed in the exhibit, the queue averaged 90% of the total production time. The queue periods ranged between 17.4 and 24.7 days, or 7.3 days. Therefore, the lead time for this assembly is 7.3 (queue) plus 2.4 (hands-on), or 9.7 days. Put 10 days into your planning system. Naturally, however, this analysis is valid only if done over several months and if the operation and/or mix of assemblies are not expected to change significantly.

Exhibit 5. Variations in Queue for an Assembly (in days)

Shop Order	Queue Time	Time in Production Hands-On-Time	Total
No. 1	22.5	2.5	25
No. 2	18.6	2.4	21
No. 3	20.7	2.3	23
No. 4	17.4	2.6	20
No. 5	24.7	2.3	27
Average	20.8	2.4	23.2

Implementing the Changes

To reduce WIP lead times beyond the point developed by queue analysis, you must increase capacity. Whether to take this action depends on the trade-off between higher manufacturing costs and lower WIP inventory plus other, less easily quantifiable benefits.

If you reduce WIP lead times by one week, you will need one week's less materials requirements to support the same scheduled output. This means that no material will be released at the "gateway" work centers (the first ones in the manufacturing process) for a week.

Because this suspension relieves the work load of the personnel assigned to the gateway centers, the best time to implement lead time reductions is when you increase the production schedules. Thus the schedule boost offsets the lead time reduction.

As in most organization changes, successful implementation of assembly lead time reductions requires selling the people affected on the benefits to them personally. The best selling points to Industrial Engineering and Production Operations are the minimization of schedule changes and the stabilization of the work load, which should improve efficiency. The move also will facilitate priority control, which is a big benefit for Production Operations because the department is obliged to react to changing priorities. With less total work in process, managing the remainder is easier.

Operators used to seeing a big backlog of work piled behind them feel insecure if they suddenly see it dwindle.[3] Unless they are informed about what is happening, operators slow down until the backlog reaches their "security level." They must understand that lower backlog levels do not mean that schedules are slowing. Showing them output rates frequently will help.

Production Operations may oppose the move on the ground that some of the lead time is contingency against late receipt of materials. Take advantage of this argument. Ask the managers there how much the lead time could be trimmed if the material were released to them promptly. If, for example, they say the period can be cut by 10 days, tell them you will reduce the assembly lead time by 10 days and simultaneously increase the safety time (contingency time between receipt at the dock and the date material is needed) of all material used in the assembly.

This would not affect the cumulative product lead time but would minimize WIP inventory and maximize availability of purchased parts. Furthermore, the step would improve priority control because material would be released into production later, causing fewer priority changes.

Costs and Benefits

Since this kind of program involves an investment in resources, ideally it should be evaluated like any other investment. Unfortunately, this is usually difficult to do. The costs of other ways to reduce lead times, like raising productive capacity and boosting the finished goods inventory to allow a faster response, are easy to estimate. In this kind of program, however, usually the benefits can only be determined subjectively. For example, management may ask, what is it worth to cut the total product lead time from seven to five months? Sure, it will reduce the likelihood that schedule changes will be allowed that violate cumulative lead times, but what is it worth in dollars and cents?

Probably the only saving that can be determined objectively is the reduction in WIP inventory due to upgrading of manufacturing capacity in equipment or manpower, or both. If, for instance, capacity rises from 100% to 120% of the amount required to meet the schedule, WIP inventory probably would be trimmed by 20%. In this case, both the reduction in WIP inventory and the cost of increasing capacity can be quantified.

In trying to quantify the benefits, the manager can develop a curve relating additional costs to the lead time reduction. If obliged to make a trade-off between the two, the curve will help the manager put the issue in perspective. It could like like Exhibit 6. As in any endeavor, lead time management requires an investment in resources. The managers of each organization must determine what is in it for them. In many instances,

Exhibit 6. Curve Relating Costs to Lead Time Reduction

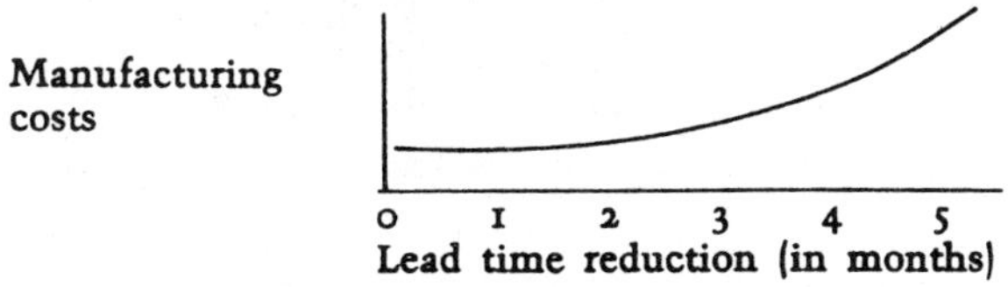

Manufacturing costs

0   1   2   3   4   5
Lead time reduction (in months)

however, lead times can be reduced without any out-of-pocket expenditure. The major investment may be only the time needed to sell people on the benefits.

In spite of the potential advantages for most manufacturers and distributors of tightly controlling lead times, most administrators let them happen. Consequently, managing lead times can provide an enormous edge on competition through lower costs and faster responses.

Notes

1. For an account of how one company bought capacity, see R. David Garwood, "Delivery as Promised," *Production and Inventory Management Journal*, Third Quarter 1971, p. 42.

2. This technique was developed by Oliver W. Wight; see his article, "Input/Output Control: A Real Handle on Lead Time," *Production and Inventory Management Journal*, Third Quarter 1970, p. 9.

3. See Earl R. Gomersall, "The Backlog Syndrome," *HBR*, September–October 1964, p. 105.

24
Look Beyond the Obvious in Plant Location

ROGER W. SCHMENNER

When on-site expansion has become impractical, companies must decide whether to relocate or to open branches. Although the location decision may appear straightforward, if it chiefly involves financial assessments, the company faces unexpected pitfalls, according to this author. He discusses the relative advantages of relocation and new branches in light of a company's unique problems and shows why simply relocating to the cheapest site is often the poorest solution for a growing company.

For many managers, plant location decision making merely refers to the selection of a site for a new plant, and for some the choice is straightforward: select the least costly site. Often a consultant is brought in or a management team assembled with the sole purpose of scouring the South or the Far East, Mexico or Puerto Rico, for low-wage low-cost low-tax sites so that plant location can contribute to "the bottom line." This mode of thinking invites disaster, as numerous companies have found out.

This article outlines what the typical company ought to think about before calling in the location consultants. It draws on extensive interviews and research centering on manufacturing companies with operations in either Cincinnati or New England.[1] I interviewed more than 30 companies. In addition, more than 1,000 plants in the two locales completed detailed questionnaires that asked about present operations and recent history and that captured many features of the plants' production, marketing, purchasing, and financial characteristics. Of these plants, over 200 had recently relocated, and I gathered data about their former as well as their present locations and about the differences between them. More than 150 of the plants were new, and most were new branch plants. In addition, more than 120 corporate headquarters filled out surveys about their location decision making.

This wealth of information supports plant location as an integral feature of a company's capacity planning. Deciding plant location is more than choosing a site. Indeed, the actual selection of a new plant site should come near the end of a chain of decisions concerning: (1) a company's capacity needs, (2) the extent and quality of its present capacity, (3) the way in which its existing plants fit together in a multiplant manufacturing strategy, and (4) expected future demands on manufacturing, apart from mere space requirements.

Site selection should not be separated from these other decisions in the chain and should not be delegated to the finance department or some consultant. Their decisions may be totally incompatible with the company's needs for new capacity, given its product mix and technology, or with important interactions among existing plants. Going straight for the bottom line may inadvertently harm a carefully constructed mosaic of manufacturing capabilities and may add to operating costs much more than tax breaks or low wages subtract.

Possible Options

Given a forecast of future capacity needs, a company can add space in one of three ways: by plant expansion on existing sites, by establishing new branch plants, or by plant relocation.

On-site plant expansion is by far the most popular means of adding industrial capacity. My data suggest that between 6% and 9% of all plants actually expand on-site during any one year. It is generally the cheapest way to add capacity and the least disruptive to current operations. The company does not risk dispersal of an existing and sometimes highly skilled labor force and does not have to wrestle with the separation of products or portions of the production process for location in another plant. Expansion may also lead to economies of scale, although such a benefit is too often illusory.

Although attractive, on-site plant expansion can usher in a host of diseconomies, particularly if such expansion has been a repeated practice. For example, as more and more production space is added on-site, the layout of the plant typically becomes less and less optimal. Rarely is an entire plant shifted around during an expansion. Rather, changes are made in only portions of the plant. The result, over time, is that departments once close together become separated. Materials handling and storage become more difficult, with more chances for delay or error. Managers find themselves isolated from one another and/or from the work groups they are supposed to oversee. In short, intraplant transportation and communication become strained, often to the detriment of product delivery and quality.

Staying at the same site often postpones the introduction of new process technology as well. Old equipment is kept in use, old methods are followed, and the advantages of new equipment and techniques are forgone, with consequences for both future costs and product innovation.

Continued on-site expansion means more and more workers and often more and more products to be managed. Such a layering of expanded responsibilities creates real complexities for managers at all levels. The existing cadre of managers may have to supervise more than they are readily capable of, thus lessening the attention certain problems should receive. With more products and output from the same plant, decisions on the levels, composition, and uses of inventories are likely to become more difficult and prone to error. Decisions on production control—what and when to produce, how to run it through the factory—are likely to become vastly more complex as well, just as the cost accounting system is becoming more arbitrary and thus less helpful.

With more products in the plant, management runs the risk not only of complicating supervision, inventory, and production control systems and the like but also of placing demands on managers, workers, and systems that are incompatible. For example, low-volume products of high quality demand a different mode of management, worker effort, and control than do products produced in high volume with little attention to quality. If both are manufactured in the same facility with common management, work force, policies, and systems, both products will most likely suffer in the dimensions (e.g., price, quality, delivery) that make a product competitive.

More than this incompatibility problem, the addition of workers to an existing site is likely to require the increasing formalization of the work force–management relationship. The work force is also less likely to identify strongly with the company, and labor relations within the plant may become strained. Earlier management concessions to the work force may come back to haunt operations. With increasing size as well, the plant is more likely to become a target for unionization, if it is not already organized.

For these reasons, continued on-site expansion becomes less and less desirable. The alternatives—new branch establishment and plant relocation—can obviate many of these long-term and frequently subtle pitfalls of on-site expansion, although their abilities to surmount certain obstacles differ. Exhibit 1 outlines some of the relative advantages of new branches and relocations.

The New Branch

If the plant's problems involve product proliferation, work force size, or meeting expected future growth, establishing a new trend may be advan-

Exhibit 1. Relative Advantages of Branches and Relocations Vis-à-Vis On-Site Expansion

Problem Area	New Branch Plant	Plant Relocation
Plant layout and materials handling	Radical improvements possible. Some possibilities of improving base plant as operations are placed in branch.	Radical improvements possible.
New process technology	New technology for branch possible; likely that base plant will keep much of old technology.	Scrapping of old plant, equipment, and methods possible; new technology can supplant it readily.
Production and/or inventory control	Can mean radical change to production control procedures and policies in new plant, though not much change to be expected for old plant. Inventories can build up.	Can mean radical changes in production and inventory control. Inventory levels more likely to be unaffected.
Managerial impact	Additional managers required to open and run branch. Staff demands increased to coordinate plant-to-plant interactions.	Old set of managers can generally run new plant without stretching the themselves too thin.
Product proliferation	Can easily manage new products, especially if branch plants are organized as product plants.	New products less easily managed.
Size of work force	Keeps work force levels at all plants under desired ceilings.	Little or no effect.
Financial burdens	Extra overhead demanded to cover more than one location, new plant start-up expenses.	Moving costs, new plant start-up expenses.
Ease of meeting future growth	Relatively easy. Geographic growth met best with new market area plants; product introductions with product plants; vertical integration with process plants.	Not easy. Shares many future capacity problems with on-site expansion alternative.

tageous. By branching, a company can avoid overloading one plant with either too many products or too many workers. At the same time, the new branch can exploit the latest production technology and the most sensible plant design. The company can ensure that operating policies and systems of the branch are carefully meshed with the product chosen for manufacture and with the competitive priorities attached to it.

Plant Relocation

If the plant's problems chiefly involve plant layout, materials handling and storage, new process technology, production and inventory control, and lack of management depth, then plant relocation may be the answer. Relocation by definition means closing one facility and opening another, which implies that relocation can readily scrap old capital, technology, and policies for new. Thus relocation gains in standing when the plant's problems are less related to large size and more to process technology and control.

Research Findings

Given this background of diseconomies of plant scale and relative advantages of branching and relocation, one should expect to find that the growing plant views on-site expansion, branching, and relocation not so much as substitutes but as distinct choices.

My research confirms these expectations. Overwhelmingly, it is the small growing plants, often independent of particular suppliers, markets, or labor sources and pressed for more production space, that move to larger modern quarters and in the process alter their production technology, sometimes in fundamental ways. The vast majority of relocations are over short distances (less than 20 miles), which helps to ensure continuity of labor force and retention to customer and supplier contacts. To a lesser degree, relocations also occur to consolidate two or more plants into a single new facility and to escape from high site costs (wages, land values, taxes).

It is the plants whose profits are hurting the most that see relocation chiefly as a means of lowering costs. These plants are also the ones most likely to move distances of greater than 20 miles in search of these lower costs.

Plant relocations are traumatic experiences for many managers and hence are likely to be avoided if at all possible. Only about a third of the relocations seriously contemplated are actually carried through, and actual relocations occur at a rate of only 3% per year for manufacturing establishments of all sizes, and less than 1% per year for plants of at least 100 employees.

More common, especially within larger companies, is the establishment of new branch plants. Each year, between 3% and 6% of the existing stock of plants is added on as new branch plants, and, of those branches contemplated, more than two-thirds are actually established, which is double the rate of relocations.

New branches start out small (only 40% of the size, on average, of their existing sister plants) and are simply organized. They are less likely to be unionized and more likely to enjoy simple logistics. Although often located in modern facilities with the latest technology, they are also frequently dependent on the corporate services provided by the plant or plants from which the branches were spun off. The products they make are commonly mature ones, technically well established, and in need of few engineering changes, although, for a quarter to a third of new branches, the product line and/or technology is new.

Multiplant Strategies

Analysis of these new branch plants and of the base plants from which they typically spring reveals that the new branch plant fits into a prescribed place in a multiplant company's scheme of things. It is possible to identify five general types of multiplant manufacturing strategies, and behind each one are compelling cost or managerial considerations.

Product Plant Strategy

Perhaps the most popular strategy is the product plant strategy, in which separate plants manufacture distinct products or product lines, each plant serving the company's entire domestic market area. Roughly 40% of all the multiplant corporations surveyed (or the autonomous divisions of the largest companies) claimed such a strategy, which involved about one-third of all their plants.

The product plant strategy permits each plant to concentrate on a limited set of products, generally within a well-defined market niche. This strategy has the advantage of permitting the plant management to select the process technology, equipment, labor force, manufacturing policies, and organization that are consistent with the particular competitive priorities (e.g., cost, quality, product flexibility, speed of delivery) associated with the plant's products. In this way, the company can avoid much of the complexity and congestion that plague many oversized multipurpose factories. In addition, a product plant strategy can take advantage of any possible economies of scale. Product plants can also make use of any raw materials or expertise of a particular geographic area.

A product plant strategy is likely to correspond to a decentralized manufacturing organization with a relatively small staff at the corporate level. Plant locations may be far-flung, though more often they are clustered within one or two broad regions of the country. Within such a strategy, a significant challenge to management lies in recognizing when a plant has simply become too large. What constitutes "too large" varies from industry to industry, from technology to technology, and from company to company, but I found that the most frequently quoted figures lie between 500 and 1,000 employees, with few companies stating figures in excess of 2,000.

In many industries, companies can divide operations according to a product plant strategy because the products manufactured are many and varied. Colt Industries, Fairchild Industries, and Insilco are large companies whose basic multiplant strategy is product plant. For smaller companies, the product plant strategy is even more prevalent.

Market Area Plant Strategy

Plants serve particular subnational market areas under this strategy. The plants themselves manufacture all or most of the corporation's product line. About a quarter of the responding corporations follow this strategy, which they use in just a little less than a quarter of all their plants.

The market area plant is perhaps the classic notion of the branch plant. When freight costs are significant because of high product weight or volume relative to value, it makes sense to spread plants apart geographically. This is all the more true if products are consumed over wide areas and if the market requires a quick response by manufacturing.

A market area plant strategy is likely to require more corporate coordination than the product plant strategy. The corporate staff is likely to be larger and to carry considerable clout. Plant managers, however, are less likely to be able to act autonomously. A different management challenge confronts the market area plant—namely, the sequencing and regional authority of new plants. For instance, should an East Coast company's second plant be in the Midwest, West, or South, and how should the market be split between plants? If the second plant is placed in the West, where and when should the company locate a third plant?

The national breweries are classic examples of market area plants, as are many glass, can, food, and building products companies. All involve products consumed in quantity everywhere and are subject to significant transport costs as a fraction of product values.

Product-Market Plant Strategy

Sometimes a corporation is so large that it is possible to assign market area plants within a product division organization. This is termed a product-market plant strategy, and although it prevails in only about one-sixth of the responding corporations, about one-third of all these companies' plants fall into this category.

The product-market plant strategy combines elements of both the product and the market area strategies and thus must make both size and sequencing decisions at the same time. For many of these companies, however, experience with past plant location decisions and a clear-cut organization often help to lessen what might otherwise be an exceedingly taxing series of decisions.

The large consumer products companies like Procter & Gamble or Standard Brands and diversified companies in standard product industries such as Georgia-Pacific are examples of product-market plant strategies. Many other large companies may pursue a market area plant strategy in the largest divisions and a product plant strategy in the smaller or more specialized divisions.

Process Plant Strategy

Rather than separate their manufacturing into individual plants by product, some companies, notably those with complex products, separate their production process by plant. These plants are often viewed as feeders to one or more final assembly plants. A process plant strategy, involving roughly one-tenth of the responding corporations and perhaps one-twelfth of their total number of plants, is less prevalent than the other strategies.

Like the product plant, the process plant exists to simplify an inherently complex and confusing managerial situation. For such complex products as automobiles, large machine tools, and computer systems, a number of plants usually make components of the completed product. The manufacturer faces a rash of make-or-buy choices for many of these components, but to be able to produce one or the other competitively may require different raw materials, labor skills, control systems, or management skills and organization.

This situation, coupled with the already discussed diseconomies introduced by large size, argues for a division of the complete manufacturing process into stages, with a separate plant for each stage.

This stage-by-stage division may lead to many feeder plants shipping to one or more assembly plants, or it may lead to one or few feeder plants (e.g., for a critical component) shipping to many other manufacturing plants. In any event, the concept of plant separation to simplify operations persists.

In fact, for any one stage, there may be economies of scale. Diverse manufacturing requirements explain why some plants may be located in the South or the Far East (for lower labor costs), or in resource or expertise-rich areas (e.g., "Silicon Valley" in California for the semiconductor industry), or merely in a separate location to provide surrounding plants with a special service that they could not provide for themselves economically.

The process plant strategy is even more demanding of high-level corporate coordination than the market area plant strategy. A manufacturing organization that is highly centralized, technically well versed, and responsible for the control and coordination of materials and products between plants generally accompanies the process plant strategy. For this reason, process plants are often located within easy commuting distance of one another.

General Purpose Plant Strategy

Some companies do not establish specific plant charters. Rather, such companies prize plants for their flexibility in adapting to constantly changing product needs. Defense contractors, among others, typically follow a general purpose plant strategy. Roughly one-tenth of the responding corporations claimed this strategy, which involved about one-twentieth of all their plants.

The general purpose plant strategy demands a considerable degree of centralized control. Coordination of plants is a real management challenge, as is the smooth staging of transitions in plant use and in employee assignments.

Consequences of Strategy

What is striking and important about these five multiplant strategies is that almost all of a company's new branch plants will and should conform to the prevailing strategy. Management, particularly manufacturing management, should be suspicious of suggested new plants or charters for existing ones whose roles and/or locations fall outside the company's established strategy.

Suspicion should be high, not because the role or location may not make sense but because the change is likely to have some significant and subtle implications for corporate and/or for plant management.

The following common situations bear particularly close scrutiny:

1. As to the first suggested market area plant within a company's product division organization—Would it be easier to split out a product instead? Can area-specific demand really be sustained over time? How would order taking and plant loading occur?

2. Concerning a process plant whose suggested location may take it far away from existing plants—What are the logistics involved and their costs? How will new product introduction be supervised? How will inventory levels and controls change? Coordinating such plants may be more difficult than first envisioned.

3. In starting production on a vacant site or adding products to an existing plant with slack capacity or space for low-cost expansion—Do the production and the new site really fit together? Does the new product dilute the established plant's "charter"? Does the new product draw on the same management and labor skills as do prevailing products, or is it qualitatively

different? Like nature abhorring a vacuum, manufacturing managers abhor unused space. For one reason or another, many companies find themselves owning vacant tracts of land here or there and are often seeking ways to fill them up. Too often the idea is, "What can we put at that site?" rather than, "What site makes sense for this product, market, or technology?"

Lower costs at certain sites due to lower wages, land values, or taxes, or to better and cheaper materials are likely to be behind such departures from prevailing manufacturing strategy. Attractive cost savings are frequently highly visible and enticing. However, evidence from my research suggests that most companies locate new branch plants not to take advantage of lower site costs but rather to take into consideration broader factors such as technology, logistics, personnel management, and organization. The key question seems to be, "Is this a location at which the company can remain competitive for a long time?" rather than, "Is it cheaper to do business here?" The answers to these questions may not necessarily be the same, particularly if the company expects to undergo considerable change over time.

I do not mean to imply that lower cost sites should be avoided. Rather, my research suggests careful review of any new site that pulls the company away from its established, and sometimes implicit, plant location strategy. Plant sites in rural areas or tax havens may work well for many companies, but a host of companies have found rural areas, Mexico, Puerto Rico, or other intuitively appealing locations difficult places with which to communicate or to which to attract the management talent or labor skills needed to foster product development, engineering changes, or coordination with other manufacturing branch plants.

Selecting a Site

Once a company has decided on a multiplant manufacturing strategy and on plant size, site selection follows. The multiplant strategy can frequently imply a lot about the choice of region. For example, clustering of plants in a particular region is most likely to occur under the process or the general purpose plant strategy and is least likely under the market area or the product-market strategy. The choice of where within a region to locate, however, is sometimes very straightforward and at other times baffling.

Many people, including some location consultants, try to simplify the decision making by introducing elaborate rating schemes to measure everything imaginable about a particular location. To my mind, much of this is false rigor. There are, of course, a number of costs that can be usefully estimated—among them labor costs; construction, rental, or remodeling costs; taxes and other government payments; transportation cost savings or pen-

SELECTING A SITE

alties for both inputs and finished goods; expenditures for needed services such as energy, pollution control, roads, sewerage, water, parking, and the like; insurance costs; moving costs; and costs associated with expected plant start-up inefficiencies or time delays due to startup or to government approvals.

It is important to evaluate these costs, but they seldom tell the complete story nor do they sometimes differ significantly enough to make a location choice strictly on their merits. A company should not expect any quantitative analysis to isolate a single area or site as clearly optimal. Rather, a company should expect that a number of sites will show more or less the same cost structure.

I would argue that the next phase of site selection should be an exploration of the intangible and qualitative features of a location that could be expected to contribute to the company's competitive success. It may be difficult or even impossible to quantify these factors, but they are no less real, and companies should thus resist the temptation of letting hard numbers drive out reasoned but qualitative analysis.

The intangibles can be of many varieties: risks associated with any of the quantitatively evaluated costs or the sales potential of the site; the area's prevailing "business climate" (which means different things to different people but which is a euphemism for long-term competitiveness); educational and training strengths of the area; attitudes of the work force toward productivity, change, and unionization; the aesthetic and cultural attributes of the area (important aspects for attracting and holding managers); the cooperation of the local and the state government for resolving public service or other public matters faced by industry; the commuting distances for workers and managers; and the impact of other, perhaps competitive, industry in the area.

Frequently, a careful point-by-point comparison of these difficult-to-quantify factors against the real demands that a particular product, area, or process will make on the manufacturing function can argue decisively for a particular site. A site need not rate highly on all factors, but it should rate highly on those that truly make a difference in the plant's competitiveness.

The company should be prepared as well for location analyses that, in the end, do not favor one site over another. If careful analysis ends in a toss-up, a company should not be disturbed if a seemingly inconsequential item tips the scale toward one site. After all, in such a case, the company stands to gain or lose little by the location choice itself.

The company should also be prepared to take a long time deciding plant location. My research suggests that the typical management team immediately involved with the location decision (two to four people, even in large companies) takes about five or six months simply deciding whether to move or to branch, another three to six months searching for a site, and still another three to six months planning the move or branch start-up. I have heard too many stories in which hasty location decisions were also those most regretted.

Notes

1. See my pamphlet, *The Manufacturing Location Decision: Evidence from Cincinnati and New England*, report to the Economic Development Administration (Washington, DC, U.S. Department of Commerce, March 1978).

25
Capacity Strategies for the 1980s

ROBERT A. LEONE and JOHN R. MEYER

The faltering competitiveness of American industry has now become a topic of broad national discussion. Out of that discussion has emerged a renewed awareness that sound production management is of crucial importance to our industrial health.

In this article the authors take a careful look at one strategic production issue: the decision to add new plant capacity. Whether the costs of new capacity are rising or falling, identifiable strategies exist for making profitable long-term decisions. Properly understood, today's competitive environment offers abundant opportunities for success, not merely survival. The trouble comes when managers attempt to make decisions about additions to capacity without first checking to see if their strategic assumptions are appropriate to the present economic climate.

It's 1960. You are the president of virtually any investor-owned electric utility in the United States. Your customers are happy with declining electricity prices. You and your fellow executives in the industry savor the prospect of all-electric living, for the commodity on which your business rests has a 40-year history of declining prices. Regulators are happy with your amenability to requests for lower rates. Environmentalists are happy with your increasing use of clean oil, natural gas, and—in time—nuclear power. Even your investors are happy. Why shouldn't they be? Your common stock is selling well above book value, your bond rating has never been higher, and you have just raised your dividend again.

Your capacity strategy? Expand as rapidly as possible. Preempt your competition by offering inducements to residential and industrial development. Price aggressively to encourage consumption. Construct large capital-intensive generating facilities to squeeze every last economy of scale out of new technology. And your strategy works. Declining costs keep prices down and customers and regulators happy. New technologies improve environmental quality and reward investors.

It's 1980. You are now chairman of the board of the same utility. Your customers are outraged at rising electricity prices. They have responded by sharply curtailing overall demand—but not, of course, during the peak times when electricity is most costly for you to generate. Regulators are outraged at the frequency of your requests for rate increases. Rates in the past 10 years have risen so rapidly that they have completely offset the 50 preceding years of rate decreases. Environmentalists are outraged at your increasing dependence on coal or nuclear power. Even your investors are outraged. And they are right to be. Your common stock is selling at less than 80% of book value, your bond rating was recently lowered, and you have even contemplated a reduction in dividends.

Your old capacity strategy will not work. Rapid expansion is neither politically possible nor economically attractive. Preemptive competitive moves merely increase the number of disgruntled customers. Even your intuition—conditioned by years of experience with strategic decisions and their consequences—is under challenge. To pursue economies of scale seems more like throwing good money after bad than the sound economics it once was. Conservation, perhaps the only strategy now palatable to all your constituencies, is at best a holding action. It's hard for you to believe, but even well-managed growth can be unprofitable.

The Lessons of U-Shaped Costs

Your dilemma is not unique. The circumstances just described are specific to the utility industry, but the problems they represent are not. In one industrial sector after another, costs that had been falling are now rising; once satisfied customers are now vocal in their criticism; communities that once sought an expanded economic base now erect barriers to industrial development. Strategies that worked in the 1960s will not work in the 1980s. Why?

In the past decade, the U.S. economy has run an uneasy course between excessive inflation and high levels of unemployment. It has experienced both the externally imposed shock of escalating energy costs and the internally imposed constraints on economic decision making associated with a regulatory boom. As a result, energy efficiency is now a top priority, daily attention to regulatory issues is commonplace, worker attitudes have changed as real incomes fail to keep up with expectations, and, as prices rise, the public is increasingly suspicious of business intentions. These changes in industrial economics need not by themselves invalidate existing strategies. Cumulatively, however, they have yielded another, virtually unnoticed economic change that does: in industry after industry, new production facilities no longer represent low-cost capacity. Thus U.S. industry enters the 1980s confronting an economic reality both unfamiliar and unwelcome, yet rife with profound implications for corporate strategy.

In a wide variety of industries, unit costs associated with capacity additions using the best most up-to-date technology have followed what we call a U-shaped cost-development pattern over time. Frequently in current dollars, and to a lesser extent in deflated dollars, production costs have first declined, then bottomed out, and finally risen over time in the manner stylized in Exhibit 1.

During the 1950s and early 1960s, productivity improvements associated with increasing volume, new technologies, learning curve effects, and the like commonly outpaced inflation or other cost increases. Computers and integrated circuits are only the most familiar examples of such declining-cost industries. There are many others: advances in oxygen technology helped keep steel costs in check for decades; economies of scale and improvements in distribution (e.g., in electricity generation) kept productivity up for many vital commodities; learning curve efficiencies along with advances in data processing yielded substantial productivity improvements in a variety of service industries from fast foods to banking.

These developments often resulted in a pattern of stable or even declining costs, creating the left-hand side (LHS) of the U-shaped pattern in Exhibit 1. In the late 1960s, however, this situation began to change. Many industries found it ever more expensive to replace or expand capacity. Productivity improvements no longer offset cost increases due to inflation, energy and capital costs, or regulatory constraints. Production costs associated with new installations tended to be higher than for existing capacity. Today, as a consequence, a growing number of industries are positioned on the right-hand side (RHS) or rising-cost portion of the U-shape.

Cost Advantages and Disadvantages

The LHS, so characteristic of many industries in the 1950s and 1960s, represents a situation in which the newest plant brought onstream typically has unit costs that are low for its industry. When an industry is on the LHS, new facilities are not severely handicapped by initial capital, environmental, or safety costs that are high relative to those of predecessors. In such circumstances, it is more profitable for management, say, to build a spanking new Burns Harbor facility than to rebuild older steel-making facilities in Bethlehem, Pennsylvania. It is more profitable to install a huge new thermal plant at Ravenswood, Queens, than to update old electricity-generating facilities around the periphery of Manhattan.

All of this changes dramatically, however, when management encounters rising costs with new capacity on the RHS. Here inflation or some other adverse development can so escalate the costs of even the least expensive

Exhibit 1. U-Shaped Cost-Development Pattern

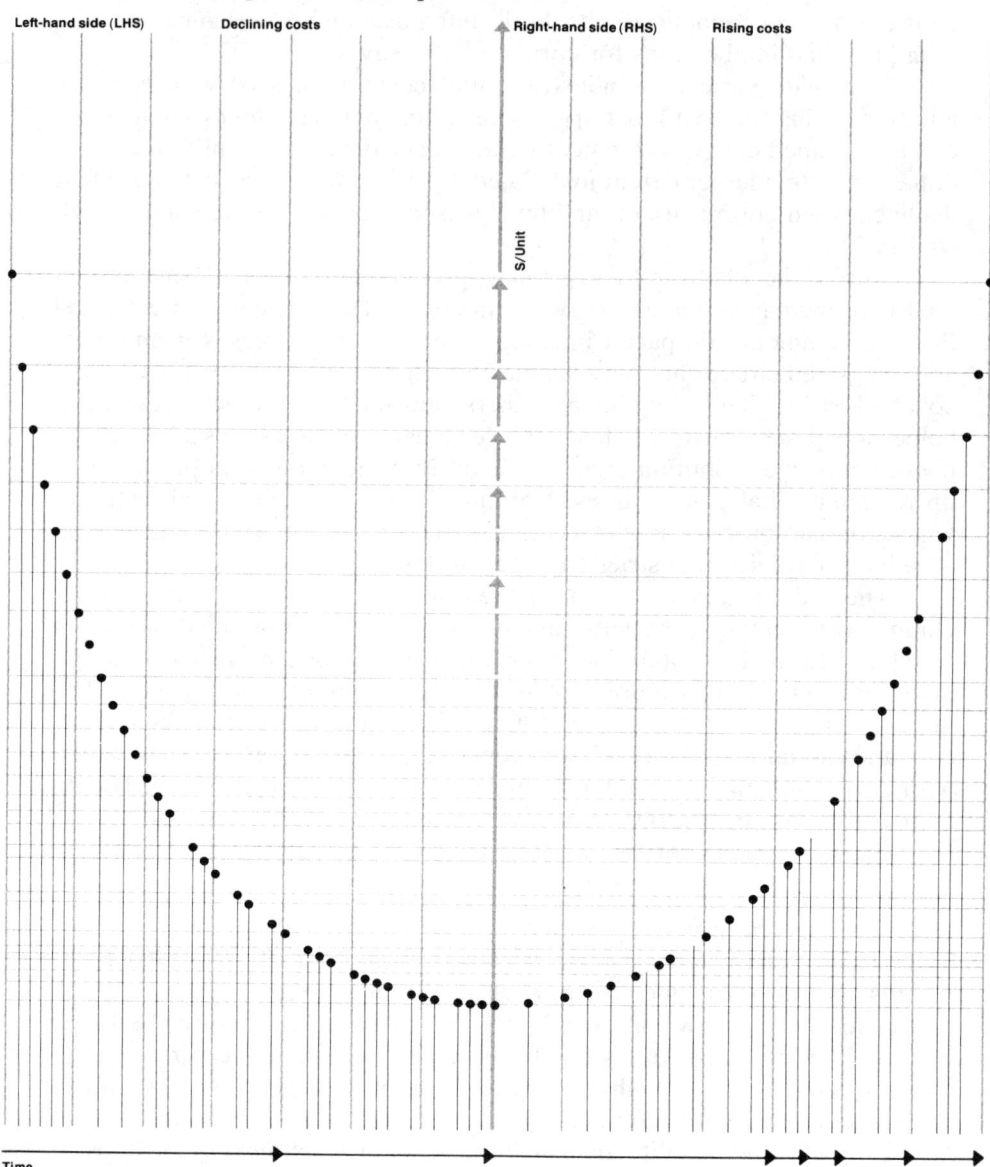

new plant that any efficiencies flowing from new technology may not be sufficient to create unit costs lower than those achieved by facilities already in place. When inflation is rampant, the technologies of older palnts, even if relatively inefficient, are often not so inefficient as to offset totally their historical or embedded capital cost advantage. Renovated buildings, for example, can rarely be made quite as energy efficient as their new counterparts, but this disadvantage can often be overcome by their lower embedded capital cost.

Moreover, when government-mandated "new source performance standards" for meeting various pollution and safety regulations are substantially more stringent for new than for old facilities, new plants can be even further disadvantaged. In such circumstances, cost increases can easily outpace technological improvement, and the total unit costs of production in new or replacement facilities are likely to be well above historical levels. In point of fact, this is what did occur in many U.S. industries during the 1970s.

Implications for Strategy

An industry's position on the U-shape has, therefore, significant implications for a number of key managerial decisions—especially those regarding the timing, scale, location, and technology of new production facilities. As summarized in Exhibit 2, these implications vary dramatically on the two sides of the curve. Consider first the declining-cost or LHS situation so familiar to business managers in the 1950s and 1960s.

The LHS Situation

Timing. From a strategic standpoint, a management confronted with LHS conditions will typically find it economically attractive to build capacity in anticipation of growth in demand. Building ahead of demand when on the LHS is, after all, a relatively inexpensive and risk-free means of preempting entry by others. Perhaps the most obvious example of this strategy in action is the aggressive expansion of the Japanese steel industry after World War II. Moreover, the surpluses accruing to such low-cost installations, over and above their unit cost advantage, provide enough of a cushion against adversity to make further investment attractive under a very wide set of future circumstances.

Under LHS conditions a tendency thus exists for industry capacity to lead industry growth. This explains, at least partially, the experience of paper and aluminum producers in the 1950s and 1960s for whom bouts with excess capacity were a recurrent problem.

Exhibit 2. Strategic Implications of U-Shaped Cost Patterns

Although there are no hard-and-fast rules for managers on either the LHS or RHS, tendencies are:

In Declining-Cost Situations to:	In Rising-Cost Situations to:
1 Build large scale	1 Build small scale
2 Build new or greenfield plants	2 Renovate existing facilities
3 Lead growth in demand with preemptive addition to capacity	3 Make more frequent addition to capacity to better track or even lag behind demand
4 Exploit economies of scale and compete on the basis of price	4 Avoid the risk associated with the exploitation of economies of scale and compete on the basis of service, quality, and other dimensions
5 Locate in developing areas and less-developed countries	5 Locate in developed areas with existing markets
6 Exploit operating leverage by choosing capital-intensive technologies	6 Avoid operating risk by choosing technologies with a high ratio of variable to total costs
7 Debt finance new facilities to exploit their favorable risk profiles	7 Debt finance existing facilities to exploit their favorable expectations for use
8 Forecast demand using relatively simple trend-projection methods	8 Forecast demand using sophisticated analytic methods
9 Expand by building new capacity	9 Expand by acquisition of existing capacity

Scale and Location. Not only will capacity tend to lead growth in demand under LHS conditions, new capacity will often be added in the form of large-scale production facilities. Such facilities are intended both to exploit the opportunities for cost reduction and to preempt entry by competitors. Since these large-scale facilities characteristically represent new or "greenfield" plants, management tends to locate them in developing regions where the best sites are not already occupied. By implication, then, the Sunbelt in particular and less-developed regions (or nations) in general become major beneficiaries of LHS industrial conditions. Should a recession take hold, the older regions with their higher-cost facilities will bear the primary burden of idle or underutilized capacity.

Technology. Since new capacity is low-cost capacity, its use is readily assured. In this situation, high operating leverage constitutes a less serious

IMPLICATIONS FOR STRATEGY

risk than it otherwise might. Hence, management will find it attractive to pursue the cost advantages that are often associated with capital-intensive (but high fixed-cost) technologies. Indeed, under LHS circumstances, a good deal of financial leverage is also justified. This fact helps explain, for example, the attractiveness of very high rates of debt financing in Japanese industries such as steel during their period of aggressive capacity expansion.

The RHS Situation

Scale and Timing. The strategic implications of RHS conditions are substantially more difficult for management to sort out. At the least, being on the right dictates a rather more conservative capacity investment policy than is appropriate to the LHS situation. Specifically, when an industry is on the RHS, capacity additions are closer to the margin of the industry's supply and, therefore, should be undertaken with more hesitancy, be smaller in scale, and occur more frequently. Put simply, RHS conditions make smaller increments of capacity attractive because they risk less and are relatively easily accommodated by market growth.

In practice, this phenomenon helps explain the current success of "minimills" in the steel industry—mills which, though not necessarily as cost-efficient as their larger counterparts when operating at full capacity, need only minimal capital commitments. As part of a strategy to "nibble" away at a growing steel market, they can effectively undercut the economic arguments for constructing large greenfield mills. Larger facilities, by virtue of their dependence on volume for operating economies, lack this strategic capability.

In an industry like steel that is marked by substantial scale economies, a continuing pattern of small increments to existing capacity can easily destroy those economies or, at best, postpone them. Thus, the dynamics of the RHS situation tend both to cause and to perpetuate a suboptimal scale of production—particularly in relatively competitive industries.

This phenomenon also helps explain the relative attractiveness in recent years of expanding capacity by acquisition. Such a strategy, for example, has allowed airlines to buy existing aircraft with low embedded costs. Expanding capacity with new equipment or construction is likely to incur today's high capital replacement costs at the same time that it creates the very conditions of excess supply that make high fixed-cost investments unprofitable in the first place.

Technology. In a rising-cost situation, management tends to adopt production methods with relatively high variable costs and low capital costs for the simple reason that facilities built to this rule tend to be smaller in scale and risk less capital. Management will find this risk-reducing strategy even more effective if the prices of raw materials swing with the market demand for the final product.

Consider, for example, the use of secondary fiber—that is, wastepaper—in paper-recycling facilities. The use of wastepaper as a resource successfully avoids many of the capital costs associated with a fully integrated pulp and paper facility. The price of wastepaper, moreover, is highly variable, shifting with the demand for the recycled product; this variability lessens profits in the upturns of the business cycle. More to the point, the converse is also true, since declining wastepaper prices stabilize profits on a downturn—a primary consideration under RHS conditions.

The same arguments apply, of course, to minimills in the steel industry or reprocessing facilities in the aluminum industry, which rely on metal scrap as a major raw material. In RHS situations, these small-scale facilities have a double advantage: (1) they have few economies of scale to lose in a downturn, and (2) their raw material inputs tend to fall in price as demand slackens.

Increased Importance of Demand Forecasting. When the costs of significant new capacity are high and rising, management has no easy rationale for undertaking capacity expansion. Even building for replacement, often a standard justification under LHS conditions, is extremely difficult. Both new and replacement capacity will have costs that are high relative to the facilities already in place or to be replaced. In such circumstances, demand takes on a magnified importance in any strategic capacity decision. Management must be able to analyze demand carefully and forecast it accurately.

On the RHS, simple extrapolation, a method of forecasting historic demand trends sufficient to LHS conditions, is likely to prove seriously inadequate. Thus, a more sophisticated method of demand forecasting, one closely tied to the microeconomists' notion of price elasticity, becomes necessary. Just as the electric utilities gave demand forecasting a low priority in their planning when the industry faced LHS conditions, they must emphasize sophisticated demand analysis now that costs are rising.

This phenomenon is by no means limited to electric or other utilities. Any management facing rising costs and a stable or declining business—whether in steel, black-and-white TVs, or even public school enrollments—must base all capacity decisions on a very close analysis of demand. Under these conditions, accurate forecasting is not just helpful; it is absolutely essential.

Plan to Exploit the RHS Situation

Faced with the complex, confusing, and often counterintuitive facts of business life on the RHS, a good number of managers have been sorely tempted to resign themselves to a capacity strategy designed merely to keep their heads above water.

This is unnecessary and unwarranted defeatism. Of course, the RHS situation is unpleasant—it goes deeply against the grain and violates the familiar dictates of common sense. But it is not so unpleasant nor disturbing nor inexplicable that sound management cannot turn it to strategic advantage.

It may, for instance, seem counterintuitive that the economic advantages of new large-scale capacity can be *less* attractive strategically in an RHS than in an LHS situation. There are, however, two straightforward reasons for this. First, in a rising-cost situation, the cost advantages of scale may be more than offset by the added risk associated with the operation of facilities that are high cost relative to existing facilities. Even though a large-scale fully integrated petrochemical facility may produce chemicals at a lower unit cost than a small-scale facility, if demand cannot sustain the profitable use of the larger capacity, its cost advantage is not worth very much.

Second, since rising costs make it very difficult for new installations to compete on price, the basis of competition for new capacity often shifts to such nonprice dimensions as service or quality. The operators of minimills in the steel industry have successfully employed service and delivery times as competitive weapons. Even the management of new entrants into the fast-food industry, as the industry reached market saturation and found profitable new sites increasingly costly, turned toward competition based on service, larger portions, and variety—factors that minimized an established competitor's embedded cost advantage. Price, after all, is not the only basis for competition.

The Virtues of "Lagging"

Some will argue, of course, that inflation is here to stay and that building ahead of demand, even in rising-cost circumstances, is better than building tomorrow at inflated prices. However appealing, this can be a dangerous path of action. For one thing, if very many competitors choose it, excess supply will make the strategy unattractive for all—even if inflation persists. Furthermore, a disciplined competitor who avoids the temptation to overbuild will not be saddled with the high embedded costs of new facilities if inflation subsides or other competitors overexpand. When and if additional demand actually materializes, the disciplined competitor will still have the option to compete for that market as then-current prices and costs dictate.

The point is that there is limited risk to a lagging capacity strategy in RHS circumstances and much real economic risk to a more aggressive strategic posture. To illustrate, many of the domestic airlines, tempted by the deregulation of the industry, expanded aggressively into new markets only to discover that unanticipated increases in the cost of jet fuel made their preemptive demand-leading strategies highly unprofitable.

The most commonly successful strategies for preempting tomorrow's inflation by investing today have been in the real estate market—particularly the market for single-family residential dwellings. Remember, however, that such investment has been accomplished more often by acquisition than by expansion. The most frequent success stories in real estate involve the appreciation of existing dwellings with their low embedded capital costs. Speculative gains to new high-cost housing have been more elusive and far less spectacular. And this is precisely what one would expect in RHS conditions.

Success, Not Survival

Overall, the most troublesome reaction among managers to the strategic implications of rising costs is the pervasive feeling that the only tenable blueprint is for survival, not for profitability. Not so. We cannot stress enough that quite the opposite is true.

In the steel industry, for example, which is unquestionably facing rising costs, competitors with traditional strategies based on large-scale, capital-intensive production methods are in serious financial difficulty. By contrast, the profitable performers are those using small-scale facilities to compete on the basis of specialty products or service in regional markets. The profits of these companies are typically high not only for the steel industry but for the manufacturing sector as a whole.

Similarly, among electric utilities the small-scale producers using agricultural wastes, process steam from manufacturing, or low-head hydro power are outperforming their more traditional competitors. Of equal importance, they are doing so by earning a return on their investment well above the norm for American industry generally.

These examples underscore our basic proposition: just as there are strategies that can successfully exploit the opportunities created by declining costs, there are strategies that can successfully exploit the opportunities created by rising costs. The challenge for management is, as always, to recognize the specific economic reality with which it must deal and to adapt capacity strategies accordingly.

Public Policy Issues

There is nothing inevitable about this pattern of U-shaped costs. It represents an empirical fact for several industries at the present time and may or may not persist. Nevertheless, given that RHS conditions are fairly widespread today and given as well their relevance to capacity strategies in the private sector, it is appropriate to ask what effect the phenomenon may have on the broader issues of public policy. Stated somewhat differently, policy analysts and economists frequently advise managers about the implications of public policy for corporate strategy. Our discussion of capacity strategies in LHS and RHS situations suggests turning the tables for a moment. Let us ask instead what these changes in business policies might mean for public policy.

Pricing Policy

Government regulatory agencies frequently establish prices on the basis of embedded average costs. This, of course, avoids the creation of visible "windfalls" for industry and tends to keep overall price levels stable. In LHS situations, this practice keeps customers, politicians, and investors happy since declining costs keep rates down, avoid political confrontations, and yet leave room for profitable investment in new and still lower-cost facilities.

In RHS situations, however, using historical costs to set prices retains its political appeal but at the expense of discouraging investment in new facilities. Indeed, such regulatory pricing policies have in recent years discouraged investment in new energy-efficient manufacturing technologies, retarded the nation's conversion to coal, and inhibited numerous other productivity-enhancing capital investments.

"Grandfather Exceptions"

A common regulatory practice exempts existing facilities from costly environmental and safety regulations and imposes relatively more stringent standards on new facilities. The apparent rationale is to protect established jobs and communities. Clearly, though, such exemptions also discourage investment, as the embedded capital cost advantages of existing facilities will be enhanced, not reduced, by a grandfather regulatory advantage.

Timing

One of the more predictable consequences of government regulation is that it almost inevitably extends the planning horizon imposed on business. In RHS circumstances, short planning horizons facilitate strategies aimed at matching investment in new facilities as closely as possible with growth in demand. This delicate balancing act risks, however, a perpetuation of suboptimal manufacturing scales and capabilities. On the other hand, longer planning horizons, by frustrating small-scale capacity additions, may help bring new large-scale facilities on stream.

Though we believe that the exploitation of such subtle distinctions in timing is presently beyond the state of bureaucratic art, we would note that questions of timing are being addressed by some policy-makers in their discussion of sophisticated "industrial policies" and economic planning.

Macroeconomic Policy

When the economy is generally experiencing declining costs, macroeconomic policy choices are relatively painless. Stimulation to move out of a recession is not quickly dissipated in higher prices; deflationary policies to avoid "over-heating" at the peak of the cycle will not totally abort management's rationale for productive plant and equipment investment.

Under RHS conditions, by contrast, stimulating demand (say, in a period of so-called stagflation) will drive prices up to the replacement cost levels necessary to justify further investment but will also intensify any inflationary tendencies in the economy. Suppressing demand when the economy becomes overheated runs the risk of lowering productivity growth (to the extent this is reliant on investment), again intensifying inflationary tendencies. At a minimum, supply bottlenecks should appear rather more quickly in an RHS upturn than has historically been the case under LHS conditions.

In general, RHS conditions simply do not admit of easy or painless public policy choices. The appropriate public policy actions may be hard not only for regulators to swallow, but for politicians, the public, and business as well.

☐ Pricing at current replacement costs will mean that windfalls will be created, which in turn could encourage further political intrusion into the affairs of business.

☐ Abandoning grandfather regulatory clauses will stimulate investment in new plant and equipment, but it will also drive up the costs of maintaining existing facilities and increase problems of economic dislocation as old facilities are forced to close.

☐ Shorter lead times in planning will mean that new smaller-scale facilities can be brought on-line less expensively, but this may preclude exploitation in the long term of the economies inherent in new large-scale productive facilities.

☐ A less-stringent monetary policy will necessitate more responsible fiscal policy controls, but fiscal policy offers no painless alternatives for business, government, or the general public.

A Concluding Thought

In the private sector, the high production costs of new capacity overthrow a host of familiar strategic assumptions, assumptions that came into vogue during a prolonged era of LHS conditions. The RHS world of today necessitates different, more conservative investment strategies. It also requires facilities of different scale, geographic location, and technical configuration.

Here lies the central challenge for management, both public and private. The RHS situation will not likely change soon. Its consequences will persist just as long as new capacity experiences total unit costs of production that are high relative to the total costs of existing facilities. This is an inescapable reality—until and unless inflation is contained or technology provides breakthroughs that greatly accelerate productive efficiency. It will be a mark of good management, again both public and private, to turn this reality to advantage.

PART SIX
THE FACTORS OF PRODUCTION (LABOR)

AN OVERVIEW

This final group of articles needs only the briefest word of introduction. Ever since Karl Marx identified the alienating effects of factory labor on workers as the Achilles heel of capitalism, learning to use the production work force well has been a central challenge for manufacturing managers. Their record of success has been mixed. In the past, however, when the necessary skills were unsophisticated and labor costs were low, indifferent work force management had relatively little competitive impact. Today, of course, the situation is radically changed.

The companies best able to hold their own in domestic and international markets are precisely those that have deliberately viewed their work force as a potential competitive advantage. They have integrated their people into production systems not by treating them as machines but by finding ways to enlist their eager cooperation in the work at hand. How to do so on a large and consistent scale remains the great unanswered riddle for this generation of management; for of all forms of wealth, human capital is now rightly seen as by far the most precious.

26
The Anachronistic Factory

WICKHAM SKINNER

Today's economic conditions, new technologies, and societal demands are impinging on the "old" factory system to the extent that the conventional production plant is fast becoming an anachronism. The problem, contends this author, is to somehow change the time-hardened image of the factory as an undesirable place for the work of intelligent, independent, and resourceful people. Overhauling this obsolete institution, he emphasizes, cannot be done piecemeal; the profound changes needed must be focused on increasing both its mechanization and humanization throughout the entire factory structure.

The conventional factory is fast becoming an anachronism. Many of the values and assumptions on which its productivity has depended are now running head-on into changing beliefs and expectations in our society. The effect of this collision is rising worker dissatisfaction and repugnance toward the factory as a place to work. Conventional methods of managing and making decisions in manufacturing are equally out of touch with the times. In many instances, the result is low utilization and efficiency of expensive equipment. As a final measure of industrial ineffectiveness, total productivity is frequently inadequate for meeting return-on-investment needs amidst the facts of worldwide competition.

Some call the problem one of "productivity."[1] Others label it as "blue-collar blues."[2] Or it is described as, "Can the U.S. stay competitive?"[3] The fact is that U.S. industry is in trouble on all three related counts. In my opinion, unless U.S. managers begin to recognize this and take corrective action, the situation may gradually spiral into a genuine national industrial emergency.

Combining to produce a powerful impact on U.S. industry are three environmental factors: (1) accelerating foreign competition, (2) technological changes in production and information-handling equipment, and (3) social changes in the work force. The massive effect of these rapidly moving simultaneous changes is rendering the typical factory an obsolete institution. Now, urgently, changes in our conventional management methods of accomplishing improved manufacturing plant performance are becoming mandatory.

In this article, I shall attempt to report on the anachronistic status of the factory system by first arguing that changes are essential in the factory infrastructure. In so doing, I shall show that the normal approach of attempting to improve factory results by pecking away at the various elements of the plant complex—that is, making modifications one by one—can no longer be tolerated by owners, employees, and society at large. Then, in the balance of the article, I shall offer my recommendations on the changes needed in (a) conventional concepts of managing manufacturing and (b) meeting human needs in manufacturing careers.

Pressure for Change

An indisputable fact is that as worldwide competition spreads, U.S. companies in a steadily increasing number of industries are finding the going rough, with high wages placing producers at a comparative disadvantage. It is also clear that U.S. industry is wrestling with some puzzling and stubborn internal problems, such as assimilating new technology, the will to work, and shortages of highly skilled workers—all key elements in achieving better productivity.

Like it or not, we are being forced to challenge from the ground up all pieces of conventional wisdom concerning every facet of industrial management from individual job definitions, work force management, the foreperson's job, and equipment and process design to scheduling and inventory control.

In sum, innovative, even radical, changes in the factory as a total social and technological institution are already necessary because rapid obsolescence of the factory as an institution has already set in. And wholesale broad sweeping changes are in order because whatever is done must be internally consistent.

"Piecemeal Syndrome"

U.S. industrial leadership and competitive productivity are eroding so quickly, in my opinion, that manufacturing executives in many industries can no longer permit themselves the luxury of what I call the "piecemeal syndrome." Let me illustrate what I mean.

The XXX Company, concerned over low profit, set out to modernize its plant. Over a two-year period new automated highly mechanized machines were analyzed, justified, and purchased one by one. But productivity improved very little. Since low utilization of equipment was one obvious culprit, a computer-based information, planning, and scheduling system was installed. This system clearly revealed that changes in plant layout and materials handling were needed.

All this took several more years, and profit margins improved somewhat. But absences, workmanship, effort, and morale were being adversely affected by the earlier changes in physical facilities and the information system.

Further analysis suggested that the pay system was apparently inappropriate to the new production and scheduling methods, and that an inconsistent span of individual jobs was contributing to poor morale. Supervisory assumptions and practices were challenged, along with employment procedures. These changes spanned another year and a half.

About that time, the company's strategic approaches to competing in worldwide markets were revised, placing an emphasis on fewer standard items and on more customer specials and model changes. Management realized that not only would the scheduling and information system need changes but much of the basic production equipment as well, if the plant was to fulfill the revised manufacturing task imposed by the new corporate strategy.

The entire period of time represented six and a half years of frustration, inadequacy, and the constant pressure of making changes. In the end, the system needed as much revision as it had in the beginning. During no single year were results even marginally satisfactory. Stockholders, managers, employees, and engineers shared only one mutual sentiment—that of unrelenting dissatisfaction.

This common example represents a reasonably accurate model of how most factories have been—and still are being—managed. To manage manufacturing differently will be a difficult undertaking because of the obvious problems in developing planned and coordinated systems that require long lead times and heavy capital investments, and involve little-understood sociological phenomena. And it will also be difficult because of the problem of keeping the whole "show" going while changing it.

These are not impossible tasks. They seem entirely "doable" once a manager knows what to do. What appears necessary first, however, is that manufacturing executives begin to develop—admittedly at some personal and corporate risk—new concepts in organizing and managing factories as complete social and technical institutions.

But what is to be done, more precisely, to update our industrial system and to improve our productivity?

Slow Progress

It is puzzling to many people that increased mechanization, automation, and computerization in industry have not been more effective to date in boosting industrial productivity. The temptation of seizing on new technology as the answer to our industrial dilemmas is appealing. For surely one way out of the growing difficulties in remaining competitive lies in the possibilities of increased mechanization and automation. James Bright wrote a decade ago that our problem is not that we are mechanizing too fast but that we are mechanizing too slowly.[4]

Thus, if mechanization, automation, and computerization can do any good at all in the factory, they should help to reduce costs and improve quality. They should also help to reduce boredom from dull jobs, and by their very complexity to attract, as the factory formerly did, bright and able young people into new knowledge and skill-oriented jobs in industry.

This sounds promising—and it is—but the gap between promise and payoff is proving to be very wide. Increased mechanization is coming about neither smoothly nor quickly enough to meet the cost and productivity improvements that are apparently needed. Automation is not a consistent success, nor does it lack confusing and paradoxical elements. Consider the following:

☐ In the face of a pressing need to change the factory, increasing both its mechanization and its humanization, we are apparently making slow progress.

☐ In the face of an increasing rate of technological change and potential for automation, actual applications are surprisingly cautious.

☐ In the face of increasing corporate demands on manufacturing to meet marketing and strategic objectives and a promise of rich rewards for those companies which forge their manufacturing function into a formidable competitive weapon, many corporations find that the factory continues to be a millstone.

☐ In the face of expanding uses for the computer, its effects in reducing lead times and costs and in improving quality of output are disappointing.

☐ In the face of what appear to be enormous opportunities for retooling with modern numerically controlled gear, we see a slowdown in orders.

In the meantime, a combination of growing competition and changing social expectations threatens to make obsolete many plants and many industries. One effect is on the appeal of factory life to able men and women. I am concerned that the problem of attracting better employees to the factory will multiply unless industrial managers are able to perform several orders of magnitude better in introducing computer-based systems and automated industrial equipment. They must also somehow change the time-hardened image of the factory as an undesirable workplace for intelligent, independent, and resourceful people. But changing over the American factory is proving to be a sticky and sluggish problem, fraught with stubborn internal resistances which block progress.

What is going wrong? Why is progress so slow and painful? Why is it so difficult to meet the problems, to change over and renovate the factory, and to employ without nightmare the fruits of amazing technologies?

Research Findings

I have analyzed many situations that involve the introduction of numerically controlled machine tools and other complex automated equipment, and the use of the computer in the factory. I would like to offer some tentative findings which are beginning to emerge from this research.

First, the complexities involved in achieving successful large-scale increases in mechanization and computerization are simply enormous—in number as well as in potentially devastating effects—and they are typically much greater than anticipated. This finding may hardly be news to industrialists, but its significance is not inconsequential.

The warning is clear: automation and computer-aided production must not be undertaken without extensive and exhaustive planning. Even then, start-up problems and side-effect falldowns are going to occur. More is involved than mere technology. Side effects are often more important (for better or worse) than the primary goals contemplated for the technological change.

Interesting Patterns

My study of the anatomy of automation/mechanization/computerization experiences is turning up some interesting patterns as follows:

1. A typical problem is the case of one company in which expensive, new, automated equipment took a year and a half to become fully operational, and even then its utilization was about half of that on which acceptable paybacks had been based. Why? The reason was a complex myriad of cause-and-effect relationships: inadequate operator and programming skills, unrealistic demands for precision, and difficulties in matching market demands with shop scheduling.

2. In another company, a computer-aided automated line of process equipment proved unable to handle the process it was designed to control. The problem was finally traced to the operators, who prior to mechanization had been handling certain material and process-introduced variables with a kind of experience-developed intuition that was too complex for the computer and sensor to handle.

3. In still another company, a new multimillion-dollar plant performed per specifications, but it was ruining the company's ability to compete. The problem was a lack of flexibility in the process that resulted in lead times for new products and special product variations that were significantly longer than those offered by the competition.

Case examples such as those just cited prove a kind of Murphy's Law—if something can go wrong, it will. An inconsistency or lack of congruence in any one of dozens of ingredients in the system will often ruin the performance and utility of the whole. These are not just technical or engineering problems, but also problems of marketing, scheduling, engineering, inventory, changeover, cost control, accounting, volume sensitivity, worker acceptance, training, supervision, safety, wage system, motivation, union contract, utilities, maintenance, pollution/effluents, community relations, vendor requirements, plant organization structure, executive performance evaluation, and communications and information flows.

In short, everything counts. One subtle flaw may immobilize or neutralize the benefits of an otherwise marvelously planned and conceived project.

This interconnectedness signals the need for a "total systems" approach, which will surprise few. But the massive inertia and complexities attendant to bringing about change also say something about the kind of system the factory is: a complex network of social and technological factors with both economic and strategic payoffs.

"Infrastructure" Problem

My analysis of companies that have invested in new technology as a means of overcoming competitive disadvantage suggests that the potentially positive results of automation and computer technology are being largely neutralized by failings or inconsistencies in other elements of the U.S. factory institution. By this, I mean the internal systems through which work is carried on—what I call the "infrastructure" of the factory. The infrastructure includes such elements as organizational levels, wage systems, supervisory practices, production control and scheduling approaches, and job design and methods concepts.

By analogy, we are learning that a new engine does not make an old automobile new. Any one part—such as the transmission, body, suspension, or electrical system—dates the vehicle's performance and can render it inadequate. To carry on this analogy, the new engine may, in fact, bring out new problems that make total performance worse than before the old engine was replaced.

The entire factory needs to be planned and renovated as a unit lest any one element undermine the entire structure. In order to successfully introduce advanced mechanization and to achieve full productivity, the entire warp and woof of the factory in all its interconnected intricacies must be retooled to make it internally consistent with the new process.

Without substantial changes in equipment and technology, we will not be able to withstand foreign competition; but without changes in methods of work, concepts of supervision, control and direction, and promotion and salary practices, I doubt very much whether the factory can ever again have the appeal it once did to sufficient numbers of competent employees. In a nutshell, our methods of decision making, communicating, scheduling, and supervising make up the infrastructure of our plants; these internal elements are proving more resistant to change than the purely technological ingredients on which factory managers and engineers tend to focus.

One way of looking at the present situation is shown in Exhibit 1. Changes in technology, society, and the economic situation are impinging on the "old" factory system—and all at the same time.

By no means is it surprising that production executives with orders to fill, schedules to meet, budgets to hold, and unions to negotiate with are hesitant to "start changing everything around." The stability of evolutionary change is demanded by the practical man, and this is eminently reasonable. But my view of the scene today is that there is a great deal of paralysis and hesitancy, a real sense of crisis and floundering in many industries, and frequently a sluggishness and failure of nerve among top managements. All of this augurs poorly for the overhauling of our factory institutions and the raising of productivity levels.

Recommended Changes . . .

How might top managers of manufacturing go about making profound changes on the stubborn infrastructure of the conventional U.S. factory to make it less anachronistic, more productive, and more relevant to today's social and economic facts of life?

Any analyst of the current scene approaches such a difficult question with a humble confession of personal inadequacies and uncertainties. Who knows, really, how to solve the complex problems of our times? Nevertheless, I shall now move to the other side and offer my opinion that there is a great deal that managers responsible for manufacturing can do to make their factories more productive and less anachronistic.

The recommendations I shall offer are simple, yet vital, and fall into the following groups:

1 Changes *in conventional concepts* of managing manufacturing.
2 Changes *in meeting human needs* in manufacturing careers.

In the balance of this article, I shall take a closer look at each of these recommendations.

Exhibit 1. How Pressures Impinge on the "Old" Factory System

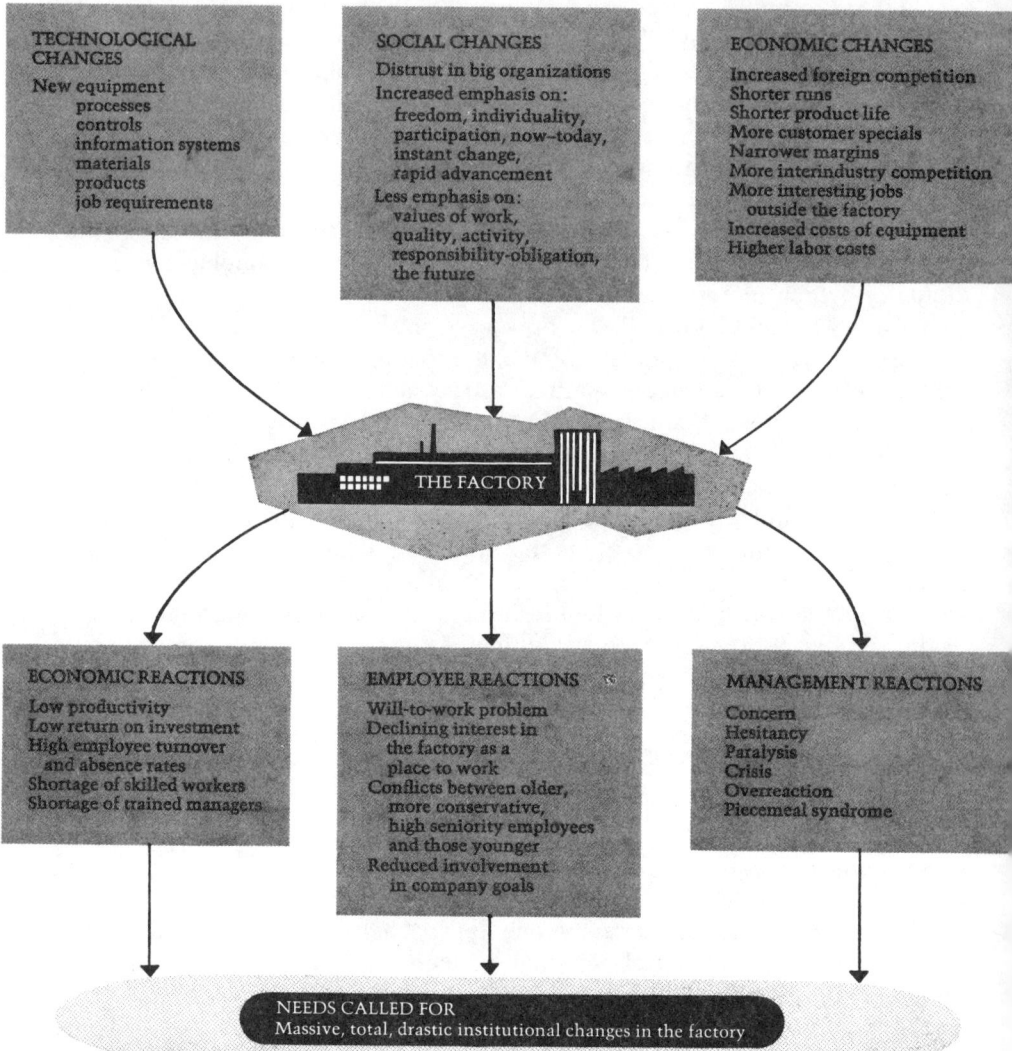

... In Conventional Concepts

Manufacturing management was derived in a conceptual sense from engineering and technologically oriented variables. Because manufacturing requires specialized expertise and constant improvement of often complex equipment and processes, its foci as a sector of management have been on technology, efficiency, and equipment. As a result of this legacy, manufacturing executives have typically been more expert in those areas of their work than in other parts.

RECOMMENDED CHANGES... 443

Indeed, the potential of manufacturing as a competitive weapon and the concept of using manufacturing as a strategic asset have been almost always overlooked in management's single-minded attention to efficiency, costs, and engineering.

Manufacturing can be managed quite differently from the way most companies manage it. What is required are fundamental changes to bring about (1) the recognition and banishment of a number of fallacious myths and assumptions about manufacturing, (2) the management of manufacturing as a corporate strategic weapon, and (3) the widespread acceptance of a concept of manufacturing as an institution, with an extensive and influential infrastructure of technological and sociological elements that are internally consistent.

Let me take each of these conceptual changes in manufacturing management in turn.

Myths and Assumptions. These have seriously hurt our progress by having led us into planning and managing plants in ways that result in disappointments and unnecessary hard work, and away from more fruitful approaches.

> The main criteria for evaluating factory performance are efficiency and cost.

This statement is wrong. Manufacturing can also be a competitive weapon when it is less "efficient" but more flexible in terms of product change, in managing inevitable ups and downs in volume, in getting new products into production quickly, in providing for and consistently meeting short-delivery promises, and in producing with a minimum investment in inventory and fixed assets.

Criteria for judging a factory should not be limited to efficiency and cost, for these criteria ignore the fact that in the context of a particular company's competitive strategy, other criteria may be vastly more important.

> A good factory can simultaneously accomplish low costs, high quality, minimum investment, short-cycle times, high flexibility, and rapid introduction of new products.

Wrong again. A factory system—like an airplane or a building—can only be designed to do certain things well. The failure to clearly identify design objectives or to compromise among many criteria results in manufacturing systems which do not perform well by any criteria.

> The management of factories is essentially a task for engineers.

This grievously mistaken assumption—blindly employed since the turn of the century and now made even more seductive by advancing technology—has generally entrusted the direction of manufacturing to men conditioned with a technical point of view. The technical dimension is important, but time is proving that social and strategic dimensions are at least equally important. Moreover, the technical obsession often delegates the production function to people who are inadequately trained and oriented toward human and social factors, financial problems, and the strategy and markets of the entire firm.

> Increasing mechanization is a job for industrial engineers and operations researchers.

Another wrong assumption. Tackling complex multidimensional problems with the limited array of disciplines offered by even those broadly intentioned professionals is simplistic.

> The systems approach and a high level of conceptualization are a substitute for experience and substantive knowledge.

This fallacy is implicit in excessively theoretical and conceptual planning exercises that have caused a multitude of errors in judgment and swarms of "bugs" in automated factories.

> The ultimate objective of automation is to reduce the numbers of people required; problems with and costs of people can be avoided and overcome with automation and mechanization; people problems can be bypassed with good equipment.

These three interrelated misconceptions should have been demolished by the experiences of the last five years.

> Economics always favors machines.

This is a myth because the fantastic abilities of human beings to plan, remember, and use judgment, wisdom, and intelligence extend far beyond the capabilities of computers and mechanization. To try to make such facilities substitute for people has repeatedly proved expensive, especially when reliable back-ups are built in to achieve a hands-off operation. When a skilled worker is to be replaced by a machine, the cost of the equipment replacing the worker may run into hundreds of thousands of dollars. Therefore, economics often favors the use of people.

In total, these myths and assumptions about plants and people have led us into an excessively technically oriented point of view of the factory. They have allowed us to overlook key dimensions in industrial change and to attempt to introduce machines and equipment without changing organizations, responsibilities, job contents, information systems, promotion and pay systems, and control and motivational approaches—in short, the stubborn total infrastructure of the factory as an institution.

The simplistic view of the factory as measured largely by efficiency not only drives away good men and women, but fails to use the factory as a competitive weapon to meet specific manufacturing tasks demanded by corporate strategy. Delegation of their own responsibility by top managers allows too many plants to be managed by technologists who do not have a general management point of view.

The wise manager recognizes the multidimensional complexity of the problems with which he or she deals. To bring about change in the infrastructure of manufacturing involves a great deal more than new technology and technological innovation. Production managers are asking for heartache, frustration, and frequent defeat when they attempt to go it alone.

We walk innocently into an ambush when we attempt to develop new production systems without looking at their strategic and social implications as well as their technological aspects. Present know-how and skills will be multiplied enormously and failures and delays prevented when we recognize that factory problems are just as complex and demanding as all the other problems involved in renewing major social institutions. They require a multidimensional team approach.

Strategic Weapon. Here, I shall be more brief, for I have already discussed this subject in a previous article.[5] Suffice it to say at this point that the concept of management as a strategic weapon is powerful in my experience because, once understood and assimilated, the concept has a dynamic effect on a manager. Its use automatically lifts the manager out of any narrow parochial corner into a broad total view of the production system and its relation to the corporation and its strategy. The concept gives a means and a framework for thinking about the design of manufacturing and requires the manager to think of the production process in policy—rather than solely operational—terms.

Concept of Manufacturing. Seen as a major institution, manufacturing at once takes on new dimensions which have existed often unrecognized all along. Certain conclusions then follow:

- Elements of the infrastructure must be mutually and internally consistent.
- Everything counts, since one overlooked element may ruin the total.
- Manufacturing decisions must span the infrastructure; changes can no longer be made piecemeal if they are to be successful.
- The span of changes must be broader and take in more elements.

The interaction between the various elements of the infrastructure is complex and often not easily understood, but their resulting effects warrant attention and improved expertise.

. . . In Meeting Human Needs

A different kind of recommendation from those representing conceptual changes involves the organization and operation of production systems in terms of societal and personal values. If an institution is to be productive in the short run and viable over the long run, it must (1) meet or change the felt needs and expectations of employees so as to be generally satisfying, and (2) develop an image that attracts sufficient numbers and varieties of people to allow for the selection of an able total cadre of employees and managers.

As stated earlier, we have much evidence that the factory as a social institution may be rapidly growing outdated. Who, after all, wants to work in a factory these days? And what does the common answer "Not very many" mean?

To me, it suggests that the values and demands that today's factory institution imposes on its members are beginning to conflict with the values and expectations of an increasing fraction of modern Americans.

Specifically, Exhibit 2 suggests a number of these conflicts and growing incongruencies and anachronisms.

What can be done with this vital "people segment" of the factory infrastructure? Although it is probably the most difficult element with which to cope, I would like to suggest, albeit cautiously, that the people area is not as impossible to deal with as is often assumed. It can be resolved more satisfactorily, but it will take some daring and innovative management nerve, for changes in people policies can be explosive; this means that top management must take responsibility and be involved.

But the picture is not all negative. For the factory can offer a great deal that employees want and need. Employees, particularly in metropolitan big city environments, are often lonely in the crowd; do feel needs for group memberships, and cooperative, nonaggressive, nondefensive, and fulfilling experiences; wish to identify with a successful organization and quality products; seek outlets for their ideas and opinions.

Seen in this sense, the factory can be attractive if it meets some of these needs. Some factories are already doing a superb job in certain facets. In fact, it appears to me that the factory is in an ideal position to meet many of today's unfulfilled social needs and expectations.

But to do so, what needs to be changed? Consider these anachronistic elements of many conventional factories:

☐ Pay systems based on hours worked.

☐ Physical arrangements that treat employees with disrespect and supervisory assumptions that fail to treat them as individuals.

RECOMMENDED CHANGES... 447

Exhibit 2. Conflicts Between Current Factory and Societal Viewpoints

Factory Expectations and Values	Social Expectations and Values
Employees are to perform jobs designed by management.	Employees know better than the boss how to do their own work.
Advancement is to be by seniority and long-proven performance.	Employees want continued and steady advancement.
Experience is important.	Experience is overemphasized.
Time is important.	Time is pressure.
Work, activity, achievement on one's job are to come first.	Family, leisure, and balanced life are most important.
Decisions are to be made quickly and efficiently.	Employees don't want anyone to decide anything that concerns them as individuals without first getting their opinion.
Employees are to adjust to the demands of expensive machinery.	Employees don't want to be treated like machines.
Following orders is essential.	Freedom is essential.
The individual is to be paid what he or she is worth.	Employees are entitled to a decent standard of living.
Productivity is essential to economic well-being.	Friends, conversation, and social interaction are essential to human well-being.
Employees are to perform well (even under adverse physical conditions).	Employees don't want to work under adverse physical conditions.
Seniority entitles employees to job protection and privileges.	One person has one vote.
Loyalty to the company is owed by employees.	Loyalty to one's beliefs is more important than loyalty to the corporation.
The corporation cares for its people.	The corporation cares little about its employees.
Employees are to perform work per schedules, quotas, and budgets.	Schedules, quotas, and budgets are mechanisms to exert control over people.

☐ Decision-making processes that leave out the opinions and ideas of involved employees.

☐ Promotion and job security policies that emphasize only experience and seniority.

☐ Communications practices that withhold information or present only one point of view.

☐ Job designs and work content that focus solely on motor-mechanism/physiological aspects of an employee's capacities and leave out the emotional and spiritual dimensions.

☐ Union contracts and governance systems that restrict change and stifle initiative.

Current Examples

Lest the foregoing discussion strikes the reader as recommendations from an ivory tower, let me cite several real-life examples of changes going on now in manufacturing management. These are typical of what some few innovative companies are doing in the light of the kinds of problems I have been discussing in this article.

Company A. This is a $50 million annual sales manufacturer of capital equipment whose manufacturing vice president and president became concerned enough about late deliveries, high costs, shortages of skilled technicians, and rising labor problems to decide that total organization—rather than piecemeal—changes were in order. Their factory is now being overhauled from top to bottom.

The changeover process started with a determination of the specific manufacturing task required by the company's competitive strategy, which the executives identified as offering short lead times on an ever increasing number and variety of products with a trend toward shorter runs of more customer specials. Subsequently, they tackled each element of the factory infrastructure, such as analyzing scheduling and information systems, supervisory and wage policies, equipment, and layout.

In short, all of this factory's operations were reexamined and rethought in order (1) to be mutually consistent, (2) to provide short lead times on new product development and delivery, and (3) to cope with today's social and economic environments.

Company B. This is one of our industrial giants. At one decentralized division where labor productivity has been marginal at best, a totally new approach to supervision and work force management has been installed on a pilot basis. The approach features a "self-determining work group," consisting of about 30 workers in a general purpose jobshop machine area who are permitted to govern themselves. The group members set their own rules and regulations within the framework of only the general and functional company objective of making parts as needed, per blueprint, and on schedule. Quality controls, scheduling of machines, discipline and work rules, and productivity are all under the control and direction of the group itself with the help of a "trainer," who functions as a nondirective consultive coordinator.

Companies C and D. These two are pursuing a less drastic approach to a new kind of supervision and work force management. Entirely independent of each other—they are located 1,200 miles apart and are in different industries—both have restructured traditional supervisor jobs.

Concluding that the typical supervisor's job is "impossible," Company C took four sections of 30 workers each under four supervisors and set up an enlarged section of 120 workers with a team of the four former supervisors in charge. One member of the team was asked to focus on quality, a second on training, a third on technical problems, and the fourth on scheduling, planning, and reporting.

In Company D, the same kind of change took place but with a three-person team in which the role of the quality specialist was omitted.

In each of these four companies, positive responses to its innovative approaches and changes are taking place. Perhaps a kind of "Hawthorne effect" (in which experiment and change always seem to produce beneficiary results regardless of the particular change) is at work. Then, again, perhaps the experiments are sound in themselves and will become models for other companies.

In any event, the climate for innovation and experimentation in manufacturing management has never been better. The recommendations in this article are derived in large part from actual cases. Real progress is taking place among a relatively small number of companies whose managers are recognizing the seriousness of problems in U.S. industry and courageously taking the risks of bringing about substantial change.

Conclusion

Our factories and industrial system are under economic and societal attack. The pressing task is to redesign ways of producing goods and services. Our job is to overhaul an archaic system of thinking about and managing the production system of the nation. The time we have to accomplish it is short, not only because of the pressures of foreign competition, but because of a vicious cycle in which an obsolete system based on misconception and unacceptable assumptions about people deteriorates and drives away able men and women.

We may need to revise much of the industrial know-how established over the last 150 years. Our technological tools are growing by great leaps, but they cannot be employed without making equivalent and appropriate changes in all the other aspects of our industrial system. An attack on this stubborn infrastructure is essential to the whole problem.

Changes in the factory infrastructure are as essential as they are difficult and as necessary in this vital area as they are in many other U.S. institutions.

The failure to bring about and plan coordinated changes in the total structure of manufacturing accounts to a great extent for our slow and miserable performance in changing over the U.S. factory so that it can continue to compete successfully. Not only are there economic pressures for change, but there are also relentless social and political pressures that are equally inescapable.

People in corporations charged with the job of renewal of the factory are under some of the greatest pressure in our high-pressure environment. This pressure will probably grow with further foreign competition and strident demands for fairness, participation, freedom, and instant change. To individual managers, this should spell opportunity as well as pressure. But an individual, "lone-wolf," or technically centered approach to any complex problem such as the overhauling of this obsolete institution is inadequate.

The U.S. factory system is anachronistic on these counts:

1 Its management concepts are outdated, focusing on cost and efficiency instead of strategy, and on making piecemeal changes instead of changes that span and link the entire system.
2 Its infrastructure contains such conflict and paradox that the expectations and desires of its people are too often incongruent with the imperatives of its technology, the demands of its markets, and the strategies of its managers.

This internal inconsistency marks a failure to adapt to environmental change in a key functional area of U.S. business—the production function.

How ironic that in production, where scientific management techniques began, these conventional approaches now seem out of date and out of tune with the social and economic facts of the times. Production management is perhaps bringing to an end a long cycle that began with innovation and new concepts for accomplishing productivity, developed in maturity of ideas, subsequently grew into a "conventional wisdom," and finally arrived at the point where we now see obsolescence.

Looking ahead, the changes in economics, technology, and society that now have an impact on the factory may, if we dare, lead us to new kinds of production infrastructures that could absorb and harness new technology and new social values. With creative and substantial change, led by the more intrepid, the U.S. factory institution could begin to achieve the productivity breakthrough our economy so sorely needs.

Notes

1. The productivity of American industry has been studied by a National Committee on Productivity appointed by President Nixon; his concerns were stated in June 1970: "In order to achieve price stability, healthy growth, and a rising standard of living, we must find ways of restoring growth to productivity.''

2. Judson Gooding, ''Blue-Collar Blues on the Assembly Line,'' *Fortune*, July 1970, p. 69.

3. Kenneth Hopper, ''Can the U.S. Stay Competitive?'' *American Machinist*, Special Report No. 644, July 27, 1970.

4. ''Are We Falling Behind in Mechanization?'' *HBR*, November–December 1960, p. 93.

5. ''Manufacturing—Missing Link in Corporate Strategy,'' *HBR*, May–June 1969, p. 136. Chapter 5, this volume.

27

The Man on the Assembly Line

CHARLES R. WALKER and ROBERT H. GUEST

The age of mass production has been with us for some time, but many basic questions remain unanswered about the best way to integrate a human work force with production machinery in a factory setting. As the authors put it, "To what degree can—or should—people be 'adjusted' to the new environment of machines, and to what degree is it possible to adjust or rebuild the environment to fit the needs and personalities of people?" Two years of on-the-spot research in a modern automobile assembly plant provide the authors with the human data to offer some beginning answers to these longstanding questions.

> There are a lot of good things about my job. The pay is good. I've got seniority. The working conditions are pretty good for my type of work. But that's not the whole story. . . . You can't beat the machine. They have you clocked to a fraction of a second. My job is engineered, and the jigs and fixtures are all set out according to specifications. The foreman is an all right guy, but he gets pushed, so he pushes us. The guy on the line has no one to push. You can't fight that iron horse.[1]

> Machines alone do not give us mass production. Mass production is achieved by both machines *and* men. And while we have gone a long way toward perfecting our mechanical operations, we have not successfully written into our equation whatever complex factors represent man, the human element.[2]

The principal social and psychological problems connected with mass production and human nature have been stated many times and in many different forms. Their importance in an age of advancing technology is hardly in dispute. The question has become rather: What shall we do about them?

Here are a few of the common problems. Since individuals react very differently to industrial occupations, what are the personality characteristics of those who adjust quickly to—and appear to thrive on—mechanically paced and repetitive jobs? What, on the other hand, are the personality characteristics of those who suffer mentally and physically on such jobs—and who, therefore, tend to perform them badly? Can the adjustment problem, in other words, be solved by selection? Or is the modern work environment simply *wrong* for the normal human being?

Or to take an engineering and management approach: In the present state of the mechanical arts, what part of a worker's skill and power can the engineer build into a machine? What must be left out? Precisely how and to what extent in the most mechanized sectors of our economy does the human equation still affect quantity and quality?

Or again, granted that the principles of mass production such as breakdown of jobs into their simplest constituent parts are sound and vital to efficient manufacture, have we yet found how to combine these principles with equally well-authenticated principles of human behavior?

Or taking still another approach, if someone spends a third of his or her life in direct contact with a mass-production environment, why should we not consider important (to that person and to society) the hours of living time spent inside the factory—as important and valuable, for example, as the product that person produces which is consumed outside the factory? We talk of a high standard of living, but frequently we mean a high standard of consumption. People consume in their leisure, yet fulfill themselves not only in their leisure but in their work. Is our mass-production work environment making such fulfillment more difficult?

A short way to sum up these and a great many more questions is: To what degree can—or should—people be "adjusted" to the new environment of machines, and to what degree is it possible to adjust or rebuild that environment to fit the needs and personalities of people?

Need for Systematic Study

Despite the tremendous contribution of mass-production methods to the productiveness of the economic system under which we live, and notwithstanding the fact that editors, philosophers, and propagandists have long speculated and written about the beneficent or injurious effects of highly mechanized jobs on human behavior, there has been singularly little systematic effort to discover "whatever complex factors represent man, the human element" in the mass-production method as such. The relatively small number of studies which have been made of assembly-line and other types of repetitive work have been mostly laboratory experiments, not explorations of experience in actual industrial plants.

A notable exception is the series of monographs which for some 25 years have been published from time to time under the auspices of the British Medical Council on the effects of mechanization and the repetitive job on productivity and *mental* fatigue. Even these, however, have only touched occasionally on the subject of assembly lines, and have never at all—to the best of our knowledge—dealt specifically with that advanced sector of a mass-production economy, the final assembly line of a plant making a large complex product like automobiles.

Survey of Automobile Assembly Plant

For these reasons the authors undertook two years ago an exploratory survey of a modern automobile assembly plant.[3] This is intended as the first of a series of studies designed to define more clearly the several "human equations" involved in assembly work, to prepare and sharpen tools of research, and to look for proximate and empirical answers to the more acute practical problems posed for people and management.

In this article we shall emphasize how an assembly line looks and feels to the people who work on it, rather than its importance to the engineers who designed it, the executives who manage it, or the public who buys its product.

In order to preserve the anonymity of those who freely supplied information—managers, workers, and union leaders—the plant in question has been called Plant X. Over a period of months 180 workers were interviewed in their homes about all phases of their life on "the line." These workers constituted a substantial—and representative—sample of the total number of productive workers in the plant.

Nearly 90% of the people working at Plant X came from jobs where the pace of work was not machine-governed in a strict sense, and from jobs over 72% of which were not repetitive. In short, the area from which they were recruited had few mass-production factories. One might say, then, that these people were like the majority of workers who in the past 30 years have made the transition from occupations characteristic of the first industrial revolution to work environments characteristic of a mass-production era. Their attitudes should be all the more revealing.

Most people, in thinking about an assembly line and the workers on it, focus only on the effect of the line on what a person does hour by hour, even minute by minute, with his or her mind and muscles. Any serious study of the human effects of the mass-production method, however, must extend its field of vision. For the method not only impinges directly on a person's immediate or intrinsic job but molds much of the character of the in-plant society of which that person is a part, including both relations with fellow workers and relations with management. Accordingly we shall discuss the impact of the mass-production method not only directly but indirectly on human nature.

Definition of Mass-Production Method

But what is the "mass-production method?" We must have a definition if our discussion and our findings are to be understandable.

Although the methods of mass production or, more accurately and specifically for our purposes, the methods of *progressive manufacture* have been defined and discussed in different ways by different writers, it is agreed by nearly everyone that these methods derive from at least two fundamental and related ideas: (1) standardization and (2) interchangeability of parts.

Given these basic ideas, plus the accurate machining methods that make them applicable to manufacture, Ford was able to work out and apply the three following additional "principles" of progressive manufacture: (3) the orderly progression of the product through the shop in a series of planned operations arranged so that the right part always arrives at the right place at the right time; (4) the mechanical delivery of these parts and of the product as it is assembled to and from the operators; and (5) a breakdown of operations into their simple constituent motions.[4]

Let us look now at how these principles translate themselves into job characteristics from the standpoint not of the engineer but of the person on the assembly line. In the first place, most automobile assembly jobs are *mechanically paced* (especially those on the main line). In the second place, since the engineer has broken the jobs down into simple and separate elements and assigned only a few to each worker they are clearly *repetitive*. Among other characteristics of most jobs are these: they have a low skill requirement, permit work on only a fraction of the product, severely limit social interaction, and predetermine for nearly every worker any use that may be made of tools and methods.

Taken together, automobile assembly-line jobs exemplify all these characteristics, but not every job exemplifies all of them. Put another way, in spite of many common characteristics, automobile assembly jobs are far from being equal—either as to the quantity or quality of job content or as to the satisfaction or dissatisfaction that workers derive from them. They differ both in the number of the several assembly-line characteristics they exemplify and in the degree of impact of any one characteristic. An understanding of this point must mark the beginning of any serious inquiry into the relation of human behavior to assembly-line work.

Attitude Toward Jobs

But that is enough of making distinctions. Now let the people on the assembly line tell us themselves about their jobs, and tell us also what they like and what they do not like about them. Here are six jobs by way of illustration: two on the main moving line, one off the main line but on a moving conveyer, one off the main line and not on a moving conveyer, one repair job on the line, and one utility job on the line. These six will illustrate at least the principal differences in human impact of mass-production, assembly-line jobs. (It should be remembered, however, that these six are not representative of the distribution of jobs in the whole plant, where one-half the jobs are on the *main moving assembly line*. Specifically the distribution of jobs in our sample was as follows: main assembly line, 86; subassembly on moving belt, 28; subassembly not on moving belt, 38; repairpersons, 14; utility people, 11; and other, 3.)

On the Main Moving Line

Here is the way the assembler of the baffle windbreaker in the trim department describes the job:

> As the body shell moves along the line, I start putting on a baffle windbreaker (two fenders fit on it) by putting in four screws. Then I put nine clips at the bottom which hold the chrome molding strip to the body. On another type of car there is a piece of rubber which fits on the hood latch on the side and keeps the hood from rattling. I drill the holes in the rubber and metal and fit two screws in. Also I put four clips on the rubber in the rear fender. On another type of body, I put the clips on the bottom molding, and in the trunk space I put two bolts which hold the spare tire clamp. I repeat these things all the time on the same types of car.

How does this person's job measure up in terms of some of the characteristics we have mentioned, particularly pace and repetitiveness?

To begin with, the job is on the main line and the worker rides along on the conveyer, completing the cycle of operations in less than two minutes while the conveyer is moving over a distance of about 30 feet. The worker then walks to the starting point and begins over again. In short, the pace is directly determined by the moving belt. On the other hand, the worker is sometimes able to work back up the line and so secure a breather.

The job is clearly repetitive, but there is some element of variety since between five and 10 operations are required to complete the job cycle. There are also different models to be worked on. Comparing the repetitiveness of this job with that of other assembly jobs, it is somewhere in the middle range—far less repetitive than a single-operation job and far more repetitive than the job of a repairperson.

Similarly, in the matter of skill it is in the middle as assembly-line jobs go. Because of the number of parts handled, learning time is slightly longer than that for many assembly jobs. The worker reported that it took a month to do the job properly. As for the expenditure of physical energy, it is a light job.

Also on the Main Moving Line

Or consider the job of the worker who installs toe plates and who performs operations typical of short-cycle, on-the-main-line jobs:

ATTITUDE TOWARD JOBS

> I put in the two different toe plates. They cover the holes where the brake and clutch pedals are. I am inside the car and have to be down on the seat to do my work. On one kind of car I put in the shift lever while another man puts in the toe plates.

While doing this job this worker rides along in the car and must complete the job before being carried too far. After finishing the work cycle the worker returns to the station, climbs into another car, and begins another installation. Thus the pace is strictly governed by the moving line. This particular worker told the interviewer that he did not mind the pace.

Such a job which demands but two operations in a two-minute cycle is highly repetitive. Only slight variety is introduced when the worker installs a shift lever instead of a toe plate on certain cars.

The job demands very little skill and has a learning period of just two days. Although the worker gets in and out of cars 20 or 30 times an hour, the expenditure of physical energy on the actual assembly operation is slight.

Off the Main Line but on a Moving Conveyer

The job of a seat-spring builder is typical of those off the main line but on a moving belt:

> I work on a small conveyer which goes around in a circle. We call it a merry-go-round. I make up zig-zag springs for front seats. Every couple of feet on the conveyer there is a form for the pieces that make up the seat springs. As that form goes by me, I clip several pieces together, using a clip gun. I then put the pieces back on the form, and it goes on around to where other men clip more pieces together. By the time the form has gone around the whole line, the pieces are ready to be set in a frame, where they are made into a complete seat spring. That's further down the main seat cushion line. The only operation I do is work the clip gun. It takes just a couple of seconds to shoot six or eight clips onto the spring, and I do it as I walk a few steps. Then I start right over again.

This job is clearly paced by a moving conveyer quite as much as if it were on the main line. A comment by the worker regarding a previous job emphasized the point: "I liked the piecework system on my old job. If I wanted to stop for a few minutes, I could. You can't do that here."

As for variety, there is none. The job is highly repetitive, consisting of one set of operations repeated every few seconds on a part that is standard for all models.

The skill requirement is minimum. This worker gave two days as the learning time, with a few days more "in order to do it like I do it now."

As for physical energy, the job would probably be rated as light since the worker guides an automatic hand gun. But there is considerable fatigue because the worker performs the operation standing up.

The worker's over-all estimate of the job is typical. As to what was liked about the job, the worker mentioned good pay, steady work, and good working hours—in that order of priority. As to what was disliked, the worker said that he could not set his own pace, that he did not have interesting work, and that his job was physically tiring.

Off the Main Line but Not on a Moving Conveyer

We turn to a blower-defroster assembler who works off the main line and not on a moving belt:

> I work at a bench on blower defrosters. The blowers come in two parts. I take one part and attach the blower motor to it. I then connect the fan to the motor shaft. Then I take the other half on the air pipe and put two parts together with fourteen screws. I test the motor to see if it works, and if it does, I put in a fifteenth screw which grounds it to the pipe. The materials are brought to me and put in a pile by a stock chaser. After I finish, I put each assembled blower on one of six shelves.

Here is an example of a job where pace is only indirectly determined by the main line. The worker must keep the shelves stocked with a supply of blower defrosters, but has some choice of pace in doing so. The worker may work fast and "build up a bank," then slow down and take a breather, or may choose to work quite steadily. The demands of the stockchaser who brings materials and takes away the finished assembly are the determinants of the work pace, rather than the moving conveyer.

There is not much variety since there are only three operations. However, a slight variation is introduced through differences in models. The worker called the job completely repetitive but did not mind it.

The job operations require a minimum of skill: "I learned it in a couple of hours, though it took me about a week to get up speed." The worker does not move around, and the materials handled are light, so very little physical energy is demanded.

Summing up the job, this worker gave good bosses, good pay, and good working conditions as the first three reasons for liking the job. The worker mentioned only one thing disliked: "I cannot do different things."

Repairperson

Here is a job description by a repairperson in the car-conditioning section of the chassis department:

> I work in a pit underneath the final line. The cars move along over the pit. On the previous assembly operations, the inspectors for the under parts of the car have indicated where parts were missing or damaged or not properly attached. There are any number of things which can be wrong, and they are usually different for each car. Sometimes we have a run of the same thing which we have to work on until they get at the

bug earlier in assembly operations. The shock absorbers may be bad, gas line in wrong, brake lines or spring attachments off. I fix whatever I see checked by the inspector. The others in the pit do the same thing. I just work down the line until I get it cleared up. Sometimes I have to work down a long way on one thing. Other times it's just a simple problem on a number of different things.

This worker is on the main line, but the pace is not strictly governed by the moving conveyer. "We don't feel the pressure of the line since we don't have to do just one thing in a given area and length of time."

The variety the job offers is derived from the nature of the work. "There are any number of things which can be wrong, and they are usually different for each car. . . . There is something different all the time."

As for skill, the job as repairperson requires manual skill and mechanical experience. A garage repairperson's job would be a good preparation. (The worker whose job description is given here had, in fact, worked as a repairperson in a garage before coming to Plant X.)

The job varies between light and medium-heavy work, with the expenditure of physical energy called for changing appreciably from job to job and from day to day.

The worker's personal satisfaction with the job was clear. Three reasons were given for liking the job: "I can set my own pace, I have good working conditions, and I have steady work." The worker also commented favorably on being able to "use my brains," "do different things," and "choose how the job is to be done."

Utility Person

A utility person in the chassis department describes the job as follows:

> I work on the whole length of that part of the chassis line beginning with motor drop up to where the wheels are mounted. My job is to fill in wherever I am needed. A man might be absent or away from the job or may need help on the job.

> We start where the motor is lowered onto the frame (motor mount). The clutch assembly is installed and hooked up. Then the exhaust system is attached and the bolts tightened. The clutch assembly bolts and the motor mount bolts are also tightened. In the next area on the line the brake chambers are filled and bled.

> Off to the side, the subassembly men put the steering column together. The steering post and the Pittman arm assembly are put in. Further down the line, men put in air cleaners and inject hydraulic fluid for the transmission.

> Next, the brakes are tested and the clutch linkage hooked up. The bumper brackets are put on; a serial number is attached next; and then the bumper brackets are tightened up. Finally, the chassis is sprayed, mounted on

wheels, and moved on toward body drop. All in all, about 28 men work on these jobs, each man with his own special operation. I go on each of these jobs, depending on where I am needed most. It is different each day. Some of the jobs are hard to learn, so when I take over one on which I haven't had much experience, it's hard to keep up. I have been learning how to do the work ever since I've been in the plant. I can never learn everything because new changes are always being made.

The pace of this utility person's work, since it is on the main line, is as strictly governed as that of any assembly worker. In certain ways this worker may feel the pressure more acutely than some of those for whom this worker substitutes, since this worker has less practice on any single job than its regular holder.

To compensate, however, there is plenty of variety, for, as pointed out, this worker shifts about among 28 different jobs. Notice how in describing the many tasks this utility person gives a very clear account of a whole segment of assembly operations in the chassis department.

Notice, too, the character of a utility person's skill. It is the sum of many little skills of many repetitive jobs. The learning time is six months to a year. The worker said: "Sometimes I walk up and down checking the line. I ask questions of the different workers. I rarely stay on the same job more than a couple of days." That this job is not easy is suggested by an additional comment:

> Some days you feel like learning, other days you don't. On jobs that take time to learn, you get disgusted because it's hard to keep up. A utility man, when on a job, has more trouble keeping up than the regular man."

This worker mentioned good pay, steady work, and good bosses as the three main reasons for liking the job, in that order. Other items bearing on the immediate job which were liked were "having interesting work, having to use my brains, doing many different things," as in the case of the repairperson, and also "talking with others." This worker had only one complaint about the job: that it was "physically tiring."

Summary of Attitudes Toward Jobs

In all of this classification of the automobile assembly workers' jobs, we have clearly been concerned not with an engineering analysis but with factors that have an effect on satisfaction or dissatisfaction with the immediate job. Mechanical pace, repetitiveness, minimum skill requirement, and the other factors were all found reflected in attitudes and feelings.

These examples underline some of the commonest facts and feelings which are part of the daily experience of the productive worker in an assembly plant. To recall a few:

1. Contrary to popular belief, all jobs on an assembly line are not alike, either in skill, variety, learning time, or the degree of satisfaction or dissatisfaction that they offer the average wage earner.
2. There are definite ways on certain jobs to get a break or a breather, such as "working back up the line," or "bank building."
3. There is a general, though not a unanimous, desire to move from highly paced jobs to jobs which are less highly paced, and "off the line."
4. It is evident from the statements of the six workers—which for illustrative purposes we have selected from 180—that other factors such as good pay, a good foreperson, and a secure job must be considered in appraising the total index of a worker's satisfaction or dissatisfaction.

Major Reactions of Workers

Looking over the range of factors connected with their immediate jobs by all workers interviewed, we see that the two that were given greatest prominence were (1) mechanical pacing and (2) repetitiveness.

To Mechanical Pacing

We asked no direct attitude questions on the first and central characteristic of any automobile assembly plant—the moving conveyer—but nearly every worker expressed opinions about it when describing his or her job, when talking about the company, or at some other point in the interview. These free-association comments on pace as governed by the moving conveyer showed that: (1) A large majority of the workers regarded the moving line or belt as an undesirable feature of the job. (2) A small minority expressed themselves as enjoying the excitement of the moving line.

Following are typical comments of workers who were highly critical of the line:

> The bad thing about assembly lines is that the line keeps moving. If you have a little trouble with a job, you can't take the time to do it right.
>
> On the line you're geared to the line. You don't dare stop. If you get behind, you have a hard time catching up.
>
> The line speed is too great. More men wouldn't help much. They'd just expect more work out of an individual. There's an awful lot of tension.
>
> I don't like rushing all the time. . . . I don't mind doing a good day's work, but I don't like to run through it.
>
> The work isn't hard; it's the never-ending pace. . . . The guys yell 'hurrah' whenever the line breaks down. . . . You can hear it all over the plant.

In contrast, a minority liked the challenge and excitement of keeping up with the line:

> I do my job well. I get some satisfaction from keeping up with a rapid-fire job. On days when the cars come off slowly, I sometimes get bored.
>
> I get satisfaction from doing my job right and keeping up with the line.
>
> It makes you feel good . . . when the line is going like hell and you step in and catch up with it.

To Repetitiveness

Turning now to the job characteristic, repetitiveness, our findings are that: (1) a majority of the workers were critical of the repetitive character of their jobs; (2) a minority preferred the repetitive character of their work or were indifferent to it; (3) a large number of workers compared on-the-line jobs unfavorably with off-the-line jobs, because off-the-line jobs offered more variety.

We found we were able to correlate the number of operations a worker performed (which can serve as a rough measure of repetitiveness) with expressions of interest or lack of interest in the job. The number of operations performed on any given job was determined not by direct questioning but by analysis of the job descriptions. The workers, however, were asked directly: "Would you say your job was very interesting, fairly interesting, not at all interesting?" The correlation with number of operations was as follows:

Operations Performed	Very or Fairly Interesting	Not Very or Not At All Interesting
1	19	38
2–5	28	36
5 or more	41	18

In the column of workers giving a positive rating to "interest," the number of workers increases as the number of operations increases. In other words, there is a tendency for interest in work to vary directly with the number of operations performed.

Following are typical comments of those workers who were critical of the repetitive nature of their jobs:

> I dislike repetition. One of the main things wrong with this job is that there is no figuring for yourself, no chance to use your brain. It's a grind doing the same thing over and over. There is no skill necessary.
>
> I'd rather work for a small company any day. They're interested in doing good work, and they are willing to allot enough time for it. The assembly

line is no place to work, I can tell you. There is nothing more discouraging than having a barrel beside you with 10,000 bolts in it and using them all up. Then you get a barrel with another 10,000 bolts, and you know every one of those 10,000 bolts has to be picked up and put in exactly the same place as the last 10,000 bolts.

I'd like to do different things on this job. I get bored. It's the same thing all the time. Cars always coming down the line endlessly every time I look up.

I would like to perform different operations, but I do the same thing all the time. I always know what I'm going to do when I come in. There's nothing to look forward to like there was on my old job.

The monotony is what I don't like. It's pretty noisy, but you get used to that. I'd never get used to the monotony. I dislike the plant for this reason.

It's not a matter of pace. It's the monotony. It's not good for you to get so bored. I do the same thing day after day; just an everlasting grind.

The job gets so sickening—day in and day out plugging in ignition wires. I get through with one motor, turn around, and there's another motor staring me in the face.

A minority of workers who declared that they were indifferent to or preferred doing the same thing over and over again commented as follows:

I keep doing the same thing all the time, but it doesn't make any difference to me.

Repeating the same thing you can catch up and keep ahead of yourself. I like the routine. You can get in the swing of it.

We do the same thing all the time, but I don't mind it really.

I like doing the same thing all the time. I'd rather stay right where I am. When I come in in the morning, I like to know exactly what I'll be doing.

I like to repeat the same thing, and every car is different anyway. So my job is interesting enough.

Explanation of why this minority group either preferred or was indifferent to the factor of repetitiveness in contrast to the majority of workers in our sample would appear to lie in the pattern of their individual personalities. An investigation of the psychological characteristics of people who react this way is clearly suggested. We sought but found no other unique characteristics in the group as regards education, age, or any of the other categories of information we used.

Effect of Human Equation

In the introductory paragraphs of this article we reviewed some of the typical questions on which it was hoped research into the human equation of assembly-line work might throw light, including some of special interest to both the production manager and the engineer: What part of a worker's skill and power can the engineer build into a machine? What must be left out? Precisely how and to what extent in the most mechanized sectors of our economy does the human equation still affect quantity and quality?

Influence of Workers on Quality

So far as assembly lines go, there is still a widespread belief on the part of *outsiders* that the machine has completely taken over and that on mechanized conveyer-line jobs the individual has no influence on quality. There is also a belief widely held by *insiders* (employers and production managers) that, even though the quality of individual performance on a mechanized job may still be important for the final product, the average worker no longer cares or gets satisfaction from doing a good job.

In Plant X, both beliefs were shown to be unfounded.

As many as 79 workers in the sample of 180 felt that it was difficult to sustain the kind of quality performance that was expected of them or which they themselves wanted to sustain. To most of the 79, *this was a discouraging and negative feature of the job.*

About half the workers felt it was possible to do the kind of quality job expected of them. Few of these workers, however, had jobs which were strictly line-paced. Rather they included most repairpersons, utility persons, workers on off-line jobs, or workers on the line who had longer time cycles or greater freedom to move up and down the line. Typical comments among this group were:

> No time limit is set on my job, so I can do it right. I get satisfaction out of really fixing a job. I can usually get this, but sometimes the company doesn't want the cars fixed as well as I'd like to.
>
> I get satisfaction and quality because I have time to complete my job right.
>
> I never let a car go by with my number on it unless it is done right. Maybe some of the men on the line don't get quality.
>
> You can take time to get quality. It's not like on the line when you have to rush so much. And I get satisfaction. It makes me feel good when I put out a good day's work and get no kickbacks.

The effects of poor-quality work on job satisfaction were reflected in many of the comments of workers on conveyer-paced jobs:

> The cars come too fast for quality. It's quantity instead of quality. I'm doing the best I can, but could do a neater job slower.
>
> On an assembly line you just do it once; if it's wrong, you have no time to fix it. I get no satisfaction from my work. All I do is think about all

the things that went through wrong that should have been fixed. My old job was nothing like this.

I try to do quality work, but I'm too rushed. This keeps me from getting pleasure from the work. They say "haste makes waste," and they're getting plenty of both.

I'd rather do less work and do it right. How can you get quality when they don't give you time? The "quality" signs they have mean nothing.

These comments tend to show that the characteristics or components of the assembly person's immediate job do have a significant bearing upon the quality of the product, and that mass production restricts rather than eliminates the "human factor" as a determinant of quality for any given part or for the total product. Most workers were conscious of this fact. For a substantial number, inability to put out quality was a source of irritation whereas putting out quality was a source of job satisfaction.

Constructive Measures by Management

Are there any measures that management can take to modify on-the-job conditions of work in the interest of greater efficiency and of increased satisfaction for the individual operator?

One answer to this question may be sought in the elements of satisfaction or of compensation which some workers already found in their jobs. To begin with, it should be remembered that there was a minority of workers who preferred or were indifferent to repetitiveness and mechanical pacing. Presumably by improved methods of recruiting and selection this minority could be increased. Then there were a number of workers who found their immediate jobs on and off the line satisfying—actually all the repairpersons and utility persons interviewed with one exception. The only measures needed here are protective—to make sure that the content of these jobs is not diluted.

This still leaves the majority of the production workers. Here the clue to constructive action lies in the fact that many of them reacted favorably to particular features of their jobs:

1 Social interaction breaking the monotony.
2 Enough operations on their particular jobs to give variety.
3 Opportunity to work back up the line and get a breather.
4 Opportunity to build up a bank and get a breather.
5 Opportunity to alternate one set of operations with another set of a substantially different character.
6 Opportunity to alternate jobs with other workers within the same section.
7 A long time cycle encompassing a larger number of operations than usual and of a more interesting character.

A practical directive for management would appear to be exploration of the possibility of extending these and other desirable features, so that more assembly workers could share in them. The degree of that extension would necessarily vary with the special circumstances—physical and organizational—of individual plants, and with the ingenuity of management; but there would be few plants where something could not be done in this direction.

Detailed discussion of such measures is beyond the scope of this article, but the tenor of our thinking may be indicated by reference to two of the seven features to which Plant X workers reacted favorably.

Job Rotation

Take Number 6—alternation of jobs between workers, a technique often called "rotation." At Plant X we were struck with the unusually high degree of job satisfaction expressed by the members of one work group under a particular foreperson. With the permission and encouragement of their foreperson, the workers were working under a system of job rotation. It was to this system that the members of the group ascribed their relatively high job satisfaction. And to the same system the section foreperson owed in part a smoothly running and efficient work unit. Top plant management is now encouraging a more widespread application of this practice.

In connection with any system of job rotation the question immediately comes to mind: Since it requires some effort to learn several jobs instead of one, will not the worker—unless exceptional—object? Many managers seem to find it difficult to get workers to change jobs frequently.

The best answer to this question about worker resistance is the pragmatic one. In certain sectors on the line at Plant X rotation *is* working. Moreover, in other industries and on other types of assembly lines the practice of rotation is steadily gaining ground. For most people learning to do something new is hard work, and it is only undertaken when an adequate reward is held out. For a considerable number of assembly-line workers the rewards of variety and of possessing a repertory of skills will be sufficient.

Of course, some resistance to an experiment in rotation is to be expected. The key to the situation lies, we suggest, in the word "experiment." Where rotation has been successfully installed on other types of assembly lines, it has usually been started as an experiment, with management guaranteeing to the work group or to any single individual a return to stationary assignments if desired—and rarely have the workers wished to return.

Another question is: Will the work be done as well or as fast under job rotation? The answer for the Plant X section which practices it is an affirmative one. For other work groups in other industries with which the authors are familiar, the answer has also been "yes." Of course there are work situations where job rotation appears either altogether impractical or less efficient. But always the real test is in the over-all and long-term performance of the group. Gains in quality and a drop in turnover or absenteeism may balance some decrease in output, if it occurs.

Job Enlargement

Or consider Number 7—a long-time cycle encompassing a larger number of operations than usual and of a more interesting character, sometimes called "job enlargement." Here is a concept and a practice that has proved successful in decreasing monotony without impairing efficiency in certain sectors of other industries. We here suggest that it be introduced experimentally into automobile assembly work.

Job enlargement is simply the recombining of two or more separate jobs into one. Certain plant managers in other industries have been finding that a law of diminishing returns applies to the subdivision of jobs and that a recombination of certain fractured parts has increased efficiency. This points toward a lengthening of time cycles. Job enlargement in the sense in which we suggest it does not mean turning automobile assembly back into the hands of master mechanics with one worker assigned to the assembly of one car. It does mean paying greater attention to psychological and social variables in the determination of time cycles and, by the same token, paying more attention to the *content* of individual jobs.

To one unfamiliar with assembly-line work experience, the difference between a job with five operations and a job with 10, or between a job taking two minutes to perform and a job taking four minutes, might seem a matter far too trivial to concern anyone. Our data have shown that this is not true. Management has a vital interest in such matters; the proper assignment of time cycles throughout an assembly plant will make an important difference in the efficiency of the plant. As for the worker, one of the most striking findings of this study is the psychological importance of even minute changes in the immediate job experience.

At the risk of oversimplification, the point may be summarized this way: Other things being equal, the difference between a satisfied and a dissatisfied worker may rest on whether the worker has a 10-operation or a five-operation job.

Relationship among Workers

Another place to look for possibilities of improvement is in the area of indirect influences—the impact of mass-production methods on the plant's social structure. Ever since the early studies of Elton Mayo, it has been widely accepted that the character of the "work group" frequently exercises a decisive influence on a worker's efficiency—not to mention on satisfaction on the job. How did the technology of the automobile assembly line affect the grouping of workers at Plant X?

Most workers are located along the "main line" according to the particular manpower requirements of each segment of the assembly process. Each operator works in a limited area completing operations independently of others as the car is carried by the conveyer down the line. A particular individual may talk with the workers immediately around him or her but these coworkers cannot be said to comprise a bona fide work group in the usual sense of the term. Take as an illustration the polishing line. Exhibit 1 shows in diagrammatic form an actual interaction pattern of a left-front-door polisher, Worker E.

The 10 workers from A to J comprise a work group of which Worker E is a part, and there is some social contact with all the other nine. The really close contacts, however, are only with C, D, F, and G. Note that these four workers comprise a group—*but only from E's point of view.* As to the social relationship pattern of G, the immediate group would consist of E, F, H, and I; it would not include C and D, who were clearly members

Exhibit 1. Social Interaction Pattern of Typical Main Assembly Line Worker—Polisher Paint Department

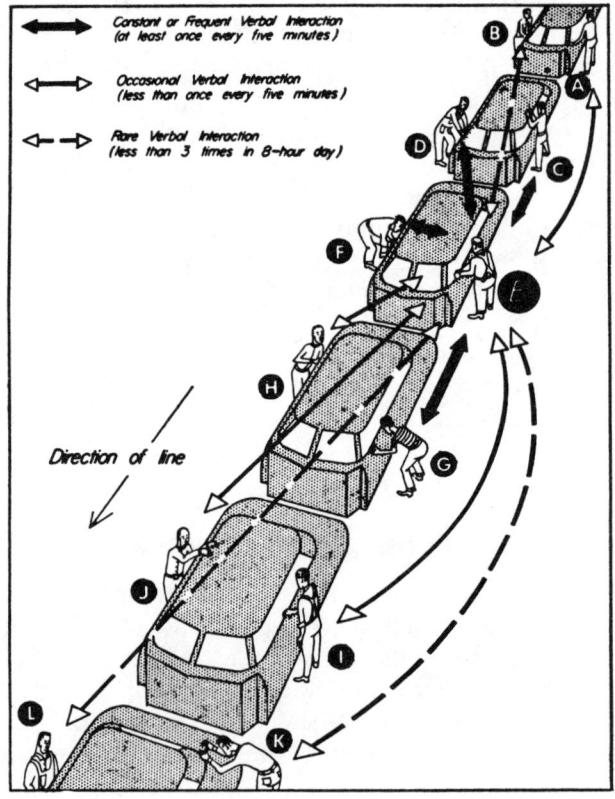

of E's group. Further variations occur, for example, when a line makes a bend or loop and brings workers in different sections closer together. Thus each worker, because of the nature of conveyer operations, has a slightly different circle of associates from that of the person next to him or her. So it goes along the entire stretch of a line, a line well over two miles long.

In our interviews these workers exhibited little of what the sociologist would call "in-group awareness." Rarely, for example, did they talk about "our team" or "our group" or "the people in our outfit." Instead, the following remark was typical: "I've been here over a year, and I hardly know the first names of the people in the section where I work."

In sharp contrast, however, to the majority of line workers, a minority—principally off-line operators—worked on bona fide teams or crews; that is, they were members of a close working group, were functionally interdependent, and frequently assisted their fellows or exchanged operations with them. On charting the interaction pattern of such groups it was found that the frequency of conversational exchange was high and constant for nearly all members of the group. Of greater significance, the group exhibited a marked *esprit-de-corps* not found among the bulk of line operators.

It is clear that the present technology of an automobile assembly line limits social interaction and does not lend itself to the arrangement of workers in bona fide teams or crews. It is suggested, however, that in the design of *new* plants, and at periods of retooling or of layout revisions, an effort be made to maximize the opportunities for social interaction and for team relationships.

Relations with Management

Still another area of social relationships—that of worker to supervisor—is crucial to an intelligent understanding of social organization.

The formal organizational structure of the various production departments in Plant X was similar to that found in many plants. In interviews with workers we came to know the quality of relationship between workers and supervisors.

Forepersons

Qualitative comments by workers about their forepersons suggested a relatively informal and friendly relationship on the part of the majority. The average foreperson had from 15 to 25 workers under him or her, and talking between worker and foreperson was generally frequent, friendly, and informal. The sort of remarks one hears about any good foreperson were also heard here, as for example: "Our foreperson is a real good guy. We're lucky. If she got into trouble, the whole department would back her right up."

There were criticisms of forepersons, but usually these were not directed at the individual. Rather they were aimed at the "line" and the role the foreperson had to play with reference to the line. As one worker said: "After all, the foreperson has to be a pusher, and nobody likes to be pushed. He's got to hold his job. If he doesn't push, somebody else will get his job."

Often workers exonerated forepersons for "pushing" since they recognized that the compulsion of line production was not the fault of the forepersons. One worker put it this way: "I guess you'd say the foreperson gets along with the workers. But they don't need a foreperson. *The line is the foreperson.* You have to keep up with the line."

Higher Supervisors

An interesting finding that came out of the study was the relationship, or lack of it, between workers and management above the foreperson level. The 180 workers in our sample were asked to indicate contacts with supervisors in their department at the general foreperson and department-head levels. Only 59 reported that they talked with their general foreperson as often as once a week; 15 put it at one to three times a month; and 88 said less than once a month. Contact between workers and upper departmental supervisors was even less, with 70% saying they spoke with their department heads less than once a month. (Departments ranged in size from 200 to 400.)

It is significant in this connection that in a steel fabricating plant which we recently studied the workers talked far more frequently with supervisors above the foreperson level. There the nature of the process and the high degree of worker skills made for a closer relationship. It was an everyday experience to find a superintendent in charge of 400 workers talking with an individual worker or group of workers. The superintendent did this because the technical and skilled judgment of the individual worker was important in the production process.

On the automobile assembly line, on the other hand, because of the high degree of mechanization and fractional assembly there appears to be less need for supervisors to discuss production matters with individual workers. Management relies on the judgment of the engineer, not the worker. Thus the basic factor that determines the rate and quality of worker-supervisor interaction is the technology of mass production.

Impact on Wage Structure

Not the least important secondary effect of the mass-production method has been its impact on the wage structure. A leveling of workers' skills has inevitably resulted in a narrowing of differentials between wage grades, in contrast to industries where the latest mass-production methods have not been applied. For example, in the steel fabricating plant which we investigated—a seamless tube mill—the differential between the rates of the lowest and of the highest paid workers was over a dollar an hour. At Plant X, however, the differential between the lowest paid and the highest paid was around 10 cents for the major categories of production workers, and over half the workers in the production departments received exactly the same hourly wage.

It is obvious that changes in skill levels and in wage categories affect what the wage administrator calls the "system of job progression." Before the application of mass-production methods most industries had many well-defined steps in their ladders of promotion. Mass-production methods, although often raising the general level of wages and bringing other benefits, have knocked out a good many rungs in these promotion ladders. To turn again to the steel mill for contrast: there were as many as seven or eight steps from laborer to roller, each one associated with progressively higher wages, skills, and prestige.

This system of promotion, with its connotations of growth, incentive, and progress, has been weakened or virtually eliminated on the assembly line. Almost any assembly worker can—and some do—say: "There are hundreds of jobs like mine, not much better, not much worse. The differences are so slight—or seem so slight to management—that I am interchangeable." Consequently, to escape a resulting sense of anonymity as much, perhaps, as to escape monotony, the average worker at Plant X does not aspire to climb into another slightly better production job, but rather into a utility person's job or a repairperson's job or out of production altogether, where the worker can be recognized, and can recognize him or herself as an individual.

Most of the benefits of the mass-production method are obvious and have often been celebrated. If we are to continue to enjoy them and to expand and refine the method, we should understand more fully its impact on the traditional organization of industry. Surely the problems as well as the promises of mass production are worthy of study.

Conclusion

It is obviously impossible in a single article to do more than sketch some of the problem areas in the broad field of relations between mass production and human nature. Concerning the direct impact of the method on the individual we made a few empirical suggestions and tried to point out at least one direction in which management might seek practical solutions.

But what can be said about the *indirect* impact of mass production on human nature through the character of work groups, the wage structure, and the promotion system? In a negative sense, at least, all these phenomena appear to be related: At Plant X they tended to increase the workers' sense of anonymity within the production enterprise of which they were functional parts. In fact, one way to express the net result of these several influences might be to say that little sense of membership in a common work community existed. (Our evidence showed that to some extent membership in the union gave the worker the feeling of personal identity and "belonging" which neither the shop nor relations with management supplied.)

It seems to us significant that the average worker appeared to be oppressed by this sense of anonymity *in spite of the fact that the workers declared themselves well satisfied with their rate of pay and the security of their jobs.* The answer to this problem in the most general terms would appear to be a program designed to re-create the sense *and also* the reality of a bona fide work community. And for such a program to be successful we believe that both union and management would have to agree on the measures to be taken.

A comment by a worker on the line will suggest the nature of the problem more clearly than many paragraphs of exposition:

> There is a different feeling in this plant. It's much bigger than people around here have ever seen. It's just like the kid who goes up to a grownup man and starts talking to him. There doesn't seem to be a friendly feeling. At the plant I used to work in there was a different feeling. Everyone spoke to everyone else. . . . Nobody goes to other departments in this plant. The understanding could be better—happier and much easier. Here a man is just so much horsepower.

Perhaps the human needs in Plant X are merely an expression in more explicit terms of the needs of our industrial civilization. The problem of reintegrating the several faculties of people into a significant unity presents itself in many fields—in industry, science, and government, to name but three—in an age of overspecialization.

It is striking that throughout the survey of Plant X both union and management agreed with the authors that the more basic problems to be explored were not those connected with a particular plant, industry, or corporation. Rather they were problems related to technological and organizational trends common to modern industry. Both agreed that modern American civilization as we know it rests upon mass-production principles quite as much as upon the natural resources of the United States. The attitude of both, therefore, was a simple and heartening one: *Since these problems exist, let us get all the facts we can. In time we shall be able to solve them.*

As Saint-Exupéry, the French aviator and author wrote:

> The Machine is not an end. . . . It is a tool . . . like the plough.
>
> If we believe that it degrades Man, it is possibly because we lack the perspective for judging the end results of transformations as rapid as those to which we have been subjected. What are two hundred years in the history of the Machine when compared with two hundred thousand

years in the history of Man? We have scarcely established ourselves in this country of mines and of central electricity. It is as if we had hardly begun to live in the new house that we have not yet finished building. Everything has changed so rapidly around us: human relations, conditions of work, customs. . . . Every step in our progress has driven us a little further from our acquired habits, and we are in truth pioneers who have not yet established the foundations of our new country.[5]

Notes

1. Worker on an assembly line, interviewed by the authors.

2. Henry Ford II, in a talk before the American Society of Mechanical Engineers, shortly after he was made President of the Ford Motor Company.

3. The full details of this survey were published in book form, *The Man on the Assembly Line*, by the Harvard University Press (June 1952).

4. This is a rephrased and slightly more explicit statement of the three principles of mass production as set down in "Mass Production" by Henry Ford in the *Encyclopaedia Britannica*, Fourteenth Edition, Vol. 15, pp. 38–39.

5. Antoine de Saint-Exupéry, *Terre des Hommes* (Paris, Gallimard, 1939), p. 58.

28
"By Days I Make the Cars"

JOHN F. RUNCIE

Arriving at a final assembly plant early in the morning, workers spend time in undefined activities such as talking and setting up concession stands. Once the line starts, the workers start; when it stops, they stop. During that eight-hour day, workers adapt to the endless sameness of their jobs in numbers of innocent ways—playing games, working slowly to force themselves to catch up, trading jobs—and some not so innocent ways—dope, liquor, sabotage, and theft. The quality of work life solutions that sociologists and human relations experts proffer pale beside the workers' need for conditions that enable them to perform their jobs well. When these conditions are satisfied, writes the author—a sociologist who spent five months working on the line—workers might become more interested in how decisions are made. Although the author had tried to maintain his objectivity, life on the line became as real and as inexorable for him as it is for people who work on it day after day. He feels the real problem in the plant stems not from bad stock or favoritism but from the view that people ought to be as identical as the cars they make.

The automobile assembly line has been the subject of songs, movies, and, more recently, articles in the business press that describe and decry the alienation of the worker in a job that causes "blue collar blues." The singer of a popular country and western song laments, "By days I make the cars and by night I make the bars."[1] Is working on the line as bad as it is made out to be? The answer is yes—and no.

A large percentage of the workers on the line today use drugs or alcohol or both. To put up with the stresses and problems of the line, many workers

---

Author's Note. This research was supported in part by funds from the C.S. Mott Foundation and the Chancellor's Special Fund of the University of Michigan—Flint.

take unauthorized absences; others resort to sabotage and theft. On the other hand, if you ask workers how long they intend to work in the plant, most will tell you that they expect to remain there until they retire. Many workers told me that they like to work on the line, and many remain on the line even though they have enough seniority to move into other jobs. Some even return to the line after trying out other jobs in the plant because they like line work better than the alternatives.

Clearly, the line can be many things to many people, but for the assembly line worker in an automobile plant, the line is the central focus of the day. It is the reason he or she is working; *it* governs the day. When the line starts, the worker starts; when the line stops, the worker stops. The line is a fact of life.

In this article, I present a picture of the life of the assembly line worker from two points of view—that of the people who work and live on the line and my own. For five months I worked on the line as an "objective" researcher, trying not to be so involved in the subject of the research as to distort it. (For a description of the research methodology, see the Appendix.) But I often found myself responding to situations as any other worker in the plant might and, for all intents and purposes, I was a worker first and a researcher second. Although I may not completely go along with all the other workers' opinions, I am in general agreement with their overall tone and implications.

The Job

Arriving in the early morning darkness, workers must pass a protection checkpoint at the plant gate. Some days the guard will stop you and ask you to show your plant pass; on other days you can just walk past, flashing the card as you enter. It always seemed to me that the guards chose the coldest or rainiest days to stop us, which didn't endear the plant guards to anyone.

Once inside the plant, the early arriver finds many workers already waiting for the start of the shift. Some arrive well before the line starts and stand around talking with the others who arrive early. These same workers may well be the ones who hang around after work talking with others in the parking lots. As Robert Schrank found in his time in a plant, "schmoozing" with other workers is an important part of any worker's day.[2] Several workers arrive early for a different purpose: to set up their small concessions to sell coffee, doughnuts, or other items. These on-the-job moonlighters have adapted to assembly line work by becoming entrepreneurs, subsidized in their pursuits by the unknowing auto companies.

Shortly before the scheduled start of the line, workers begin to congregate near their work stations—putting on aprons, getting their materials ready for the day, and building up reserves of their "stock," the assembled pieces they build into cars. By building stock ahead of time, you can make the day a bit easier for yourself.

For example, in my first job on the line I was responsible for installing the stabilizer bars, which give the car additional stability in cornering, on the underside of the front end of the car's chassis. To do the stabilizer bar job, I had to build two pieces of stock for each car, take one of three possible stabilizer bar models, move to the line as the chassis came by upside down, place the bar on it so it would not slip, put down one of the pieces of stock, and, finally, install the other piece on the chassis to secure the bar.

Each piece of stock was composed of a bolt approximately eight inches long on which I had to place, in order, a metal ring much like a washer, two rubber bushings that had to face each other, another ring, a bar to keep the sections separate, a third ring, two more rubber bushings facing each other, one more metal ring, and, finally, a nut to keep the whole assembly together. To install the piece of stock, I had to disassemble it so that only one rubber bushing and one metal ring remained on the bolt.

While holding the rest of the pieces, I'd insert the bolt through a hole in the chassis, replace the parts on the bolt, insert the bolt through a hole in the stabilizer bar, and finger-tighten the nut. Unless I did it just right, my carefully constructed piece of stock would come apart and fall on the floor, and I'd have to start over. By the time I'd finish, I could see the next chassis arriving, so I'd go back to the bench and start the whole process again.

The entire process—build stock, select bar, install bar—was supposed to be completed in 75 to 80 seconds. Because it was impossible to do the job in the time allotted, I would often arrive early and build up a backlog of stock in case I got behind, which I did regularly. If there was any stock left at the end of a shift, I'd hide it to use the next day. (The job was so hard that workers from one shift would not leave their extra stock for workers on the next shift. It was every man for himself.)

The people in the area generally acknowledged that the stabilizer bar job was the most difficult of all. In fact, one of the workers whose job it was to fill in for me during rest periods did not want to do it. That reliefperson offered to pay me $10 if I would not take a rest period because he didn't want the foreperson to know that he couldn't do the stabilizer bar job.

After I had complained to the foreperson about the difficulty of the job, and after other workers had also complained to both the foreperson and the union committeeperson, the company clocked the job. When the time study was completed, the company seemed surprised to discover what we had known all along—that the job required 150% of the time the engineers had alloted to it. No wonder I was always behind! The company then removed some of the tasks from the job, which made it slightly easier. The job was still difficult, however, and required building stock ahead of time each day. In terms of the number of tasks required and the amount of time necessary to do them, the stabilizer bar job was the most difficult of all my jobs in the plant.

It is hard to imagine doing the stabilizer bar job over and over each day, each week, but until I was moved to another part of the plant, I did: 368 times in an eight-hour day. The first few days on the job I even found myself dreaming about it at night and doing the job in my sleep. One man told me that his job bothered him so much that his wife woke him up one night and told him that in his sleep he had imagined he was still doing the job, but he was doing it on her forehead.

In the course of my stay, I worked on approximately 20 different jobs in the plant. I worked on so many jobs because (1) I was of low seniority and got moved around as needed and (2) I wanted as wide a scope of experience as possible, and those persons in upper management who knew of my research obliged me by helping to move me to as many new and different jobs and shifts as possible without revealing my true purpose in the plant. Some of the jobs lasted only a few minutes as the foreperson tried to decide where best to use me; others lasted two to three weeks—long enough to discover that illusive sense of rhythm that allows a worker to do the job and still have time to rest in between cars. I found that the easiest jobs are not always that easy, the most difficult jobs not always that hard.

My most boring, monotonous, and, therefore, hard job was as a driver in the repair section. In this job, along with two others I was expected to ferry cars from one section of the repair floor to another. Although three of us were assigned to the task, most of the time two were sufficient; we were only needed if a car had to be moved. We worked out a schedule so that two of us were available at any one time, with the third hiding out of sight, reading a newspaper, napping, or eating lunch.

If you subtract the relief time given to each worker during a normal eight-hour day (a total of 46 minutes according to the union contract), as well as the other official and unofficial time off from my paid eight hours, I actually worked a total of about two and one-half hours. Most workers I talked to wanted this type of job and looked forward to the time when their seniority would give them access to such a position.

One of my easiest jobs in the plant was one that no one else wanted because it was "so hard." On this job I had to kneel down next to the car and ride along with it as it moved down the assembly line. From this position I had to reach in through the open door and carefully place a small clip on the emergency brake cable up under the dashboard. This job was difficult because it was impossible to see what you were doing. Once I had the rhythm, I could do the job in about 30 seconds, leaving me almost a minute in between cars to rest, read the paper, look out the window, or talk to the workers around me. In fact, I often let myself fall behind so that I then had to work fast to catch up. On other occasions I would stay with a car longer than necessary so that the foreperson would not realize how easy the job really was.

By the end of that particular job, I could work an entire shift and not make a mistake, whereas I never was able to master some other jobs and, to this day, do not know how the regular operators handle them.

Once the worker has the rhythm of the job, it is not nearly as hard to do as it is to describe. You become adapted to the flow of the job and begin to find other things to do with your mind. Some workers try to find shortcuts to make the jobs even easier. Others read books, magazines, or newspapers in between cars. Still others (I was one of these) try to calculate how many cars have already been completed and how many more are still to come.

Counting cars was one conscious method I used to pass the time; other methods came unconsciously. One time I realized that I was doing my job to the rhythm of an aria from an opera I had heard the last weekend. Another time I found myself a thousand miles away, driving an imaginary automobile down a highway I had not been on for years. How many chassis went by during my mental lapses—and whether I even did my job—I don't know and never found out.

Adapting to the Line

Workers generally adapt to boredom and monotony in one of two ways: remain in the plant and find a way to get along or take off. Absenteeism is an extremely big problem. As one utilityperson said, "People take time off because they're bored. They get tired of the same old routine." During hunting season, for instance, so many take off that other workers are often asked to "work a double," that is, to work two shifts back to back. Even during the rest of the year, on many mornings the line could not start due to the shortage of workers. Often we would stand around waiting for the company to find people to fill the holes in the line.

For those who remain on the job, adaptation takes many and often ingenious forms. Although not all workers became bored with their jobs, enough do so that shutting one's mind to the surroundings becomes common. I remember one day when I was inadvertently in another worker's way, the other worker walked into me, backed up, walked into me again, and did the same a third time, until the worker realized that there was something or someone in the path.

One worker said: "I'm pretty good at blocking things out. I sing songs. One day I recited my multiplication tables. You get like a computer, you do the job automatically." What workers do about the monotony and boredom is as individual as the workers themselves.

Another worker told me: "I throw stock, I throw gloves, I bullshit about everything. I lie about how many hours we're working. I daydream a lot."

A third said:

> [There's] not much you can do, I guess. You just do the work. Daydream, that's the best. [*What do you dream about?*] Gettin' out of this place. Gettin' off the line for about six hours. Just put your mind in a different place, say you're not here. I daydream about when I was a kid. Then you sit and laugh, and people look at you like you're crazy or something.

Talking, gossiping, or becoming an entrepreneur are only some of the techniques workers use to overcome the boredom of the line. We also played numerous games to make the time pass more quickly. We played "football" with a ball made out of foam rubber wrapped in electrical tape; in "basketball" we threw screws, bolts, nuts, or washers into a styrofoam cup taped to a girder. Another game we played was "hooting": when a worker hoots at the top of his or her lungs, others pick up the cry and the hooting goes up and down the line until it dies out sometime later.

Other means for decreasing the boredom and monotony are trading jobs (where two people agree to trade jobs for some specified period of time); doubling or tripling up (where one worker does the work of two or three workers for some period of time, after which he or she rests and another person does the jobs for a while); alternating jobs (where two people agree that one will do both jobs on cars no. 1,3,5, and 7 and the other will cover for cars no. 2,4,6, and 8); and working up the line (where workers work as fast as possible to get ahead and actually work "up the line" from their assigned work stations); or, as mentioned earlier, letting work fall far behind so that extraordinary effort is required to catch up.

Not all of the techniques the workers use to decrease the boredom and monotony are quite so benign, of course. Workers often block out monotony and boredom with alcohol or drugs. When I asked one young worker why he used drugs, particularly marijuana (which tends to be the drug of choice in the plant), he answered, "If I smoke [marijuana], I can stare at a spot on the floor all day long and not get bored." Another worker said:

> I know a few guys that get completely messed up and they can run their job as good as when they're straight. There's a lot who couldn't. On second shift I've seen them take a guy and hide him 'cause he was so messed up. I don't like to get stoned when I'm working 'cause I don't know if I've done the whole car or not.

Although the incidences of outright sabotage and theft are not great, a number of workers told me that they occasionally let a car go by without doing their jobs. Sometimes they take their frustrations out on the car or the tools themselves—breaking tools, banging tools against the bench, or causing air wrenches to emit high-pitched shrieks.

Feelings about Work

Most of the workers I met had strong feelings about their work. These feelings centered mainly around the job itself and the company, as well as the union. (See Exhibit 1 for a summary of workers' feelings about work in the plant.)

The Company

Although the benefits and wages are high in the plants, if the quality of work life were not okay, one would expect that workers would want to leave. When I asked one 22-year-old woman how long she planned to remain with the company, she said, "I plan to put in my time and be a retiree." A 22-year-old man said:

> Till I retire. I think that the company is the best place for me to work in [this town]. There is a lot of potential here if you want to make it. There's a lot of things I can do here to make me happy. I like to be able to say I accomplished something.

Exhibit 1. Workers' Feelings about Work in the Plant*

	Yes	No	Uncertain
Do you have to take a day off every once in a while?	54.3%	43.3%	2.4%
Is absenteeism a big problem in the plant?	86.1	9.1	4.8
Do you ever drink at lunchtime?	40.4	59.6	—
Have you ever gotten high while working on the line?	32.7	66.3	—
Have you seen others in the plant get high while working on the line?	50.9	49.1	—
Do you think it's not important how much you know but whom you know that counts?	78.4	12.0	9.6
Does your supervisor treat everyone fairly?	43.8	48.1	8.2
Would the company be better off without a union?	2.9	88.0	9.1

Note: Several of the statements presented to the workers have been edited into question form for this article, but the substance remains the same.

*These are only some of the attitudinal questions used in the larger research project. In the questionnaire, attitudes were measured on a five-point scale rather than on the three-point scale shown here, and the percentages represent only those workers who actually answered each question.

Another man said: "Thirty years and then I'm gonna retire. I hate it, but what else are you gonna do for a living? What else is there to do? Thirty years in the shop is enough for anybody." (At which point his wife added, "It's better than anything he's done before.") Most workers believe that, although work in the plant is not everything one might want, it presents better opportunities, better pay, and better fringe benefits than other jobs in the area.

If one assumes that workers would not remain long if the job were not agreeable, then you would expect the seniority levels of the workers in the final assembly plant to be below the minimum needed to transfer. (This indirect measure of their relative feelings toward working for the company has to be qualified, though, because the workers I talked to were in the final assembly plant, where the lower seniority workers predominate.)

In fact, the average seniority of the workers in the plant is quite a bit above the minimum needed to transfer out to the easier jobs, where the workers make "easy money." (The average for the entire plant is a little under eight and one-half years on the job; the minimum to transfer is two years.) Of course, other departments may well have high seniority levels, and it may be that the workers in the final assembly plant are waiting until they have even higher seniority so they can get a job in a particular plant.

Although many prefer them, not all workers want to move to the easier jobs. One reliefperson who had nine and one-half years of seniority and who still worked in the same area of final assembly told me:

> That's the only zone I ever worked in. I could go anywhere I want to with my service, but I like that zone. I was in [another and easier job] for five years, but I couldn't hack it. The doctor told me to get off it 'cause I wasn't active enough, always [feeling sick].

This same repairperson said "a lot of people go in there and they don't want to work. I want to work."

Although the majority of the workers think the company is a good place to work, some feel ambivalent:

> The company wants cars. If you drop dead, they'll pull you out of the way and somebody else will be there the next day. That line has to run no matter what. As for our benefits, they're hard to beat—medical insurance, time off, and they're trying to get more time off. [*Is the company a good place to work?*] To me it could be better. I think it's a good place to work, but I want better than where I'm at right now.

Or, as another worker said:

> The shop can be anything you make it. I'm looking forward to a future there. You can climb the ladder there higher than any other place I could go with my education. I think the biggest plus in the shop is security.

There're layoffs and stuff, but compared to the outside, there's a lot of security.

The Union

For the workers, the union exists and is there when you need it. But, as in the old joke, many of them would "not want my son or daughter to marry a union official."

Very few of the workers feel they would be better off without a union in the plant. At the same time few had much good to say about the union. One reliefperson summed up feelings about the union this way:

> I don't have a lot to say about the union. I think they charge way too much money for what we get out of it. Unions are good but you don't see what you pay for. When you get penalized, it just seems management and the union get together on it. The committeeperson we have is too buddy-buddy with all the forepersons and G-Fs [general forepersons]. A lot of the guys have to settle with what the foreperson and committeeperson come up with.

Workers generally see the union as they see the company: large, impersonal, and probably all right. The committeeperson, like the supervisor, is someone with whom you must work all the time, and he or she is either good or bad.

One worker said his committeeperson is

> . . . excellent. . . . Some people say he's been there so long he's slacking off and that we need another one. He's friends with all the uppers at the union, and he knows a lot of people. He is the best one I've ever seen. He never forgets it if you ask him something.

Another committeeperson was considered ". . . worthless as tits on a piece of bacon" by one worker but held in high regard by others.

Most workers do not know what the union has done for them in the recent past. Thinking that nothing important occurs there, most union members do not attend union meetings. Between 2% and 4% of the total membership attended union meetings in the local of which I was a member. Attendance at union meetings is sufficiently unusual that once, when I attended a meeting and a picture of me sitting next to one of the union officers was taken and published in the union newspaper, I was rumored to be a union spy sent to see what my fellow workers were up to. Even meetings called to discuss new and important contract developments aren't attended. A recent meeting of my local to discuss the latest contract with the automobile manufacturer, which contained some important changes over the previous version, managed to draw less than 1% of its membership.

The workers I knew viewed union officials much the way most people see other elected officials, as suspicious but necessary. Because union officials are privy to secret material and socialize with the top managers of the company, the workers don't completely trust them. At the same time workers are quite adamant that they need a union in the plant, and they are quick to call for the committeeperson to intercede for them when they are in trouble.

Quality of Work Life

Although sociologists, psychologists, and human relations specialists may make suggestions on how assembly lines could be made more humane and less boring, the workers probably know best what it will take to make them happier, more contented, and, most important perhaps, more productive. When discussing the possibility for change, most workers I talked to commented either on management or supervisory style in the plant or on other general modifications the company could make. Workers see only a few places where changes they could make would be effective.

One thing that bothers most workers about their jobs is what they call "bad stock," material that does not meet specifications or is in some way defective, which causes the worker to fall behind. In the stabilizer bar job, for example, it was maddening to open a box of rubber bushings and find them useless because the majority didn't have holes drilled through them. Others agreed with me:

> Any repair I send is because of defective parts. The screws would strip out [early in the model year], but they are getting that straightened around finally.
>
> As long as I get good stock, there's no hassle with the job.
>
> Half the time the parts don't fit right.
>
> One day the stock is good, the next day it's bad, and you got to fight it. That's poor economy, the rejected stock. The stuff gets cheaper every day, the stock does. A guy's gonna pay so much money for the car, it ought to have real good stock on the car.

Whether the concern about stock is sincere or manifests a deeper feeling that something else is wrong, I don't know. I do know, however, how frustrating it is continually to have parts that do not fit, especially when it makes the job move more slowly and makes you fall farther and farther behind, getting more in the hole with every passing chassis.

Another distinct problem in the plant is the favoritism supervisors show toward certain workers. My own experience confirms that it's really destructive. Although the official policy of the plant is nondiscriminatory, discrimination does in fact exist. Thus although women are supposed to be given the same jobs as men, it does not usually happen that way. Almost universally, women are given easier jobs than are given to the men in the same plant. In some situations, it seemed that the easier jobs were given to women in exchange for sexual favors. One worker told me about the girlfriend of one of the general supervisors who had a meteoric rise in the job hierarchy. The girlfriend may well have been a good worker but having good connections did her no harm.

Workers who have relatives in "high places" can also get away with behavior for which other workers would be disciplined. In one section of the plant where I was, two workers had higher-up relatives in the company. One worker had been disciplined so many times that, were it not for his connections, he would have been fired long ago. I saw this worker openly drinking liquor on the job, sharing a drink with the supervisor, smoking marijuana, coming in late, leaving early, and so forth. The other workers knew of his connections and resented them.

The supervisor did not seem in the least concerned about the morale problems the favoritism shown the worker was generating. Rather, the supervisor seemed more concerned about the long-term consequences for the supervisor's own career than the effect the favoritism was having on the other workers in that area.

I responded to the other case of favoritism in that department as a worker, not as a dispassionate observer. One of the young workers apparently felt that he should be a supervisor, even though he worked on the line. Apparently, he felt this way because his father had an important position in the company. This young man did what he wished, when he wished. Often at the expense of the job he was supposed to be doing, he "supervised" other workers. He would leave his work station and move to another part of the area when he thought something was going wrong that needed his immediate attention.

One day this young man and I almost came to blows over his assertion that he could do what he wanted, when he wanted, even if it meant that I could not do my job. Knowing that I would be fired for physically removing this worker, I told the foreperson that the young man was in imminent danger of being placed upside down in a large parts bin if he did not get out of my way. The foreperson realized that I was quite upset and caused him to stay out of my way for the remainder of the shift.

I think the young worker was quite nonplussed at my reaction. Other workers later told me that no one else had ever spoken to him quite so strongly and that he was somewhat put off by my not realizing that I should defer to him. I suspect that the foreperson had had to screw up his courage to tell the young worker to be careful, because this was also the first time I had ever seen the supervisor stand up to him.

Above and beyond the more general problem of favoritism, the workers

I talked to generally felt that supervisors do not treat all workers fairly. For example, at one point I was asked to learn a new job, was given one-half day of training, and was then told to "run" it by myself. The other workers told me that you are normally given three days of training to learn a job, during which time an experienced worker works alongside the trainee showing him or her the tricks of the trade.

During my first day alone on the job, one of the supervisors criticized me rather severely. When I informed the supervisor that I had not been given three days to learn the job and that I thought the union representative should be present to hear the criticism, the supervisor apologized and said I would be given some help. The assistance I received was from another worker who had little more idea of what the job was than I had, and this "training" lasted for only another half day.

Shortly after my run-in with the foreperson, I was told that a rumor was going around that I was an undercover operative for the plant security forces sent to spy on the workers to see if they were engaging in sabotage or using drugs on company property. I later found out that the rumor was started by the foreperson who had criticized my work.

My experience was common. Many workers told me similar stories:

> I can't say I've had any problems with any of the forepersons in there except one. He doesn't like me 'cause he doesn't like women. He came up to me one day when I was bent over a car and said my jeans were too tight. I said, "Stop looking at my ass, and you won't have any problems. Nobody else is complaining."

> I would say the supervisors are just like any other employee, 95% of them; 3% are the overreactive type, and the other 2% are the hard-core— the ones who laugh about penalizing people. Never showing a guy when he's wrong . . . just stickin' it to him. . . .

(Some supervisors are proud of such reputations. The supervisor who started the rumor about me often referred to himself as a "gold-plated bastard" who would send workers home for the smallest rule violation.)

> As a whole they're pretty good. The general foreperson on second shift is great. He goes out of his way to be friendly. Some of them would go out of their way to fire their mothers. Some of them, if they get down on you, will go after you. If you're a good worker, they'll go out of their way for you. If there's a clash of personalities with them, you could be in trouble.

> You're gonna have a few that are real assholes here and there. [He] is the lowest thing that walks as far as I'm concerned. He and I never see eye-to-eye or get along very good. I think some do a pretty good job. There's too many things that have to be changed for him to be effective. He catches too much shit from both directions to be any good. I don't

think I personally dislike anyone. I dislike their methods of handling their management relationships.

One of my supervisors had a unique attitude toward working with his people—he was known to tell new hires (as he told me in our first discussion) that he did not care if they smoked (marijuana) or if they drank, all that concerned him was that there be no fighting in his area. He may have been one of the few supervisors who realized that the workers used drugs or alcohol and accepted the fact. How useful such an attitude is I can't say, except that it's extremely realistic.

Practically all workers are confronted with impersonality. When a new worker enters some departments, the first question the supervisor asks is, "What's the social?"—meaning the worker's social security number. It seems that no one cares what your name is, only your number. Workers are often referred to as "heads," not people, as when one supervisor calls another and asks if there are any extra heads that can be sent over to help out.

Management also tends to ignore workers' suggestions about jobs. I have seen engineers ignore comments from workers that could improve the productivity of an individual job. At one point I noticed that two air hoses were crossed, creating a potentially dangerous situation. When I suggested they be uncrossed, the foreperson said they had been designed that way by the engineers, who clearly knew better than I how the plant works.

On another occasion I submitted a suggestion concerning means for alleviating the bad stock problem. It was not until a year later, after I had left the company, that I received a check and a notification that my suggestion had been accepted. During the time my suggestion was under consideration, I never received even a postcard telling me that my comments had reached them.

Impersonality, favoritism, and bad stock are all problems that management might do something about. In addition, workers noted a number of more general conditions they thought should be corrected, such as trash and dirt:

> An assembly plant is going to be greasy. But I mean the overall conditions, the housekeeping. If there was some color in the plant. You go in and you have to kick the trash out of the way. General housecleaning. I can't accept the fact, the conditions, like it is now as far as paper all over. Half the time it looks like hell. If the floor was clean around where you work, I get a better attitude.

I certainly agree about the conditions in the plant. Some of us were occasionally asked to stay after the rest had left for the night to sweep up around our production area. As some people's sole responsibility in the plant was to sweep, you might think that the assembly line workers shouldn't have to. The cafeteria and restrooms also received their share of justified criticism for dull food and lack of cleanliness, respectively. Many workers told me that they do not come to work to be entertained, but they do feel they should be given at least minimal amenities.

What Do Workers Really Want?

The workers want changes in the plant, but they are not certain what the mechanisms for the changes should be. Not long before I began my work at the plant, the company and the union had agreed that they should jointly attempt to improve the quality of work life (QWL). To accomplish the stated goals, a number of joint management and labor committees were set up to monitor quality of work life and to solicit suggestions for improving the situation in the plant.

At one membership meeting of the local union to discuss the cooperation, the union representatives said they felt they should be paid from the union treasury for their attendance. A number of other union members at the meeting questioned the attendance payments but, more significant, challenged the entire concept of the QWL meetings and raised questions as to whether the union should involve itself in joint meetings with the management to try to solve the problems.

Ultimately, the experiment met with only limited success at best. Workers in the plant distrusted the committees. Workers felt that improvements in the quality of work life on the line would simply bring with them what other improvements had brought in the past—a faster line speed. A number of first-line supervisors thought that, by attempting to improve the quality of work life, the company was simply "mollycoddling" workers who needed a good kick in the pants rather than lace curtains in the windows.

By far the greatest majority of the workers I talked to had not heard of the committees and, once they were acquainted with the work of the committees, were not convinced that they would help anyway. To workers quality of work life is not an abstraction; it affects their jobs. If a workbench is too close to a pillar, if a hose connection is loose, if the work area is too cold, if a pair of gloves is not available in the morning, the quality of work life is diminished. Once these problems are eliminated, workers would be able to enjoy the luxury of deciding the degree to which they really want to be involved in either overall company decision making or in simply choosing the color for the walls.

Accompanying the individual nature of the QWL problems is the fact that, although many workers know what it is they do and what their own job title is, most do not really know how their jobs fit into the whole. Some additional orientation for all workers—new and old—might increase their feelings of belonging to the company.

Workers do care about the company well beyond the paycheck they bring home each week. Workers may say that all they care about is the paycheck, but they know that the quality of the automobiles they build determines largely what they take home. Although intrinsic work satisfaction is important, it is also important to know that you are making enough money to live comfortably, are covered by extremely comprehensive medical and dental insurance, and can leave the job and not worry about it.

What is extremely important for the company, the union, and the workers to understand (and it has become more obvious to me the more I have thought about the situation) is the need to deal with workers as human beings. Workers do not want something for nothing. Most people are interested in making a living; they want to come to work and be treated with the respect normally accorded to adults. F.J. Roethlisberger and William Dickson made the same point more than 40 years ago.[3] They concluded that each worker:

> . . . is bringing to the work situation a different background of personal and social experiences. No two individuals are making the same demands of their job. The demands a particular employee makes depend not only upon his physical needs but upon his social needs as well.

Many years, many studies, and many people later, industrial relations still has not become human relations.

The technology of the assembly line fosters the idea that the people should be like the products rolling off the line. All workers should think the same, act the same, do the same things. When a person comes along who does not play by the rules and wants simply to be seen as an individual, the members of the system react to bring the person back to the norm. But no one person totally fits the mold. Everyone is different, and people can only adapt so far. Maybe how they are treated has to change. Some supervisors, union officials, and workers realize this—but, sadly, not enough do.

Notes

1. Mel Tillis and Danny Dill, "Detroit City," Cedarwood Publishing Co., Inc., copyright © 1962, 1977.

2. Robert Schrank, *Ten Thousand Working Days* (Cambridge, MA, MIT Press, 1978).

3. F.J. Roethlisberger and William J. Dickson, *Management and the Worker* (Cambridge, MA, Harvard University Press, 1939), p. 553.

Appendix

Research Methodology

Using three separate methods, I gathered the data for this study from the workers in an automobile assembly plant in a medium-sized city in the Midwest.

First, I spent five months as an employee on the line, working on numerous different assembly operations. Although certain persons in both the management and the union hierarchy knew who I was and the general purpose of my research, no one in the plant itself knew. Once my observation period was completed, I interviewed 22 workers. These were extensive interviews, taking on the average two hours. Finally, I distributed a questionnaire to all workers in the final assembly complex of the plant on both shifts of a particular day. I received 209 usable responses, which represents a return rate of approximately 24%.

Such a three-pronged approach, although often seen as "methodological overkill," allows us to compare findings from one approach with findings from another to see if they are similar. If the findings differ, the complementary approaches allow for a greater probability of discovering why there is a difference and also for reconciling the difference.

29
How to Counter Alienation in the Plant

RICHARD E. WALTON

A plant where work teams perform without supervisors, where many decisions are based on employee consensus, and where most of the staff functions are assigned to line operators—in what future organization would such a phenomenon exist? "Probably in most," says this author, "because such radical innovations are part of the emerging answer to alienation in the workplace." He argues that total, "systemic" restructuring of the way work is done is required to both meet the changing expectations of employees and increase productivity. Some companies, in fact, have already used this approach with considerable success—and they have the productivity and high morale to prove it. After analyzing the employee dissatisfaction that dictates the innovations he recommends, the author draws lessons from a redesign effort implemented in a pet-food plant by a particularly forward-looking organization.

Managers don't need anyone to tell them that employee alienation exists. Terms such as "blue-collar blues" and "salaried drop-outs" are all too familiar. But are they willing to undertake the major innovations necessary for redesigning work organizations to deal effectively with the root causes of alienation? My purpose in this article is to urge them to do so, for these reasons:

1 The current alienation is not merely a phase that will pass in due time.

Author's Note. An earlier version of this article was prepared for the Work in America Project, sponsored by the Secretary of the Department of Health, Education, and Welfare, as a basis for assessing the nature of problems and potential crises associated with work in the United States.

2 The innovations needed to correct the problem can simultaneously enhance the quality of work life (thereby lessening alienation) and improve productivity.

In the first part of the article, I shall risk covering terrain already familiar to some readers in order to establish that alienation is a basic, long-term, and mounting problem. Then I shall present some examples of the comprehensive redesign that I believe is required.

I also hope to provide today's managers with a glimpse at what may be the industrial work environment of the future, as illustrated by a pet-food plant which opened in January 1971.

In this facility, management set out to incorporate features that would provide a high quality of work life, enlist unusual human involvement, and result in high productivity. The positive results of the experiment to date are impressive, and the difficulties encountered in implementing it are instructive. Moreover, similar possibilities for *comprehensive* innovations exist in a wide variety of settings and industries.

The word "comprehensive" is important because my argument is that each technique in the standard fare of personnel and organization development programs (e.g., job enrichment, management by objectives, sensitivity training, confrontation and team-building sessions, participative decision making) has grasped only a limited truth and has fallen far short of producing meaningful change. In short, more radical, comprehensive, and systemic redesign of organizations is necessary.

Anatomy of Alienation

There are two parts to the problem of employee alienation: (1) the productivity output of work systems, and (2) the social costs associated with employee inputs. Regarding the first, U.S. productivity is not adequate for the challenges posed by international competition and inflation; it cannot sustain impressive economic growth. (I do not refer here to economic growth as something to be valued merely for its own sake—it is politically a precondition for the income redistribution that will make equality of opportunity possible in the United States.) Regarding the second, the social and psychological costs of work systems are excessive, as evidenced by their effects on the mental and physical health of employees and on the social health of families and communities.

Employee alienation *affects* productivity and *reflects* social costs incurred in the workplace. Increasingly, blue and white-collar employees and, to some extent, middle managers tend to dislike their jobs and resent their bosses. Workers tend to rebel against their union leaders. They are becoming less concerned about the quality of the product of their labor and more angered about the quality of the context in which they labor.

In some cases, alienation is expressed by passive withdrawal—tardiness, absenteeism and turnover, and inattention on the job. In other cases, it is expressed by active attacks—pilferage, sabotage, deliberate waste, assaults, bomb threats, and other disruptions of work routines. Demonstrations have taken place and underground newspapers have appeared in large organizations in recent years to protest company policies. Even more recently, employees have cooperated with newsmen, Congressional committees, regulatory agencies, and protest groups in exposing objectionable practices.

These trends all have been mentioned in the media, but one expression of alienation has been underreported: pilferage and violence against property and persons. Such acts are less likely to be revealed to the police and the media when they occur in a private company than when they occur in a high school, a ghetto business district, or a suburban town. Moreover, dramatic increases in these forms of violence are taking place at the plant level. This trend is not reported in local newspapers and there is little or no appreciation of it at corporate headquarters. Local management keeps quiet because violence is felt to reflect unfavorably both on its effectiveness and on its plant as a place to work.

Roots of Conflict

The acts of sabotage and other forms of protest are overt manifestations of a conflict between changing employee attitudes and organizational inertia. Increasingly, what employees expect from their jobs is different from what organizations are prepared to offer them. These evolving expectations of workers conflict with the demands, conditions, and rewards of employing organizations in at least six important ways:

1. Employees want challenge and personal growth, but work tends to be simplified and specialties tend to be used repeatedly in work assignments. This pattern exploits the narrow skills of a worker, while limiting his or her opportunities to broaden or develop.

2. Employees want to be included in patterns of mutual influence; they want egalitarian treatment. But organizations are characterized by tall hierarchies, status differentials, and chains of command.

3. Employee commitment to an organization is increasingly influenced by the intrinsic interest of the work itself, the human dignity afforded by management, and the social responsibility reflected in the organization's products. Yet organization practices still emphasize material rewards and employment security and neglect other employee concerns.

4. What employees want from careers, they are apt to want *right now*. But when organizations design job hierarchies and career paths, they con-

tinue to assume that today's workers are as willing to postpone gratifications as were yesterday's workers.

5. Employees want more attention to the emotional aspects of organization life, such as individual self-esteem, openness between people, and expressions of warmth. Yet organizations emphasize rationality and seldom legitimize the emotional part of the organizational experience.

6. Employees are becoming less driven by competitive urges, less likely to identify competition as the "American way." Nevertheless, managers continue to plan career patterns, organize work, and design reward systems as if employees valued competition as highly as they used to.

Pervasive Social Forces. The foregoing needs and desires that employees bring to their work are but a local reflection of more basic, and not readily reversible, trends in U.S. society. These trends are fueled by family and social experience as well as by social institutions, especially schools. Among the most significant are the following:

- ☐ *The rising level of education.* Employees bring to the workplace more abilities and, correspondingly, higher expectations than in the past.
- ☐ *The rising level of wealth and security.* Vast segments of today's society never have wanted for the tangible essentials of life; thus they are decreasingly motivated by pay and security, which are taken for granted.
- ☐ *The decreased emphasis given by churches, schools, and families to obedience to authority.* These socialization agencies have promoted individual initiative, self-responsibility and control, the relativity of values, and other social patterns that make subordinacy in traditional organizations an increasingly bitter pill to swallow for each successive wave of entrants to the U.S. work force.
- ☐ *The decline in achievement motivation.* For example, whereas the books my parents read in primary school taught them the virtues of hard work and competition, my children's books emphasize self-expression and actualizing one's potential. The workplace has not yet fully recognized this change in employee values.
- ☐ *The shifting emphasis from individualism to social commitment.* This shift is driven in part by a need for the direct gratifications of human connectedness (for example, as provided by commune living experiments). It also results from a growing appreciation of our interdependence, and it renders obsolete many traditional workplace concepts regarding the division of labor and work incentives.

Exhibit 1 shows how these basic societal forces underlie, and contribute to, the problem of alienation and also sums up the discussion thus far. Actually, I believe that protests in the workplace will mount even more rapidly than is indicated by the contributing trends postulated here. The latent dissatisfaction of workers will be activated as (1) the issues receive public attention and (2) some examples of attempted solutions serve to raise expectations (just as blacks' expressions of dissatisfaction with social and economic inequities were triggered in the 1950s, and women's discontent expanded late in the 1960s).

Revitalization and Reform

It seems clear that employee expectations are not likely to revert to those of an earlier day. As Exhibit 1 shows, the conflicts between these expectations and traditional organizations result in alienation. This alienation, in turn, exacts a deplorable psychological and social cost as well as causing worker behavior that depresses productivity and constrains growth. In short, we need major innovative efforts to redesign work organizations, efforts that take employee expectations into account.

Over the past two decades we have witnessed a parade of organization development, personnel, and labor relations programs that promised to revitalize organizations.:

- ☐ *Job enrichment.* Would provide more varied and challenging content in the work.
- ☐ *Participative decision making.* Would enable the information, judgments, and concerns of subordinates to influence the decisions that affect them.
- ☐ *Management by objectives.* Would enable subordinates to understand and shape the objectives toward which they strive and against which they are evaluated.
- ☐ *Sensitivity training or encounter groups.* Would enable people to relate to each other as human beings with feelings and psychological needs.
- ☐ *Productivity bargaining.* Would revise work rules and increase management's flexibility with a quid pro quo whereby the union ensures that workers share in the fruits of the resulting productivity increases.

Each of the preceding programs *by itself* is an inadequate reform of the workplace and has typically failed in its more limited objectives. Although application is often based on a correct diagnosis, each approach is only a partial remedy; therefore, the organizational system soon returns to an earlier equilibrium.

The lesson we must learn in the area of work reform is similar to one

Exhibit 1. Diagnosis of Alienation

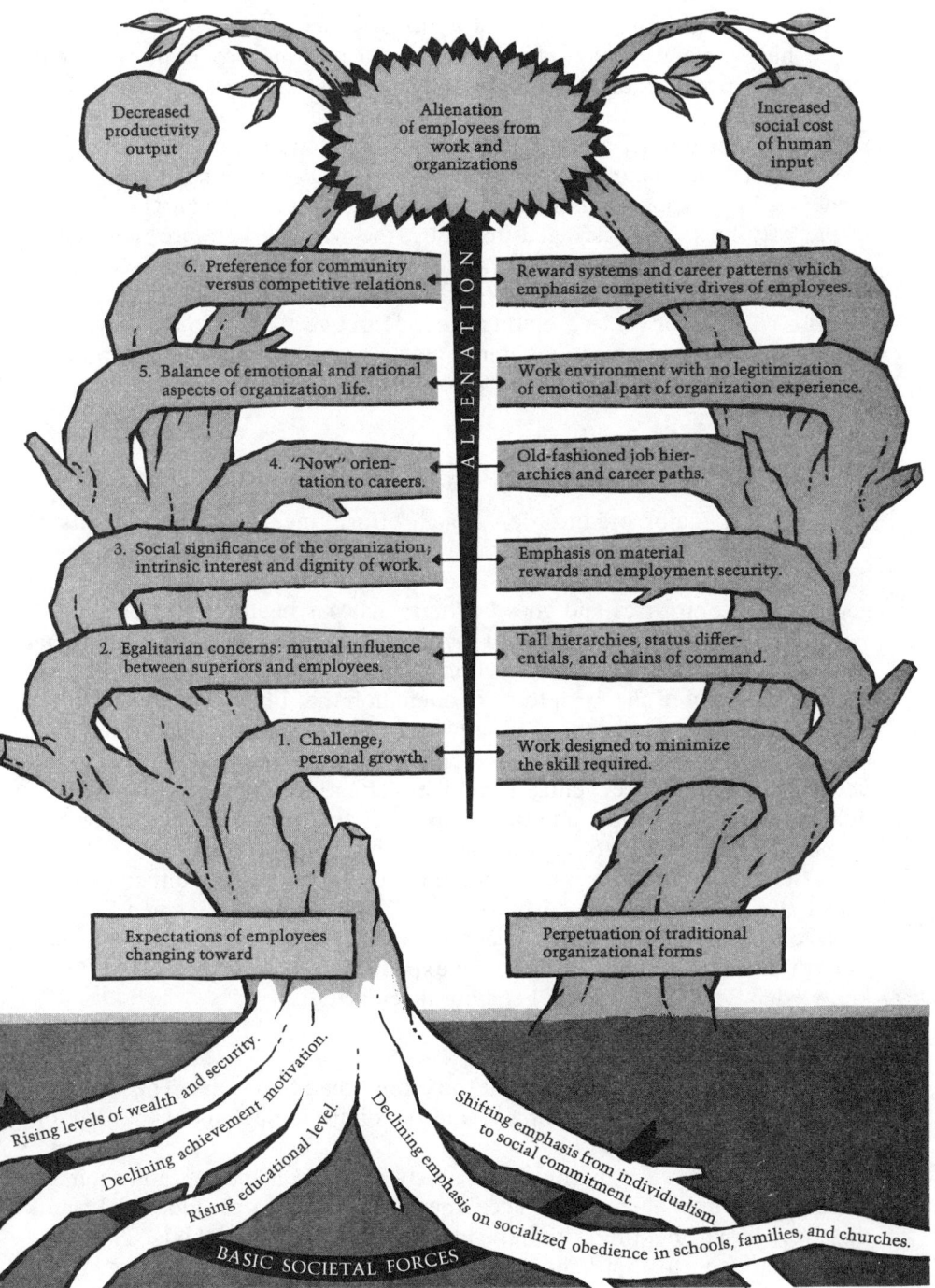

we have learned in another area of national concern. It is now recognized that a health program, a welfare program, a housing program, or an employment program alone is unable to make a lasting impact on the urban-poor syndrome. Poor health, unemployment, and other interdependent aspects of poverty must be attacked in a coordinated or systemic way.

So it is with meaningful reform of the workplace: we must think "systemically" when approaching the problem. We must coordinate the redesign of the way tasks are packaged into jobs, the way workers are required to relate to each other, the way performance is measured and rewards are made available, the way positions of authority and status symbols are structured, and the way career paths are conceived. Moreover, because these types of changes in work organizations imply new employee skills and different organizational cultures, transitional programs must be established.

A Prototype of Change

A number of major organization design efforts meet the requirements of being systemic and comprehensive. One experience in which I have been deeply involved is particularly instructive. As a recent and radical effort, it generally encompasses and goes beyond what has been done elsewhere.

During 1968, a large pet-food manufacturer was planning an additional plant at a new location. The existing manufacturing facility was then experiencing many of the symptoms of alienation that I have already outlined. There were frequent instances of employee indifference and inattention that, because of the continuous-process technology, led to plant shutdowns, product waste, and costly recycling. Employees effectively worked only a modest number of hours per day, and they resisted changes toward fuller utilization of manpower. A series of acts of sabotage and violence occurred.

Because of these pressures and the fact that it was not difficult to link substantial manufacturing costs to worker alienation, management was receptive to basic innovations in the new plant. It decided to design the plant to both accommodate changes in the expectations of employees and utilize knowledge developed by the behavioral sciences.

Key Design Features

The early development of the plant took more than two years. This involved planning, education, skill training, and building the nucleus of the new organization into a team.

During this early period, four newly selected managers and their superior met with behavioral science experts and visited other industrial plants that were experimenting with innovative organizational methods. Thus they were stimulated to think about departures from traditional work organizations and given reassurance that other organizational modes were not only possible but also more viable in the current social context. Although the consultations and plant visits provided some raw material for designing the new organization, the theretofore latent knowledge of the five managers played the largest role. Their insights into the aspirations of people and basically optimistic assumptions about the capacities of human beings were particularly instrumental in the design of the innovative plant. In the remainder of this section, I shall present the nine key features of this design.

Autonomous Work Groups. Self-managed work teams are given collective responsibility for large segments of the production process. The total work force of approximately 70 employees is organized into six teams. A processing team and a packaging team operate during each shift. The processing team's jurisdiction includes unloading, storage of materials, drawing ingredients from storage, mixing, and then performing the series of steps that transform ingredients into a pet-food product. The packaging team's responsibilities include the finishing stages of product manufacturing—packaging operations, warehousing, and shipping.

A team is comprised of from 7 to 14 members (called "operators") and a team leader. Its size is large enough to include a natural set of highly interdependent tasks, yet small enough to allow effective face-to-face meetings for decision making and coordination. Assignments of individuals to sets of tasks are subject to team consensus. Although at any given time one operator has primary responsibility for a set of tasks within the team's jurisdiction, some tasks can be shared by several operators. Moreover, tasks can be redefined by the team in light of individual capabilities and interests. In contrast, individuals in the old plant were permanently assigned to specific jobs.

Other matters that fall within the scope of team deliberation, recommendation, or decision making include:

- ☐ Coping with manufacturing problems that occur within or between the teams' areas of responsibilities.
- ☐ Temporarily redistributing tasks to cover for absent employees.
- ☐ Selecting team operators to serve on plantwide committees or task forces.
- ☐ Screening and selecting employees to replace departing operators.
- ☐ Counseling those who do not meet team standards (e.g., regarding absences or giving assistance to others).

Integrated Support Functions. Staff units and job specialties are avoided. Activities typically performed by maintenance, quality control, custodial, industrial engineering, and personnel units are built into an operating team's responsibilities. For example, each team member maintains the equipment he or she operates (except for complicated electrical maintenance) and housekeeps the area in which he or she works. Each team has responsibility for performing quality tests and ensuring quality standards. In addition, team members perform what is normally a personnel function when they screen job applicants.

Challenging Job Assignments. Although the designers understood that job assignments would undergo redefinition in light of experience and the varying interests and abilities on the work teams, the initial job assignments established an important design principle. Every set of tasks is designed to include functions requiring higher-order human abilities and responsibilities, such as planning, diagnosing mechanical or process problems, and liaison work.

The integrated support functions just discussed provide one important source of tasks to enrich jobs. In addition, the basic technology employed in the plant is designed to eliminate dull or routine jobs as much as possible. But some nonchallenging, yet basic, tasks still have to be compensated for. The forklift truck operation, for example, is not technically challenging. Therefore, the team member responsible for it is assigned other, more mentally demanding tasks (e.g., planning warehouse space utilization and shipping activities).

Housekeeping duties are also included in every assignment, despite the fact that they contribute nothing to enriching the work, in order to avoid having members of the plant community who do nothing but menial cleaning.

Job Mobility and Rewards for Learning. Because all sets of tasks (jobs) are designed to be equally challenging (although each set comprises unique skill demands), it is possible to have a single job classification for all operators. Pay increases are geared to an employee mastering an increasing proportion of jobs first in the team and then in the total plant. In effect, team members are paid for learning more and more aspects of the total manufacturing system. Because there are no limits on the number of operators that can qualify for higher pay brackets, employees are also encouraged to teach each other. The old plant, in contrast, featured large numbers of differentiated jobs and numerous job classifications, with pay increases based on progress up the job hierarchy.

Facilitative Leadership. Team leaders are chosen from foreperson-level talent and are largely responsible for team development and group decision making. This contrasts with the old plant's use of supervisors to plan, direct, and control the work of subordinates. Management feels that in time the teams will be self-directed and so the formal team leader position might not be required.

A PROTOTYPE OF CHANGE

"Managerial" Decision Information for Operators. The design of the new plant provides operators with economic information and managerial decision rules. Thus production decisions ordinarily made by supervisors can now be made at the operator level.

Self-Government for the Plant Community. The management group that developed the basic organization plan before the plant was operational refrained from specifying in advance any plant rules. Rather, it is committed to letting these rules evolve from collective experience.

Congruent Physical and Social Context. The differential status symbols that characterize traditional work organizations are minimized in the new plant. There is an open parking lot, a single entrance for both the office and plant, and a common decor throughout the reception area, offices, locker rooms, and cafeteria.

The architecture facilitates the congregating of team members during working hours. For example, rather than following the plan that made the air-conditioned control room in the process tower so small that employees could not congregate there, management decided to enlarge it so that process team operators could use it when not on duty elsewhere. The assumption here is that rooms that encourage ad hoc gatherings provide opportunities not only for enjoyable human exchanges but also for work coordination and learning about others' jobs.

Learning and Evolution. The most basic feature of the new plant system is management's commitment to continually assess both the plant's productivity and its relevance to employee concerns in light of experience.

I believe pressures will mount in this system with two apparently opposite implications for automation.

On the one hand, people will consider ways of automating the highly repetitive tasks. (There are still back-breaking routine tasks in this plant; for example, as 50-pound bags pile up at the end of the production line, someone must grab them and throw them on a pallet.)

On the other hand, some processes may be slightly de-automated. The original design featured fully automated or "goof-proof" systems to monitor and adjust several segments of the manufacturing process; yet some employees have become confident that they can improve on the systems if they are allowed to intervene with their own judgments. These employees suggest that organizations may benefit more from operators who are alert and who care than from goof-proof systems.

Implementation Difficulties

Since the plant start-up in January 1971, a number of difficulties have created at least temporary, and in some cases enduring, gaps between ideal expectations and reality.

The matter of compensation, for example, has been an important source of tension within this work community. There are four basic pay rates: starting rate, single job rate (for mastering the first job assignment), team rate (for mastering all jobs within the team's jurisdiction), and plant rate. In addition, an employee can qualify for a "specialty" add-on if the employee has particular strengths—for example, in electrical maintenance.

Employees who comprised the initial work force were all hired at the same time, a circumstance that enabled them to directly compare their experiences. With one or two exceptions on each team, operators all received their single job rates at the same time, about six weeks after the plant started. Five months later, however, about one third of the members of each team had been awarded the team rate.

The evaluative implications of awarding different rates of pay have stirred strong emotions in people who work so closely with each other. The individual pay decisions had been largely those of the team leaders who, however, were also aware of operators' assessments of each other. In fact, pay rates and member contributions were discussed openly between team leaders and their operators as well as among operators themselves. Questions naturally arose:

☐ Were the judgments about job mastery appropriate?
☐ Did everyone have an equal opportunity to learn other jobs?
☐ Did team leaders depart from job mastery criteria and include additional considerations in their promotions to team rate?

Thus the basic concepts of pay progression are not easy to treat operationally. Moreover, two underlying orientations compete with each other and create ambivalences for team leaders and operators alike:

☐ A desire for more equality, which tends to enhance cohesiveness.
☐ A desire for more differential rewards for individual merit, which may be more equitable but can be divisive.

Similar team and operator problems have also occurred in other areas. Four of these are particularly instructive and are listed in the Appendix following this article.

Management, too, has been a source of difficulty. For example, acceptance and support from superiors and influential staff groups at corporate headquarters did not always come easily, thus creating anxiety and uncertainty within the new plant community.

Management resistance to innovative efforts of this type has a variety of explanations apart from natural and healthy skepticism. Some staff departments feel threatened by an experiment in which their functions no longer require separate units at the plant level. Other headquarters staff who are not basically threatened may nevertheless resist an innovation that deviates from otherwise uniform practices in quality control, accounting, engineering, or personnel. Moreover, many managers resent radical change, presuming that it implies they have been doing their jobs poorly.

Evidence of Success

Although the productivity and the human benefits of this innovative organization cannot be calculated precisely, there have nevertheless been some impressive results.

Using standard principles, industrial engineers originally estimated that 110 employees should operate the plant. Yet the team concept, coupled with the integration of support activities into team responsibilities, has resulted in a manpower level of slightly less than 70 people.

After 18 months, the new plant's fixed overhead rate was 33% lower than in the old plant. Reductions in variable manufacturing costs (e.g., 92% fewer quality rejects and an absenteeism rate 9% below the industry norm) resulted in annual savings of $600,000. The safety record was one of the best in the company and the turnover was far below average. New equipment is responsible for some of these results, but I believe that more than half of them derive from the innovative human organization.

Operators, team leaders, and managers alike have become more involved in their work and also have derived high satisfaction from it. For example, when asked what work is like in the plant and how it differs from other places they have worked, employees typically replied: "I never get bored." "I can make my own decisions." "People will help you; even the operations manager will pitch in to help you clean up a mess—he doesn't act like he is better than you are." I was especially impressed with the diversity of employees who made such responses. Different operators emphasized different aspects of the work culture, indicating that the new system had unique meaning for each member. This fact confirms the importance of systemwide innovation. A program of job enrichment, for example, will meet the priority psychological needs of one worker, but not another. Other single efforts are similarly limited.

Positive assessments of team members and team leaders in the new plant are typically reciprocal. Operators report favorably on the greater influence that they enjoy and the open relations that they experience between superiors and themselves; superiors report favorably on the capacities and sense of responsibility that operators have developed.

Although the plant is not without the occasional rumor that reflects some distrust and cynicism, such symptomatic occurrences are both shorter-lived and less frequent than are those that characterize other work organizations with which I am familiar. Similarly, although the plant work force is not without evidence of individual prejudice toward racial groups and women, I believe that the manifestations of these social ills can be handled more effectively in the innovative environment.

Team leaders and other plant managers have been unusually active in civic affairs (more active than employees of other plants in the same community). This fact lends support to the theory that participatory democracy introduced in the plant will spread to other institutional settings. Some social scientists, notably Carole Pateman, argue that this will indeed be the case.[1]

The apparent effectiveness of the new plant organization has caught the attention of top management and encouraged it to create a new corporate-level unit to transfer the organizational and managerial innovations to other work environments. The line manager responsible for manufacturing, who initiated the design of the innovative system, was chosen to head this corporate diffusion effort. The manager can now report significant successes in the organizational experiments under way in several units of the old pet-food plant.

What It Cost

I have already suggested what the pet-food manufacturer expected to gain from the new plant system: a more reliable, more flexible, and lower-cost manufacturing plant; a healthier work climate; and learning that could be transferred to other corporate units.

What did it invest? To my knowledge, no one has calculated the extra costs incurred prior to and during start-up that were specifically related to the innovative character of the organization. (This is probably because such costs were relatively minor compared with the amounts involved in other decisions made during the same time period.) However, some areas of extra cost can be cited.

Four managers and six team leaders were brought on board several months earlier than they otherwise would have been. The cost of outside plant visits, training, and consulting was directly related to the innovative effort. And a few plant layout and equipment design changes, which slightly increased the initial cost of the new plant, were justified primarily in terms of the organizational requirements.

During the start-up of the new plant, there was a greater than usual commitment to learning from doing. Operators were allowed to make more decisions on their own and to learn from their own experience, including

A PROTOTYPE OF CHANGE

mistakes. From my knowledge of the situation, I infer that there was a short-term—first quarter—sacrifice of volume, but that it was recouped during the third quarter when the more indelible experiences began to pay off. In fact, I would be surprised if the pay-back period for the company's entire extra investment was greater than the first year of operation.

Why It Works

Conditions Favorable to the Pet Food Experiment. Listed below are the factors that facilitated the success of the new plant.

1. The particular technology and manufacturing processes in this business provided significant room for human attitudes and motivation to affect cost; therefore, by more fully utilizing the human potential of employees, the organization was able to both enhance the quality of work life and reduce costs.
2. It was technically and economically feasible to eliminate some (but not all) of the routine inherently boring work and some (but not all) of the physically disagreeable tasks.
3. The system was introduced in a new plant. It is easier to change employees' deeply ingrained expectations about work and management in a new plant culture. Also, when the initial work force is hired at one time, teams can be formed without having to worry about cliques.
4. The physical isolation of the pet-food plant from other parts of the company facilitated the development of unique organizational patterns.
5. The small size of the work force made individual recognition and identification easy.
6. The absence of a labor union at the outset gave plant management greater freedom to experiment.
7. The technology called for and permitted communication among and between members of the work teams.
8. Pet foods are socially positive products, and the company has a good image; therefore, employees were able to form a positive attitude toward the product and the company.

I want to stress, however, that these are merely facilitating factors and are *not* preconditions for success.

For example, although a new plant clearly facilitates the planning for comprehensive plantwide change (Factor 3), such change is also possible in ongoing plants. In the latter case, the change effort must focus on a limited part of the plant—say, one department or section at a time. Thus, in the ongoing facility, one must be satisfied with a longer time horizon for plant-wide innovation.

Similarly, the presence of a labor union (Factor 6) does not preclude innovation, although it can complicate the process of introducing change. To avoid this, management can enter into a dialogue with the union about the changing expectations of workers, the need for change, and the nature and intent of the changes contemplated. Out of such dialogue can come an agreement between management and union representatives on principles for sharing the fruits of any productivity increases.

One factor I do regard as essential, however, is that the management group immediately involved must be committed to innovation and able to reach consensus about the guiding philosophy for the organization. A higher-level executive who has sufficient confidence in the innovative effort is another essential. He or she will act to protect the experiment from premature evaluations and from the inevitable reactive pressures to bring it into line with existing corporate policies and practices.

Management and supervisors must work hard to make such a system succeed—harder, I believe, than in a more traditional system. In the case of the pet-food group, more work was required than in the traditional plant, but the human satisfactions were also much greater.

The Other Innovators

Although the pet-food plant has a unique character and identity, it also has much in common with innovative plants of such U.S. corporations as Procter & Gamble and TRW Systems. Moreover, innovative efforts have been mounted by many foreign-based companies—e.g., Shell Refining Co., Ltd. (England), Northern Electric Co., Ltd. (Canada), Alcan Aluminum (smelting plants in Quebec Province, Canada), and Norsk-Hydro (a Norwegian manufacturer of fertilizers and chemicals). Related experiments have been made in the shipping industry in Scandinavia and the textile industry in Ahmedabad, India. Productivity increases or benefits for these organizations are reported in the range of 20% to 40% and higher, although I should caution that all evidence on this score involves judgment and interpretation.

All of these experiments have been influenced by the pioneering effort made in 1950 in the British coal mining industry by Eric Trist and his Tavistock Institute colleagues.[2]

Procter & Gamble has been a particularly noteworthy innovator. One of its newer plants includes many design features also employed in the pet-food plant. High emphasis has been placed on the development of "business teams" in which organization and employee identification coincides with a particular product family. Moreover, the designers were perhaps even more ambitious than their pet-food predecessors in eliminating first-line supervision. In terms of performance, results are reportedly extraordinary, although they have not been publicized. In addition, employees have been unusually active in working for social change in the outside community.[3]

Progressive Assembly Lines

Critics often argue that experiments like those I have discussed are not transferable to other work settings, especially ones that debase human dignity. The automobile assembly line is usually cited as a case in point.

I agree that different work technologies create different opportunities and different levels of constraint. I also agree that the automotive assembly plant represents a difficult challenge to those who wish to redesign work to decrease human and social costs and increase productivity. Yet serious experimental efforts to meet these challenges are now under way both in the United States and overseas.

To my knowledge, the most advanced projects are taking place in the Saab-Scandia automotive plants in Södertälje, Sweden. Consider, for example, these major design features of a truck assembly plant:

☐ Production workers have been included as members of development groups that discuss such matters as new tool and machine designs before they are approved for construction.

☐ Workers leave their stations on the assembly line for temporary assignments (e.g., to work with a team of production engineers "rebalancing" jobs on the line).

☐ Responsibility for in-process inspection has been shifted from a separate quality-inspection unit to individual production workers; the separate quality section instead devotes all its efforts to checking and testing completed trucks.

☐ Work tasks have been expanded to include maintenance care of equipment, which was previously the responsibility of special mechanics.

☐ Individuals have been encouraged to learn several jobs; in some cases, a worker has proved capable of assembling a complete engine.

Encouraged by the results of these limited innovations, the company is applying them in a new factory for the manufacture and assembly of car engines, which was opened in January 1972. In the new plant, seven assembly groups have replaced the continuous production line; assembly work within each group is not controlled mechanically; eventually the degree of specialization, methods of instruction, and work supervision will vary widely among the assembly groups.

In effect, the seven groups fall along a spectrum of decreasing specialization. At one end is a group of workers with little or no experience in engine assembly; at the other end is a group of workers with extensive experience in total engine assembly. It is hoped that, ultimately, each group member will have the opportunity to assemble an entire engine.[4]

In addition to the improvements that have made jobs more interesting and challenging for workers, management anticipates business gains that include: (1) a work system less sensitive to disruption than is the production line (a factor of considerable significance in the company's recent experience); and (2) the twofold ability to recruit workers and reduce absenteeism and turnover. (The company has encountered difficulty in recruiting labor and has experienced high turnover and absenteeism.)

Another Swedish company, Volvo, also has ambitious programs for new forms of work systems and organization. Especially interesting is a new type of car assembly plant being built at Kalmar. Here are its major features:

- ☐ Instead of the traditional assembly line, work teams of 15–25 people will be assigned responsibility for particular sections of a car (e.g., the electrical system, brakes and wheels, steering and controls).
- ☐ Within teams, members will decide how work should be divided and distributed.
- ☐ Car bodies will be carried on self-propelled carriages controlled by the teams.
- ☐ Buffer stocks between work regions will allow variations in the rate of work and "stock-piling" for short pauses in the work flow.
- ☐ The unique design of the building will provide more outside windows, many small workshops to reinforce the team atmosphere, and individual team entrances, changing rooms, and relaxation areas.

The plant, which opened in 1974, cost 10% more than a comparable conventional car plant, or an estimated premium of $2 million. It employs 600 people and has a capacity to produce 30,000 cars each year. Acknowledging the additional capital investment per employee, with its implication for fixed costs, Volvo nevertheless justifies this experiment as "another stage in the company's general attempt to create greater satisfaction at work."[5]

Question of Values

The designers of the Procter & Gamble and pet-food plants were able to create organizational systems that both improved productivity and enhanced the quality of work life for employees. It is hard to say, however, whether the new Saab-Scandia and Volvo plants will result in comparable improvements in both areas. (As I mentioned earlier, the assembly line presents a particularly difficult challenge.)

In any event, I am certain that managers who concern themselves with these two values will find points at which they must make trade-offs—that is, that they can only enhance the quality of work life at the expense of productivity or vice versa. What concerns me is that it is easier to measure productivity than to measure the quality of work life, and that this fact will bias how trade-off situations are resolved.

Productivity may not be susceptible to a single definition or to precise measurement, but business managers do have ways of gauging changes in it over time and comparing it from one plant to the next. They certainly can tell whether their productivity is adequate for their competitive situation.

But we do not have equally effective means for assessing the quality of work life or measuring the associated psychological and social costs and gains for workers.[6] We need such measurements if this value is to take its appropriate place in work organizations.

Conclusion

The emerging obligation of employers in our society is a twin one: (1) to use effectively the capacities of a major natural resource—namely, the manpower they employ; (2) to take steps to both minimize the social costs associated with utilizing that manpower and enhance the work environment for those they employ.

Fulfillment of this obligation requires major reform and innovation in work organizations. The initiative will eventually come from many quarters, but I urge professional managers and professional schools to take leadership roles. There are ample behavioral science findings and a number of specific experiences from which to learn and on which to build.

Furthermore, the nature of the problem and the accumulating knowledge about solutions indicate that organizational redesign should be systemic; it should embrace the division of labor, authority and status structures, control procedures, career paths, allocation of the economic fruits of work, and the nature of social contacts among workers. Obviously, the revisions in these many elements must be coordinated and must result in a new internally consistent whole.

This call for widespread innovation does *not* mean general application of a particular work system, such as the one devised for the pet-food plant. There are important differences within work forces and between organizations. Regional variances, education, age, sex, ethnic background, attitudes developed from earlier work experiences, and the urban–rural nature of the population all will influence the salient expectations in the workplace. Moreover, there are inherent differences in the nature of primary task technologies, differences that create opportunities for and impose constraints on the way work can be redesigned.

Notes

1. *Participation and Democratic Theory* (Cambridge, England, Cambridge University Press, 1970).

2. See E.L. Trist et al., *Organizational Choice* (London, Tavistock Publications, 1963).

3. Personal correspondence with Charles Krone, Internal Consultant, Procter & Gamble.

4. For a more complete description of this plant, see Jan-Peter Norstedt, *Work Organization and Job Design at Saab-Scandia in Södertälje* (Stockholm, Technical Department, Swedish Employers' Confederation, December 1970).

5. Press release from Volvo offices, Gothenburg, Sweden, June 29, 1972.

6. For the beginning of a remedy to this operational deficiency, see Louis E. Davis and Eric L. Trist, *Improving the Quality of Work Life: Experience of the Socio-Technical Approach* (Washington, DC, Upjohn Institute, scheduled for publication in 1973).

Appendix

Implementation Problems in the Pet Food Plant

Here are four team and operator problems encountered in the design of the innovative plant.

The expectations of a small minority of employees did not coincide with the demands placed on them by the new plant community. These employees did not get involved in the spirit of the plant organization, participate in the spontaneous mutual-help patterns, feel comfortable in group meetings, or appear ready to accept broader responsibilities. For example, one employee refused to work in the government-regulated product-testing laboratory because of the high level of responsibility inherent in that assignment.

Some team leaders have had considerable difficulty *not* behaving like traditional authority figures. Similarly, some employees have tried to elicit and reinforce more traditional supervisory patterns. In brief, the actual expectations and preferences of employees in this plant fall on a spectrum running from practices idealized by the system planners to practices that are typical of traditional industrial plants. They do, however, cluster toward the idealized end of the spectrum.

The self-managing work teams were expected to evolve norms covering various aspects of work, including responsible patterns of behavior (such as mutual help and notification regarding absences). On a few occasions, however, there was excessive peer group pressure for an individual to conform to group norms. Scapegoating by a powerful peer group is as devastating as scapegoating by a boss. The same is true of making arbitrary judgments.

Groups, however, contain more potential for checks and balances, understanding and compassion, reason and justice. Hence it is important for team leaders to facilitate the development of these qualities in work groups.

Team members have been given assignments that were usually limited to supervisors, managers, or professionals: heading the plant safety committee, dealing with outside vendors, screening and selecting new employees, and traveling to learn how a production problem is handled in another plant or to troubleshoot a shipping problem. These assignments have been heady experiences for the operators, but have also generated mixed feelings among others. For example, a vendor was at least initially disappointed to be dealing with a worker because he judged himself in part by his ability to get to higher organizational levels of the potential customer (since typically that is where decisions are made). In another case, a plant worker attended a corporationwide meeting of safety officials where all other representatives were from management. The presence and implied equal status of the articulate knowledgeable worker was at least potentially threatening to the status and self-esteem of other representatives. Overall, however, the workers' seriousness, competence, and self-confidence usually have earned them respect.

30
Doing Away with the Factory Blues

DONALD N. SCOBEL

When one thinks of a factory, images of a Dickensian sort often spring to mind: soot-coated windows, row upon row of downtrodden employees, and a stern fat-bellied boss sitting in a window-office high above the work floor where no one can reach him. Although these stereotypes are no longer realities, and most factories are clean healthy places in which to work, many plants are still inhospitable to most people. Is this situation unavoidable in a factory? In reporting on a new approach to revitalize the factory's work climate that is being carried out in some plants of Eaton Corporation, the author of this article says no. He asserts that by simply replacing many discriminatory personnel policies and practices which assume that the factory employee is untrustworthy and antiproductive and by instituting new ones, management can create a workplace where the aims of the business are congruent with the employees' desires for a happy work experience. The aim of the new approach is not to enrich employees' jobs, but rather to create a responsive work climate where desires for job enrichment can arise and be fulfilled along the way. The author also reports on how efforts to implement the new approach in older plants do meet with some resistance at first, but how it appears that they too will be successful.

During the past few decades, the financial lot of the U.S. factory employee has been enhanced immeasurably by beneficial laws, organized and persuasive representation, economic clout, and, until recently, a generally increasing economy. The factory employee now also has more avenues than ever before to lodge specific protests and to achieve some social equity through grievance procedures, courts, labor boards, equality commissions, safety councils, and arbitration hearings.

Despite these social and economic advances for the factory employee, however, the factory itself has retained much of its classism and discrimination. Even with the dissections of academia, decades of behavioral science, theories of job enrichment and of human relations, new styles of management, and concepts of organizational development, the factory remains the kind of place *non*factory people hope their children never have to work in as well as the kind of place factory people hope their children can get out of. Why?

Why must the U.S. factory cause unhappiness for so many of its inhabitants? Why is it that an average of a few hundred people spending more than a third of their lives under a common roof cannot seem to find there a sustaining measure of equity, understanding, or even friendship? How can this minisociety called the workplace, where members are truly dependent on each other for economic security, remain so socially and emotionally sterile?

Part of the problem is that most people concerned with improving the lot of "people at work" fail to see the workplace holistically. Behavioral scientists, managements, unions, consultants, and legislators often concern themselves with separate segments of the industrial complex. Those who are concerned with styles of management do not worry about how the job is separate from the environment. Those concerned about worker alienation generally leave problems of the white collar force to others. Still other groups work to improve laws for the nonexempt. Yet these individual efforts rarely succeed in establishing a work culture where internal social values and business objectives are congruent.

In the past six years, however, considerable work has been done at several U.S. Eaton Corporation locations to provide the foundation for a workplace culture quite different from the more common industrial environment. At the outset, management did not form work teams, thrust a system of enriched jobs on the workplace, or even presume that the participation of people in decisions directly affecting them is a necessary ingredient of a healthy work culture. The thrust at the Eaton plants was simply for a climate of responsible industrial freedom, where the respect, dignity, and trust due a "man at work" is not culturally different from those due a man at church, a man bowling, or a man in tune with his own family. Management's effort was to achieve a happy responsive work culture that would respond constructively to job enrichment, decision participation and involvement, or whatever grassroots needs, as they emerged.

The "Eaton story" may at times seem as if it were a fairy tale. Indeed, the approach used at Eaton has been spawned and nurtured more by innocence than by behavioral analysis, and that may have been part of its magic. Regardless, since 1968 about 13 Eaton manufacturing plants, involving over 5,000 people, have tried and succeeded in establishing a responsive workplace. Each plant's approach is tailored to the needs of its employees, which include foundry workers, truck transmission and axle makers, lift truck and auto parts makers, and forestry equipment and hardware builders.

It all began seven years ago when the manager of Eaton's Battle Creek, Michigan engine valve plant decided to build a new facility in Kearney, Nebraska. He asked his managerial staff and the Cleveland headquarters employee relations people how he might avoid the deterioration in employee/management relationships in Nebraska that had occurred over the decades in the Michigan plant.

In response to this challenge, a few managerial people representing the full spectrum of functional disciplines at Eaton isolated themselves to discuss and evaluate traditional policies and practices that affect employee relations. They summarized their composite critique in a report to the Battle Creek manager that took the form of a letter written as if by a factory employee who is explaining why he brings so little of himself to his workplace.

The Employee's Letter

Beginning in the Nebraska cornfields and spreading to other new facilities and, more recently, to some older plants, Eaton's revolt against the factory blues began with this "letter."

Dear Sir:

What you are asking me, as I see it, is why am I not giving you my best in exchange for the reasonable wages and benefits you provide me and my family.

First, I'm not trying to blame anybody for why you don't see the "whole" me. Some of the problem is company policy, some is union thinking, some is just me. Let me tell you why, and I'll leave it to bigger minds than mine to figure out blames and remedies.

I'll begin with my first day on the job eleven years ago—my first factory job, by the way. I was just 19 then. Incidentally, my cousin started work in your office as a clerk typist on the same day. We used to drive to work together. She still works for you, too.

The first thing I was told that day by the personnel manager and my foreman was that I was on 90 days' probation. They were going to measure my ability and attendance and attitude and then make up their minds about me. Gee, that surprised me. I thought I'd been hired already—but I really wasn't. Although the foreman tried to make me feel at home, it was still sort of a shock to realize I was starting out kind of on the sidelines until I proved my worth. In fact, the only person who told me I "belonged," without any strings attached, was my union steward.

You know, that first day my foreman told me all about the shop rules of discipline as if I were going to start out stealing or coming to work drunk or getting into fights or horseplay. What made it even worse was when I later found out that no one told my cousin she was on probation. I asked her if she had seen the rules, and here it is eleven years later and she still doesn't know there are about 35 rules for those of us working in the factory.

What it boils down to is that your policies—yes, and the provisions of our union contract—simply presume the factoryman untrustworthy, while my cousin in the office is held in much higher regard. It's almost like we work for different companies.

After I had been here about eight months, a car hit my car broadside on the way to work. My cousin and I were both taken to the hospital right away and released several hours later. As soon as I was released by the hospital, I called the plant to tell them what happened. I couldn't get through to my foreman, so I told my tale to a recording machine. When my cousin didn't show up by nine o'clock, her boss got worried and called the house and then the hospital. When he found out my cousin had a broken arm and some cuts, but was basically okay, he sent for a taxi to take her home.

Both my cousin and I ended up missing four days' work. On each of the next three days, I called and told the tape recorder I would not be in. I never heard from anybody in the company and when I got back to work later that week, my supervisor said, "Sure glad to see you're okay . . . it's a shame you spoiled your perfect attendance record. . . ."

Sir, I don't come to work to be worried about by someone. But I have some difficulty understanding why, when I'm absent, nobody really cares. It seems as if the company's just waiting for me to do something wrong. When I got back to work from that car accident, you started getting another little chunk less from me. Does that sound crazy? Or does it seem selfish?

Sir, why must I punch a time clock? Do you think I'd lie about my starting and quitting times? Why must I have buzzers to tell me when I take a break, relieve myself, eat lunch, start working, go home? Do you really think I can't tell time or would otherwise rob you of valuable minutes? Why doesn't the rest room I must use provide any privacy? Why do I have to drive my car over chuck holes while you enjoy reserved, paved parking? Why must I work the day before and after a holiday to get holiday pay? Are you convinced I will extend the holiday into the weekend—while, by the way, my cousin is thought to have more sense than that?

I guess I'm saying that when you design your policies for the very few who need them, how do you think the rest of us feel?

Sir, do you really think I don't care or don't know what you think of me? If you are convinced of that, then you will never understand why I bring less than all of myself to my workbench.

You know, sir, in my eleven years, I've run all kinds of machinery for you, but your company has never even let me look at what the maintenance man does when he has to repair one of my machines. No one has ever really asked me how quality might be better or how my equipment or methods might be improved. In fact, your policies drum it into me good and proper that you really want me to stay in my place. And now, *you* want to know why *I* don't pour it on? Wow! Don't you realize that I may want to contribute more than you let me? I know the union may be responsible for some of this—but again, I'm trying to explain why, not whose fault it is.

You know, sir, I would like a more challenging job, but that isn't the heart of the matter, not for me at least. If there were a sense of dignity around here, I could not hold back the effort and ideas within me, even if my particular job was less than thrilling. Many of my buddies do not want a greater job challenge, but they do want their modest contributions respected.

You know, my neighbor is a real quiet, sweet old man who just retired from here last month. When I ask him how he sums up his life's work, he says—and I can almost quote him exactly—"A pretty good place to work—only thing that really bothered me was that warning I got 26 years ago for lining up at the clock two and one-half minutes early."

Well, sir, I suspect that 26 years ago, you may have corrected this quiet, nice guy for lining up early at your clock. But the price you paid was making him a "clock watcher" for 26 years. I wonder—was that warning all that necessary? Why couldn't you have just told him why lining up early isn't a good idea and then relied on him to discipline himself? I wonder.

It has been said, sir, that factory people look upon *profit* as a dirty word. I don't feel that way, but you know, it's almost as if *love* is the dirty word here.

Why don't I give my best? Well, I guess I have a kind of thermostat inside me that responds to your warmth. Do you have a thermostat inside you?

Very truly yours,

The Company's Answer

The above letter all but spells out its own solutions. The epilogue of the report to the Michigan manager said: "To avoid industrial decay, build a plant around the presumed correctness of the letter writer." And this is what the manager of the new plant in Nebraska, and all managers of new Eaton plants built since then, set out to do. Critical to solving inequities and problems cited in the letter is that management's commitment to the new approach be made explicit from the very beginning and that supervisors reexamine factory relationships.

The First Steps

At the new Eaton plants, management puts out a written handbook in which it commits itself to a counseling rather than a rules-penalties process; to weekly departmental meetings where employee inputs are sought; to manager roundtables and an "open floor" concept; to a uniform office-factory benefit system; and to a foundation of concern, trust, and participation. The handbook states that

> ... an important concept here is that people are individuals ... and a company must relate to uniqueness if there is to be a full measure of personal growth and contribution to organizational objectives. The emphasis is upon employee involvement in matters that affect him and sharing the responsibility for an effective operation. It's a mutual fulfillment.

What Eaton does in the formal training of supervisors under the new model is remarkably minimal. In a two-day seminar, the group of supervisors spends the first day just talking about why people work and what they want out of life. The consensus usually is that "we are all into this for pretty much the same reasons." The group invariably believes there are personal differences in motivational priorities, but does not believe these differences can be categorized for any class or group of employees, or that different categories of motivational factors are inherently more important. Although behavioral scientists have dissected this premise almost to death, it is true that most people desire a sense of community at work. Recognizing this fact helps supervisors and managers see that treating employees under the same roof with different value systems does not make much "human" sense.

During the second day of the seminar the supervisors review the basic components of the new approach and consider how that approach helps build a common value system of respect and participation. The reason training can be minimal is that the supervisor steps from the seminar into a workplace where the new commitments and ground rules are in effect immediately. Another plus is that it is not necessary to have "behavioral science superstars" to understand or apply the new approach. Supervisors of varying competencies are usually at ease with this approach after only brief exposure. Very few clamor for the old regimentation, or see it as essential to their ability to supervise. One supervisor simply said, "Nothing fancy about this. It's just being human with biblical roots." Eaton is trying to resurrect fairness through identifiable policy changes that are fundamentally fair.

Policy Changes

Space prohibits listing all aspects of this new approach. In essence, personnel policies and presumptions that are based on mistrust and lack of care are discarded and replaced, where necessary, with ones that reflect concern and mutual respect. The following are a few examples of how this attitude is applied to actual policies and processes.

At the new Eaton plants, the hiring process is a meaningful two-way exchange, which replaces the structured interview and the more common "get-me-twelve-warm-bodies-by-Tuesday" factory-hiring syndrome. Applicants and their spouses are invited in small groups to an after-dinner "coffee" where the plant's products, processes, and philosophy are discussed. Both factory and office employees take the group on a plant and office tour and encourage the applicants to spend additional time in departments that seem most attractive to them. Personnel people ask the newcomers to express their job preferences within their general skill levels for initial placement or for later transfer if there is no opening in the department selected. The people conducting the tour introduce applicants to people they may be working for and with. With this open review of the job, job seekers end up knowing more about the company and its people than they do about them. This process extends to a drill press operator or a file clerk the concern and dignity that industry usually extends only to its applicants for managerial posts.

There is no probationary period. Supervisors evaluate individually any problem that might arise with a new person. Although it can happen that supervisors may have to let someone go, the policy presumes that people are eager to work and to be dependable employees, rather than the opposite.

The plants do not use time clocks, buzzers, or similar controls. Although the company needs records of time allocations for many legal as well as good business reasons, it assumes that individuals can accurately record their own times.

The dual value system mentioned by the "letter writer" no longer exists. Many companies, including Eaton, have traditionally maintained reasonable responsible relationships with their office and supervisory staffs and have solved problems with these employees by carefully appraising the facts of each case, counseling employees according to individual circumstances, and assuming that the employees are able to direct themselves rather than relying on a rigid penalty schedule for correcting behavior. This approach is now being used for all factory employees who once were subjected to a formal disciplinary system that had numerous posted rules and a sliding scale of penalties that went with them.

All factory and office people also share the same benefit package. Levels of certain benefits vary with salary, but the system is uniform. Payment for casual absence is often a dynamic distinguisher between office and factory status. At the newer Eaton facilities, all people are paid for both casual and long-term absences and are under the same pay system for long-term absences.

Office and factory supervisors hold departmental meetings at least once every two weeks to discuss issues that the employees themselves raise. Often the supervisor will have an employee lead the discussion.

The plant manager chairs a periodic roundtable with representatives from all office and factory departments who are selected in whatever way the department decides. The participants prepare the agenda of concerns and the minutes, as well as post follow-up action notices on central and departmental bulletin boards.

An "open floor" concept replaces the old "open door" policy. The "open door" implied to a factoryperson, "If you want to do business with a staff person, you must come up to the front office." The new approach makes the factoryperson's workplace as important an "office" as anyplace else in the facility. So that territorial barriers are specifically torn down, the personnel department and other staff people make a point of conducting business at the employee's workplace as well as at their own.

In a variety of ways, factory, supervisory, and lower-level office people participate in managerial meetings and functions. For example, the manager invites some factory and office people to weekly staff meetings. Similarly, there is regular factory representation at production planning meetings, as well as factory participation on methods, products, and process engineering committees.

At some locations, factory and lower-level office people are editors of the plant's newssheets. Often the recreational, social, and community affairs activities are independently managed, including direction of the fiscal aspects, by joint committees of factory and office people. Special committees (little ad hocracies) are formed from time to time to handle contingencies.

It is common for factory people to volunteer to be plant tour guides, to be involved with food service, plant safety, and fire protection matters, even to the extent of codirection of these activities.

I hope the above list gives the reader some idea of what Eaton is trying to do. In addition to these items, there are two important kinds of experiences that flow from this approach. For employees who want them, there are opportunities to be involved in developing the scope of their jobs or in increasing their participation in decision making.

Job Involvement. From the beginning of the workplace renaissance, Eaton has not tried to implement new work structures or process designs. Each of the newer plants began with updated versions of the same basic technologies and procedures used at its older counterparts. Management wanted first to restructure the work climate and then to be responsive to spontaneous employee drives for greater job involvement as these drives emerged. What followed clearly, and almost quantifiably, resulted from the new work culture.

In the new plants, almost all employees seek better and more rapid performance inspection and feedback. In some cases, some of the inspection duties have been taken over by the employees themselves and blended into their own manufacturing responsibilities and operations. Interestingly, until people achieve job proficiency, they want guidance on how to improve their performance.

About one third of the people seek some involvement in their equipment repair. A significant number do not seek this enrichment, but for those who do, it is meaningful, and most maintenance people are willing trainers. Although maintenance time does sometimes rise briefly, it soon goes down, and preventive maintenance practices become more routine.

On the average, three-quarters of the factory employees want to learn more about the whole production process, and those familiar with the process sequence soon develop an "early alert" system that warns them of trouble elsewhere on the line. Often these employees ask for temporary reassignment to help resolve the production holdups. It is startling how quickly employees become familiar with the total manufacturing process and how many of them aid the supervisor in product flow planning and problem solving.

Almost a third of the work force diagnoses its own job methods and scopes. At one plant, a janitor persuaded his boss that he, rather than the purchasing department, could order local cleaning supplies because he would give it higher priority than they would. He was allowed to do so, whereas other janitors wanted no part of the telephoning and paper work. At another plant the lathe operators insisted they be allowed to join a meeting of equipment engineers to learn why their lathes were malfunctioning. Many times people come forth with combinations of jobs or changes in sequences that can improve output. Some improvements require that the job and pay structure be changed, but many can be accommodated by the existing system.

These experiences in job involvement result from a specific policy of laissez-faire. Management responds positively to involvement but does not attempt to structure it.

Participation in Decision Making. It is integral to many aspects of the new approach that employees should participate in decisions. This extends to specific decisions that affect work and the work life. For example, if a plant is on a two-shift five-day operation, and business expands, the different departments will discuss different work-schedule options, such as weekend work, extended daily hours, or a third shift that could be used to handle the increase. Often management will express its thoughts and invite reactions; more often, the options are put to a vote. In either case, employee inputs are specifically invited before any decision is made.

At one plant several employees suggested the company try a four-day week. The suggestion was put to a vote—and passed; in another plant, it failed. Elsewhere, management asked the employees in one departmental unit to restructure their own job contents and assignments when the current system was obviously inequitable. At a few locations, employees have nominated and selected candidates for supervisory positions, and in one situation, the employees said another supervisor was not necessary!

Even in layoff circumstances, decision participation is invited. Although people do not like to vote on only negative alternatives, such as a reduction of the work force versus a reduction in working hours, if the company submits its preferred course to employee consideration, it will often find the attitudinal "pulse" and more often than not receive ideas for policy redirection. During one temporary layoff, plantwide discussion brought forth more layoff volunteers than were needed! In almost all cases, when the employees participate in decisions, they cooperate to the full with the final decision. As one manager put it, "I can no longer conceive of making a decision of major impact on any segment of that work force without first inviting meaningful dialogue."

The Response

Although some problems have arisen under the new approach (I will discuss these below), nothing so far indicates that the basic concepts are off the mark. In fact, there are some interesting comparisons that can be drawn between the new model facilities and the older plants, indicating that the new approach increases both productivity and worker satisfaction.

Measures of Success

At the new plants, absenteeism (casual as well as sick leaves) ranges from 0.5% to 3%, compared with 6% to 12% at traditional locations. Turnover is similarly reduced. With the new approach, voluntary separations average under 4% annually, compared with up to 60% at traditional plants.

In the new plants the hourly product output (for identical blueprints of products run on similar equipment) will range from parity to 35% more than at the traditional plants. Of more importance to Eaton, however, is the longer range performance where trends are comparable. Management in the new locations actually hopes that productivity will fall off at times. A dip in productivity indicates that improvements are being made in the manufacturing process, which will lead to greater gains in the long run. It is interesting that some new locations report up to 15% less scrap and rework costs. Nevertheless, those plants that have the highest output gains report the least savings (if any) in the quality area. Most report reduced maintenance costs per unit of output once start-up problems are resolved.

On the other hand, new facilities often have a worse plant safety record than the older plants. Management speculates that this decline in safety is caused partly by the new work force's unfamiliarity with industrial hazards and by the fact that carelessness creeps in when people strive so hard to increase production. In any event, the safety problem has led employees to involve themselves more in plant and departmental safety activities.

Actions Speak Louder than Words. These measurements are interesting, but are subject to all the problems involved in accurately comparing even seemingly like facilities. Although many of the plants compared are "paired" in terms of product and basic machinery, there are crucial differences, such as age of equipment; length of production runs; availability and quality of raw materials, parts and supplies; climate; and reliance on a parent plant for services. These differences make it difficult to isolate and measure the involvement and effectiveness of people. One can tell what is happening at the new plants and what the work force's effect is on productivity more by examining actual events than by measuring output.

At one plant an employee literally broke in to go to work. The first day her shift went to ten hours, requiring a 5:00 A.M. starting time, she arrived at 3:30 A.M., as was her usual habit of showing up an hour and a half early. Finding the whole place dark, unoccupied, and locked, and even though she lived nearby and could have returned home until the plant officially opened, she climbed a fence, pried open a window, turned on the lights, cleaned her area, and started up the heating equipment to warm her "plating" bath.

At another facility, a significant number of day-shift people, while taking the family out for an evening "Dairy Queen," stop by the plant just to make sure everything is going all right on the night shift.

A plant manager at one of the older plants visited a new model facility and reported to a vice-president,

> . . . I'd sum it up by reporting that when the first shift ended you couldn't tell it was quitting time! No clocks to line up at! No rushing to cars! No tires screeching! Some people finished the last piece in their machine. Many casually took showers. Some went out to the picnic area and gossiped over a bottle of pop. Several stayed to play baseball or horseshoes in the back field. Some went to a variety of committee meetings. The point is that the exodus was so gradual it went unnoticed. Unbelievable!

A group of employees, on their own time, used company materials to build a special scooter to enable an employee who had become permanently handicapped in an automobile accident to return early to the job.

At a facility where overtime work is assigned on a voluntary basis, for three months 97% of the people worked seven days a week with less than 2% absenteeism *during* the week, even though casual weekday absence would have been paid for.

There have been no employee-initiated EEO or OSHA complaints at any facility where this approach to employee relationships is practiced.

At a southern plant where 30% of the work force is black, the factory people selected five supervisors; three of them were black.

Although there are not many transfers between office and factory positions, it is just as common to have office people apply for transfer to the factory as the other way around. At one plant, five office people volunteered to run factory machinery so five avid hunters could catch the first day of the season!

At one location, a high-ranking visitor reported, among other things

> ... the most remarkably constructive graffiti I have ever read ... the few cartoons, poems and song parodies are genuinely witty and poignant and prideful. What a difference from the traditional back walls of industry!

One New Year's Day, almost all the employees at one plant responded to a TV news bulletin that the plant was within an unexpected flood area. Most labored around the clock so the plant could be fully operational the next day.

At one plant, if at the beginning of the shift an employee registers a choice of lunch food, a tray will be waiting for the worker at lunchtime. A cafeteria employee who thinks that "people's lunch break should be spent eating and gabbing and not waiting in line or kicking a vending machine" introduced the idea and carried it out.

These examples show how the new approach affects employees at work, and were perhaps best summarized by one manager: "On those especially frustrating days I still know in my bones that nothing intentionally destructive is going on around here."

Problems of Implementation

Although the humanistic approach to employee relationships has not failed at any location, there have, nevertheless, been growing pains. With varying degrees of severity, most of the following problems have occurred at one or more plants.

Initially, Eaton concentrated its effort on employee relations in the factory. Although very few office people were averse to bringing dignity and fairness to the factory employees, when the factories were filled with camaraderie, the office people became envious of the "feeling." The office people did not have the sense of involvement with their workplace that management had assumed they did, and once the issue was raised it was clear why. Some plant managers did not include the office people in their roundtable discussions, and when they did conduct departmental meetings, which was infrequently, the meetings seemed pallid in comparison to factory meetings.

Management in the new plants solved these problems by stressing participation in the offices and ensuring more meaningful interaction between the office and factory employees so that all could share the same work climate. What Eaton had seen originally as a factory revitalization now involves the entire workplace.

Another related problem is what Eaton now calls the "up-the-ladder" disease. The first symptom appeared at a retreat that the manager of the new Nebraska plant held so that the supervisors could talk in a relaxed atmosphere about how things were going. This quasi-recreational gathering turned out to be a pressure cooker for the plant manager. The supervisors said most discreetly that their relationships with the factory employees were more spirited and participative than their rapport with higher management. They felt they were "short circuited" up the hierarchy. The plant manager realized the need to be more awake and responsive to the supervisors and their ideas. Invariably, the cure for this disease is exposing higher management levels to the plant culture itself.

At one very small location, the plant manager ignored the espoused policies. The hiring orientation process fell short of the commitment, and departmental meetings did not occur. In reacting angrily to an employee soliciting money for a "cause," a department manager ignored individualized consideration and posted a mass denouncement on the bulletin board. As was immediately evident from the horrendous absentee and turnover experience, the managers were not treating the employees with respect and dignity. Luckily, the plant manager recognized what was happening and called the work force together to admit the hypocrisy and to pledge a speedy "new beginning," which has taken place.

There are different problems that arise when things go almost too smoothly. At a few places, for instance, the sense of goodwill was so pervasive that the company did not react to a few individuals who were exploiting the trust placed in them. The other employees became restless and brought pressure on these people directly as well as on management to deal with these individuals. In most cases, the peer pressure and counseling procedure has been effective, and the individuals responded positively.

Despite the implementation problems I have cited, the approach has been accepted in most new locations. Although not without its skeptics, the concept is now a familiar idea throughout the company, and many managers of traditional plants, which have varied histories of problems with factory and office employees, are searching out ways to apply the new approach at their own plants, where practices, policies, and attitudes are already firmly established.

The Backward Glance

Eaton's efforts at some older plants are still in early stages, and it is too soon to report significant successes or failures. It is already apparent, however, that remodeling is slower and more complex than building anew. It is equally evident, nevertheless, that meaningful changes can be made at traditional locations without great risk or investment. As at new locations, the company must express its commitment; the absence of commitment makes the ideas seem vague and philosophical rather than action oriented.

Understandably, it is much more difficult to convince supervisors, employees, and their unions in the older plants that change is not threatening and can take place with fairness and dignity. This task has become easier at Eaton since the word has now spread that the new plants are such fulfilling places to work in. It is still, however, a great challenge to managers in the traditional plants to bring everyone together without fanfare into a common constructive process, to get them to believe that management means what it is saying. If management tries to impose the new approach, it runs the risk of appearing as if it were just another management attempt to impose its will upon the employees. Because of these problems, managers in some older plants are using different approaches to attain the same ends.

At one old plant, there is a joint company–union initiated effort to transform the workplace climate through a variety of participative endeavors. These include such experiences as employees themselves rearranging an entire stockroom area more efficiently or management entrusting employees in a certain department with the responsibility of resolving their own absentee problems. At another location, the company has approached the union to recast the provisions of the labor agreement in language that assumes trust and respect between parties. The point is to see whether constructive relations can emerge from changes in legalistic language and principles previously inscribed in stone.

More commonly, however, Eaton is trying to adapt its new plant experiences to traditional places. There is no theoretical reason that the new hiring procedure, the "open floor" policy, departmental meetings, the manager's roundtable, and the counseling approach to discipline cannot be initiated by managers in the plants. In fact, some of these changes are in process at older places and seem to attract voluntary union involvement and cooperation.

The union, of course, must be integrally involved in the entire change process. As management takes on a new role, so must the union and the employees. All three must involve themselves in some new processes that have them working together toward some common objectives. Working together seems to bring about change far sooner than does eons of dialogue.

From our early efforts to reduce alienation at traditional workplaces, it seems that decision participation must come into play early in the process. This comes slowly at first for people not accustomed to participating, but the encouragement to participate begins to narrow the credibility gap and most people join in after a few invitations.

Lastly, management must discard traditional policies and practices that presume or embody mistrust. Where these policies are rooted in provisions of a labor agreement such as the probationary concept or a host of other rigid systems, the company and union must work these out together. And this teamwork is not likely to occur unless the union and employees are playing a part in the entire change process.

P.S.

What Eaton is doing is not complex. When one observer suggested we were only getting the "Hawthorne effect," we glowed and said that was exactly right. All we are trying to do is "bottle" the Hawthorne effect, and share respect and concern with employees.

It is significant that about a quarter of the companies that research the Eaton approach and visit a facility adapt some form of the process for one or more of their own locations. Of equal significance, however, are some of the reasons cited by those who do not make changes in their own organizations. In some cases, the inquirers are personally enthusiastic but see no chance to influence traditional higher management in their companies. This happens mostly with people from small companies where the chief executive officer is seen as having a negative attitude that dominates the entire organization. In larger, multiple plant facilities, such as Eaton, the change is often introduced at an interested branch, and then spreads throughout the organization.

Conversely, in some cases the chief executive officer, impressed by the concept, expresses doubt that other key people in the organization could implement these new processes.

Some people say they are hesitant to propose such an approach in their own companies because there are so many seemingly complex theories of behavior now on the shelf that the company fears embarking on any particular course when it may soon be outdated. Some inquirers are actually startled to find that Eaton people are not steeped in any particular behavioral school.

Those companies that have tried the Eaton approach have confirmed our experiences. They report:

1. This approach is fundamentally fair and makes sense even if it doesn't prove to be a panacea.
2. It is based on some very specific and simple actions that can be implemented by existing personnel.
3. The company can rely on its own innovators, and not, as one inquirer put it on "a behavioral guru."
4. The approach does not require a large financial investment, and even a 1% increase in plant utilization or a 2% drop in absenteeism brings a substantial return on investment.

At Eaton we are convinced that concern, respect, and trust in people produce a cohesive and effective workplace. Complex evaluation procedures, behavioral science theories and analyses, job design, and individual consultations are not primary and often not necessary. In fact, the process is more akin to an attitude than to a detailed intellectual plan. Most supervisors and managers boast of the esprit de corps and excitement that builds as the approach takes hold. One manager, when asked by a visitor just beginning a tour, "What will I see different out there?" responded, "A feeling."

Perhaps behavioral science's gallop is leaping over some very simple and moving truths. When bird hunters spontaneously prepare a duck casserole luncheon for the entire work force; when a fifty-seven-year-old man boasts how his wife of thirty-seven years has finally got him bowling and dancing " 'cause I come home so rarin' "; when a plant's annual aspirin consumption is down to a small bottle; when hospitalized employees are visited by about 20% of the work force; when the plant community spontaneously plants trees and shrubs to create its own wooded picnic area; and when a guitar-playing employee sits in that picnic area and sings an original folk song about a "workplace havin' soul," then something constructive and productive is truly happening somehow.

31
Work Innovations in the United States

RICHARD E. WALTON

What have ten years of work innovations taught us? For one thing, these efforts are usually neither extreme successes nor extreme failures. For another, people who sponsor these projects are neither villains nor saints. Also, the quality of work life projects may add to productivity but not necessarily. In other words, work innovations are not absolute solutions to any set of problems; rather, they represent an approach to looking at problems. In this article, the author, a well-known authority in the area of work innovation, sets out to examine some of the myths that surround it. To do this, he puts forth his own three-level conception of work innovation showing how techniques, outcomes, and culture relate to each other. Using this conception, managers can better approach improving work in their own operations. One of his main conclusions from looking at the past ten years of experience is that work improvement efforts that have both productivity and quality of work life as goals are more likely to succeed on both counts than projects that stress one goal to the exclusion of the other.

Americans tend to do things by trial and error, and in dealing with changes in the way they work, they are no different. Whereas changes in European workplaces tend to be guided by government intervention and ideological rationalizations and involve an explicit transfer of authority, innovations in American workplaces are voluntary and pragmatic and involve no such transfer.[1] Despite its random nature, however, much change that has been planned has occurred in American workplaces during the past ten years.

Author's Note. I wish to express my special thanks to Leonard Schlesinger, who has reviewed this manuscript at different stages of its development and made helpful suggestions for improving it.

Observers differ about whether work improvement is a fad or a long-term transformation in the nature of work organizations. Scientists differ in their theoretical explanations of why it works or when the conditions are right for it. Managers invariably wonder whether it has application in their organizations, and some union officials are concerned about its implications for the union as an institution. These concerns imply varying conceptions of work innovation and hence indicate the amount of confusion that exists about what work improvement is.

In this article, I want to look at what has actually changed in workplaces, find out what we can learn from these work improvement activities, and derive some principles from what is reflected in the most successful ones. First, though, let us clarify what "work improvement" means and how I will be using it in the remainder of this article.

What Work Improvement Is

The planned changes called "work improvements" have appeared in workplaces in many guises—as "quality of work life," "humanization of work," "work reform," "work restructuring," "work design," and "sociotechnical systems."

Although some of these terms have special connotations for the professionals who employ them, in method and goals the actual activities pursued under the various labels are not very different. I find it useful to distinguish three separate aspects of a work improvement effort.

Design Techniques

The element of work improvement activities that is most apparent is the specific changes in the way work is organized and managed. For instance, the content of tasks changes when jobs are enriched, work teams affect the way tasks are organized and how they relate to each other, and consultative management gives workers the opportunity to influence decisions that affect them. The techniques may also affect the information provided workers as well as their compensation, security, physical environment, and access to due process.

The techniques employed and their possible combinations are many. For example, in changing assembly methods, auto plants have assigned related tasks to work teams, allowed them to decide how to allocate the work among themselves (provided they meet quality and quantity requirements), and created buffer inventories between adjacent work teams to increase latitude in the rhythm of their work. Also, management and unions in competitive manufacturing situations have designed plantwide schemes to share productivity increases and have structured mechanisms to ensure that workers' ideas for improvement are considered.

Intended Results

Another aspect of work improvement is the results it is intended to produce. They can be either economic (for the benefit of the organization) or human (for the benefit of employees). The business benefits can take many forms—quality, delivery, materials usage, machine capacity utilization, and labor efficiency. The human benefits can take form as real income, security, challenge, variety, advancement opportunity, dignity, equity, and sense of community. The relative importance of these depends on the needs and aspirations of the employees in question.

Most of the work improvement labels focus narrowly on either techniques or results. For example, "job enrichment" directs attention to the techniques level and only to one technique. The connotation of "job design" is only slightly broader. "Quality of work life" has the same limitations. It refers directly to an objective that can be served in innumerable ways. Moreover, as labels, "quality of work life" and its first cousin, "humanization of work," have serious drawbacks; they refer only to human gains, which in today's business environment need to be closely coupled with improved competitive performance.

In my experience, I have found that organizations can improve business results in a humane way and improve the quality of the human experience in a businesslike manner by identifying the work cultures that promote both improvements simultaneously. Such work cultures are the links between technique and results in my three-level conception of work improvements.

Work Culture: The Intermediate Effects

The combination of attitudes, relationships, developed capabilities, habits, and other behavioral patterns that characterize the dynamics of an organization is a work culture.

Some changes in the culture, such as high-cost consciousness, responsiveness to authority, and high activity norms, may promote performance but do little or nothing for people. Conversely, under some circumstances, high sensitivity to feelings and concern for the personal growth of the individual are cultural attributes that may be appreciated by the people affected but may not by themselves contribute to business performance.

In the most successful work improvement efforts, the culture simultaneously enhances business performance and the quality of human experience. In one food plant, for instance, management sought to promote employee identification with goals. Such positive identification increases not only workers' motivation to work but also their sense of belonging in the workplace and their pride in the plant's achievement. Similarly, a behavior pattern that influences both employee self-esteem and the soundness of business decisions is another desirable cultural attribute.

Identification and mutual influence are ideals common to many work improvement projects, but no single culture is ideal for all businesses or all people. What particular set of attitudes, capabilities, and relationships a company should emphasize will depend on its industry's strategic performance indexes and its employees' work life values. Whatever the work culture sought, it cannot be mandated by anyone. It can only be shaped over time by a combination of things—including the techniques by which work is organized and managed.

Let us review how these three aspects of work improvement activities relate to each other.

Techniques are the elements of the work organization that people can alter directly; intended results are the fundamental business and human criteria by which to judge effectiveness; and the work culture mediates the impact of the former on the latter. The techniques create the culture, which strongly influences business performance and the human experience at work.

According to this conception, one's choice of techniques is guided by continuously referring to the type of work culture that they promote, and in turn to projected business and human outcomes. For example, in a paper manufacturing plant, the business ends required that the manpower be flexible, and employees wanted the opportunity to acquire new skills. The plant adopted a design in which teams are responsible for a cluster of tasks and members are rewarded for acquiring the skills to perform all the team tasks. Such a design promotes both flexibility and opportunity. (The three-level conception of work improvement is shown in Exhibit 1; the arrows indicate influence.)

The exhibit illustrates how important it is to specify the proper business and work life outcomes for a particular company.

Applying this concept, one is also guided in the quality of choice one should make at each level. As one moves backward in the exhibit from intended results through work culture to design techniques, one's stance should become increasingly pragmatic. If the desired outcomes are clear and one's commitment to both business and human values is firm, then one can evaluate cultural attributes and in turn design techniques in terms of their efficacy in achieving the desired results.

Some principles that arise out of the three-level conception of work innovation are outlined in the Appendix following this article.

Interest in Work Innovation

Over the past decade, media attention has gradually shifted from focusing on the symptoms of disaffection with work to possible solutions. The amount of work improvement activity in plants and offices throughout the United States has grown steadily, appearing to be on the path of a classical S growth

Exhibit 1. Three-Level Conception of Work Improvement

Level I Design techniques	Level II Work culture ideals	Level III Intended results
Job design	High skill levels and flexibility in using them	*For business:*
Pay	Identification with product, process, and total business viewpoint	Low cost
Supervisor's role	Problem solving instead of finger pointing	Quick delivery
Training	Influence by information and expertise instead of by position	High-quality products
Performance feedback	Mutual influence	Low turnover
Goal setting	Openness	Low absenteeism
Communication	Responsiveness	Equipment utilization
Employment stability policies	Trust	*For quality of work life:*
Status symbols	Egalitarian climate	Self-esteem
Leadership patterns	Equity	Economic well-being
		Security

Note: The design techniques, cultural ideals, and intended results listed above are presented as illustrative, not as comprehensive or even universally applicable. Also, the items in the three columns are not horizontally lined up to relate to each other. The arrows indicate influence.

curve, in which growth climbs slowly at first, accelerates, and then slows again. Today, the rate of growth in these experiments continues to increase annually, suggesting that we are approaching the steeper portion of the curve.

Extrapolating from available information, I estimate that an important minority of the *Fortune* "500" companies are attempting some significant work improvement projects. And, not surprisingly, the companies that have greater commitment to and experience with such projects are among the leaders in their respective industries: General Motors, Procter & Gamble, Exxon, General Foods, TRW, and Cummins Engine. Less prominent but similarly well-managed manufacturing companies such as Butler Manufacturing and Mars, Inc. have also become increasingly active in this area. Citibank is one company with major work improvement efforts in the office environment.[2] Prudential Insurance is another.

All of the manufacturing companies I have listed have regarded new plant start-ups as opportunities to introduce major new work structures. In recent years, major projects have begun in organizations of various sizes (from 100 to over 3,000), with varying technologies (from simple hand assembly to sophisticated continuous flow processes) and in different geographical locations (from upstate New York to the deep South and the West). As these companies extend their innovative work systems to other new plant sites, managers learn from the experience of the pioneers, and the systems cease to be regarded as experimental. Although the diffusion generally occurs slowly, the principles that underlie these new designs usually spread to companies' established plants as well. Let us look at some of these work innovations in detail.

Individual Projects

HBR readers have been exposed to a number of accounts of individual efforts (e.g., the Topeka Pet Food Plant) and to the distinctive approaches of several U.S. companies (e.g., Donnelly Mirrors and Eaton Corporation).[3] Although not fully representative of the diverse practices that one can observe, these experiments do illustrate the growing work improvement activity in the United States.

To my knowledge, the activity of General Motors is the most extensive of any company in the United States and may be more extensive than that of Volvo, whose pioneering efforts have been well publicized internationally. GM's dozens of projects take a variety of forms. One long-term effort at GM began in the early 1970s in an assembly plant in Tarrytown, New York. What began as a "What-have-we-got-to-lose?" experiment in which workers and the union were involved in redesigning the hard and soft-trim departments' facilities has blossomed into a plantwide quality of work life program involving over 3,500 people.

A different type of project at GM began in 1974 at a new battery plant in Fitzgerald, Georgia, where the pay system was set up to reward knowledge and skills acquisition. After four years, almost all workers there have become familiar with a wide range of jobs and have detailed knowledge of the production process. Initially, inspectors evaluated the workers' performance, but eventually the production teams themselves acquired the responsibility to ensure high-quality performance. Since 1977, work teams have prepared their own departmental budgets for materials and supplies. Managers provide workers with information such as cost data, which is traditionally not shown to them. The sparse and functional offices reveal the prevailing attitude about status symbols.

The pay system, self-supervision, and other design techniques have been combined at the Fitzgerald plant to create a work culture characterized by flexibility, mutual trust, informality, equality, and commitment. Reportedly, the Fitzgerald plant's performance has been very favorable, compared both with other plants and with its own plan. Those familiar with the plant attribute much of its superior performance to the work structure and to the fact that workers take pride in establishing new levels of output and quality.

Another innovator in this field is as much a leader in nondurable consumer goods as GM is in durable goods but shuns publicity of any of its work improvements. It regards the knowledge it has developed about implementing innovative work systems as proprietary, similar to other types of know-how that give it a competitive edge.

In the late 1960s in one plant of a major division, this company introduced a new work system designed around the idea that workers would be paid according to their skill levels. Under this system, the company does not impose quotas to limit the number who could advance to higher levels. The work system promotes the development of relatively self-supervising work teams. The basic features of this system have been adapted to the six new plants built subsequently as well as to departments in the preexisting unionized plants of the division.

Because successful work improvement approaches have not always spread to other plants within the same company, it is worth noting why transfer did occur in this case. The acceptance of change in the existing plants has been fueled by their need to remain competitive with the newer plants, which employ more productive work structures. The change has been facilitated by transferring managers with experience from the innovative plants to the established ones. Also, whenever a new technology or project has been launched or major physical renovations planned, work innovations have been introduced in the old plants.

I have observed many of the plants in this company. Without a doubt, their innovative work systems have contributed significantly to the impressive performance of these plants and to the fact that by a wide margin the plants are usually regarded as the best places to work in their respective communities.

Although GM and the manufacturer of nondurable goods are leaders in the field of work improvements, they are not typical. Most companies, such as Butler Manufacturing, have only a few projects. In 1976, Butler introduced innovative work structures similar to the one at GM's Fitzgerald plant in two new plants. In one plant, the program is working exceptionally well; participants are enthusiastic about the work system and think it contributes strongly to their performance. According to pertinent internal criteria, this plant is 20% more productive and 35% more profitable than comparable plants in the same company.

The other new plant has experienced difficulties, and it is less clear that it has benefited from the work innovations.

The experience of a large paper company is also typical. With encouragement and support from the company's chairman, management launched two major facilitywide projects at the time of the plants' start-ups. When I last heard, the paper mill project was regarded as successful, but the other, in a converting plant, was not. Extenuating circumstances in the marketplace have contributed to the lack of profitability of the converting plant. Also, misjudgments in design reportedly have not been remedied, and optimism is declining.

Most companies experience both success and failure. One large company with four major plantwide projects has experienced almost the full spectrum. A plant that started up with a bold and imaginative work structure three and a half years ago has been very disappointing in terms of economic performance and the work system itself. Local management and union officials judge a second plant to be only somewhat more effective than it would have been without the innovations. A third is solidly effective, and a fourth is a big success according to both human and economic criteria.

The examples I have discussed so far are plant projects, but comparably conceived work improvement efforts have been occurring in office settings as well. In 1972, the clerical work in the Group Policyholders' Service Department of the Guardian Life Insurance Company was fragmented. To process a case file required several steps, each performed by a different person at a different desk in assembly line fashion. Files were hard to find, and responses to client inquiries were delayed. No one person performed or had responsibility for a whole job. Consequently, there was little basis for meaningful recognition of achievement, and morale was low.

The work improvement effort created natural units of work by combining policyholder services and accounting functions for a particular geographic area. The new "account analyst" became identified with a limited and stable set of clients with whom he or she maintained contact and for whom he or she provided a number of services previously assigned to different desks. Control over individual aspects of the work was removed, and individual accountability for overall results was increased.

Although the new work system at Guardian required people to go through complex training, with the result that 6 out of 120 employees could not meet the demands of the redesigned jobs, management reports that the system was effective in producing cumulative increases in productivity of about 33% in four years.

Top Management Interest

Part of the evidence supporting my projection of a continued acceleration of the growth rate of new projects goes beyond concrete activities; it is found in the trend toward increased top management attention to work innovation. Whereas five years ago it was plant or division level managers who invariably sought educational or consultative assistance for potential projects, today it is equally likely that inquiries will come from top corporate managers who are interested in advancing their own understanding of the field, formulating appropriate policies, and promoting constructive corporate activity.

Also, whereas before managers would invite professors to meet with them and report on developments in the field, today it is equally likely that managers with direct experience in promoting work innovations will address these management groups. For example, the chairman of the board of a major packaging company recently assembled the company's top corporate and divisional executives to learn about the work innovations of a major automobile company by a firsthand report of the auto company's vice chairman.

A particularly striking example of the trend toward top management interest in work innovations and toward more manager-to-manager consultation on the subject is provided by a November 1977 conference sponsored by the American Center for the Quality of Working Life. Convened for the purpose of exchanging experiences and examining from the "practical viewpoint of operating executives the principles underlying quality of work life efforts and their efficacy in society," the conference was attended by 40 senior executives from Xerox, General Motors, Nabisco, and Weyerhaeuser.

The "blue collar blues" may promote the adoption and diffusion of innovative work designs in a wide range of industries, from blue collar manufacturing work to white collar and service work and in both the private and the public sector, but a major reason companies are trying work improvement projects is competition. Another is the changing expectations of workers, whose consciousness of quality of work life issues continues to rise. Another is the implicit threat of legislation that might set new more embracing quality of work environment standards or that might require workers to participate in the governance of private industry.

Asking the Right Questions

Despite the many good reasons for attempting work improvement systems, their future depends on how managers approach some fundamental issues and whether they reject the myths surrounding these efforts. Some misconceptions yield easily to more valid assumptions; others appear to need more direct challenge.

Have Work Improvements Been Effective?

There has been a tendency for people to assume that work innovation projects are either spectacular successes or abject failures. At the expense of some widely held myths, however, people active in the field have become increasingly realistic, recognizing that, in fact, projects can and do fall at every point along a broad spectrum of effectiveness.

I have been deeply involved in four major projects and am familiar with aspects of another 30 or so. In terms of their effectiveness in achieving excellence in business and quality of work life outcomes, my impression is that these three dozen projects represent roughly a normal distribution around the mean, just as the effectiveness of more conventionally organized plants would be expected to form a normal distribution.

I believe that the average effectiveness of these innovative work systems is higher than the average of more conventionally organized but otherwise comparable plants. Certainly, however, the poorly managed innovative plants are less effective than the better managed conventional ones. I cannot offer proof that these assumptions are valid, but the mixed experiences of the companies I have discussed illustrate my observations.

Despite the evidence, the myths persist. I have visited a few innovative plants that were advertised as significantly successful, only to discover that they were at best marginally more effective than they would have been without the work innovations. And I have read reports of the "failures" of previously publicized projects, which, on investigation, I found were faulty. People had blown some difficulties encountered in the design or implementation of the projects way out of proportion.

Why these exaggerations? First, people view such efforts with emotion—some being deeply committed to work improvement activities, others being basically hostile to them. Second, where they are involved, the media deem dramatic successes and failures to be newsworthy. Third, because their expectations are high, people readily see any shortfall as a failure.

Even assuming that work innovations have merit, managers and researchers need to have the realistic expectation that their effectiveness will conform to some normal distribution.

What Are the Sponsors' Motives?

Myths have surrounded the motives of those promoting or undertaking work improvement activities. People see sponsors as narrowly interested in either productivity or the human condition, each at the expense of the other. During the early 1970s, when much interest in work improvement was stimulated by one of the two objectives, these beliefs had some basis in reality, but the situation has gradually changed.

In the successful innovations, managers behave as if both economic and human values count. I am familiar with several major innovative work systems that have taken a long time to become effective (and in one plant remain not very effective today) because management's choices were too heavily influenced by quality of work life considerations in the beginning.

In one case, for example, although stability of assignments and mastery of jobs was necessary to get the plant's new technology under control, employees were permitted to move among jobs and learn multiple skills that would advance their pay. Management later recognized that it had erred in not continuously keeping economic as well as human considerations in mind.

Conversely, I am aware of some abortive job redesign efforts in which management strictly viewed worker satisfaction either as a means to improve productivity or as an incidental by-product. Not surprisingly, management's orientation affected not only what changes were made but also workers' attitudes toward the changes. Many union officials believe it unwise to be publicly committed to productivity as well as to quality of work life goals lest the former be identified with speedups and other activities that achieve productivity at the workers' expense. Nevertheless, union officials often implicitly acknowledge the legitimacy of improved business results.

A commitment to dual outcomes is congruent with the values increasingly held by knowledgeable people, but also it has proved to be the most practical approach to making significant advances toward either end. Consider the point negatively. When changes in the work structure do not improve the work environment from a human perspective, they will not increase employees' contribution to the business; likewise, changes in work structure that require managers to relate differently to workers but do not also benefit the business are not as likely to be sustained by those managers over time.

One should not confuse a dedication to achieving both results with the assumption that meeting one will guarantee the other; morale and productivity are not necessarily linked. Morale can be enhanced in any number of ways. Rather, a commitment to dual objectives sets in motion a search for the limited set of changes that will promote both human and economic ends.

Some issues will inevitably not yield to dual orientation. Planners and managers will have to make trade-off decisions in areas where achieving human goals can occur only at the expense of the business, and vice versa. Nevertheless, it is more important for those involved in work improvement to recognize that in most work structures there is an abundance of opportunities to make changes that will advance both objectives.

What Do Workers Really Want from Work?

Individuals and groups will always express broad differences in the types of work structure they prefer. Therefore, as the multiple-level framework indicates, the ideal culture and the design features of the work structure need to be responsive to the employee population at a given location. Even though researchers and managers are learning which questions about employees' needs and preferences will provide good guidelines to practice, they continue to ask a few either–or questions, which are more confusing than helpful.

Observers often ask variations of the following question: "Are people motivated more by intrinsic factors, such as tasks that use and develop their skills, or by extrinsic factors, such as variable pay for performance and the prospect of advancement?" Both kinds of factor are important, albeit one may be more important to any one group at any one time. The most significant question is how to integrate both extrinsic and intrinsic factors in a practical way.

My observation is that workers in innovative systems have not had to choose between more interesting work and more pay; and that where intrinsic satisfaction has increased, the pay has been improved, reflecting the workers' greater contribution. As Irving Bluestone of the UAW has said of the American worker,

> While his rate of pay may dominate his relationship to his job, he can be responsive to the opportunity for playing an innovative, creative, and imaginative role in the production process.[4]

A related question people often ask is: "Are people more interested in finding meaning in the workplace or in minimizing the time spent there?" Although the answer to this question may add to our understanding of the sociology of work today, it is not a productive question for improving current practice. It is better to assume that the work force as a whole would like both in some measure.

But, even if some workers care more about time off than a meaningful work life, it may still pay to heed the lower priority issue because improving the meaning of the workplace may be much more feasible than reducing the workweek. Speculating about workers' desires also leads to the related myths about regional differences and the need for selective hiring. Each myth is built on the assumption that a relatively small subset of the work force has attitudes and talents compatible with work restructuring. I have heard managers assert, "It may work in a plant located in a small town in the Midwest, but workers in the South (or the Northeast, California, big cities, etc.) are different."

If an innovative plant is located in an abundant labor market where supervisors screen, say, six times as many applicants as they actually hire, then their myth may be: "Only one in six is a high achiever who will be receptive to the new work structure. It is okay to redesign work if you can be selective but not if you are in a tight labor market."

Fortunately, since projects are launched in all regions of the country, in both rural and urban areas, in both tight and abundant labor markets, and appear to have a degree of effectiveness not determined by these factors, belief in these myths is weakening.

What Economic Benefits Can One Expect?

Managers frequently ask: "How much productivity gain can one expect from work redesign?" Unfortunately, some advocates answer: "One should be able to achieve 15% to 20% improvement in productivity." The question itself is emphatically misdirected, and the response just cited is meaningless without knowing what index of productivity the questioner has in mind and whether it is appropriate. For example, the number of output units per work-hour may not be an important index when labor is a low fraction of total costs. Moreover, prior to analysis of the operations in question, one cannot assume a basis for the estimates.

An inquiry and response should focus on methods by which managers can answer the question for themselves. The form of potential gains will vary significantly according to the technology used. The magnitude of possible gains will depend on how well the unit is already performing and on whether the aspects of performance that can be improved are strongly influenced by employees' attitudes and skills. Finally, whether potential gains ever materialize depends on the quality of redesign ideas and their implementation.

The following examples illustrate how productivity indexes can take different forms:

1. A facility that warehouses and supplies engine parts to dealers and dealer chains could gain new accounts by speeding up its delivery response; it could add very profitable business if it could promise certain large national chains 48 hours versus 72 hours for delivery.

2. In a capital-intensive plant that machines casted parts, management determined that it was technically feasible to increase by 15% the maximum throughput of a $10 million segment of the technology manned by 10 employees. This rate has, however, been achieved only for brief periods of time because of the limitations of operating personnel. Running speeds and machine downtime play a similarly important role in other parts of this plant and strongly affect its competitiveness.

3. In a relatively high labor-intensive business, management was experiencing a high rate of turnover. The particular tasks, mostly assembly line jobs, did not require great skill, but learning the idiosyncracies of the company's many different products took a lot of time. While the new employees were learning to deal with these peculiarities, their higher scrap rates and lower labor efficiency significantly affected unit costs. As a result, the turnover costs were significant.

ASKING THE RIGHT QUESTIONS

To assess the potential of work improvements in the foregoing operations, one should ask: "How much difference would it make if workers cared more and knew more about this work?" Let us examine the first example in light of this question to show how one can begin to analyze the situation.

First, one needs some facts: the replacement engine parts center employs about 100 hourly workers; the pay is good for this type of work in the area; turnover is relatively low; and labor relations are amicable. Although workers do not especially identify with management and many are known to goof off whenever possible, they are not antagonistic.

After a preliminary analysis of the various ways in which performance is sensitive to employee motivation and knowledge, the management of the center estimated that:

1. Employees could reasonably handle a 10% additional volume, even allowing for increased time to be devoted to training and regular meetings. But the 10% savings would not create a net economic benefit because the wage increases reflecting greater job scope and skills would offset them.
2. The cost of errors (orders lost, wrong parts pulled, overages, underages, or damages in shipment due to carelessness) could be reduced by $100,000 per year.
3. The work system could reliably handle up to 25% of the facility's volume within a 48-hour response time, enabling the management to win over some additional accounts and increase the margins on some existing ones and thereby to add an estimated $200,000 more profit per year.
4. The potential benefits of $300,000 assumes a work force that cares more and knows more and that is amenable to flexibility in work assignments based on the needs of the business, the latter point being especially critical to reducing the center's response time.

The foregoing analysis illustrates good practice.

First, management identified particular points in the system where poor labor utilization, errors, and limitations in response time occurred. It did not rely on global hunches.

Second, by converting potential gains to annual dollar amounts, management could see the relative importance of error reduction and improved response time. Moreover, management could relate the benefits to other factors; for example, $300,000 would be a savings equal to 25% of the annual payroll.

Third, management understood these were potential benefits and not certain gains that would automatically flow from the adoption of some set of design techniques. Its ability to achieve any of these benefits depended on its ingenuity and skill. It always ran the risk that it would not be able to modify the work culture as intended.

Fourth, management knew that for any changes to be effective from a business standpoint, it would also have to improve the work from the workers' point of view.

Managers in the machining operation and assembly unit followed procedures similar to the one just outlined. However, their estimate of benefits took a different form. Because they could spread the large fixed interest and depreciated expenses, managers in the capital-intensive machining operation figured that increasing the output rate of finished parts by 15% would result in lower unit costs. The estimated annual savings represented 150% of the $140,000 payroll for the unit—that is, $210,000.

In the assembly line unit, the managers concluded that it was not feasible to reduce turnover significantly, that only modest improvements in scrap and labor efficiency were possible, and that costs associated with any changes contemplated would largely offset the estimated gains.

In cases such as those just described, management's analyses are limited by the same difficulties encountered in estimating the costs and benefits of untried technologies or management systems—that is, the estimates can prove to be incomplete, too optimistic, too conservative, and so on. Nevertheless, the analytic approach presented here illustrates the systematic and realistic efforts managers should make to assess the potential performance gains.

Which procedures a manager actually uses and the level of detail of the analysis is not the point. The important point is that planners have some systematic approach for assessing potential benefits that might accrue if the cultural ideals are actually realized. The methodology need not be elaborate.

Some Lessons from Experience

For those who consider undertaking new initiatives and promoting the spread of successful innovations to other units in the organization, I offer the following four guidelines. Though not comprehensive, they are nonetheless derived from observations of the contrasts between relatively effective work improvement efforts and less effective ones.

Attempt Work Improvement Because of Its Intrinsic Positive Values, Not Because It Might Be a Way to Avoid Unionization

Apart from the fact that I believe in the institution of collective bargaining, trying to avoid unionization has several drawbacks. One is that unions are more likely to join in efforts to adapt innovations to existing facilities if work patterns are not being used as an antiunion device in the new plants. Another is that, although most projects in the United States have been in nonunionized offices and plants, the amount of joint union–management cooperation is increasing. Such projects as Harman Industries, Weyerhaeuser, Tennessee Valley Authority, the Rushton Coal Mines, and Rockwell International attest to the benefit of cooperation.

As I stated earlier, GM and UAW have a very active program of work improvement. The approach contractually agreed on by the parties is oriented to quality of work life, but as the Tarrytown experience illustrates, management, union officials, and workers are all genuinely interested in the business results. Irving Bluestone, international vice-president of the UAW, describes the joint GM–UAW program as follows:

> The objective of our quality of work life program is to create a more participative and satisfying work environment. If, as a result of increased participation, unit costs are improved because turnover rates go down and product quality goes up, that is fine.
>
> But if a plant manager is thinking of a quality of work life project as a means for increasing productivity, we don't proceed. There are certain other constraints—people must not be compelled to work harder, changes must not result in workers getting laid off, and the local and national agreements remain inviolate. The projects must be from the ground up and participation voluntary on the part of workers. The first phase of all projects is to improve the climate of mutual respect between union and management; if this doesn't succeed, there is no basis to proceed on. Plant management and the local union must both be committed.[5]

During the past half dozen years, as work improvement activities have been growing in number, diversity, and visibility, both labor and management have encountered doubt within their own ranks. UAW officials have not found it easy to convince union members that the program is not a management gimmick to increase productivity and perhaps weaken the union.

At GM, managers at certain levels express concern that the program will result in a loss of authority and prestige. These fears are diminishing gradually but can flare up at any event that seems to support them. Still, the commitment at the top of both organizations has been extraordinary and is bolstered by a growing constituency of local managers and union officials who have had positive experiences.

According to Bluestone, very few projects have actually failed, but more time must pass before the majority of projects currently under way can be declared successes.

Recognize the Basic Difference Between Opportunities in New Facilities and Opportunities in Existing Ones

Once, most people assumed that the major innovations introduced in new plant start-ups could serve as inspirational and instructive examples for managements and union officials of established plants. I have concluded that providing examples of what was done in a new organization is not helpful in enabling managers of established units to visualize alternative futures for their units and is not an effective stimulus for developing a program for transforming them.

The reasons are severalfold and go beyond the fact that a particular work structure that is successful in a new plant may be inappropriate in an old one. More fundamentally, the processes of innovation (diagnosing, planning, inventing, and implementing) are significantly different for new and existing units. In established facilities, the level of aspiration for change and the time frame allotted for achieving it must be much more modest than in new facilities.

In selecting aspects of work structure that can be changed, planners need to be opportunistic—doing what they can when they can. Also, the main job of planners in old facilities is defrosting the old work culture and creating a sense of the potential for change. To do this, they need to give careful attention to the participative processes for deciding the direction and method of the change.

Fortunately, the literature is providing us with a growing number of instructive examples of productive change in established organizations. The Tarrytown plant is one such example.

Avoid Either-Or Conceptions of Work Organization

An example of this faulty thinking relates to the sources and types of controls: "Traditional systems rely on hierarchical controls. The innovative system is the opposite; therefore, it must rely on individual or team self-management." Another example of this thinking is: "If we need to rely on self-discipline and peer group pressure to minimize counterproductive behavior, then there is no place for management-administered discipline."

Indeed, as managers in these work systems have sooner or later discovered, a selective emphasis and sensible mixture of management techniques are called for. A number of organizations have had to go through a period of permissiveness before management discovered the need to set and enforce certain boundaries on the behavior of members of the company.

Managers make a related mistake when they assume that an organization at start-up can be at an idealized advanced state of development. Some plans for new plant organization neglect the important distinction between conceiving of the steady state design and designing the initial organization. These plants start up with workers and supervisors having roles and responsibilities that reflect the planners' idealized view of the mature organization. Workers lack the technical and human skills as well as the problem-solving capacities to perform effectively. Supervisors cannot merely "facilitate"—they must provide directive supervision.

Delegation is the cornerstone of new plant development. Such delegation must be rooted in careful diagnosis of the existing base of skills and capabilities in the work force and a realistic view of their ability to develop over time.

Do Not Advocate One Answer

Spread a way of looking for answers. Managers and planners need to inculcate their people with a way of thinking about the diagnosis and designing of innovative work structures, not the work structures themselves. This is a major implication of my three-level conception of work improvement activity. It is less appropriate (and sometimes counterproductive) to promote the spread of particular techniques—for example, enriched jobs, team concepts, productivity gain sharing—than it is to promote the diffusion of a diagnostic and innovative planning process.

Notes

1. See Ted Mills, "Europe's Industrial Democracy: An American Response," *HBR*, November–December 1978, p. 143.

2. See Richard J. Matteis, "The New Back Office Focuses on Customer Service," *HBR*, March–April 1979, p. 146.

3. See my article, "How to Counter Alienation in the Plant," *HBR*, November–December 1972, p. 70 (Chapter 29, this volume); "Participative Management at Work," an interview with John F. Donnelly, *HBR*, January–February 1977, p. 117; and Donald N. Scobel, "Doing Away with the Factory Blues," *HBR*, November–December 1975, p. 132 (Chapter 30, this volume).

4. See Irving Bluestone, "The Next Step Toward Industrial Democracy" (Detroit, UAW Paper 1972), p. 4.

5. Irving Bluestone, in personal conversation with the author.

Appendix

Principles Reflected in the Three-Level Conception of Work Innovation

Most effective work improvement efforts have reflected the following principles. I have induced them largely from experience rather than deduced them from social science theory.

1. In designing work structures, it is imperative to be absolutely committed to the results one chooses (shown on the far right of Exhibit 1). One

should become pragmatic in the choice of techniques to achieve these ends (shown on the far left of Exhibit 1).

2. Recognize that no universally applicable set of human preferences and priorities regarding quality of work life exists. Hypotheses about what would enhance human experience at work may be useful, provided that they are tested with the people in question and are revised or discarded and replaced on the basis of that experience. The same points apply to the determination of the business results that the work culture should promote.

3. Accept that most techniques affect business and human results indirectly, altering first the culture of the organization. Even if in their designs planners ignore cultural considerations, the latter will nevertheless surface as the most important elements of the operation. Participants and visiting observers are quick to appreciate the motivation, cooperation, problem solving, openness, and candor that often mark a successful effort in practice.

4. Imagine the attitudes, relationships, and capabilities that would promote both business achievement and quality of work life in a particular setting, and then use these cultural attributes as proximate criteria for guiding the design of the work structure. In many cases, duality of goals is absent, or the step of idealizing a work culture is omitted, or both. An elaborate methodology is not required, but a certain type of thinking is advantageous.

5. Be sure that at the technique level the many different elements of design and management practice—reward scheme, division of labor, performance reporting scheme, status symbols, and leadership style—are consistent with each other, each reinforcing or complementing the other. When these elements of the work structure send common or compatible signals, the culture will be internally consistent; if they send "mixed signals," people will feel ambivalent. Also, the more comprehensive the planned work structure and the more the design elements are aligned with each other, the more powerful the structure will be in shaping a distinctive work culture.

32
Quality of Work Life: Learning from Tarrytown

ROBERT H. GUEST

Currently, when business people and researchers talk or write about the beginnings of the human relations era in management, the name Hawthorne is invariably mentioned. In the future, when they talk about quality of work life, they will refer to Topeka, Kalmar, and Tarrytown. Each plant's experience with a quality of work life effort, essentially a structured program to involve workers in decisions affecting how they work, is unique. Each plant had different problems and different reasons for beginning a quality of work life program. Tarrytown, a GM car assembly plant in New York state, is perhaps the plant with the greatest number of people ever to have undergone such a program and is perhaps one that had the most to gain, for it was in a fairly sad economic state when the program began. This is the story of the developing and ongoing quality of work life program at Tarrytown, accented by quotes from the people involved.

Imagine that an executive of one of our largest corporations is told that one of the plant managers wants to spend over $1.6 million on a program that has no guarantee of any return in greater efficiency, higher productivity, or lower costs. Then imagine the reaction if the executive were told that the union is in on the program up to its ears and that the purpose of the program is referred to as "improving the quality of work life."

If the reader imagines that the average top corporate manager would say the plant manager had lost his or her senses and ought to be fired, the reader is probably in the majority. The striking fact, however, is that one particular executive, the head of what is probably the largest division of any manufacturing company in the world (18 plants and almost 100,000 employees) knew just what was going on and approved the idea enthusiastically.

This is the story of the General Motors car assembly plant at Tarrytown, New York. In 1970, the plant was known as having one of the poorest labor relations and production records in GM. In seven years, the plant turned around to become one of the company's better run sites.

Born out of frustration and desperation, but with a mutual commitment by management and the union to change old ways of dealing with the workers on the shop floor, a quality of work life (QWL) program developed at Tarrytown. "Quality of work life" is a generic phrase that covers a person's feelings about every dimension of work including economic rewards and benefits, security, working conditions, organizational and interpersonal relationships, and its intrinsic meaning in a person's life.

For the moment, I will define QWL more specifically as a *process* by which an organization attempts to unlock the creative potential of its people by involving them in decisions affecting their work lives. A distinguishing characteristic of the process is that its goals are not simply extrinsic, focusing on the improvement of productivity and efficiency per se; they are also intrinsic, regarding what the worker sees as self-fulfilling and self-enhancing ends in themselves.

In recent years, the QWL movement has generated wide-scale interest. Just since 1975, more than 450 articles and books have been written on the subject, and there are at least four national and international study and research centers focusing on quality of work life as such. Scores of industrial enterprises throughout the United States are conducting experiments, usually on a small scale; and in an eight-month world study tour a few years back of more than 50 industrial plants in Japan, Australia, and Europe, I found great interest in "industrial democracy."

So what is special about the Tarrytown story? First, it has the earmarks of success. Second, it illustrates some underlying principles of successful organizational change that can be applied in a variety of work environments. Third, although a number of promising experiments are going on in many General Motors plants and in other companies, this QWL program has involved more human beings—more than 3,800—than any other I know of. Finally, and this is speculative, I believe that Tarrytown represents in microcosm the beginnings of what may become commonplace in the future—a new collaborative approach on the part of management, unions, and workers to improve the quality of life at work in its broadest sense.

Tarrytown—the Bad Old Days

In the late 1960s and early 1970s, the Tarrytown plant suffered from much absenteeism and labor turnover. Operating costs were high. Frustration, fear, and mistrust characterized the relationship between management and labor. At certain times, as many as 2,000 labor grievances were on the docket. As one manager puts it, "Management was always in a defensive posture. We were instructed to go by the book, and we played by the book. The way we solved problems was to use our authority and impose discipline." The plant general superintendent acknowledges in retrospect, "For reasons we thought valid, we were very secretive in letting the union and the workers know about changes to be introduced or new programs coming down the pike."

Union officers and committeepersons battled constantly with management. As one union officer describes it, "We were always trying to solve yesterday's problems. There was no trust and everybody was putting out fires. The company's attitude was to employ a stupid robot with hands and no face." The union committee chairperson describes the situation from a personal viewpoint:

> When I walked in each morning I was out to get the personnel director, the committeeman was shooting for the foreman, and the zone committeeman was shooting for the general foreman. Every time a foreman notified a worker that there would be a job change, it resulted in an instant '78 (work standards grievance). It was not unusual to have a hundred '78s hanging fire, more than 300 discipline cases, and many others.

Another committeeperson adds,

> My job was purely political. It was to respond instantly to any complaint or grievance regardless of the merits, and just fight the company. I was expected to jump up and down and scream. Every time a grievance came up, it lit a spark, and the spark brought instant combustion.

Workers were mad at everyone. They disliked the job itself and the inexorable movement of the high-speed line—56 cars per hour, a minute and a half per operation per defined space. One worker remembers it well, "Finish one job, and you always had another stare you in the face." Conditions were dirty, crowded, and often noisy. Employees saw their forepersons as insensitive dictators, whose operating principle was "If you can't do the job like I tell you, get out."

Warnings, disciplinary layoffs, and firings were commonplace. Not only did the workers view the company as an impersonal bureaucratic machine, "They number the parts and they number you," but also they saw the union itself as a source of frustration,

> The committeeman often wrote up a grievance but, because he was so busy putting out fires, he didn't tell the worker how or whether the grievance was settled. In his frustration, the worker would take it out on the foreman, the committeeman, and the job itself.

In the words of both union and management representatives, during this period "Tarrytown was a mess."

Beginnings of Change

What turned Tarrytown around? How did it start? Who started it and why?

Because of the high labor turnover, the plant was hiring a large number of young people. The late 1960s was the time of the youth counterculture revolution. It was a time when respect for authority was being questioned. According to the plant manager,

> It was during this time that the young people in the plant were demanding some kind of change. They didn't want to work in this kind of environment. The union didn't have much control over them, and they certainly were not interested in taking orders from a dictatorial management.

In April 1971, Tarrytown faced a serious threat. The plant manager saw the need for change, and also an opportunity. The manager approached some of the key union officers who, though traditionally suspicious of management overtures, listened. The union officers remember liking what they heard, "This manager indicated that he wanted to create a philosophy of management different from what had gone on before. He felt there was a better way of doing things."

The plant manager suggested that if the union was willing to do its part, he would put pressure on his own management people to change their ways. The tough chairman of the grievance committee observed later that

> this guy showed right off he had a quality of work life attitude—we didn't call it that at that time—inside him. He was determined that this attitude should carry right down to the foremen, and allow the men on the line to be men.

The company decided to stop assembling trucks at Tarrytown and to shuffle the entire layout around. Two departments, Hard Trim and Soft Trim, were to be moved to a renovated area of the former truck line.

At first, the changes were introduced in the usual way. Manufacturing and industrial engineers and technical specialists designed the new layout, developed the charts and blueprints, and planned every move. They then presented their proposals to the supervisors. Two of the production supervisors in Hard Trim, sensing that top plant management was looking for new approaches, asked a question that was to have a profound effect on events to follow: "Why not ask the workers themselves to get involved in the move? They are experts in their own right. They know as much about trim operations as anyone else."

The consensus of the Hard Trim management group was that they would involve the workers. The Soft Trim Department followed suit. The union was brought in on the planning and told that management wanted to ask the workers' advice. Old-timers in the union report "wondering about management's motives. We could remember the times management came up with programs only to find there was an ulterior motive and that in the long run the men could get screwed." Many supervisors in other departments also doubted the wisdom of fully disclosing the plans.

Nevertheless, the supervisors of the two trim departments insisted not only that plans *not* be hidden from the workers but also that the latter would have a say in the setup of jobs. Charts and diagrams of the facilities, conveyors, benches, and materials storage areas were drawn up for the workers to look at. Lists were made of the work stations and the personnel to operate them. The supervisors were impressed by the outpouring of ideas: "We found they did know a lot about their own operations. They made hundreds of suggestions and we adopted many of them."

Here was a new concept. The training director observes,

> Although it affected only one area of the plant, this was the first time management was communicating with the union and the workers on a challenge for solving *future* problems and not the usual situation of doing something, waiting for a reaction, then putting out the fires later.

The union echoes the same point: "This demonstrated how important it is to solve problems before they explode. If not solved, then you get the men riled up against everything and everybody."

Moving the two departments was carried out successfully with remarkably few grievances. The plant easily made its production schedule deadlines. The next year saw the involvement of employees in the complete rearrangement of another major area of the plant, the Chassis Department. The following year a new car model was introduced at Tarrytown.

Labor–Management Agreement

In 1972, Irving Bluestone, the vice president for the General Motors Department of the United Automobile Workers Union (UAW), made what many consider to be the kick-off speech for the future of the quality of work life movement. Repeated later in different forms, he declared:

> Traditionally management has called upon labor to cooperate in increasing productivity and improving the quality of the product. My view of the other side of the coin is more appropriate; namely, that management should cooperate with the worker to find ways to enhance the dignity of labor and to tap the creative resources in each human being in developing a more satisfying work life, with emphasis on worker participation in the decision-making process.[1]

In 1973, the UAW and GM negotiated a national agreement. In the contract was a brief "letter of agreement" signed by Bluestone and George

Morris, head of industrial relations for GM. Both parties committed themselves to establishing formal mechanisms, at least at top levels, for exploring new ways of dealing with the quality of work life. *This was the first time QWL was explicitly addressed in any major U.S. labor–management contract.*

The Tarrytown union and management were aware of this new agreement. They had previously established close connections with William Horner of Bluestone's staff and with James Rae, the top corporate representative in the Organization Development Department. It was only natural that Tarrytown extend its ongoing efforts within the framework of the new agreement. Furthermore, Charles Katko, vice president and general manager of the GM Assembly Division, gave his enthusiastic endorsement to these efforts.

Local issues and grievances, however, faced both parties. In the past, it had not been uncommon for strike action to be taken during contract negotiations. The manager and the union representatives asked themselves, "Isn't there a better way to do this, to open up some two-way communication, gain some trust?" The union president was quick to recognize

> that it was no good to have a "love-in" at the top between the union and management, especially the Personnel Department. We had to stick with our job as union officers. But things were so bad we figured "what the hell, we have nothing to lose."

The union president's observation about that period is extremely significant in explaining the process of change that followed:

> We as a union knew that our primary job was to protect the worker and improve his economic life. But times had changed and we began to realize we had a broader obligation, which was to help the workers become more involved in decisions affecting their own jobs, to get their ideas, and to help them to improve the whole quality of life at work beyond the paycheck.

The negotiations were carried out in the background of another effort on management's part. Delmar Landen, director of organizational research and development at General Motors, had been independently promoting an organizational development effort for a number of years. These efforts were being carried out in many plants. Professionally trained communication facilitators had been meeting with supervisors and even some work groups to solve problems of interpersonal communication.

What General Motors was attempting to do was like the OD programs that were being started up in many industries and businesses in the United States. But, as with many such programs, there was virtually no union involvement. As the training director put it,

Under the influence of our plant manager, the OD program was having some influence among our managers and supervisors, but still this OD stuff was looked upon by many as a gimmick. It was called the "happy people" program by those who did not understand it.

And, of course, because it was not involved, the union was suspicious.

Nevertheless, a new atmosphere of trust between the union and the plant manager was beginning to emerge. Local negotiations were settled without a strike. There was at least a spark of hope that the Tarrytown mess could be cleaned up. Thus the informal efforts at Tarrytown to improve union–management relations and to seek greater involvement of workers in problem solving became "legitimatized" through the national agreement and top level support. Other plants would follow.

The Testing Period

In April 1974, a professional consultant was brought in to involve supervisors and workers in joint training programs for problem solving. Management paid the fees. The consultant talked at length with most of the union officers and committeemen, who report that "we were skeptical at first but we came to trust him. We realized that if we were going to break through the communications barrier on a large scale, we needed a third party."

The local union officials were somewhat suspicious about "another management trick." But after talking with Solidarity House (UAW's headquarters), they agreed to go along. Both parties at the local level discussed what should be done. Both knew it would be a critical test of the previous year's preliminary attempts to communicate with one another on a different plane. Also, as one union person says, "We came to realize the experiment would not happen overnight."

Management and the union each selected a coordinator to work with the consultant and with the supervisors, the union, and the workers. The consultant, with the union and the management coordinators, proposed a series of problem-solving training sessions to be held on Saturdays, for eight hours each day. Two supervisors and the committeepersons in the Soft Trim Department talked it over with the workers, of whom 34 from two shifts volunteered for the training sessions that were to begin in late September 1974. Management agreed to pay for six hours of the training, and the workers volunteered their own time for the remaining two hours.

Top management was very impressed by the ideas being generated from the sessions and by the cooperation from the union. The regular repairpersons were especially helpful. Not long after the program began, the workers began developing solutions to problems of water leaks, glass breakage, and molding damage.

Layoff Crisis

In November 1974, at the height of the OPEC oil crisis, disaster struck. General Motors shut down Tarrytown's second shift, and laid off half the work force—2,000 workers. Workers on the second shift with high seniority "bumped" hundreds of workers on the first shift. To accommodate the new schedule, management had to rearrange jobs and work loads the entire length of the two miles of main conveyors, feeder conveyors, and work stations. A shock wave reverberated throughout the plant, not just among workers but supervisors as well. Some feared the convulsion would bring on an avalanche of '78s—work standards grievances—and all feared that the cutback was an early signal that Tarrytown was being targeted for permanent shutdown. After all, it was one of the oldest plants in General Motors and its past record of performance was not good.

However, the newly developing trust between management and the union had its effects. As the union president puts it, "Everyone got a decent transfer and there were surprisingly few grievances. We didn't get behind. We didn't have to catch up on a huge backlog."

What did suffer was the modest and fragile quality of work life experiment. It was all but abandoned. Many workers who had been part of it were laid off, and new workers "bumping in" had not been exposed to it. Also, a number of persons in the plant were not too disappointed to see it go. Some supervisors, seeing worker participation as a threat to their authority, made wisecracks such as "All they are doing is turning these jobs over to the union." Some committeepersons felt threatened because the workers were going outside the regular political system and joining with representatives of management in solving problems.

In spite of the disruption of plant operations, the quality of work life team, the plant manager, and the union officials were determined not to give up. Reduced to a small group of 12 people during 1975, the team continued to work on water leaks and glass breakage problems. This group's success as well as that of some others convinced both parties that quality of work life had to continue despite a September 1975 deadline, after which management would no longer foot the bill on overtime.

During this period all parties had time to reflect on past successes as well as failures. The coordinators (one from the union and one from management) had learned a lesson. They had expected too much too soon: "We were frustrated at not seeing things move fast enough. We got in the trap of expecting 'instant QWL.' We thought that all you had to do was to design a package and sell it as you would sell a product."

Also, during this period, the grapevine was carrying a powerful message around the plant that something unusual was going on. The idea of involving workers in decisions spread and by midyear the molding groups were redesigning and setting up their own jobs. Other departments followed later.

THE TESTING PERIOD

At this time everyone agreed that if this program were to be expanded on a larger scale, it would require more careful planning. In 1975, a policy group made up of the plant manager, the production manager, the personnel manager, the union's top officers, and the two QWL coordinators was formed. The program was structured so that both the union and management could have an advisory group to administer the system and to evaluate the ideas coming up from the problem-solving teams. Everyone agreed that participation was to be entirely voluntary. No one was to be ordered or assigned to any group. Coordinators and others talked with all of the workers in the two departments.

A survey of interest was taken among the 600 workers in the two volunteering departments; 95% of these workers said they wanted in. Because of the large number that wanted to attend, pairs of volunteers from the ranks of the union and management had to be trained as trainers. Toward the middle of the year, a modified program was set up involving 27 off-time hours of instructional work for the 570 people. Four trainers were selected and trained to conduct this program, two from the union and two from management.

A second crisis occurred when the production schedule was increased to a line speed of 60 cars per hour. Total daily output would not be enough to require a second shift to bring back all the laid-off workers. Instead, the company asked that 300 laid-off workers be brought in and that the plant operate on an overtime schedule. Ordinarily the union would object strongly to working overtime when there were still well over 1,000 members out on the street. "But," as the union president puts it, "we sold the membership on the idea of agreeing to overtime and the criticism was minimal. We told them the survival of the plant was at stake."

Full Capacity

Despite the upheavals at the plant, it seemed that the quality of work life program would survive. Then, a third blow was delivered. Just as 60 workers were completing their sessions, the company announced that Tarrytown was to return to a two-shift operation. For hundreds of those recalled to work, this was good news. Internally, however, it meant the line would have to go through the same musical chair game it had experienced 14 months earlier when the second shift was dropped.

Workers were shuffled around according to seniority and job classification. Shift preferences were granted according to length of service. With a faster line speed than before, the average worker had fewer operations to perform but those the worker did perform were done at a faster pace. In short, because of possible inequities in work loads, conditions were ripe for another wave of work standards grievances. Happily, the union and management were able to work out the work-load problems with a minimum of formal grievances.

But again the small partially developed QWL program had to be put on ice. The number of recalled workers and newly hired employees was too great, and turnover was too high among the latter for the program to continue as it had been. Capitalizing on the mutual trust that had been slowly building up between them, management and the union agreed to set up an orientation program for newly hired employees—and there were hundreds of them. Such a program was seen as an opportunity to expose new workers to some of the information about plant operations, management functions, the union's role, and so forth. At one point, the union even suggested that the orientation be done at the union hall, but the idea was dropped.

The orientation program was successful. Some reduction in the ratio of "quits" among the "new hires" was observed. The union president did feel that "we had set a new tone for the new employee and created a better atmosphere in the plant."

Brave New World

Early the next year, 1977, Tarrytown made the "big commitment." The QWL effort was to be launched on a plant-wide scale involving approximately 3,800 workers and supervisors. Charles Katko, vice president for the division and UAW's top official, Irving Bluestone, gave strong signals of support. The plant manager retired in April and was replaced by the production manager. The transition was an easy one because the new manager not only knew every dimension of the program but also had become convinced of its importance.

The policy committee and the quality of work life coordinators went to work. In the spring of 1977, all the top staff personnel, department heads, and production superintendents went through a series of orientation sessions with the coordinators. By June, all middle managers and first-line supervisors (general foreperson and forepersons) were involved. Thus by the summer of 1977 more than 300 members of Tarrytown management knew about the QWL approach and about the plans for including 3,500 hourly employees. All union committeepersons also went through the orientation sessions.

Also, during mid-1977, plans were underway to select and train those people who would eventually conduct the training sessions for the hourly employees. More than 250 workers expressed an interest in becoming trainers. After careful screening and interviewing, 11 were chosen. A similar process was carried out for supervisors, 11 of whom were subsequently selected as trainers, mostly from among forepersons.

The two coordinators brought the 22 designated trainers together and exposed them to a variety of materials they would use in the training itself.

The trainers conducted mock practice sessions which were videotaped so they could discuss their performance. The trainers also shared ideas on how to present information to the workers and on how to get workers to open up with their own ideas for changing their work environment. The latter is at the heart of the quality of work life concept.

The trainers themselves found excitement and challenge in the experience. People from the shop floor worked side by side with members of supervision as equals. At the end of the sessions, the trainers were brought together in the executive dining room for a wrap-up session. The coordinators report that "they were so charged up they were ready to conquer the world!"

Plant-Wide Program

On September 13, 1977 the program was launched. Each week, 25 different workers (or 50 in all from both shifts) reported to the training rooms on Tuesdays, Wednesdays, and Thursdays, for nine hours a day. Those taking the sessions had to be replaced at their work stations by substitutes. Given an average hourly wage rate of more than $7 per attendee and per replacement (for over 3,000 persons), one can begin to get an idea of the magnitude of the costs. Also, for the extra hour above eight hours, the trainees were paid overtime wages.

What was the substance of the sessions themselves? The trainee's time was allocated to learning three things: first, about the concept of QWL; second, about the plant and the functions of management and the union; third, about problem-solving skills important in effective involvement.

At the outset, the trainers made it clear that the employees were not to use the sessions to solve grievances or to take up labor–management issues covered by the contract itself. The presentation covered a variety of subjects presented in many forms with a heavy stress on participation by the class from the start. The work groups were given a general statement of what quality of work life was all about. The union trainer presented materials illustrating UAW Vice President Bluestone's famous speech, and the management trainer presented a speech by GM's Landen stressing that hourly workers were the experts about their own jobs and had much to contribute.

The trainers used printed materials, diagrams, charts, and slides to describe products and model changes, how the plant was laid out, how the production system worked, and what the organizational structures of management and the union are. Time was spent covering safety matters, methods used to measure quality performance, efficiency, and so forth. The work groups were shown how and where they could get any information they wanted about their plant. Special films showed all parts of the plant with a particular worker "conducting the tour" for his or her part of the operation.

To develop effective problem-solving skills, the trainers presented simulated problems and then asked employees to go through a variety of some experiential exercises. The training content enabled the workers to diagnose themselves, their own behavior, how they appeared in competitive situations, how they handled two-way communications, and how they solved problems. By the final day "the groups themselves are carrying the ball," as the trainers put it, "with a minimum of guidance and direction from the two trainers."

Trainers took notes on the ideas generated in the sessions and at the end handed out a questionnaire to each participant. The notes and questionnaires were systematically fed back to the union and management coordinators, who in turn brought the recommendations to the policy committee. The primary mode of feedback to their forepersons and fellow workers was by the workers themselves out on the shop floor.

Continuing Effort

Seven weeks after the program began in September 1977, just over 350 workers (or 10% of the work force) had been through the training sessions. The program continued through 1978, and by mid-December more than 3,300 workers had taken part.

When all the employees had completed their sessions, the union and management immediately agreed to keep the system on a continuing basis. From late December 1978 through early February 1979, production operations at Tarrytown were closed down to prepare for the introduction of the all-new 1980X model. During the shutdown, a large number of workers were kept on to continue the process.

In preparation for the shift, managers and hourly personnel together evaluated hundreds of anticipated assembly processes. Workers made use of the enthusiasm and skills developed in the earlier problem sessions and talked directly with supervisors and technical people about the best ways of setting up various jobs on the line. What had been stimulated through a formal organized system of training and communication (for workers and supervisors alike) was now being "folded in" to the ongoing planning and implementation process on the floor itself.

In evaluating the formal program, the trainers repeatedly emphasized the difficulties they faced as well as the rewards. Many of the men and women from the shop floor were highly suspicious at the start of the sessions. Some old-timers harbored grudges against management going back for years. Young workers were skeptical. Some of the participants were confused at seeing a union trainer in front of the class with someone from management.

In the early period, the trainers were also nervous in their new roles. Few of them had ever had such an experience before. Many agreed that their impulse was to throw a lot of information at the worker trainee. The trainers found, however, that once the participants opened up, they "threw a lot at us." Although they understood intellectually that participation is the basic purpose of the QWL program, the trainers had to experience directly the outpouring of ideas, perceptions, and feelings of the participants to comprehend emotionally the dynamics of the involvement process.

But the trainers felt rewarded too. They describe example after example of the workers' reactions once they let down their guard. One skeptical worker, for example, burst out after the second day, "Jesus Christ! You mean all this information about what's going on in the plant was available to us? Well, I'm going to use it." Another worker who had been scrapping with a foreperson for years went directly to the foreperson after the sessions and said, "Listen, you and I have been butting our heads together for a long time. From now on I just want to be able to talk to you and have you talk to me." Another worker used the free relief time to drop in on new class sessions.

Other regular activities to keep management and the union informed about new developments parallel the training sessions. Currently, following the plant manager's regular staff meetings, the personnel director passes on critical information to the shop committee. The safety director meets weekly with each zone committeeperson. Top union officials have monthly "rap sessions" with top management staff to discuss future developments, facility alterations, schedule changes, model changes, and other matters requiring advance planning. The chairman of Local 664 and the zone committeepersons check in with the personnel director each morning at 7:00 A.M. and go over current or anticipated problems.

After the Dust Settles

What are the measurable results of quality of work life at Tarrytown? Neither the managers nor union representatives want to say much. They argue that to focus on production records or grievance counts "gets to be a numbers game" and is contrary to the original purpose or philosophy of the quality of work life efforts. After all, in launching the program, the Tarrytown plant made no firm promises of "bottom line" results to division executives or anyone else. *Getting the process of worker involvement going was a primary goal with its own intrinsic rewards. The organizational benefits followed.*

There are, however, some substantial results from the $1.6 million QWL program. The production manager says, for example,

> From a strictly production point of view—efficiency and costs—this entire experience has been absolutely positive, and we can't begin to measure the savings that have taken place because of the hundreds of small problems that were solved on the shop floor before they accumulated into big problems.

Although not confirmed by management, the union claims that Tarrytown went from one of the poorest plants in its quality performance (inspection counts or dealer complaints) to one of the best among the 18 plants in the division. It reports that absenteeism went from 7¼% to between 2% and 3%. In December 1978, at the end of the training sessions, there were only 32 grievances on the docket. Seven years earlier there had been upward of 2,000 grievances filed. Such substantial changes can hardly be explained by chance.

Does this report on Tarrytown sound unreal or euphoric? Here are the comments of the most powerful union officer in the plant, the chairman of Local 664:

> I'm still skeptical of the whole thing but at least I no longer believe that what's going on is a "love-in" at Tarrytown. It's not a fancy gimmick to make people happy. And even though we have barely scratched the surface, I'm absolutely convinced we are on to something. We have a real and very different future. Those guys in the plant are beginning to participate and I mean really participate!

By May 1979 the Tarrytown plant, with the production of a radically new line of cars, had come through one of the most difficult times in its history. Considering all the complex technical difficulties, the changeover was successful. Production was up to projected line speed. The relationship among management, union, and the workers remained positive in spite of unusual stress conditions generated by such a change.

As the production manager puts it, "Under these conditions, we used to fight the union, the worker, and the car itself. Now we've all joined together to fight the car." Not only were the hourly employees substantially involved in working out thousands of "bugs" in the operations, but plans were already under way to start up QWL orientation sessions with more than 400 new workers hired to meet increased production requirements.

Tarrytown, in short, has proved to itself at least that QWL works.

Learning from Tarrytown

Although the Tarrytown story is, of course, unique, persons responsible for bringing about change in an organization might derive some useful generalizations and important messages from it. (See the Appendix following this article for a list of general observations on quality of work life.)

Bringing about change—any kind of change—is extraordinarily difficult in our modern organizations. It is challenge enough to introduce new machines, computers, management information systems, new organizational structures, and all the bureaucratic paraphernalia required to support our complex production systems. It is even more difficult to organize and stimulate people to accept innovations directed at greater efficiency. Perhaps most difficult of all, as one looks at the quality of work life process and Tarrytown as an example, is for managers, union officials, and even workers themselves to adjust to the idea that certain kinds of changes should be directed toward making life at work more meaningful and not necessarily toward some immediate objective measures of results.

Even when people become committed to this idea, starting the process is not easy. Witness, for example, how long it took to turn the Tarrytown ship around. Look at the roadblocks its people had to overcome; deep-seated antagonisms between management and labor and the impact of changes beyond the control of the organization itself—new facilities, new products, and personnel changes at all levels, especially among hourly workers. Just when the quality of work life efforts gained some momentum, an unanticipated event intervened and the program was stopped dead in its tracks—almost. Indeed, one gets the impression that the only constant was change itself.

Some observations are in order. Developing this climate for change takes extraordinary patience. It takes time. It calls for sustained commitment at all levels. In most of the efforts to change human behavior that I have observed directly, these characteristics are lacking. Managers and leaders are under pressure to change things overnight. They draw up a program, package it, press the authority button, set deadlines, then move. It all sounds so easy, so efficient, so American.

In changing the way Americans work, we have, as the chairman of Local 664 said, "barely scratched the surface." What went on at Tarrytown was only a beginning. The intrinsic nature of repetitive conveyor-paced jobs has not substantially changed. The commitment to quality of work life is strong at the local level and among some people at division and corporate levels, but it is not universal. Changes in management or new crises could threaten further developments. Nevertheless, a new atmosphere about change, and the worker's role in it, is clearly emerging. People feel they have some "say," some control over their work environment now and in the future.

The Tarrytown story may, however, reflect something important about quality of work life efforts springing up in many other places in the United States. Studies are showing that workers in our large rationalized industries and businesses are seeking more control over, and involvement in, the forces affecting their work lives. Due in part to the rising levels of education, changing aspirations, and shifts in values, especially among young people, I believe we are witnessing a quiet revolution in what people expect from work, an expectation that goes beyond the economic and job security issues that led to labor unrest in an earlier day.[2]

In parts of Europe, the response to this quiet revolution is manifest in broad-scale political efforts on the part of labor and government to gain greater control over the management of the enterprise itself. In the United States, the response is different.[3] Workers or their unions have given no indications that they wish to take over basic management prerogatives. As the Tarrytown story illustrates, what they want is more pragmatic, more immediate, more localized—but no less important.

The challenge to those in positions of power is to become aware of the quiet revolution at the workplace and to find the means to respond intelligently to these forces for change. What management did at Tarrytown is but one example of the beginnings of an intelligent response.

Notes

1. Irving Bluestone, "A Changing View of Union–Management Relationships," *Vital Speeches*, December 11, 1976.

2. For recent confirmation based on survey data over a period of 25 years, see M.R. Cooper et al., "Changing Employee Values: Deepening Discontent," *HBR*, January–February 1979, p. 117.

3. For a fuller discussion of the differences between American and European responses to labor today, see Ted Mills's "Europe's Industrial Democracy: An American Response," *HBR*, November–December 1978, p. 143.

Appendix

Quality of Work Life—Things to Consider

What generalizations or principles might one derive from the Tarrytown story? The list below combines those of the participants themselves with my own observations about quality of work life experiments here and abroad. The list is not exhaustive. The first six are limited in general to organizations with collective bargaining agreements. The others have more universal applications.

1. For quality of work life to succeed, management must be wholly competent in running the business as a profit-making enterprise. When management lacks organizational competence and adequate technical expertise, no amount of good intentions to improve worker–union–management communication will succeed. Workers will not be willing to become involved knowing management lacks the competence to do anything about their ideas.

2. The union must be strong. The members must trust their leadership.

and this trust must exist within the framework of a democratic "political" process.

3. In most instances, management has to be the first party to initiate change, to "hold out the olive branch."

4. Quality of work life should never be used by either party to circumvent the labor–management agreement. The rights, privileges, and obligations of both parties should remain inviolate. Dealing with grievances and disputes can be made easier through quality of work life efforts, but at no time should management give up its right to manage nor the union its right to protect its members on matters related to wages, hours, benefits, and general conditions of employment.

5. Top management and top union officials must make an explicit commitment to support quality of work life.

6. Even with agreement at high levels and a demonstrated concern on the part of rank-and-file employees, it is essential that middle management and front-line supervisors (and shop stewards) not only know what is taking place but also feel they have a say in the change process. Supervisors naturally feel threatened by any moves to give subordinates greater power in determining how work is to be performed. Union representatives can perceive unilateral work participation as a threat to their political position.

7. A quality of work life program is unlikely to succeed if management's intention is to increase productivity by speeding up the individual worker's work pace or, if it uses the program *as such*, to reduce the work force through layoffs. Workers will quickly see such actions as unfair exploitation. This is not to say that cost savings from better quality performance, lower absenteeism and turnover, and better production methods should not be an expected consequence of the effort.

8. A program should be voluntary for the participants.

9. Quality of work life should not be initiated with a detailed master plan. It should start on a limited scale focused on the solution of specific problems, however small. It should be flexible.

10. At each step in developing a program, all small bottlenecks or misunderstandings must be talked out and solved on the spot. If set aside simply to get on with the "important" plans, the little misunderstandings can later explode with enough force to destroy the entire program.

11. It is not enough to expose employees to the principles of effective interpersonal communication and problem-solving skills. There must be immediate opportunities available for them to use these skills in practical ways right in the job situation itself. Further follow-up action of some kind is necessary to serve as positive reenforcement to the employees.

12. Quality of work life efforts should not be thought of as a "program" with a finite ending. There must be a built-in momentum that is dynamic, on-going, and that can continue regardless of changes in the personnel in the organization. Once employees come to believe that they can

participate and do in fact become involved in solving problems, the process gains a momentum of its own.

There is an implied warning here. Management may have the *formal* power to drop quality of work life efforts summarily. Union officers may have the *political* power to scuttle such efforts. Both would be acting at their peril for, under quality of work life, the workers will have gained a unique power to influence substantially the quality of their own lives at work. To them there is no turning back.

33

Let First-Level Supervisors Do Their Jobs

W. EARL SASSER, JR. and FRANK S. LEONARD

Performing well as a first-level supervisor is like walking the circus high wire. In both positions, the ability to maintain one's balance when shifting forces pull in opposite directions is a measure of one's success. First-level supervisors must be able to harmonize the demands of management, the demands of the collective work force (often represented by unions), and the demands of workers with the requirements for doing the tasks at hand. These needs are more often than not conflicting and even at times mutually exclusive. First-level supervisors usually have mixed emotions about their situation and often lose their sense of identity as they try to perform this precarious balancing act. Today these supervisors are part of management, but chances are they were once among the employees they are now trying to supervise. Although first-level supervisors have the responsibility for implementing the goals of upper management, their organizational authority to carry out the necessary actions is frequently unclear and often insufficient. By allowing these lowest-level managers to use the levers of influence inherent in their position, higher-level managers will be improving the performance of the whole organization.

"Our supervisors can probably have more influence on our productivity, worker absenteeism, product quality, morale of our work force, labor relations, and cost reduction than any other group in the company," the vice president of personnel at a manufacturing company recently told us. We were there to do research on the function of first-level supervisors.

"If we don't do something soon, we're going to lose our best foremen—it's no wonder that they're turned off, given the pressures they have to live with," the plant manager at the same company said.

Being a first-level supervisor is one of the most difficult, demanding, and challenging jobs in any organization. Buried in an organizational web, this person must be adroit at administering a unit and at perceiving which, among all the daily tasks delegated downward, are the most important to accomplish. Through such administrative competence, he or she must be able to link the unit's accomplishments to the functioning of other organizational subunits.

Even at the first level, a supervisor must be able to think and act in terms of the total system of operation.[1] This includes defining and assigning priorities, planning and organizing, and programming and coordinating the operating tasks of a department so that the objectives of both the department and the company as a whole are achieved.

Furthermore, the first-level supervisor must excel in interpersonal skills. More and more, the trend is for employees to be a heterogeneous group of individuals, many of whom are not especially dedicated to their jobs, their departments, or their companies. Handling the variety of attitudes and values in this multiple-generation worker base has become extremely difficult. Also, the work force is aging as the post-World War II babies reach middle age, and challenges to mandatory retirement are widening the age spread.

Along with age, the increase in working women and minorities has become a factor in the work force. Supervisors must learn to deal with these new workers and yet guard against discriminatory practices. Also, the fact that the educational level of the work force has continued to rise means that the supervisor does not often maintain an educational advantage over the worker. (In 1977, more than 90% of the U.S. population between 20 and 29 were high school graduates, and 8 million Americans were enrolled in colleges and universities.)

Challenge of the First Level

In addition to the increasing pressure for administrative and clerical efficiency at the first level, two areas of supervisory competence that are continually problematic are human relations and technical knowledge. Workers are no longer conformists who without question accept the rules and procedures that management lays down. No longer do they take authority at face value.

Human Relations

Many workers view their jobs as necessary evils to provide the resources for fulfilling their lives in leisure time, which they are pressing harder and harder to increase. It is the first-level supervisor who must cope with such workers face to face and day to day. Being able to communicate effectively is vital. In a recent study of 25 middle managers, the materials manager of an electrical company expressed a theme common to the group: "Being able to work with people is the most important characteristic a first-level supervisor can have. I can buy technological expertise, but it's hard to find someone with good basic communication skills."[2]

Technical Competence

First-level supervisors must of course have technical competence in the areas they supervise. The supervisors must be able to perform the specific tasks they ask their workers to do and must, to some degree, understand the equipment and the process technology they manage.

Technological changes continue to occur rapidly, though, and supervisors can no longer hope to understand completely all the complex equipment and processes of which they are in charge. New products and new processes abound—computers, plastic molding, electronic test equipment, temperature and pressure-sensitive distillation, component machining, complex metal alloy foundries, acoustic devices, and synthetic rubber, to name but a few.

Having good technical skills gives supervisors both enough understanding to deal with the many specialists brought in to accomplish the units' objectives and the ability to train subordinates in their tasks.

Mix of Skills

Despite the difficulty and challenge of the first-level supervisor's job, many upper-level managers fail to appreciate its merits or its requirements. Although most of them agree that the human relations aspect of the job is important, they often promote a supervisor for such skills as record keeping. Although the mix of skills needed for each position varies from situation to situation, managers often fail to perceive the particularity of the task required, the type of people being supervised, or the stage the organization is going through.

One general supervisor at an auto manufacturing plant said: "For some reason, our supervisors just aren't able to switch between our departments; they may be great in materials handling, but they have a hell of a time in welding. It's almost like it's a different job!" Supervising highly skilled welders requires a different blend of skills than supervising semiskilled laborers.

To overcome the growing pains and technical difficulties of starting up production or of making a major product changeover, the supervisor must emphasize technical skills rather than interpersonal relations, which must be downplayed in the rush to finish technical tasks. During stable periods, however, administrative and interpersonal skills rise in importance in the first-level supervisor's order of priorities.

Decline of the Position

Although a person serving as a first-level supervisor is performing a major function, the position has often been labeled "the man in the middle," "the forgotten man," "the master and victim of double talk," and "the marginal man." Such descriptions not only indicate the male domination of the position but also its degeneration to one of "being on the edge," "being victimized," and "fading in importance."[3]

Confusion of Roles

The causes for the decline of the first-level position are manifold. Over the years confusion has developed about what to expect of supervisors and what role to give them. The position has two very separate roots.

One root is the master craftsperson of the past. This person was a real entrepreneur—bidding on jobs, hiring employees to perform required tasks, and managing their progress. Like the subcontractor of today, the master craftsperson took on the difference between the revenues for jobs completed and the costs associated with those jobs as personal profits or losses. The master craftsperson's skill and knowledge of the job were the key ingredients on which these profits or losses depended.

The other root is the "lead man," the foreperson of a gang of workers performing manual labor. Like the lead dog or lead horse of a work team, the lead man served as an example for other work-crew members. He often set the pace by calling out a cadence to synchronize the crew's physical movements. The lead man was part of the actual work, and yet he was responsible for the behavior of the whole group.

The amalgamation of these two roles has resulted in today's confusing hybrid. Peter Drucker notes: "From the master craftsman the supervisor of today has largely inherited what is expected of him. From the lead man he has, however, largely inherited his actual position."[4]

The word *supervisor* has conflicting connotations. A supervisor not only commands, directs, controls, and inspects but also takes responsibility for, leads, shepherds, administers, guides, consults, and cares for. Just how the connotation varies from situation to situation and from person to person is in itself a reason for the ambiguity—and the decline—of the first-level supervisor's role.

Specialization of Skills

Another cause of the decline is the rise of staff service departments in such fields as quality control, production planning and control, industrial engineering, personnel, maintenance, and cost accounting. Most of these staff service departments were created to handle the new demands of scientific management in the 1920s and 1930s. The more recent growth of specialization and professionalization within companies has been noted as an important trend of the twentieth century.[5]

Each staff group wants to have a say in the job, to establish a power base, and to protect its area of expertise. Its success in meeting these needs has eroded the authority of first-level supervisors. As Thomas Patten points out:

> The foreman found himself in effect surrounded by specialists who were taking over parts of what had formerly been his job. He was left with little to do except administer the plans and programs devised by the service departments.[6]

Rise of Unions

A further influence has been the rise of the unions, which have stripped supervisors in unionized plants of much of their remaining authority. Rather than always dealing directly with workers, the supervisors have become more dependent on, and are quite often the target of, the union. It has become increasingly difficult to hire or fire without union involvement. Hiring often has to come from the union list; firing has to follow a strict interpretation of the contract, often requiring a number of warnings. Layoffs are normally by seniority, not according to productivity. Disciplinary action was formally taken away from the prerogative of the first-level supervisor's judgment and set down in black and white.

And, even when the strict letter of the contract is followed, grievances are often filed by the union steward. The company, in some instances, has failed to support the supervisor in a legitimate claim against the union. When such actions have eroded the power base of first-level supervisors, they have been bypassed by workers and union officials, and workers have taken their problems to the union steward instead. The first stage of any grievance procedure—talking with the supervisor in charge—has become lip service. "Don't talk to him, he doesn't know anything" has become a self-fulfilling prophecy on the shop floor.

The union has been a coconspirator in usurping the first-level supervisor's prerogative to set work standards. Setting work standards—the one domain supervisors had prided themselves on and that had been considered *their* territory—has become the domain of the industrial engineering and industrial relations departments working with the union.

The union has also served to lower the prestige of the first-level supervisor by winning large wage increases, improved working conditions, and job security for its members. First-level supervisors have seen workers' wages rise more rapidly than their own; they have not had the same job security that the workers have fought for; they can be fired or demoted at a moment's notice; and the Taft-Hartley Act effectively precludes them from organizing.

Crossfire of Demands

The first-level supervisor is a "person caught between"—primarily between middle management and the work force. Both groups have very different values and priorities. Middle managers tend to be interested in cost, efficiency, and performance; workers tend to be more interested in wage rates, security, and comfort. Managers usually believe that hard work leads to advancement; workers often see little point in exerting themselves. To management, the labor contract and work rules seem restrictive; to labor, they seem protective from unreasonable management demands. Managers are concerned about the status of their positions; workers want recognition for work well done. Managers usually identify strongly with the company; workers often have little company loyalty.

The first-level supervisor is caught directly in a crossfire of values and priorities:

☐ The supervisor often does not know the objectives and policies of top management but heavily influences what management can accomplish.

☐ The supervisor is not part of the work force but depends heavily on its acceptance.

☐ The supervisor is in the first line of management but has little authority.

☐ The supervisor is a member of management but is far removed from the locus of decision making.

☐ The supervisor is limited by precedents and company culture but serves as the agent of change, without whose action little occurs in the company.

☐ The supervisor establishes standards and precedents but has little information or knowledge on which to base decisions.

☐ The supervisor is supposed to spend much time on interpersonal relationships but finds that much of that time is needed for record keeping.

☐ The supervisor is supposed to have a position of leadership but feels that leadership traits are suppressed because of the low self-image associated with the position.

☐ The supervisor is asked to identify with the values and aspirations of management but is at a dead end in career progress and development.

☐ The supervisor is usually young and deals with a young diverse new type of working person but is evaluated, trained, and rewarded by older, more conservative, more authoritarian supervisors.

This combination of role confusion, increase in staff services, overlap of power with the unions, and conflicting demands has reduced the position of first-level supervisor to just a shadow of its earlier form.

Success at the First Level . . .

As we can see from the often ambiguous and contradictory findings, success is difficult to identify. Sometimes it means productivity, sometimes satisfaction, and sometimes quality of work life. What is successful to employees is not always the same as what is successful to management, and that is not necessarily the same as what is successful to the first-level supervisor.

. . . According to Outside Observers

Our knowledge of what makes a successful supervisor is still quite incomplete. However, several studies have been carried out since the end of World War II.

A pioneering effort was a three-year study (1947–1949) conducted by Aaron Q. Sartain and Alton W. Baker in the offices of Prudential Insurance Company in Newark, New Jersey.[7] Two samples of matched pairs of work groups, 12 in each sample, were carefully selected. The samples were statistically alike with regard to number of men and women, marital status, average age, education, years of experience, salary grade, average distance from job to home, and average score on a battery of psychological tests for each pair of work groups.

However, the productivity differences between the two samples of work groups were statistically significant. Prior to the study, characteristics of the group leaders (supervisors) such as age, education, experience, and salary were thought to explain the differences in group productivity, but the study did not show that any of these factors makes a difference.

What it did show is that the high-productivity groups had more pride in their work than the low-productivity groups. Supervisors of high-productivity groups usually supervised in a more general manner than did supervisors of low-productivity groups. These latter supervisors closely watched their workers and gave greater amounts of instruction to them. Overinstruction was an easy way to oversupervise.

The supervisors of the low-productivity groups made a larger number of requests for promotions and salary increases, but a lower percentage of their requests was approved. The supervisors of the high-productivity groups were more critical than their counterparts.

Finally, and perhaps most important, the high-productivity supervisors talked about their people; the low-productivity supervisors talked about their jobs. The researchers classified the former group as "employee oriented," the latter as "work centered."

Sartain and Baker concluded their analysis of this study by noting that there are no ironclad rules for supervising.

The Institute for Social Research, under the direction of Rensis Likert, followed the Prudential study with a number of similar studies in a variety of settings. The findings from these studies can be summarized as follows:

☐ Supervisors viewed themselves more favorably than did their subordinates.

☐ Employees in the high-productivity groups liked their work less than their counterparts in the low-productivity groups. (A happy worker is not always the most productive worker.)

☐ As a general rule, the better supervisors spent more time in meetings with their employees.

☐ The supervisors of the more productive groups were judged by their employees to have greater influence with top management.

☐ Keeping subordinates informed, thinking of them as individuals, taking an interest in them, soliciting their opinions, and developing an atmosphere of trust were traits of the better supervisors.

In a later study, Saul W. Gellerman analyzed the jobs of 12 first-line supervisors in the packaging plant of a major food-processing company.[8] Gellerman followed each of the supervisors through the plant for an entire shift, noted every move, and questioned each course of action.

Gellerman found three supervisors (A, B, and C) particularly interesting. For each of these supervisors Gellerman detected a number of important elements of substance (what is done) and style (how it is done). How their superiors described their ways of supervising is shown in Exhibit 1.

What is certain is that the job of first-line supervisor is an extremely difficult and demanding one that requires shifting sets of information, skills,

Exhibit 1. Gellerman's Study on Quality of Supervision

	Supervisor		
	A	B	C
Rating by superiors	Mediocre	Good	Excellent
Substance	Checks location but not activity of subordinates; avoids insistence on prescribed procedures.	Frequently checks that employees are following correct procedures.	Concentrates attention where it will be most valuable.
Style	Regularly (albeit mechanically) uses first names in all employee contacts, tends to stay on foot rather than sit, and does much energetic rushing about.	Mixes gentle humor and reassurance with genuine pride in subordinates and has an easy positive relationship with people.	Reassures the discouraged, jollies along the angry, and leaves those who need no help pretty much alone; gives support as it is needed and only where it is needed.

and abilities. A successful supervisor seems to have the ability to balance the demands of task, employees, union, and management with his or her own needs for esteem and respect. But this balancing act takes place in a ring where not all of these demands can be met at once.

. . . According to Subordinates

Employees' attitudes often reveal the quality of supervision. To see what good first-level supervisors are like, it is useful to hear what subordinates want from their leaders. And to see what kind of supervision encourages the development of first-level supervisors, it is helpful to hear what they think of their managers.

A 1969–1970 survey of working conditions shows workers' satisfaction to be significantly correlated with the adequacy of resources and the competence of their supervisors.[9] Workers said that "people orientation" is important to them but is not the only thing that contributes to their satisfaction and productivity. Supervisors whom the workers viewed as effective combined "people management" with competence at the job, maintenance of high performance standards, and ability to supply workers with adequate help, equipment, and information related to their jobs.

In 1977, a national restaurant chain we interviewed undertook a confidential survey of its employees as part of an attempt to find the cause of a corporate sales plateau. The results of the survey were quite revealing.

The employees felt they had little job security since most of their rights depended on the esteem in which particular managers held them. The rate of turnover was high because the company had a policy of moving managers throughout the organization.

This rapid turnover of management personnel created another concern—each new manager seemed to expect a different standard or a different type of performance from employees.

There was a general feeling that managers who had been hourly employees in the past could deal better with the hourly employees than managers without hourly experience who had come straight through the corporate training program.

Managers were very quick to correct but slow to reward. Employees felt a definite lack of encouragement and praise.

Most employees felt that their performance had never been evaluated and that they did not know where they stood with the managers.

Several employees felt that it was common for them to get "bad shifts" as punishment and that they never found out whether they had done something wrong until the schedule was posted. Only when they inquired of management did they find out what had gone wrong.

Some expressed the feeling that they would like to go into management except that they saw the constant squeeze on managers—the conflict between the desire to be a "good guy" and the ability to produce the results that upper management demanded.

Overall, there was a strong correlation between how the employees ranked their unit managers (supervisors) and the performance of their units. The better supervisors produced better operating results.

. . . According to First-Level Supervisors

James W. Driscoll, Daniel J. Carroll, Jr., and Timothy A. Sprecher, in recent research, asked first-level supervisors about the amount of control they had over factors that motivated their subordinates. Their findings reaffirm the generalizations we presented earlier:

> Unfortunately, these first-level supervisors are still "the man in the middle." (The only change is a semantic update in gender.) They report no more control over the things they consider important than over the things they consider unimportant. It is quite likely this lack of control generates very high levels of frustration in first-level supervisors. They are held responsible for producing organizational results through their subordinates, but they lack control over the means to motivate these workers.[10]

Research we recently completed at several plants confirms that this attitude is widespread. A quote from a general foreperson summarizes a common complaint:

> They [upper management] have completely taken away our ability to get things done. We are still responsible for things that we have little control over—absenteeism, purchasing parts, quality, labor relations, maintenance. When we go to them with some problem, to get some help, all we get is, "Fix it, make it go away."

By giving control of these factors to first-level supervisors, middle and top management could help the supervisors motivate their subordinates. Driscoll, Carroll, and Sprecher discovered that the higher-level managers very accurately perceived this control discrepancy between what is important and what the first-level supervisors control: "Basically, these first-level supervisors seem to be in an unwinnable situation. They need help, and their bosses seem to know it."

Such a finding suggests that an important starting point in designing a program to make supervision effective is not changing the behavior of first-level supervisors but convincing those who manage them to yield some control.

Several researchers have recently studied what first-level supervisors want from their jobs. In their sample of 300 first and second-level supervisors at Allied Chemical Company, Michael J. Abhoud and Homer Richardson found that, out of 10 factors evaluated, first-level supervisors ranked interesting work first and salary second.[11] The second-level managers ranked salary first and interesting work second. Other factors ranked evenly by both levels of managers include, in descending order, chance for promotion, appreciation for work done, good working conditions, job security, loyalty of supervisors, "feeling in on things," tactful discipline, and help on personal problems.

In a survey of 65 first-level supervisors, Paul W. Cummings asked the respondents to list their motivations for accepting a first-level position. He noted that 90% of the respondents listed more money as a reason for accepting, 38% listed advancement, 48% listed the challenge of a new position, and 40% said they enjoy leadership positions.[12]

In a study of the attitudes of plant supervisors and salespeople, Sartain and Baker found that 78% of the salespeople rated their work favorably, whereas only 56% of the supervisors did so. The survey also indicated that the supervisors felt that they had fewer opportunities in their jobs for personal growth, development, and advancement than the salespeople.[13]

Obviously, the background of first-level supervisors has a lot to do with what they expect of this position, and their aspirations change as their service lengthens. A young process engineer, placed in a first-level supervisory position to be groomed for management, wants different things from the job than the 40-year-old lathe operator who finally cracks this lower rung of management.

Getting onto the lower rung is a time for remolding, but managers must be careful not to foster it in the form of stagnation. To expect that good wages is all that first-level supervisors want is a gross misleading simplification. They may learn, however, that this is all they can expect from management. The opportunity is there for management to encourage these individuals to see the first-level job as a transition and to expect some career development from it.

Improving the Situation

If first-level supervisors are to succeed, they must first establish the informal authority and interpersonal influence to back up the responsibility that comes with their position. Then first-level supervisors must continue to deal with their immediate supervisors and their work force in a manner that minimizes the conflicts between the two groups and permits them to retain the authority to perform effectively.

A major reason that a first-level supervisory job seems so difficult to master is the decrease in its traditional authority, an increase in dependency on other people to get the job done, and an apparent lack of other operating levers. Many see this erosion of formal authority and increasing dependence as a condition to be straightened out by increasing the first-level supervisor's authority. This is an unrealistic remedy. The decreasing power base of this lower-level manager is due to two pervasive organizational phenomena—division of labor into specializations and scarce resources of all types. Influencing people has to take forms other than exercising formal authority.

Supervisors to Use New Levers

Levers can be thought of as tools for influencing people in specific situations; none are applicable, however, to every situation. Levers such as job assignment, overtime, work conditions, equipment repair, and even hiring and firing are now often out of the supervisors' control. Very few discretionary items exist in the operating budget. What are some of the available levers today? How can first-level supervisors exercise influence and get the job done without using the more traditional levers? They can:

- ☐ Use positive reinforcement in the form of incentive schemes, job redesign, and awareness of psychological needs, including peer group acceptance and pride.

- ☐ Try negative reinforcement—both the traditional type (write up, fire, suspend) and more indirect means (job reassignment, job redesign, forced overtime).

- ☐ Delegate the resolution of a sticky problem to a shop steward or another union official.

- ☐ Appeal to workers for support on the basis of having gone out on a limb for them or having given over some prerogative to them in the past.

- ☐ Appeal to workers on the basis of understanding their position, since first-level supervisors once stood in their shoes.

- ☐ Appeal to workers on the basis of previously agreed-on goals and plans for achieving them.

As can be seen from this list, the available levers have shifted from administrative and technical competence to competence in interpersonal and group relations. This employee-oriented area requires the development of nontraditional authority and power bases and an understanding of the subtle processes of influence and persuasion. The first-level supervisor must have the ability to analyze and resolve the various dependencies that management and workers have.

As one director of production for a large defense subcontractor we visited said:

> I know in my gut that the real key to productivity that the general manager is pushing on and [the key] to better labor relations that the union is

IMPROVING THE SITUATION

yelling about is my supervisors. Any investment in them in training, communications, time, energy, attention, or plain listening gets one of the best returns in this company.

Managers to Shore Up the Position

Rather than contribute to the continued erosion of the first-level supervisory position, upper management should shore up the position by encouraging and training first-level supervisors to use available power sources to energize their situation. The end result would be an environment in which satisfaction and productivity abounds.

Upper management should recognize the difficulties associated with the position and help these supervisors develop a power base. Power can come from many sources: a mandate from management, personal confidence, a reputation for being able to tackle tough situations, loyalty of the work force, and dependence of the work force and management on the first-level supervisor's knowledge and skills.

Both middle and top managers should strive to create an organizational environment in which first-level supervisors can perform their function most effectively. There are a number of steps that managers above first-level supervisors can take to help:

1. Become aware of the actual working conditions of first-level supervisors. Don't assume that the key to present-day first-level supervisory effectiveness is the same as it was 10 or 20 years ago. "When *I* ran that assembly line, I did things this way" is a meaningless and misleading appeal. Things aren't the same!

2. Keep first-level supervisors informed about the corporate perspective as it relates to their operation. To relate to upper-level management and to present the management viewpoint to the work force, first-level supervisors must know some of the long-term goals of the corporation.

3. Keep first-level supervisors aware of upper-level managers' priorities. Without a clear idea of these priorities, first-level supervisors risk disapproval of their actions.

4. Educate first-level supervisors about new technological developments that might affect their job. Knowledge of the equipment and process technology they are supervising is essential for gaining credibility with both management and the work force and for exposing areas of potential improvement.

5. Provide feedback on how well first-level supervisors are meeting management's expectations.

6. Provide first-level supervisors an opportunity on company time to work together on specific problems affecting their job. Such teamwork not only generates solutions where the problems are but also allows peer inter-

action and learning as part of the job—something that most managers take for granted and that first-level supervisors' day-to-day routines lack.

7. Assist first-level supervisors in keeping the work force up to date on any information that may affect their job. A good in-plant communications program administered through first-level supervisors can pay handsome dividends.[14]

8. Provide training for first-level supervisors to improve their skills in dealing with people. Such a training program should include sessions on topics like being an effective listener, performance appraisal, motivation, disciplinary procedures, and labor relations.

9. Encourage first-level supervisors to stand up for and express their beliefs to upper management.

In essence then, the first-level supervisor must become more political in both skill and outlook. The real key is the ability to understand, influence, and merge the two worlds of management and workers. First-level supervisors are forced to walk the high wire and, like the circus, their act is now in the center ring.

Notes

1. See Robert Dubin et al., *Leadership and Productivity: Some Facts of Industrial Life* (Novato, CA, Chandler & Sharp, 1965), p. 75.

2. See Thomas De Long, "What Do Middle Managers Really Want from First-Line Supervisors?" *Supervisory Management*, September 1977, p. 8.

3. See F.J. Roethlisberger, "The Foreman: Master and Victim of Double Talk," *HBR*, September–October 1965, p. 22; Thomas A. Patten, Jr., *The Foreman: Forgotten Man of Management* (New York, American Management Associations, 1968); and Donald E. Wray, "Marginal Man of Industry: The Foreman," *American Journal of Sociology*, January 1949, p. 298.

4. Peter F. Drucker, *The Practice of Management* (New York, Harper & Row, 1954), p. 321.

5. See James G. March and Herbert A. Simon, *Organization* (New York, John Wiley, 1958); H.L. Wilensky, "The Professionalization of Everyone?" *American Journal of Sociology*, vol. 70, 1964, p. 137; and Charles A. Myers and John G. Turnbull, "Line and Staff in Industrial Relations," *HBR*, July–August 1956, p. 113.

6. Patten, *The Foreman*, p. 18.

7. See Aaron Q. Sartain and Alton W. Baker, *The Supervisor and His Job* (New York, McGraw-Hill, 1972) for a description and analysis of this study.

8. Saul W. Gellerman, "Supervision: Substance and Style," *HBR*, March–April 1976, p. 89.

APPENDIX

9. *The 1969–1970 Survey of Working Conditions: Chronicles of an Unfinished Enterprise*, edited by Robert P. Quinn and Thomas W. Mangione (Ann Arbor, University of Michigan, 1973).

10. James W. Driscoll, Daniel J. Carroll, Jr., and Timothy A. Sprecher, "The First-Level Supervisor: Still the Man in the Middle," *Sloan Management Review*, Winter 1978, p. 34.

11. Michael J. Abhoud and Homer Richardson, "What Do Supervisors Want from Their Jobs?" *Personnel Journal*, June 1978, p. 308.

12. Paul W. Cummings, "Occupation Supervisor," *Personnel Journal*, August 1975, p. 448.

13. See Sartain and Baker, *The Supervisor and His Job*.

14. Louis J. Gelfand, "Communicate Through Your Supervisors," *HBR*, November–December 1970, p. 101.

Appendix

When You Become Management*

I'm probably the youngest general foreman in the plant. . . . I'm in the chassis line right now. There's 372 people working for us, hourly. And thirteen foremen. I'm the lead general foreman. . . .

If you're a deadhead when you're an hourly man and you go on supervision, they don't have much use for you. But if they know the guy's aggressive and he tries to do a job, they tend to respect him. . . .

When I came here I wanted to be a utility man. He goes around and spot relieves everybody. I thought that was the greatest thing in the world. When the production manager asked me would I consider training for a foreman's job, boy! My sights left utility. I worked on all the assembly lines. I spent eighteen months on the lines, made foreman, and eighteen months later I made general foreman. . . .

A lot of the old-timers had more time in the plant than I had time in the world. Some of 'em had thirty, thirty-five years' service. I had to overcome their resentment and get their respect. I was taught one thing: to be firm but fair. Each man has got an assignment of work to do. If he has a problem [derived from the work], correct his problem. If he doesn't have a problem, correct him.

If an hourly man continued to let the work go, you have to take disciplinary action. You go progressively, depending on the situation. If it

---

*From Wheeler Stanley, quoted in *Working: People Talk about What They Do All Day and How They Feel about What They Do*. Copyright © 1972, 1974 by Studs Terkel. Reprinted by permission of Pantheon Books, a division of Random House, Inc.

was me being a young guy and he resented it, I would overlook it and try to get him to think my way. If I couldn't, I had to go to the disciplinary route—which would be a reprimand, a warning.

If they respect you, they'll do anything for you. Be aggressive. . . . I have to know each and every one of my foremen. I know how they react, all thirteen.

There's a few on the line you can associate with. I haven't as yet. . . . The more you get to know somebody, it's hard to distinguish between boss and friend. This isn't good for my profession. We work together, we live together. But they always gotta realize you're the boss.

I want to get quality first, then everything else'll come. The line runs good, the production's good, you get your cost and you get your good workmanship. When they hire in, you gotta show 'em you're firm. We've got company rules . . . that we try to enforce from the beginning.

The case begins with a reprimand, a warning procedure. A lotta times they don't realize this is the first step to termination. . . . If you catch a guy stealing, the first step *is* a termination. In the case of workmanship, it's a progressive period. . . .

There's an old saying: The boss ain't always right but he's still the boss. He has things applied to him from top management, where they see the whole picture. A lot of times I don't agree with it. . . .

Prior to going on supervision, you think hourly. But when you become management, you have to look out for the company's best interests. You always have to present a management attitude.

Out here, it's a big job. There's a lot of responsibility. It's not like working in a soup factory, where all you do is make soup cans. If you get a can punched wrong, you put it on the side and don't worry about it. You can't do that with a five-thousand-dollar car.

About the Authors

William J. Abernathy *is professor of business administration at the Harvard Business School. He is a leading authority on the automobile industry. Mr. Abernathy is the author of* The Productivity Dilemma: Roadblock to Innovation in the Automobile Industry *(Johns Hopkins Press, 1978) and co-author of the forthcoming* Wheels of Change: The De-Maturity of the U.S. Auto Industry.

Robert L. Banks *is Senior Vice President, Administration, for Americana Hotels Corporation (formerly Pick Hotels Corporation) in Chicago. His areas of responsibility include corporate development, personnel and training, central purchasing, central reservations, insurance, public relations, the gift shops division, and Americana Dining, a restaurant management group. He previously held responsibility for the corporate data center as well. Prior to joining Americana, Mr. Banks had been a consultant in the field of the management of service operations with clients in the hotel, restaurant, banking, educational, communications, and other industries. He began working with Americana in 1978 as a consultant, concentrating on corporate strategy and organizational development. Mr. Banks is the recipient of a B.S. degree from Lehigh University and a master's degree from Harvard University. He has co-authored articles in the* Harvard Business Review, *the* M.I.T. Sloan Management Review, *and the* Cornell Hotel Administration Quarterly.

John E. Bishop *is professor of business administration at the Harvard Business School, where he is a member of the production and operating management area. A specialist in decision theory and operations research, he has been involved in the Harvard Business School development of quantitative techniques in the analysis of business decisions. Currently he is doing research in manufacturing planning and control.*

ABOUT THE AUTHORS

Kim B. Clark *is an assistant professor at the Harvard Business School. He received the B.A., M.A. and Ph.D. degrees in economics from Harvard University. Mr. Clark served as an economist on the staff of John Dunlop during Mr. Dunlop's term as Secretary of Labor (1975–1976), and he has participated in consulting and executive teaching activities with numerous organizations. He is currently a research associate of the National Bureau of Economic Research. Mr. Clark's research interests are in the areas of industrial relations, technology and productivity, and operations strategy. He is currently involved in a major study of technology and the international competitive status of the U.S. auto industry for the National Academy of Engineering. A book,* Wheels of Change: The De-Maturity of the U.S. Auto Industry *(with William J. Abernathy and Alan M. Kantrow), is in preparation. His recent publications include "The Impact of Unionization on Productivity: A Case Study"* (Industrial and Labor Relations Review, *July 1980).*

David A. Garvin *is assistant professor of business administration at the Harvard Business School, where he specializes in industrial economics and production and operations management. He is the author of numerous articles on regulatory policy and industry analysis, and has also written* The Economics of University Behavior *(Academic Press, 1980). His current research focuses on the determinants and management of product quality.*

Donald Gerwin *is professor of business administration at the University of Wisconsin–Milwaukee. His research interests are in the management of technology, especially the problems of adopting and implementing new manufacturing equipment. Research appointments in France, Norway, and West Germany have provided opportunities to study these issues from an international perspective. Currently, he is participating in a joint international project to learn how computerized automation affects the structure and effectiveness of automobile factories. Mr. Gerwin is an associate editor of* Management Science, *and is on the editorial board of* Human Systems Management.

Peter Gilmour's *major interests are in the field of production and operations management, physical distribution, management/business logistics/materials management, and computer simulation. He teaches at Macquarie University (Australia) and is a past president of the Australian Physical Distribution Management Association. Professor Gilmour has conducted research into the relationships between corporate structure for business logistics and performance and between logistics structures and corporate strategy at the Harvard Business School. He has had extensive consulting experience in Australia and overseas. He has also held positions in systems analysis and distribution planning with Mobil Oil Australia in Melbourne and New York.*

ABOUT THE AUTHORS

Professor Gilmour has acted as coordinator of the Harvard Business School's Business Logistics Educators Workshop and is a member of the National Advisory Panel on Physical Distribution to the Productivity Promotion Council of Australia. He is a prolific writer and has published seven books, including The Management of Distribution, Physical Distribution Management in Australia, *and* Moving Goods and People, *eight monographs, and more than 25 professional papers.*

Robert H. Guest *is Professor Emeritus at the Amos Tuck School of Business Administration, Dartmouth College. He is the co-author of* The Man on the Assembly Line *(Harvard University Press, 1952; republished by Arno Press in 1979), one of the first books to outline the questions that quality of work programs attempt to solve. Mr. Guest's latest work is* Innovative Work Practices *(Pergamon Press, 1982).*

William K. Hall *is vice president of North American Marketing Operations at the Cummins Engine Company. He is responsible for the areas of parts and service, North American automotive and industrial business, North American field sales and service advertising and sales promotion, and the Lowest Total Cost Program. Previously he was a professor at the Graduate School of Business, University of Michigan. Mr. Hall has been a consultant on corporate strategy, general management problems, and executive development to a variety of corporations and government agencies. He received his Ph.D in business administration from the University of Michigan.*

Robert Hayes *is professor of business administration at the Harvard Business School, where he teaches courses in manufacturing strategy and production and operations management. Before his appointment to the Harvard faculty in 1966, he worked for I.B.M. and McKinsey and Company. He received his B.A. from Wesleyan University and his M.S. and Ph.D. degrees from Stanford University. Mr. Hayes' current research is concerned with the facilities investment and productivity improvement activities of manufacturing companies, both here and abroad. He recently completed two years as the Faculty Chairman for Harvard's International Senior Managers' Program in Vevey, Switzerland, where he studied and worked with a number of European companies.*

James L. Heskett *is Senior Associate for Educational Programs and 1907 Foundation Professor of Business Logistics, Graduate School of Business Administration, Harvard University. He has been a member of the faculty of The Ohio State University, having completed his Ph.D. at the Graduate School of Business, Stanford University. Professor Heskett is a member of the Board of Directors of Brooks Fashion Stores, Inc., the* Des Moines Register and Tribune, *and Distribution Centers, Inc.; the Scientific Advisory Board of ISTUD, an Italian business school; the Advisory Board of IPADE,* a Mexican business school; he has also served as a consultant to a number of companies. In 1974 Professor Heskett was the recipient of the John Drury Sheehan Award of the National Council of Physical Distribution Management for outstanding contributions to the field of physical distribution management. Professor Heskett was for a number of years on the editorial board of the Journal of Marketing Research and is now a member of the editorial boards of the Journal of Business Logistics and the Transportation Journal. Mr. Heskett is the author of Marketing (Macmillan, 1976), and co-author of Business Logistics (3rd edition, Wiley, 1983). He has also published articles in the Harvard Business Review, Journal of Marketing, Transportation and Distribution Management, and others.

William K. Holstein was a faculty member at the Harvard Business School from 1964 to 1972. From 1972 to 1981 he was the dean of the School of Business at the State University of New York at Albany. He is currently a professor of business administration at SUNY-Albany and the senior partner of Management Decision and Training Associates. In addition to continuing his interest in large-scale production planning and control systems, Mr. Holstein is currently doing research on computer-integrated manufacturing systems and serves on the National Academy of Sciences' Committee on Computer-Aided Manufacturing.

Ernest L. Huge is materials manager at Clark Equipment Co.'s Statesville, North Carolina plant, which produces axles for Clark's industrial and construction equipment as well as for other companies. Formerly he worked in all aspects of production and inventory control at a plant of NCR Corporation. Active in the American Production and Inventory Control Society, Mr. Huge is a frequent contributor to its publication, Production and Inventory Management Journal, and is a columnist for Purchasing World. He is co-author of Manufacturing Resources Management.

Frank S. Leonard is a management educator and researcher in the areas of manufacturing management, quality, and business strategy. He is currently involved in several projects with large American firms.

Robert A. Leone is a lecturer at the Kennedy School of Government at Harvard University. His research focuses on the consequences of business regulation and government policy for strategic business decisions. Mr. Leone served in Washington with the President's Council of Economic Advisers and has consulted with numerous private firms and government agencies. His most recent articles include "Toward a More Effective Industrial Policy" (Harvard Business Review, November–December 1981) and "Energy Policy and Corporate Strategy in the Automobile Industry" (Annual Review of Energy, 1982), both with S. Bradley.

ABOUT THE AUTHORS

John R. Meyer, 1907 Professor in Transportation, Logistics, and Distribution at the Harvard Business School, is also a member of Harvard's Faculty of Arts and Sciences and the Kennedy School of Government. He is currently on leave from Harvard serving as vice chairman of the Union Pacific Corporation. His most recent book, Autos, Transit, and Cities *was published by Harvard University Press in the fall of 1981.*

Jeffrey G. Miller is professor and chairman of the Operations Management Department at Boston University's School of Management. He has also served on the faculty of the Harvard Business School and Purdue University's Krannert Graduate School of Industrial Administration. Prior to his career in education, he worked for the Dow Chemical Company in both operations and corporate staff positions. He holds B.A. and M.B.A. degrees from UCLA, and received his Ph.D. from Purdue. Professor Miller maintains active interests in operations policy, logistics, and manufacturing control. He is co-author of two textbooks and has written numerous articles in journals such as Harvard Business Review, Decision Sciences, Management Science, Journal of Operations Management, Organizational Behavior and Human Performance, *and* AIEE Transactions. *He is currently heading the Manufacturing Futures research project, a survey of the plans and strategies of over 150 large manufacturing companies. At Boston University, Professor Miller teaches operations management in both the M.B.A. and the doctoral programs. He also consults and develops and teaches in executive education programs for private clients and other schools around the world. He is a member of the editorial boards of the* Journal of Operations Management *and the* Academy of Management Journal, *and is a member of the Curriculum and Certification Council of APICS.*

John F. Runcie is currently with the Organization Development and Research Department of Anheuser-Busch Companies, Inc., St. Louis. Prior to joining Anheuser-Busch, he was a senior researcher with Public Systems Evaluation, Inc., Cambridge. Mr. Runcie's recent publications include Experiencing Social Research *(2nd ed., Dorsey Press, 1980) and, with Richard C. Larson,* A Controlled Preventive Patrol Experiment *(forthcoming), which describes research on police patrol practices and was funded by the National Institute of Justice.*

W. Earl Sasser, Jr. is professor of business administration at the Harvard Business School, where he specializes in the management of operations. He currently teaches in the Advanced Management Program at Harvard and is chairman of a three-week executive seminar, "Manufacturing in Corporate Strategy" held on campus each summer. Mr. Sasser is the author of several Harvard Business Review *articles including "Managers with Impact: Versatile and Inconsistent."*

Roger W. Schmenner *is currently an associate professor at the Fuqua School of Business, Duke University. He teaches production/operations management there to both the M.B.A. and Executive M.B.A. programs. Before joining the Duke faculty, Mr. Schmenner taught at the Harvard Business School and at Yale University. Mr. Schmenner's research interests are focused primarily on industrial location, multiplant manufacturing management, manufacturing strategy, and productivity. His work on the industrial location decision making of the* Fortune 500 *and on the industrial location decisions around Cincinnati and New England was recently published as* Making Business Location Decisions *(Prentice-Hall). Mr. Schmenner is also the author of* Production/Operations Management: Concepts and Situations *(published by SRA). His articles have appeared in* Quarterly Journal of Economics, Harvard Business Review, Journal of Operations Management, Journal of Regional Science, Review of Economics and Statistics, Journal of Transport Economics and Policy, Journal of Urban Economics, Policy Analysis, *and* Public Policy. *Mr. Schmenner holds an A.B. degree from Princeton University and a Ph.D. in economics from Yale University.*

Donald N. Scobel *is now director of the Creative Worklife Center, in Mentor, Ohio. He consults with a variety of organizations on improving both the worklife experience and the performance of the workplace. Mr. Scobel spent 25 years with the Eaton Corporation in a variety of capacities involving human resource relationships. He is author of* Creative Worklife *(Gulf Publishing Company, 1981). Mr. Scobel's most recent* Harvard Business Review *article is "Guidelines to Labor–Management Cooperation."*

Benson P. Shapiro *is a professor at the Harvard Business School, where he is head of the required M.B.A. marketing course. He has previously taught sales management, industrial marketing, and creative marketing strategy. He is the author of eleven* Harvard Business Review *articles,* Sales Program Management *(McGraw-Hill, 1977), and numerous other pieces. Professor Shapiro has taught in several executive programs and has been a consultant to over 60 companies.*

Wickham Skinner *is James E. Robison Professor of Business Administration at the Harvard Business School. Before coming to Harvard in 1958 he worked at the Honeywell Corporation for ten years. Mr. Skinner's current research interests include manufacturing policy and corporate strategy and the management of human resources. His many publications include* Manufacturing in the Corporate Strategy *(Wiley, 1978).*

Linda G. Sprague *is professor of operations management at the Whittemore School of Business and Economics, University of New Hampshire, and director of their Executive Programs. In 1980 she was a founding professor at the National Center for Industrial Science and Technology Management*

ABOUT THE AUTHORS

Development at Dalian, China. Mrs. Sprague received her doctorate in Business Administration from the Harvard Business School; she also has an M.B.A. from Boston University and an S.B. in Industrial Management from M.I.T. Her consulting and research interests include capacity management and operations scheduling for manufacturing enterprises and for community general hospitals, and production information systems. She has published articles on material requirements planning, the four-day week, applications of management science and production management in China. Mrs. Sprague is president of the American Institute of Decision Sciences and is a Past Chair of the Production/Operations Management Division of the Academy of Management. She is a member of the faculty of the Harvard Introduction to Business Program for Ph.D.'s.

Philip M. Thurston *is the Richard P. Chapman Professor of Business Administration at the Harvard Business School, where he teaches courses in production and general management. He worked in industry, including ten years with the General Electric Company, before joining Harvard. His other articles published in the* Harvard Business Review *include "Requirements Planning for Inventory Control" (1972), one of the early writings introducing MRP. Professor Thurston holds bachelor's and master's degrees from Columbia and a doctorate from Harvard.*

Charles R. Walker, *as a young man, held skilled and unskilled jobs in the steel, copper, and rubber industries. He resolved at the time that, if he ever had the opportunity, he would make a thorough study of the neglected human equations in work situations such as the assembly line. Mr. Walker was Director of Research in Technology and Industrial Relations at Yale University's Institute of Human Relations when "The Man on the Assembly Line" was published.*

Richard E. Walton *is professor of business administration at the Harvard Business School, where he conducts research and teaches in the area of organizational behavior. He is the author of numerous books and articles on work innovation.*

Steven C. Wheelwright *received his Ph.D. from Stanford University, where he now teaches at the School of Business. He has taught at Harvard University and in a variety of executive programs at such companies as AT&T, Citibank, Digital Equipment, Corning Glass, General Electric, SCM, Tektronix, and TRW. Mr. Wheelwright has written or been co-author of numerous cases, articles, and books in the areas of manufacturing strategy, operations management, and forecasting. His research interests are primarily in policy and strategy for manufacturing firms as well as forecasting. He is working on a book on manufacturing strategy and pursuing research dealing with facilities focus and plant rationalization.*

Author Index

Abernathy, William J., 152, 357

Baker, Alton W., 571
Bluestone, Irving, 539, 543, 551, 556, 557
Blumberg, Mel, 357
Bradley, Omar N., 289–290
Bright, James, 440

Carroll, Daniel J., 574
Crosby, Philip, 260

Dhalla, N. K., 132
Dickson, William, 490
Driscoll, James W., 574

Ford, Henry, 91

Galbraith, John Kenneth, 243
Gellerman, Saul W., 572
Graham, Edward M., 87
Grayson, C. Jackson, 28

Hamilton, Alexander, 6
Hayes, Robert H., 357
Horner, William, 552

Iacocca, Lee A., 76

Katko, Charles, 552, 556
Katz, Abraham, 78
Klahorst, H. Thomas, 361

Landon, Delmar, 552, 557
Lawrence, Paul R., 223

Levitt, Theodore, 284
Likert, Rensis, 571
Lorsch, Jay W., 223
Lynas, Robert, 239

Malkiel, Burton, 19–20, 44
Mayo, Elton, 469
Morris, George, 552

Packard, David, 197
Pateman, Carol, 504
Patten, Thomas, 569
Patton, George S., 289–290

Rae, James, 552
Reiter, Stanley, 320
Roethlisberger, F. J., 490

Sartain, Aaron Q., 571
Schumpeter, Joseph, 24
Skinner, Wickham, 137, 201, 207, 229–230, 339
Sloan, Alfred P., 60, 91, 122, 152
Sprecher, Timothy A., 574
Starr, Martin K., 229

Tarondeau, Jean Claude, 361
Taylor, Frederick W., 109
Trist, Eric, 506

Von Hipple, Eric, 27

Yuspeh, S., 132

Subject Index

Admiral, 73
Air compressors, 75
Allis Chalmers, 70
American business, 15–34
  auto industry, U.S. *vs.* Japanese, 75–95
  cash generated rate, 44
  competition, international, 2, 54, 72–75
  deterioration, 15–16
    rate, 44–45
  foreign competition and, 2, 54, 72–75
  hurdle rate, 45–46
  labor productivity growth, 18 (exhibit)
  management:
    behavior, 23
    failure, 16–22
    neglect of, 4–5
    manufacturing, problems and, 4–5, 15–17
  new management orthodoxy, 22–24
  pressures in 1980s, 52
  R & D expenditures, 20–21
  rate of return for past 30 years, 44
  "rediscovery of factory," 3
  study of strategic and structural changes in, 52–71
  technology, use of new, 51
  trends, present, 37–38
  see also Basic Industries study
American Center for Quality of Working Life, 536
American goods:
  demand changes, 249
  foreign competitors, 248–249
  management and, 250–260
  quality, 240–261. *See also* Quality
  sources of quality problems, 250
American Printed Circuit Company, study of, 180–181
American Production/Inventory Control Society (APICS), 367
American Productivity Center, 28
Armco Steel, 57, 67–68, 70
Assembly lines, progressive, 507–508. *See also* Automobile assembly plant study; Automobile assembly line
Assembly schedule, 369
Automation, innovative plant and, 501
Automobile assembly line, 476–491
  favoritism at plant, 486–487
  jobs, description of, 477–480
  management, 488
  quality of work life improvements, 489–490
  research methodology for study, 491
  supervisors, 487–488
  union, view of, 484–485
  women and, 486
  workers, 476–491
    adaptation to job, 480–481
    feelings about work, 482–485
Automobile assembly plant study, 456–475
  blower-defroster assembler, 460
  job:
    characteristics, assembly line, 457
    enlargement, 469
    favorable features, 467–468
    rotation, 468–469
  main moving line workers, 458–459
  management's constructive measures, 467–468
  moving conveyor workers, 459
  repair person, 460–461
  utility person, 461–462
  workers':
    attitudes toward jobs, 457–463
    influence on quality, 466–467
    reactions:
      to mechanical pacing, 463
      reactions to repetitiveness, 464–465
    relations:

with forepersons, 471–472
with supervisors, 472
relationships, 469–471
sense of anonymity, 474
social interaction patterns, 470 (exhibit)
Autonomous work groups, 499

Basic industries study, 52–71
business level returns and revenue growth rates, 64 (exhibit)
comparative strategies, 60 (exhibit)
compound annual real growth rates in demand, 54 (exhibit)
failing competitors in each basic industry, 66–69
financial returns:
and growth rates, 57 (exhibit)
and revenue growth rate, 55 (exhibit)
foreign competition, 54
growth, projected, 53
heavy-duty truck manufacturing, 55–56, 61, 63 (exhibit), 66
investment decisions, 65–66
leadership position movement, 62–66, 69–70
managers, implications for, 71
marginal or failing companies, 67 (exhibit)
product/market diversification, 67–68
strategic and performance subgroups, 69–70 (exhibit)
success, 56
strategies, 59–62
Batch manufacturers, equipment, 352. *See also* CAM
Bethlehem Steel, 56
B. F. Goodrich, 67, 68, 70
Bill-of-material processor, 315–316
Bill-of-materials file, 369, 371
"Bill-of-materials structuring decisions," 340
Business:
environment, pressures in 1980s, 52
European, 32–33
reinvestment, decline in, 37–41
trends, recent, 37–38
see also American business

CAM (Computer-aided manufacturing):
adoption problems, 354–357
batch manufacturing and, 358–360
current version, 354
do's and don'ts for adoption and implementation, 362
forerunners, 353–354
implementation, 357–361

infrastructure support for, developing, 360–361
research study, 361–362
selection, basis for, 357
selling techniques, 356
workers' attitudes toward, 357
Capacity planning, 216, 218
long-term, 310 (exhibit)
new plant decision-making, 423–434
see also U-shaped costs
Caterpillar, 60–61, 69
Census of Manufacturers, material and transport costs, 381
"Channel vision," 284
Chrysler, 55–56, 67, 70, 126
Cigarette manufacturing, 61
Companies:
communications and planning, 165–166
market- and product-oriented, 196
see also American business
Competition, choice of priorities, 197–198
Computer-aided manufacturing (CAM), 352–362. *See also* CAM
Computer numerical control, 353–354
Computers, 74
capacity planning, 310–311
ferromagnetic memory core prices, 116
manufacturing and, 345–346
materials management and, 392
Computer specialist, 109–110
Consolidation, of services, 276–277
Consumer Reports, Japanese autos, 81
Corporate:
attitudes, 195–198
strategy, manufacturing and, 99–113, 195–198
Cost:
effect of learning curve, 116
reduction, innovation and, 124–126
Cost minimization strategies:
Douglas Aircraft, 127
Model T, 118–126
pattern of change, 128–129
risks of success, 129–130
Creeping breakdown phenomenon, 157
Crompton & Knowles, 127
Customer service, cuts to, 163–164

Daimler Benz, 61
Dependent demand, 369
Deterioration, use of term, 40
Diamond Reo, 56
Digital Equipment, 58
Direct numerical control (DNC), 354, 356

SUBJECT INDEX

Discounting approach, 37, 43
  threats of, 46–49
Disinvestment:
  logic of, 47–49
  spiral, 48–49
Dispatching:
  daily:
    reports, 326, 327 (exhibits)
    status system, 325–327
  functions of well-designed system, 330–331
  job sequence schedule, 328–330
    detailed, 329 (exhibit)
  rules 321–331
  shop control and, 323–331
Diversification, ways of, 196
Douglas Aircraft, 127
Draper, 74
DuPont, 116

Eastman Kodak, 58, 150
Eaton approach, 512–527
  benefits of, 518
  employee:
    decision making, 520–521
    discontent, 514–516
    job involvement, 519–520
  employees' letter, 514–516
  handbook content, 516–517
  hiring process, 518
  initial problems, 523–524
  measures of success, 521–523
  number of plants involved, 513
  old plant response, 524–525
  open floor concept, 519
  reactions of other companies, 526
  union's role, 525
Eaton Corporation, work climate revitalition, 512–527. *See also* Eaton approach
Economic lot size, 291–292
  mathematical formal, 301–304
  required production time *vs*. setup cost, 295 (exhibit)
Economic order quantity (EOQ), 291–293, 314–316
  failure of, 294–295
  lot size and, 295–296
"Economics of scale," 100, 191, 203
Emerson Electric, 139
Employee alienation, 492–511
  diagnosis, 497 (exhibit)
  manifestations, 494
  programs to revitalize organization, 496–498
  prototype of change (pet food manufacturer), 498–506
  social forces and, 495–496
  worker expectations *vs*. organizational design, 494–495
  see also Innovative plant
Employee relations, humanistic approach, 512–527
Endangered industries, 75
Entrance-exit strategies, 148–150 (exhibit)
Environmental factors, impact on U.S. industry, 438
Experience curve:
  Ford Motor Co., 120 (exhibit)
  failure at, 122
  Model T, 118–126
  TV picture tubes, 127

Factory:
  as anachronism, 437–453. See also Tarrytown Project
  automobile, 456–475, 476–491. *See also* Tarrytown Project
  employee alienation in, 492–511. *See also* Employee alienation
  focused, 179–192. *See also* Focused manufacturing
  innovative, 498–507
  Japanese, 231–247
  low cost, 183–184
Factory system:
  automation/mechanization/computerization patterns, 441–442
  automation results, 440
  changes:
    in conventional concepts, 444–446
    in meeting human needs, 448–450
    recommendations for, 443–451
  employees, 440–441, 448–450, 512–527
    Eaton Corp. revitalization approach, 512–527
    reasons for discontent, 513–516
  factory society viewpoints, 449 (exhibit)
  infrastructure problem, 442–443
  management changes, examples of, 450–451
  "piecemeal syndrome," 439–440
  plant modernization examples, 439
  pressures impinging on old system, 444 (exhibit)
First-level supervisor, 565–580
  conflicts of, 570
  decline of position, 568–569
  employees' attitudes, 573–574
  foreman speaks about, 579–580

592 SUBJECT INDEX

Gellerman study, 572
Likert study findings, 571–572
managers, suggestions for, 576–578
needs and wants of, 574–575
productivity study, 571
quality of supervision, 572 (exhibit)
research studies and conclusions, 575
skills needed, 566–567
union and, 569
Flexible manufacturing systems (FMS), 354–355 (exhibit), 356
Focused manufacturing, 179–192
basic concepts, 181–182
characteristics of, 182–183
four-step approach, 188–191
mission, 198, 207
rarity of, 180
rules of approach, 187
Ford Motor Company, 56, 61, 66, 70, 76, 78–80, 116–117 (exhibit)
experience curve, 120 (exhibit)
innovation and process change, 125–126
Model A, 119, 126
Model N, 119
Model T, 116–126, 152
design changes in, 121–122
era, 118–126
progressive manufacture principles, 457
vital statistics, 1910–1931, 123 (exhibit)
Foreign competition, Japanese auto industry, 72–95
Freightliner, 61
Fujitsu, 74
Furniture, marketing strategy for, 103–104

General Motors, 56, 60, 65, 70, 71
strategy (1920s), 121–122, 126
work improvement programs, 533–535, 543
see also Tarrytown project
General Tire, 57, 67–68, 70
Germany:
productivity, 16
tool and automotive production, 33
Goodyear, 58
Government and industry, positive adjustment, 87
Guardian Life Insurance Co., work improvement program, 535

Hewlett-Packard, 197
Hitachi, 74
Hokuetsu, 75
Honeywell Tradeline program, 281

IBM, 59, 74
System/360 delivery schedule, 127
Industrial engineers, 109
Industry, present problems of, 2
Ingersoll Milling Machine Company, 51
Ingersoll-Rand, 75
Inland Steel, 58, 65, 66
Innovative plant, 498–507
automation, implications for, 501
autonomous work groups, 499
challenging job assignments, 500
cost of new, 504–505
facilitating factors, 505–506
facilitative leadership, 500
implementation difficulties, 502–503
integrated support functions, 499–500
job mobility, 500
managerial decision rules, 501
physical features, 501
Procter & Gamble, 506, 508
results, 503–504
rewards for learning, 500
Saab-Scandia automotive, 507–508
self-government, 501
Volvo at Kalmar, 508
International corporations:
air compressor field, 75
computers, 74
endangered industries, 75
machine tools, 33, 74
television products, 33, 73–74
textile machinery, 74
International Harvester, 56, 61, 66
Inventories, MRP and lowering of, 373
Inventory:
control, 314–316
manpowered plan, 316
vs. demand, 297 (exhibit)
differentiated service levels, 279 (exhibit)
effect of demand on, 295–297
effects of capacity on, 297–300
sales volume and turnover rates of, 278 (exhibit)
status file, 369, 371
turnover rates, 277–278
Investment, decline of long-term, 38–41

Japanese auto industry, 75–95
cost advantage, 93 (exhibit)
factors affecting productivity, 84–85 (exhibit)
Jidoka, 86
Kanban ("just in time" production), 83
manufacturing excellence, 82–86

SUBJECT INDEX 593

Japanese factories, 231–247
 equipment, monitoring systems, 235–236
 manager's role, 235
 minimal inventory in, 234–235
 myths about, 232–233
 product changes, 236
 production schedules, 236–237
 quality circles, 232–233
 sense of order in, 233–234
 use, 235
 see also Japanese management
Japanese management, 237–245
 codestiny, 240
 in-house production equipment fabrication, 242–243
 lifetime employment, 241–242
 parallels to U.S. industries, 243–245
 quality consciousness, 238–239
 success, reasons for, 231–247
 time consciousness, 240–242
 "zero defects," 237, 239–240
Japanese Ministry of International Trade and Industry (MITI), 2
Japanese people, character of, 237
Jidoka, 86
Job mobility, 500

Kaiser, 56, 70
Kanban ("just in time" production), 83
Kodak, Eastman, 58, 150

Landsdowne, 127
"Lateral relations", 392
Leadership, facilitative, 500
Lead times, 369, 371, 398–410
 exhibits, 401, 403, 406–409
 management programs for inventory control, 402–409
 problems, facets of, 399–402
Learning curve:
 approaches, 115
 cost reduction/volume increase patterns, 115–118
 Douglas Aircraft, 127
 economic effects of, 116
 IBM, 127
 limits of, 114–131
 possible strategies, 154 (exhibit)
 product-process matrix, 153–155
 see also Experience curve
Learning, rewards for, 500
Liggett & Myers, 68
Litton Industries Atherton Division, 149

Loading approaches, 318–320
Logistics, 271–290
 corporate strategy questions, 280–290
 80/20 relationships, 277–280
 future considerations, 288–290
 importance for large companies, 272
 influence in business, 274
 life cycle, 283
 liquid bleach company (example), 271–272
 long-term action, 286–288
 milk products (example), 272
 process of, 273 (exhibit)
 strategic decision-making, participation in, 287 (exhibit)
 strategy, 274
 strategy audit, 281–286
 system redesign, 286
 uncommon logistical responses, 274–277
Lot size, 291–292
Lynchburg Foundry, 141

Machine loading, 317
Machinery centers, 353
Machine tools, 33, 74
Machinists, demand for, 38
Mack, 56
Management:
 automobile assembly line and, 476–491
 computer specialist, 109–110
 corporate portfolios, 22–23
 current behavior, 23
 efficiency experts' approach, 109
 financial control, 22
 focused manufacturing, 187–192
 innovative plant and, 498–506
 interest in work improvements, 536
 lead times, 398–410
 product orientation, 23–24
 quality of goods and, 250–260
 see also Tarrytown project
Manager:
 corporate materials, 393–394
 as "cost center," 203
Managers:
 backward integration decisions, 25–26
 career pattern changes, 28–29
 decisions, 24–28
  of division level, 165–166
 discounting approach, 37, 43
 European, 32–33
 evaluation of performance, 164–165
 failure of American, 16–22
 general, 250–251

manufacturing control systems and, 339–340, 343
materials, 379–397. *See also* Materials managers
merger activity and, 30–31
process development decisions, 27–28
product design choices, 24–25
production, 307
"pseudo-professionalism," 29–30
quality improvement, steps toward, 257–260
reinvestment decisions, 36–49
reporting relationships, 382 (exhibit)
salvage of profits, 159–160
S/L tradeoffs, 161–173
Manufacturer, pet food, 498–506
Manufacturing:
  American neglect of, 4–5
  backward integration decisions, 25–26
  changes required for improvements, 445–448
  computer specialist, 109–110
  constraints of industry, 112–113 (exhibit)
  corporate:
    attitudes related to, 195–198
    strategy and, 99–113
    weapon, 447
  cost minimization strategies, 118–131. *See also* Cost minimization strategies
  design tradeoff, 105–108 (exhibit)
  differing views, 101–102
  disconnected line flow process, 134
  efficiency-centered orientation, 109
  executives' perceptions, 102
  facilities decisions, 199–200
  focused, 179–192
  focused units, 201–202
  growth of organization, 211–214
  infrastructure decisions, 200
  key elements in competitiveness, 77 (exhibit)
  lead times, 398–410
  line-policies and demands, 103–104
  management's role and, 4–5
  marketing and, 215–230. *See also* Marketing/manufacturing interface
  mission of, 198, 207
  myths and assumptions, 445–446
  neglect of, 4–5
  patterns of change and, 128–129
  "plant within a plant," 191
  policy determination, 110–113
  priorities, 199–201

process-focused organization, 202, 204–205
product:
  focused organization, 202–204
  vs. process focus, 202–211
  proliferation, 186–187
production operations and corporate strategy, 103–105
purpose for company, 105
single plant approach, 201
specialized units, 141
technological changes and, 130–131
testing organizational focus, 210–211
Manufacturing company:
  causes of problems, 145–146
  entrance-exit strategies, 148–150 (exhibit), 149
  planning for growth, 147–157
Manufacturing control systems, 336–350
  causes of failure, 337–339
  choices in development of, 340–348
  focused factory, 345
  information system design, 349
  management's job and, 339–340, 345
  responsibilities for, 347–348
  system architecture, 341 (exhibit)
  types of technologies used in, 345–347
Manufacturing function, examples of problems, 194
Manufacturing mission, 198, 207
Manufacturing policy:
  elements of, 184
  negative effect of, 185
  noncongruent system, causes, 185–187
Marketing data, 221
Marketing/manufacturing interface, 215–230
  adjunct services, 220
  balancing, 225–228
  breadth of product line, 219–220
  capacity planning, 216, 218
  conflicts in, 216–231
    causes of, 221–225
    lessening of, 228–230
  cost control, 220
  delivery and physical distribution, 218–219
  management as adversary, 221–223
  new product introduction, 220
  production scheduling, 218
  quality assurance, 219
  R & D *vs*. engineering function, 223–224
  sales forecasts:
    long-range, 216, 218
    short-range, 218

SUBJECT INDEX

Marketing strategy:
  high-quality furniture, 104
  low-price line furniture, 103–104
Mass production method:
  automobile assembly plant study, 456–475
  definition, 457
  human nature and, 454–455
  impact on wage structure, 472–473
  need for systematic study, 455–456
  worker sense of anonymity, 474
  see also Automobile assembly plant study
Master schedule, 311–314, 369, 371
  estimating shoploads, 312–313
  information flows for, 313 (exhibit)
  objectives of, 311
Materials functions, tradeoffs matrix, 390 (exhibit)
Materials management:
  corporate level, 393–394
  departments, 347
  organization, 381, 383 (exhibit), 384
    major structures, 385–387 (exhibit)
    material tradeoffs, 389–392
    options for, 392–393
  survey, 395–397
Materials managers:
  emergence of, 380–385
  hiring decisions (examples), 388–389
  job of, 381
  proponents, 384
  reporting relationships, 383 (exhibit)
  types, 384–385
Materials requirements planning (MRP), *see* MRP
Materials specialist, definition, 385
Mead Corporation, 141
Mechanical technologies, 346 (exhibit)
Mercedes-Benz, 197
Mergers, 30–31, 39
Micro-Lam, 156
MITI (Japanese Ministry of International Trade and Industry), 2
Mitsubishi, 74
Model T, 116–117, 152
  cost minimization strategy, 118–126
  design changes, 121–122
  prices of, 117 (exhibit)
Motorola, 73
MRP (Materials Requirements Planning), 367–378
  advantages, 372–374
  analysis of manufacturing operations for success, 374–377
  bill of materials file, 369, 371
  company examples, 374–377
  comparison to PERT, 371
  de-expediting, 372–373
  determining value, 377–378
  elements, 369–370 (exhibit)
  inventory status file, 369, 371
  logic of, 368–369, 371
  management survey of materials, 395–397
  system, 348–350
    example, 371
Murphy's law, 235, 237, 442

National Commission on Productivity, 179
Nippon Electric, 74
Nissan, Zama facility, 83
Numerical control (NC) machine tools, 353, 360

Objectives, short-term *vs.* long-term, 159–173
OPEC, 145
Order quantity, 291–292
Organization:
  effects of growth, 211–214
  types of growth, 212
Organizational technologies, 345, 346 (exhibit), 347

Paccar, 56, 61
Pet food manufacturer, example, 498–506
Philip Morris, 61, 65
Phillips Petroleum, 58
Plant location:
  advantages of branches and relocation, 414 (exhibit)
  consequences of strategy, 419–420
  deciding about, 411–422
  general-purpose strategy, 419
  market area strategy, 417
  multiplant strategies, 416–419
  new branch, 413–416
  options for adding space, 412–413
  process-plant strategy, 418–419
  product-market strategy, 417–418
  product strategy, 416–417
  relocation, 415
  site selection, 420–422
"Plant within a plant" (PWP), 191
Polaroid, 148
Postponement, practice of, 275 (exhibit)
"Process champion," 354, 356
Process change, innovation and, 125

Process-focused organization, 202–211
Process life cycle, see Product-process life
    cycle; Product-process matrix
Process yield, 83–86
  determinants of, 85 (exhibit)
Process-product life cycles:
  dynamics of, 144–158
  impact of external forces, 145
Procter & Gamble, innovations of, 506
Product:
  development, cuts in, 163
  innovation, cost reduction and, 124–128
Product-focused organization, 202–211
Production planning:
  capacity, 310–311
  control systems and, 306–335
    information flows, 332 (exhibit)
    integration and, 331–335
    progress, 333–334
  economic lot size, 291–292. See also
      Economic lot size; Economic order
      quantity
  EOQ, 294–295, 315–316
    failure of, 294–295
    reorder point system vs. time, 315–316
  future demand forecasts, 308–309
  inventory:
    control, 314–315
    effect of capacity on, 297–300
    effect of demand on, 295–297
  managers, 307
  phased requirements, 314–315
  scheduling:
    master, 311–314
    short-term, 317–321
  steps for, 300–301
Product life cycle:
  shortcomings of, 132–133
  see also Product-process life cycle
Product/market diversification, 67–68
Product-process life cycle:
  effects on management, 137–140
  implications for corporate strategy, 142
  manufacturing problems, 140
  use of concept, 136–142
Product-process matrix, 132–143
  advantages, 157–158
  change of position on, 146
  company plan for growth, 147–157
  disconnected line flow process, 134
  examples of competitive approaches,
      139–140
  expanded, 138 (exhibit)
  interaction of product and process life
      cycle stages, 134 (exhibit)

learning curve strategy, 153–155
manufacturing companies, problems of,
    145–147
new markets, 156–157
no-progress industries, 152–153
paths, 150–153
product growth, 155–156
simple growth, 147–155
vertical integration, 156–157
Production system:
  concept, 265–270
  definition, 265
  exhibits, 268–269
  interrelationship of problems, 267
  material flow, 266
  suggestions for managers, 270
Productivity:
  study of group leaders and, 571
  work improvement programs and, 540–542
  see also Tarrytown project
Products:
  breadth of lines, 219–220
  imitative vs. innovative design, 24–25
    tradeoffs, 25 (exhibit)
  learning curve approaches to, 114–131
  line growth, 155–156
  managers approach to new, 23
  market analysis of, 24
  market-driven strategy, 23–25
  new, introduction of, 220
  outlets for, 282
  proliferation, 186–187
  quality of American, 248–261
  see also American goods
Profit:
  Impact of Market Strategies (PIMS), 65
  margins vs. high-output volumes, 197–198
  pressure on management, 160
  S/L tradeoffs, 161–173
Progress function, see Learning curve
Progressive manufacture, 457

Quality:
  attributes for improvement of, 257–260
  decisions that affect, 252–253 (exhibit)
  improvement of (examples), 255
  investments to yield higher, 256
  levers for, 255–257
  management, 250–260
  problems, causes of, 254–255
  productivity and, 256–257
  responsibility for, 254–255
  views of quality for, 250–257 (exhibit)
Quality Is Free (Crosby), 260
Quality of work life (QWL), 489–490

SUBJECT INDEX 597

definition of, 548
General Motors Tarrytown project, 547–564
movement in U.S., 548, 561–562
principles of programs, 562–564
see also Tarrytown project

Reinvestment:
  decline in, 37–41
  gradual disinvestment, 43 (exhibit)
  process, example of, 40–43
  rates, 42 (exhibit)
Reliance electric, 139
Report on Manufactures (Hamilton), 6
River Rouge, 116
Rockwell International, 74, 150
ROI-control system, 25–26
Rolls-Royce, Ltd., 135

Saab-Scandia automotive plant, 507–508
Sales:
  inventory turnover rates and volume of, 278
  long-range forecasts, 216–218
  short-range forecasts, 218
Sanyo, 75
Scheduling:
  master, 311–314
    estimating shoploads, 312–313
    information flows for, 313 (exhibit)
    objectives of, 311
  short-term, 317–321
Schlitz, 70
Service levels, 278–281
  accounting, 280
  customer expectation, 281
Short-term scheduling:
  capacity loading, 318–319
  information flows, 322 (exhibit)
  loading to infinite capacity, 319–320
  machine loading, 317
  see also Dispatching
S/L tradeoffs, 161–173
  assessment of corporate situation, 167
  capital outlay postponement, 162
  controls on, most effective, 168 (exhibit)
  customer service cuts, 163–164
  managers, reasons for, 164–166
  minimizing detrimental tradeoffs, 167–171
  operating expense:
    deferrment, 162–163
    reduction, 163–164
  price changes, 164
  product development cuts, 163

research methods, 172–173
structural and variable controls, 166–167
Sony, 73
Specialty fields, 185
Standardization, of products, 275–276
Startup function, *see* Learning curve
Stock Keeping Unit Location (SKUL), 278
Strategy, meaning, 103
Structural controls, meaning, 166
Supervisor:
  connotations of word, 568
  first-level, 565–580. *See also* First-level supervisor
System, definition, 306, 347

Tappan, 67
Tarrytown project, 547–564
  employee training sessions, 557–558
  labor-management agreement, 551–553
  layoff crisis, 554–555
  plant before project, 548–551
  program beginnings, 553
  QWL effect, 556–558
  results of program, 559–560
Technology, manufacturing strategy and, 130–131
Television products, 33, 73–74
Texas Instruments, 58, 197
  jewelry line digital watch, 139–140
Textile machinery, 74
3M, 59
Time phased requirements, 314–316
  examples of planning, 315 (exhibit)
Toshiba, 75
Toyo Kogyo (Mazda), 79–80
  estimated per-vehicle employee cost, 94 (exhibit)
  product mix adjustment, 95
Toyota, 74, 78, 234
  inventory, 234
Trade, balance of trade, 3 (figure)
Tradeoff decisions, in manufacturing, 105–108 (exhibit)
Tradeoffs, material functions, 389–392
Transient economic misfortune, 87
Trus Joist Corp., 156–157
TV picture tubes, price reduction, 127

Union, supervisors and, 569
Uniroyal, 70
United Automobile Workers Union (UAW), 539, 543, 551
United States auto industry:
  brake drum instruments, 26

cost advantage of subcompact cars, 78
customer loyalty, 82 (exhibit)
estimated pre-vehicle employee cost
    (Ford), 94 (exhibit)
interpretation of industry's crisis, 87-88
Japanese competition, 75-95
management:
    approach, 78
    challenge to, 91
oil price effects, 87-88
organizational focus, 211
poor quality of vehicles, 76
productivity costs, 79-80
product mix adjustment (Ford), 95
    (exhibit)
product quality, 81-82
renewal elements, 89-91
United States factories, economic batches,
    234
United States industry:
    impact of environmental factors, 438
    problems of, 437-438
    see also American business; United States
        auto industry
United States Steel, 68
United States manufacturing:
    pessimists' view of, 179-180
    manufacturing attitudes, basic changes
        needed, 180
    productivity crisis, 179
    work improvements in, 512-546
United Technologies, 58
U-shaped costs, 424-434
    advantages and disadvantages, 425-427
    cost development pattern, 426 (exhibit)
    effect on public policy, 432-434
    lagging capacity strategy, 431
    LHS conditions, 427-429
    RHS conditions, 429-430
    strategic implications of patterns, 428
        (exhibit)

Variable controls, meaning, 167
Volkswagen, 127

Warwick, 73
Whirlpool, 65, 69
White Motor, 56, 61, 66, 68
"Work group," 469
Work improvements, 528-546
    Butler Manufacturing, 535
    company's interest in, 532-533
    Eaton approach, 512-527
    effectiveness of, 537
    effects of work culture, 530-531
    General Motors programs, 533-535, 543,
        547-564
    Guardian Life Insurance Co., 535-536
    guidelines for beginning programs,
        524-545
    job enrichment techniques, 529-533
    management interest in, 536
    motives of management for, 538
    pet food plant, 448-506
    productivity and, 540-542
    results produced by, 530
    three-level conception of, 532 (exhibit),
        545-546
    UAW programs, 539, 543
    Volvo, 508
    workers' motivations and needs
        considered, 539
Work in progress inventory:
    costs and benefits of management
        program, 409-410
    exhibits of, 401, 403, 406-409
    management programs for, 402-409
    reducing lead times, 408-409
    WIP inventory, 400, 406
Work teams, 499

Xerox, 58, 148
    service program, 281

Youngstown, 56

Zenith Radio Corporation, manufacturing
    strategy, 136

12/2-3